DICTIONARY OF LITERARY BIOGRAPHY

DOCUMENTARY SERIES

AN ILLUSTRATED CHRONICLE
VOLUME FIVE

Depicting The American
Transcendentalist Movement
Including Photographs,
Manuscript Facsimiles, Letters,
And Contemporary Assessments

DICTIONARY OF LITERARY BIOGRAPHY

DOCUMENTARY SERIES
AN ILLUSTRATED CHRONICLE
VOLUME FIVE

AMERICAN
TRANSCENDENTALISTS

EDITED BY
JOEL MYERSON

A BRUCCOLI CLARK LAYMAN BOOK

GALE RESEARCH COMPANY • BOOK TOWER
DETROIT, MICHIGAN 48226

Manufactured by Edwards Brothers, Inc.
Ann Arbor, Michigan
Printed in the United States of America

Library of Congress Cataloging-in-Publication Data

(Revised for v. 5)

Dictionary of literary biography documentary series.

"A Bruccoli Clark Layman book."
Vol. 5: "A Bruccoli Clark Layman book."
Contents v. 1. Sherwood Anderson, Willa Cather,
John Dos Passos, Theodore Dreiser, F. Scott Fitzgerald,
Ernest Hemingway, Sinclair Lewis/edited by Margaret A.
Van Antwerp—v. 2. James Gould Cozzens, James T.
Farrell, William Faulkner, John O'Hara, John Steinbeck,
Thomas Wolfe, Richard Wright/edited by Margaret A.
Van Antwerp—[etc.]—v. 5. American transenden-
talists/edited by Joel Myerson
1. Authors, American—Biography—Sources
2. American literature—History and criticism—Sources
I. Van Antwerp, Margaret A.   II. Bruccoli, Mary.
III. Johns, Sally.   IV. Documentary series.
PS129.D48   1982   810'.9 [B]   82-1105
ISBN 0-8103-1112-7 (v. 1)

CONTENTS

CONTENTS

FOREWORD

DLB: Documentary Series (1982-) is a reference source with a twofold purpose: 1) it makes significant literary documents accessible to students and to scholars as well as to nonacademic readers: and 2) it supplements the *Dictionary of Literary Biography* (1978-). The *Documentary Series* was conceived to provide access to a range of materials that many students never have the opportunity to see. By itself it is a portable archive. Used with *DLB,* it expands the biographical and critical coverage of the essays by presenting key documents on which these essays are based. *DLB* places authors' lives and works in the perspective of literary history; the *Documentary Series* chronicles literary history in the making.

American Transcendentalists brings together many basic texts of American Transcendentalism to fulfill the aim of the *DLB Documentary Series* to chronicle "literary history in the making." Literary history was not made by convenient, anthology-sized snippets; the complete texts of works are here reprinted whenever possible. This decision has meant the omission of some important longer documents of Transcendentalism (such as Ralph Waldo Emerson's *Nature,* most of Henry David Thoreau's *Walden,* and Margaret Fuller's *Woman in the Nineteenth Century*); but these texts are easily available. Many of the pieces in this volume have not been reprinted in their entirety since their first appearances in hard-to-find nineteenth-century periodicals.

Because Transcendentalism was such a diverse movement that even its participants could not agree on their common principles or even to be designated Transcendentalists–as one of them put it, they were called "'the club of the like-minded' . . . because no two of us thought alike"–any attempt to assemble the entire movement between two covers is impossible. What I have done, then, is to concentrate, first, on the main period of Transcendentalist activity from 1836 to 1844, and, second, on the controversial documents of the movement and the responses they brought forth. Transcendentalism was primarily a religious movement, and many of the documents in this volume deal with religious questions and the two great works putting forth the Transcendentalists' ideas, Emerson's Divinity School Address and Theodore Parker's *A Discourse on the Transient and Permanent in Christianity.* Most Transcendentalist writing at this time was expository prose–Emerson's *Poems* was not published until 1847–and this emphasis is reflected in the selections. Although Thoreau was active during the Transcendentalist period, his great writings did not come until later; nevertheless, his omission would be a serious error, for so many of the ideas of this period bore their greatest expression in writings such as *Walden* or "Resistance to Civil Government," and both are therefore represented here. Besides literary, philosophical, religious, and social writings, the Transcendentalists were also involved in two communitarian ventures, the Brook Farm and Fruitlands communities; special sections are given to each. Two appendixes print an excellent survey-discussion of Transcendentalism by Alexander Kern and a list of books for further reading. Biographical information on individual Transcendentalists may be found in Kern's essay or in other *DLB* volumes (as cross-referenced in headnotes to the selections).

Transcendentalism was a Boston-based movement that flourished between 1836 and 1844. Its period of greatest influence began with the publication of Ralph Waldo Emerson's *Nature* in 1836 and with the first meeting of the Transcendental Club one day earlier. By 1844 whatever unity had existed among the Transcendentalists was no longer present, and formal recognition of this growing-apart came when the semi-official journal of the movement, the *Dial,* ceased publication in April. Most Transcendentalists were Harvard-educated Unitarian ministers dissatisfied with the conservative Unitarians who were the leaders of their church, and all were unhappy about the conservative tenor of the times. This conservatism is best described by Henry Adams, who, though educated at Harvard in the 1850s, had many of the conservative Unitarians as his teachers: "For them, difficulties might be ignored, doubts were waste of thought; nothing exacted solution. Boston had solved the universe; or had offered and realized the best solution yet tried. The problem was worked out" (*The Education of Henry Adams*).

The Transcendentalists found themselves in conflict with the conservative Unitarians and society in general in four particular areas: literature, philosophy, religion, and man's place in society.

In literature, the Transcendentalists championed English and continental writers such as Thomas Carlyle and Johann Wolfgang von Goethe. Emerson served as Carlyle's agent in America, and George Ripley introduced continental authors in his series of *Specimens of Foreign Standard Literature* (1838-1842). Yet critical dissension existed within the ranks of the Transcendentalists. Some, led by Emerson, believed that a few "representative men" should set an example and lead the way; others, such as Orestes Brownson, held that literature should "appeal to the mass, wake up just sentiments, quicken elevated thoughts in them, and direct their attention to great and noble deeds; the literature will follow as a necessary consequence" ("American Literature").

In philosophy, the Transcendentalists followed the German Immanuel Kant in believing that man had an innate ability to perceive that his existence transcended mere sensory experience, as opposed to the prevailing belief of John Locke that the mind was a blank tablet at birth which registered only those perceptions received through the senses and experience. From the writings of Sampson Reed came the idea of "correspondence," that every object was a microcosm– or world in miniature–of the vast spiritual source named by some the "Oversoul", and an early formulation of the concept of organic style, that the artist produces his work by giving expression to the forms of nature rather than by imposing an artificial arrangement upon nature. The Transcendentalists also took much from the idealism of the Frenchman Victor Cousin. And because man was seen as basically good, to some Transcendentalists evil did not exist; in Emerson's words, "Evil is merely privative, not absolute; it is like

cold, which is the privation of heat" (Divinity School Address).

In religion, the Transcendentalists were holding dangerous ground. In 1828, the Reverend William Ellery Channing had said that "man has a kindred nature with God, and may bear the most important and ennobling relations with him." Now, less than a decade later, Channing and his fellow Unitarians were being accused of perpetrating a monstrous duplicity, centering on the question of the accuracy or believability of the miracles of Christ. William Henry Furness proposed in 1836 that if all nature were truly seen as miraculous, then no specific phenomenon could be more so; hence, to believe in the miracles of the New Testament was to deny the miraculous everywhere and was also a mere skepticism based upon Locke's ideas. In response, Orville Dewey described man as too fallible a creature to discern the truth of Christianity without the evidences provided for by miracles. The conservative Unitarians were now caught in the middle; they had, in denying Calvinism (with its acceptance of depravity, original sin, and the idea of predestination), dedicated themselves to a lofty concept of man, but they refused to glorify him as did the Transcendentalists by believing that he could attain religion without miracles or supernatural assistance. By placing their elders in this position, the Transcendentalists were also indirectly accusing them of robbing man of his dignity even more shamefully–because more slyly–than had the Calvinists. The Unitarian response avoided the main issues: Andrews Norton loftily announced that the Transcendentalists, many of whom had taken his courses in the Harvard Divinity School, were simply not competent to speak on such matters and that their movement was characterized by "the most extraordinary assumption, united with great ignorance, and incapacity for reasoning." Francis Bowen called Transcendentalism an un-American fad, and its adherents arrogant and dogmatic. Ripley led the counterattack by responding to Norton with a plea for intellectual freedom and by answering Bowen that Harvard was itself so isolated that it failed to see Transcendentalism was indeed the sentiment of the land. Brownson carried the idea of Harvard's isolation one step further: he called the battle social as well as religious. To Brownson, the aristocratic institutions of the Unitarian church were arrayed against the democratic principles of the Transcendentalists; the Unitarians themselves were now accused of being anti-American. The battle then raged, lasting into the

1840s, when Theodore Parker summed up the Transcendentalists' position thus:

> Their [miracles'] connection with Christianity appears accidental: for if Jesus had taught at Athens, and not at Jerusalem; if he had wrought no miracle, and none but the human nature had ever been ascribed to him; if the Old Testament had forever perished at his birth,–Christianity would still have been the word of God; it would have lost none of its truths. . . . So if it could be proved–as it cannot–in opposition to the greatest amount of historical evidence ever collected on any single point, that the Gospels were the fabrication of designing and artful men, that Jesus of Nazareth never lived, still Christianity would stand firm, and fear no evil. (*A Discourse on the Transient and Permanent in Christianity*)

In short, the word and spirit–the teachings–of Christ gave Christianity its validity, and not any mere– and unprovable–"supernatural" actions.

In viewing man's position in society, the Transcendentalists also challenged beliefs. They attacked the religious and social formalism of the day, proposing in its place freedom and spontaneity in all ways of life. Commercialism, too, disturbed them, and they countered the traditional view of success as measured by monetary or materialistic standards with a belief that the dollar should be replaced by personal morality as the standard of conduct. Finally, in opposition to what they saw as a false democracy in which legislation was enacted through the will of the majority, the Transcendentalists held that the individual should oppose laws he feels are unjust. As Thoreau put it, the government "is not armed with superior wit or honesty, but with superior physical strength," and "It costs me less in every sense to incur the penalty of disobedience to the state, than it would to obey."

Transcendentalism had a major impact on subsequent American literature and thought. Although no single document represents all aspects of the movement the sum of its participants' influence has been great.

In literature, the Transcendentalists provided later writers with models that stressed experimentation and freedom from the conservatism of the early nineteenth century. Walt Whitman, for example, at one time credited Emerson for making it possible for him to be a poet. In general, numerous studies have argued that Transcendentalism was a major source for experimental poetry in America, from Whitman and Emily Dickinson to Wallace Stevens and Allan Ginsberg. Studies of Romanticism in America have generally seen Transcendentalism as partially responsible for that movement by shaping the beliefs of its followers, or serving as a convenient focal point for its detractors.

While no Transcendentalist produced an organized philosophical system, many of their ideas have entered American life and culture. Emerson's concept of self-reliance has been seen widely as the most influential statement of that belief in the nineteenth century, and his educational ideas greatly influenced Charles W. Eliot in his shaping of the curriculum at Harvard University. Thoreau's idea of civil disobedience influenced Mahatma Gandhi and Martin Luther King, Jr., in their practice of passive resistance. Margaret Fuller's pleas for women's rights have been echoed (and often quoted) from the Women's Rights Convention of 1851 to the present. Theodore Parker was partially responsible for the changes that took place in the Unitarian church in the mid-nineteenth century. The communitarian impulse, as seen at Brook Farm and Fruitlands, was mirrored in the communal experiments of the 1960s. And any movement which has been praised as a positive influence by people as diverse as the architect Frank Lloyd Wright and the musician Charles Ives must surely be considered to have had an effect which outlasted its own lifetime.

—Joel Myerson

ACKNOWLEDGMENTS

My research has been supported by Carol McGinnis Kay, Dean of Humanities and Social Sciences, of the University of South Carolina. Armida Gilbert assisted in preparing the manuscript and was primarily responsible for reading proofs. Marcia Moss helped me in using the collections of the Concord Free Public Library, and I am once again in her debt. Joseph M. Bruccoli did the photographic work for this book.

I am grateful to Ohio State University Press for permission to reprint part of Hawthorne's *American Notebooks* and to *Resources for American Literary Study* for permission to reprint part of my edition of Charles Lane's letters about Fruitlands. I also wish to thank the Concord Free Public Library and the Houghton Library of Harvard University for permission to reproduce materials from their collections. All other illustrations in this book are from photographs or original materials in the Myerson Collection.

This book was produced by Bruccoli Clark Layman, Inc. Karen L. Rood is the senior editor for the *Dictionary of Literary Biography* series. The production coordinator is Kimberly Casey. Photographic work was done by Joseph Bruccoli. The production staff includes Cheryl Crombie, Gabrielle Elliott, Sarah Estes, Kathleen Flanagan, Cynthia Hallman, Sheri Neal, and Elizabeth York. Typesetting was supervised by Mary Louise Shevlin and Robert T. Shevlin.

Dictionary of Literary Biography

DICTIONARY OF LITERARY BIOGRAPHY

DOCUMENTARY SERIES

AN ILLUSTRATED CHRONICLE
VOLUME FIVE

[Frederic Henry Hedge]

"Coleridge's Literary Character," *Christian Examiner*, 14 (March 1833): 108-129.

Frederic Henry Hedge's article on English poet, critic, and philosopher Samuel Taylor be-gins this volume because, in Perry Miller's words, it "marks the point at which Transcendental-ism went over to the offensive" against conservative Unitarians. Earlier writers on were apolo-gists who spent most of their time defending him from charges of obscurity; Hedge, on the other hand, offers "no apology." In fact, he says, "To those only is [Coleridge] obscure who have no depths." Those who appreciate , then, are the ones who are on intellectually sound footing, not those who attack him. Because was one of the main popularizers of the transcendental philosophy of Kant, legitimizing was a major step in making the German philosophy a subject for serious study. (For further information on this Unitarian minister and Harvard professor, see the entry for Hedge in DLB 1, The American Renaissance in New England.*)*

There is no writer of our times whose literary rank appears so ill-defined as that of Mr. Coleridge. Per-haps there is no one whose true standing in the liter-ary world it is so difficult to determine. For ourselves we know not a more doubtful problem in criticism than this author and his works present. If it were lawful to judge men by what they are, rather than by what they have done, by the evidence they give of what they might accomplish, rather than by the value of that which they have accomplished, few would stand higher than Mr. Coleridge. His talents and acquirements, the original powers, and the exceeding rich cultivation of his mind, place him among the foremost of this genera-tion. But this method of estimating a man's merit will hardly be thought righteous judgment in an age which is peculiarly prone to try every man by his works. Tried by his works, Mr. Coleridge, we fear, must ulti-mately fall, not only below the rank which nature and ed-ucation had fitted him to maintain, but even below that which he now actually holds in the estimation of liter-ary men.

As a prose-writer he has never been popular, though skilled beyond most men in the use of lan-guage, and writing on subjects of the deepest interest. As a poet, though gifted in no common degree with the essentials of the poetic character, he has not been successful. As a philosopher, though at once both sub-tile and profound, and deeply versed in all the myster-ies of the inner man, he has gained little else than smiles of compassion and ominous shaking of heads by his metaphysical speculation. For a reconciliation of these several antitheses we must have recourse to the history of the man. In the "Biographia Literaria," by far the most entertaining, and in our opinion the most in-structive of his works, we have that history in part; the influences which operated most powerfully on our au-thor's youth, and the elements both of thought and feel-ing which entered most largely into the formation of his literary character, are there set before us with great clearness and precision; and from the data which this book furnishes we are enabled to account for much that would otherwise be unintelligible in the doings and not-doings of this remarkable man. Nature, it would seem, had endowed Mr. Coleridge with a singularly fer-tile and creative mind,–a mind which, if left to itself with no other training than opportunity might supply, would have enriched the world with manifold and pleas-ing productions. The marks of this creative tendency are still visible in some of his poetical productions; we would mention in particular the "Ancient Mariner," and the tragedies.

But at an early period of his education, our au-thor's mind acquired a bias which proved injurious to its productive faculty, and which, by changing the ten-dency of his intellect from the creative to the reflec-tive, in process of time seduced him from the open high-way of literary fame, into more devious and darksome paths. We refer to the discipline which he received at

Photograph of Frederick Henry Hedge, a founder of the Transcendentalist Club

freer field in deep and comprehensive speculations on topics of national and universal interest, particularly those which agitated Europe at the commencement of the present century. It has been employed on knotty questions in politics, philosophy, and religion, it has canvassed the rights and duties of civil government, criticized the movements of nations, and passed judgment on the tendencies and characteristics of the age. The results of these speculations were first given to the world in "The Morning Post," and afterwards in "The Friend," a collection of original essays, which for depth of thought, clearness of judgment, sound reasoning, and forcible expression, have few rivals in the English language. For the American edition of this work, as also for the republication of the "Aids to Reflections," and "The Statesman's Manual," we take this opportunity of expressing our obligations to President Marsh. Next to the writer of a good book, he most deserves our gratitude, who in any way helps to increase its circulation. This praise is due, in an eminent degree, to Mr. Marsh; nor does this comprise the whole of his claims to our regard and good wishes; and in the valuable dissertation which accompanies the "Aids to Reflection," he has done much to illustrate Mr. Coleridge's philosophical opinions, and has evinced a philosophical talent of his own, which we cannot but hope will some day be employed in more extensive undertakings.

To return to our author. After finding him engaged in the desultory and patch-work business of journal composition and essay writing, we are no longer surprised that he should have produced nothing of a more lofty and epic character. Whether the habit of small writing (under which name we include essays, reviews, and critiques of all kinds) be cause or effect, we shall not undertake to say; but certain we are, that this habit is always connected with an indisposition for more dignified and sustained efforts. From a skillful essayist we might expect excellence in small matters,–a spirited ode or a pointed epigram,–but never should we expect from such a one a well sustained epic poem, or perfect drama, a complete history, or system of philosophy. That species of talent which leads to fragmentary composition, will generally be found to be the offspring of a mind which loves rather to dwell on particulars than to contemplate universals, and is more accustomed to consider things in their special relations and minutest bearings, than to expatiate in large and comprehensive views. In such minds the centrifugal force is out of all proportion to the centripetal; they

the grammar school at Christ's-Hospital, as described in his life.[1] Such a discipline, though admirably adapted to invigorate the understanding, and to strengthen the judgment, was ill-suited to unfold a poet's talent, or to nourish creative genius of any kind. It was precisely the training to make a critic; and although we are unwilling to ascribe any irresistible influence to education alone, we cannot help believing that the strong tendency to criticism which has ever marked Mr. Coleridge's literary pursuits, is in part the effect of early discipline. We do not mean that Mr. Coleridge has at any period of his life been a writer of critiques, as that business is generally understood, but that he has ever inclined to comment upon the sayings and doings of others, rather than to say and do himself. This propensity, however, has not been exercised on literary subjects alone; it has found a wider scope and a are ever losing themselves in endless diffusion, without the ability to recover themselves in systematic results, or to concentrate their powers into regular and definite forms. Such a habit of mind is decidedly anti-creative, and therefore fatal to success in the higher departments of literary production. In proportion as the mind accustoms itself to dwell on particulars, it loses sight of unity and totality, and becomes incapable of contemplating or producing a whole. And herein, we conceive, lies the secret of Mr. Coleridge's failures. Here we have the answer to the oft repeated question, why a mind of such copious resources, so filled and overflowing with various and rich material, should have produced so little, and that little so loose and desultory.

Something more than abundance of material is wanted to constitute a perfect literary production. In every intellectual, as well as in every material creation, there are two essential elements, substance and form. Of substance Mr. Coleridge has enough, but in respect to form he is strikingly deficient, and being deficient in this, he wants that which constitutes the perfection of genius.

The characteristics of genius have been variously defined. To us it has always seemed, that, as there are two degrees of this mental quality, so there are so two characteristics, the one common to both degrees, the other peculiar to, and, indeed, constituting the highest. The first characteristic is originality. By this we mean not merely a disposition to think and act differently from the rest of mankind, but the power of imparting novelty, and a sense of freshness to common thoughts and familiar objects. In poetry this faculty constitutes what is called the poetical feeling; it is that which distinguishes genuine poetry, whether metrical or unmetrical, from mere eloquence. In this quality Mr. Coleridge is by no means deficient. The following quotation may serve to illustrate our meaning; it is from the story of an orphan girl, contained in "The Friend."

"Maria followed Harlin, for that was the name of her guardian angel, to her home hard by. The moment she entered the door she sank down and lay at her full length, as if only to be motionless in a place of rest had been the fulness of delight. *As when a withered leaf that has long been whirled about by the gusts of autumn is blown into a cave or the hollow of a tree, it stops suddenly, and all at once looks the very image of quiet.* Such might this poor orphan girl appear to the eye of a meditative imagination."

AIDS TO REFLECTION,

IN THE

FORMATION OF A MANLY CHARACTER,

ON THE SEVERAL GROUNDS OF

PRUDENCE, MORALITY, AND RELIGION:

ILLUSTRATED BY

SELECT PASSAGES FROM OUR ELDER DIVINES, ESPECIALLY
FROM ARCHBISHOP LEIGHTON.

BY S. T. COLERIDGE.

FIRST AMERICAN, FROM THE FIRST LONDON EDITION ;
WITH AN APPENDIX, AND ILLUSTRATIONS FROM OTHER WORKS OF THE SAME
AUTHOR; TOGETHER WITH A

PRELIMINARY ESSAY, AND ADDITIONAL NOTES,

BY JAMES MARSH,
PRESIDENT OF THE UNIVERSITY OF VERMONT.

BURLINGTON:
CHAUNCEY GOODRICH.
MDCCCXXIX.

Title page of the first American edition for the volume which introduced Coleridge's writings to most of the Transcendentalists

In the words which are here marked with Italics we have a plain but accurate description of an incident familiar to all of us. Nothing can be simpler,–perhaps some will think nothing could be less indicative of genius than the mention of such a circumstance. And yet it is this faculty of seizing upon a natural incident, of presenting it exactly as it is, without embellishment or emotion, yet at the same time making it impressive by gently emphasizing its most distinctive feature, and by diffusing over the whole a kind of ideality,–it is this faculty which gives life to poetry; it is this which gives to the poetry of the ancients in particular, its strange and peculiar charm. Who has not seen a leaf whirled about by the wind, and then lodged in the hollow of a tree? but who except a poet would have recalled the circumstance? who but a poet would have found in it an analogy to any thing in the moral world? This is to look upon nature with a poet's eye, and to interpret nature with a poet's sense. This is to clothe with new beauty, and as it were to sanctify, a common sight, so that it can never more seem common, nor pass unnoticed again. An incident thus selected from the daily spectacle of nature, and associated with a particular state of mortal being, becomes thenceforward and for ever a poetical image; by the poet's magic synthesis a natural object has become inseparably linked with a human feeling, so that the one must thenceforth always suggest the other. We feel assured that after reading this passage we shall never again behold the thing there described without a new sensation. We shall add a few extracts from Mr. Coleridge's poetry for the purpose of further illustrating what we mean by the *poetical feeling*.

The first is a description of nocturnal silence from the "Frost at Midnight."

"'Tis calm indeed, so calm that it disturbs
And vexes meditation with its strange
And extreme silentness.
                              Sea, hill, and wood,
    With all the numberless goings-on of life
Inaudible as dreams,
Only that film which fluttered on the grate
Still flutters there, the sole unquiet thing.
Methinks its motion in this hush of nature
Gives it dim sympathies with me, who live
Making it a companionable form."

The following is from the same piece:

"Therefore all seasons shall be sweet to thee,
Whether the summer clothe the general earth
With greenness, or the redbreast sit and sing
Betwixt the tufts of snow on the bare branch
Of mossy apple-tree, while the nigh-thatch
smokes in the sun-thaw. Whether the eave-drops fall
Heard only in the trances of the blast,
Of if the secret ministry of frost
Shall hang them up in silent icicles,
Quietly shining to the quiet moon."

How aptly is a well known state of mind described in the following passage from the ode, entitled, "Dejection."

"A grief without a pang, void, dark, and drear,
A stifled, drowsy, unimpassioned grief,
Which finds no natural outlet, no relief
In word or sigh or tear.

"The Ancient Mariner" is so full of beauties that we find it difficult to make a selection. The description of a vessel becalmed near the equator is probably familiar to many of our readers.

"All in a hot and copper sky
The bloody sun at noon
Right up above the mast did stand
No bigger than the moon.
Day after day, day after day
We struck, nor breath nor motion,
As idle as a painted ship
Upon a painted ocean."

The effects of a sudden breeze are set forth with the same nervous and graphic power.

"But in a minute she 'gan stir
With a short uneasy motion,
Backwards and forwards half her length
With a short uneasy motion:
Then, like a pawing horse let go,
She made a sudden bound."

The influence of superstitious fears is portrayed with great truth.

"Like one who on a lonesome road
Doth walk in fear and dread,
And having once turned round, walks on
And turns no more his head,
Because he knows a frightful fiend
Doth close behind him tread."

Sometimes the poetical merit consists solely in a happy choice of epithets.

"The moonlight *steeped* in *silentness*
The *steady* weathercock."

In the following passage from "Christabel," the poetical feeling is equally diffuse over the whole.

"There is not wind enough to twirl
The one red leaf, the last of its clan
That dances as often as dance it can,
Hanging so light and hanging so high
On the topmost twig that looks up at the sky."

The second characteristic of genius, that which distinguishes its highest degree, relates to form. It may be termed completeness, or the power of producing a well-proportioned whole. By a well-proportioned whole, we mean a work of art in which one central idea pervades, connects, and determines all the parts; where the greatest diversity of matter is nicely balanced by unity of purpose; where the same leading thought shines visibly through every variety of attitude and scene;—a work which, originating in a happy conception, and grounded upon a rational plan, has all its parts proportioned to that plan, pursues a consistent course, has beginning, middle, and end, moulds itself, as it were, by the self-determining power of its subject, into a compact and pleasing form, and produces, when finished, a simple and undivided impression. Thus a good literary composition may be known by the same test by which we judge of an architectural work, unity of design and totality of effect. Some of Shakespeare's plays, "Othello," for example, or "Romeo and Juliet," will illustrate our meaning. Indeed, the greatest literary productions of ancient and modern times, whether dramatic, epic, or didactic, whether they be histories, orations, or systems of philosophy, all are marked with this characteristic. And not only literary production, but all that is great in every department of intellectual exertion, a good painting, a masterpiece of sculpture, or in active life a masterpiece of policy, or in mechanics a useful invention, a well-contrived machine, any and every creation of the human mind, so far as it conforms to this standard,—unity and completeness,—is a work of genius. Genius then, in its most perfect state, is known by its *"perfect work."* A writer in whom this quality is wanting, betrays the defect in the loose and disjointed character of his composition. The difference between such a writer and one who possesses the quality we have described, is like the contrast we may suppose between the *coup d'oeil* of an eagle who surveys whole landscapes from his perch amid the clouds, and the vision of an insect to whose microscopic eye the minutest object divides itself into numberless fragments. The difference in the productions of these men resembles that which distinguishes the growth of an organic from that of a mineral product;—the one developes itself into determinate forms by the evolution of a single germinal principle, the other irregularly swells its bulk by heterogeneous accretions. Mr. Coleridge is one of those in whom this quality of completeness, the power of producing a whole, is entirely wanting. We have never met with a writer whose works are so patched and ill made up. There does not occur to us at this moment a single production of his, which has the least pretensions to shape.

As to the charge of obscurity, so often and obstinately urged against Mr. Coleridge's prose writings, we cannot admit it in any thing like the extent in which it has been applied. So far as there is *any* ground for this complaint, it is owing to the author's excessive anxiety to make himself intelligible, an anxiety which leads him to present a subject in so many points of view, that we are sometimes in danger of losing the main topic amid the variety of collateral and illustrative matter which he gathers round it. We are inclined, however, to suspect that the greater part of this alleged obscurity exists in the mind of the reader, and not in the author. In an age when all classes read, and when a consequent demand for popular works has rendered every thing superficial that could be made superficial, and excluded almost every thing that could not, when the best books in the language are the least read, when such works as Butler's Analogy and others of the same stamp are confined within the narrow circle of professional reading,—while at the same time complaints are heard that we have no good books to put into the hands of infidels,—when in religion and philosophy superficial treatises and books of amusement have almost supplanted scientific inquiry,—when, even in the department of taste, novels and tales supersede Shakespeare and Milton;—in such an age, we are not surprised to hear the charge of obscurity preferred against books whose only fault is that they deserve, and therefore require, a little more study than we are compelled to bestow upon a novel or a tract. It is to be feared that the men of this generation have been spoiled by the indulgence shown to their natural indolence, and made tender by the excessive pains which have been taken to render every thing easy and smooth. Our intellects are dwarfed and stunted by the constant stimulus of amusement which is mixed up with all our literary food. There is no taste for hardy application, no capacity for vigorous and manly efforts of the understanding. Whatever taxes the mind, instead of exciting it, is deemed a burden. A hard word scares us; a proposition, which does not explain itself at first glance, troubles us; whatever is *supersensual* and cannot be made plain by images addressed to the senses, is denounced as obscure, or beckoned away as mystical and extravagant. Whatever lies beyond the limits of ordinary and outward experience, is regarded as the ancient geographers regarded the greater portion of the globe,—as a land of shadows and chimaeras. In a treatise on mechanics or astronomy, many things would be unintelligible to one who is ignorant of mathematics; but would it be fair in such a one to charge the author with a difficulty which arises from his own ignorance? Some writers are clear because they are shallow. If it be complained that Mr. Coleridge is not one of these, we shall not deny a charge which is applicable also, and in a much greater degree to much wiser men. He is certainly not a shallow writer, but, as we think, a very profound one, and his style is for the most part as clear as the nature of his thoughts will admit. To those only is he obscure who have no depths within themselves corresponding to his depths, and such will do well to consider, as Bishop Butler has said in reference to his own work,—"that the question is not whether a more intelligible book might have been written, but whether the subjects which he handles will admit of greater perspicuity in the treatment of them."

In a review of Mr. Coleridge's literary life, we must not omit to notice that marked fondness for metaphysics, and particularly for German metaphysics, which has exercised so decisive an influence over all his writings. Had it been given to him to interpret German metaphysics to his countrymen, as Mr. Cousin has interpreted them to the French nation, or had it been possible for him to have constructed a system of his own, we should not have regretted his indulgence of a passion which we must now condemn as a source of morbid dissatisfaction with received opinions, unjustified by any serious attempt to introduce others and better. From his vigorous understanding, his acute dialectic powers, his complete knowledge of the subject, his historical research, and power of expression, something more might have been expected than the meager sketch contained in his autobiography.[2] That Mr. Coleridge has done so little in the way of original production in his department, we ascribe to the same mental defect which has already been remarked upon, namely, the preponderance of the reflective over the creative faculty, and the consequent inability to collect, and embody in systematic forms, the results of his inquiries. But though so ill-qualified for the work of production, one would think the translator of Wallenstein might have interpreted for us all that is most valuable in the speculation of Kant and his followers. It has been said that these works are untranslatable, but without sufficient grounds. That they are not translatable by one who has not an intimate acquaintance with the transcendental philosophy, is abundantly evident from the recent attempt which has been made in England to translate Tenneman. But in this respect, and indeed in every respect, Mr. Coleridge is eminently fitted for such a task; and it is the more to be regretted that he has not undertaken it, as the number of those who are thus fitted is exceedingly small, while the demand for information on this subject is constantly increasing. We are well aware that a mere translation, however perfect, would be inadequate to convey a definite notion of transcendentalism to one who has not the metaphysical talent necessary to conceive and reproduce in himself a system whose only value to us must depend upon our power to construct it for ourselves from the materials of our own consciousness, and which in fact exists to us only on this condition.

While we are on this ground, we beg leave to offer a few explanatory remarks respecting German metaphysics,[3] which seem to us to be called for by the present state of feeling among literary men in relation to this subject. We believe it impossible to understand fully the design of Kant and his followers, without being endowed to a certain extent with the same powers of abstraction and synthetic generalization which they possess in so eminent a degree. In order to become fully master of their meaning, one must be able to find it in himself. Not all are born to be philosophers, or are capable of becoming philosophers, any more than all are capable of becoming poets or musicians. The works of the transcendental philosophers may be translated word for word, but still it will be impossible to get a clear idea of their philosophy, unless we raise ourselves at once to a transcendental point of view. Unless we take our station with the philosopher and proceed from his ground as our starting-point, the whole system will appear to us an inextricable puzzle. As in astronomy the motions of the heavenly bodies seem confused to the geocentric observer, and are intelligible only when referred to their heliocentric place, so there is only one point from which we can clearly understand and decide upon the speculations of Kant and his followers; that point is the interior consciousness, distinguished from the common consciousness, by its being an active and not a passive state. In the language of the school, it is a free intuition, and can only be attained by a vigorous effort of the will. It is from an ignorance of this primary condition, that the writings of these men have been denounced as vague and mystical. Viewing them from the distance we do, their discussions seem to us like objects half enveloped in mist; the little we can distinguish seems most portentously magnified and distorted by the unnatural refraction through which we behold it, and the point where they touch the earth is altogether lost. The effect of such writing upon the uninitiated, is like being in the company of one who has inhaled an exhilarating gas. We witness the inspiration, and are astounded at the effects, but we can form no conception of the feeling until we ourselves have experienced it. To those who are without the veil, then, any *exposé* of transcendental views must needs be unsatisfactory. Now if any one chooses to deny the point which these writers assume, if any one chooses to call in question the metaphysical existence of this interior consciousness, and to pronounce the whole system a mere fabrication, or a gross self-delusion,–to such a one the disciples of this school have nothing further to say; for him their system was not conceived. Let him content himself, if he can, with "that compendious philosophy which talking of mind, but thinking of brick and mortar, or other images equally abstracted from body, contrives a theory of spirit, by nicknaming matter, and in a few hours can qualify the dullest of its disciples to explain the *omne scibile* by reducing all things to impressions, ideas, and sensations." The disciples of Kant wrote for minds of quite another stamp, they wrote for minds that seek with faith and hope a solution of questions which that philosophy meddles not with,–questions which relate to spirit and form, substance and life, free will and fate, God and eternity. Let those who feel no interest in these questions, or who believe not in the possibility of our approaching any nearer to a solution of them, abstain for ever from a department of inquiry for which they have neither talent nor call. There are certain periods in the history of society, when, passing from a state of spontaneous production to a state of reflection, mankind are particularly disposed to inquire concerning themselves and their destination, the nature of their being, the evidence of their knowledge, and the grounds of their faith. Such a tendency is one of the characteristics of the present age, and the German philosophy is the strongest expression of that tendency; it is a striving after information on subjects which have been usually considered as beyond the reach of human intelligence, an attempt to penetrate the most hidden mysteries of our being. In every philosophy there are three things to be considered, the object, the method, and the result. In the transcendental system, the *object* is to discover in every form of finite existence, an infinite and unconditioned as the ground of its existence, to refer all phenomena to certain *noumena*,[4] or laws of cognition. It is not a *ratio essendi*, but a *ratio cognoscendi;* it seeks not to explain the existence of God and creation, objectively considered, but to explain our knowledge of their existence. It is not a skeptical philosophy;[5] it seeks not to overthrow, but to build up; it wars not with the common opinions and general experience of mankind, but aims to place these on a scientific basis, and to verify them by scientific demonstrations.

The method is synthetical, proceeding from a given point, the lowest that can be found in our consciousness, and deducing from that point, "the whole world of intelligences, with the whole system of their representations." The correctness or philosophical propriety of the construction which is to be based upon this given point, this absolute thesis, must be assumed for a while, until proved by the successful completion of the system which it is designed to establish. The test by which we are to know that the system is complete, and the method correct, is the same as that by which we judge of the correct construction of the material arch,–continuity and self-dependence. The last step in the process, the keystone of the fabric, is the deduction of time, space, and variety, or, in other words, (as time, space, and variety include the elements of all empiric knowledge) the establishing of a coincidence between the facts of ordinary experience and those which we have discovered within ourselves, and scientifically derived from our first fundamental position. When this is accomplished, the system is complete, the hypothetical frame-work may then fall, and the structure will support itself.[6]

We have called the method synthetical; we should rather say that it is an alternation of synthesis and antithesis. Every synthesis, according to Fichte in the "Wissenschaftslehre,"[7] presupposes an antithesis; every antithesis, by limitation of the terms opposed, must be reconciled into a synthesis; in every new synthesis thus obtained, new antitheses are found; these again must be reconciled, and so on, till we come to a stand. The first proposition in the "Wissenschaftslehre" is stated thus, A = A. In this proposition the first term is something, A unconditionally proposed; the second term is the same A reflected upon. I propose A, and then, reflecting upon it, find that it is A. This identity arises not from any quality in the thing proposed; it exists solely in my own consciousness. A = A, because I, the being who proposed it, am the same with I, the being who reflects upon it. Consequently the proposition, A = A, is equivalent to the proposition, I = I. Again, I propose A = A, or A unconditionally denied not equal to A unconditionally proposed; consequently not equal to A, the object of reflection in the former proposition. Now the possibility of my denying A presupposes and depends upon my power of proposing or affirming A.-A is relative, and can exist only so far as A exists in my consciousness. Consequently, I, the being who now denies A, must be the same with I, the being who first proposed or affirmed A, otherwise-A might be equal to A. This is what is meant by identity of consciousness. I find then in consciousness, two opposites apparently incompatible with each other, absolute affirmation, and absolute negation. Here then is the first antithesis. Now how can these two things exist together? Why does not the one exclude the other? They can be reconciled only by the introduction of a new term.[8] This new term is the idea of divisibility or limitation. It is than no longer absolute, but partial affirmation and negation. What was first unconditionally affirmed to exist, and if allowed unconditional existence must of course exclude its opposite, is now allowed to exist only so far as its opposite does not exist, and the opposite exists only so far as this does not exist, i.e. they coexist by mutual limitation; they define and determine each other. The *I* proposes itself as divisible or limitable, and determined by the *not-*, and it proposes the *not-I* as divisible and determined by the *I*, and here we have the first synthesis. In this synthesis we find new antitheses, which, by further qualification must be reconciled as the first was reconciled into new syntheses, and so on till we arrive at absolute unity, or absolute contradiction.

This mode of proceeding is peculiar to Fichte, but it is a form of the method used to a greater or less extent by all the philosophers of that school. Defining it by that which is common to all its forms, we may call it the method of synthetic conclusions from opposite terms. Kant first suggested this method in his treatise entitled "The use of Negative Quantities in Metaphysics." To *him,* the father of the critical philosophy, we are indebted for the successful cultivation of the preparatory, or, to use his own expression, the "propaideutic" branches of the science. He did not himself create a system, but he furnished the hints and materials from which all the systems of his followers have been framed. In his preface to the second edition of the "Critique of pure Reason," he makes us acquainted with the train of reasoning which led to the course he has adopted in his metaphysical inquiries. He had been struck with the fact, that, while other departments of knowledge, availing themselves of scientific method, were constantly and regularly advancing, intellectual philosophy alone, although the most ancient of all sciences, and the one which would remain, though all the rest should be swallowed up in the vortex of an all-ingulphing barbarism,–intellectual philosophy alone, appears to be still groping in the dark, sometimes advancing and sometimes receding, but making on the whole little actual progress. How are we to account for this fact? Is a science of metaphysics impossible? Why then has nature implanted within us this ardent longing after certain and progressive knowledge on subjects of all others the most interesting to the human soul; or how can we place any confidence in our reason, when it fails us in the investigation of such topics as these? But perhaps the fault lies with us. May not our want of success be owing to a wrong method? The science of geometry was probably for some time in the same condition that metaphysical inquiry is now; but ever since the demonstration of the equilateral triangle commonly ascribed to Thales, it has advanced in regular and rapid progression. Physical science has done the same since Bacon. It is evident that both these branches of knowledge are indebted for the success with which they have been cultivated, to the fortunate discovery of a right method. May not the want of such a method constitute the sole obstacle to the progress of metaphysical science? Hitherto philosophers have assumed that our cognitions are determined by the objects they represent. On this assumption it is evident that every attempt to establish any thing *a priori* concerning them (the objects) must be vain. Let us therefore try whether, in metaphysical problems, we may not succeed better by assuming that the objects without us are determined by our cognitions. Copernicus, when he found that he could not explain the motions of the heavenly bodies on the supposition that the starry host revolves around the observer, changed his theory and made the observer revolve, and the stars stand still. Reversing this process, let us, since the supposition that our intuitions depend on the nature of the world without, will not answer, assume that the world without depends on the nature of our intuitions. Thus perhaps we shall be enabled to realize that great desideratum–*a priori* knowledge.

We have here the key to the whole critical philosophy, the very essence of which consists in proposing an absolute self as unconditionally existing, incapable of being determined by any thing higher than itself, but determining all things through itself. On this fundamental position, Fichte, in his "Wissenschaftslehre," endeavoured to found a system of consequential deductions, explanatory of the grounds of all human belief; a system which should serve as a foundation-science for all other sciences. With whatever success this attempt was attended in the author's own estimation, it has never been generally satisfactory to others. The system is altogether too subjective. The possibility of any knowledge of the absolute or self-existing, is denied; we can know only concerning our knowledge; man's personal freedom is the basis of all reality; with many other assertions of like character.

Next to Fichte in the order of time, but differing widely from him as it respects the tendency of their respective systems, appears Schelling, the projector of the "natural philosophy" so called; a branch of transcendentalism which was afterwards more fully developed, and reduced to a system by Oken. If Fichte confined himself too exclusively to the subjective, Schelling on the other hand treats principally of the object, and endeavours to show that the outward world is of the same essence with the thinking mind, both being different manifestations of the same divine principle. He is the ontologist of the Kantian school. All knowledge, according to him,[9] consists in an agreement between an object and a subject. In all science, therefore, there are these two elements or poles, subject and object, or nature and intelligence; and corresponding to these two poles there are two fundamental sciences, the one beginning with nature and proceeding upward to intelligence, the other beginning with intelligence and ending in nature. The first is natural philosophy, the second transcendental philosophy. Of all the Germans who have trod the path of metaphysical inquiry under the guidance of Kant, Schelling is the most satisfactory. In him intellectual philosophy is more ripe, more substantial, more promising, and, if we may apply such a term to such speculations, more practical than in any of the others. Though in one sense a follower of Kant, he begins a new period, and may be considered as the founder of a new school. Of the other successors of Kant, Hegel, Oken, Fries, Reinhold, Krug, Plattner and others, our information would not enable us to say much, and our limits forbid us to say any thing. The three whom we have particularized are the only ones who appear to us to possess much individuality; or to have exercised much influence in the philosophical world. In designat-

ing these, we have done all that this brief sketch requires. We need only add, that the best histories of philosophy, and, with the exception of Cousin's, the only good ones we have, are productions of German philosophers.

If now it be asked, as probably it will be asked, whether any definite and substantial good has resulted from the labors of Kant and his followers, we answer, Much. More than metaphysics ever before accomplished, these men have done for the advancement of the human intellect. It is true the immediate, and if we may so speak, the calculable results of their speculations are not so numerous nor so evident as might have been expected: these are chiefly comprised under the head of method. Yet even here we have enough to make us rejoice that such men have been, and that they have lived and spoken in our day. We need mention only the sharp and rightly dividing lines that have been drawn within and around the kingdom of human knowledge; the strongly marked distinctions of subject and object, reason and understanding, phenomena and noumena;–the categories established by Kant; the moral liberty proclaimed by him as it had never been proclaimed by any before; the authority and evidence of law and duty set forth by Fichte; the universal harmony illustrated by Schelling. But in mentioning these things, which are the direct results of the critical philosophy, we have by no means exhausted all that that philosophy has done for liberty and truth. The preeminence of Germany among the nations of our day in respect of intellectual culture, is universally acknowledged; and we do fully believe that whatever excellence that nation has attained in science, in history, or poetry is mainly owing to the influence of her philosophy, to the faculty which that philosophy has imparted of seizing on the spirit of every question, and determining at once the point of view from which each subject should be regarded,–in one word, to the transcendental method. In theology this influence has been most conspicuous. We are indebted to it for that dauntless spirit of inquiry which has investigated, and for that amazing erudition which has illustrated, every corner of biblical lore. Twice it has saved the religion of Germany,–once from the extreme of fanatic extravagance, and again, from the verge of speculative infidelity. But, though most conspicuous in theology, this influence has been visible in every department of intellectual exertion to which the Germans have applied themselves for the last thirty years. It has characterized each science and each art, and all bear witness to its quickening power. A philosophy which has given such an impulse to mental culture and scientific research, which has done so much to establish and to extend the spiritual in man, and the ideal in nature, needs no apology; it commends itself by its fruits, it lives in its fruits, and must ever live, though the name of its founder be forgotten, and not one of its doctrines survive.

We have wandered far from the subject of our critique. It is time we should return and take our final leave. It was not our intention in this brief review of Mr. Coleridge's literary merits to criticize in particular any one of the works whose titles stand at the head of this article. But the "Aids to Reflection," as containing an account of the author's religious views, demand a passing notice in a work like this. In his biography, Mr. Coleridge describes the state of his mind, with respect to religion, previous to his leaving England, by saying that his head was with Spinoza, and his heart with Paul and John; which means, we presume, that he found it impossible to reconcile his religion with his philosophy. In another passage, he tells us that he was at this time a Unitarian, "or more accurately a *Psilanthropist,*" which term he chooses to consider as synonymous with the former. We understand it very differently. Psilanthropism, according to our definition, mens Humanitarianism,–a doctrine which has no more necessary connexion with the Unitarian faith than with the Roman Catholic. In the "Aids to Reflection," our author would have us believe that he has accomplished at last the wished for reconciliation between his head and his heart. To us the breach seems as wide as ever. In this work he appears as a zealous Trinitarian, and a warm defender of the doctrines of the English church. We have no doubt of his sincerity; but unless we err greatly, he has either misunderstood his own views, or grossly misinterpreted the doctrines of his church. His view of the Trinity, as far as we can understand it, is as consistent with Unitarianism, to say the least, as his former psilanthropic scheme. His opinion of the atonement is far from Orthodox; the idea of vicarious suffering he rejects with disdain. The strong expressions used by St. Paul in reference to this subject, he tells us are not intended to designate the *act* of redemption, but are only figurative expressions descriptive of its effects. The *act* of redemption he calls a "mystery," which term, as it may mean any thing, means, in reality, nothing. The other doctrines fare in the same way. Every thing is first mystified into a sort of imposing indis-

tinctness, and then pronounced to be genuine Orthodoxy. The truth is, Mr. Coleridge, though a great scholar, was not qualified in point of biblical learning for an undertaking like this. Many of his assertions, we are persuaded, would not have been hazarded, had he not taken his understanding of the New Testament for granted, but studied that book with the same diligence and perseverance which he appears to have bestowed upon other works. With these exceptions, however, we consider the "Aids to Reflection" as a very valuable work. The distinctions between prudence and morality, and between natural and spiritual religion, are sound and important.

On the whole, in summing up Mr. Coleridge's merits, we cannot but regard him as endowed with an intellect of the highest order, as a profound thinker, and a powerful writer, though not a successful poet or an amiable critic. As a translator, he has no equal in English literature. His prejudices are strong,[10] his tastes confined, his pedantry often oppressive, his egotism unbounded. Yet we can never read a chapter in any one of his prose works, without feeling ourselves intellectually exalted and refined. Never can we sufficiently admire the depth and richness of his thoughts, the beauty of his illustrations, the exceeding fitness and force of all his words. If he is too minute in details to shine in the higher walls of literature, too anxious in the elaboration of single parts, to succeed in the total effect, it must be allowed that few compositions will bear so close an inspection, and still maintain their color and their gloss so well as his. If he divides nature and life and human art into too many particulars, it cannot be denied that his divisions, like those of the prism, give to each particular an individuality and a glory, which it did not possess while merged and lost in the whole to which it belonged. If he has produced far less than might have been expected from a mind so ready and so rich, we will nevertheless cheerfully accord to him the credit which he claims in his own appeal against a similar charge. "Would that the criterion of a scholar's utility were the number and moral value of the truths which he has been the means of throwing into the general circulation, or the number and value of the minds whom by his conversation or letters he has excited into activity, and supplied with the germs of their after-growth. A distinguished rank might not even then be awarded to my exertions, but I should dare look forward with confidence to an honorable acquittal."[11]

1. See Biographia Literaria, Chapter 1.
2. See Biographia Literaria, Chapter 12.
3. When we speak of *German* metaphysics we wish to be understood as referring to the systems of intellectual philosophy which have prevailed in Germany since Kant. Our remarks do not apply to Leibnitz, Wolf, or any of Kant's predecessors.
4. Kant, Kritik der renen Vernunft.
5. Perhaps the writings of Fichte may be considered as an exception to this statement.
6. We give the *ideal* of the method proposed; we are by no means prepared to say that this idea has been realized, or that it can be realized.
7. translates this word, "lore of ultimate science;" it means the science of knowing.
8. It was found necessary to abridge the process so much, that perhaps the conclusions may not appear strictly consequential. Let it be understood, then, that affirmation and negation stand for existence and non-existence,-the *I* and *not-I*,-which, of course, when absolute must eventually exclude each other.
9. Schelling. Transcendentaler Idealismus.
10. Mr. Coleridge's prejudices against the French nation, and all that belongs to them, are unreasonable and absurd in the extreme. He is said, upon one occasion, during the delivery of a public lecture, in the presence of a numerous assembly, to have thanked God in the most serious manner for so ordering events, "that he was entirely ignorant of a single word of that frightful jargon, the French language."
11. Biographia Literaria, Chapter 10.

[Elizabeth Palmer Peabody]

Preface to *Record of a School: Exemplifying the General Principles of Spiritual Culture,* 2d ed. (Boston: Russell, Shattuck; New York: Leavitt, Lord, 1836), pp. 1–10.

Elizabeth Palmer Peabody served as an assistant in Bronson Alcott's Temple School in Boston, and her transcripts of the class meetings formed the basis for the Record *of that school. Alcott believed that the source of truth was to be found within each child's consciousness, and therefore he used inductive, Socratic methods to unfold the intuitive powers of his charges. He re-created a pleasant, home–like atmosphere in his classroom and deplored corporal punishment, merely excluding problem children from the group until they had demonstrated a desire to return by settling down. Peabody's explanation of Alcott's educational practices in the first edition of* Record of a School *(1835) was considered unclear by many, and in the second edition (the text of which is reprinted below) she clarified her comments. (For further information on these educators and reformers, see the entries for Alcott and Peabody in* DLB 1, The American Renaissance in New England.)

Plans.

Mr. Alcott re–commenced his school in Boston, after four years interval, September, 1834, at the Masonic Temple, No. 7.

Believing that the objects which meet the sénses every day for years, must necessarily mould the mind, he felt it necessary to choose a spacious room, and ornament it, not with such furniture as only an upholsterer can appreciate, but with such forms as would address and cultivate the imagination and heart.

In the four corners of the room, therefore, he placed upon pedestals, fine busts of Socrates, Shakspeare, Milton, and Sir Walter Scott. And on a table, before the large gothic window by which the room is lighted, the Image of Silence, "with his finger up, as though he said, beware." Opposite this gothic window,

was his own table, about ten feet long, whose front is the arc of a circle, prepared with little desks for the convenience of the scholars. On this, he placed a small figure of a child aspiring. Behind was a very large bookcase, with closets below, a black tablet above, and two shelves filled with books. A fine cast of Christ, in basso–relievo, fixed into this bookcase, is made to appear to the scholars just over the teacher's head. The bookcase itself, is surmounted with a bust of Plato.

On the northern side of the room, opposite the door, was the table of the assistant, with a small figure of Atlas, bending under the weight of the world. On a small bookcase behind the assistant's chair, were placed figures of a child reading, and a child drawing. Some old pictures; one of Harding's portraits; and several maps were hung on the walls.

The desks for the scholars, with conveniences for placing all their books in sight, and with black tablets hung over them, which swing forward, when they wish to use them, are placed against the wall round the room, that when in their seats for study, no scholar need look at another. On the right hand of Mr. Alcott is a sofa for the accommodation of visitors, and a small table, with a pitcher and bowl. Great advantages arise from this room, every part of which speaks the thoughts of Genius. It is a silent reproach upon rudeness.

About twenty children came the first day. They were all under ten years of age, excepting two or three girls. I became his assistant, to teach Latin to such as might desire to learn.

Mr. Alcott sat behind his table, and the children were placed in chairs, in a large arc around him; the chairs so far apart, that they could not easily touch each other. He then asked each one separately, what idea he or she had of the purpose of coming to school? To learn; was the first answer. To learn what? By pursuing this question, all the common exercises of school were brought up by the children themselves; and various subjects of art, science, and philosophy. Still Mr. Alcott intimated that this was not all; and at last some one said "to behave well," and in pursuing this expression into its meanings, they at last decided that they came to learn to feel rightly, to think rightly, and to act rightly. A boy of seven years old suggested, and all agreed, that the most important of these three, was right action.

Simple as all this seems, it would hardly be believed what an evident exercise it was to the children, to be led of themselves to form and express these conceptions and few steps of reasoning. Every face was eager and interested. From right actions, the conversation naturally led into the means of bringing them out. And the necessity of feeling in earnest, of thinking clearly, and of school discipline, was talked over. School discipline was very carefully considered; both Mr. Alcott's duty, and the children's duties, also various means of producing attention, self–control, perseverance, faithfulness, Among these means, punishment was mentioned; and after a consideration of its nature and issues, they all very cheerfully agreed, that it was necessary; and that they preferred Mr. Alcott should punish them, rather than leave them in their faults, and that it was his duty to do so. Various punishments were mentioned, and hurting the body was decided

upon, as necessary and desirable in some instances. It was universally admitted that it was desirable, whenever words were found insufficient to command the memory of conscience.

After this conversation, which involved many anecdotes, many supposed cases, and many judgements, Mr. Alcott read "The Peaches," from Krummacher's fables, a story which involves the free action of three boys of different characters; and questioned them respecting their opinion of these boys, and the principles on which it was seen by analysis that they acted. Nearly three hours passed away in this conversation and reading; and then they were asked, how long they had been sitting; none of them thought more than an hour. After recess Mr. Alcott heard them read; and after that, spell. All could read in such a book as Miss Edgeworth's Frank. Each was then asked what he had learned, and having told, they were dismissed one by one. The whole effect of the day seemed to be a combination of quieting influences, with an awakening effect upon the heart and mind.The next day, a conversation somewhat like the former was commenced; and Mr. Alcott showed that he intended to have profound attention. When any one's eyes wandered he waited to have them return to him, and he required that they should sit very still in their comfortable chairs. The questions, by interesting them very much, aided them in this effort. After recalling the conclusions of the day before, more fables from Krummacher were read. These he paraphrased, interrupting himself continually, to enforce what was read, by addressing it particularly to individuals; requiring them now to guess what was coming next, and now to tell what they thought of things said and done. Then they all read, and spelled, and, after recess, were replaced in their seats; where each found a rule blank–book and a lead pencil; with a printed volume, from which they were directed to copy a passage. Only half a dozen could write. He told the rest, even the youngest, to copy the words in printed letters, and this occupied them very diligently until school was done.

Mr. Alcott's mode of teaching the art of writing is the result of a good deal of thought; having grown out of his own experience as a teacher. He early discovered how to obtain a ready command of his pen, without instruction from others; and, having reasoned on the methods which necessity suggested to himself, he has reduced them very happily to their principles, and

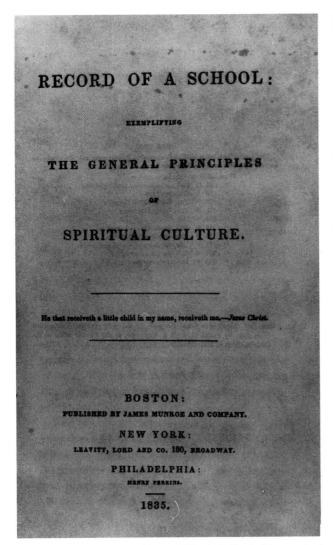

RECORD OF A SCHOOL:

EXEMPLIFYING

THE GENERAL PRINCIPLES

OF

SPIRITUAL CULTURE.

He that receiveth a little child in my name, receiveth me.—*Jesus Christ.*

BOSTON:
PUBLISHED BY JAMES MUNROE AND COMPANY.

NEW YORK:
LEAVITT, LORD AND CO. 180, BROADWAY.

PHILADELPHIA:
HENRY PERKINS.

1835.

Title page for the first edition of Elizabeth Peabody's report of Bronson Alcott's teaching methods in his Temple School

constructed them into a natural system, whose results are worth noticing in this place.

When children are committed to his charge very young, the first discipline to which he puts them, is of the eye; by making them familiar with pictures. The art of Drawing has well been called the art of learning to see; and perhaps no person ever began to learn to draw, without astonishment at finding how imperfectly he had always been seeing. He finds that the most common forms are not only very falsely defined on his sense, but a vast deal that is before the eyes, is entirely overlooked. The human mind seems very gradually to descend from its own infinity into the details of the finite; and the senses give but little help when unaided by a developed mind. It has been demonstrated,

not only by the acute reasonings of philosophers, but by observations made on persons,[1] who have begun to see at late periods of life, that the eye sees scarcely any thing but what the mind has suggested beforehand. Yet by a reciprocal influence of the mind and the organ, this "avenue of wisdom," may become very broad. By attention to children's habits, and by exercise, their minds may very early attain great perfection in the use of this instrument, than which none is finer of all that are given to us; and none more effective in bringing to our fixed point in the universe that variety of the Almighty's manifestation of himself, to which it is necessary for us to have access, in order to be able to clothe our inward life with forms, by which it may manifest itself to kindred beings; carrying them and ourselves on, into harmony with the Divine intellect, and sympathy with his spirit. The Phrenologists say it was their first discovery, that persons who had prominent eyes were remarkable for their powers of learning and using language. Now, as all language is founded on imagery, it follows that fine and perfect organs of sight, giving to the mind vivid impressions of the forms of things, would, in this way, make the language of the individual picturesque and lifely, and thus, even without resorting to the theory of Phrenology, the fact of prominent or fine eyes, connected with great powers of language, has an explanation. But without reference to this influence of clear vision upon expression, there can be no doubt of its effect upon thought. The forms of things are God's address to the human soul. They are the first incitements to activity of mind; or to speak more accurately, they are the first supporters of that Activity which is the nature of the mind, and which can only be checked by the soul's being starved of nature.

It is from considerations of this kind, that Mr. Alcott very early presents to children pictured forms of things; and he selects them in the confidence that the general character of these forms will do much towards setting the direction of the current of activity, especially if we attend to and favour those primal sympathies, with which nature seems to wed different minds to different portions of the universe. But the practice of the eye, in looking at forms, and that of the hand in imitating them, should be simultaneous. Mr. Alcott thinks the slate and pencil, or the chalk and blackboard can hardly be given too early. The latter is even better than the former; for children should have free scope, as we find that their first shapings are always gigantic.

Francis Graeter's drawing of Bronson Alcott's Temple School, which appeared in the second edition of Record of a School

And is it not best that they should be so? Miniature, when it appears first in the order of development, seems to be always the effect of checked spirit or some artificial influence.

With such education of the eye, as a preliminary, reading and writing are begun simultaneously; and the former will be very much facilitated, and the latter come to perfection in a much shorter time, than by the usual mode. By copying print, which does not require such a sweep of hand as the script character, a clear image of each letter is gradually fixed in the mind; and while the graceful curves of the script are not attained till afterwards, yet they are attained quite as early as by the common method of beginning with them; and the clearness and distinctness of print, is retained in the script, which, from being left to form itself so freely, becomes also characteristic of each individual's particular mind.

When the pages were presented to Mr. Alcott after their first trial, the hieroglyphics were sufficiently unintelligible it must be confessed. But, (and this is another proof of how slowly the mind appreciates the arbitrary and finite,) the serious looks of the children, especially of the younger ones, as they exhibited their strange copies, betrayed no misgivings as to the want of resemblance; nor did Mr. Alcott rudely point it out.

He took the writing for what it was meant to be; knowing that practice would at once mend the eye and hand; but that criticism would check the desirable courage and self–confidence.

In the course of a few days, cards were placed at the desk of each child, on which were very large forms of the letters; and they were encouraged to imitate them. It soon became a regular arrangement for the children to pass their first school hour at this employment, and to return to it after the recess. After some weeks, they were taught the small script letter, but not to supersede the exercises in printing. Indeed, throughout the whole teaching, Mr. Alcott recommends that this system of printing should be retained, (especially in all those written exercises, which children are tempted to slight;) for it prevents the habit of indistinct writing, by keeping the imagination wonted to the original forms of the letters.

The ultimate and sure result of this plan, is a simple unflourishing choreography, whose great and characteristic merit is intelligibleness; and constant practice in writing the script, gradually adds to this merit the grace of beauty. When a child begins on this plan of writing, at five years of age, by the time he is seven or eight, he has much of the ease of the practised penman, combining considerable rapidity with perfect intelli-

[A. Bronson Alcott]

Record of Conversations on the Gospels, 2 vols. (Boston: James Munroe, 1836-1837), 1:60-73, 228-237.

Even before the publication of the first volume of Alcott's Conversations, *Boston was worried. Rumors spread that he was discoursing about religion and sex before young children. He was, but only in the most general ways, trying to elicit his students' feelings about those matters so as to make them fit subjects for conversation and contemplation, not dark secrets beyond their comprehensions. The publication of the first volume of his book in December 1836 brought immediate reaction. Elizabeth Palmer Peabody, who had recorded the Conversations, distanced herself from Alcott in a letter in which she requested him to state "that your Recorder did not entirely sympathize or agree with you." Andrews Norton, the leading conservative Unitarian, was quoted in print as saying that one-third of the book was absurd, one-third blasphemous, and one-third obscene. Emerson came to Alcott's defense, publishing a letter in his behalf in the* Boston Courier *and writing him that "I hate to have all the little dogs barking at you," but the public outcry sent the Temple School into a decline: Many people withdrew their children and after Alcott racially integrated the school in 1839, only two students were left. Alcott quit the school and moved to Concord in 1840.*

Amos Bronson Alcott in 1857 as drawn by Caroline Hildreth

[19]

CONVERSATION VIII.

NATIVITY OF SPIRIT.

FAMILY RELATION.

Birth and Naming of John the Baptist, from the Sacred Text. — Ideas of Birth-place and Birth. — Birth. — Sacredness of Birth. — Travail of Body with Spirit. — Emblems of Birth. — Naming of Spirit incarnate. — Influence of Nature on Imagination. — Analysis of Zacharias' Prophecy. — Emblems of John and Jesus. — Prejudice. — Subject.

Review. Mr. Alcott began by asking, What was our conversation upon the last time? CHARLES and OTHERS. The journey of Mary. The visit to her cousin Elisabeth. Their conversation. Mr. Alcott then read

THE BIRTH AND NAMING OF JOHN THE BAPTIST.

LUKE i. 57 to the end.

Before the Vulgar Æra, 5, Julian Period, 4709.

Birth and Naming.

Hebron.

57 Now Elisabeth's full time came that she should be delivered: and she brought forth a son.

58 And her neighbours and her cousins heard how the Lord had showed great mercy upon her; and they rejoiced with her.

59 And it came to pass, that on the eighth day they came to circumcise the child; and they called him Zacharias, after the name of his father.

60 And his mother answered and said, Not so; but he shall be called John.

61 And they said unto her, There is none of thy kindred that is called by this name.

62 And they made signs to his father, how he would have him called.

63 And he asked for a writing-table, and wrote, saying, His name is John. And they marvelled all.

64 And his mouth was opened immediately, and his tongue loosed, and he spake and praised God.

FAMILY RELATION.

61

Before the Vulgar Æra, 5, Julian Period, 4709.

Hebron.

65 And fear came on all that dwelt round about them: and all these sayings were noised abroad throughout all the hill country of Judea.

66 And all they that heard them laid them up in their hearts, saying, What manner of child shall this be! And the hand of the Lord was with him.

67 And his father Zacharias was filled with the Holy Ghost, and prophesied, saying,

68 Blessed be the Lord God of Israel;
For he hath visited and redeemed his people,

69 * And hath raised up an horn of salvation for us,
In the house of his servant David;

70 † As he spake by the mouth of his holy prophets,
Which have been since the world began:

71 That we should be saved from our enemies,
And from the hand of all that hate us:

72 To perform the mercy promised to our fathers,
And to remember his holy covenant;

73 ‡ The oath which he sware to our father Abraham,

74 That he would grant unto us,
That we, being delivered out of the hand of our enemies,
Might serve him without fear,

75 In holiness and righteousness before him,
All the days of our life.

76 And thou, child, shalt be called the prophet of the Highest,
For thou shalt go before the face of the Lord to prepare his ways;

77 To give knowledge of salvation unto his people,
By the remission of their sins,

78 Through the tender mercy of our God;
Whereby the day-spring from on high hath visited us,

79 To give light to them that sit in darkness and in the shadow of death;
To guide our feet into the way of peace.

80 And the child grew, and waxed strong in spirit, and was in the deserts till the day of his showing unto Israel.

Ps. cxxxii. 17.

† Jer. xxiii. 6. xxx. 10.

‡ Gen. xxii. 16.

Idea of Birth-place and Birth.

Now what came into your minds while I was reading?

JOSIAH. The deserts seemed to me a great space covered with sand, like that in the hour-glass. The sun was shining on it, and making it sparkle. There were no trees. John was there alone.

VOL. I. 6

62   RECORD OF CONVERSATIONS.

EDWARD J. I thought the deserts meant woods, with paths here and there.

LUCY. I thought of a space covered with grass and some wild flowers, and John walking about.

CHARLES. I thought of a prairie.

ALEXANDER. I thought of a rocky country.

AUGUSTINE. I thought of a few trees scattered over the country, with bees in the trunks.

GEORGE K. I thought of a place without houses, excepting John's; and flowers, trees, and bee-hives.

Birth.

MR. ALCOTT. I should like to hear all your pictures, but as I have not time, you may tell me now what interested you most? (See Note 83.)

CHARLES. The prophecy of Zacharias.

LUCIA. Elisabeth's saying the child's name must be John.

LUCY. Zacharias finding his speech again.

ANDREW. The birth of the child.

MR. ALCOTT. How was it?

ANDREW. I thought, one night, as Elizabeth was sleeping, an angel brought her a child, and made her dream she had one, and she awoke and it was lying at her side.

WILLIAM B. I think he was born like other children except that Elisabeth had visions. (See Note 84.)

GEORGE K. I thought God sent an angel to give her a child. It cried as soon as it came and waked up its mother to give it something to eat.

LUCIA. When John was first born, his mother did not know it, for he was born in the night; but she found it by her side in the morning.

CHARLES. Elisabeth must have had some vision as well as Zacharias, or how could she know the child was theirs? Zacharias could not speak.

NATHAN. I don't see why John came in the night. All other children come in the day.

FAMILY RELATION.   63

Sacredness of Birth.

MR. ALCOTT. No; more frequently in the night. God draws a veil over these sacred events, and they ought never to be thought of except with reverence. The coming of a spirit is a great event. It is greater than death. It should free us from all wrong thoughts. (See Note 85.)

What is meant by "delivered"?

Travail of Body with Spirit.

WILLIAM B. She delivered her child to Zacharias.

OTHERS. No; God delivered the child to Elisabeth.

CHARLES. Elisabeth's thoughts made the child's soul, and when it was fairly born she was delivered from the anxiety of the thought.*

Emblems of Birth.

MR. ALCOTT. You may give me some emblems of birth.

ALEXANDER. Birth is like the rain. It comes from heaven.

LUCIA. I think it is like a small stream coming from a great sea; and it runs back every night, and so becomes larger and larger every day, till at last it is large enough to send out other streams.

LEMUEL. Lives streamed from the ocean first; now smaller streams from the larger ones, and so on.

SAMUEL R. Birth is like the rising light of the sun; the setting is death.

* MR. ALCOTT. Yes, the deliverance of the spirit is the first thing. And I am glad to find, that you have so strong an impression of that. The physiological facts, sometimes referred to, are only a sign of the spiritual birth. You have seen the rose opening from the seed with the assistance of the atmosphere; this is the birth of the rose. It typifies the bringing forth of the spirit, by pain, and labor, and patience. (See Note 86.) ED.

64   RECORD OF CONVERSATIONS.

ANDREW. God's wind came upon the ocean of life, and washed up the waters a little into a channel, and that is birth. They run up farther, and that is living.

MR. ALCOTT. I should like to have all your emblems but have not time. There is no adequate sign of birth in the outward world, except the physiological facts that attend it, with which you are not acquainted.

Naming of Spirit Incarnate.

Why did they call the child John?

SEVERAL. Because the angel told them to.

RECORDER. The Hebrew word *John* means gift of God. They felt he was so kindly given that they called him Gift. (See Note 87.)

MR. ALCOTT. Why did the people marvel?

FRANKLIN and OTHERS. Because it was the custom to name children from relations.

JOSEPH. And the people did not know that the angel had told them to name him John.

MR. ALCOTT. What loosed Zacharias' tongue?

EDWARD J. The power of God.

ANOTHER. His faith.

LUCIA. The child was born, and it was said that he should speak then.

CHARLES. It was promised that he should speak.

FRANK. Because God did not want to make the angel tell a lie.

FRANKLIN. It was a reward of his obedience.

WILLIAM B. He gave up a natural desire to name him from himself.

Influence of Nature on Imagination.

MR. ALCOTT. Why was it "noised abroad"?

SEVERAL. It was a great event to have a child born from such old parents.

MR. ALCOTT. And in the country, especially a hilly country, the people being imaginative, seem quite disposed to look beyond external things. They are apt

FAMILY RELATION.   65

to think singular events typify, or are a sign of, something supernatural. (See Note 88.) They wondered what kind of child this would be.

Analysis of the Prophecy of Zacharias.

How had the Lord "visited his people"? (See Note 89.)

LEMUEL. He had visited their spirits.

FRANKLIN. By sending John to tell that Jesus was coming.

MR. ALCOTT. What is it to redeem a people?

LUCIA. To make them good.

EDWARD B. To save them from sin.

MR. ALCOTT. A man who loves to eat and drink, an intemperate man, a passionate man, is a slave to the body; and when his spirit is released from his body, by renewing thoughts, that withdraw his attention from his body, he is redeemed, just as a prisoner taken out of a dungeon is said to be redeemed from captivity. (See note 90.) What is meant by "horn of salvation"?

CHARLES. A great deal of mercy.

MR. ALCOTT. What is meant by "house of David"?

FRANKLIN. Jesus was a descendant of David.

MR. ALCOTT. What enemies are mentioned here?

CHARLES. Spiritual enemies.

MR. ALCOTT. What fathers are meant here?

CHARLES. All good people who went before.

MR. ALCOTT. What is "holy covenant"?

(No answer.)

It is a promise, on condition of holiness, of giving blessings. And the oath?

(*Here it was found necessary to discriminate between profane swearing and judicial oaths, which they had confounded.* (See Note 91.)

Is there any such promise to us, as was made by that covenant?

6*

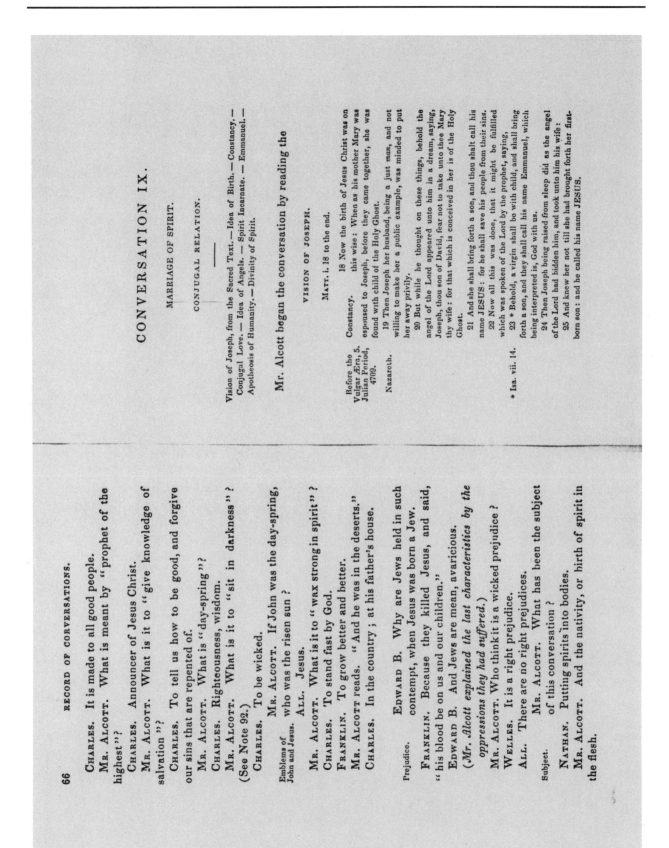

66   RECORD OF CONVERSATIONS.

CHARLES. It is made to all good people.

MR. ALCOTT. What is meant by "prophet of the highest"?

CHARLES. Announcer of Jesus Christ.

MR. ALCOTT. What is it to "give knowledge of salvation"?

CHARLES. To tell us how to be good, and forgive our sins that are repented of.

MR. ALCOTT. What is "day-spring"?

CHARLES. Righteousness, wisdom.

MR. ALCOTT. What is it to "sit in darkness"? (See Note 92.)

CHARLES. To be wicked.

Emblems of John and Jesus.

MR. ALCOTT. If John was the day-spring, who was the risen sun?

ALL. Jesus.

MR. ALCOTT. What is it to "wax strong in spirit"?

CHARLES. To stand fast by God.

FRANKLIN. To grow better and better.

MR. ALCOTT reads. "And he was in the deserts."

CHARLES. In the country; at his father's house.

EDWARD B. Why are Jews held in such contempt, when Jesus was born a Jew.

FRANKLIN. Because they killed Jesus, and said, "his blood be on us and our children."

EDWARD B. And Jews are mean, avaricious.

Prejudice.

(*Mr. Alcott explained the last characteristics by the oppressions they had suffered.*)

MR. ALCOTT. Who think it is a wicked prejudice?

WELLES. It is a right prejudice.

ALL. There are no right prejudices.

Subject.

MR. ALCOTT. What has been the subject of this conversation?

NATHAN. Putting spirits into bodies.

MR. ALCOTT. And the nativity, or birth of spirit in the flesh.

CONVERSATION IX.

MARRIAGE OF SPIRIT.

CONJUGAL RELATION.

Vision of Joseph, from the Sacred Text. — Idea of Birth. — Constancy. — Conjugal Love. — Idea of Angels. — Spirit Incarnate. — Emmanuel. — Apotheosis of Humanity. — Divinity of Spirit.

Mr. Alcott began the conversation by reading the

VISION OF JOSEPH.

MATT. i. 18 to the end.

Before the Vulgar Æra, 5, Julian Period, 4709. Nazareth.

Constancy.

18 Now the birth of Jesus Christ was on this wise: When as his mother Mary was espoused to Joseph, before they came together, she was found with child of the Holy Ghost.

19 Then Joseph her husband, being a *just man*, and not willing to make her a public example, was minded to put her away privily.

20 But while he thought on these things, behold the angel of the Lord appeared unto him in a dream, saying, Joseph, thou son of David, fear not to take unto thee Mary thy wife: for that which is conceived in her is of the Holy Ghost.

21 And she shall bring forth a son, and thou shalt call his name JESUS: for he shall save his people from their sins.

22 Now all this was done, that it might be fulfilled which was spoken of the Lord by the prophet, saying,

23 * Behold, a virgin shall be with child, and shall bring forth a son, and they shall call his name Emmanuel, which being interpreted is, God with us.

24 Then Joseph being raised from sleep did as the angel of the Lord had bidden him, and took unto him his wife:

25 And knew her not till she had brought forth her first-born son: and he called his name JESUS.

* Isa. vii. 14.

68   RECORD OF CONVERSATIONS.

After the reading Mr. Alcott asked what interested them most.

Idea of Birth.   JOSIAH. I thought most of Jesus' being born.*

EDWARD C. I thought I saw Jesus come down from heaven, when you read.

WILLIAM B. When mothers have children they are always good, better than at other times. Mary's vision had made her good—better than other people, and so her child was better.

LUCY. I liked the angel's appearing to Joseph and telling him not to be afraid.

SAMUEL T. It was beautiful where the angel came to Joseph in a dream.

AUGUSTINE. The birth was so peculiar, because the child was different, more holy than other children. If such a child should come again, there would be the same signs and wonders, that the father and mother might get ready to take care of it. (See Note 94.)

ALEXANDER. The angel came, so that Mary and Joseph might become good; so that they could teach their child, lest he should have faults.

JOHN B. I imagined the angel, but I cannot put my idea into words.

Constancy.   FRANK. The angel ought to have told Joseph that it would be wrong for him not to marry Mary, after he had promised to. (See Note 95.)

* Mr. Alcott. And what did you think being born was?
Josiah. It is to take up the body from the earth. The spirit comes from heaven, and takes up the naughtiness out of other people, which makes other people better. And these naughtinesses, put together, make a body for the child; but the spirit is the best part of it. (See Note 93.) Ed.

CONJUGAL RELATION.   69

Mr. Alcott. That is just what the angel did tell him.

Edward B. I thought of Joseph lying on a splendid bed in a splendid room. And the angel had on a white glistening robe, flowing round his feet, and a golden girdle round his waist, and a glittering crown and wand, and flaxen hair over his shoulders, and he told Joseph to keep his promise.

Recorder. How could a poor carpenter in Nazareth, have a splendid room?

Edward B. An angel would not come into a poor looking room. It would not be appropriate.

Recorder. Do they never visit poor men's huts?

(After some conversation, Edward seemed to think, that such outward splendors were not particularly appropriate to angels, at least, upholstery.)

Mr. Alcott. Was this angel in Joseph's mind or out of it?

Edward B. There was a real angel, but different persons' imaginations would have shaped him differently. I believe there are different kinds of angels:—Some are to be born as men; some are ministering angels, who had lived in bodies once; some who like Gabriel, have never had a body, and never will have one. These are called visiting angels.

Edward J. I wonder why the angel did not tell Joseph to marry Mary before?

Mr. Alcott. Did he not tell him what to do, as soon as he began to inquire what he should do?*

*Edward J. I should think the father would know about the child's coming, as soon as the mother.
Mr. Alcott. Mothers always know first. (See Note 96.)
Edward J. Yes; because they have most to do with the children. Ed.

70   RECORD OF CONVERSATIONS.

Conjugal Love. GEORGE K. I thought about Joseph's kindness to Mary. I think that he always let her choose about things, what they should have for dinner, and such things (See Note 97); and when he had any thing, he always gives it to her, and would go any where to carry things when she asked him to. I think Joseph had a good room, because he was a carpenter, and could make every thing; but I think an angel would be more likely to go to a poor person's house, because the poor are generally happier.

MR. ALCOTT. Do any of the rest of you think as George does, that the poor are the happiest.

(*All held up their hands but Edward B.*) (See Note 98.)

CHARLES. I was interested in the angel's coming to tell Joseph that he need not fear to marry Mary.

MR. ALCOTT. Why do you think Joseph doubted about it?

CHARLES. Because he thought Mary was too holy for him, and he did not want to have the child be the son of a carpenter's wife, lest people should not think so much of him.

ANDREW. I think the reason the angel told him to marry Mary was, because she was going to have such a holy child, who would make him a better man.

LUCIA. I though of Joseph walking in the fields, where there was grass and flowers. He was thinking about marrying Mary, and he lay down and went to sleep, and an angel came, with glistening hair and robes, and a dove on each shoulder, and told him to marry Mary.

MR. ALCOTT. Was he alone?

LUCIA. Yes; there was no other person holy enough to know any thing about it.

MR. ALCOTT. How did the angel look to you?

CONJUGAL RELATION.   71

LUCIA. As small as an infant, and had a smile like a child, and his words sounded like music.

Idea of Angels. MR. ALCOTT. Do you generally think of angels as infants?

ALL. I do! I do! (See Note 99.)

Spirit Incarnate. EMMA. I was interested in the name "God with us." I thought it meant that Jesus was God, though on earth.

CHARLES. I think it means that God will be with the parents of Jesus, because God's spirit is in Jesus, and so with them.

MR. ALCOTT. Is God's spirit always in Children?

CHARLES. God's spirit was in him more than in any other; because he was more pure.

ANDREW. I think it means that God had faith in them all.

JOHN B. It means that God was in the child and his mother.

EDWARD J. I thought of greatness and goodness in Jesus Christ; and that Jesus Christ would be with men. So he was God with us.

EDWARD B. It means Jesus was more like God than any one else.

Emmanuel. Do the words Jesus and Emmanuel mean the same?

MR. ALCOTT. One of the prophets, speaking of a great era, a renovation of things by the spirit, said it would bring God among men. And Matthew quoted these words, saying, that they were fulfilled, when Jesus was born, for he was a God among men. (See Note 100.)

GEORGE K. He was called God because he was so much like God, and was with his disciples, so he was Emmanuel.

MR. ALCOTT. What disciples was he with?

72 RECORD OF CONVERSATIONS.

GEORGE K. Luke and John and those; but he is spiritually with all good men. It says, in a book which I have at home,—

"If I could find some cave unknown,
Where human feet had never trod,
Yet there I should not be alone,
On every side there would be God."

JOSIAH. I think Emmanuel means, that God was so very good as to send Jesus to make men repent, and so when he came, it was said that God was with us.

Apotheosis of Humanity.
FRANK. If you call Jesus God, and God God, I think there would be two Gods, and that is the same as worshipping statues.

AUGUSTINE. I think that Jesus and God are not two but one. If we were to say Jesus, or to say God, we should mean the same thing, only Jesus is God in a body.

JOHN B. I think the same.

GEORGE K. God is God; Jesus is godlike. (See Note 101.)*

Divinity of Spirit.
MR. ALCOTT. Is there any one word which may express this idea of God with us?

* It will be observed that Mr. Alcott does not decide between such differing views. All opinions seem to be represented by the different children, and there is something characteristic in the views which they take. Very few seem indoctrinated at home. The same original difference of mind, which originates different creeds, originates them here. They have formed their own creeds; and these sometimes differ from those of their parents. Mr. Alcott leads them to express their views, and then leaves these to make their own impression, confident that truth will prevail in the end. REC.

CONJUGAL RELATION. 73

AUGUSTINE. Spirit.
ANDREW. Conscience.
FRANK. Immortality.
MR. ALCOTT. Is God with us?
(*All held up hands.*) (See Note 102.)
How many think our life is God?
AUGUSTINE. God makes our life.
MR. ALCOTT. How many think our love is God?
GEORGE K. Some of God, not all.
MR. ALCOTT. How many think our faith is God?
AUGUSTINE. The spirit is flowing over us, and what we get is God in us.
MR. ALCOTT. Is our body God in any sense?
GEORGE K. It is God's work. (See Note 103.)

Subject
MR. ALCOTT. Our next conversation will be on the birth of Jesus, which point in his history we have now reached. We have seen what preparations God makes in order to bring a spirit into the world, and make it visible to our eyes, by clothing it in flesh.

VOL. I.   7

CONVERSATION VIII.

NOTE 83, PAGE 62.

(*Here Charles changed his picture, and supposed John dressed in a camel's hairy hide, with his tail for a belt.*)

MR. ALCOTT. You make him quite a savage. Who was John the Baptist like?

CHARLES. Dr. Graham.

NOTE 84, PAGE 62.

MR. ALCOTT. Do any of you think your mothers had visions of you?

(Several.)*

Restored by the Editor.

NOTE 85, PAGE 63.

MR. ALCOTT. And now I don't want you to speak; but to hold up your hands, if you have ever heard any disagreeable or vulgar things about birth.

(*None raised hands.*)

Men have been brought before Courts of Justice for saying vulgar things about the birth of Christ; and all birth is sacred as Jesus Christ's. And I have heard of children saying very profane things about it; and have heard fathers and mothers do so. I hope that none of us will ever violate the sacredness of this subject.

NOTE 86, PAGE 63.

MR. ALCOTT. Edward B., it seems, had some profane notions of birth, connected with some physiological facts; but they were corrected here. Did you ever hear this line,

"The throe of suffering is the birth of bliss?"

GEORGE K. Yes; it means that Love, and Joy, and Faith, lead you to have suffering, which makes more happiness for you.

NOTES.

229

NOTE 87, PAGE 64.

(*Here Mr. Alcott asked if every child was not a gift of God. They assented, and then there was some conversation upon names, and their own names were traced.*)

NOTE 88, PAGE 65.

CHARLES. Why in a hill country more than any where else?

GEORGE K. Because they see more and have more imagination.

NATHAN. One can't have imagination in a city.

CHARLES. Some country fellows are very stupid.

MR. ALCOTT. That is true; but still the country affords advantages which the city does not. Should you not like to have more mountains and valleys and streams about Boston?

ANDREW. Yes; a great many more.

(*Mr. Alcott spoke of the effect of the Ocean on himself, seen first, when he was twelve years old.*)

NOTE 89, PAGE 65.

MR. ALCOTT. Does the Lord visit his people now?

CHARLES. Yes; in little babies.

MR. ALCOTT. Yes; you have the thought. And a mother suffers when she has a child. When she is going to have a child, she gives up her body to God, and he works upon it, in a mysterious way, and with her aid, brings forth the Child's Spirit in a little Body of its own, and when it has come, she is blissful. But I have known some mothers who are so timid that they are not willing to bear the pain; they fight against God, and suffer much more.

CHARLES. I should think it ought to be the father, he is so much stronger.

MR. ALCOTT. He suffers because it is his part to see the suffering in order to relieve it. But it is thought, and with good reason, that if there were no wrong doing there would be no suffering attending this mysterious act. When Adam and Eve did wrong, it was said that Adam should earn bread by the sweat of his brow, and Eve have pain in bringing her children into the world. We never hear of trees groaning to put forth their leaves.

CHARLES. They have no power to do wrong.

MR. ALCOTT. True; God only gives them power to put forth, and they do it without pain. A rose has no pain in being born.

VOL. I.   20

230

NOTES.

MR. ALCOTT. Every one is a visiter on the Earth from the Lord. I hope you will all be pleasant visiters. Some visiters are very unpleasant; they do not like what is given them to eat and drink; they do not like the beds they lie on. Do you think a drunkard is a pleasant visiter? Is he doing what he is sent to do?

(They all laughed.)

EMMA. I am not a very pleasant visiter, but I have a very pleasant visit.

NOTE 90, PAGE 65.

MR. ALCOTT. How many of you are redeemed?
NATHAN. I am not quite, but almost.

NOTE 91, PAGE 65.

(Here Mr. Alcott repeated that to speak of God without having a holy feeling was profanity; but an oath in a Court of Justice was sacred. It was speaking of God seriously, with a holy feeling.)

NOTE 92, PAGE 66.

MR. ALCOTT. Tell me what the shadow of death means. Would there be any shadow without light? Which was made first, light or darkness?
CHARLES. Darkness. It seems to me that there was darkness first; I can't think otherwise.
MR. ALCOTT. Is darkness real, positive? I thought darkness was the shadow of light. What if the sun should be put out?
ANDREW. Then there would be darkness.
NATHAN. When there is darkness we would not know it if light had not been first.
MR. ALCOTT. Which of you think light came first? If light made the darkness, then if there had been no light there would have been no darkness. When the light goes out of this room does any thing come in?

NOTES.

231

CHARLES. Yes; darkness comes in.
MR. ALCOTT. Nothing comes in; and I cannot conceive of there not being light. Darkness is the absence of light to our external senses.

NOTE 94, PAGE 68.

Mr. Alcott. Suppose you knew all that happened before you were born, and all the interest God took in it, and all that the angels took in it; do you think you should have known any thing as wonderful as these things?

Charles. I don't think near so much would happen.

Mr. Alcott. Who knows but the same wonders are going on in every case of birth, and that we are mistaken in supposing that this account of birth belonged to Jesus alone, rather than was an emblem of all birth?

Emma. I think the outward facts were different, because he was born in a different place and under different circumstances; but there was no other difference.

Nathan. I don't think they all felt the same when I was born as when Jesus Christ was, because I am not as good as Jesus was.

Mr. Alcott. All may rise, who think with Emma, that some outward circumstances were different.

(All rose.)

Charles. I should think Mary would feel rather more, because she knew what a great son she was going to have.

Mr. Alcott. Perhaps it was Mary's idea that she was going to have a Saviour in her son; and her faith in the thought, that brought this message to her, made him what he was, or helped to do so, together with Joseph's constancy to her.

Charles. I don't know any better way to say, than the old way in the Bible, that it was made out of the dust.

Mr. Alcott. Which is as much as to say you have no opinion at all of your own.

George K. It is a spirit coming into the body. God makes the body. The spirit always was. It was not made at that time. When you do wrong and repent, you are born again.

Mr. Alcott. I will now tell you what I think. The spirit makes the body just as the rose throws out the rose leaves. I cannot tell you how the rose leaves come out of the rose. But I think the spirit throws the body out. The body is the outside of the spirit — the spirit made visible. I don't think God made my spirit and then my body, and brought them together, but I think that God makes my soul, and my soul all the time makes my body, just as something in the rose seed makes the rose leaves.

20*

CONVERSATION IX.

NOTE 93, PAGE 68.

(Here Mr. Alcott asked if there was any thing to be said on Josiah's idea.)

Nathan. I think Jesus was good at first, body and all, and he made the body better while he lived.

Mr. Alcott. Yes; I know that some of you thought that Jesus was so good that his body went to heaven.

George K. I don't think there was any naughtiness in him, or in any babies, but when they do wrong it comes, and they repent, and are born again.

Mr. Alcott. Does Repentance make the body perfect again? Temperance would keep it good.*

* Restored by the Editor.

Mr. Alcott. I want to ask you about Josiah's idea, which is, that the body is made out of the naughtiness of other people.

Andrew. I can't think that it takes the naughtiness away from other people, because it is all good at first.

Martha. I think just as Andrew does.

Charles. I don't see what Josiah means.

Samuel R. I don't think bodies are either bad or good.

Nathan. It don't take the bad away from other people, but gets bad itself.

Mr. Alcott. What is birth?

Charles. Putting the spirit into a body; having the body put round the spirit.

Mr. Alcott. But where is the body taken from?

Charles. I don't know.

George B. I think people get bad, and when they get bad they throw away their goodness, and God takes the goodness and makes it up into little babies.

Nathan. God makes the body and does not put any goodness into it, and then the spirit comes and makes the body better.

Mr. Alcott. I want all of you to account for the origin of the body. How is the body made, Charles, what does it come from?

284   NOTES.

CHARLES. I don't think it is so, because it says, Joseph was going to put off Mary.

MR. ALCOTT. But he did not put her off.

CHARLES. Because an angel came to him in a dream.

MR. ALCOTT. And he trusted in the inward thought and feeling of his dream. Suppose your parents had thought, before you were born, that you were to be a Reformer, and had kept this thought unwaveringly uppermost, and their friends had sympathized with them in this, and all circumstances had been arranged in reference to it?

CHARLES. I do not think I should have been a Messiah.

NOTE 95, PAGE 68.

MR. ALCOTT. Frank is very decided; he tells what God ought to do; he thinks God does wrong, for he does not see the spiritual fact.

NOTE 96, PAGE 69.

(Here Mr. Alcott spoke of the Maternal Sense, and made it one with the Maternal Love that watches over infancy like a second Providence—God made visible to protect; and asked them if they felt differently towards their fathers and mothers. None thought they loved one better than the other; but some said they felt differently. Charles, and Nathan, and others, said they felt exactly alike about them.)

MR. ALCOTT. How do you know, Charles, which you are feeling about?

CHARLES. I know which I am thinking about. I feel about them exactly alike.

NOTE 97, PAGE 70.

GEORGE K. I don't think so much about dinner as I did then.

MR. ALCOTT. Do you think Jesus thought about his dinner?

NATHAN. I don't think he cared about it much; he eat what was given to him.

NOTES.   285

NOTE 98, PAGE 70.

(Here Mr. Alcott repeated the question, and all expressed the Idea that the poor were happier than the rich—why?)

CHARLES. Because they have not so many chances, and anxieties, and do not have to think about so many hills.

GEORGE K. The poor are not tempted so much to do wrong.

EMMA. I think the rich can be as happy as the poor.

MR. ALCOTT. Those, who think neither riches nor poverty make happiness, may stand up.

(All rose.)

What does happiness depend on?

CHARLES. On the state of mind.

MR. ALCOTT. Name the state of mind.

SAMUEL R. Conscience must be at peace.

MR. ALCOTT. Happiness depends on the state of mind first, and secondly on the use we make of it. But should you go out in the street and ask people as you meet them, thus—Man! are riches essential to happiness? Certainly, he would say. Madam! are riches essential to happiness? Why, how can you ask such a question! Boy! do you think riches essential to happiness? Oh yes!—how could I have good dinners and 'rich clothes, without riches?

I am very glad that you, so early in life, have learnt the true view of this subject. And now I want each of you to ask yourselves this,—Are my father and mother spiritual persons—are they devoted to the culture of their own and other people's spirits, as much as they should be, or do they care more than I wish about outward things? I do not wish you to tell me.

NATHAN. I am sure I don't know.

(None of the rest answered.)

NOTE 99, PAGE 71.

(Here most of them confirmed the old idea.)

EMMA. Mr. Alcott, I always think of all angels looking like Jesus Christ.

NOTE 100, PAGE 71.

MR. ALCOTT. Is God with you?

MARTHA. I think "God with us" means that we have Spirit, and God is in our spirit.

ANDREW. God is in our Conscience.

MR. ALCOTT. Does God come to every Parent when the Baby comes?

(*Most rose.*)

How many of you have lost the God you brought with you? Do those that sit around me now, have as much of God in them as they would have had?

(*No answer.*)

Is God with us when we walk out and see the ocean, and mountains, and streams?

(*All assented.*)

God is with us even in our passion; we take his strength to destroy ourselves; we turn God round against himself.

NOTE 101, PAGE 72.

MARTHA. I think Jesus is Godlike.

CHARLES. I think he is God.

MR. ALCOTT. Who think Jesus is Godlike?

(*All rose.*)

Who think Jesus is God?

(*Martha, Nathan, and George K. sat down.*)

You, who are standing, think Jesus is Godlike and God also?

GEORGE K. I think he is *only* Godlike.

NOTE 102, PAGE 73.

MR. ALCOTT. What is the most striking fact that proves God is with us?

EMMA. God is with us, because he speaks to us through our Conscience.

NOTE 103, PAGE 73.

MR. ALCOTT. All may rise who think there is any sense in which the body is God.

(*No one rose.*)

All may rise who think there is no sense in which that can be said.

(*All rose.*)

I think there is a sense in which the body may be called God.

CHARLES. I wish you would explain how.

MR. ALCOTT. I cannot, because you cannot look through Physiology; and the language is liable to misconstruction. George spoke very well, when he called it God's work.

[James Freeman Clarke]

"Mr. Furness' New Book," *Western Messenger,* 2 (December 1836, January 1837): 341-349, 371-382.

William Henry Furness's Remarks on the Four Gospels *(1836) raised serious speculations about the validity of miracles in the Bible. Contrary to the established Unitarian view that the miracles of the New Testament were performed as God's way of convincing man of the truth of Christianity, Furness argued that man has an intuitive perception of religious truths that requires no such confirmation, thus making Christianity depend upon the teachings of Christ, rather than His supposed deeds. Published the same year as Emerson's* Nature, *Furness' book was an excellent application of Transcendental philosophy to biblical writings.*

James Freeman Clarke was one of a group of young Harvard Divinity School graduates who had headed West to spread Unitarianism, settling in Louisville, Kentucky. There, they founded the Western Messenger *in June 1835, promoting liberal theology in the region. (For further information, see the entries for Clarke and Furness [a Unitarian minister in Philadelphia] in* DLB 1, The American Renaissance in New England.)

Inestimable, no doubt, are the benefits which have resulted from the invention of printing–infinite the blessings of an age in which useful knowledge is diffused by quartos, octavos, and duodecimos; by quarterlies, monthlies, weeklies, and dailies; by republications, penny magazines, and family libraries. Yet one slight difficulty attends this profusion of mental knowledge which should not be wholly lost sight of. We mean the difficulty of distinguishing a real book from an apparent book. Has it never fallen to the lot of any reader to be attracted by a flaming advertisement, setting forth the merits of a new volume on some interesting subject, and when he has hurried away to the nearest book store and procured it, and sat himself down by his fire for a good evening's reading shortly found that his cake was dough? Has he not felt like one, who, cracking a nut between his teeth, suddenly finds his mouth full of ashes instead of the expected kernel? how often has a like experience befallen us. Tell us not of wooden nutmegs, speak not of horn gun flints. How much greater the cheat of writing page after page of sounding inanity, having it printed and bound up in a neat looking gold lettered volume, with a recommendatory preface, by the Rev. Scriblerius, and a number of testimonial letters from Professor This and Doctor That, and palming it on an innocent and unsuspecting public as a BOOK. A book was once supposed to contain ideas, thoughts, arguments, opinions, bearing upon some great point of difficulty. It was the repository of mental treasures, carefully gathered and painfully elaborated. Long days of observation, multiplied enquiries, much travel, nights of stern thought had matured it, till at last it rose like a sun into the heaven of thought, scattering the fogs, and leaving clearness and beauty where once was obscurity and entanglement. But now many so called books are such in appearance only. To the outward eye, they have the semblance of real books–the civil shopman as he hands them over the counter, receives in lieu solid coin. They occupy a visible, definite space on your table and shelf. But for all other uses they prove, on trial, wholly unfitted. They are shew books, phenomenal books, appearances with merely a subjective existence. In fact, to speak with philosophical rigor, they are no books, but phantasms, or shadows of books.

It may not therefore be wholly needless to declare at the outset, that this work of our friend Furness is in fact a book. Its first great merit is, that it is something. He who shall read it, will find in it not a vapid reproduction of commonplace thoughts, but something wholly new, something he never met before. He will find himself in company with a man who has thoughts which he struggles to express, feelings which he labours to inspire, a bright and living idea whose glory he longs to communicate to all whom he can gather together, out of the highways and hedges to his marriage feast. That we should have a real book be-

[32]

Photograph of William Henry Furness,
Philadelphia clergyman

fore us in these "Remarks," is noteworthy, but especially encouraging in this when we consider the subject, namely, "The Four Gospels." Of all vapid and tiresome books, commentaries and expositions of scripture are usually the most empty. They seem to be written by men whose eyes are closed and ears stopped, and hearts dulled–who cannot see with their eyes, nor understand with their hearts the beauty and sublimity of the living oracles of God. They discourse in the same humdrum strain on things great and small– on St. Paul's cloak and the crucifixion of their Savior. They consider it a duty to dispense with all feeling, to stifle all emotion, to quench every spark of genial enthusiasm, while walking their dry and dusty path of comment and exposition. Every verse, whether important or trifling, must have its comment–so much and no more time must be bestowed on every line. Then every thing which has been ever said before must be brought forward and considered. If the true meaning of a passage is obvious, all the absurd meanings which have ever been ascribed to it, must be put by the side

of it, with the express design, one would judge, of confusing the mind of the reader, and making him doubt whether the truth could ever be found out. Sometimes a quantity of pious moralizing is added, but always of the same formal, studied, unnatural character. Such is the prevailing style of scripture commentaries. They darken counsel with words without knowledge. Instead of helping us to *understand*, i.e. get at the essential meaning, the deeper significance of scripture, they direct the attention to outward unimportant particulars, which only tend to confuse and dissipate the feeling. The last effect of most commentaries is to make us feel that there is nothing significant or intelligible in the whole matter they treat of. They appear, in short, to have been written by dead men.

Long, therefore, has it been our wish that a book might be written on the New Testament which could bear some comparison with Herder's Letters on the Old.[1] Of such a work Enthusiasm should be the basis. Let it be an intelligent self-possessed enthusiasm; we want no sentimentalism, no bombast, no empty emotion; but without a deep and thrilling sense of the importance of the work, no one is qualified to explain the Bible. The man who undertakes to explain the Scripture, should be pervaded with a sense of its divine truth and beauty, and his book should have for its motto, "Put off thy shoes from off thy feet, for the place where thou standest is holy ground." Such a man is W. H. Furness; such a book, so far as it undertakes to go, is the work before us.

After having carefully read the work to its last chapter, and analysed the impression made on our own mind, the conclusion we came to was–"This is a new revelation of the character of Christ." Then, when we begin to consider how it would affect others, what would be its adaptation to the community, what wants it would meet, we said, "This is what was needed." And with a few remarks to illustrate these two judgments, and a few extracts to justify them, we will conclude our criticism, and take another opportunity for the fault-finding part of our duty.

The vague and mysterious reverence paid to Christ, has hitherto prevented a just appreciation of his real character. Regarding him as the Infinite God, men have shrunk from an examination of his personality, counting it irreverent to apply any human standard of excellence to Jehovah. How could they indeed dare to analyze and criticise the character of God? And though admitting his humanity, they could not regard him as in any sense really human, while the common doctrine of the two Natures in the God-Man was believed–a doctrine which confuses and mystifies every enquiry. The utter looseness and inadequacy of all past Trinitarian expositions of our Master's character justifies the assertion, that neither the depths of his human excellence, nor the heights of his divine attributes, can be appreciated, while the Trinitarian dogma lies, like a shapeless mist, in the path of vision. The doctrine of Christ's Deity prevents us from recognising the Son of Man. The doctrine of the two Natures obscures our view of the Son of God.

In the volume before us the mist is cleared away; the veil is lifted. The Christ of this volume is no mystical personage, wrapping himself in the cloud of undefined and undefinable attributes of an unexplained and inexplicable nature. He comes to us like a brother and friend, a man like ourselves, made in all respects like his brethren. As the mountain which carries its gleaming summit above the clouds, sinks its foundations far beneath the bosom of the common earth, so the divine and transcendent excellencies of Jesus have their basis in the very depths of his humanity. In all the dazzling glory of his appearance on the Mount of Transfiguration, the lineaments of the man were not extinguished or obscured. They were lighted up and ennobled, and shone through the radiances with a new distinctness of beauty.

But we are tired of interposing our own words between our readers and this book. We will close this part of our notice of the "Remarks by extracting the last thirteen pages of the volume. We recommend to all our readers who are able (the book has not reached the West) to get a copy. When they have read it, we should like to talk with them again about it in our next number.

**The books which we have now been examining are invaluable for the saving knowledge which they give us of Jesus Christ, of whose life they are the record, and of whose spirit they are an unconscious illustration. In him I see a revelation of religious truth, and consequently a disclosure of the will of God, a representation of the perfection and destiny of man. When we see Jesus Christ as he is, we have come to the knowledge and possession of Christianity. He shows us what God is and what He would have us to be. In the spiritual and immortal lineaments of Jesus, we discover our own immortality, and in sympathy with him we come to feel and know ourselves to be immortal. To estimate him is to grow in Christian knowledge, and to become worthy of the Christian name.

"It is a character of no ordinary force which has for eighteen hundred years commanded the respect of the world. Christianity, in the forms in which it has been for ages extensively represented, has shown but few features of a heavenly origin. It has been set forth before the world as a religion identified with a most magnificent and complicated structure of outward ceremonies. Its sanction has been claimed for the exercise of a power, which knew hardly any limit, over national affairs and the rights of private opinion. At one time it was promulgated by bishops clad in mail and demanding faith at the point of the sword. And in all periods of its history, the appeal for its security and its triumphs has been directly made to the civil arm, or to those prejudices and passions which for ever war against human liberty. Under the banner of the Cross, that symbol of the divine power of an unresisting spirit, acts of the bloodiest violence have been perpetrated; the most merciless persecutions have been carried on. Opinions concerning God and man have been published under the name of Christianity, contradicting not only the first dictates of the understanding, but every natural sentiment of justice and mercy; and the terrors of this world and the next have been threatened upon the faintest whisper of dissent. In fine, that which has been called Christianity instead of taking its place in the van of human interests, has been found opposing the progress of our race by all the weapons which ignorance and passion could supply. Not by one only, but by all denominations of its friends, has our religion been made to occupy more or less decisively this position.

"When these things are considered, the question arises, how comes it–by what means–by what principle of vitality–has Christianity maintained itself for long ages in the world? Forced through the unwise zeal of its friends, to ally itself with the worldly interests and passions of men, taking so little pains to address the better principles of our nature,–how is it that amidst all vicissitudes, and the various and increasing lights of civilization, it has not long ago been mistaken to its foundations, levelled with the dust, and swept away with the fragments of many preceding and contemporaneous empires! I find the principal answer to this inquiry in the person of its Founder, in the simple force of his character.

"It was this which wrought the most powerfully for Christianity at its first introduction, when it came, unarmed with any worldly power, to rebuke the passions of the selfish, and dissipate the darkness which men loved. The great spring of action in the hearts of the first promulgators of our religion was the sentiment of ardent affection and reverence with which Jesus Christ inspired them. The love of Christ constrained them. It was for his sake that they accounted it joy and triumph to toil and suffer, and with the kindling idea of him were blended their best hopes and aims. And this it was, by the way, which constituted the wide differences between him and them, and which makes his fortitude so much more wonderful than theirs. He had no human precedent to which he could look, and from which he might draw strength and animation. No one had gone before him by whose memory his human sympathies might be encouraged, and whose example might cheer him onward. Only the highest source of inspiration was open to him–the simple thought of God, and to appreciate this so that it might stand in the place of all other supports, an elevation of mind was necessary, of which we can but faintly conceive. His successors on the contrary were aided by all those human affections which found an all-animating object in him, and the devoted love which he awakened was their efficient motive to do and endure.

"It may be asked whether those, who were active in the first establishment of his religion, were not moved by those great moral principles which he taught. Undoubtedly they were. But then it was these principles, not merely, nor chiefly, as they were presented in words to their understandings, but as they were far more divinely expressed in his character to their hearts. Truth, not abstractedly, but as it filled and transfigured his whole being–this it was that kindled in them a noble zeal, "the light of the knowledge of the glory of God in the face of Jesus Christ." What words could convey to them such a sentiment of love as was expressed in his Cross!

"Or again it may be intimated that it was the miracles he wrought, that operated so powerfully in convincing and urging onward his followers. It is true his works of power did much; they filled an important and indispensable place in producing that state of feeling in his disciples, requisite for them to carry on what he had begun. But then the main power of his miracles lies not in their mere power, but in their relation to his character, which they help far more strikingly than any thing else to glorify. What a depth of tenderness is laid open, how touching his meekness, what a new lustre is added to all the virtues he exemplified, when we consider them as the virtues of one, endowed with more than regal gifts; with powers exceeding all that Fortune or Genius has ever bestowed on man! Look at the case whichever way you will, the result is the same. It was by the force of his character that the apostles were swayed.

"And it has been and must be always. No cause, religious or political, good or bad, has ever gained a foothold in the world, except by the impulse of a leading mind, the energy of some prominent character, some one individual, who has been to its adherents the embodiment of the object at which they had aimed. Individuals of this description, have so often and so mournfully abused their influences to selfish purposes, they have been so ready to take advantage of the idolatrous attachment of their fellow men that it has failed to be seen how deeply this mode of influence is founded in the nature of man. Thus the maxim has gone forth–"principles, not men," a sound maxim but only in a qualified sense. The truth is, principles at best are but imperfectly set forth in a verbal form. Language is an artificial sign and an inadequate one. It may meet and satisfy the understanding, and answer important purposes,

but it reaches the great springs of human action only indirectly by aid of association. The conduct, the life of a human being is the true, natural, divine symbol, whereby great truths are made to kindle our strongest affections. So that in the very nature of things, men, living men are required to express in their lives to other men, the great purposes with reference to which they are to be moved.

"I make these remarks to show that the stamp of divinity is as visible upon the mode in which Christianity has been communicated to man as upon its substance. The great truths, the paternal providence of God and another life, have been acknowledged to be great and important, worthy of God to teach. But the manner in which they have been revealed, has not been recognised, as equally worthy of Deity. 'Why,' it has often been asked, 'why were not these truths written out upon the firmament, so that all men might read without the possibility of mistake, or proclaimed, as by an arch-angel's trump, so that the whole world might hear." Alas! there is much written from of old in unfading characters all over the sky, the earth and the sea. There are myriads of voices sounding on from eternity to eternity through all the heights and depths of the universe,–but where is the seeing eye, the hearing ear? Such methods of revelation as I now refer to, are mere human propositions. The mode actually adopted in the Christian dispensation, harmonizes perfectly with the deepest principles of human nature, and displays the same wisdom by which that nature was fashioned. Man has been addressed through man. One has been raised up to communicate the life of truth through his own life, to point men, not into space but into their own souls, there to read the will and behold the countenance and feel the spirit of God. In his spiritual features beams the glory of God. The character of Christ is the Rock of Christian faith, the high tower which cannot be hid by the thickest clouds which steam up from the ignorance and corruption of earth, and which assures us that the city of God is there, the dwelling place of unchanging Truth.

"As it was from the character of its Founder, that Christianity received its first impulse, so by the same force has it been sustained under the crushing weight of the corruptions by which its brightness has been darkened and its beauty deformed, and from the enormity of these corruptions we may form some idea of the force by which they have been resisted. This has been its shield amidst the deep wounds which it has received in the house of its friends. The common impression is, that it owes the influence it has retained, amidst the errors of its adherents, to its great moral principles. True. But to repeat what I have said, these principles in an abstract, verbal form, separated from the life of him, by whom they were promulgates, lose nearly all their peculiar power. A moral system of almost equal excellence might be gathered from the records of ancient wisdom. Gibbon has remarked in one of his notes that he finds the great social law of Christian love stated in the plainest terms by a writer who flourished ages before Christ. Take from Christianity the original exposition of truth which it presents in its Founder, suppose it to have been first taught by one whose life gave no significance to his words, and it is evident at once how much it must lose. On the contrary, we might erase from the Christian Records every general precept, yet so long as the acts and sufferings of Jesus were remembered they would retain an all-commanding influence. The superiority of actions to words has passed into a proverb. But where is it so strikingly shown as in the religion of Jesus Christ? His precepts recommend themselves to our reason; but the application we allow them is narrow or comprehensive according as we appreciate him. We understand them no further than we understand him. When men, outraged by its corruptions, have been disposed to abjure Christianity altogether, the pure and generous character of its author, dimly discerned indeed, but yet seen in something of its truth, has commanded their respect and prevented them from rejecting a religion promulgated by lips so pure and eloquent. The greatest skeptics have confessed that the character of Christ is too great and too natural not to be a reality.

"When we turn from the past to the present and the future, and inquire by what means the improvement of mankind individually and collectively is to be most effectually promoted, we find in the character of Christ untold resources of wealth and power. 'Political reform, pressingly enough wanted, can indeed root out the weeds; but it leaves the ground *empty,* ready either for noble fruits, or new worse tares! And how else is a moral reform to be looked for but in this way, that more and more good men are, by a bountiful Providence, sent hither to disseminate Goodness; literally to show it, as in seeds shaken abroad by the living tree! For such in all ages and places is the nature of a good man; he is ever a mystic, creative centre of goodness; his influence, if we consider it, is not to be measured; for his works do not die, but being of eternity, are eternal; and in new transformation and ever wider diffusion, endure, living and life-giving. Then let him whose character is acknowledged to be the best and purest ever exhibited on earth–let him live in the faith and imagination of men. To ascertain our destiny–to know the hidden aim of our being, we need not gaze into the sky, or pry fruitlessly into Futurity. The end of life is revealed in Jesus Christ. He is the model whereby all men may fashion themselves. When he appears, not personally, but morally, not to the outward eye, but to the inward sense, we shall become like him for we shall see him as he is.

"When the character of Christ is felt, then exists that principle of action denominated in the Scriptures, faith, the faith that saves the soul. Then will the destiny of man be realized. He who contemplates Jesus Christ, as he is presented in the brief and simple sketches of his life, as a pattern of disinterestedness, self-command, and piety, before whose imagination and affections that wonderful being stands distinctly revealed, such a one must feel the force of the character of Christ. He beholds a being, the greatest that ever trod this earth, not merely for the extraordi-

nary powers he possessed, but for the uniform humility, the touching self-forgetfulness, with which he bore his great gifts, one who disregarded all the seductions of ambition and power, in whom the hosannas of multitudes never excited one throb of vain glory, whose tenderness, overflowing all artificial distinctions, poured a tide of mercy into the hearts of the degraded and miserable; one who suffered fatigue and hunger and thirst, and contumely and violence, that he might comfort, correct, and bless our race; out of whose heart, in the very agonies of death, broke words of affection for his mother, and prayers for those who tortured him. Such was the man of Nazareth: But how vain are words to describe his original excellence! Could we only bring up before our minds, the spotless and venerable idea of him; could our cold and sluggish imaginations only picture him in his youth, in the serenity of that blessed countenance, in that attitude of unspeakable love, yearning to gather the whole family of the suffering and afflicted, even as a bird gathereth her young under her wings;–could the eye of the soul be so cleansed as to see him as he was, then we should not need to be told of the power of his character. In the reverence, gratitude, and love which would overflow our minds, gushing up from a thousand hidden springs, we should have a present proof of his moral force, of his power to sweep away from the heart all the false idols and temples we erect there, and to cover it with the unfading verdure, and the immortal fruits of true and evergrowing goodness. If we have ever been in any degree impressed with the wisdom and excellence of Jesus, by the emotions we have sometimes felt, let us pause and consider what a transformation must be wrought in him, who discerns this illustrious being not partially and by glimpses transient and far between, but who cherishes his pure idea in the inner-most recesses of his mind, amidst his best sensibilities, studying all the beautiful details of his life with an ever-present conviction of reality, learning to conform all his ideas of greatness to him as an unerring standard! Must not a mind, thus occupied, be strong in the goodness which it loves? And if strong in goodness, then saved, yes, saved–O, how truly saved! Being delivered from all corrupting passions, from all those false prepossessions, to which those who live in the world without a pure object to look at and to love, are ever so exposed,–being redeemed from all iniquity, and inspired with an affection for all that is holy in imagination, upright and benevolent in the act.

"If a great and good man were now to appear, such as this age, and many preceding ages, had not produced nor approached, a great public benefactor, an example of every private virtue, and it were our privilege to be associated with him daily, intimately, by the respect and love he would inspire, would not every generous and virtuous sentiment be called into action? Would not our cheeks be crimsoned with shame as the bare thought of doing any thing abhorrent to the nature of our revered friend? Could any thing act upon us so powerfully as such a fellowship with living virtue! Of precisely this nature is the force of the character of Christ, and this is the way in which he who believes in Christ, attains to that blessedness, which the Scriptures describe as the presence of God; Heaven, Salvation. To live in a Christian land, among Christian institutions; to profess the Christian faith in one or another form,–this is not faith in Christ, although thousands hug the delusion. It is to have the sacred images of his excellence set up at the very fountain-head of ones spiritual being,–this is faith, living, Christian, saving faith. He who cherishes it will, aye, must be saved. The decree is writ in the very constitution of the soul.

"The world has suffered from nothing so much as from false ideas of greatness. The passion for military glory has been the fruitful cause of slavery, bloodshed and crime. How little has the experience of its fatal results hitherto done to teach men wisdom! How is this deadly charm ever to be broken, save by the formation of a nobler idea, the creation of a better taste, the erection of the true standard! In Jesus Christ, the real greatness of our nature–the glory of a pacific, all enduring temper–is revealed. Let him then be lifted up before all eyes and all hearts will be touched, and the sword and the spear, and the banner bathed in blood will be buried at the foot of his cross, and it will be felt that all other courage is fear, all other glory shame, in comparison with that spirit which subdues by mercy and reigns by suffering.

"Once more. There is a wide and mournful need of confidence in the omnipotence of moral truth. This it is that the wise in all ages have most seriously wanted. They have had, as it has been said of a certain political party, "more of the wisdom of experience than the wisdom of hope," and they have "looked for their Future–only in the direction of the Past." Look at the wise and the educated and the thinking at the present day. How faint and sickly are their hopes of the moral improvement of our race! Things are deemed impossible, for the instant accomplishment of which only that single energy of will is required, which a sure faith in the vitality of moral truth would immediately create. In these circumstances how unspeakably precious, (could it only be brought home to the heart!) the memory of one in whom no trait is more conspicuous than a calm and unfaltering confidence in truth, and this too in a condition of things apparently the darkest and most hopeless! Without a single decisive token of success, he uniformly looked upon the great revolution he commenced as already consummated. In no respect is his example more original and inspiring. In nothing does he stand so pre-eminently alone, far above all other teachers, as in his perfect faith in human nature. He scattered fearlessly abroad the seeds of truth, and trusted in God that they would germinate and grow. Whereas all other teachers have divided their doctrines into *esoteric* and *exoteric*–philosophy for the initiated, and fables for the vulgar. And at the present day, how frequently is it said in regard to any new and more rational view of religion–'It is all very true. I understand and believe it. But it will not do to disseminate such views. The generality of men cannot appreciate them.' I

say nothing of the modesty of this sentiment. It reveals the very worst kind of infidelity, and our sabbaths, our churches, and our multitudinous institutions of religion are but a dead and delusive show, so long as man believes not in man. Jesus Christ went down directly among the most ignorant and degraded, and well did he describe it as the most decisive attestation to his divine authority, that he delivered the glad messages of Truth "to the Poor."

"But I have done. To bring the man of Nazareth, the elder brother of our race, the chosen son of God, the Revealer of God and man, more within the reach of human sympathies; to show that such, in the unspeakable grace of God, are the Records of his life, that the remotest generation may cherish, not merely a traditional, but a personal faith in him; that in the very form and structure of the Gospels there are the means by which every man may be brought into personal intimacy with him, beholding him, as it were, face to face, is the ultimate aim of the present work; and gives it whatever value it may be found to possess. How imperfect it is, how all-inadequately I have touched upon the great subject, I feel deeply. Still it has been a delightful employment. If it fail to awaken interest in other minds, I do not say I shall not be disappointed. But I shall be ungrateful to the Giver of all good if I ever cease to acknowledge with fervent thankfulness the confirmation it has afforded to my own faith."

SECOND NOTICE.

Speaking of this work in our last number, we said, that we thought it just the book that was needed. We will now give our reasons.

1. This book will make people *think* about Christ. This is sorely needed. As we intimated in our last number, the mysterious doctrines of his Deity and the two Natures in his person, have stopped all enquiry and investigation of his character. If he sometimes spoke as God and sometimes as man, and there is no criterion to distinguish when he spoke in one character and when in the other, it is obviously useless to study his words as exponents of his feelings. His character is a sealed book.

But Mr. Furness does not scruple to think, and thus excites his reader to a like exertion. There is something fascinating in the exhibition of a free and active mind, which quickens our own sluggish faculties. The rich results too of such enquiries excite our longing desire to partake of them. When we come in contact with an intellect, which is full of life and action, plunging into the depths of hidden knowledge, heaping up rich stores of learning and science, garlanded with the fair flowers which it has plucked by the way, and feasting on rich fruits which have rewarded its adventurous expedition into new regions of thought; we feel a generous emulation, a wish to do the like, not to let our God-given powers rust unused, not to be left so far behind in the heavenly race of mind. The view of such ardour comes to the shackled mind, like the thought of his native hills to the home sick student in the University.

> And yet, if I the truth might say,
> I would I were again away.
> Walls like these, and halls like these,
> Will, I fear, in no wise please.
> The narrow gloom of this low room,
> Where nothing green is ever seen,
> No tree, no bush, no flowers bloom,
> I mourn the hour I came hither,
> Ear, and eye, and heart, will die,
> Thought and the power of thought will wither.

2. This book will produce faith in Jesus Christ. This also is very much wanted. There is among those who call themselves Christians, a great lack of real belief in the divine mission of Jesus. They believe Christianity a good thing, and religion useful for the people. They have a kind of vague and uncertain faith in the reality of the Gospel History, but it is all too ignorant and dim a vision. They are not acquainted with Jesus Christ. They do not know him with any personal knowledge. Their faith is a matter of hear say altogether. Flesh and blood have revealed it to them, and not their heavenly Father, through the deep convictions of their own hearts. Hence their faith differences them in no respect from the thoughtful and serious Deist. Hence calamity keeps its burden and death retains its sting, they sorrow as without hope for their friends, they look on the evil and wickedness of earth without hope, they look on mankind without any belief in the moral power of Christianity to regenerate and save them, they look on themselves and feel the weight of their sins, unassuaged by the divine love which shines in the merciful face of Jesus Christ. What they want is not to believe on another's testimony, but to see Jesus for themselves, and know that he is indeed the Christ, the Savior of the world. This book will help them to such a faith. It expands the page of the gospels, and points to each particular trace of the divine presence of the Savior. Its author does not interpose himself dogmatically between his readers and his Savior. He is but a more ardent disciple, declaring that he has found Him of whom

the prophets did write, and telling the doubter to "come and see" the Master he so reverences.

3. We think this book will produce a better mode of interpreting Scriptures. Its *exegesis,* as Professor Stewart would call it, is wonderfully good. Take as an illustration the following exposition, which we consider one of the finest criticisms to be found, and which is so alive with the spirit of the scene and circumstances:

> "In the most public manner Jesus had, by his word, relieved a man, who had lost the powers both of sight and of speech, and who, according to the current belief of the times, was under the influence of a malignant spirit. Certain Pharisees, who were among the spectators, charged Jesus with being in league with the very prince of the evil spirits. By this charge, they virtually admitted that the cure he had just wrought transcended the power of man. One cannot but feel that such inveterate perverseness of mind must have shocked him deeply. After replying to the charge in various ways, he went on to make those solemn declarations which have so often struck terror into the minds of readers: "All manner of sin and blasphemy will be forgiven unto men, but the blasphemy against the Holy Spirit will not be forgiven unto men. And whosoever speaketh against the Son of man, it will be forgiven him, but whosoever speaketh against the Holy Spirit, it will not be forgiven him, neither in this world, nor in the world to come." Now in the very form of these sentences, I think I perceive that they must have been uttered with great feeling–with the deepest emotion. They are in the shape of general propositions. They are couched in unqualified language. Deep feeling always craves this mode of expression. It delights to leap at once, from the particular circumstances which have excited it, to the annunciation of a general or universal truth, or rather, such is the magnifying power, that it immediately swells out the incident or object which has awakened it, whether it be joyous or otherwise, into a world-embracing light, or an all-obscuring darkness. It loses sight of all qualifications of time or circumstance.

> "And here I cannot but mourn, to think how the thrilling life of the Christian scriptures has been concealed through the irrecognition of this mode of expression, so characteristic of intense feeling. Passages, from being expressed in universal terms, have been understood as cold, formal, creedlike statements of theological dogmas, when in fact they assumed their particular form because those by whom they were originally uttered or written, spoke or wrote from hearts bursting with emotion. Thus, for instance, a dry, doctrinal character has been given to the language of the Apostle Paul, when he says "In Jesus Christ neither circumcision availeth anything nor uncircumcision, but a new creation." And yet, when I consider the connexion of these words, I cannot help feeling that in this general way, he was giving expression to his own burning experience. He acclaims just before, "God forbid that I should

glory, save in the Cross of our Lord Jesus Christ, by whom the world is crucified unto me, and I unto the world." And then he adds, "For in Jesus Christ, neither circumcision is of any importance, nor uncircumcision, but a new creation."[2] What an immense change had taken place in the mind of Paul! The Cross, that instrument of suffering–that symbol of the deepest shame, had become, in its spiritual aspects, its moral manifestations, his central light, and a glory streamed from it, which was as the glory of God! Well did he say, and he must have uttered it from the fervent feeling of his own soul–'To be a Christian, is to be ushered into a new creation.' In eyes, illuminated by the moral light of the Cross of Christ, all things are changed. The old world with its artificial standards of judgment and thought, its superficial distinctions, vanishes utterly away, and a new world appears, a world not of outward observance, but bound together by the moral influences, and irradiated by the spiritual light of the Cross of Christ.

"But to return. On the occasion mentioned above, they who cavilled at the astonishing work wrought by Jesus, betrayed a moral blindness, hopeless to the last degree. A work which they confessed to be superhuman, and in which power and benevolence were miraculously displayed, they refused to refer to the agency of God. As I conceive, and as I have already said, Jesus was shocked at the impenetrable hardness of their hearts. And it is as if he had said, 'any other sin or blasphemy, of which men may be guilty, they may be forgiven, for they may repent of it; but you are past repentance, you, who speak against the Spirit of God, so overpoweringly manifested. There is no hope of you. You cannot be moved, and of course you cannot be forgiven. He who speaks against me as a man, without knowledge of my words or works, as, no doubt, many do, may be forgiven, for he may repent; but when a man sets himself against God, against the most striking exhibitions of God's presence and agency, there is no hope for him, now, or ever.' Such I believe to be substantially the meaning of this passage. It was uttered with direct reference to a peculiar case, and in that general and unqualified manner, which the deep feeling, excited by the case, naturally prompted.

"The Pharisees immediately asked Jesus for a sign. And this request in connexion with the peculiar circumstances, intimates, as I have suggested in another place, that the Pharisees were momentarily impressed by what he had done, and were ready to believe in him, if he would only do a work which should prove him to be such a Christ as they expected. That this was their state of mind is implied by what follows. For, after saying that no sign of his authority would be given them except his death and resurrection, he goes on to describe the condition of a man suffering under one of those violent maladies, which in those days were ascribed to evil spirits, and which come on by paroxysms; evidently hinting in this description at the moral condition of the Pharisees. They might appear for a little while to be forsaken by the evil spirit of unbelief which possessed them. But its departure

was only temporary. It would return like other diseases with seven-fold fury and violence.

"We come now to the point which I wish to make prominent. The narrative proceeds to inform us that while he was speaking, speaking, as I have represented, with the greatest earnestness and solemnity, one said to him, "Thy mother and thy brethren stand without, desiring to speak with thee," Some thoughtless individual, insensible to the import of his words and to common decorum, or, it might have been, some one, who disliked the direction his remarks were taking, and was glad of an opportunity to break them off, interrupted him, telling him that his mother wanted to see him. Now it seems to me he was disturbed at the interruption ("aegre ferens interpellationem," says Kuinoel) and that the exclamation, "Who is my mother, and who are my brethren!" reveals a momentary excitement of mind. So full was he of what he was saying, and so offended, if I may be allowed the expression, that he utters himself as if he had forgotten that he had either mother or brethren.

"I am unable to understand the feelings of those who can consider this incident, thus regarded, as indicating any defect in the character of Jesus. It reveals his humanity, it is true, but in so doing, in showing him affected by human feelings,–weaknesses, if you please, it heightens my reverence for him and makes him live more vividly in my faith and affections. With not a trace of human weakness his character might have been beautiful, but its beauty would have been unreal and visionary, appealing only to the imagination. It could have had no foundation in nature, no power over the deep and active sympathies of the human soul. There is none absolutely good but one, God. We want not a character absolutely good in the person of a man, for that would be an inconsistency in the nature of things, but we want a specimen of the perfection of a nature, still seen and felt to be a human nature, possessing the inherent, ineradicable principles of humanity. My mind does not pause with the least regret over the hasty feeling which prompted the exclamation, "Who is my mother, and who are my brethren!" but I feel all the more deeply the touching manner in which he corrects himself, the evidence he immediately gives of the tenderness of his filial and frathenal affections, when, extending his hand towards his disciples, and, as if he could say nothing more affectionate, he adds, "Behold my mother and my brethren! For whosoever will do the will of my Father in Heaven, the same is my brother and sister and mother."

"In commenting upon this passage I have followed the Gospel of Matthew.–Luke relates the circumstances of the same occasion, but he does not mention that the mother of Jesus desired to see him. He only mentions that a woman of the company lifted up her voice and said unto him, "Blessed is the womb that bare thee, and the breasts that gave thee nourishment!"[3] Is there not a probable coincidence here between the two narratives! Some one, as we learn from Matthew, told Jesus that his

Letter from Furness to Emerson with a caricature of Thoreau (Records of a Lifelong Friendship 1807–1882: Ralph Waldo Emerson and William Henry Furness, *edited by Horace Howard Furness [1910]*)

mother was waiting for him. Upon the mention of his mother, a woman, herself probably a mother, exclaimed in effect, "Thy mother! what a blessed woman thy mother must be!" The whole passage is redolent of nature and life. Is it looking at it too curiously to see in the introduction of the word, "sister," a little fraction as it were, a bright but delicate hue of truth! Observe, according to Matthew, Jesus says, "Whoever will do the will of my Father in Heaven, the same is my brother and *sister* and mother." Bringing before the imagination the whole group, keeping in view the sensibility of the woman who had just broken forth in blessing her who had born such a son, may we not suppose that he was led, unconsciously as it were, to increase the point and emphasis of the sentiment, by the introduction of the sisterly relation–turning his eyes as he spake towards the woman!"–pp.59–76.

This piece of criticism illustrates a remark, which we once found in the "Wanderjahre," to the following effect: "I am convinced that the Bible will ever be more highly valued, the more it is *understood;* that is, the more we consider that every thing which we take in a general sense, had originally a special local application, under particular circumstances, to a particular occasion." Here too is another beautiful specimen of insight into the deeper meaning of a simple word:

"When Jesus had cried aloud, " 'Lazarus, come forth,' he that was dead came forth, bound hand and foot with grave-clothes, and with a cloth about his face. *And Jesus said, 'Loose him and let him go. ' "* At first view we cannot help feeling that there is an abrupt falling off here in the narrative, a sudden descent to a trifling particular–to an observation apparently and comparatively insignificant. We instantly ask how came Jesus to give this trifling direction! Or, if he did give it, how happened the narrator to recollect it and to think it worth while to put it on record! These queries are silenced the instant we recur to the probable circumstances. If the dead man actually appeared, into what consternation must the by-standers have been thrown! Some shrieked, some fainted, and all, transfixed and bereft of their composure, and doubting whether they beheld an apparition or real flesh and blood, left Lazarus to struggle and stagger in the grave-clothes in which he was wrapt 'hand and foot.' It is impossible that any one present could have failed to be most deeply impressed with that sublime self-possession which Jesus alone preserved, and with which he quietly bade them go and loose the grave-clothes, and set Lazarus at Liberty. That simple sentence–"And Jesus said, 'Loose him, and let him go,'"–thus considered, in connexion with the circumstances, how full is it of truth and nature! To my mind, it furnishes evidence the most decisive, because entirely incidental, of the reality of the restoration of Lazarus. It is a slight circumstance in itself, but in its perfect naturalness there is an indelible stamp of truth. *Ex pede Herculem.*"–pp. 138-139.

We can only give more example of the excellent insight which our author has into the meaning of Scripture, and this shall be in relation to the Lord's rebuke given to Peter.–Matt. XVI.

"Again. In the sixteenth chapter of Matthew, we have the following: 'From that time forth began Jesus to show unto his disciples, how that he must go unto Jerusalem, and suffer many things of the elders and chief priests and scribes, and be killed, and be raised again the third day." Is it suspected that this passage is a mere fabrication, inserted into the history with a view to invest Jesus with the character and reputation of a Prophet! Every trace of such a suspicious vanishes when we observe the beautiful, because unconscious, consistency of this portion of the history with what precedes and what follows. "From that time forth," so this passage commences, "began Jesus to show his disciples how he must go to Jerusalem, and suffer and die." From what time? Why, immediately after he had ascertained that his disciples acknowledged him as the anointed messenger of God. As soon as he found that they explicitly recognized his authority, he began to disclose to them what was about to take place. So that this passage comes in just where it ought to come in, in order to harmonize with the connexion. But this is not all. The disclosure of his approaching sufferings and death on this occasion, is incidentally connected with a striking and most natural illustration of the character of Peter. When Jesus spake of what he must suffer, "Peter took him," we are told. "and began to rebuke him, saying, 'Be it far from thee, Lord; this shall not be done unto thee.' But he turned and said unto Peter, 'Get thee behind me, Satan; thou art a stumbling-block to me; for thou savourest not the things that be of God, but those that be of men.' " What! Is this Peter–the Rock, as Jesus a moment before named him, saying, that upon this Rock he would build his church, and the gates of Hell should not prevail against it–is this the man who is now addressed in the severest language of reproof, and pronounced a stumbling-block, a rock of offence!

"O, tell me not there has been any garbling–any forgery here! If this portion of the history had not its deep foundations in truth and nature–if it were a fiction, its author would never have dreamed of venturing apparently so gross an inconsistency, or, if he had, he would not have permitted it to go unexplained. In reality, there is here not only no inconsistency, but the most exquisite keeping, as I proceed to show.

"Shortly before, as we read in the same chapter, Jesus had inquired of his disciples what the people thought of him–whom they supposed him to be. They replied, "Some say thou art John the Baptist, some Elias, and others Jeremiah, or one of the old prophets." He then put the question directly to the disciples themselves, "Whom do you think me to be?" Peter, with his characteristic forwardness, answers without hesitation, "Thou art the Anointed, the Son of the living God." It disclosed great openness to the truth in Peter, to have come so speedily and confidently to the conviction, that in the humble man of Nazareth he beheld the long-looked for, magnificent Messiah. There was nothing in the external appearance of Jesus which proved him to be that illustrious personage, but much to the contrary. Since Peter then recognized him as the Christ, it could only have been through the moral, spiritual credentials which he gave in his beneficent words and

works. Accordingly, Jesus breaks forth in blessing upon Peter, exclaiming, "Blessed art thou, Simon, son of Jonas,[4] flesh and blood hath not revealed it unto thee, but my father who is in Heaven!" i.e. "it is not from men, or from any earthly source, that thou hast discovered me to be the Messiah. It has been revealed unto thee by that true spirit in thine own soul, which is the Spirit of God." How naturally must the warm commendation of Jesus have tended to elate the ardent mind of Peter! This it was, we perceive, that emboldened him to contradict and rebuke Jesus, when the latter immediately afterwards proceeded to speak of his sufferings. Although he acknowledged Jesus to be the Christ, he was not at all prepared to believe that the Christ could suffer indignity and violence. Therefore he sought to silence Jesus, saying, "Be it far from thee, Lord, this shall not be done unto thee," and so drew upon himself that severe rebuke, "Away! thou enemy! Thou art a stumbling-block to me, for thou savourest not the things that be of God, but the things that be of men.""–pp. 220–222

These examples will show how we expect this work to improve the style of our Scripture commentaries. The bare meaning of the words of a text, stated in a dry and abstract manner, do not give us half of their original significance. The look and tone of the speaker, the state of mind of his auditors, preceeding events, surrounding scenery, impending and expected occurrences–all tend to modify, and deepen the significance of the words spoken. We cannot have all of these accessories, but by an effort of the imagination,–we may transport ourselves to the place, and bring before us the images and circumstances which belong to it. Mr. Abbott, in his Young Christian, recommends and exemplifies this, very successfully, and the preceeding quotations are admirable specimens of a better style of commentary than we have yet had. To young theological students we especially recommend it as a means of quickening their own powers to a more active study of Scripture. The only commentary which we now recollect written in this manner, is that of Olshausen. We have been told that Paulus is also an example, but have never read his work. Olshausen's commentary, we have seen advertised at Princeton as about to be translated by some theological student. He can render no better service to the cause of scriptural knowledge.

4. This book will tend to alter and correct our opinions with respect to Miracles.

It is high time, so it seems to us, that we should somewhat modify our ways of talking on the subject of miracles. There is something very unsatisfactory in the common theological account of the nature and object of miracles. Every one who has had to do with sceptical or inquiring minds, knows this. In a limited experience, we have found that among the young men, graduates of our Universities, many who have attended to the arguments, have had their belief destroyed, instead of being fortified by their course of study. Where the religious feeling is stronger than the speculative bias, this does not take place, but this is because the heart instructed by God, is wiser than the head taught of men. And though in these cases one is preserved from infidelity, he is yet left destitute of faith. He has not the clear calm conviction of the reality of Christ's wonderous works, which results from a rational apprehension of their consistency with all the laws of Nature and of God. We are therefore glad to see this great subject brought into discussion by Mr. Furness in this volume, and by the author of an article in the last Christian Examiner, upon Martineau's lectures. We are by no means certain that these gentlemen have expressed a perfectly correct view of the matter, but they have set a discussion on foot, from which much light may be elicited.

There are two points especially in the common notion of miracles which seem to us to need modifying. First, that they are violations of the laws of Nature—and second, that their object is to compel an assent to the truth of Christian Revelation. Against the first of these views Mr. Furness contends, against the second the Reviewer in the Examiner.

Supposing miracles violations of the laws of Nature, we meet with inseparable difficulty in contending for them. They are unnatural and monstrous by our very statement. There is something opposed to our trust in God as a faithful Creator and unchanging Guardian of the universe. Without, however, entering on this discussion, we can only remark here, that scripture authorizes no such idea, but repeatedly intimates that miracles have their conditions and laws, and are part of the great system of things. *Above* nature, they are not *violations* of nature, they are the manifestations of high spiritual powers which are now full of mystery and wonder to us, but in a higher state of being, will seem natural. This view of miracles, which might be explained and defended at great length, is, as far as we know, the only now received by German Theologians of the school opposed to Rationalists and Naturalists.

Then as to the other view as regards the object of miracles. That they are not intended to force men to believe in Christianity, appears so plainly on the face of Scripture that it is a matter of surprise to us, that

so learned a theologian as Mr. Andrews Norton, should have thought this opinion injurious to Christianity, as he has in a lately published letter. The Reviewer of Martineau seems to us to have proved very clearly that his view is that of the most orthodox theologians in all ages of the church. And the most cursory glance at the gospels will show us, that in a vast majority of cases, Jesus required faith *before* he would work the miracle, and that in no one case does he demand it *after* the miracle has been performed. He leaves it then, to work its due influence on the soul prepared by faith for its reception, kindling inner fires of awe, love and trusting reverence, producing convictions of the superiority of the soul to material laws, and bringing out feelings and convictions which can never pass away or be forgotten:

Truths, which wake, to perish never.

"Believest thou that I am able to do this?" is the usual preface to the working of a miracle. How extraordinary this demand, if the miracle itself was to be the evidence! "He did not many mighty works there, because of their unbelief." If the object of miracles be to produce faith, this would have been the very place where they should be performed.

Let these remarks be regarded as mere hints and suggestions with respect to these two points. For a more full discussion, we refer our readers to the work before us, and the Christian Examiner for November 1835, article on Martineau. It seems to us that a free examination of these great subjects will help us to a higher, as well as a deeper faith in the spiritual world.

We must, however, bring forward some objections which have occurred to us, while perusing certain passages in the "Remarks on the Gospels."

On the 44th and 45th pages, we find an explanation of the incident of the woman who came and touched the hem of Christ's garment, and was healed of an issue of blood. Our author says that the evangelists "all tell us that when the woman came forward, Jesus addressed her in a cheering tone, assuring her that her faith had cured her. By this assurance, as I conceive, he intended to correct the impression she had evidently entertained, that there was a miraculous power of healing in his very garments. It was through the power of her own faith—the influence of her own mind, that so instantaneous a cure had been effected." Now there seems to us no difficulty in believing, that she was cured by her own faith, *aided by* a real influence from the Savior. And as the Savior declares, according to Luke, that "virtue had gone out of him," this appears the only conclusion possible. But our author goes on to say, that it was "purely an inference of the historians, that Jesus ascertained that some one had touched him, by the departure of a medical virtue from his body." "And one of them (Luke)" continues he, "has gone so far as to put words to this effect into his mouth." It seems to us that in this short sentence, is a complete contradiction of all which he so eloquently declares of the inspiration of the Evangelists. If they can so far be mistaken as to make Jesus say the very opposite of what he means to say, expressly teach what he intended expressly to deny, where has gone that single purpose of seeing and stating things exactly as they were, on which we are to rely for our only proof, that the gospels contain only what really happened. A sharp sighted enquirer finds, that Jesus meant to teach the very opposite of what the historians represent him as teaching—what is our security that other searchers may not find them equally mistaken, in many other of their representations?

Our author goes on further to remark, that "probably the woman did not merely touch the garments, but seized them with a quick convulsive grasp, and so he felt something peculiar in the movement." But the three evangelists evidently mean, to convey that it was a *touch* and no more. It was the "hem" and the "border" of his garment, which she sought to reach. If then, after all, she did not touch it but grasped it, the historians have given a wrong impression of the event.

In the same way, where, on page 58, our author supposes that Jesus, when driving the money-changers from the temple, only used the whip of small cords to *drive the cattle,* not the men, and says also that he probably *found* the whip there and did not make it—he violates the obvious construction of the passage. It is expressly said, that he *"made* a scourge of small cords." and that he drove out them who sold oxen and doves and the money changers—*and the sheep and the oxen.* Why then torture the passage to another meaning? Indeed it infinitely heightens our conceptions of the *compass,* so to speak, of the character of Jesus, that he was led like a sheep to the slaughter, and was meek and gentle toward his own persecutors, could in a moment when the violated majesty of Heaven required it, gather the sternness and awful bearing of the most terrible of the ancient prophets. His meekness then was no mere natural gentleness or physical good-nature. He could be severe and terrible, but he *chose* to be tender and meek as a child. Yet even though it should seem inconsistent and unaccountable, better let it stand as it is for some future interpreter to explain, than put the smallest violence on the construction of the passage.

These two examples will illustrate a fault which, however, is very rare indeed with our author; a tendency to bend the language to suit his own explanation. We cannot bear the slightest tendency of this kind. If we wish to learn anything from these gospels, it must be by opening our minds fully to the exact impression they choose to make. We must be first wholly receptive, then we may scrutinize the impression as much as we will, and try fully to understand it.

In the chapter on the prophetic character of Jesus, our author seems not to have fully expressed his thought. To many readers, he will appear to say, that our Lord foresaw, by an exercise of common human sagacity, the desertion of his friends, the denial of Peter, his own death, and the destruction of Jerusalem. He does not mean to say this, but he seems to say it.

Much more might be said in behalf of this production, something more perchance against it. But here we must leave the matter, concluding, however, as we began, that it contains, on the whole, a new revelation of Christ. And so we wind up our labor of love, with the following noble description of the manner of the great Teacher:

"I apprehend that in this respect he has never yet been understood. He so uniformly represented himself as speaking and acting by the express command of God, that he is too much regarded as a mere passive instrument, the mechanical agent of another and higher being. We are not aware of the strong personal interest which the whole style of his teaching undesignedly shows he must have cherished in his work. I believe the principal force of the Divine command was felt by him in the free and inner force of his own convictions. The voice of his own soul, clear and imperative—this it was that he reverenced as the commanding voice of his Father. This was to him the most intimate and solemn expression of the Divine authority. His words were continually modified and suggested by external circumstances. And what does this indicate but the fulness of his heart, the inexhaustible abundance of his spirit? Must it not have been with him even as I have said, that he was full of spiritual life, and that when he spoke he spoke from within. He could not have held his peace, and he needed no outward inducement to speak, but such as was offered at the moment. The vessel was filled to the brim, and every breath made it overflow, and like the precious ointment upon the head of the High-priest that ran down, down to the skirts of his garments, the costly streams from the full heart of Jesus, fell upon the world cleansing and sanctifying.

"Here was the unequalled power of the words of Jesus. This it was that gave them a victorious influence. They were uttered simply and earnestly as the natural expression of thoughts and sentiments, which he himself cherished and felt far more deeply than it was in the power of any language to express. This is true Eloquence,—when a man speaks not for the sake of effect, not from any outward necessity, but from an impulse within which he cannot resist,—from the concentrated force of his own convictions. Then words are words no longer. They are acts. They exhibit and convey the life's life, that energy of human thought and feeling which is of eternity and of God. Of all the powers of nature, the power of a human spirit, thoroughly persuaded in itself, penetrated with faith, is the most vital and intense. When the force of such a spirit is bodied forth either by word or deed, it acts upon all surrounding spirits–on all other minds. A brief sentence, a single articulate sound of the voice, coming from the heart, or rather bringing the heart along with it, possesses a resistless power. It is like "the piercing of a sword," like "a winged thunderbolt," prostrating all opposition, inflaming all souls. Such are the sympathies between man and man. It was this that gave to Peter the Hermit the power to arouse all Europe, nobles and their vassals, priests and kings, the rich and the poor men, women and children, and lead them to the recovery of the Holy Land. The historian Gibbon sneers at his fanaticism and confesses his power, observing that "the most perfect orator of Athens might have envied his eloquence." Ignorant though he was, mean and contemptible in appearance, still his words expressed the burning convictions of his own soul, and so he created the same convictions in other men.

"Seldom, alas! have human words exerted this influence. The reason how obvious! They have seldom shown themselves to be the inspiration of the living heart. They, who have enjoyed the opportunity and the privilege of teaching, have taught from self-interest or for reputation's sake, or to produce upon others an effect which has never been wrought upon themselves. They have been sworn to maintain and advocate certain established systems of religious opinion. They have consequently spoken, because they were required to speak and must say something, and take good care not to deviate from a track before appointed. How widely opposite to all this, the spirit of a true teacher, of one in whom the truth lives and works as in Jesus of Nazareth, stimulating every power, inspiring every affection, commanding his whole being, and who therefore speaks because something within–the voice of the living God, commands and will not be disobeyed. He must utter himself even if he perish in the act.

He neither thinks to please nor to offend, to conciliate nor to shock. His feeling is–Let me speak out my own heart or let me die! He that hath the word of the Lord, hath it stamped upon his inmost being, sounding for ever through the secret chambers of the soul, let him speak that word faithfully. What is the chaff to the wheat?"–pp. 128.

---

1. Lately translated Professor Marsh.
2. Not 'a new creature.'
3. To this benediction, Jesus replied, "Yes, rather blessed are they who hear the word of God and keep it." Here, by the way, we have an instance of that mode of speaking, upon which I was just remarking–a proposition general in its terms, but prompted by and applying to a peculiar case. It was not a formal declaration, but a spontaneous and sudden exclamation. We cannot doubt that when Jesus uttered these words, he fastened his eyes upon the woman whose language had called them forth. And it is as if he had said, "Dost thou deem my mother happy? Rather most blessed art thou if thou but know thy present privilege, and hearing what I say, bear thyself accordingly." How deeply absorbed he was with what he had just been saying, we may infer from the sensitiveness he evinces to the least disposition on the part of his hearers to think of any thing else.

When the woman uttered this benediction on the mother of Jesus, little did she dream that she uttered a sentiment to which, in the worship of the Virgin, the world was for ages to respond; and which was to be embodied in the finest efforts of Art. In the adoration of the infant Jesus and his mother, have we not a touching tribute to the power with which Christianity has appealed to some of the best and tenderest affections of our nature? With the manhood of Jesus, the world has yet to learn to sympathize.

4. "Simon, son of Jonas." The intense fervour with which this benediction was uttered, is incidentally and strikingly displayed in this mode of address. How natural, when a friend communicates any unexpected sentiment or intelligence, do we express our surprise in a similar way, uttering the whole name of our friend, with fervent emphasis?

[James Freeman Clarke]
"New Views of Christianity," *Western Messenger,* 3 (March 1837): 529-539.

Orestes A. Brownson's New Views of Christianity, Society, and the Church *(1836) argued for an eclectic world view that incorporated the best of past religions in an attempt to base social reform on Christian teachings. Although Brownson's book was well-received by the Transcendentalists, with whom he had at that time allied himself, Brownson later broke with them. The Transcendentalists placed too great an emphasis upon man's intuition and the freedom it called forth, Brownson felt, and he feared that wrongly applied this could lead to anarchy. In his later years, Brownson became a staunch Catholic. Clarke's review in the* Western Messenger *is another example of that journal's support of Transcendentalist ideas. (For further information on this reformer and editor, see the entry for Brownson in* DLB 1, The American Renaissance in New England.)*

We were prepared for something good from Mr. Brownson, but this work has far exceeded our expectations. While in eloquence of style it equals the writings of the Abbé de la Mennais and Victor Cousin, it surpasses the first in philosophic depth and the last in condensation. In fact we look upon this book as calculated to make a deeper and wider impression than any thing of the sort since "The Words of a Believer."

The following passage, from the preface, will tend to remove a prejudice which the name naturally excites:

"It must not be inferred from my calling this little work New Views, that I profess to bring forward a new religion, or to have discovered a new Christianity. The religion of the Bible I believe to be given by the inspiration of God, and the Christianity of Christ satisfies my understanding and my heart. However widely I may dissent from the Christianity of the Church, with that of Christ I am content to stand or fall, and I ask no higher glory than to live and die in it and for it.

"Although I consider the views contained in the following pages original, I believe the conclusions, to which I come at last, will be found very much in accordance with those generally adopted by the denomination of Christians, with whom it has been for some years my happiness to be associated. That denomination, however, must not be held responsible for any of the opinions I have advanced. I am not the organ of a sect. I do not speak by authority, nor under tutelage. I speak for myself and from my own convictions. And in this way, better than I could in any other, do I prove my sympathy with the body of which I am a member, and establish my right to be called a Unitarian.

"With these remarks I commit my little work to its fate. It contains results to which I have come only by years of painful experience; but I dismiss it from my mind with the full conviction, that He, who has watched over my life and preserved me amidst scenes through which I hope I may not be called to pass again, will take care that if what it contains be false it shall do no harm, and if it be true that it shall not die."

We will now attempt to give our readers a brief summary of the book. Yet we fear we shall do it injustice; for where all is so condensed, any omission breaks the course of thought.

He sets forth with two propositions, on which, as upon firm foundation stones, the whole work is based. The first is, that "Religion is natural to man, and he ceases to be man the moment he ceases to be religious." The second declares, that as man is a creature of growth, the institutions, forms, and embodyments of religion must necessarily be always changing.

Christianity, therefore, he goes on to say, as given by Christ, is always "the same, yesterday, today and forever." But Christianity as taught by the Church, is quite another thing. It is defective, mutable, improveable. Christianity as it exists now, is very far from being what Christ meant it to be. What, then, did he mean? Let Mr. Brownson answer.

"To comprehend Jesus, to seize the Holy as it was in him, and consequently the true idea of Christianity, we must, from the heights to which we have risen by the aid of the church, look back and down upon the age in which he came, ascertain what was the work which there was for him to perform, and from that obtain a key to what he proposed to accomplish.

"Two systems then disputed the Empire of the World; spiritualism[1] represented by the Eastern world, the world of Asia, and Materialism represented by Greece and Rome. Spiritualism regards purity or holiness as predicable of Spirit alone, and Matter as essentially impure, possessing and capable of receiving nothing of the Holy,—the prison house of the soul, its only hindrance to a union with God, or absorption into his essence, the cause of all uncleanness, sin, and evil, consequently to be contemned, degraded, and as far as possible annihilated. Materialism takes the other extreme, does not recognise the claims of Spirit, disregards the soul, counts the body every thing, earth all, heaven nothing, and condenses itself into the advice, 'Eat and drink, for to-morrow we die.'

"This opposition between Spiritualism and Materialism presupposes a necessary and original antithesis between Spirit and Matter. When Spirit and Matter are given as antagonist principles, we are obliged to admit antagonism between all the terms into which they are respectively convertible. From Spirit is deduced by natural generation, God, the Priesthood, Faith, Heaven, Eternity; from Matter, Man, the State, Reason, the Earth, and Time; consequently to place Spirit and Matter in opposition, is to make an antithesis between God and Man, the Priesthood and the State, Faith and Reason, Heaven and Earth, and Time and Eternity.

"This antithesis generates perpetual and universal war. It is necessary then to remove it and harmonize, or unite the two terms. Now, if we conceive Jesus as standing between Spirit and Matter, the representative of both—God-Man—the point where both meet and lose the antithesis, laying a hand on each and saying, 'Be one, as I and my Father are one,' thus sanctifying both and marrying them in a mystic and holy union, we shall have his secret thought and the true Idea of Christianity.

"The Scriptures uniformly present Jesus to us as a mediator, the middle term between two extremes, and they call his work a mediation, a reconciliation—an atonement. The Church has ever considered Jesus as making an atonement. It has held on to the term at all times as with the grasp of death. The first charge it has labored to fix upon heretics has been that of rejecting the Atonement, and the one all dissenters from the predominant doctrines of the day, have been most solicitous to repel, is that of 'denying the Lord who bought us.' The whole Christian world, from the days of the Apostles up to the moment in which I write, have identified Christianity with the Atonement, and felt that in admitting the Atonement they admitted Christ, and that in denying it they were rejecting him."

Mr. Brownson we perceive appropriates to his own use the very famous orthodox word, Atonement. It is very certain, however, that its original meaning was that which he gives it—"to make at one"—"to reconcile." He goes on to say that Jesus and John (he might have added Paul) repeatedly declare Love to be the essence of Christianity.

"The nature of love is to destroy all antagonism. It brings together; it begetteth union, and from union cometh peace. And what word so accurately expresses to the consciousness of Christendom, the intended result of the mission of Jesus, as that word peace? Every man who has read the New Testament feels that it was peace that Jesus came to effect,—peace after which the soul has so often sighed and yearned in vain, and a peace not merely between two or three individuals for a day, but a universal and eternal peace between all conflicting elements, between God and man, between the soul and body, between this world and another, between the duties of time and the duties of eternity. How clearly is this expressed in that sublime chorus of the angels, sung over the manger-cradle—'Glory to God in the highest, on earth peace and good-will to men!'

"Where there is but one term there is no union. There is no harmony with but one note. It is mockery to talk to us of peace where one of the two belligerent parties is annihilated. That were the peace of the grave. Jesus must then save both parties. The Church has, therefore, with a truth it has never comprehended, called him GOD MAN. But if the two terms and their products be originally and essentially antagonist; if there be between them an innate hostility, their union, their reconciliation cannot be effected. Therefore in proposing the union, in attempting the Atonement, Christianity declares as its great doctrine that there is no essential, no original antithesis between God and man; that neither Spirit nor Matter is unholy in its nature; that all things, Spirit, Matter, God, Man, Soul, Body, Heaven, Earth, Time, Eternity, with all their duties and interests, are in themselves holy. All things proceed from the same Holy Fountain, and no fountain sendeth forth both sweet waters and bitter. It therefore writes 'HOLINESS TO THE LORD' upon every thing, and sums up its sublime teaching in that grand synthesis. 'Thou shalt love the Lord thy God with all thy heart and mind and soul and strength, and thy neighbor as thyself.' "

The next chapter deals with the church, and we are beginning to despair, since our limits prevent us from extracting the whole of it, the only way of doing it justice. Its sum is that the church did not succeed in taking the idea of Jesus, and instead of understanding him to assert the holiness of spirit and matter, it understood him to say that matter was cursed, and to predicate holiness of spirit alone. He is therefore no more an Atoner, but a Redeemer. He redeems spirit from the curse of the flesh.

From this original mistake proceeded the Gnostic and Manichæan errors, original sin, total depravity, vicarious sacrifice, human inability, supremacy of the church, a Pope, Creeds, Inquisitions, Implicit Faith, Celibacy of the Clergy, Monks, Nuns, and contempt for all earthly interests.

"But every thing," so begins the next chapter, "must have its time. The church abused, degraded, villified matter, but could not annihilate it. It existed in spite of the church. It increased in power, and at length rose against spiritualism and demanded the restoration of its rights. This rebellion of Materialism, of the material order against the spiritual, is Protestantism."

His reasons for this assertion are briefly these. The revival of classic literature and art, was confessedly an immediate cause of Protestantism. But classic Greece and Rome were wholly material in their character. In protestantism, as in classic antiquity, religion becomes a function of the state, and is valued as a useful help in keeping the people in order. In both, reason or government determine the belief of the people, and not church authority. The tendency now is toward perfect freedom of opinion and conscience. Protestant philosophy also is material. The senses are made the source of knowledge, and scepticism of all which cannot be perceived by the senses is the result. Strictly speaking, there is no religion in Protestantism. "As protestants,

Engraving of Orestes Brownson in 1843

people are not religious, but co-existing with their Protestantism, they may indeed retain something of religion." Protestant religion is Catholicism continued.

"The same principle lies at the bottom of all Protestant churches, in so far as they are churches, which was at the bottom of the Church of the middle ages. But Materialism modifies their rites and dogmas. In the practice of all, there is an effort to make them appear reasonable. Hence Commentaries, Expositions, and Defences without number. Even where the authority of the reason is denied, there is an instinctive sense of its authority and a desire to enlist it. In mere forms, pomp and splendor have gradually disappeared, and dry utility and even baldness have been consulted. In doctrines, those which exalt man and give him some share in the work of salvation have gained in credit and influence. Pelagianism, under some thin disguises or undisguised, has become almost universal. The doctrine of man's inherent

Total Depravity, in the few cases in which it is asserted, is asserted more as a matter of duty than of conviction. Nobody, who can help it, preaches the old-fashioned doctrine of God's Sovereignty, expressed in the dogma of unconditional Election and Reprobation. The Vicarious Atonement has hardly a friend left. The Deity of Jesus is questioned, his simple Humanity is asserted and is gaining credence. Orthodox is a term which implies as much reproach as commendation; people are beginning to laugh at the claims of councils and synods, and to be quite merry at the idea of excommunication."

The same material tendency shows itself in Literature, Art, Government and Industry. There is however, in this century, a slight reaction in favor of spiritualism, in consequence of the excessive materialism of the eighteenth century. Here is a beautiful description of the events which accompanied this reaction.

"The Eighteenth Century will be marked in the annals of the world for its strong faith in the material order. Meliorations on the broadest scale were contemplated and viewed as already realized. Our Republic sprang into being, and the world leaped with joy that 'a man child was born.' Social progress and the perfection of governments became the religious creed of the day; the weal of man on earth, the spring and aim of all hopes and labors. A new paradise was imaged forth for man, inaccessible to the serpent, more delightful than that which Adam lost, and more attractive than that which the pious Christian hopes to gain. We of this generation can form only a faint conception of the strong faith our fathers had in the progress of society, the high hopes of human improvement they indulged, and the joy too big for utterance, with which they heard France in loud and kindling tones proclaim LIBERTY and EQUALITY. France for a moment became the centre of the world. All eyes were fixed on her movements. The pulse stood still when she and her enemies met, and loud cheers burst from the universal heart of Humanity when her tri-colored flag was seen to wave in triumph over the battle field. There was then no stray thought for God and eternity. Man and the world filled the soul. They were too big for it. But while the voice of hope was yet ringing, and *Te Deum* shaking the arches of the old Cathedrals, –the Convention, the reign of Terror, the exile of patriots, the massacre of the gifted, the beautiful and the good, Napoleon and the Military Despotism came, and Humanity uttered a piercing shriek, and fell prostrate on the grave of her hopes!

"The reaction produced by the catastrophe of this memorable drama was tremendous. There are still lingering among us those who have not forgotten the recoil they experienced when they saw the Republic swallowed up, or preparing to be swallowed up, in the Empire. Men never feel what they felt but once. The pang which darts through their souls changes them into stone. From that moment enthusiasm died, hope in social melioration ceased to be indulged, and those who had been the most sanguine in their anticipations, hung down their heads and said nothing; the warmest friends of Humanity apologized for their dreams of Liberty and Equality; Democracy became an accusation, and faith in the perfectibility of mankind a proof of disordered intellect."

The signs of this reaction on behalf of spiritualism are many. It shows itself in philosophy, art and literature. "Materialism in philosophy is extinct in Germany. It is only a reminiscence in France, and it produces no remarkable work in England or America. Phrenology, which some deem materialism, has itself struck materialism with death in Gall's work." Protestantism ceases to gain ground in this century in what is peculiar to itself. Rationalism in Germany, England and America, retreats before the Evangelical party. Unitarianism on the plan of Priestly and Belsham, is on the decline. Catholicism has revived, offered some able apologies for itself, made some eminent proselytes, and alarmed Protestants. "Men who a few years ago were staunch Rationalists, now talk of spiritual communion; and many who could with difficulty be made to admit the inspiration of the Bible, are now ready to admit the inspiration of the sacred books of all nations, and instead of stumbling at the idea of God's speaking to a few individuals, they see no reason why he should not speak to every body." Money getting and utilitarianism are spoken of with contempt. "Protestantism died in the French revolution, and we are beginning to get disgusted with its dead body. Spiritualism revives, will it again become supreme? Impossible."

We have thus accompanied our author through his survey of the past. He began by stating the Idea of Jesus to be the reconciliation of Heaven and earth, or founding the Kingdom of Heaven below. This the Church did not understand. Through long ages Spiritualism triumphed. But in the Reformation of Luther the Material became ascendant. There was a reaction from Spiritualism to Materialism. But just now there is another reaction in favor of Spiritualism. The question now comes what is to be the result of it–what are the prospects of our own and coming ages?

According to our author, neither the Catholic nor the Protestant ideas are to have exclusive supremacy hereafter, but there is to be a reconciliation between them, and the Christianity of Christ is to take the place of the Christianity of these two churches. To bring this about is the mission of the present. Humanity never goes back; to go back either to exclusive Spiritualism or exclusive Materialism, is impossible. The world is tired of both, it desires something better than either. All this is expounded minutely and confirmed by appeal to facts. We should be glad to insert here, had we space, our author's remarks on Calvinism, Universalism and Unitarianism, but we really must stop extracting somewhere, and as these are not absolutely essential to the argument, we pass on to the

Results Of The Atonement.

"The influence of this doctrine cannot fail to be very great. It will correct our estimate of man, of the world, of religion and of God, and remodel all our institutions. It must in fact create a new civilization as much in advance of ours, as ours is in advance of that which obtained in the Roman Empire in the time of Jesus.

"Hitherto we have considered man as the antithesis of all good. We have loaded him with reproachful epithets and made it a sin in him even to be born. We have uniformly deemed it necessary to degrade him in order to exalt his creator. But this will end. The slave will become a son. Man is hereafter to stand erect before God as a child before its father. Human nature, at which we have pointed our wit and vented our spleen, will be clothed with a high and commanding worth. It will be seen to be a lofty and deathless nature. It will be felt to be Divine, and Infinite will be found traced in living characters on all its faculties.

"We shall not treat one another then as we do now. Man will be sacred in the eyes of man. To wrong him will be more than crime, it will be sin. To labor to degrade him will seem like laboring to degrade the Divinity. Man will reverence man.

"Slavery will cease. Man will shudder at the bare idea of enslaving so noble a being as man. It will seem to him hardly less daring than to presume to task the motions of the Deity and to compel him to come and go at our bidding. When man learns the true value of man, the chains of the captive must be unloosed and the fetters of the slave fall off.

"Wars will fail. The sword will be beaten into the ploughshare and the spear into the pruning hook. Man will not dare to mar and mangle the shrine of the Divinity. The God looking out from human eyes will disarm the soldier and make him kneel to him he had risen up to slay. The war-horse will cease to bathe his fetlocks in human gore. He will snuff the breeze in the wild freedom of his native plains, or quietly submit to be harnessed to the plough. The hero's occupation will be gone, and heroism will be found only in saving and blessing human life.

"Education will destroy the empire of ignorance. The human mind, allied as it is to the Divine, is too valuable to lie waste or to be left to breed only briars and thorns. Those children, ragged and incrusted with filth, which throng our streets, and for whom we must one day build prisons, forge bolts and bars, or erect gibbets, are not only our children, our brother's children, but they are children of God, they have in themselves the elements of the Divinity and powers which when put forth will raise them above what the tallest archangel now is. And when this is seen and felt, will these children be left to fester in ignorance or to grow up in vice and crime? The whole energy of man's being cries out against such folly, such gross injustice.

"Civil freedom will become universal. It will be every where felt that one man has no right over another which that other has not over him. All will be seen to be brothers and equals to the sight of their common Father. All will love one another too much to desire to play the tyrant. Human nature will be reverenced too much not to be allowed to have free scope for the full and harmonious development of all its faculties. Governments will become sacred; and while on one hand they are respected and obeyed, on the other it will be felt to be a religious right and a religious duty, to labor to make them as perfect as they can be.

"Religion will not stop with the command to obey the laws, but it will bid us make just laws, such laws as befit a being divinely endowed like man. The Church will be on the side of progress, and Spiritualism and Materialism will combine to make man's earthly condition as near like the lost Eden of the Eastern poets, as is compatible with the growth and perfection of his nature.

"Industry will be holy. The cultivation of the earth will be the worship of God. Workingmen will be priests, and as priests they will be reverenced, and as priests they will reverence themselves and feel that they must maintain themselves undefiled. He that ministers at the altar must be pure, will be said of the mechanic, the agriculturist, the common laborer, as well as of him who is technically called a priest.

"The earth itself and the animals which inhabit it will be counted sacred. We shall study in them the manifestation of God's goodness, wisdom, and power, and be careful that we make of them none but a holy use.

"Man's body will be deemed holy. It will be called the temple of the Living God. As a temple it must not be desecrated. Men will beware of defiling it by sin, by any excessive or improper indulgence, as they would of defiling the temple or the altar consecrated to the service of God. Man will reverence himself too much, he will see too much of the Holy in his nature ever to pervert it from the right line of Truth and Duty."

We will close our extracts from this remarkable work with the concluding passage. Many parts which we had marked for extracting, we are obliged to omit. As respects the truth or falsehood of the views contained in this work, we hardly feel able as yet to pronounce a judgment. Carried away by the stream of the author's eloquence, we know not yet how to perform our office of critical discrimination. We will however say thus much, that the Eclectic Philosophy upon which these views are based, has long seemed to us the only one which can gain the conviction of the present age. Its method we believe the true and right one, however erroneous some of its present results may be. The leading ideas of this work of Mr. Brownson we feel compelled to admit. It appears to us that there is no middle ground between the optimism of this work, and the creed of despair of Augustine and Calvin. And when the question fairly comes before us in this shape, we cannot hesitate a moment. If Christianity is a gospel of glad tidings, it does not teach those black doctrines of total depravity, and an unending, predetermined Hell, which are more gloomy and horrible than that which may be known of God by the light of Nature. It teaches that evil, though suffered for a time, is surrounded by good and will be at last overcome, and swallowed up in it. It teaches that Love is stronger than Hate, Good than Evil, and that Christ shall reign till all enemies shall be subdued under his feet, and death and hell cast together into the lake of fire. Christianity is in some sense or other a doctrine of Hope, of

Reconciliation, of Optimism. It teaches that every thing is for the best, that our God is a Father, and that he only suffers evil for the sake of Good. If there is danger in this view, of fostering lax and careless sentiments with regard to evil and sin, we say there is a like danger in every system of grace ever preached. The Calvinistic doctrine of Election is equally dangerous. Make a system as stern as you will, you must have a door of hope open somewhere, and then false hopes will always intrude themselves. That, on the whole, is the safest system which gives the most lovely and noble views of God's character and providence, thus creating no hypocritical service, but genuine love.

It seems to us that our author underrates the practical influence of existing sects. When he says on the first page, that the Christian institution must be spoken of as what was, not as what is, as a shadow of a sovereign and an empire in ruins; when he says that Protestantism is dead, &c. &c.; he says what should be qualified. Philosophically, it may be true–but we are so apt to confound the form with the spirit, that he should have stated, perhaps, that the Church is still capable of producing Christians and saving souls.

We bid our friend farewell, thanking him for this work, and praying that we may share his strong faith in the prospects of man.

"Here I must close. I have uttered the words UNION and PROGRESS as the authentic creed of the New Church, as designating the whole duty of man. Would they had been spoken in a clearer, a louder and a sweeter voice, that a response might be heard from the universal heart of Humanity. But I have spoken as I could, and from a motive which I shall not blush to own either to myself or to him to whom all must render an account of all their thoughts, words and deeds. I once had no faith in Him, and I was to myself 'a child without a sire.' I was alone in the world, my heart found no companionship, and my affections withered and died. But I have found Him, and he is my Father, and mankind are my brothers, and I can love and reverence.

"Mankind are my brothers,–they are brothers to one another. I would see them no longer mutually estranged. I labor to bring them together, and to make them feel and own that they are all made of one blood. Let them feel and own this, and they will love one another; they will be kindly affectioned one to another, and 'the groans of this nether world will cease;'

the spectacles of wrongs and outrages oppress our sight no more; tears be wiped from all eyes, and Humanity pass from death to life, to life immortal, to the life of God, for God is love.

"And this result, for which the wise and the good every where yearn and labor, will be obtained. I do not misread the age. I have not looked upon the world only out from the window of my closet; I have mingled in its busy scenes; I have rejoiced and wept with it; I have hoped and feared, and believed and doubted with it, and I am but what it has made me. I cannot misread it. It craves union. The heart of man is crying out for the heart of man. One and the same spirit is abroad, uttering the same voice in all languages. From all parts of the world voice answers to voice, and man responds to man. There is a universal language already in use. Men are beginning to understand one another, and their mutual understanding will beget mutual sympathy, and mutual sympathy will bind them together and to God."

---

1. I use these terms, Spiritualism and Materialism, to designate two social, rather than two philosophical systems. They designate two orders, which, from time out of mind, must have been called *spiritual* and *temporal* or carnal, *holy* and *profane, heavenly* and *worldly,* &c.

[James Freeman Clarke]
"Religious Education of Children," *Western Messenger,* 3 (March 1837): 540-545.

Clarke's review of Alcott's Conversation on the Gospels *(which is continued in the May issue, reprinted below) continued the* Western Messenger's *string of positive comments on the emerging Transcendentalist philosophy. By comparing Alcott to Socrates, and pledging to uphold "the power of truth and its adaption to the human mind to allow of free inquiry and examination," Clarke hoped to counter the many negative remarks then appearing in the Boston press.*

James Freeman Clarke, an editor of the Western Messenger

Photograph of Amos Bronson Alcott

[52]

Bronson Alcott's letter of 20 May 1862 to Thoreau's mother about Henry's death: "Nor do I think of a contemporary who has done so much in so short a time as he has." (Sophia Thoreau's Scrapbook, edited by Walter Harding [1964])

Religious Education of Children.   **540**

ART. 8.—RELIGIOUS EDUCATION OF CHILDREN.

We regard it not the least favorable sign of the state of our country, that so much attention has been paid of late to this important subject. We are beginning to understand that any education which does not awaken the spiritual nature of a child is of little value, and that a merely intellectual education may be positively injurious. We begin to perceive that the fear of the Lord is the beginning of all wisdom, and that without religion the most intellectual man is incomplete in his character. Hence the great interest felt in Sunday schools, hence the increasing anxiety among parents to fulfil their duties toward their child's soul as well as its body and intellect, hence public lectures to children on religion, hence the growing custom of introducing it into week day schools as a regular branch of instruction, hence, in fine, works upon this special subject like the one now lying before us.*

To teach children religion is understood to be difficult as well as important. The difficulties however, are not inherent, but extraneous. To communicate religion to the mind of a child is easy enough, when you once set about it in the right way. But here lies the difficulty. We have done so little of this work, that we hardly know any thing about the right way. We have not learnt that what we have to do is, to suffer them to approach Jesus and forbid them not. We have put ourselves between the Savior and the infant mind with our catechisms and dogmatics, our theological speculations and refinements. Our duty was very easy and simple, had we only known it. It was merely to bring the children to their Savior, to put them into his arms, and let them see his benign and heavenly face. In other words, instead of cramming their minds with our own conclusions and opinions, we were to excite them to act, freely and naturally, upon the Savior's words and the facts of his life, and induce them to draw their own conclusions.

The success of Mr. Alcott, as recorded in the book before us, would, we should think, satisfy the most sceptical, of the practicability and excellence of such a method. A more interesting series of conversations we have never seen. A more natural and beautiful exposition of some great religious principles has not fallen in our way. As an historical document, showing the adaptation of the young mind to religion, it is of inestimable value. It would not gratify, we grant, sectarians

---

* *Conversation with Children on the Gospels; conducted and edited by A. Bronson Alcott. Volume I. Boston: James Munroe & Co. 1836.*

50

541   *Religious Education of Children.*

of any name; for it is eclectic and liberal, and truths belonging to all parties are freely expressed, and remain uncontradicted. In this respect it appears like a running commentary on the work of Mr. Brownson, noticed in the previous article. His philosophic views are here experimentally verified. We see that all forms of faith and opinion have their truth, and that only by including all, can we arrive at perfect Christianity. It argues well for Eclecticism that these two works should issue at the same time, from the same press, in the same city. It is Theory and Practice walking hand in hand.

Those parents should be counted very fortunate who have an opportunity of placing their children in a school like Mr. Alcott's. When we consider how the natures of children are twisted and perverted and spoiled by mismanagement and ignorance on the part of teachers, and that no money can buy for a child that understanding sympathy which alone enables a teacher to unfold the moral nature, it should always be a matter of special gratitude to God on the part of parents when their children come under influences like those set before us in this volume. Parents, however, seldom understand their privileges, and we see by the preface to this volume, that even Mr. Alcott's school is very fluctuating. Many of the children remained with him, it appears, but a short time, and were then taken away. Why this should be, we cannot understand, except the parents thought they would grow too wise and spiritual; a thing we consider quite unlikely to happen in this world of temptation. We have indeed heard fears expressed lest the child's vanity should be excited by the deference shown to his opinions in this method. But the book shows that a rigid self-scrutiny is constantly in action, by which exhibitions of vanity or pride, and other faults, are detected and repressed. After carefully reading the whole book, we are forced to say, that we do not see how a child could go through such a discipline, and bring away habits of vanity or conceit.

We therefore cordially recommend this book to all who desire a knowledge of the method of addressing the young mind on religious truth. With the works of Gallaudet and Jacob Abbott, we shall keep it as a manual in this important department of science. To parents and Sunday school teachers especially, it is a valuable present, the study of which must enable them to abound more and more in that true work of the Lord — the blessed work of bringing the lambs into his fold of safety and peace.

To give some idea of the book, we add extracts from the various conversations.

Religious Education of Children. 542

The following is part of a conversation upon the first chapter of John — "In the beginning was the Word, &c."

Ontological Evidence. Now those who have some dim idea of what these words mean may hold up their hands.

(Several did.)

Now, those who think they have a clear sense of their meaning :

(Several hands fell.)

Now, let each who can express it tell what idea these words convey to him.

Generation of Nature from Spirit. JOSIAH. They seemed to me to mean there was nothing without God.

JOSEPH. Nothing ever would have been without God.

EDWARD B. God made every thing that was and would be.

AUGUSTINE. There could be no life without God, for all life comes from God. He is the fountain of life.

WILLIAM B. God is in every thing.

GEORGE K. God was the first thing, then he made things. If he had not been first, there would have been no other things.

CHARLES. God made every thing, is in every thing, and will continue in every thing to the end.

LUCIA. There must have been spirit before there was any thing else. There must have been spirit to make the world before there could be any world.

Idea of Divinity and Creation. ALEXANDER. Every thing was God, first.

WILLIAM B. Every thing is God, now.

JOSIAH. I think all spirits are emblematic of God. Just as images of stone are copies of men's bodies, so the souls of men are copies of God. I mean all good souls.

FRANK. I think the body is the shadow of the spirit.

LEMUEL. If, as Josiah says, all good spirits are emblems of God, what must bad spirits be the emblems of?

MR. ALCOTT. We will not begin on that subject now, Lemuel. It will come bye and bye.

LUCIA. God must have thought within his mind before any thing could be made, and it was his thought that shaped things.

MR. ALCOTT. Was his thought the word then?

CHARLES. First there was God ; then he thought, then he spoke the thought in a WORD ; and so there was a World.

The following paragraph is an example of an appeal to conscience, and its answer.

Spiritual Experience. Do you think these emblems could be applied to what passes within yourselves ; can it be said of you that the baptism of repentance has been in your soul, and the dove has descended upon it?

(They hesitated.)

Can you say to yourself, I have repented of doing wrong ; I have turned away from my sins ; I have gone down into the deep waters of baptism and washed away my sins ; I have felt a spirit of holiness, gentleness, sweetness, come upon me, and seem to call me child, and tell me to hear and obey?

EMMA. I have felt so, somewhat.

ELLEN. I never felt so sorry as I ought.

The following seems as clear an explanation of Eternity as can be given:

MR. ALCOTT. Eternity is the abolition of all Time. No dial plate can measure it.

EMMA. A dial plate marks off Time.

MR. ALCOTT. The flow of Eternity shall not cease, though centuries are marked off endlessly.

LEMUEL. Eternity has no hours, no spaces.

GEORGE K. I cannot imagine it.

MARTHA. I cannot imagine any thing without an end.

LEMUEL. There is nothing without an end.

CHARLES. My mind is too small to imagine any thing without an end.

MR. ALCOTT. No; your mind is so large that no finite thing can seem to you infinite. The reason you cannot imagine any thing without an end is, because your thought is larger than any thing, and more comprehensive. Every thing is finite, thought is infinite, and you feel this; no thing can measure this feeling.

A very useful part of these conversations is the exercise of imagination. By means of this the children are led to realize the scene or persons concerning which they read. For example, here are two of the pictures which they made in their mind of the massacre of the Innocents.

CHARLES. I imagined Herod, just as his anger was raging, and his passionate order was given to the soldiers to kill every child. And they went out and did as he commanded; and the mothers were so frantic, that they tried to kill the soldiers themselves. I imagined there were stone steps to the houses, and both mothers and children were pitched down the stone steps and killed. And all this while, Herod was looking out at the window, and seeing the slaughter; and at last he could bear it no longer, and stopped it. But when he found Jesus was not killed, he repented of this mercy.

WILLIAM B. I thought of a place ten times as large as this temple. And there was a large room and a beautiful throne, with golden steps, very high, and a great window, and a door open into the street; and soldiers were standing round, waiting; and Herod was waiting for the wise men, till at last he was in such a rage, that he did not know what he was saying, and he told the soldiers to go and kill all the children in the town. And they were afraid to disobey him, and went. And Herod clapped his hands as he saw the massacre go on, looking out of his great window. And he saw one mother, with a child crying, praying; and Herod thought it must be the mother of Jesus, and he sent for it, and had it brought in, and killed it himself. The soldiers were flying about, and the mothers were also flying about frantically, and throwing stones; and now and then a soldier fell dead. And when Herod afterwards found Jesus was not dead, he killed all the soldiers.

Here is a description of Joseph and Mary that might assist a painter in his representation of the Holy Family.

MR. ALCOTT. Have you ever imagined what kind of a person the father of Jesus was?

FRANCIS. I think he had a long beard, and was rather old.

CHARLES. I think he was a plain man, and went to church, and was very decided in his manner about things; not but that he was perfectly kind, but he would set his foot down, and say things should be so and so.

ANDREW. I think he looked like the bust of Plato. (*Pointing to the corner of the room.*)

MR. ALCOTT. How does Mary represent herself to you?

MARTHA. I think she was young, and her hair fell over her neck.

EMMA. I think she was very beautiful.

MR. ALCOTT. Do you mean inward or outward beauty.

EEMA. Both.

CHARLES. I think she was an angel before she was a woman. It seems to me, as if she must have been.

ANDREW. I think she looked like an angel, and a woman too.*

[* "I saw her upon nearer view
An angel, yet a woman too."—*Ed.*]

Religious Education of Children.   **544**

SAMUEL R.   I thought she was very beautiful.

CHARLES.   I thought she had a great deal of maternal feeling, and that made her beautiful; and that she looked like the Circassian women, very simple. and when not engaged in cleaning up her house, Jesus was sitting by, reading to her.   Her eyes were dark blue.

FRANK.   I think they were light blue.

CHARLES.   And her hair was black.

EMMA.   I thought it was brown.

MR. ALCOTT.   I always have imagined her of light complexion, with delicate features, full blue eyes and light hair; and that the Son resembled the Mother.

CHARLES.   I think of Jesus reading to her, and when he could not pronounce a word, his mother would take a needle and point out the letters, and show him how the word was spelt.

MR. ALCOTT.   Well! I never thought of Jesus as learning to read, but as a quiet, meditative Child, who observed his own Nature, and Creation.

EMMA.   When he was not engaged for his parents, I think his usual occupation was to go out into the woods to walk.

MARTHA.   Sometimes I think he had a book in his walks.

CHARLES.   I think he had a garden, and every day he went into it and gathered flowers for his mother.

MR. ALCOTT.   Yes; I have seen a very beautiful picture of Jesus in his childhood, with flowers in his hands.   He liked to be influenced by Nature; he was imaginative; he had a magnificent imagination; he was poetical; he seemed to have every thing in his mind: it was a perfect mind — good Sense, just Judgment, entire Faith.   He grew up like a tree in the midst of Nature.   The scenery around Nazareth was very impressive.   Nazareth was not a city, but a town.

EMMA.   I think if I could draw, I could show exactly how the house looked in which he lived, I seem to see it so clearly.

And here is the idea of "sojourners and pilgrims" happily familiarized:

MR. ALCOTT.   Every one is a visiter on the Earth from the Lord.   I hope you will all be pleasant visiters.   Some visiters are very unpleasant; they do not like what is given them to eat and drink; they do not like the beds they lie on.   Do you think a drunkard is a pleasant visiter?   Is he doing what he is sent to do?

They all laughed.

EMMA.   I am not a very pleasant visiter, but I have a very pleasant visit.

Repentance and Spiritual aid are forcibly taught by a child's image in the following extract:

Emblems of Repentance.   LEMUEL.   A person doing wrong but once, is a foul spring; but the foul particles may settle down, and then it will be clear again.

MANY.   And they need do wrong no more.

MR. ALCOTT.   That would prevent more foul matter from getting in.   But what is to be done with the particles that are there?

(A long pause.)

ANDREW.   You can flow away from them and leave them.

LUCIA.   I think there is pure water under the mud and sand, which springs up, and softens it, and carries off the muddy particles, and leaves them somewhere, and so flows clear, and the spring is clear too.

MR. ALCOTT.   What makes the water spring up and flow away?   Whence comes the current?

LEMUEL.   It comes from God.   God is always helping.

The temptation and its application are thus pithily set forth:

FREDERIC.   I think the temptation was to show the devil that he could never get any advantage over Jesus.   Jesus settled the matter with him.

50*

545 *Religious Education of Children.*

MR. ALCOTT. Have you settled with the devil in this respect?

FREDERIC. No.

And finally, we will close with the following extract, which shows what manner of faith in Christ this system produces.

MR. ALCOTT. As many of you as think you have as high evidence, that these words of the written Gospels are a true record of what Jesus Christ did, as you have of any thing that is put into language, may rise.

(All rose.)

As many as think they have as high evidence that Jesus Christ lived, as that they live themselves, may rise.

(All rose.)

How do you know that this record of Jesus Christ's action is true?

CHARLES. Because the principles and truths of the Gospel are acted out every day; and when we do the same kind of things Jesus did, we have proofs within ourselves that it is as Jesus said. I feel perfectly sure that Jesus lived and did just as it says there.

SEVERAL. So do I.

SUSAN. I am sure of it, because Luke would not say so, if it was not true. There are a great many things that are said there, which we know are true, because we find them in ourselves.

MR. ALCOTT. You mean by experience?

SUSAN. Yes; and so we believe that all the rest of the things said there are true.

CHARLES. And we see there is nothing there, that does not happen every day, and so there is no reason why we should not believe.

MR. ALCOTT. Is Lazarus raised, and are demons cast out every day?

CHARLES. There is resurrection, as we know in other ways, every day, and men are possessed by appetites and passions; and their demons are cast out by faith, and love, and truth.

MR. ALCOTT. There are many men among us, Charles, who do not feel this evidence that you speak of. Yes; some ministers, I fear, go into the pulpit and preach, who do not.

CHARLES. Then they have not risen from their graves — the graves of their bodies.

MR. ALCOTT. Which set of senses do they set up to judge truth, their external or internal senses.

CHARLES. Their external senses.

MR. ALCOTT. Can we always trust our external senses.

CHARLES. No; never.

MR. ALCOTT. Not even when we are perfectly good, or, if we were perfectly good?

CHARLES. Yes; if we were perfectly good, and had never done wrong, nor inherited any disease, to spoil our temper, I suppose we could.

MR. ALCOTT. As many as are perfectly convinced, and cannot doubt, that there is a Spirit within you, may rise.

(All rose up.)

Yesterday I saw a man who said he knew of no evidence of spirit.

ELLEN How large a man!

MR. ALCOTT. A grown up man, and learned.

CHARLES. Why did you not talk to him and tell him?

MR. ALCOTT. Faith and knowledge of spirit is something which cannot come by the hearing of the ear; it comes by living, by a pure and holy life. If any man will have faith, he must first be pure, both in body and mind. *Ed.*

[James Freeman Clarke]
"Mr. Alcott's Book," *Western Messenger,* 3 (May 1837): 678–683.

In our March number, under the head, "Religious Education of Children," we reviewed the first volume of a work upon that subject by Mr. Alcott. We spoke of the book with high respect, as we thought it merited. Since then, however, we have seen severe criticisms upon it, in quarters which show that it has met with strong opposition and grave objections. This was not wholly unexpected by us. We could easily imagine that the views contained in it would be misunderstood and disliked by many. For these views were new. This opposition, too, was likely to come from the wise and good. For feeling a deep interest in the preservation of sound opinions on religious and moral subjects, the good and wise are always ready to begin the attack on any reformer in religion and morals. They mistake him for a rash and foolish innovator, and until they find out their mistake, they are his worst enemies, afterward his staunchest friends. The Conservatives are a good party, but they are always the first to stone the Prophets and hale them into the prison of misrepresentation and abuse.

Now we are very ready to grant that Mr. Alcott's system and Mr. Alcott's book may have many errors in it; but for all that we maintain him to be a prophet. He has made discoveries, so we think, and poured light on the most important subjects of human interest. His *theories* have been of the greatest practical use to us, and we doubt not that he is a lever by which Providence designs to lift to a higher ground the whole business of education. Thinking this, we cannot stop to find fault till we have said it. Thinking this, we feel bound to say a word in reply to some current objections made to the book by those who, we think, do not yet appreciate its high and extraordinary merits.

The worthy editor of the Christian Monitor asks whether we were not extravagant in our praise of Mr. Alcott, and says it is the last book he could speak well of. The very respectable editor of the Boston Daily Advertiser also has a long and severe criticism in his editorial columns under the date of March 21. The charges brought by this article against the book are so very weighty, as to make it necessary for all who take any interest in the matter, to see whether they can be sustained. If they can, Mr. Alcott's whole system should go by the board. If not, he ought to be defended against such a severe attack, the effects of which would naturally be to ruin him altogether in the opinion of the community, and destroy his professional prospects in life. Common justice therefore to the man, as well as the importance of the subject, demand that both sides be heard.

The editor of the Advertiser speaks of Mr. Alcott's system as "radically false and mischievous," as one which he "could not have supposed it possible that any teacher would adopt or any parent would tolerate"–and the effect of the whole upon the children he thinks must be "to impress on their minds many erroneous notions, to puzzle and perplex them with a thousand useless and inexplicable fancies, to accustom them to trifling and irreverent habits of reflection upon the most grave and solemn subjects, to excite them in a degree injurious to their bodily health, as well as the proper and healthful exercise of their minds, and to impress them with a degree of self–esteem, quite unfavorable to the future development of their understanding, as well as to the improvement of their manners."

Now these objections are the very ones which are likely to arise in the mind of a person who opens the book without much previous thought on the subject, and without any practical acquaintance with the difficulties of getting at the minds of children, and what success or failure is in this department. Accordingly, to sustain his charges the Editor of the Advertiser merely selects and extracts a number of those passages which would strike a superficial reader as most objectionable. And we have no doubt that most of those who read them agreed that it was a clear mass of nonsense–a perfect farrago of absurdity. But we do not think that they would appear in this light to any zealous and practical teacher of the young. All these objections, it seems to

Bronson Alcott's study in Orchard House at Concord

us, spring from a misapprehension of the nature of teaching and the nature of a child. Let us look at them one by one.

He thinks this system will "accustom them to trifling and irreverent habits of reflection upon the most grave and solemn subjects." This would be indeed an evil–but what makes him fear it? The answers of the children are childish, we grant, but far from being trifling. Is it not evident that they are always *in earnest,* from the connexion and closeness of application of all which is said? If any thing is clear, this is so, that these children are exercising the whole force of their attention upon the subjects before them. Mr. Alcott, it will be seen, does not suffer the conversation to go on when any sign of carelessness appears. The illustrations are, no doubt, familiar, and drawn from common place objects. We are very apt to think and call this irreverent. Wesley and Whitfield and all popular preachers have been accused of irreverence because their illustrations were familiar and drawn from common life. The illustrations which the Savior used are sanctified to our minds now, but at first they seemed very irreverent to the for-

mal Pharisee and traditional worshipper. Calling God his Father was the most shocking irreverence in their eyes, and they were going to stone him for it, yet now all our prayers begin "Our Father." The fact is that if religion is to be any thing more than a form, it must be spoken of familiarly as a household thing, and when thus spoken of, men will always cry out "How irreverent." Most people's respect for religion consists in keeping at a respectful distance from it. They pay it all outward homage and respect, but take care that it never comes into their homes and hearts. It is the beauty of Mr. Alcott's plan that religion becomes a familiar, dear and constant inmate in the heart and thoughts of the child.

This is perhaps the strongest objection brought against Mr. Alcott's plan, and therefore we have noticed it first. It is an objection to which all reformers are liable–all who wish to change a formal and ceremonious worship into a living and real one. Another which is dwelt upon a good deal lies against the method. Mr. Alcott is blamed because he does not teach his own opinions directly, but rather leads on the mind of the child. This method is unusual we know, but not unprece-

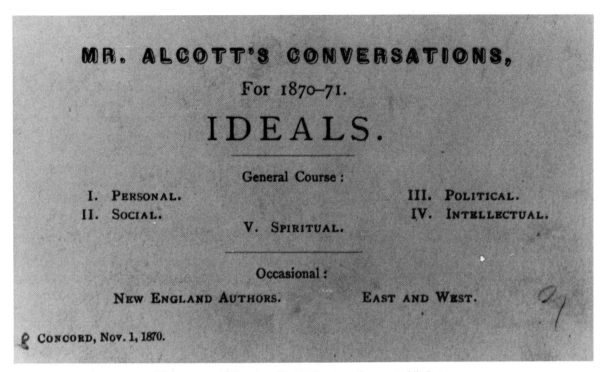

Ticket to one of Bronson Alcott's Conversations or public lectures

dented. The dogmatic style of teaching is the most common, and on most subjects the right one. But Mr. Alcott has at least one illustrious precedent to justify him—namely, Socrates. Those who remember the admirable conversations of that great sage preserved by Xenophon, will be struck to see how closely and successfully Mr. Alcott has copied his plan of teaching. The object of Socrates was to lead on and bring out the mind of his pupil rather than to impress his own opinions, and we certainly think it the best method of teaching morality. It makes the impression deep, vivid, and permanent.

Another objection on which stress is laid is, that by this plan self–esteem is fostered. This also appears at first sight a plausible view, yet by a closer study we find that the very opposite effect is and must be produced by the system before us. It was the main object of Socrates we know to cure vanity and conceit in his disciples. How did he do it? He first let it *come out*. He gave it a chance to appear, and then exposed it to the light of truth till it withered. He made his pupils ashamed of their vanity. So does Mr. Alcott. Proofs of this are to be found in every part of these volumes. Moreover a strict personal application is constantly made by the children to themselves. For example, is such a conversation as the following likely to impress children "with a self–esteem quite unfavorable to the future development of their understanding as well as to the improvement of their manners?"

Confession of Faults. What is the grave of the Soul of each particular one of you? Each one of you think within yourself, into what particular grave your spirits are most liable to fall. I shall require an answer from each.

ELLEN. Temper–love of vexing. I sometimes love to say things to plague my little sister.

MR. ALCOTT. Oh, Ellen! to try to give pain! It will need the voice of the Son of God to lift you out of that grave.

GEORGE K. My grave is something like Ellen's.

(*This very unwillingly, as if ashamed.*)

HALES. Mine is passion, I think.

MARTHA: I don't know the principal one, but impatience is one of mine.

FRANCIS. The appetites are mine, and I like to thump and hurt.

MR. ALCOTT. Yes; and it has almost buried you. At first you had not a very strong constitution, and you have indulged yourself till it is weaker still, and weaker and weaker it will grow, until your mortal body, which has been the grave of the spirit, itself finds a grave in the earth.

FRANCIS. To–day I only mean to eat a piece of ham for my dinner, so big. (*Showing his two fingers.*)

CORINNA. My grave is passion.

ANDREW. Mine is anger.

NATHAN. Laziness and eating are mine.

MR. ALCOTT. You mean eating more than you ought. How does your head feel afterward–does it not feel heavy? How is it with you Lucia?

(*Lucia did not speak.*)

Perhaps there is not any.

WILLIAM. Mine is anger.

MR. ALCOTT. Anger is more than the grave. The raging of anger is like fire; it originated the pictures of hell. Hell is the state of raging passions.

LEMUEL. My grave is appetites and passions.

CHARLES. Passions. Anger is a hot grave.

SAMUEL R. Tantalizing–a love of playing unkind tricks; and I have a great many more.

MR. ALCOTT. I should like to have the deepest grave told.

SUSAN. Disobedience and thoughtlessness.

MR. ALCOTT. Disobedience is the spade that digs the graves; and sometimes it digs very deep graves.

W. AUGUSTUS. Passions and appetites.

SAMUEL R. Love of tantalizing is the deepest in me.

(*All the rest confessed to this sin, and Mr. Alcott made some observations upon the malignity that has its germ in this habit of tantalizing.*)

MR. ALCOTT. But Lucia, you have not told.

LUCIA, (*hesitating.*) Impatience, I believe.

Quickening Agency of Conscience.

MR. ALCOTT. How does the voice of the Son of God come to us in our graves?

MARTHA. By Conscience.

GEORGE K. In repentance. Conscience is the voice of the Son of God.

MR. ALCOTT. As many as think that they have heard the voice of the Son of God may rise.

(*Several did.*)

Tell an instance.

CHARLES. After I came from fishing the last time I went, when you talked to me about it.

ANDREW. When I put a little kitten's feet into the water to frighten it.

GEORGE K. After I have plagued my sister.

LEMUEL. Once I put a little puppy, just born, into the frog pond.

(*He seemed distressed in telling this, and all the others seemed to think it was particularly bad.*)

MR. ALCOTT. All, who are in the habit of troubling your brothers and sisters knowingly, wilfully, may rise.

(*A great many rose.*)

And all this time you were burying your brother and sister in the grave of anger and ill temper. Ellen does not know how much sin in her sister may have its origin in her want of patience and her unkindness.

(*Considerable conversation arose here on their responsibility for the tempers of others, especially of those younger than themselves, which seemed to impress the children very seriously.*)

Another apprehended danger is lest this mode of questioning should "excite them in a degree injurious to their bodily health." We hardly know what to make of this objection. If the "habits of reflection" are "trifling," which is one assertion, they can hardly excite the mind in this extraordinary manner. One of these objections therefore must needs destroy the other. We have heard this age called one of excessive mental excitement, and can easily understand that injury may result both to mind and body by severe studies prosecuted under the spur of strong ambition. But that cheerful and unpremeditated conversations like those recorded here, should have such tendencies ascribed to them, only shows, to our mind, the very hasty manner in which the critic has looked at the subject. It is so trivial an objection, that it tends to vitiate the whole argument.

Another great fear is of errors of opinion, false views, &c. &c. This is the great bugbear with which we, of this magazine, have to be constantly contending. We have to be always saying what we now say again, that the great danger is rather that men shall not think at all, than that they should think erroneously; that the great error is sluggishness of mind and indifference to the truth; that if the mind is suffered to act freely on great subjects, truth must be in the end the gainer by it. These are the principles to which all cheerfully assent in the abstract, but unanimously object to in practice. Few have faith enough in the power of truth and its adaptation to the human mind to allow of free inquiry and examination. The author of this book is one of that few. We also are pledged to these principles in theory, and we shall aim as far as in us lies to uphold and protect their practical application.

Ralph Waldo Emerson

An Oration, Delivered Before the Phi Beta Kappa Society, at Cambridge, August 31, 1837 (Boston: James Munroe, 1837).

> *One of Emerson's most famous works, this was not known as "The American Scholar" until its inclusion in his* Nature; Addresses, and Lectures *(1849). Delivered before the best students at what many considered was the best college in America, it was called by Oliver Wendell Holmes America's "literary Declaration of Independence." In it, Emerson argued for the scholar to be "Man Thinking"; to trust his Reason or intuition over what his Understanding or senses can tell him; to beware of allowing books to become too great an influence and thus stifle originality; and to ignore European models in the search for a truly American literature. The address received few but favorable reviews. The next year, with his Divinity School Address, Emerson brought down upon himself the highly negative criticisms that are popularly associated with his early career. (For further information, see the entry for Emerson in* DLB 1, The American Renaissance in New England.*)*

Harvard undergraduate catalogue for 1820, showing Emerson as a senior

MR. PRESIDENT, AND GENTLEMEN,

I greet you on the re-commencement of our literary year. Our anniversary is one of hope, and, perhaps, not enough of labor. We do not meet for games of strength or skill, for the recitation of histories, tragedies and odes, like the ancient Greeks; for parliaments of love and poesy, like the Troubadours; nor for the advancement of science, like our contemporaries in the British and European capitals. Thus far, our holiday has been simply a friendly sign of the survival of the love of letters amongst a people too busy to give to letters any more. As such, it is precious as the sign of an indestructible instinct. Perhaps the time is already come, when it ought to be, and will be something else; when the sluggard intellect of this continent will look from under its iron lids and fill the postponed expectation of the world with something better than the exertions of mechanical skill. Our day of dependence, our long apprenticeship to the learning of other lands, draws to a close. The millions that around us are rushing into life, cannot always be fed on the sere remains of foreign harvests. Events, actions arise, that must be sung, that will sing themselves. Who can doubt that poetry will revive and lead in a new age, as the star in the constellation Harp which now flames in our zenith, astronomers announce, shall one day be the pole-star for a thousand years.

In the light of this hope, I accept the topic which not only usage, but the nature of our association, seem to prescribe to this day,–the AMERICAN SCHOLAR. Year by year, we come up hither to read one more chapter of his biography. Let us inquire what new lights, new events and more days have thrown on his character, his duties and his hopes.

It is one of those fables, which out of an unknown antiquity, convey an unlooked for wisdom, that the gods, in the beginning, divided Man into men, that he might be more helpful to himself; just as the hand was divided into fingers, the better to answer its end.

The old fable covers a doctrine ever new and sublime; that there is One Man,–present to all particular men only partially, or through one faculty; and that you must take the whole society to find the whole man. Man is not a farmer, or a professor, or an engineer, but he is all. Man is priest, and scholar, and statesman, and producer, and soldier. In the *divided* or social state, these functions are parcelled out to individuals, each of whom aims to do his stint of the joint work,

First page of Emerson's first publication

whilst each other performs his. The fable implies that the individual to possess himself, must sometimes return from his own labor to embrace all the other laborers. But unfortunately, this original unit, this fountain of power, has been so distributed to multitudes, has been so minutely subdivided and peddled out, that it is spilled into drops, and cannot be gathered. The state of society is one in which the members have suffered amputation from the trunk, and strut about so many walking monsters,–a good finger, a neck, a stomach, an elbow, but never a man.

Man is thus metamorphosed into a thing, into many things. The planter, who is Man sent out into the field to gather food, is seldom cheered by any idea of the true dignity of his ministry. He sees his bushel and his cart, and nothing beyond, and sinks into the farmer, instead of Man on the farm. The tradesman

A

HISTORICAL DISCOURSE,

DELIVERED BEFORE THE CITIZENS OF CONCORD,

12TH SEPTEMBER, 1835.

ON THE

SECOND CENTENNIAL ANNIVERSARY

OF THE INCORPORATION OF THE TOWN.

BY RALPH WALDO EMERSON.

PUBLISHED BY REQUEST.

CONCORD:
G. F. BEMIS, PRINTER.
1835.

Title page for Emerson's "Concord Discourse" his first separately published work.

scarcely ever gives an ideal worth to his work, but is ridden by the routine of his craft, and the soul is subject to dollars. The priest becomes a form; the attorney, a statute-book; the mechanic, a machine; the sailor, a rope of a ship.

In this distribution of functions, the scholar is the delegated intellect. In the right state, he is, *Man Thinking*. In the degenerate state, when the victim of society, he tends to become a mere thinker, or, still worse, the parrot of other men's thinking.

In this view of him, as Man Thinking, the whole theory of his office is contained. Him nature solicits, with all her placid, all her monitory pictures. Him the past instructs. Him the future invites. Is not, indeed, every man a student, and do not all things exist for the student's behoof? And, finally, is not the true scholar the only true master? But, as the old oracle said, "All things have two handles. Beware of the wrong one."

In life, too often, the scholar errs with mankind and forfeits his privilege. Let us see him in his school, and consider him in reference to the main influences he receives.

I. The first in time and the first in importance of the influences upon the mind is that of nature. Every day, the sun; and, after sunset, night and her stars. Ever the winds blow; ever the grass grows. Every day, men and women, conversing, beholding and beholden. The scholar must needs stand wistful and admiring before this great spectacle. He must settle its value in his mind. What is nature to him? There is never a beginning, there is never an end to the inexplicable continuity of this web of God, but always circular power returning into itself. Therein it resembles his own spirit, whose beginning, whose ending he never can find–so entire, so boundless. Far, too, as her splendors shine, system on system shooting like rays, upward, downward, without centre, without circumference,–in the mass and in the particle nature hastens to render account of herself to the mind. Classification begins. To the young mind, every thing is individual, stands by itself. By and by, it finds how to join two things, and see in them one nature; then three, then three thousand; and so, tyrannized over by its own unifying instinct, it goes on tying things together, diminishing anomalies, discovering roots running under ground, whereby contrary and remote things cohere, and flower out from one stem. It presently learns, that, since the dawn of history, there has been a constant accumulation and classifying of facts. But what is classification but the perceiving that these objects are not chaotic, and are not foreign, but have a law which is also a law of the human mind? The astronomer discovers that geometry, a pure abstraction of the human mind, is the measure of planetary motion. The chemist finds proportions and intelligible method throughout matter: and science is nothing but the finding of analogy, identity in the most remote parts. The ambitious soul sits down before each refractory fact; one after another, reduces all strange constitutions, all new powers, to their class and their law, and goes on forever to animate the last fibre of organization, the outskirts of nature, by insight.

Thus to him, to this school-boy under the bending dome of day, is suggested, that he and it proceed from one root; one is leaf and one is flower; relation, sympathy, stirring in every vein. And what is that Root? Is not that the soul of his soul?–A thought too bold–a dream too wild. Yet when this spiritual light shall have revealed the law of more earthly natures,–

when he has learned to worship the soul, and to see that the natural philosophy that now is, is only the first gropings of its gigantic hand, he shall look forward to an ever expanding knowledge as to a becoming creator. He shall see that nature is the opposite of the soul, answering to it part for part. One is seal, and one is print. Its beauty is the beauty of his own mind. Its laws are the laws of his own mind. Nature then becomes to him the measure of his attainments. So much of nature as he is ignorant of, so much of his own mind does he not yet possess. And, in fine, the ancient precept, "Know thyself," and the modern precept, "Study nature," become at last one maxim.

II. The next great influence into the spirit of the scholar, is, the mind of the Past,—in whatever form, whether of literature, of art, of institutions, that mind is inscribed. Books are the best type of the influence of the past, and perhaps we shall get at the truth–learn the amount of this influence more conveniently–by considering their value alone.

The theory of books is noble. The scholar of the first age received into him the world around; brooded thereon; gave it the new arrangement of his own mind, and uttered it again. It came into him–life; it went out from him–truth. It came to him–short-lived actions; it went out from him–immortal thoughts. It came to him–business; it went from him–poetry. It was–dead fact; now, it is quick thought. It can stand, and it can go. It now endures, it now flies, it now inspires. Precisely in proportion to the depth of mind from which it issued, so high does it soar, so long does it sing.

Or, I might say, it depends on how far the process had gone, of transmuting life into truth. In proportion to the completeness of the distillation, so will the purity and imperishableness of the product be. But none is quite perfect. As no air-pump can by any means make a perfect vacuum, so neither can any artist entirely exclude the conventional, the local, the perishable from his book, or write a book of pure thought that shall be as efficient, in all respects, to a remote posterity, as to contemporaries, or rather to the second age. Each age, it is found, must write its own books; or rather, each generation for the next succeeding. The books of an older period will not fit this.

Yet hence arises a grave mischief. The sacredness which attaches to the act of creation,—the act of thought,—is instantly transferred to the record. The poet chanting, was felt to be a divine man. Henceforth the chant is divine also. The writer was a just and wise spirit. Henceforward it is settled, the book is perfect; as love of the hero corrupts into worship of his statue. Instantly, the book becomes noxious. The guide is a tyrant. We sought a brother, and lo, a governor. The sluggish and perverted mind of the multitude, always slow to open to the incursions of Reason, having once so opened, having once received this book, stands upon it, and makes an outcry, if it is disparaged. Colleges are built on it. Books are written on it by thinkers, not by Man Thinking; by men of talent, that is, who start wrong, who set out from accepted dogmas, not from their own sight of principles. Meek young men grow up in libraries, believing it their duty to accept the views which Cicero, which Locke, which Bacon have given, forgetful that Cicero, Locke and Bacon were only young men in libraries when they wrote these books.

Hence, instead of Man Thinking, we have the bookworm. Hence, the book-learned class, who value books, as such; not as related to nature and the human constitution, but as making a sort of Third Estate with the world and the soul. Hence, the restorers of reading, the emendators, the bibliomaniacs of all degrees.

This is bad; this is worse than it seems. Books are the best of things, well used; abused, among the worst. What is the right use? What is the one end which all means go to effect? They are for nothing but to inspire. I had better never see a book than to be warped by its attraction clean out of my own orbit, and made a satellite instead of a system. The one thing in the world of value, is, the active soul,—the soul, free, sovereign, active. This every man is entitled to; this every man contains within him, although in almost all men, obstructed, and as yet unborn. The soul active sees absolute truth; and utters truth, or creates. In this action, it is genius; not the privilege of here and there a favorite, but the sound estate of every man. In its essence, it is progressive. The book, the college, the school of art, the institution of any kind, stop with some past utterance of genius. This is good, say they,—let us hold by this. They pin me down. They look backward and not forward. But genius always looks forward. The eyes of man are set in his forehead, not in his hindhead. Man hopes. Genius creates. To create,—to create,—is the proof of a divine presence. Whatever talents may be, if the man create not, the pure efflux of the Deity is not his:—cinders and smoke, there may be, but not yet flame. There are creative manners, there are creative actions, and creative words; manners, actions, words, that is, indicative of no custom or authority, but springing spontaneous from the mind's own sense of good and fair.

On the other part, instead of being its own seer, let it receive always from another mind its truth, though it were in torrents of light, without periods of solitude, inquest and self-recovery, and a fatal disservice is done. Genius is always sufficiently the enemy of genius by over-influence. The literature of every nation bears me witness. The English dramatic poets have Shakspearized now for two hundred years.

Undoubtedly there is a right way of reading,—so it be sternly subordinated. Man Thinking must not be subdued by his instruments. Books are for the scholar's idle times. When he can read God directly, the hour is too precious to be wasted in other mens' transcripts of their readings. But when the intervals of darkness come, as come they must,—when the soul seeth not, when the sun is hid, and the stars withdraw their shining,—we repair to the lamps which were kindled by their ray to guide our steps to the East again, where the dawn is. We hear that we may speak. The Arabian proverb says, "A fig tree looking on a fig tree, becometh fruitful."

It is remarkable, the character of the pleasure we derive from the best books. They impress us ever with the conviction that one nature wrote and the same reads. We read the verses of one of the great English poets, of Chaucer, of Marvell, of Dryden, with the most modern joy,—with a pleasure, I mean, which is in great part caused by the abstraction of all *time* from their verses. There is some awe mixed with the joy of our surprise, when this poet, who lived in some past world, two or three hundred years ago, says that which lies close to my own soul, that which I also had well nigh thought and said. But for the evidence thence afforded to the philosophical doctrine of the identity of all minds, we should suppose some pre-established harmony, some foresight of souls that were to be, and some preparation of stores for their future wants, like the fact observed in insects, who lay up food before death for the young grub they shall never see.

I would not be hurried by any love of system, by any exaggeration of instincts, to underrate the Book. We all know, that as the human body can be nourished on any food, though it were boiled grass and the broth of shoes, so the human mind can be fed by any knowledge. And great and heroic men have existed, who had almost no other information than by the printed page. I

only would say, that it needs a strong head to bear that diet. One must be an inventor to read well. As the proverb says, "He that would bring home the wealth of the Indies, must carry out the wealth of the Indies." There is then creative reading, as well as creative writing. When the mind is braced by labor and invention, the page of whatever book we read becomes luminous with manifold allusion. Every sentence is doubly significant, and the sense of our author is as broad as the world. We then see, what is always true, that as the seer's hour of vision is short and rare among heavy days and months, so is its record, perchance, the least part of his volume. The discerning will read in his Plato or Shakspeare, only that least part,—only the authentic utterances of the oracle,—and all the rest he rejects, were it never so many times Plato's and Shakspeare's.

Of course, there is a portion of reading quite indispensable to a wise man. History and exact science he must learn by laborious reading. Colleges, in like manner, have their indispensable office,—to teach elements. But they can only highly serve us, when they aim not to drill, but to create; when they gather from far every ray of various genius to their hospitable halls, and, by the concentrated fires, set the hearts of their youth on flame. Thought and knowledge are natures in which apparatus and pretension avail nothing. Gowns, and pecuniary foundations, though of towns of gold, can never countervail the least sentence or syllable of wit. Forget this, and our American colleges will recede in their public importance whilst they grow richer every year.

III. There goes in the world a notion that the scholar should be a recluse, a valetudinarian,—as unfit for any handiwork or public labor, as a penknife for an axe. The so called "practical men" sneer at speculative men, as if, because they speculate or *see*, they could do nothing. I have heard it said that the clergy,—who are always more universally than any other class, the scholars of their day,—are addressed as women: that the rough, spontaneous conversation of men they do not hear, but only a mincing and diluted speech. They are often virtually disfranchised; and, indeed, there are advocates for their celibacy. As far as this is true of the studious classes, it is not just and wise. Action is with the scholar subordinate, but it is essential. Without it, he is not yet man. Without it, thought can never ripen into truth. Whilst the world hangs before the eye as a cloud of beauty, we can not even see its beauty. Inaction is cowardice, but there can be no scholar with-

Miniature painting of Ralph Waldo Emerson in 1829 (Journals of Ralph Waldo Emerson, edited by Edward Waldo Emerson and Waldo Emerson Forbes [1904-1914])

out the heroic mind. The preamble of thought, the transition through which it passes from the unconscious to the conscious, is action. Only so much do I know, as I have lived. Instantly we know whose words are loaded with life, and whose not.

The world,—this shadow of the soul, or *other me,* lies wide around. Its attractions are the keys which unlock my thoughts and make me acquainted with myself. I launch eagerly into this resounding tumult. I grasp the hands of those next me, and take my place in the ring to suffer and to work, taught by an instinct that so shall the dumb abyss be vocal with speech. I pierce its order; I dissipate its fear; I dispose of it within the circuit of my expanding life. So much only of life as I know by experience, so much of the wilderness have I vanquished and planted, or so far have I extended my being, my dominion. I do not see how any man can afford, for the sake of his nerves and his nap, to spare

any action in which he can partake. It is pearls and rubies to his discourse. Drudgery, calamity, exasperation, want, are instructers in eloquence and wisdom. The true scholar grudges every opportunity of action past by, as a loss of power.

It is the raw material out of which the intellect moulds her splendid products. A strange process too, this, by which experience is converted into thought, as a mulberry leaf is converted into satin. The manufacture goes forward at all hours.

The actions and events of our childhood and youth are now matters of calmest observation. They lie like fair pictures in the air. Not so with our recent actions,—with the business which we now have in hand. On this we are quite unable to speculate. Our affections as yet circulate through it. We no more feel or know it, than we feel the feet, or the hand, or the brain of our body. The new deed is yet a part of life,—remains for a time immersed in our unconscious life. In some contemplative hour, it detaches itself from the life like a ripe fruit, to become a thought of the mind. Instantly, it is raised, transfigured; the corruptible has put on incorruption. Always now it is an object of beauty, however base its origin and neighborhood. Observe, too, the impossibility of antedating this act. In its grub state, it cannot fly, it cannot shine,—it is a dull grub. But suddenly, without observation, the selfsame thing unfurls beautiful wings, and is an angel of wisdom. So is there no fact, no event, in our private history, which shall not, sooner or later, lose its adhesive inert form, and astonish us by soaring from our body into the empyrean. Cradle and infancy, school and playground, the fear of boys, and dogs, and ferules, the love of little maids and berries, and many another fact that once filled the whole sky, are gone already; friend and relative, profession and party, town and country, nation and world, must also soar and sing.

Of course, he who has put forth his total strength in fit actions, has the richest return of wisdom. I will not shut myself out of this globe of action and transplant an oak into a flower pot, there to hunger and pine; nor trust the revenue of some single faculty, and exhaust one vein of thought, much like those Savoyards, who, getting their livelihood by carving shepherds, shepherdesses, and smoking Dutchmen, for all Europe, went out one day to the mountain to find stock, and discovered that they had whittled up the last of their pine trees. Authors we have in numbers, who have written out their vein, and who, moved by a

Miniature painting of Emerson's first wife, Ellen Tucker Emerson (Journals of Ralp Waldo Emerson, edited by Edward Waldo Emerson and Waldo Emerson Forbes [1909-1914])

self in the inspiring and expiring of the breath; in desire and satiety; in the ebb and flow of the sea, in day and night, in heat and cold, and as yet more deeply ingrained in every atom and every fluid, is known to us under the name of Polarity,—these "fits of easy transmission and reflection," as Newton called them, are the law of nature because they are the law of spirit.

The mind now thinks; now acts; and each fit reproduces the other. When the artist has exhausted his materials, when the fancy no longer paints, when thoughts are no longer apprehended, and books are a weariness,—he has always the resource to *live*. Character is higher than intellect. Thinking is the function. Living is the functionary. The stream retreats to its source. A great soul will be strong to live, as well as strong to think. Does he lack organ or medium to impart his truths? He can still fall back on this elemental force of living them. This is a total act. Thinking is a partial act. Let the grandeur of justice shine in his affairs. Let the beauty of affection cheer his lowly roof. Those "far from fame" who dwell and act with him, will feel the force of his constitution in the doings and passages of the day better than it can be measured by any public and designed display. Time shall teach him that the scholar loses no hour which the man lives. Herein he unfolds the sacred germ of his instinct screened from influence. What is lost in seemliness is gained in strength. Not out of those on whom systems of education have exhausted their culture, comes the helpful giant to destroy the old or to build the new, but out of unhandselled savage nature, out of terrible Druids and Berserkirs, come at last Alfred and Shakspear.

I hear therefore with joy whatever is beginning to be said of the dignity and necessity of labor to every citizen. There is virtue yet in the hoe and the spade, for learned as well as for unlearned hands. And labor is every where welcome; always we are invited to work; only be this limitation observed, that a man shall not for the sake of wider activity sacrifice any opinion to the popular judgments and modes of action.

I have now spoken of the education of the scholar by nature, by books, and by action. It remains to say somewhat of his duties.

They are such as become Man Thinking. They may all be comprised in self-trust. The office of the scholar is to cheer, to raise, and to guide men by showing them facts amidst appearances. He plies the slow, unhonored, and unpaid task of observation. Flamsteed and Herschel, in their glazed observatory, may cata-

commendable prudence, sail for Greece and Palestine, follow the trapper into the prairie, or ramble around Algiers to replenish their merchantable stock.

If it were only for a vocabulary the scholar would be covetous of action. Life is our dictionary. Years are well spent in country labors; in town—in the insight into trades and manufactures; in frank intercourse with many men and women; in science, in art; to the one end of mastering in all their facts a language, by which to illustrate and embody our perceptions. I learn immediately from any speaker how much he has already lived, through the poverty or the splendor of his speech. Life lies behind us as the quarry from whence we get tiles and copestones for the masonry of to-day. This is the way to learn grammar. Colleges and books only copy the language which the field and the workyard made.

But the final value of action, like that of books, and better than books, is, that it is a resource. That great principle of Undulation in nature, that shows it-

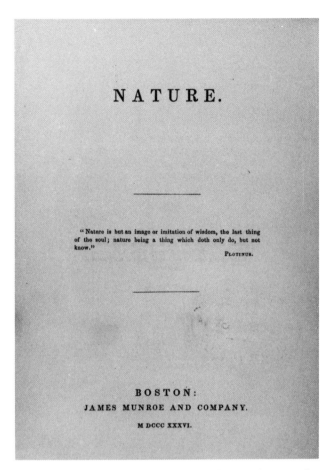

NATURE.

"Nature is but an image or imitation of wisdom, the last thing of the soul; nature being a thing which doth only do, but not know."

PLOTINUS.

BOSTON:
JAMES MUNROE AND COMPANY.
M DCCC XXXVI.

Title page for the work that established Emerson's reputation as a leader in the Transcendentalist movement

logue the stars with the praise of all men, and, the results being splendid and useful, honor is sure. But he, in his private observatory, cataloguing obscure and nebulous stars of the human mind, which as yet no man has thought of as such,—watching days and months, sometimes, for a few facts; correcting still his old records;—must relinquish display and immediate fame. In the long period of his preparation, he must betray often an ignorance and shiftlessness in popular arts, incurring the disdain of the able who shoulder him aside. Long he must stammer in his speech; often forego the living for the dead. Worse yet, he must accept—how often! poverty and solitude. For the ease and pleasure of treading the old road, accepting the fashions, the education, the religion of society, he takes the cross of making his own, and, of course, the self accusation, the faint heart, the frequent uncertainty and loss of time which are the nettles and tangling vines in the way of the self-relying and self-directed; and the state of virtual hostility in which he seems to stand to society, and especially to educated society. For all this loss and scorn, what offset? He is to find consolation in exercising the highest functions of human nature. He is one who raises himself from private considerations, and breathes and lives on public and illustrious thoughts. He is the world's eye. He is the world's heart. He is to resist the vulgar prosperity that retrogrades ever to barbarism, by preserving and communicating heroic sentiments, noble biographies, melodious verse, and the conclusions of history. Whatsoever oracles the human heart in all emergencies, in all solemn hours has uttered as its commentary on the world of actions,—these he shall receive and impart. And whatsoever new verdict Reason from her inviolable seat pronounces on the passing men and events of to-day,—this he shall hear and promulgate.

These being his functions, it becomes him to feel all confidence in himself, and to defer never to the popular cry. He and he only knows the world. The world of any moment is the merest appearance. Some great decorum, some fetish of a government, some ephemeral trade, or war, or man, is cried up by half mankind and cried down by the other half, as if all depended on this particular up or down. The odds are that the whole question is not worth the poorest thought which the scholar has lost in listening to the controversy. Let him not quit his belief that a popgun is a popgun, though the ancient and honorable of the earth affirm it to be the crack of doom. In silence, in steadiness, in severe abstraction, let him hold by himself; add observation to observation; patient of neglect, patient of reproach, and bide his own time,—happy enough if he can satisfy himself alone that this day he has seen something truly. Success treads on every right step. For the instinct is sure that prompts him to tell his brother what he thinks. He then learns that in going down into the secrets of his own mind, he has descended into the secrets of all minds. He learns that he who has mastered any law in his private thoughts, is master to that extent of all men into whose language his own can be translated. The poet in utter solitude remembering his spontaneous thoughts and recording them, is found to have recorded that which men in "cities vast" find true for them also. The orator distrusts at first the fitness of his frank confessions,—his want of knowledge of the persons he addresses,—until he finds that he is the complement of his hearers;—that they drink his words because he fulfils for them their own nature; the deeper he dives into his privatest secretest presentiment,—to his

A Harvard academic procession in 1836

wonder he finds, this is the most acceptable, most public, and universally true. The people delight in it; the better part of every man feels, This is my music: this is myself.

In self-trust, all the virtues are comprehended. Free should the scholar be,–free and brave. Free even to the definition of freedom, "without any hindrance that does not arise out of his own constitution." Brave; for fear is a thing which a scholar by his very function puts behind him. Fear always springs from ignorance. It is a shame to him if his tranquillity, amid dangerous times, arise from the presumption that like children and women, his is a protected class; or if he seek a temporary peace by the diversion of his thoughts from politics or vexed questions, hiding his head like an ostrich in the flowering bushes, peeping into microscopes, and turning rhymes, as a boy whistles to keep his courage up. So is the danger a danger still: so is the fear worse. Manlike let him turn and face it. Let him look into its eye and search its nature, inspect its origin–see the whelping of this lion,–which lies no great way back; he will then find in himself a perfect comprehension of its nature and extent; he will have made his hands meet on the other side, and can henceforth defy it, and pass on superior. The world is his who can see through its pretension. What deafness, what stone-blind custom, what overgrown error you behold, is

there only by sufferance,–by your sufferance. See it to be a lie, and you have already dealt it its mortal blow.

Yes, we are the cowed,–we the trustless. It is a mischievous notion that we are come late into nature; that the world was finished a long time ago. As the world was plastic and fluid in the hands of God, so it is ever to so much of his attributes as we bring to it. To ignorance and sin, it is flint. They adapt themselves to it as they may; but in proportion as a man has anything in him divine, the firmament flows before him, and takes his signet and form. Not he is great who can alter matter, but he who can alter my state of mind. They are the kings of the world who give the color of their present thought to all nature and all art, and persuade men by the cheerful serenity of their carrying the matter, that this thing which they do, is the apple which the ages have desired to pluck, now at last ripe, and inviting nations to the harvest. The great man makes the great thing. Wherever Macdonald sits, there is the head of the table. Linnaeus makes botany the most alluring of studies and wins it from the farmer and the herb-woman. Davy, chemistry: and Cuvier, fossils. The day is always his, who works in it with serenity and great aims. The unstable estimates of men crowd to him whose mind is filled with a truth, as the heaped waves of the Atlantic follow the moon.

For this self-trust, the reason is deeper than can be fathomed,–darker than can be enlightened. I might

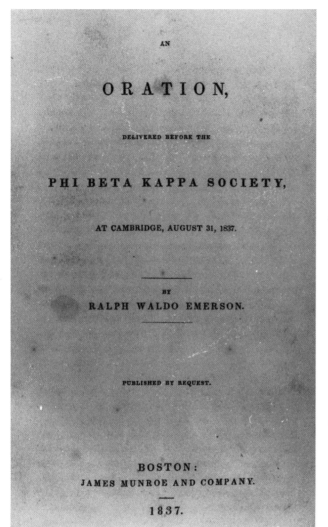

AN

ORATION,

DELIVERED BEFORE THE

PHI BETA KAPPA SOCIETY,

AT CAMBRIDGE, AUGUST 31, 1837.

BY

RALPH WALDO EMERSON.

PUBLISHED BY REQUEST.

BOSTON:
JAMES MUNROE AND COMPANY.
—
1837.

Title page for the "American Scholar" address (1837), called by Oliver Wendell Holmes "America's literary declaration of independence"

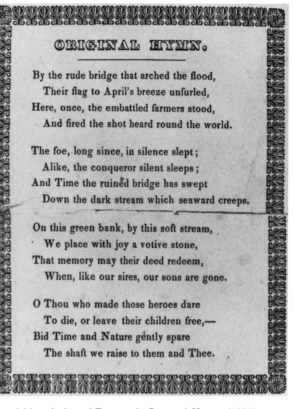

ORIGINAL HYMN.

By the rude bridge that arched the flood,
   Their flag to April's breeze unfurled,
Here, once, the embattled farmers stood,
   And fired the shot heard round the world.

The foe, long since, in silence slept;
   Alike, the conqueror silent sleeps;
And Time the ruinèd bridge has swept
   Down the dark stream which seaward creeps.

On this green bank, by this soft stream,
   We place with joy a votive stone,
That memory may their deed redeem,
   When, like our sires, our sons are gone.

O Thou who made those heroes dare
   To die, or leave their children free,—
Bid Time and Nature gently spare
   The shaft we raise to them and Thee.

Broadside printing of Emerson's Concord Hymn *(1837), sung at the dedication of a monument memorializing the Revolutionary War battle in Concord*

not carry with me the feeling of my audience in stating my own belief. But I have already shown the ground of my hope, in adverting to the doctrine that man is one. I believe man has been wronged: he has wronged himself. He has almost lost the light that can lead him back to his prerogatives. Men are become of no account. Men in history, men in the world of to-day are bugs, are spawn, and are called "the mass" and "the herd." In a century, in a millenium, one or two men; that is to say—one or two approximations to the right state of every man. All the rest behold in the hero or the poet their own green and crude being—ripened; yes, and are content to be less, so *that* may attain to its full stature. What a testimony—full of grandeur, full

of pity, is borne to the demands of his own nature, by the poor clansman, the poor partisan, who rejoices in the glory of his chief. The poor and the low find some amends to their immense moral capacity, for their acquiescence in a political and social inferiority. They are content to be brushed like flies from the path of a great person, so that justice shall be done by him to that common nature which it is the dearest desire of all to see enlarged and glorified. They sun themselves in the great man's light, and feel it to be their own element. They cast the dignity of man from their downtrod selves upon the shoulders of a hero, and will perish to add one drop of blood to make that great heart beat, those giant sinews combat and conquer. He lives for us, and we live in him.

Men such as they are, very naturally seek money or power; and power because it is as good as money,—the "spoils," so called, "of office." And why not? for they aspire to the highest, and this, in their sleep-walking, they dream is highest. Wake them, and they shall quit the false good and leap to the true, and leave governments to clerks and desks. This revolution is to be wrought by the gradual domestication of the idea of Culture. The main enterprise of the world for splendor, for extent, is the upbuilding of a man. Here are the materials strewn along the ground. The private life of one man shall be a more illustrious monarchy,–more formidable to its enemy, more sweet and serene in its influence to its friend, than any kingdom in history. For a man, rightly viewed, comprehendeth the particular natures of all men. Each philosopher, each bard, each actor, has only done for me, as by a delegate, what one day I can do for myself. The books which once we valued more than the apple of the eye, we have quite exhausted. What is that but saying that we have come up with the point of view which the universal mind took through the eyes of that one scribe; we have been that man, and have passed on. First, one; then, another; we drain all cisterns, and waxing greater by all these supplies, we crave a better and more abundant food. The man has never lived that can feed us ever. The human mind cannot be enshrined in a person who shall set a barrier on any one side to this unbounded, unboundable empire. It is one central fire which flaming now out of the lips of Etna, lightens the capes of Sicily; and now out of the throat of Vesuvius, illuminates the towers and vineyards of Naples. It is one light which beams out of a thousand stars. It is one soul which animates all men.

But I have dwelt perhaps tediously upon this abstraction of the Scholar. I ought not to delay longer to add what I have to say, of nearer reference to the time and to this country.

Historically, there is thought to be a difference in the ideas which predominate over successive epochs, and there are data for marking the genius of the Classic, of the Romantic, and now of the Reflective or Philosophical age. With the views I have intimated of the oneness or the identity of the mind through all individuals, I do not much dwell on these differences. In fact, I believe each individual passes through all three. The boy is a Greek; the youth, romantic; the adult, reflective. I deny not, however, that a revolution in the leading idea may be distinctly enough traced.

Our age is bewailed as the age of Introversion. Must that needs be evil? We, it seems, are critical. We are embarrassed with second thoughts. We cannot enjoy any thing for hankering to know whereof the pleasure consists. We are lined with eyes. We see with our feet. The time is infected with Hamlet's unhappiness,–

"Sicklied o'er with the pale cast of thought."

Is it so bad then? Sight is the last thing to be pitied. Would we be blind? Do we fear lest we should outsee nature and God, and drink truth dry? I look upon the discontent of the literary class as a mere announcement of the fact that they find themselves not in the state of mind of their fathers, and regret the coming state as untried; as a boy dreads the water before he has learned that he can swim. If there is any period one would desire to be born in,–is it not the age of Revolution; when the old and the new stand side by side, and admit of being compared; when the energies of all men are searched by fear and by hope; when the historic glories of the old, can be compensated by the rich possibilities of the new era? This time, like all times, is a very good one, if we but know what to do with it.

I read with joy some of the auspicious signs of the coming days as they glimmer already through poetry and art, through philosophy and science, through church and state.

One of these signs is the fact that the same movement which effected the elevation of what was called the lowest class in the state, assumed in literature a very marked and as benign an aspect. Instead of the sublime and beautiful, the near, the low, the common, was explored and poetised. That which had been negligently trodden under foot by those who were harnessing and provisioning themselves for long journies into far countries, is suddenly found to be richer than all foreign parts. The literature of the poor, the feelings of the child, the philosophy of the street, the meaning of household life, are the topics of the time. It is a great stride. It is a sign–is it not? of new vigor, when the extremities are made active, when currents of warm life run into the hands and the feet. I ask not for the great, the remote, the romantic; what is doing in Italy or Arabia; what is Greek art, or Provencal Minstrelsy; I embrace the common, I explore and sit at the feet of the familiar, the low. Give me insight into to-day, and you may have the antique and future worlds. What would we really know the meaning of? The meal in the firkin; the milk in the pan; the ballad in the street; the news of the boat; the glance of the eye; the form and the gait of the body;–show me the ultimate reason of these matters,–show me the sublime presence of the highest spiritual cause lurking, as always it does lurk, in these suburbs and extremities of nature; let me see every trifle bristling with the polarity that ranges it instantly on an eternal law; and the shop, the plough, and the ledger, referred to the like cause by which

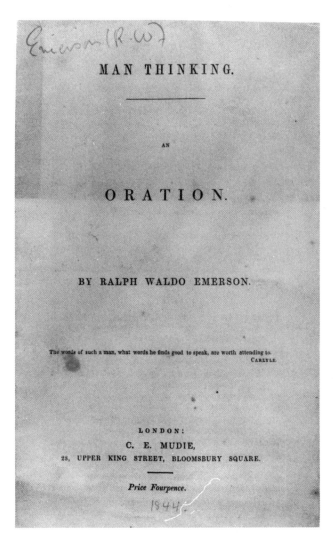

MAN THINKING.

AN

ORATION.

BY RALPH WALDO EMERSON.

The words of such a man, what words he finds good to speak, are worth attending to.
CARLYLE.

LONDON:
C. E. MUDIE,
23, UPPER KING STREET, BLOOMSBURY SQUARE.

Price Fourpence.

1844.

Title page for the English edition of the "American Scholar" address (1843)

light undulates and poets sing;—and the world lies no longer a dull miscellany and lumber room, but has form and order; there is no trifle; there is no puzzle; but one design unites and animates the farthest pinnacle and the lowest trench.

This idea has inspired the genius of Goldsmith, Burns, Cowper, and, in a newer time, of Goethe, Wordsworth, and Carlyle. This idea they have differently followed and with various success. In contrast with their writing, the style of Pope, of Johnson, of Gibbon, looks cold and pedantic. This writing is blood-warm. Man is surprised to find that things near are not less beautiful and wondrous than things remote. The near explains the far. The drop is a small ocean. A man is related to all nature. This perception of the worth of the vulgar, is fruitful in discoveries. Goethe, in this very thing the

most modern of the moderns, has shown us, as none ever did, the genius of the ancients.

There is one man of genius who has done much for this philosophy of life, whose literary value has never yet been rightly estimated,—I mean Emanuel Swedenborg. The most imaginative of men, yet writing with the precision of a mathematician, he endeavored to engraft a purely philosophical Ethics on the popular Christianity of his time. Such an attempt, of course, must have difficulty which no genius could surmount. But he saw and showed the connexion between nature and the affections of the soul. He pierced the emblematic or spiritual character or the visible, audible, tangible world. Especially did his shade–loving muse hover over and interpret the lower parts of nature; he showed the mysterious bond that allies moral evil to the foul material forms, and has given in epical parables a theory of insanity, of beasts, of unclean and fearful things.

Another sign of our times, also marked by an analogous political movement is, the new importance given to the single person. Every thing that tends to insulate the individual,—to surround him with barriers of natural respect, so that each man shall feel the world is his, and man shall treat with man as a sovereign state with a sovereign state;—tends to true union as well as greatness. "I learned," said the melancholy Pestalozzi, "that no man in God's wide earth is either willing or able to help any other man." Help must come from the bosom alone. The scholar is that man who must take up into himself all the ability of the time, all the contributions of the past, all the hopes of the future. He must be an university of knowledges. If there be one lesson more than another which should pierce his ear, it is, The world is nothing, the man is all; in yourself is the law of all nature, and you know not yet how a globule of sap ascends; in yourself slumbers the whole of Reason; it is for you to know all, it is for you to dare all. Mr. President and Gentlemen, this confidence in the unsearched might of man, belongs by all motives, by all prophecy, by all preparation, to the American Scholar. We have listened too long to the courtly muses of Europe. The spirit of the American freeman is already suspected to be timid, imitative, tame. Public and private avarice make the air we breathe thick and fat. The scholar is decent, indolent, complaisant. See already the tragic consequence. The mind of this country taught to aim at low objects, eats upon itself. There is no work for any but the decorous and the complaisant.

Young men of the fairest promise, who begin life upon our shores, inflated by the mountain winds, shined upon by all the stars of God, find the earth below not in unison with these,–but are hindered from action by the disgust which the principles on which business is managed inspire, and turn drudges, or die of disgust,– some of them suicides. What is the remedy? They did not yet see, and thousands of young men as hopeful now crowding to the barriers for the career, do not yet see, that if the single man plant himself indomitably on his instincts, and there abide, the huge world will come round to him. Patience–patience;–with the shades of all the good and great for company; and for solace, the perspective of your own infinite life; and for work, the study and the communication of principles, the making those instincts prevalent, the conversion of the world. Is it not the chief disgrace in the world, not to be an unit;–not to be reckoned one character;–not to yield that peculiar fruit which each man was created to bear, but to be reckoned in the gross, in the hundred, or the thousand, of the party, the section, to which we belong; and our opinion predicted geographically, as the north, or the south. Not so, brothers and friends,–please God, ours shall not be so. We will walk on our own feet; we will work with our own hands; we will speak with your own minds. Then shall man be no longer a name for pity, for doubt, and for sensual indulgence. The dread of man and the love of man shall be a wall of defence and a wreath of love around all. A nation of men will for the first time exist, because each believes himself inspired by the Divine Soul which also inspires all men.

Ralph Waldo Emerson

An Address Delivered Before the Senior Class in Divinity College, Cambridge, Sunday Evening, 15 July, 1838
(Boston: James Munroe, 1838).

Emerson's Divinity School Address (also first given its present title in Nature; Addresses, and Lectures *[1849]) was called by William R. Hutchison "the first Transcendentalist attack upon Unitarianism which left no avenue of escape from open conflict." Emerson directly confronted the question of the genuineness of miracles with such statements as "To aim to convert a man by miracles, is a profanation of the soul." Throughout the address, Emerson argued the importance of Reason over Understanding, the necessity for self-reliance, the duties and rights of free speech, and the importance of the German theologians who opposed a fundamentalist interpretation of the Bible. The publication of the address drew down upon Emerson both wrath and praise. Conservative Unitarians, led by Andrew Norton, charged that Emerson lacked clarity in his literary expression and a sense of decorum in criticizing Unitarianism in its stronghold at Harvard, made him guilty by association with the "infidel" Germans, and complained about the democratic tendencies of his ideas. One immediate result of Emerson's address was that the Divinity School students, who had secured him as their orator, were no longer allowed to extend invitations to commencement speakers.*

In this refulgent summer it has been a luxury to draw the breath of life. The grass grows, the buds burst, the meadow is spotted with fire and gold in the tint of flowers. The air is full of birds, and sweet with the breath of the pine, the balm-of-Gilead, and the new hay. Night brings no gloom to the heart with its welcome shade. Through the transparent darkness pour the stars their almost spiritual rays. Man under them seems a young child, and his huge globe a toy. The cool night bathes the world as with a river, and prepares his eyes again for the crimson dawn. The mystery of nature was never displayed more happily. The corn and the wine have been freely dealt to all creatures, and the never-broken silence with which the old bounty goes forward, has not yielded yet one word of explanation. One is constrained to respect the perfection of this world, in which our senses converse. How wide; how rich; what invitation from every property it gives to every faculty of man! In its fruitful soils; in its navigable sea; in its mountains of metal and stone; in its forests of all woods; in its animals; in its chemical ingredients; in the powers and path of light, heat, attraction, and life, is it well worth the pith and heart of great men to subdue and enjoy it. The planters, the me-chanics, the inventors, the astronomers, and builders of cities, and the captains, history delights to honor.

But the moment the mind opens, and reveals the laws which traverse the universe, and make things what they are, then shrinks the great world at once into a mere illustration and fable of this mind. What am I? and What is? asks the human spirit with a curiosity new-kindled, but never to be quenched. Behold these outrunning laws, which our imperfect apprehension can see tend this way and that, but not come full circle. Behold these infinite relations, so unlike, so unlike; many, yet one. I would study, I would know, I would admire forever. These works of thought have been the entertainments of the human spirit in all ages.

A more secret, sweet, and overpowering beauty appears to man when his heart and mind open to the sentiment of virtue. Then instantly he is instructed in what is above him. He learns that his being is without bound; that, to the good, to the perfect, he is born, low as he now lies in evil and weakness. That which he venerates is still his own, though he has not realized it yet. *He ought.* He knows the sense of that grand word, though his analysis fails entirely to render account of it. When in innocency, or when by intellectual perception, he attains to say,–'I love the Right;

Emerson's letter to his aunt Mary Moody Emerson showing his early reading
(facsimile distributed to visitors at the old Manse, Concord)

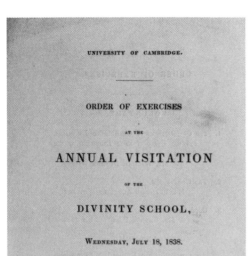

UNIVERSITY OF CAMBRIDGE.

ORDER OF EXERCISES

AT THE

ANNUAL VISITATION

OF THE

DIVINITY SCHOOL,

WEDNESDAY, JULY 18, 1838.

CAMBRIDGE:
FOLSOM, WELLS, AND THURSTON,
PRINTERS TO THE UNIVERSITY.
1838.

ORDER OF EXERCISES.

VOLUNTARY.

1. The Characteristics of the Shemitic Languages, and the Utility of those Languages to the Biblical Interpreter.
    MR. WILLIAM DEXTER WILSON.

2. The Good Pastor.
    MR. FREDERIC AUGUSTUS WHITNEY.

3. Good Sense and Eloquence.
    MR. GEORGE FREDERIC SIMMONS.

ANTHEM.

Sanctus, sanctus, sanctus Dominus Deus Sabaoth, pleni sunt cœli et terra gloriâ tuâ ; hosanna in excelsis. Benedictus qui venit in nomine Domini ; hosanna in excelsis.

4. The Certainty of Present and the Credibility of what Christianity teaches respecting Future Retribution.
    MR. CRAWFORD NIGHTINGALE.

5. Christianity in the Middle Ages.
    MR. THEODORE HASKELL DORR.

3

HYMN.

Of old on Priest and Prophet came
Thy spirit's light, thy spirit's power ;
Of old the altar's kindled flame
Declared thy blessing on the hour.
Thy servants, Lord,
That power require,
That light beam ever o'er their way ;
On waiting hearts
A holier fire
Than fell on Carmel, fall this day.

In death as faithful Pastors sleep,
On us their mantling spirit spread ;
While whitened harvests still we reap,
Where lived and toiled the sainted dead.
Be ever nigh,
All grace impart,
To teach thy truth, to speed thy will ;
Lord, purify
The worldly heart,
The empty, famished spirit fill.

Then bear our Leader's standard high,
Wide let it wave o'er land and sea ;
Till tongues shall cease, till time shall die,
Its blessed folds unfurled and free
Be found where care
And doubt and strife,
Where sin and death their shadows fling ;
Who wins shall wear
A crown of life,
While heavenly choirs their pæan sing.

4

6. Exposition of John v. 17–30.
    MR. HARRISON GRAY OTIS BLAKE.

7. Faith in the Efficacy of Moral Means, Important to the Christian Minister.
    MR. BENJAMIN FISK BARRETT.

ANTHEM.

Lord of all power and might, thou that art the Author, thou that art the Giver of all good things, graft in our hearts the love of thy name, increase in us true religion, nourish us in all goodness, and of thy great mercy keep us in the same, through Jesus Christ our Lord. Amen.

Program for Emerson's ordination as a minister

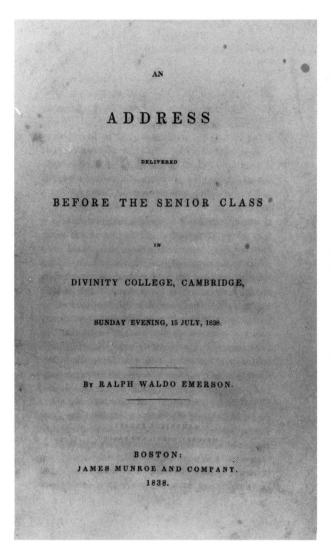

AN

ADDRESS

DELIVERED

BEFORE THE SENIOR CLASS

IN

DIVINITY COLLEGE, CAMBRIDGE,

SUNDAY EVENING, 15 JULY, 1838.

By RALPH WALDO EMERSON.

BOSTON:
JAMES MUNROE AND COMPANY.
1838.

Title page for the "Divinity School Address" Emerson's most controversial publication

Truth is beautiful within and without, forevermore. Virtue, I am thine: save me: use me: thee will I serve, day and night, in great, in small, that I may be not virtuous, but virtue;'–then is the end of the creation answered, and God is well pleased.

The sentiment of virtue is a reverence and delight in the presence of certain divine laws. It perceives that this homely game of life we play, covers, under what seem foolish details, principles that astonish. The child amidst his baubles, is learning the action of light, motion, gravity, muscular force; and in the game of human life, love, fear, justice, appetite, man, and God, interact. These laws refuse to be adequately stated. They will not by us or for us be written out on paper, or spoken by the tongue. They elude, evade our persevering thought, and yet we read them hourly in each other's faces, in each other's actions, in our own remorse. The moral traits which are all globed into every virtuous act and thought,–in speech, we must sever, and describe or suggest by painful enumeration of many particulars. Yet, as this sentiment is the essence of all religion, let me guide your eye to the precise objects of the sentiment, by an enumeration of some of those classes of facts in which this element is conspicuous.

The intuition of the moral sentiment is an insight of the perfection of the laws of the soul. These laws execute themselves. They are out of time, out of space, and not subject to circumstance. Thus; in the soul of man there is a justice whose retributions are instant and entire. He who does a good deed, is instantly ennobled himself. He who does a mean deed, is by the action itself contracted. He who puts off impurity, thereby puts on purity. If a man is at heart just, then in so far is he God; the safety of God, the immortality of God, the majesty of God do enter into that man with justice. If a man dissemble, deceive, he deceives himself, and goes out of acquaintance with his own being. A man in the view of absolute goodness, adores, with total humility. Every step so downward, is a step upward. The man who renounces himself, comes to himself by so doing.

See how this rapid intrinsic energy worketh everywhere, righting wrongs, correcting appearances, and bringing up facts to a harmony with thoughts. Its operation in life, though slow to the senses is, at last, as sure as in the soul. By it, a man is made the Providence to himself, dispensing good to his goodness, and evil to his sin. Character is always known. Thefts never enrich; alms never impoverish; murder will speak out of stone walls. The least admixture of a lie,–for example, the smallest mixture of vanity, the least attempt to make a good impression, a favorable appearance,–will instantly vitiate the effect. But speak the truth, and all nature and all spirits help you with unexpected furtherance. Speak the truth, and all things alive or brute are vouchers, and the very roots of the grass underground there, do seem to stir and move to bear you witness. See again the perfection of the Law as it applies itself to the affections, and becomes the law of society. As we are, so we associate. The good, by affinity, seek the good; the vile, by affinity, the vile. Thus of their own volition, souls proceed into heaven, into hell.

ORDER OF SERVICES

AT THE

ORDINATION OF MR RALPH WALDO EMERSON,

AS JUNIOR PASTOR

OF THE

Second Church and Society

IN BOSTON,

ON WEDNESDAY, MARCH 11, 1829.

VOLUNTARY.—ANTHEM.

ORIGINAL MUSIC BY MR I. ALLEN.

GREAT GOD, whose universal sway
All heaven reveres, all worlds obey,
Now make the Saviour's glory known,
Extend his power, exalt his throne.

Through Him shall endless prayers be made,
And praises throng to crown his head;
His name, like sweet perfume, shall rise,
With every daily sacrifice.

every creature rise and bring
ar honors to our King!
escend with songs again,
repeat the long Amen.

INTRODUCTORY PRAYER,

AND SELECTIONS FROM SCRIPTURE,

HYMN.

How beautiful the feet of those
Who publish Peace from heaven!
How glad the message they disclose
From Him, to save us given!
Glory to God, good will to men,
And Peace on earth, attend his reign.

The world was dark with wo and strife;
Pain, sin, and death bore sway;
And souls, ordain'd to nobler life,
In fear and bondage lay.
His word went forth—earth's evils cease,
And ransom'd spirits rest in peace.

That Peace, which earth can never give,
And never take away,
Shall conquer time and death, and live
Through heaven's eternal day.
Praise to the Lord! whose boundless grace
Redeems and saves our sinful race.

SERMON.

ORDAINING PRAYER.

HYMN.

FATHER! we bow in fervent prayer
In this, thy holy place,
That we, thy children, here may share
The blessings of thy grace.

On HIM, thine eye benignant bend,
The herald of thy truth,
Who, in thy service, vows to spend
The treasures of his youth.

For HIM we humbly crave thy care;
Thy faith and hope to cheer;
Thy strength, the pains and toils to bear
Of every coming year.

Here may the gospel of thy Son,
Pure, as when Jesus taught,
A full, unfetter'd current run,
With joy and healing fraught.

Here may the young and thoughtless learn
To walk in Wisdom's path;
And here the aged spirit burn
With love and perfect faith.

Here may the mourner's heart rejoice
In hopes of promised heaven,
And sorrowing sinners hail the voice,
That tells of sins forgiven.

May souls, beneath thy servant's care,
To truth and glory brought,
In joyful numbers, witness bear
How faithfully he wrought.

And, when the final hour shall come,
That sunders earthly ties,
May he and they a happier home
Enjoy beyond the skies.

CHARGE.

RIGHT HAND OF FELLOWSHIP.

ADDRESS TO THE SOCIETY.

CONCLUDING PRAYER.

ANTHEM.

The Lord will comfort Zion, he will comfort her waste places and make her like Eden, like the garden of the Lord.
Joy and gladness shall be found therein, Thanksgiving and the voice of melody.
We praise thee, O God, we acknowledge thee to be the Lord. All the earth doth worship thee, the Father everlasting. To thee all angels cry aloud, the Heavens and all the powers therein, to the Cherubim, to the Seraphim continually do cry, Holy, holy, holy Lord, God of Sabaoth, Heaven and earth are full of the majesty of thy glory.

BENEDICTION.

BOSTON—PRESS OF ISAAC R. BUTTS.

Order of exercises for the graduation at Harvard divinity School in 1838, at which Emerson delivered his "Divinity School Address"

DIVINITY HALL, ERECTED IN 1826.

Divinity Hall at Harvard College, erected 1826

These facts have always suggested to man the sublime creed, that the world is not the product of manifold power, but of one will, of one mind; and that one mind is everywhere, in each ray of the star, in each wavelet of the pool, active; and whatever opposes that will, is everywhere baulked and baffled, because things are made so, and not otherwise. Good is positive. Evil is merely privative, not absolute. It is like cold, which is the privation of heat. All evil is so much death or nonentity. Benevolence is absolute and real. So much benevolence as a man hath, so much life hath he. For all things proceed out of this same spirit, which is differently named love, justice, temperance, in its different applications, just as the ocean receives different names on the several shores which it washes. All things proceed out of the same spirit, and all things conspire with it. Whilst a man seeks good ends, he is strong by the whole strength of nature. In so far as he roves from these ends, he bereaves himself of power, of auxiliaries; his being shrinks out of all remote channels, he becomes less and less, a mote, a point, until absolute badness is absolute death.

The perception of this law of laws always awakens in the mind a sentiment which we call the religious sentiment, and which makes our highest happiness. Wonderful is its power to charm and to command. It is a mountain air. It is the embalmer of the world. It is myrrh and storax, and chlorine and rosemary. It makes the sky and the hills sublime, and the silent song of the stars is it. By it, is the universe made safe and habitable, not by science or power. Thought may work cold and intransitive in things, and find no end or unity. But the dawn of the sentiment of virtue on the heart, gives and is the assurance that Law is sovereign over all natures; and the worlds, time, space, eternity, do seem to break out into joy.

This sentiment is divine and deifying. It is the beatitude of man. It makes him illimitable. Through it, the soul first knows itself. It corrects the capital mistake of the infant man, who seeks to be great by following the great, and hopes to derive advantages *from another,* — by showing the fountain of all good to be in himself, and that he, equally with every man, is a door into the deeps of Reason. When he says, "I ought;" when love warms him; when he chooses, warned from on high, the good and great deed; then, deep melodies wander through his soul from Supreme Wisdom. Then he can worship, and be enlarged by his worship; for he can never go behind this sentiment. In the sublimest flights of the soul, rectitude is never surmounted, love is never outgrown.

This sentiment lies at the foundation of society, and successively creates all forms of worship. The principle of veneration never dies out. Man fallen into superstition, into sensuality, is never wholly without the visions of the moral sentiment. In like manner, all the expressions of this sentiment are sacred and permanent in proportion to their purity. The expressions of this sentiment affect us deeper, greatlier, than all other compositions. The sentences of the oldest time, which ejaculate this piety, are still fresh and fragrant. This thought dwelled always deepest in the minds of men in the devout and contemplative East; not alone in Palestine, where it reached its purest expression, but in Egypt, in Persia, in India, in China. Europe has always owed to oriental genius, its divine impulses. What these holy bards said, all sane men found agreeable and true. And the unique impression of Jesus upon mankind, whose name is not so much written as ploughed into the history of this world, is proof of the subtle virtue of this infusion.

Meantime, whilst the doors of the temple stand open, night and day, before every man, and the oracles of this truth cease never, it is guarded by one stern condition; this, namely; It is an intuition. It cannot be received at second hand. Truly speaking, it is not instruction, but provocation, that I can receive from another soul. What he announces, I must find true in me, or wholly reject; and on his word, or as his second, be he who he may, I can accept nothing. On the contrary, the absence of this primary faith is the presence of degradation. As is the flood so is the ebb. Let this faith depart, and the very words it spake, and the things it made, become false and hurtful. Then falls the church, the state, art, letters, life. The doctrine of the divine nature being forgotten, a sickness infects and dwarfs the constitution. Once man was all; now he is an appendage, a nuisance. And because the indwelling Supreme Spirit cannot wholly be got rid of, the doctrine of it suffers this perversion, that the divine nature is attributed to one or two persons, and denied to all the rest, and denied with fury. The doctrine of inspiration is lost; the base doctrine of the majority of voices, usurps the place of the doctrine of the soul. Miracles, prophecy, poetry, the ideal life, the holy life, exist as ancient history merely; they are not in the belief, nor in the aspiration of society; but, when suggested, seem ri-

diculous. Life is comic or pitiful, as soon as the high ends of being fade out of sight, and man becomes nearsighted, and can only attend to what addresses the scenes.

These general views, which, whilst they are general, none will contest, find abundant illustration in the history of religion, and especially in the history of the Christian church. In that, all of us have had our birth and nurture. The truth contained in that, you, my young friends, are now setting forth to teach. As the Cultus, or established worship of the civilized world, it has great historical interest for us. Of its blessed words, which have been the consolation of humanity, you need not that I should speak. I shall endeavor to discharge my duty to you, on this occasion, by pointing out two errors in its administration, which daily appear more gross from the point of view we have just now taken.

Jesus Christ belonged to the true race of prophets. He saw with open eye the mystery of the soul. Drawn by its severe harmony, ravished with its beauty, he lived in it, and had his being there. Alone in all history, he estimated the greatness of man. One man was true to what is in you and me. He saw that God incarnates himself in man, and evermore goes forth anew to take possession of his world. He said, in this jubilee of sublime emotion, 'I am divine. Through me, God acts; through me, speaks. Would you see God, see me; or, see thee, when thou also thinkest as I now think.' But what a distortion did his doctrine and memory suffer in the same, in the next, and the following ages! There is no doctrine of the Reason which will bear to be taught by the Understanding. The understanding caught this high chant from the poet's lips, and said, in the next age, 'This was Jehovah come down out of heaven. I will kill you, if you say he was a man.' The idioms of his language, and the figures of his rhetoric, have usurped the place of his truth; and churches are not built on his principles, but on his tropes. Christianity became a Mythus, as the poetic teaching of Greece and of Egypt, before. He spoke of miracles; for he felt that man's life was a miracle, and all that man doth, and he knew that this daily miracle shines, as the man is diviner. But the very word Miracle, as pronounced by Christian churches, gives a false impression; it is Monster. It is not one with the blowing clover and the falling rain.

He felt respect for Moses and the prophets; but no unfit tenderness at postponing their initial revelations, to the hour and the man that now is; to the eternal revelation in the heart. Thus was he a true man. Having seen that the law in us is commanding, he would not suffer it to be concealed. Boldly, with hand, and heart, and life, he declared it was God. Thus was he a true man. Thus is he, as I think, the only soul in history who has appreciated the worth of a man.

1. In thus contemplating Jesus, we become very sensible of the first defect of historical Christianity. Historical Christianity has fallen into the error that corrupts all attempts to communicate religion. As it appears to us, and as it has appeared for ages, it is not the doctrine of the soul, but an exaggeration of the personal, the positive, the ritual. It has dwelt, it dwells, with noxious exaggeration about the *person* of Jesus. The soul knows no persons. It invites every man to expand to the full circle of the universe, and will have no preferences but those of spontaneous love. But by this eastern monarchy of a Christianity, which indolence and fear have built, the friend of man is made the jurer of man. The manner in which his name is surrounded with expressions, which were once sallies of admiration and love, but are now petrified into official titles, kills all generous sympathy and liking. All who hear me, feel, that the language that describes Christ to Europe and America, is not the style of friendship and enthusiasm to a good and noble heart, but is appropriated and formal,–paints a demigod, as the Orientals or the Greeks would desire Osiris or Apollo. Accept the injurious impositions of our early catechetical instruction, and even honesty and self-denial were but splendid sins, if they did not wear the Christian name. One would rather be

'A pagan suckled in a creed outworn,'

than to be defrauded of his manly right in coming into nature, and finding not names and places, not land and professions, but even virtue and truth foreclosed and monopolized. You shall not be a man even. You shall not own the world; you shall not dare, and live after the infinite Law that is in you, and in company with the infinite Beauty which heaven and earth reflect to you in all lovely forms; but you must subordinate your nature to Christ's nature; you must accept our interpretations; and take his portrait as the vulgar draw it.

That is always best which gives me to myself. The sublime is excited in me by the great stoical doctrine, Obey thyself. That which shows God in me, forti-

fies me. That which shows God out of me, makes me a wart and a wen. There is no longer a necessary reason for my being. Already the long shadows of untimely oblivion creep over me, and I shall decease forever.

The divine bards are the friends of my virtue, of my intellect, of my strength. They admonish me, that the gleams which flash across my mind, are not mine, but God's; that they had the like, and were not disobedient to the heavenly vision. So I love them. Noble provocations go out from them, inviting me also to emancipate myself; to resist evil; to subdue the world; and to Be. And thus by his holy thoughts, Jesus serves us, and thus only. To aim to convert a man by miracles, is a profanation of the soul. A true conversion, a true Christ, is now, as always, to be made, by the reception of beautiful sentiments. It is true that a great and rich soul, like his, falling among the simple, does so preponderate, that, as his did, it names the world. The world seems to them to exist for him, and they have not yet drunk so deeply of his sense, as to see that only by coming again to themselves, or to God in themselves, can they grow forevermore. It is a low benefit to give me something; it is a high benefit to enable me to do somewhat of myself. The time is coming when all men will see, that the gift of God to the soul is not a vaunting, overpowering, excluding sanctity, but a sweet, natural goodness, a goodness like thine and mine, and that so invites thine and mine to be and to grow.

The injustice of the vulgar tone of preaching is not less flagrant to Jesus, than it is to the souls which it profanes. The preachers do not see that they make his gospel not glad, and shear him of the locks of beauty and the attributes of heaven. When I see a majestic Epaminondas, or Washington; when I see among my contemporaries, a true orator, an upright judge, a dear friend; when I vibrate to the melody and fancy of a poem; I see beauty that is to be desired. And so lovely, and with yet more entire consent of my human being, sounds in my ear the severe music of the bards that have sung of the true God in all ages. Now do not degrade the life and dialogues of Christ out of the circle of this charm, by insulation and peculiarity. Let them lie as they befel, alive and warm, part of human life, and of the landscape, and of the cheerful day.

2. The second defect of the traditionary and limited way of using the mind of Christ is a consequence of the first; this, namely; that the Moral Nature, that

Laws of laws, whose revelations introduce greatness,– yea, God himself, into the open soul, is not explored as the fountain of the established teaching in society. Men have come to speak of the revelation as somewhat long ago given and done, as if God were dead. The injury to faith throttles the preacher; and the goodliest of institutions becomes an uncertain and inarticulate voice.

It is very certain that it is the effect of conversation with the beauty of the soul, to beget a desire and need to impart to others the same knowledge and love. If utterance is denied, the thought lies like a burden on the man. Always the seer is a sayer. Somehow his dream is told. Somehow he publishes it with solemn joy. Sometimes with pencil on canvas; sometimes with chisel on stone; sometimes in towers and aisles of granite, his soul's worship is builded; sometimes in anthems of indefinite music; but clearest and most permanent, in words.

The man enamored of this excellency, becomes its priest or poet. The office is coeval with the world. But observe the condition, the spiritual limitation of the office. The spirit only can teach. Not any profane man, not any sensual, not any liar, not any slave can teach, but only he can give, who has; he only can create, who is. The man on whom the soul descends, through whom the soul speaks, alone can teach. Courage, piety, love, wisdom, can teach; and every man can open his door to these angels, and they shall bring him the gift of tongues. But the man who aims to speak as books enable, as synods use, as the fashion guides, and as interest commands, babbles. Let him hush.

To this holy office, you propose to devote yourselves. I wish you may feel your call in throbs of desire and hope. The office is the first in the world. It is of that reality, that it cannot suffer the deduction of any falsehood. And it is my duty to say to you, that the need was never greater of new revelation than now. From the views I have already expressed, you will infer the sad conviction, which I share, I believe, with numbers, of the universal decay and now almost death of faith in society. The soul is not preached. The Church seems to totter to its fall, almost all life extinct. On this occasion, any complaisance, would be criminal, which told you, whose hope and commission it is to preach the faith of Christ, that the faith of Christ is preached.

It is time that this ill-suppressed murmur of all thoughtful men against the famine of our churches; this moaning of the heart because it is bereaved of the consolation, the hope, the grandeur, that come along out of the culture of the moral nature; should be heard through the sleep of indolence, and over the din of routine. This great and perpetual office of the preacher is not discharged. Preaching is the expression of the moral sentiment in application to the duties of life. In how many churches, by how many prophets, tell me, is man made sensible that he is an infinite Soul; that the earth and heavens are passing into his mind; that he is drinking forever the soul of God? Where now sounds the persuasion, that by its very melody imparadises my heart, and so affirms its own origin in heaven? Where shall I hear words such as in elder ages drew men to leave all and follow,–father and mother, house and land, wife and child? Where shall I hear these august laws of moral being so pronounced, as to fill my ear, and I feel ennobled by the offer of my uttermost action and passion? The test of the true faith, certainly, should be its power to charm and command the soul, as the laws of nature control the activity of the hands,–so commanding that we find pleasure and honor in obeying. The faith should blend with the light of rising and of setting suns, with the flying cloud, the singing bird, and the breath of flowers. But now the priest's Sabbath has lost the splendor of nature; it is unlovely; we are glad when it is done; we can make, we do make, even sitting in our pews, a far better, holier, sweeter, for ourselves.

Whenever the pulpit is usurped by a formalist, then is the worshipper defrauded and disconsolate. We shrink as soon as the prayers begin, which do not uplift, but smite and offend us. We are fain to wrap our cloaks about us, and secure, as best we can, a solitude that hears not. I once heard a preacher who sorely tempted me to say, I would go to church no more. Men go, thought I, where they are wont to go, else had no soul entered the temple in the afternoon. A snowstorm was falling around us. The snowstorm was real; the preacher merely spectral; and the eye felt the sad contrast in looking at him, and then out of the window behind him, into the beautiful meteor of the snow. He had lived in vain. He had no one word intimating that he had laughed or wept, was married or in love, had been commended, or cheated, or chagrined. If he had ever lived and acted, we were none the wiser for it. The capital secret of his profession, namely, to convert life into truth, he had not learned. Not one fact in all his experience, had he yet imported into his doctrine.

This man had ploughed and planted, and talked, and bought, and sold; he had read books; he had eaten and drunken; his head aches; his heart throbs; he smiles and suffers; yet was there not a surmise, a hint, in all the discourse, that he had ever lived at all. Not a line did he draw out of real history. The true preacher can always be known by this, that he deals out to the people his life,–life passed through the fire of thought. But of the bad preacher, it could not be told from his sermon, what age of the world he fell in; whether he had a father or a child; whether he was a freeholder or a pauper; whether he was a citizen or a countryman; or any other fact of his biography.

It seemed strange that the people should come to church. It seemed as if their houses were very unentertaining, that they should prefer this thoughtless clamor. It shows that there is a commanding attraction in the moral sentiment, that can lend a faint tint of light to dulness and ignorance, coming in its name and place. The good hearer is sure he has been touched sometimes; is sure there is somewhat to be reached, and some word that can reach it. When he listens to these vain words, he comforts himself by their relation to his remembrance of better hours, and so they clatter and echo unchallenged.

I am not ignorant that when we preach unworthily, it is not always quite in vain. There is a good ear, in some men, that draws supplies to virtue out of every indifferent nutriment. There is poetic truth concealed in all the common-places of prayer and of sermons, and though foolishly spoken, they may be wisely heard; for, each is some select expression that broke out in a moment of piety from some stricken or jubilant soul, and its excellency made it remembered. The prayers and even the dogmas of our church, are like the zodiac of Denderah, and the astronomical monuments of the Hindoos, wholly insulated from anything now extant in the life and business of the people. They mark the height to which the waters once rose. But this docility is a check upon the mischief from the good and devout. In a large portion of the community, the religious service gives rise to quite other thoughts and emotions. We need not chide the negligent servant. We are struck with pity, rather, at the swift retribution of his sloth. Alas for the unhappy man that is called to stand in the pulpit, and *not* give bread of life. Everything that befals, accuses him. Would he ask contributions for the missions, foreign or domestic? Instantly his face is suffused with shame, to propose to his par-

ish, that they should send money a hundred or a thousand miles, to furnish such poor fare as they have at home, and would do well to go the hundred or the thousand miles, to escape. Would he urge people to a godly way of living;–and can he ask a fellow creature to come to Sabbath meetings, when he and they all know what is the poor uttermost they can hope for therein? Will he invite them privately to the Lord's Supper? He dares not. If no heart warm this rite, the hollow, dry, creaking formality is too plain, than that he can face a man of wit and energy, and put the invitation without terror. In the street, what has he to say to the bold village blasphemer? The village blasphemer sees fear in the face, form, and gait of the minister.

Let me not taint the sincerity of this plea by any oversight of the claims of good men. I know and honor the purity and strict conscience of numbers of the clergy. What life the public worship retains, it owes to the scattered company of pious men, who minister here and there in the churches, and who, sometimes accepting with too great tenderness the tenet of the elders, have not accepted from others, but from their own heart, the genuine impulses of virtue, and so still command our love and awe, to the sanctity of character. Moreover, the exceptions are not so much to be found in a few eminent preachers, as in the better hours, the truer inspirations of all,–nay, in the sincere moments of every man. But with whatever exception, it is still true, that tradition characterizes the preaching of this country; that it comes out of the memory, and not out of the soul; that it aims at what is usual, and not at what is necessary and eternal; that thus, historical Christianity destroys the power of preaching, by withdrawing it from the exploration of the moral nature of man, where the sublime is, where are the resources of astonishment and power. What a cruel injustice it is to that Law, the joy of the whole earth, which alone can make thought dear and rich; that Law whose fatal sureness the astronomical orbits poorly emulate, that it is travestied and depreciated, that it is behooted and behowled, and not a trait, not a word of it articulated. The pulpit in losing sight of this Law, loses all its inspiration, and gropes after it knows not what. And for want of this culture, the soul of the community is sick and faithless. It wants nothing so much as a stern, high, stoical, Christian discipline, to make it know itself and the divinity that speaks through it. Now man is ashamed of himself; he skulks and sneaks through the world, to be tolerated, to be pitied, and scarcely in a thousand years does any man dare to be wise and good, and so draw after him the tears and blessings of his kind.

Certainly there have been periods when, from the inactivity of the intellect on certain truths, a greater faith was possible in names and persons. The Puritans in England and America, found in the Christ of the Catholic Church, and in the dogmas inherited from Rome, scope for their austere piety, and their longings for civil freedom. But their creed is passing away, and none arises in its room. I think no man can go with his thoughts about him, into one of our churches, without feeling that what hold the public worship had on men, is gone or going. It has lost its grasp on the affection of the good, and the fear of the bad. In the country,–neighborhoods, half parishes are *signing off,*–to use the local term. It is already beginning to indicate character and religion to withdraw from the religious meetings. I have heard a devout person, who prized the Sabbath, say in bitterness of heart, "On Sundays, it seems wicked to go to church." And the motive, that holds the best there, is now only a hope and a waiting. What was once a mere circumstance, that the best and the worst men in the parish, the poor and the rich, the learned and the ignorant, young and old, should meet one day as fellows in one house, in sign of an equal right in the soul,–has come to be a paramount motive for going thither.

My friends, in these two errors, I think, I find the causes of that calamity of a decaying church and a wasting unbelief, which are casting malignant influences around us, and making the hearts of good men sad. And what greater calamity can fall upon a nation, than the loss of worship? Then all things go to decay. Genius leaves the temple, to haunt the senate, or the market. Literature becomes frivolous. Science is cold. The eye of youth is not lighted by the hope of other worlds, and age is without honor. Society lives to trifles, and when men die, we do not mention them.

And now, my brothers, you will ask, What in these desponding days can be done by us? The remedy is already declared in the ground of our complaint of the Church. We have contrasted the Church with the Soul. In the soul, then, let the redemption be sought. In one soul, in your soul, there are resources for the world. Wherever a man comes, there comes revolution. The old is for slaves. When a man comes, all books are legible, all things transparent, all religions are forms. He is 'religious. Man is the wonderworker. He is seen amid miracles. All men bless and curse. He

saith yea and nay, only. The stationariness of religion; the assumption that the age of inspiration is past, that the Bible is closed; the fear of degrading the character of Jesus by representing him as a man; indicate with sufficient clearness the falsehood of our theology. It is the office of a true teacher to show us that God is, not was; that He speaketh, not spake. The true Christianity,–a faith like Christ's in the infinitude of man,–is lost. None believeth in the soul of man, but only in some man or person old and departed. Ah me! no man goeth alone. All men go in flocks to this saint or that poet, avoiding the God who seeth in secret. They cannot see in secret; they love to be blind in public. They think society wiser than their soul; and know not that one soul, and their soul, is wiser than the whole world. See how nations and races flit by on the sea of time, and leave no ripple to tell where they floated or sunk, and one good soul shall make the name of Moses, or of Zeno, or of Zoroaster, reverend forever. None assayeth the stern ambition to be the Self of the nation, and of nature, but each would be an easy secondary to some Christian scheme, or sectarian connexion, or some eminent man. Once leave your own knowledge of God, your own sentiment, and take secondary knowledge, as St. Paul's, or George Fox's, or Swedenborg's and you get wide from God with every year this secondary form lasts, and if, as now, for centuries,–the chasm yawns to that breadth, that men can scarcely be convinced there is in them anything divine.

Let me admonish you, first of all, to go alone; to refuse the good models, even those most sacred in the imagination of men, and dare to love God without mediator or veil. Friends enough you shall find who will hold up to your emulation Wesleys and Oberlins, Saints and Prophets. Thank God for these good men, but say, 'I also am a man.' Imitation cannot go above its model. The imitator dooms himself to hopeless mediocrity. The inventor did it, because it was natural to him, and so in him it has a charm. In the imitator, something else is natural, and he bereaves himself of his own beauty, to come short of another man's.

Yourself a newborn bard of the Holy Ghost,–cast behind you all conformity, and acquaint men at first hand with Deity. Be to them a man. Look to it first and only, that you are such; that fashion, custom, authority, pleasure, and money are nothing to you,–are not bandages over your eyes, that you cannot see,–but live with the privilege of the immeasurable mind. Not too anxious to visit periodically all families and each family in your parish connexion,–when you meet one of these men or women, be to them a divine man; be to them thought and virtue; let their timid aspirations find in you a friend; let their trampled instincts be genially tempted out in your atmosphere; let their doubts know that you have doubted, and their wonder feel that you have wondered. By trusting your own soul, you shall gain a greater confidence in other men. For all our penny-wisdom, for all our soul-destroying slavery to habit, it is not to be doubted, that all men have sublime thoughts; that all men do value the few real hours of life; they love to be heard; they love to be caught up into the vision of principles. We mark with light in the memory the few interviews, we have had in the dreary years of routine and of sin, with souls that made our souls wiser; that spoke what we thought; that told us what we know; that gave us leave to be what we inly were. Discharge to men the priestly office, and, present or absent, you shall be followed with their love as by an angel.

And, to this end, let us not aim at common degrees of merit. Can we not leave, to such as love it, the virtue that glitters for the commendation of society, and ourselves pierce the deep solitudes of absolute ability and worth? We easily come up to the standard of goodness in society. Society's praise can be cheaply secured, and almost all men are content with those easy merits; but the instant effect of conversing with God, will be, to put them away. There are sublime merits; persons who are not actors, not speakers, but influences; persons too great for fame, or display; who disdain eloquence; to whom all we call art and artist, seems too nearly allied to show and by-ends, to the exaggeration of the finite and selfish, and loss of the universal. The orators, the poets, the commanders encroach on us only as fair women do, by our allowance and homage. Slight them by preoccupation of mind, slight them, as you can well afford to do, by high and universal aims, and they instantly feel that you have right, and that it is in lower places that they must shine. They also feel your right; for they with you are open to the influx of the all-knowing Spirit, which annihilates before its broad noon the little shades of gradations of intelligence in the compositions we call wiser and wisest.

In such high communion, let us study the grand strokes of rectitude: a bold benevolence, an independence of friends, so that the unjust wishes of those who love us, shall impair our freedom, but we shall resist for truth's sake the freest flow of kindness, and appeal to sympathies far in advance; and,–what is the highest form in which we know this beautiful element,–a certain solidity of merit, that has nothing to do with opinion, and which is so essentially and manifestly virtue, that it is taken for granted, that the right, the brave, the generous step will be taken by it, and nobody thinks of commending it. You would compliment a coxcomb doing a good act, but you would not praise an angel. The silence that accepts merit as the most natural thing in the world, is the highest applause. Such souls, when they appear, are the Imperial Guard of Virtue, the perpetual reserve, the dictators of fortune. One needs not praise their courage,–they are the heart and soul of nature. O my friends, there are resources in us on which we have not drawn. There are men who rise refreshed on hearing a threat; men to whom a crisis which intimidates and paralyzes the majority–demanding not the faculties of prudence and thrift, but comprehension, immovableness, the readiness of sacrifice,–comes graceful and beloved as a bride. Napoleon said of Massena, that he was not himself until the battle began to go against him; then, when the dead began to fall in ranks around him, awoke his powers of combination, and he put on terror and victory as a robe. So it is in rugged crises, in unweariable endurance, and in aims which put sympathy out of question, that the angel is shown. But these are heights that we can scarce remember and look up to, without contrition and shame. Let us thank God that such things exist.

And now let us do what we can to rekindle the smouldering, nigh quenched fire on the altar. The evils of that church that now is, are manifest. The questions returns, What shall we do? I confess, all attempts to project and establish a Cultus with new rites and forms, seem to me vain. Faith makes us, and not we it, and faith makes its own forms. All attempts to contrive a system, are as cold as the new worship introduced by the French to the goddess of Reason,–to-day, pasteboard and fillagree, and ending to-morrow in madness and murder. Rather let the breath of new life be breathed by you through the forms already existing. For, if once you are alive, you shall find they shall become plastic and new. The remedy to their deformity is, first, soul, and second, soul, and evermore, soul. A whole popedom of forms, one pulsation of virtue can uplift and vivify. Two inestimable advantages Christianity has given us; first; the Sabbath, the jubilee of the whole world;

whose light dawns welcome alike into the closet of the philosopher, into the garret of toil, and into prison cells, and everywhere suggests, even to the vile, a thought of the dignity of spiritual being. Let it stand for-evermore, a temple, which new love, new faith, new sight shall restore to more than its first splendor to man-kind. And secondly, the institution of preaching,–the speech of man to men,–essentially the most flexible of all organs, of all forms. What hinders that now, every-where, in pulpits, in lecture-rooms, in houses, in fields, wherever the invitation of men or your own occa-sions lead you, you speak the very truth, as your life and conscience teach it, and cheer the waiting, fainting hearts of men with new hope and new revelation.

I look for the hour when that supreme Beauty, which ravished the souls of those Eastern men, and chiefly of those Hebrews, and through their lips spoke oracles to all time, shall speak in the West also. The Hebrew and Greek Scriptures contain immortal sen-tences, that have been bread of life to millions. But they have no epical integrity; are fragmentary; are not shown in their order to the intellect. I look for the new Teacher, that shall follow so far those shining laws, that he shall see them come full circle; shall see their rounding complete grace; shall see the world to be the mirror of the soul; shall see the identity of the law of gravitation with purity of heart; and shall show that the Ought, that Duty, is one thing with Science, with Beauty, and with Joy.

Andrews Norton

"The New School in Literature and Religion," Boston Daily Advertiser, 27 August 1838, p. 2.

By far the most vituperative attack on Emerson was by Andrews Norton, the leading conservative Unitarian of the day. Norton was so incensed by the content of Emerson's address and by his audacity in delivering his criticisms before the Divinity School faculty, that he took the almost unheard-of step of sending his criticisms to a daily paper, rather than waiting for the religious monthlies or quarterlies to appear. He was so immoderate and intemperate that even some who opposed Emerson were embarrassed by being associated with Norton. Norton's opening salvo in the war of words over the Divinity School Address later brought in some two dozen notices in Boston newspapers and periodicals, as well as these pamphlets: Henry Ware, Jr.'s The Personality of the Deity *(1838); Norton's* A Discourse on the Latest Form of Infidelity *(1839); George Ripley's* "The Latest Form of Infidelity" Examined. A Letter to Mr. Andrews Norton . . . *(1839),* Defense of "The Latest Form of Infidelity" Examined. A Second Letter to Mr. Andrews Norton . . . *(1840), and* Defense of "The Latest Form of Infidelity" Examined. A Third Letter to Mr. Andrews Norton . . . *(1840); Norton's reply to Ripley,* Remarks on a Pamphlet Entitled " 'The Latest Form of Infidelity' Examined" *(1839); Theodore Parker's (writing as "Levi Blodgett")* The Previous Question Between Mr. Andrews Norton and His Alumni Moved and Handled, in a Letter to All Those Gentlemen *(1840); and* Two Articles from the "Princeton Review" Concerning the Transcendental Philosophy of the Germans and of Cousin, and Its Influence on Opinion in This Country *(1840), which Norton edited. (For further information, see the entries for Norton, Parker, and Ripley in* DLB 1, The American Renaissance in New England.)

There is a strange state of things existing about us in the literary and religious world, of which none of our larger periodicals has yet taken notice. It is the result of this restless craving for notoriety and excitement, which, in one way or another, is keeping our community in a perpetual stir. It has shown itself, we think, particularly since that foolish woman, Miss Martineau, was among us, and stimulated the vanity of her flatterers by loading them in return with the copper coin of her praise, which they easily believed was as good as gold. She was accustomed to talk about her mission, as if she were a special dispensation of Providence, and they too thought that they must all have their missions, and began to "vaticinate," as one of their number has expressed it. But though her genial warmth may have caused the new school to bud and bloom, it was not planted by her.—It owes its origin in part to ill-understood notions, obtained by blundering through the crabbed and disgusting obscurity of some of the worst German speculatists, which notions, however, have been received by most of its disciples at second hand, through an interpreter. The atheist Shelley has been quoted and commended in a professedly religious work, called the Western Messenger, but he is not, we conceive, to be reckoned among the patriarchs of the sect. But this honor is due to that hasher up of German metaphysics, the Frenchman, Cousin; and, of late, that hyper-Germanized Englishman, Carlyle, has been the great object of admiration and model of style. Cousin and Carlyle indeed seem to have been transformed into idols to be publicly worshipped; the former for his philosophy, and the latter both for his philosophy and his fine writing; while the veiled image of the German pantheist, Schleiermacher, is kept in the sanctuary.

The characteristics of this school are the most extraordinary assumption, united with great ignorance, and incapacity for reasoning. There is indeed a general tendency among its disciples to disavow learning and reasoning as sources of their higher knowledge.—The mind must be its own unassisted teacher. It discerns transcendental truths by immediate vision, and these

Andrews Norton.

Andrew Norton V. C. Blumenbach S.

A curatoribus nostra Universitatis Harvidinensis, officium est mihi demandatum, jucundissimum, agere tibi gratias pro opusculo tuo, lingua Germanica scripto de nisu formatio et generatione plantarum et animalium, quod nuper scriptum a te tuo acceperunt. Gratum est illis hoc opus accipere, viro pro eximia in rebus physicis scientia per orbem litterariam celeberrimo

Has litteras tibi tradet juvenis ingenuus, optimæ spei, Georgius Bancroft, omnibus bonis moribus, et ingenio eximio ornatus. Illi propositum est studiis litterariis dare operam in Universitate Gottingensi. Quod omnia sint illi fausta, multum est curæ viris bonis et litterarum fautoribus in hoc loco. Vale vir clarissime.

Andrews Norton

Manuscript Latin passage by Andrews Norton (Autograph Leaves of Our Country's Authors, edited by John Pendleton Kennedy *and Alexander Bliss [1864])*

truths can no more be communicated to another by addressing his understanding, than the power of *clairvoyance* can be given to one not magnetized. They announce themselves as the prophets and priests of a new future, in which all is to be changed, all old opinions done away, and all present forms of society abolished. But by what process this joyful revolution is to be effected as are not told; nor how human happiness and virtue is to be saved from the universal wreck, and regenerated in their Medea's caldron. There are great truths with which they are laboring, but they are unutterable in words to be understood by common minds. To such minds they seem nonsense, oracles as obscure as those of Delphi.

The rejection of reasoning is accompanied with an equal contempt for good taste. All modesty is laid aside. The writer of an article for an obscure periodical, or a religious newspaper, assumes a tone as if he were one of the chosen enlighteners of a dark age.–He continually obtrudes himself upon his reader, and announces his own convictions, as if from their having that character, they were necessarily indisputable.–He floats about magnificently on bladders, which he would have it believed are swelling with ideas.–Common thoughts, sometimes true, oftener false, and "Neutral nonsense, neither false nor true," are exaggerated, and twisted out of shape, and forced into strange connexions, to make them look like some grand and new conception. To produce a more striking effect, our common language is abused; antic tricks are played with it; inversions, exclamations, anamalous combinations of words, unmeaning, but coarse and violent, metaphors abound, and withal a strong infusion of German barbarians. Such is the style of Carlyle, a writer of some talent; for his great deficiency is not in this respect, it is in good sense, good taste and soundness of principle; but a writer, who, through his talents, such as they are, through that sort of buffoonery and affectation of manner which throws the reader off his guard, through the indisputable novelty of his way of writing, and through a somewhat too prevalent taste among us for an over-excited and *convulsionary* style, which we mistake for eloquence, has obtained a degree of fame in this country, very disproportioned to what he enjoys at home, out of the Westminster Review. Carlyle, however, as an original, might be tolerated, if one could forget his admirers and imitators.

The state of things described might seem a matter of no great concern, a mere insurrection of folly, a sort of Jack Cade rebellion; which in the nature of things must soon be put down, if those engaged in it were not gathering confidence from neglect, and had not proceeded to attack principles which are the foundation of human society and human happiness. "Silly women," it has been said, and silly young men, it is to be feared, have been drawn away from their christian faith, if not divorced from all that can properly be called religion. The evil is becoming, for the time, disastrous and alarming; and of this fact there could hardly be a more extraordinary and ill boding evidence, than is afforded by a publication, which has just appeared, entitled an "Address, delivered before the Senior class in Divinity College, Cambridge," upon the occasion of that class taking leave of the Institution. "By Ralph Waldo Emerson."

It is not necessary to remark particularly on this composition. It will be sufficient to state generally, that the author professes to reject all belief in Christianity as a revelation, that he makes a general attack upon the Clergy, on the ground that they preach what he calls "Historical Christianity," and that if he believe in God in the proper sense of the term, which one passage might have led his hearers to suppose, his language elsewhere is very ill-judged and indecorous. But what *his* opinions may be is a matter of minor concern; the main question is how it has happened, that religion has been insulted by the delivery of these opinions in the Chapel of the Divinity College at Cambridge, as the last instruction which those were to receive, who were going forth from it, bearing the name of christian preachers. This is a question in which the community is deeply interested. No one can doubt for a moment of the disgust and strong disapprobation with which it must have been heard by the highly respectable officers of that Institution. They must have felt it not only as an insult to religion, but as personal insult to themselves. But this renders the fact of its having been so delivered only the more remarkable. We can proceed but a step in accounting for it. The preacher was invited to occupy the place he did, not by the officers of the Divinity College, but by the members of the graduating class. These gentlemen, therefore, have become accessories, perhaps innocent accessories, to the commission of a great offence; and the public must be desirous of learning what exculpation or excuse they can offer.

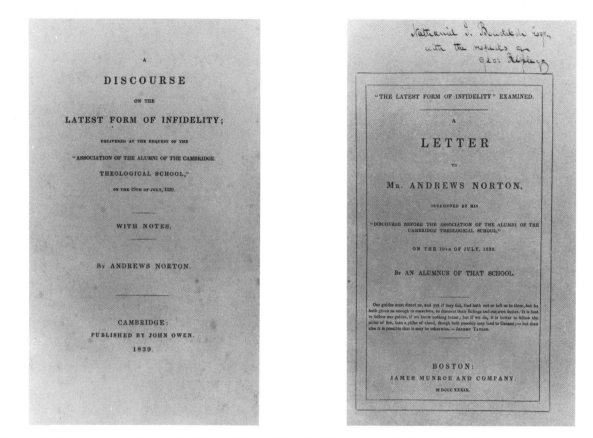

Title page for Norton's reply to Emerson's "Divinity School Address"   *Front wrapper for George Ripley's reply to Norton's pamphlet*

Title page of Norton's reply to George Ripley's pamphlet

It is difficult to believe that they thought this incoherent rhapsody a specimen of fine writing, that they listened with admiration, for instance, when they were told that the religious sentiment "is myrrh, and storax and chlorine and rosemary;" or that they wondered at the profound views of their present Teacher, when he announced to them that "the new Teacher," for whom he is looking, would "see the identity of the law of gravitation with purity of heart;" or that they had not some suspicion of inconsistency, when a new Teacher was talked of, after it had been declared to them, that religious truth "is an intuition," and "cannot be received at second hand."

But the subject is to be viewed under a far more serious aspect. The words God, Religion, Christianity, have a definite meaning, well understood. They express conceptions and truths of unutterable moment to the present and future happiness of man. We well know how shamefully they have been abused in modern times by infidels and pantheists; but their meaning remains the same; the truths which they express are unchanged and unchangeable. The community know what they require when they ask for a Christian Teacher; and should any one approving the doctrines of this discourse assume that character, he would deceive his hearers; he would be guilty of a practical falsehood for the most paltry of temptations; he would consent to live, a lie, for the sake of being maintained by those whom he had cheated. It is not, however, to be supposed that his vanity would suffer him long to keep his philosophy wholly to himself. This would break out in obscure intimations, ambiguous words, and false and mischievous speculations. But should such preachers abound, and grow confident in their folly, we can hardly overestimate the disastrous effects upon the religious and moral state of the community.

[Orestes A. Brownson]
"Alcott on Human Culture," *Boston Quarterly Review,* 1 (October 1838): 417-432.

Brownson's defense of Alcott came at an opportune time, for the press was still involved in debating Emerson's Divinity School Address. By saying that Alcott and his ideas
were worthy of serious study rather than a cursory dismissal, Brownson was indirectly arguing for a fair treatment of Emerson and other Transcendentalists. Nevertheless, here can be
seen the beginnings of Brownson's ultimate rejection of Transcendentalism because of–he felt–
too much importance being placed on individual intuition.

Conversations with Children on the Gospels; *conducted and edited by A. Bronson Alcott.*
Boston: James Munroe and Co. 1836. 2 vols. 12 mo.

This is a difficult book for Reviewers. It is not
easy to say what it is, or what it is not. It is hardly
safe to assume it as an index to the views and opinions
of its editor, or to the character and worth of the
school in which these Conversations were held. The
Conversations published are incomplete; they comprise
only one year of what was intended to be a four years'
course. The very nature of such conversations precludes the possibility of recording them with perfect accuracy, though these were recorded with great fidelity;
and then, they constituted the exercise of the scholars
for only a part of one half-day in a week, the rest of
the time being taken up with the studies common in
other schools. As it regards Mr. Alcott, these Conversations very imperfectly reveal him, or his system of instruction. One is in constant danger of misapprehend-
ing him, and of ascribing to him views and opinions
which belong solely to the children. Even his own questions, if we are not on our guard, may mislead us; for
they were frequently suggested by the remarks of the
scholars, and designed merely to induce them to carry
out their own thought.

Mr. Alcott has received much reproach, and we
fear been made to suffer in the prosperity of his school
on account of this book. He has been treated with
great illiberality, and made to undergo as severe a persecution as the times allow. As a man he is singularly evangelical, pure minded, in love with all that is beautiful
and good, and devoted soul and body to what he
deems truth, and the regeneration of mankind. He is con-

scious of being sent into this world on a high and important mission, and his great study is to discharge that mission to the acceptance of him that sent him. Yet no
man among us has been spoken of in severer tones, or
been more seriously injured, for the moment, by the misapprehension and ill-nature, the misrepresentation and
abuse, he has had to endure from those who affect to
lead public opinion. It is painful to record this fact. For
there is no man in our country who so well understands the art of education, and who is capable or desirous of doing more for establishing a system of Human
Culture, in consonance with our faith as Christians and
as republicans. And there is no fault, nor even shadow
of a fault to be found with him; save that he will be
true to the deepest and holiest convictions of his own
mind; and will never sacrifice what he holds as truth, virtue, manhood, independence, to popular opinion, to a
sickly taste, or a heartless conventionalism. It is not
much to our credit, that we condemn him for this.

Mr. Alcott may not be sound in his philosophy,
he may not be correct in all his views, and he may
carry, and we believe he does carry, some of his favorite notions to extremes; but he deserves profound reverence for his determination to be a Man; to be true to
Human Nature; for his fearless assertion of his own convictions, and for his deep and living faith in God and Humanity. He aims to be himself and not another; to
think his own thoughts and not another's; and having
done this, he will not lock up his thoughts in his own
bosom, and seem to acquiesce in reigning dogmas; but

[95]

The Alcotts in front of Orchard House in the mid 1860s

he will utter them, regardless of the reproach or injury he may sustain by so doing. Such a man in these times, when there are so few who feel that they are Men and have a part of their own to act, is not to be cast aside, to be trampled on, without great detriment to our social and moral progress. Did we know what is for our good, we should seek out such men, and honor them as prophets sent from God to foretell and to usher in a more glorious future.

Still we are not at all surprised that Mr. Alcott and his publications are so little appreciated, and so greatly misapprehended. Mr. Alcott is a reformer. He does not believe that the Past has realized the highest worth man may aspire to; he does not believe that the methods of teaching usually adopted, or the systems of education contended for by our teachers and professors generally, are at all adapted to the purpose of rearing up MEN, and of making them walk as becomes moral and intellectual beings, made in the image of God and possessing a Divine Nature; he thinks that

the aim of our systems of education, whether private, public, domestic, or social, is too low, and that the methods adopted are destitute of science, above all of vitality, that they are too mechanical, and make of our schools only commendable "treadmills." Now to think and say all this is to reflect no great credit on our thousands of school-teachers and learned professors and their friends, nor upon those who boast the efforts we have made and are making in the cause of Education. This is as much as to tell his disciples, that unless their righteousness, in this respect, exceed that of the Scribes and Pharisees, the Chief Priests and Elders in the teaching Art, they shall in no wise be qualified for undertaking to rear up men and women, fit to be the citizens of a free and Christian Republic. Can the Chief Priests and Elders, the Scribes and Pharisees, be made to believe this; or to regard him who utters it in any other light than that of a reviler, a blasphemer? Reformers are never understood and appreciated, till the reforms for which they contend are to a good degree rea-

Photograph of Bronson Alcott's wife, Abigail May Alcott

lized.

Then again, Mr. Alcott is a peculiar man. He has observed more than he has read, and reflected more than he has observed. He is man, though eminently social in his feelings and tastes, who has lived mostly in communion with himself, with children, and with Nature. His system is one which he has thought out for himself and by himself. It has therefore almost necessarily taken the hues of his own mind, and become somewhat difficult to communicate to minds not constructed like his own. The terms he has made use of in his solitary reflections to express his thoughts to himself have a special meaning, a special value in his use of them, of which those with whom he converses are ignorant, and of which it is often extremely difficult for them to conceive. In consequence of his solitary reflections, of his little intercourse with the world at large, and his limited acquaintance with books, he has framed to himself a peculiar language, which, though formed of the choicest English, is almost, if not quite wholly unintelligible to all who have not become extensively acquainted with his mode of thinking. He very easily translates the thoughts of others into his language, but it is with great difficulty that he translates his thoughts into their language. People generally in hearing him converse form no conception of his real meaning; and if they attach any meaning to what he says, it will in nine cases out of ten be a false one. This, however, though it accounts for the misapprehension of people, in regard to him, is not altogether his fault. People may misapprehend him, because they do not understand themselves. There are not many men who have thoroughly analyzed their own minds, become masters of their own ideas, and so familiar with them that they can recognise them when clothed in a new dress. We are familiar with certain words, which we suppose we use as signs of ideas, but which we use very often as substitutes for ideas. When we find these words defined, or hear them used indeed as signs of ideas, and as signs of the very ideas for which we should have used them, had we used them for any, we are at fault; we find ourselves introduced to entire strangers with whom we can hold no conversation. We know not our own ideas; and very likely are frightened at them, and run away from them as though they were the Evil One himself.

But due allowance made for men's own ignorance as it regards the ideas they really express, if any, by the words they use, it is still extremely difficult to understand Mr. Alcott's system in all its parts. In the work before us it is but partially developed, and nowhere has he to our knowledge given us a complete development of it. But as we believe he really has a system, and one which is truly his own, and withal one for which he is willing to labor and suffer reproach, privation, and, perhaps, death itself, were it necessary, we shall,—availing ourselves of all our means of arriving at a just compensation of it,—endeavor to lay it before our readers, as faithfully and as fully as we can, within the very narrow limits to which we are necessarily restricted.

Mr. Alcott is known mainly as a schoolmaster, but as a schoolmaster, as we usually think of schoolmasters, he must not be viewed. Unblessed with an abundance of this world's goods, he has often been obliged to confine himself to the drudgery of mere schoolmaster duties; but he is an original thinker, and he aspires to be an educator, not of children only, but of mankind. His system of Human Culture is designed for the human race, and is valued by him as true in itself, and as the means of raising all men to the stature of perfect men in Christ Jesus. He professes to have a whole system of Theology, Morality,—a philosophy of Man, of

Nature, of God. His method of teaching is but the means by which men are to be led ideally and actually to the Absolute. His philosophy he regards as the philosophy of the Absolute. It is as the theologian, the philosopher, the moralist, and the philanthropist, rather than as a schoolmaster, that he is to be regarded. But we proceed to develop his system.

Suppose a man who has no means of knowledge but his five senses. Such a man can take cognizance, of only material objects, of sensible qualities. Color, form, extension, solidity, sound, odor, taste, comprise all the objects of knowledge he can consistently admit. In a word, external nature is all he knows. External nature is to him what it appears. It is real, not symbolical. It indicates nothing which it is not,—nothing on which it depends, and of which it may be regarded as the sign or apparition. It is what it appears, and when seen it is known, and when known that is the end of knowledge. Nothing more is to be known.

In Nature everything, as known by this man of five senses, and of five senses only, is concrete. Nothing is abstract. There are particulars but no generals. Mankind is merely a collective name, and has no meaning beyond the number of individual men and women it designates. A tree is a tree and nothing more. Truth and virtue are abstract nouns, invented for the convenience of conversation, but void of meaning. There may be true stories, true views, but not truth, conformity to which makes the individual story or view a true one. There may be virtuous men and women, but no virtue, conformity to which makes one virtuous.

But is this true? Are all things what they appear? And does all that is appear? Is the Appearance the Thing? Or is the Thing that appears always back of the Appearance? Is it the Thing that we recognise with our senses, or is it only the sign, symbol, or shadow of the Thing? In man, is it the man that is apparent to the senses? The senses perceive the body, but is the body anything more than the symbol of the man? Take all the phenomena with regard to a man, presented us by the senses, and do they constitute the man? The man is evidently a collection of forces, moral, intellectual, and physical. We observe in him moral affections; we know that he performs the act of thinking; we see that such things as growth, decay, digestion, nutrition, and the like, are constantly going on in him. Now is there not back of these Something that produces them? Is it the feet that walk, or is it the man that walks? Does the brain think, or is it the man that thinks? The stomach, does it digest, or is it the man who digests? The heart, does it love, or is it the man that loves? Back then of the sense-phenomena lies the real Man, the Thing, the Reality, of which what is apparent to the senses is the mere symbol, or sign. The appearance, the apparition is not the man, but a mere index to point us to where the man is and to what he does.

Take a plant. The senses show us a certain number of phenomena. But in that plant are there not things which the senses do not show us, of which they can take no cognizance? Back of this sense-plant is there not the spirit-plant, that is, the real plant of which the senses show us only the appearance or symbol? The real plant is the law that is manifesting itself; the force which pushes itself out in what we call growth, in the bud, the blossom, the fruit; and which makes it precisely what it is, and not something else. It is not meant by this that the senses deceive us; it is only meant that they do not show us the Thing, but its sign; not the reality, but the phenomenon, as a word is not the idea, but its sign or symbol.

We do not give examples as demonstrations, but merely as illustrations to make our meaning obvious. Now apply the remarks we have made of man and of the plant to all nature, and you have Mr. Alcott's doctrine of Nature, or more properly of the external world. The external world is merely the world of the senses; it is not a real but an apparent world, not substantial, but phenomenal. He does not distrust the senses as do the Idealists, but he denies their power to attain to realities. They stop short of the Thing, and merely give us its sign. They show us where the Thing is, but leave it for the spirit to see what it is.

Pursuing the path in which we have started we may go much further. The Real is always the Invisible. But the invisible world which we have found lying immediately back of the sensible or apparent world, is it the ultimate world? Is there not another world which the soul may discover back of that? All effects are included in their causes, and we have not attained to the Thing till we have attained to the ultimate cause. Absolute reality of all things can then be found only in the absolute cause of all things. A cause in order to be a cause must be free, self-sufficing, and self-acting. If absolute then it must be one, for more absolute causes than one is an absurdity which the reason rejects. The world of the senses must then be resolved into the invisible world of the reason, which may for distinction's sake be called the *intelligible* world; and the intelligible world must then be resolved into the Absolute world, the world of Unity, which, if we understand Mr. Alcott in his terminology, may be called the world of Faith. In man he recognises sense, understanding, or reason, and Faith or Instinct; each of these has a world of its own. The absolute world, that is, Absolute Reality is found only by Faith or Instinct, and is the world of Absolute Unity.

Now, Absolute Unity, in the bosom of which all things exist, is God. In the last analysis all Reality resolves itself into God. God is the sum total of all that is; the only Substance, the only absolute Being, the only absolute Reality. God is the Universe, and the Universe is God;—not the sensible universe, nor the intelligible, but the Instinctive;—not the universe seen by the eye of sense, nor that seen by the eye of reason or understanding, but that seen by the inner eye of the soul, by Faith or Instinct.

Now the universe of the senses and that of the understanding are both manifestations of God. The sensible universe is God as he appears to the senses; the intelligible universe is God as he unfolds himself to the intellect; the universe beheld by Faith or Instinct, that is, by the highest in man, is God in his absoluteness; as he is in himself, the real, not the manifested God. We take our stand now on the revelations of Instinct; that is, in God himself, and from his point of view examine and interpret all phenomenal worlds and beings. In descending from him through the intelligible world and the sensible, we perceive that all laws, all forces, all things, so far forth as they have any real being, are identical with God. God is not the plant as it exists to the understanding, or the senses; nevertheless, he is all the reality, all the absolute being there is in the plant; God is not man, and man is not God, as he exists to the senses, or to the understanding; nevertheless all the real being there is in man, all that is not phenomenal, appearance merely, is God, "in whom we live, and move, and have our *being.*"

By a psychological examination of man, we find that he takes cognizance of the three worlds, or universes we have enumerated. Man must have then three orders of faculties, corresponding to these three worlds. He is not then merely endowed with five senses, as we supposed in the beginning; he has, above his five senses, reason or understanding; and above this, as that which attains to the Absolute, Faith or Instinct; which, so far as we can perceive, is very identical with what M. Cousin calls Spontaneity or the

Spontaneous Reason. Now in the business of education, we should have reference to these three worlds, or these three orders of faculties, and according to their relative importance. The education which has been and is most common has reference almost exclusively to the world of the senses; some few philosophers and teachers are laboring to make it conform to the world of the understanding; few or none labor to make it conform to the world of Instinct, to the absolute Truth and Reality of things. This last is Mr. Alcott's work. To call attention to this work, to show by his instructions what it is, and by his example how it may be and is to be done, is what he regards as his mission. As a partial experiment, as an intimation of what may under more favorable circumstances be accomplished, he had these Conversations recorded as they occurred, and has finally published them to the world.

Having thus far glanced at what may be called Mr. Alcott's metaphysical system, we may now proceed without much difficulty to seize his theory of education, and to a general comprehension of his views of Childhood and Religion. These views have struck many minds as absurd, but the absurdity, we think we find in the views of others, is often an absurdity for which we alone are responsible. We assign to others very frequently the absurd views which originate with ourselves; and it is a good rule for us to observe, that so long as a man's views appear to us to be wholly absurd, if he be a man of but tolerable understanding, we should judge ourselves ignorant of his real meaning.

Instinct, which must be carefully distinguished from Impulse, is according to Mr. Alcott's theory the Divine in Man. It is the Incarnate God. Our instincts are all divine and holy, and being the immediate actings, or promptings of the Divinity, they constitute the criterion of Truth and Duty. They are what there is in man the most real and absolute. They are then the most Godlike, the most Divine, partake the most of God; they are then to be regarded as the highest in man, to which all else in him is to be subordinated. The instincts are to be followed as the supreme law of the soul.

The instincts, inasmuch as they are the Divine in man, the Incarnate God, contain all the truth, goodness, reality there is in man. The Divine in man, or the God Incarnate, is one with the Universal, the Absolute God. There is nothing in the sensible universe, nor in the intelligible universe, that is not in the Absolute God. All things are in God, and God is in man. In our instincts then are included, in their law, their reality, both the world of sense and the world of the understanding. To know these worlds then we must look within, not abroad. To become acquainted with God and his manifestations we must study the instincts. Knowledge, truth, goodness, all that can deserve to be called by either name, must be drawn out of the soul, not poured into it. Human culture, therefore, as the word *education,* (from *e* and *duco,*) literally applies, is merely drawing forth what exists, though enveloped, in the soul from the beginning.

As the child is born with all the instincts and with them more active and pure than they are in after life, it follows that the child is born in possession of all truth, goodness, worth, human nature can aspire to. Therefore said Jesus, "Suffer little children to come unto me, for of such is the kingdom of heaven." Childhood is therefore to be reverenced. The wise men from the East do always hail with joy the star of the new-born babe, and haste to the cradle to present their offerings and to worship. The educator must sit down with reverence and awe at the feet of the child, and listen. Till this be done, little progress can be expected in human culture.

The child is pure and holy. It obeys freely and without reserve its Divine Instincts. It smiles, loves, acts, as God commands. The true end, or one of the great ends of Human Culture must be to preserve the child in the grown up man. Most people at a very early day lose the child, and go through life bewailing their lost childhood. The wholy family of man may be represented as the distracted mother, who wept with loud lamentation for her children, because they were not. The only exception to this is, that they too often lose their childhood without being conscious of their loss. Childhood is lost; the innocency, the freedom, the light of the instincts are obscured, and all but annihilated, by the false modes of life which are adopted; by the wrong state of society which prevails; by intemperance, in eating, drinking, sleeping, and the like; and by the mistaken education which men have unwisely encouraged,–an education which tends perpetually to raise sense and understanding above Divine Instinct, and to subject us to shadows and illusions, rather than to truth and reality. Hence, the necessity of strict temperance in all the habits of the body, and of early attention to the instincts, so that they may be called forth and strengthened before the senses and the understanding have established their dominion over us.

The body in its true state is to the soul what the outward universe is to God,–its veil or covering, or more properly, its symbol which marks to the senses the place where it is. What are called bodily appetites and inclinations, come from the soul, not from the body; proceeding from the soul, they should be regarded, in themselves, as of like purity and divinity, as any of the instincts of our nature. The exercise of them all, and in all cases, should be regarded as a religious exercise, and should be performed with all the feelings of awe and responsibleness, with which we accompany the most solemn act of religious worship. All the functions of the body, as we call them, but which are really functions of the soul, are holy, and should be early surrounded with holy and purifying associations. Hence the conversations in the volumes before us with the children, on the mysterious phenomena attending the production and birth of a new member to the human family, or what Mr. Alcott calls the Incarnation of Spirit,–conversations which have caused him much reproach, and done him, for the moment, we fear no little injury. His motives were pure and praiseworthy, and his theory seemed to require him to take the course he did, and he should not be censured; but for ourselves, we regard as one of the most certain instincts of our nature, that one which leads us to throw a veil over the mysterious phenomena by which the human race is preserved and its members multiplied. Mr. Alcott's theory requires him to respect all the Instincts, and why this less than others? In attempting to eradicate it, he appears to us to be inconsistent with himself, and likely to encourage more prurient fancies than he will be able to suppress. Nature in this has provided better, in our judgment, for the preservation of chastity in thought and in deed, than man can do by any system of culture he can devise.

Pursuing the rules implied in these general principles, the educator aims to call forth into full glory and activity the grace and truth with which man is endowed. He labors to train up the human being committed to his care, in obedience to the Highest, to see, and respect, and love all things in the light, not of the senses, not of the intellect even, but of Faith, of Instinct, of the Spirit of God,–the "true light, which enlighteneth every man that cometh into the world." If he succeeds in realizing his aim, the result is a perfect Man, "armed at all points, to use the Body, Nature, and Life for his growth and renewal, and to hold dominion over the fluctuating things of the Outward." Realize this in the case of every child born into the world, and you have reformed the world,–made earth a heaven, and men the sons of God in very deed. This is the end Mr. Alcott contemplates; this end he believes can be attained by his method of viewing and disciplining the soul, and by no other. Hence the magnitude of the work he is engaged in,–the importance of his doctrine, and his method of culture to the human race.

If now for the word *God,* we substitute the word *Spirit,* and call spirit absolute Being, and the absolute, the real universe, which lies back of the sensible universe and the intelligible, also spirit, and therefore regard all power, force, cause, reality, as spirit, and spirit everywhere as identical, we may, with the expositions we have made, attain to a proximate notion of Mr. Alcott's theory of God, Man, and Nature, as well as of Human Culture. He sees spirit everywhere, and in everything he seeks spirit. Spirit is regarded as the cause and law of organization is God; spirit organized is the universe; spirit incarnated is man. An identity therefore runs through God, Man, and Nature; they are all one in the fulness of universal and everlasting spirit.

Spirit, though incarnate in the case of every human being, attains rarely to anything like a perfect manifestation. A perfect manifestation, however, is not to be expected, because there are no bounds to the growth of spirit. Many bright specimens of the worth men may attain to have been exhibited at distant intervals in the world's history; among which Moses, Socrates, and Jesus are the worthiest. Of these three Jesus stands first.

With this estimate of the character of Jesus, the Records of his life must of course be regarded as the most suitable text book for the educator. They give the children for their study the model nearest to perfection, that can as yet be found. Besides all this, the identity of spirit, and therefore of human nature in all ages and countries of the world, implies an identity between Jesus, or the Instincts of Jesus, and the Instincts of the child. The coincidence, which we may discover between the manifestations of the pure Instincts of Childhood and those recorded of Jesus, becomes therefore a proof of the accuracy of the Record. If we can reproduce in children, as yet unspoiled, the phenomena recorded of Jesus, then we have a new proof, and a strong proof, that the Record is a faithful one. These Conversations on the Gospels, therefore, so far as the answers of the children may be regarded as a reproduc-

tion of Jesus, the doctrines or precepts ascribed to Jesus, constitute a class of evidence for Christianity, which the Christian theologian will find not without value.

These are, rudely and imperfectly sketched, the chief outlines of Mr. Alcott's system, so far as we have ourselves been able to comprehend it. Of the two volumes before us we will not attempt to form an estimate. Different minds will estimate them differently. That they do in part accomplish the end for which they were designed we think no one can reasonably deny. They may be read with profit by all students of the New Testament; and to minds of some quickness of apprehension they will open up, in that often read but poorly comprehended volume, many views of rich and varied beauty on which the soul may feast with delight. Parents and Sunday School teachers will find them a valuable help in their work of instructing their children, and in conversing with children on religious subjects; and to them we conscientiously commend these volumes, not for the doctrines they may be supposed to teach, but for the suggestions they contain, and for the method of approaching the young mind they in part unfold.

As it regards Mr. Alcott's religious and metaphysical system, we have not much to offer. We have aimed to state it, not to criticise it. It strikes us as neither absurd nor alarming. We see much truth in it, and we recognise in it the marks of a mind earnestly in love with truth and willing to labor to gain it. The system, though original with Mr. Alcott, is by no means new or peculiar. As a whole we do not embrace it. We differ from him in several essential particulars. We do not admit that identity between Man and God, and God and Nature, which he does. God is in his works; but he is also separate from them. Creation does not exhaust the Creator. Without Him his works are nothing; but He nevertheless *is,* and *all* He is, without them. I am in my intention, but my intention makes up no part of me. I am in the word I utter; and yet I am the same without the word that I am with it. In uttering it I have put forth a creative energy, but I nevertheless retain, after uttering it and independently of it, all the creative energy I had before. So of God. The universe is his intention, his word, and we may find him in it; but he remains independent of it, and is no more identical with it, than my resolution is identical with the power I have of forming resolutions, or than my word is identical with the power that utters it. Mr. Alcott appears to us not to distinguish with sufficient accuracy between the Creation and the Creator. The relation of the universe to God, according to him, is the relation of a word to the idea it stands for, whereas we regard it as the relation of an effect to its cause. It would be hard for us to entertain his views, without becoming more pantheistic than we believe truth and piety warrant.

But notwithstanding this, Mr. Alcott's views of education, as he reduces them to practice, are unexceptionable. If he runs into an extreme in some cases, if he dwells too much in the Inward, and insists too much on Spontaneity, he probably goes not farther than is necessary to counteract the strong tendency in an opposite direction, which is the most striking characteristic of our schools as they are. What we regard as erroneous in his theory, can in the actual state of things amongst us have no bad effect. We have overlooked the Inward; we have lost our faith in the Spiritual; and it is well that a man comes amongst us, who persists in directing our attention to the voice of God that speaks to us, is ever speaking to us, in the soul of man. The Instincts, as Mr. Alcott calls them, are no doubt from God; they deserve to be studied and reverenced; we must, however, be on our guard that we do not become exclusively devoted to them, for if we do we shall become Mystics.

[James Freeman Clarke]
"R. W. Emerson and the New School," *Western Messenger,* 6 (November 1838): 37-42.

> *Clarke's defense of Emerson in two consecutive articles in the* Western Messenger *(the second is reprinted below) showed vividly the alarm and concern of someone away from the center of the storm. Clearly, Clarke was aware that not just Emerson but all who espoused the Transcendentalist philosophy were under attack, and his replies served as not only a defense but also a plea for fairness.*

We perceive that our friends in Boston, and its vicinity, have been a good deal roused and excited by an address, delivered by the gentleman whose name stands above. Mr. Emerson has been long known as a man of pure and noble mind, of original genius and independent thought. Formerly settled as a Unitarian Preacher over the Second Church, in Boston, he left his charge, with feelings of mutual regret, on account of his having adopted the Quaker opinion in relation to the ordinance of the Lord's Supper. Since that time he has published a small volume called "Nature," and delivered various addresses and lectures on subjects of Literature, Philosophy, and Morals. All these productions have shown a mind of extreme beauty and originality. Their style, however, has been so different from the usual one, so completely Emersonian, as to confound and puzzle some, and disgust others. Many thought too, that they detected in his thoughts and doctrines the germs of dangerous errors. On the other hand, he has been surrounded by a band of enthusiastic admirers, whom the genius, life and manliness of his thoughts attracted, and his beautiful delivery as a public speaker charmed.

Matters stood thus, when he was invited to make an address to the parting class at the Cambridge Theological School. He readily accepted their offer and the result was that they heard an address quite different, we judge, from what ever fell into the ears of a Theological class before. He told them that the faith of Christ was not now preached, that "the Priest's Sabbath has lost the splendor of nature; it is unholy; we are glad when it is done; we can make, we do make, even sitting in our pews, a far better, holier, sweeter for ourselves." This was not polite to the preachers, of whom we suppose many were present, and must have been rather disagreeable to bear–especially as no exception seemed to be made in behalf of his own sect. Instead of inculcating the importance of church-going, and shewing how they ought to persuade every body to go to church, he seemed to think it better to stay at home than to listen to a formal lifeless preacher. Instead of exhorting them to be always doing the duties of a pastor, he tells them not to be too anxious, to visit periodically, each family in their parish connection. Such things as these he told them, and moreover introduced them by some general remarks, which we cannot agree with him in thinking, that "while they are general, none will contest them." Notwithstanding their generality, they seemed to excite quite as much opposition as the other part of this harrangue.

Immediately after the delivery of this address, a lively discussion and controversy sprung up with respect to its doctrines, of which the end is not yet. First, there appears an article in the Boston Daily Advertiser,[1] in which Mr. Emerson is accused of rejecting all belief in Christianity as a revelation, and as probably disbelieving in the existence of a God. The graduating class are rebuked as having become accessories to the commission of a great offense, in asking him to address them, and are called upon, in a tone of great authority, to make their exculpation or excuse before the public.

Some remarks are prefixed concerning a New School in Literature and Philosophy which we shall notice again by and by. In the same paper, there shortly appears a reply to this first attack on Mr. Emerson. This reply is well written, only a little too poetical for controversy, as his opponent observed. Its author does not, however, defend Mr. Emerson, on the whole he agrees with his opponent respecting him, but does not like the *manner* of the attack. He thinks it altogether too harsh and severe to do any good.

Then comes a good democratic article in the Morning Post, censuring Mr. Emerson for some things, and praising him for others—then follow various communications in the Courier, and in the Register, with editorials appended, lamenting that Mr. Emerson should turn out an Atheist, or enquiring whether all Unitarians think as he does which the Editor very promptly denies. Then comes a very thorough discussion of the doctrines of the Address in the Boston Review, in which, while Mr. Emerson is treated with courtesy and respect, his supposed opinions are very sharply examined. Again, we hear that Dr. Henry Ware, Jr. has published two sermons upon the subject of this Address. We are sure that his name will never be appended to any productions not written with clear thought and in a Christian Spirit.[2]

On the whole, we think that the results of this controversy will be excellent. It will show that our Unitarian plan of church union works better in a case of real or supposed heresy, than any other. How is it in those churches where they are bound together by a minute creed? A man publishes a sermon, containing some point supposed to be objectionable; he is tried by his Presbytery, condemned, appeals to his Synod, acquitted; referred to the Assembly, and deposed. He goes on preaching, his party increases, and a rent takes place in a great church, when the entering wedge was a thin pair of volumes. In our church, on the other hand, we have no creed but the Christian Scriptures. A man proclaims some strange sounding doctrine. Whoever feels most keenly that this is an Anti-Christian one, comes out against it with severity. This brings out other opinions, already formed, of various characters. This excites the attention of others. The discussion follows, but the bitterness all dies away—for men who seriously set themselves to *thinking* are not apt to get angry. But when the business is not to think it down, but to vote it down, to get together a party, and bind them together and heat them up by party conventions—there, it seems to us, things are likely to go a little warmly, and we shall hear more denunciation than argument.

For ourselves, we are convinced that if Mr. Emerson has taught any thing very wrong, it will be found out, and then he will quietly drop out of the Unitarian church, or the Unitarian church quietly fall off from him. No *excommunication* is necessary. Where people are held together by no outward bend, if the inward attraction ceases, they will soon drop apart.

The question, however, is, *has* he taught any thing wrong? Is he opposed to historical Christianity? Has he given any ground for supposing that he does not believe in the God of Christianity?

To give our opinion at length, on these points is out of the question—we have neither ability nor will to do it. To confess the truth, when we received and read the Address, we did not discover anything in it objectionable at all. We were quite delighted with it. We read it, to be sure, looking for good and not evil, and we found enough that was good to satisfy us. Parts seemed somewhat obscure, and for that we were sorry—in places we felt hurt by the phraseology, but we bounded carelessly over these rocks of offence and pitfalls, enjoying the beauty, sincerity and magnanimity of the general current of the Address. As critics, we confess our fault. We should have been more on the watch, more ready to suspect our author when he left the broad road-way of commonplace, and instantly snap

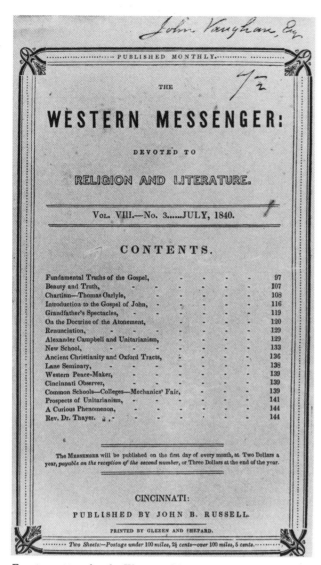

Front wrapper for the Western Messenger, *which essentially treated religious topics*

him up when he stated any idea new to us, or differing from our pre-conceived opinions.

But we must be serious—we have already, perhaps, treated this subject too ironically. The most serious charges that can be brought against a Christian man, have been laid against our author, founded on the contents of this discourse. He has been accused of Infidelity, disbelief in historical Christianity—and of probable Atheism or Pantheism. That charity which thinketh no evil, rejoiceth not in iniquity and hopeth all things, should induce every man most carefully to pause before he brings such charges against a brother. If Mr. Emerson maintains these sentiments, we can no longer hold any fellowship with him, for a wide chasm yawns between our sympathies. But not for an obscure passage in an address, would we believe this of a man whose course of life has been always open—whose opinions never lay hid, and who, being such an one, has preached and still preaches as a Christian Minister.

He is accused of opposing Historical Christianity, that is, we suppose, of disbelief in the historical account of the life of Jesus. Now he speaks very strongly against those whose faith is only an historical one—who believe in Jesus Christ, not feeling him in their own souls as a Savior and Friend, but only acquiescing in the fact of his past existence. He speaks very strongly—without perhaps sufficient care against misconstruction. But does he speak more strongly or unguardedly than Paul did, when he said that the *letter* of the New Testament KILLED, while the spirit gave life? (2 Cor. iii.6). Does this sound like doing away entirely with the letter of the New Testament? But Paul only meant, as Mr. Emerson, we suppose means, that the letter is dead weight in the mind, if the spirit does not animate it. How many things are there in the New Testament to show that a bare historical faith in Jesus Christ is not a saving faith—that we must have the witness in our own hearts—that our faith must stand, not in the will of men but the power of God—that our Father in Heaven must reveal it to us. The true doctrine undoubtedly is, that both witnesses are necessary to believe in Christ's divinity—an outward witness, coming down through history, and an inward witness of the spirit in our heart. This is beautifully shown in John xi. 26, 27. "But when the Comforter is come, which I will send unto you from the Father, even the spirit of truth, which proceedeth from the Father, *he shall testify of me; and ye also shall bear witness* because ye have been with me from the beginning."

Now if Mr. Emerson means to deny the value of this second testimony, we think him quite wrong, but we believe he only wishes to have it, as Christ put it, *second.* The common error is to be satisfied with the historical faith, and it is this error which he thought it necessary to oppose.

If Mr. Emerson disbelieves in all our present historical Christianity, how happens it that instead of opposing it, he opposes its *defects?* "The first *defect*" says he "of historical Christianity"—"the second defect." And how happened it that in this very Address he used the strongest expression we ever met with, to show the *historical influence* of Jesus Christ? "whose name is not so much written as *ploughed into the history of the world.*"

We have been taking the view of the matter, which seems to us at the same time, the most correct, and the most charitable. At the same time we freely admit that there are many expressions which we would gladly have seen altered, or not seen at all; because though not so meant, they sound like irreverence or impiety to the common ear. Thus, where he says in the passage for which he was accused of Pantheism, "If a man is at heart just, then in so far, is he God; the safety of God, the immortality of God, the majesty of God, do enter into that man with justice." Why not be satisfied with the strong language of Jesus and John, and say that if he love, God dwells *in* him, and he *in* God? or that he *partakes* of the divine nature, as Peter declares. Why go further, and seem to destroy the personality either of God or man by saying that he *is* God? The privilege of being called the *sons of God* seemed to astonish John. "Behold! what manner of love" said he "the Father has shown us, that we should be called the sons of God!" Is it not enough to dwell *in God,* and have God dwell *in us,* but that we must also aspire to *be God?*

We might go on, and find more fault with Mr. Emerson's opinions, and his expressions. But we prefer, if possible, to stand now as mediators, if it may be, to soften down a little of the harshness of the attacks he has already experienced. The Unitarians have already fully vindicated themselves from the charge of agreeing with him in opinion. He has certainly been very soundly rated by them, in some instances we think with too much harshness and dogmatism. For it is too late in the day to put a man down by shouting Atheist, Infidel, Heretic. Formerly you could thus excite a prejudice against him that would prevent men from examining the truth of the charge. Not so now. Men cannot be in this day put down by denunciation. The whole religious pulpit and religious press has united for thirty or forty years in calling Unitarians, Deists. What is the result? That their principles are rapidly spreading. In view of this fact, let us lay aside prejudice and candidly examine every new thing.

---

1. We cannot say that we like this plan of bringing Theological disputes before the world through Political and Commercial prints. There is never space for discussion, and only room to excite prejudices in the minds of those who may be supposed to be previously ignorant of the facts of the case. We do not find that Jesus Christ commands us to tell our brother's fault to the *world,* even after telling it to himself in private. He says "tell it to the Church." He does not say "tell it to the world."

2. And lastly we perceive that some college lad, writing a class-poem, wishing to lash existing abuses, and taking his direction, like the weather-cocks, from the winds, stands up "severe in youthful wisdom," tells Mr. Emerson it is very wrong to be an Infidel, and compares him to "Gibbon and Voltaire!!!" Ah! unfortunate Mr. Emerson! well may you say with the sad old king

      The little dogs and all,
      Tray, Blanch, and Sweetheart, see they bark at me.

[James Freeman Clarke]
"The New School in Literature and Religion," *Western Messenger,* 6 (November 1838): 42-47.

The writer who first publicly attacked Mr. Emerson's Address, prefaced his remarks by observations upon what he called "the New School in Literature and Religion." Thus he speaks:–

"There is a strange state of things existing about us in the literary and religious world, of which none of our larger periodicals have yet taken notice. It is the result of that restless craving for notoriety and excitement, which, in one way, or another, is keeping our community in a perpetual stir.

"It owes its origin in part to ill-understood notions, obtained by blundering through the crabbed and disgusting obscurity of some of the worst German speculatists, which notions, however, have been received by most of its disciples at second hand, through an interpreter."

Thus far we were quite at a loss to know what this new school was. But the next sentence becomes more particular:

"The Atheist Shelley has been quoted and commended in a professedly religious work, called the Western Messenger; but he is not, we conceive, to be reckoned among the patriarchs of the sect."

When in our simplicity, we inserted an article upon Shelley in the Western Messenger, we were not aware that because a man was an Atheist he might not be commended for writing good poetry. We lamented the nature of his opinions, we mourned over his want of faith, and expressly stated our aversion to his general views. We did not expect therefore to be accused of commending him, as though we had been praising him for his Atheism–least of all did we expect that we were to become members of "a new school" through the medium of that article. But let us hear more about this New School and its follies:

"But this honor is due to that hasher up of German metaphysics, the Frenchman, Cousin; and, of late, that hyper-Germanized Englishman, Carlyle, has been the great object of admiration and model of style. Cousin and Carlyle indeed seem to have been transformed into idols to be publicly worshipped, the former for his philosophy, and the latter both for his philosophy and his fine writing; while the veiled image of the German pantheist, Schleiermacher, is kept in the sanctuary."

Here then we have some means given us of detecting the members of the New School. If a man praises Shelley, he is to be suspected. If he studies Cousin, the charge is almost brought home against him. But if he admires Carlyle, and occasionally drops dark hints about Schleiermacher, he is a confirmed disciple of this new heresy.

"Hic niger est. Hunc tu, Romane, caveto?

But yet, though this seems at first an easy way of detecting these dark disorganizers, some difficulty may arise in its application. Thus, there are some who read and study Cousin, but care nothing for Carlyle, or dislike him. And again, there are admirers of Carlyle, who do not wholly admit the Eclectic philosophy. And as to the admirers of Schleiermacher, veiled or otherwise, it is rather difficult to find them. A single article on his character, translated from Dr. Lücke, appeared in the Examiner. He has been alluded to, once or twice, in the Western Messenger. One of his essays on the Trinity, translated by Moses Stuart, with copious notes of approbation, occupied several numbers of the Biblical Repository. And an essay of his upon Election, appeared in that supporter of old Calvinism, the New York Literary and Theological Review, translated by its editor, Leonard Woods, Jr., also with notes of approval. This is nearly all the notice we have seen taken of Schleiermacher in our religious periodicals. Do Professor Stuart, and the New York Calvinists, then, belong to this "New School in religion and literature?"

But our writer goes on to give some further characteristics of the New School. Let us hear:

"The characteristics of this school are the most extraordinary assumption, united with great ignorance, and incapacity for reasoning."

It is easy enough, we fear, to find men of all schools, and of no school, who would fall under this category. There is plenty of assumption, ignorance, and incapacity for reasoning, in the world. It is notorious that these traits may be found united even in those, who cherish the deadliest hostility to Transcendentalism, Carlyleism, and all new ideas. We must have some other clue then, before we can certainly distinguish this pestilent New School.

The next characteristic of the New School is thus given:–

"There is indeed a general tendency among its disciples to disavow learning and reasoning as sources of their higher knowledge. The mind must be its own unassisted teacher. It discerns transcendental truths by immediate vision, and these truths can no more be communicated to another by addressing his understanding, than the power of *clairvoyance* can be given to one not magnetized."

Now it is very true that there are those who assert that the soul is not like a sheet of white paper–that it does not acquire all knowledge by perception and reasoning, but that it is endowed by the Creator with certain ideas which arise necessarily in the mind of every sane man. The idea of cause and effect, for instance, is one–that of God another–those of time, space, infinity, and our own identity, others. We do not depend upon logic for our conviction of these things. They belong to a common sense which is back of all logic–an impartial God bestows them on all his children, and not merely on those who have been educated at Colleges and Universities.

Thus for instance, faith in God does not depend upon arguments, *a priori* or *a posteriori,* but upon a necessity of the mind. It is necessary to believe in God, just as it is necessary to believe in cause and effect, or time and space. A man may by logic so confuse himself as to think he disbelieves, but healthy minds believe by intuition, and the necessity of their own natures. To those who have never gone out of the circle of John Locke, this may seem very absurd, but it is in fact the oldest philosophy.

This belief, that all our knowledge does not come to us through the senses or from logical deduction, but that the mind itself furnishes some of the most essential convictions, as a groundwork or foundation, seems to us capable of the clearest demonstration. We know of nothing more conclusive than the train of reasoning by which Cousin establishes this, in his criticism on Locke. "Learning and reasoning," we do *not* believe to be "the sources of our higher knowledge." But observation and reasoning still have their place, though in another sphere. A man who should attempt to prove by logic his own existence, we should say, mistook the use of logic. So would every one else, yet this is all that transcendentalists say. To say that they reject *all* logic or reasoning, because they do not suffer them to be applied to those truths to which a man's own consciousness and the universal consent of the race testifies, is to mistake the matter.

This writer against the New School goes on to speak of them as announcing themselves as prophets and priests of the future–and as about to do away with old things, and abolish all the present forms of society. We do not precisely understand what this charge means. It may answer to terrify with visions of Agrarianism, respectable capitalists, but to what class of persons it applies we cannot tell. We have heard indeed of Fanny Wright and Robert Dale Owen preaching against the marriage bond, and other important institutions. The paragraph might apply to them, but then we never heard of their admiring Carlyle or Cousin, or worshipping Schleiermacher even in the most secret and veiled manner. We remain in the dark therefore as to the matter of this sentence.

This writer also says a great deal about the *bad taste* of the new school in their writings. We must remind him that *taste* is, by its nature, a very personal affair, and what to one man may seem bad taste, may appear to another very good. One man may think that good taste requires every one to write like Addison or Hume, another may think it in better taste for every man to write like himself. Bossu and Boileau thought it very bad taste to have less than five acts in a play or to violate the unities of time and space. Modern critics laugh at these rules. Voltaire used to prate about good taste perpetually, and showed his own by calling Shakespeare a barbarian. In fact, he who thinks, by rules of taste, to keep the style of writing always at one point, is as foolish as he who would hold back any other part of the great social movement.

"Labitur et labetur, in omis volubile aevum."

From all which we have said, however, we would not have it inferred that we deny the existence of a New School in Religion and Literature; but only that the characteristics as given by the writer before, do not appear to us sufficiently descriptive. They would apply to too many sorts of schools.

The truth is, our friend has failed in his definition of the New School, because he sought it in their opinions and manners, rather than in their principles and spirit. There are many who like Mr. Emerson, but do not like Cousin. Mr. E. himself, in his Dartmouth oration, finds fault with Cousin. There are others who like Cousin, who will have nothing of Emerson or Carlyle. And the admirers of Schleiermacher, (Leo. Woods, Jr. and Moses Stuart, for example) have probably no great relish for either of the others. We cannot find any certain test in these likes and dislikes.

Yet we agree with our friend that there is a new school. Perhaps we should agree with him as to those who are its chief masters and leaders. But we should describe them quite differently. We should say—there is a large and increasing number of the clergy and laity, of thinking men and educated women, especially of the youth in our different colleges, of all sects and all professions, who are dissatisfied with the present state of religion, philosophy and literature. The common principle which binds them together and makes them if you choose a school, is a desire for more of LIFE, soul, energy, originality in these great departments of thought. If they like Carlyle, it is not that they wholly agree with his opinions, or think his style perfect, but because they find in him a genuine man, full of life and originality. If they listen with delight to Mr. Emerson, and read his works with pleasure, it is not that they agree with all his speculations, but that they sympathize with his independence, manliness, and freedom. They read Mr. Brownson's writings, and perhaps they may not admit his opinions about the sub-treasury or acquiesce in all his new views of Christianity, but they honor and esteem the free and ardent energy of thought, which every paragraph displays. In the same way they sympathize with the spirit of Mr. Furness, without accepting all his results. In a word they esteem genuine, earnest, independent thought as the one thing needful in our whole life, and where they find this in a man they are drawn toward him by strong sympathies. Wherever there is reality and not appearance, substance and not form, living energy and not hollow show, sincere conviction and not traditional cant—there they feel their chief wants met and answered. They can sympathize with orthodoxy, though holding liberal opinions, when they find orthodoxy sincere, earnest and true. They can sympathize with the doubts of those who believe less than themselves, if these doubts spring from an earnest pursuit of truth. They can join heart and hand with those who never read a page of Cousin or Carlyle, if they find them earnestly laboring by Sunday schools, city missions, and benevolent associations to put more of moral and spiritual life into society. Their sympathies embrace the secluded scholar, the active preacher, the devoted school-master, the enthusiastic artist, the true poet—every man who feels that life should not be a mechanical routine, but be filled with earnestness, soul and spiritual energy. All who look, and hope, and labor for something better than now is, who believe in progress, who trust in future improvement, and are willing to spend and be spent in bringing forward that better time; all such are members of the New School.

If we are asked who is the leader of this New School, we should not name Mr. Emerson so soon as Dr. Channing. He leads on the new school, because from him has come the strongest impulse to independent thought, to earnest self-supported activity. Dr. Channing is one of those who deeply and mournfully feel the absence of life in our religion, philosophy and literature. We know not whether or not he sympathizes with the speculations of Carlyle, Emerson and Cousin; but we know that he sympathizes with earnest sincere seeking in every shape and form. And when he might condemn the results, he would still tolerate and esteem the honest seeker. He believes in progress, he sympathizes with every effort of struggling humanity to bring on by severe thought or manly action a happier and better day. And this, we take it, is the true definition of a member of the NEW SCHOOL.

[Orestes A. Brownson]
"American Literature," *Boston Quarterly Review*, 2 (January 1839): 1-26.

Brownson's essay on "American Literature" (reviewing Emerson's address on "Literary Ethics" [1838] continued the discussion Emerson began in "The American Scholar" and showed clearly the former's stronger social orientation. Brownson not only argued for the democratic impulse that Emerson had mentioned, but went further in his attacks upon the Unitarian establishment for trying to make literature their special concern. Whereas Emerson had tried to inspire and liberate, Brownson continued on to demonstrate the social implications of Emerson's ideas. This essay probably represented the last time Brownson substantially agreed with the Transcendentalists in print.

Mr. Emerson in this oration professes to discuss the subject of Literary Ethics. He speaks of the Resources, the Subject, and the Discipline of the Scholar.

The resources of the scholar are proportioned to his confidence in the intellect. They are coextensive with nature and truth. Yet can they never be his, unless claimed with an equal greatness of mind. He must behold with awe the infinitude and impersonality of the intellectual power; learn that it is not his, that it is not any man's; but the soul which made the world; that it is all accessible to him, and he, as its minister, may rightfully hold all things subordinate and answerable to it. He must feel that he stands in the world as its native king; that he may inhale the year as a vapor; and give a new order and scale to the grand events of history. He is the world; and the epochs and heroes of chronology are pictorial images in which his thoughts are told. So must the scholar feel. All things are his, and he is equal to all things, nature and its laws, life and its deeds, the world and its events.

And not only must the scholar feel his right, but he must claim and exercise it. He must assert and maintain his spiritual independence; feel that he is a new man, and that the world into which he comes is not foreclosed; is not mortgaged to the opinions and usages of Europe, Asia, or Egypt. Every man, as to his spiritual independence, comes into a new world, and may roam as freely over it, as if he were the first born of time. Every man is an Adam in the Garden, and may summon all creatures before him, distribute them into their

Painting of Brownson by G.P.A. Healy (Doran Whalen, Granite for God's House: The Life of Orestes Augustus Brownson *[1941])*

classes, and give them their names. No one is bound

to follow the classifications, or to adopt the names given by his predecessors. Creation is born anew with every new-born soul; and each new-born soul may hear the sons of the morning singing with joy over a new created world. In plain terms, the whole field of thought and action are open to the scholar, and he must, to avail himself of his resources, feel that he comes into the world as free as the first born man, that he is bound by none of the opinions, or usages of those who have preceded him; that he has the right to read all nature with his own eyes; and is in duty bound to form his own creed, his own life-plan, his own system of the Universe.

The subject offered to the scholar is as broad as his resources. His subject to-day is the same that it was yesterday. Nothing has been exhausted; science is yet in its cradle; literature is to be written; and poetry has scarcely chanted its first song. The perpetual admonition of nature to us is, "The world is new, untried. Do not believe the past. I give you the Universe a virgin to-day."

Latin and English poetry sing us ever the praises of nature, and yet poetry has hitherto conversed with only the surface of things. Its chants reveal to us nothing of the handsome things of nature. The poet has not seen and felt for himself. All is yet undescribed, almost unattempted. The man who stands on the sea-shore, or who rambles in the woods, seems to be the first man that ever stood on the shore, or entered a grove, his sensations and his world are so novel and strange. Nature still awaits her poet, and listens to catch the strains of the voice that shall sing her praises worthily.

Civil history is yet open to the labors of the scholar. The past shall wear a new aspect as each new man of genius looks upon it. Since Niebuhr and Wolf, Roman and Greek history have been written anew. May not a new Niebuhr and Wolf be needed to re-write them? Is the story told, and its lesson fixed forever? Let a man of genius pronounce the name of the Pelasgi, of Athens, of the Etrurian, of the Roman people, and under what new aspect do we instantly behold them. Are there not still new aspects under which they may be seen? Who can say what shall be the new aspect under which the next man of genius shall reveal them? As in poetry and history, so in all other departments. There are few masters or none. Religion is yet to be settled on its fast foundations in the breast of man; and politics, and philosophy, and letters, and art. As yet, we have nothing but tendency and indication.

Such are the resources and the subject of the scholar. The world is his; but he must possess it, by putting himself into harmony with the constitution of things. He must be a solitary, laborious, modest, charitable soul. He must embrace solitude as a bride. He must have his glees and his glooms alone. His own estimate must be measure enough; his own praise reward enough for him. We live in the sun and on the surface of things,–a thin, plausible, superficial existence, and talk of muse and prophet, of art and creation. But out of our shallow and frivolous way of life how can greatness ever grow? We must go and be dumb; sit with our hands on our mouths a long Pythagorean lustrum; live in corners, and do chares, and suffer, and weep, and drudge, with eyes and hearts that love the Lord; by silence, seclusion, austerity, pierce deep into the grandeur and secret of our being; and so diving, bring up out of secular darkness the sublimities of the moral constitution. How mean to go blazing, a gaudy butterfly, in fashionable or political saloons, the fool of society, the fool of notoriety, a topic for newspapers, a piece of the street, and forfeiting the real prerogative of the russet coat, the privacy, and the true and warm heart of the citizen?

But we give it up. We cannot analyze one of Mr. Emerson's discourses. He hardly ever has a leading thought, to which all the parts of his discourse are subordinate, which is clearly stated, systemetically drawn out, and logically enforced. He is a poet rather than a philosopher,–and not always true even to the laws of poetry. He must be read not for a work of art, which shall be perfect as a whole, but for the exquisite beauty of its details; not for any new or striking philosophical views, but for incidental remarks, frequent aphorisms, valuable hints, rich and original imagery and illustration. In all his productions, the decorations strike us more than the temple itself, and the shrine evidently surpasses the god. Nevertheless, he always selects an important topic for his discourses, and furnishes us subjects which well deserve our consideration. This is something.

In reading Mr. Emerson's various productions, and in listening to his lectures, we obtain the impression that he thinks very meanly of the past achievements of the human mind. No poet according to him has ever yet seen the sea-shore, or entered a grove; and nobody but himself has ever heard the "wild geese scream." As it regards American scholars, they have done nothing to redeem the pledges we made the world, when we adopted free institutions. American Literature can scarcely be said to have a being. Not that we want men who write very clever books, and make commendable verses which fill up the corner of a newspaper with much respectability, and look very decent in a scrap-book, or lady's album; but of the higher literature, which addresses itself to the higher faculties of the soul, and is the out-speaking and the embodyment of the national life, we have produced nothing worth naming. And worse than all this, we seem to have no adequate conception of what American literature should be, and what it is capable of becoming. Why is this, and what is the remedy?

This is the question which is laboring in his mind, and which he appears to be striving to answer. One of the chief causes, he thinks, is our want of faith in the intellect. Wanting faith in the intellect, we attempt no great intellectual effort, and therefore produce nothing intellectually great. We have no faith that great things may be done, and therefore do not attempt to do great things. The remedy here is to increase and confirm our faith in the intellect, to learn that the intellectual power, which develops itself within us, is the power that made the world, and therefore infinite and inexhaustible.

Another cause is our want of confidence in ourselves. We regard ourselves as born in the dotage of the world, and out of work, except to treasure up in our memories, and mimic as we may in our lives, the sayings and doings of the giants, who lived long ago, when the world was in its prime. Genius has no vocabulary; poesy has sung her swan-song; philosophy is finished; the sciences are completed; creeds are all determined; opinions made up; miracles ended, and the book of prophecy is closed. Sad creatures are we!–born long ages too late, after all the work cut out by the Almighty for thought, fancy, imagination, genius, is completed! We are doomed to idleness, and by idleness to imbecility. The spiritual nature is useless, and must be discharged. We sink our humanity, and become mere prudent, calculating animals; content to labor for a little worldly wealth, to fill the belly or clothe the back; to flutter in a saloon, or to catch a breath of empty applause from brainless fellow mortals; to be complaisant and decorous; to provide for a commendable funeral, a showy coffin, and a respectable tombstone.

To remedy this evil, we must cease to look back to learn what has been, around to learn what is, and must look into ourselves to learn what we are, and

what we can do. Man is man to-day as much as he was six thousand years ago; and every man is born with all that constitutes a man, with as rich endowments, and as creative a genius, in this age or country as in any other. Men in the past were great, were heroes. Be it so. Men in the present are also men, and may be great, may be heroes, if they will but act out the divinity that is slumbering in them. Our senses are as acute, our minds as penetrating, our bodies as finely moulded and as firmly knit, our limbs as active and as vigorous, and our souls as capable of swelling with noble thoughts, with rich affections, and of burning with as pure, as free, and intense a love for the true, the beautiful, and the good, as theirs who lived in the past, and before whose shadows we prostrate ourselves with such servile devotion. Nature is ever renewed, and is as fresh now, as when beheld by the divine bards of old; and is as open and as beautiful to us, as it was to them. We stand as near to God as did the prophets, who had "open vision" and conversed with him face to face; and we may be inspired, illuminated by his spirit, as well as they were. The whole spiritual world is ours. Truth, beauty, goodness, are not monopolized, foreclosed. God has not disinherited us, nor left us no employment. Every man has an indefeasible right to the Universe, and may labor in what part of it he pleases; in work which commends itself to his taste and genius; and be his own producer; and in his own way too. He need labor where others have labored, and be their imitators, not unless it be his choice. He may whistle his own tune, and sing his own song. Nobody has the right to insist on his obligation to imitate the tone or gestures of others. He may pitch his voice to his own key, and modulate it to his own ear. Plato, Bacon, Cousin, have philosophized; let who will philosophize also, and be a Plato, a Bacon, a Cousin, not by imitating them, but by claiming and maintaining that right to philosophize for oneself, which they claimed. We must assert our spiritual independency, or never shall our minds act freely, and show forth the divine stuff they are made of. And without free, strong, and varied action, no living literature; no original creations; no works of art, worthy of the age, of the country, of man.

This may be true, if understood in strict reference to literature, and what are usually considered the higher walks of art and science; but we are not disposed to regard the American mind as strikingly deficient in originality and independence. We doubt if there ever was a country in which the people had more faith in the intellect, or less of servility to the mind of other ages or other countries. We may not be ready at once to adopt every new notion or new doctrine, which may be set forth in metaphysics, theology, morals, aesthetics; but we are by no means backward in considering and adopting everything, which promises to be an improvement in agriculture, manufactures, the mechanic arts, commerce, and navigation. In these matters we are not wanting in faith in intellect, nor are we slaves to routine, to established usage, to fixed opinions, to the teachings of other ages, other countries, other men. We create for ourselves, and our creations are by no means despicable. The American ship is not a servile copy of a foreign model. The Yankee exercises his own original genius in its construction; and he mans and works it in his own way. The Patent Office may bear witness that we are cunning to seek out many inventions. Our political institutions can hardly be termed a copy, a tradition, a reminiscence. They are original. In whatever direction the American mind is turned, it is self-confiding, original, creative. Hitherto it has been turned almost exclusively in a material direction; to the realization of progress in our external condition; not to the realization of progress in the moral and intellectual sciences. With us, genius has come forth into practical life; instead of the marble statue, it gives us the ship; for a picture, it gives us a mule or jenney; for systems of metaphysics and ethics, it gives us railroads, canals, and steamboats; for the novel or the poem, it furnishes us with an improved system of legislation, ministries to the poor, and universal education; and for an elevated and living literature, it creates an elevated and living people. Genius has come out of the cloister and the university, and creates in the ship-yard and the smithy, reasons on change, and sings in the music of the axe, the hammer, and the loom, giving dignity to labor and the empire of the world to the laborer.

Shall we complain of this? Is this all low utilitarianism? Why is it that our minds have been carried away in an outward direction? In this world there is a reason, and usually a pretty good reason, for whatever is. Nothing is arbitrary, or the production of blind chance. It is not by accident that a people at a given epoch is wholly intent on improving its outward condition, all engrossed in useful labors; and at another epoch equally intent on spiritual progress, and engrossed with the embellishments of life. It is true that we have not, as it concerns high literary matters, that full faith in intellect which may be desirable; and it is true, that in such matters, we depend too much on the taste, criticism, and opinions of others. But what then? Our first and most urgent work in this country was not the creation of an original literature. Give the whole American people that peculiar self-trust and faith in intellect, called for in the oration before us, and every man, woman, and child would be soaring into the regions of ideas, or seeking in vain a pathway through the wilds of imagination; the useful arts would be neglected; the fields would lie fallow; commerce would languish; manufactures would fail; silence would reign in the workshops; and nakedness and starvation cover the land. Nature ordains that we provide for the body, before we provide for the soul; that we obtain those things without which life is not possible, before we attempt life's embellishments.

We have a few misgivings about the propriety of this declamation, in which some of our scholars are beginning to indulge, against the utilitarian pursuits of our age and country. We are not quite sure but we ought to be very thankful for these pursuits. Perhaps this business world on which the scholar looks down, is fulfilling a higher mission than it or the scholar dreams of. We can hardly persuade ourselves, that the young man, who has no means of living but by his daily labor, can be applauded for neglecting all useful labor and devoting his whole time to playing the flute or the fiddle. Why not? Music is one of the fine arts, and to play the flute or the fiddle well is an elegant accomplishment; and why not then applaud the young man who devotes himself to it at the expense of his wordly fortunes? What is true of individuals, is true of nations. Let a nation provide for its physical well-being, let it provide for the easy subsistence of all its citizens, before it takes itself to fiddling or flute-playing.

We commenced in this country poor; we had little beside our hands, our wits, and our self-confidence. We had a savage world to subdue, and by our labors a wilderness to convert into a fruitful field. We had this to do also for the *whole* people. In the old world the mass of the people are drudges, and we know not but always must be drudges. There a favored few may study life's embellishments, because the drudges are at hand to furnish them with subsistence. But here, all must be drudges or none; so long as drudgery is necessary, all must drudge; and when a part enter into the paths of elegant literature, the mass must enter. If at any previous epoch in our history, a number of our people sufficiently large to secure success had engaged solely in literary pursuits, and labored exclusively for progress in the spiritual order, they must have imposed an extra amount of drudgery on the rest; for scholars, all spiritual as they would have us believe them, have bodies and stomachs, and require food and raiment, as well as the drudges themselves, and in general of a somewhat superior sort too; they would have established a literary caste, which, when it is a caste, is no better than a sacerdotal caste, or a military caste; divided the community by a broad and distinct line into two classes, of which one would have been regarded as altogether superior to the other. The scholars would have constituted a nobility; they would have glorified themselves,–boasted the dignity of their pursuits; and, speaking to the mind and passions of the people, they would have had all things pretty much in their own way. The drudges, marking the leisure and apparent ease of the scholars, their freedom from many of the cares, vexations, and hardships of ordinary life, would have regarded them as a privileged class, a superior order of beings;–and in return, they would have looked upon themselves as a doomed race, lying under the curse of God, bound to the dust they cultivated, and fated to live and die mere beasts of burden. Now this would have been at war with the mission of this country. A literary class, as such, we cannot tolerate. They who call for a literary class, and labor diligently to create one, were they not impotent, should be regarded as our worst enemies. Here, no man can safely be exempted from the ordinary duties of practical life. The scholar must be a man of business, and do his own share of the drudgery.

We confess, therefore, that we are beginning, of late, to look favorably on the business habits of our countrymen, and to declaim less and less against their money-getting propensities. It is, in fact, a real cause for gratitude to God, that our whole population has been carried away in a material direction, engaged in the accumulation of material wealth. Not that literature is unimportant, not that progress in the spiritual order is not in the last degree desirable and imperative; but because it is as desirable and as imperative in the case of all men, as in the case of a few; and because it can be possible in the case of all men, only on the condition that all men be placed in such circumstances, as to their physical wants, that with moderate labor they can obtain a respectable subsistence. It was necessary then in the first instance, to cut down and clear away the eternal forest, to break the stubborn glebe, and convert the barren field into a garden, to build up our manufactures, to extend and perfect our commerce, and so to augment and distribute the wealth of the country, that all our citizens should have the requisite independence and leisure for the cultivation of their minds. And this could not have been done, had not our whole people been carried away in a material direction.

It is said, that the whole nation has been absorbed in the pursuit of wealth. We admit it, and rejoice that it has been so. It is proof of the unity of our national life; that we all move together, feel the pulsations of the heart, and engage as one man in whatever is the work for the moment. It is also a proof that we are an earnest race, and that what we attempt, we attempt with our whole heart; that we throw our whole being into our work, and live and move but in it and for it. This is a noble trait of character. It is full of promise. It assures us that whatever the nation undertakes, it shall accomplish; that when it has provided for the most pressing wants of the body, and turned its attention to the creation of a literature, it shall bend its whole soul to it, and create a literature which shall deserve and receive the world's admiration. The very intensity with which we pursue wealth is full of hope. It proves that the pursuit of wealth can be only a temporary pursuit, that we must soon satisfy our material wants, and be ready to engage with similar intenseness in providing for the wants of the soul.

The pursuit of wealth, we are told again, is a low, degrading pursuit, proceeding from a mean and sordid ambition. It can in no sense compare with the elegant and ennobling pursuit of letters. Their business man, counting dollars and cents, and balancing his losses and gains, is a low and servile being compared with the scholar, whose soul is unbound, whose thoughts are free to roam over the universe, to commune with all nature, and to rise to close intimacy with the "first Good and first Fair." "The scholar is the favorite of Heaven and Earth, the excellency of his country, the happiest of men. His duties lead him directly into the holy ground, where other men's aspirations only point. His successes are occasions of the purest joy to all men. Eyes is he to the blind; feet is he to the lame." Is there no "optical illusion" in all this? Is there not here, in this estimate of the comparative dignity of literature and business, no want of independence? Is there no slavishness to what we have been taught,–to the mind of the past? What occasion is there for the men of letters to scorn the men of business? Is this business world as contemptible as the literary world would fain make us believe? Genius has not hesitated to weave a garland of fadeless flowers around the brows of ancient heroism, and later chivalry, and why should it hesitate to do the same for modern business, since there is many a merchant moved by as heroic and chivalric aspirations, as ever moved an ancient hero or a modern knight? We often suppose that the merchant is moved by mere love of gain, that his ruling motive is avarice; but we are greatly mistaken. The merchant fits out his ships with as lofty feelings, as those with which an ancient monarch led forth his armed followers to make conquests. He loves excitement; he has a taste for the adventurous; and he longs to act a conspicuous part in great events. The great and active man is in him; the soul of the chivalric knight is in him; and it is only in immense business calculations and business enterprises, that the spirit of the age allows him to act out what is in him. It is not the littleness, but the greatness, of his soul, that leads him to cover the ocean with his rich "argosies," and to lay every clime under contribution. Now we ask, wherein is this merchant-prince less honorable, less glorious, than the warrior-prince, around whom men of letters love to cluster, and whom they conspire to deify? His enterprises are infinitely more serviceable to Humanity.

In all ages of the world, business pursuits have been regarded as ignoble. Kings and military chieftains, tyrants and "man-killers," royal and noble hunters, have passed for the representatives of God on earth; while the honest laborer has been accounted low and vulgar, a menial, a slave. Is not this contempt, which men of letters cast on the men of business, a tradition of the old contempt with which they looked upon all useful labor? Is it not a reminiscence of the times when all useful labor was performed by slaves, or by the ignorant and vulgar; and when the "better sort" lived in idleness and luxury, or engaged only in war or "manly sports?" If so, the business world has not yet succeeded in rendering labor perfectly honorable. The patent of its nobility bears a too recent date; the scholar remembers the time when it was plebeian and accounted vile. But does the scholar well to remember this? Has he a right to look down on the man of business? and is he aiding the cause of Humanity by sowing dissensions between those who labor to accumulate wealth for the body, and those who are seeking to create wealth for the soul? The scholar, in fact, ought to be chary of producing a disgust, a loathing for the practical duties of life, or of undervaluing those pursuits without which society and life must fail, or worse than fail. Instead of regarding the material improvements of society, efforts to perfect political institutions, and to increase the physical comforts of the people, as low, sordid, mercenary, he should elevate them to the rank of liberal pursuits. His mission is to ennoble business, and to make drudgery the path to honor, as it is to independence. He may, and he should, point out the abuses into which the business world falls,—the errors it commits,—the low standard of morals it adopts; but he should also seek to combine business with literature,—as we would practice with theory,—and make it felt to be not beneath the dignity of the most learned man, the most accomplished scholar, to enter the arena of politics, to cultivate a farm, to manage a shop, to engage in manufactures, or commerce. The business world doubtless has its errors; its morality is of too low an order; its aims are not high enough; many of its practices are injurious to society; many of its members are purely selfish, and fall far below the standard of even its own morality; its politics are short-sighted and selfish, deficient in enlarged views and true policy; but nevertheless the more closely we examine it, the more we see it in all its bearings, the more shall we find in it to approve, and the better satisfied shall we be with the mission it is fulfilling.

Moreover, we believe the charge brought against the American people, of being exclusively devoted to money-getting, of being great lovers of money, is altogether too sweeping. The American people are far, very far, from being supreme lovers of money. They have no disposition to hoard. Not a native born miser can be met with in our whole country. We pursue wealth indeed to a great extent, but not as an end. We pursue it not for its own sake, but as a means; because we crave independence and would possess what wealth alone can purchase. The majority start in life poor, obliged to depend on their own exertions for the means of living. They are obliged, for a time at least, to struggle hard; they are made to feel the evils, the slights, the inconveniences of poverty; the consideration, influence, ease, and pleasures of which it deprives them; and they seek with great earnestness, by all the means in their power, to escape it; to cease to be mere drudges, living and toiling but for the human animal; to gain independence, and a position by which they can take rank as men amongst men, and act a useful and respectable part in the affairs of society. What is there in this to blame? The end is surely honorable and elevated; and the most we can say is, that the means adopted are not the most appropriate, or that some few forget the end in the means. No doubt many among us continue the pursuit of gain, long after the original reasons which induced them to adopt that pursuit have ceased to exist; but they do it not from the mere love of money, but from the force of habit; from the pleasure they find in doing to-day what they did yesterday; from the excitement, the employment afforded by their business exercises; and because they must, in order to enjoy themselves, do something, and there is nothing else they are fitted to do. Those among us who are most absorbed in money-getting, and who acquire wealth fastest, often spend it faster than they acquire it, proving thus that they value something else more than they do money. There is nothing miserly, sordid, mercenary in the American disposition. We are fond of show and consideration, anxious to be thought well of both at home and abroad, of holding a respectable social rank, and of gathering around us the comforts and elegances of civilized life; and so far as wealth can contribute to this end, we love and seek it; but no farther. The man who seems wholly absorbed in counting dollars and cents, and balancing his losses and gains, may on close inspection be found to be moved by an honorable ambition, and to be contributing not a little to the means of moral and intellectual progress.

This general and absorbing pursuit of wealth, which seems so low and mean to the man of letters, is, moreover, essential to the existence and success of the scholar. A poor people, a people sunk in the depths of poverty, all of whose thoughts and exertions are needed to gain a mere subsistence for the human animal, can never be expected to contribute anything to the cause of letters. Men must be taught to read, and have leisure to read and reflect, before they can either become scholars or the audience of scholars. This instruction and this leisure can be obtained only on the condition that there be a certain independence as to the means of living. The scholar cannot be far in advance of his countrymen, at least not far in advance of the class to which he addresses himself. He never appears alone. He may surpass his brethren; but there will be always many near him, who reach the goal almost as soon as he. He must have competitors. He must have an audience, a public. This is always an indispensable condition of his existence. Give the audience, and the speaker will present himself; the public, and the philoso-

pher will bring forth his theories, the scholar unfold his treasures.

Now in this country the whole people must constitute the audience, the public. The scholar here must speak not to a clique, a coterie, but to the entire nation. The first thing to be done, then, is to make the whole nation a "fit audience." To talk of a "fit audience though few," betrays an entire ignorance of the age and the country. This is neither the age nor the country for scholars to consult only the tastes of scholars, and to address themselves only to a literary nobility. He who would be an American scholar must address himself to the whole American people; and his own attainments cannot far outrun the capacity of the masses to comprehend and relish his speech. It follows from this, that the first requisite to the scholar's success, in this country, is to make the whole nation a nation of readers, and to secure to the great mass of the people the leisure necessary to attend to the subjects on which the scholar discourses. The mere ability to read, however, is not enough. He who has worked all day with his hands, and sits down at night fatigued with the day's labor, and harassed in mind about the employment of the morrow, can hardly be expected to read and relish the profound and finished compositions of the true scholar. Now this very business world, against which we war, is the most active in teaching all to read, in providing the means of universal education. And how, without this general and absorbing devotion to moneygetting, is the general wealth of the country to be sufficiently augmented to allow the leisure we have determined to be necessary?

We go still further; we say that the general attention to business in this country is itself favorable to the growth of mind, to moral, spiritual progress. We could verify this assertion by history, were we so disposed. But we ask, what can more tax the mind and call forth its powers than the pursuits of commerce? Can the merchant make his calculations, extend his business to all parts of the world, without mental exertion? All industrial employments require more or less of skill and science. The desire to become rich, and quickly rich, stimulates improvements, seeks out inventions, makes perpetual demands on science to abridge the process. Many an ordinary mechanic in our city makes use of a science that a Newton might have been proud to own, and employs a mental power equal to that which discovered the law of gravitation, and determined the laws of the Universe. The more intense the desire to accumulate wealth, the more use will be made of science; consequently the more employment will be given to mind, to intellect. The business world is in no sense inferior in active intellect to the world of letters; all the difference is in the application.

Nor is American literature, as it is, to be condemned outright. True, not much is to be said of our regular built books; but we have newspapers. Our newspapers are conducted for the great mass of the people, by men who come out immediately from the bosom of the people, and they of necessity express the sentiments of the people. They constitute, therefore, in the strictest sense of the word, a popular literature. And scattered through our newspapers and popular journals, may be found more fine writing, more true poetry, genuine eloquence, vigorous thought, original and comprehensive views, than can be found in the classics of either France or England. All the elements of the soul by turns are appealed to, and in turn find their expression; all subjects are discussed, and on all sides too; and often with a clearness and depth which leave little to be desired. Your most ordinary newspaper not unfrequently throws you off an essay, that it would be impossible to match in the writings of Addison, Steele, or Johnson.

The great merit and wide circulation of our newspapers and periodicals, are doubtless the cause of the meagreness of our "book" literature. They are a ready channel through which he who thinks can communicate his thoughts to the public; and they therefore supersede the necessity, in some measure, of writing books. They answer the most urgent wants of the people, talk to the people on the topics on which they are thinking, discuss the subjects in which they feel an immediate interest; and therefore lessen the demand for more elaborate productions. At least this is their effect for the moment. But in the end they will increase the demand for more elaborate productions, by calling forth ability and giving the preliminary information necessary for understanding and relishing them. The newspaper gives us a general view of all matters, and therefore prepares us for a special view of any particular matter. Not to insist then on the newspaper as affording in fact a definitive literature, we cannot fail to perceive that it must end in creating a taste for literature; in preparing a literature; in leading directly to its creation; and that so long as we sustain it, we can by no means be said to be doing nothing for literature.

It may be alleged that our newspaper literature, whatever its excellence, is so scattered, so mixed up with what is impure and noxious, and withal presented in so frail and perishing a form, that it can neither be made available nor preserved. But it is preserved; perhaps not on the shelves of the student's library, but in the hearts and intellects of the people; in the actions it prompts, and in the public measures, the adoption of which it secures. And this is enough. A literature is of no great value any farther than it becomes absorbed into the popular mind, and constitutes an integral part of the life of the people; and a literature which becomes so absorbed, can hardly be said to be unavailable.

But passing over all we have thus far said, admitting all that may be urged against the business pursuits of our countrymen, and the meagreness of American literature; we must still call in question the soundness of the doctrine set forth in Mr. Emerson's oration. This oration teaches us, if we understand it, that the creation of a literature is a thing entirely dependent on the individual will; that a man has nothing to do but to rise up and say, Be there produced a literature that shall command the world's homage, and forthwith it shall be. Now in point of fact, few things are less dependent on mere will or arbitrariness than literature. It is the expression and embodyment of the national life. Its character is not determined by this man or that, but by the national spirit. The time and manner of its creation are determined by as necessary and invariable laws, as the motions of the sun, the revolutions of the earth, the growth of a tree, or the blowing of a flower. It is not by accident that this man sings and that one philosophizes; that this song is sung, and this system of philosophy is brought out now and in this country; and that another song is sung and another system of philosophy is broached, at another time and in another country. The thing is predetermined by the spirit of the age and nation. It depended not on Homer alone to sing. He sung because his song was in him and would be uttered. The God moved, and he must needs give forth his oracle. The choice of his subject, and the manner of treating it, depended not alone on his individual will. It was given him by the belief in which he had been brought up, the education which he had received, the spirit, habits, beliefs, prejudices, tastes, cravings of the age and country in which he lived, or for which he sung. Had he been born at the Court of Augustus, or of Louis XIV., he had not sung the wrath of Achilles and prowess of Hector; or if he had, it would have been to listless ears. His song would have taken no hold on the affections, and would have died without an echo. He might even not have been a poet at all.

This notion, which some entertain, that a national literature is the creation of a few great men, is altogether fallacious. Chaucer, Shakspeare, and Milton, Spencer, Pope, and Johnson are not the creators of English literature; but they are themselves the creatures of the spirit of the English nation, and of their times. Bacon, Hobbes, and Locke are not the authors of English philosophy, they are but its interpreters. Great men do not make their age; they are its effect. They doubtless react on their age, and modify its character; but they owe their greatness not to their individuality, but to their harmony with their age, and to their power of embodying the spirit, the reigning views of their age and country. Know the great men of a country, and you know the country; not because the great men make it, but because they embody and interpret it. A great man is merely the glass which concentrates the rays of greatness scattered through the minds and hearts of the people; not the central sun from which they radiate. To obtain an elevated national literature, it is not necessary then to look to great men, or to call for distinguished scholars; but to appeal to the mass, wake up just sentiments, quicken elevated thoughts in them, and direct their attention to great and noble deeds; the literature will follow as a necessary consequence. When a national literature has been quickened in the national mind and heart, the great man is sure to appear as its organ, to give it utterance, form, embodyment. Before then his appearance is impossible.

We find also some difficulty in admitting the notion that the scholar must be a solitary soul, living apart and in himself alone; that he must shun the multitude and mingle never in the crowd, or if he mingle, never as one of the crowd; that to him the thronged mart and the peopled city must be a solitude; that he must commune only with his own thoughts, and study only the mysteries of his own being. We have no faith in this ascetic discipline. Its tendency is to concentrate the scholar entirely within himself, to make him a mere individual, without connexions or sympathies with his race; and to make him utter is own individual life, not the life of the nation, much less the universal life of Humanity. He who retires into the solitude of his own being, in order to learn to speak, shall never find a companion to whom he can say, "How charming is this solitude!" He who disdains the people shall find the people scorning to be his audience. He who will not sympathize with the people in their sentiments and passions, their joys and sorrows, their hopes and fears, their truths and prejudices, their good and bad, their weal and woe, shall gain no power over the mind or heart of his nation. He may prophesy, but it shall be in an unknown tongue; he may sing, but he shall catch no echo to his song; he may reason, but he shall find his arguments producing no conviction. This is the inflexible decree of God. We can make the people listen to us only so far as we are one of them. When God sent us a Redeemer, he did not make him of the seed of angels, but of the seed of Abraham. He gave him a human nature, made him a partaker of flesh and blood, in like manner as those he was to redeem were partakers of flesh and blood, so that he might be touched with a sense of human infirmities, sympathize with our weakness, and through sympathy redeem us. So he who would move the people, influence them for good or for evil, must have like passions with them; feel as they feel; crave what they crave; and resolve what they resolve. He must be their representative, their impersonation.

He who has no sympathies with the people, and who finds himself without popular influence, may console himself, doubtless, with the reflection that he is wiser than the people; that he is above and in advance of his age; that a few choice minds understand and appreciate him; and that a succeeding generation shall disentomb him,–posterity do him justice and dedicate a temple to his memory. Far be it from us to deprive any man of such consolation as this; but for ourselves, it we cannot succeed in commanding to some extent the attention of our own age, we have no hope of succeeding better with a future and more advanced age. He who is neglected by his own age, is more likely to be below his age than above it. We recollect not an instance on record of remarkable posthumous literary fame, in opposition to the decision of the people during the man's life time. Posterity often reverses the judgments our own age renders in our favor; rarely, if ever, the judgments rendered against us. We speak not here of the judgments rendered by professional judges, but by the real, living, beating heart of the people. We therefore, notwithstanding we have experienced our full share of neglect, derive very little consolation from the hope that a coming age will do us better justice. Alas, it is that "better justice," we most dread. If we have failed to interest our own age, how can we hope to interest the age to come? Is it not as likely to be our fault as that of the age, that we do not reach its heart? We always distrust the extraordinary merits of those, who attribute their failures not to their defects, but to their excellence, to the fact that they are above the vulgar herd, and too profound to be comprehended, till the age has advanced and called into exercise greater and more varied intellectual powers. We are disposed to believe that of our scholars the greater part may attribute their failures to the fact, that they have drawn their inspirations from books, from the past, from a clique or coterie, and not from the present, not from the really living, moving, toiling and sweating, joying and sorrowing people around them. Did they disdain the people less, did they enter more into the feelings of the people, and regard themselves strictly as of the people, and as setting up for no superiority over them, they would find their success altogether more commensurate with their desires, their productions altogether more creditable to themselves, and deserving of immortality.

Moreover, we doubt whether we show our wisdom in making direct and conscious efforts to create an American literature. Literature cannot come before its time. We cannot obtain the oracle before the Pythoness feels the God. Men must see and feel the truth before they can utter it. There must be a necessity upon them, before they will speak or write, at least before they will speak or write anything worth remembering. Literature is never to be sought as an end. We cannot conceive anything more ridiculous than for the leading minds of a nation to set out consciously, gravely, deliberately, to produce a national literature. A real national literature is always the spontaneous expression of the national life. As is the nation so will be its literature. Men, indeed, create it; not as an end, but as a means. It is never the direct object of their exertions, but a mere incident. Before they create it, they must feel a craving to do something to the accomplishment of which speaking and writing, poetry and eloquence, logic and philosophy are necessary as means. Their souls must be swelling with great thoughts–struggling for utterance; haunted by visions of beauty they are burning to realize; their hearts must be wedded to a great and noble cause they are ambitious to make prevail, a far-reaching truth they would set forth, a new moral, religious, or social principle they would bring out and make the basis of actual life, and to the success of which speech, the essay, the treatise, the song

are indispensably necessary, before they can create a national literature.

We feel a deep and absorbing interest in this matter of American literature; we would see American scholars in the highest and best sense of the term; and we shall see them, for it is in the destiny of this country to produce them; but they will come out because we seek them, and they will be produced not in consequence of any specific discipline we may prescribe. They will come when there is a work for them to do, and in consequence of the fact that the people are everywhere struggling to perform that work. How eloquently that man speaks! His words are fitly chosen; his periods are well balanced; his metaphors are appropriate and striking; his tones are sweet and kindling; for he is speaking on a subject in which his soul is absorbed; he has a cause he pleads, an idea he would communicate, a truth he would make men feel, an end he would carry. He is speaking out for truth, for justice, for liberty, for country, for God, for eternity; and Humanity opens wide her ears, and her mighty heart listens. So must it be with all men who aspire to contribute to a national literature.

The scholar must have an end to which his scholarship serves as a means. Mr. Emerson and his friends seem to us to forget this. Forgetfulness of this is the reigning vice of Goethe and Carlyle. They bid the scholar make all things subsidiary to himself. He must be an artist, his sole end is to produce a work of art. He must scorn to create for a purpose, to compel his genius to serve, to work for an end beyond the work itself. All this which is designed to dignify art is false, and tends to render art impossible. Did Phidias create but for the purpose of creating a statue? Was he not haunted by a vision of beauty which his soul burned to realize? Had the old Italian masters no end apart from and above that of making pictures? Did Homer sing merely that he might hear the sound of his own voice? Did Herodotus and Thucydides write but for the sake of writing, and Demosthenes and Cicero speak but for the purpose of producing inimitable specimens of art? Never yet has there appeared a noble work of art which came not from the artist's attempt to gain an end separate from that of producing a work of art. Always does the artist seek to affect the minds or the hearts of his like, to move, persuade, convince, please, instruct, or ennoble. To this end he chants a poem, composes a melody, laughs in a comedy, weeps in a tragedy, gives us an oration, a treatise, a picture, a statue, a temple. In all the masterpieces of ancient and modern literature, we see the artist has been in earnest, a real man, filled with an idea, wedded to some great cause, ambitious to gain some end. Always has he found his inspiration in his cause, and his success may always be measured by the magnitude of that cause, and the ardor of his attachment to it.

American scholars we shall have; but only in proportion as the scholar weds himself to American principles, and becomes the interpreter of American life. A national literature, we have said, is the expression of the national life. It is the attempt to embody the great idea, or ideas, on which the nation is founded; and it proceeds from the vigorous and continued efforts of scholars to realize that idea, or those ideas, in practical life. The idea of this nation is that of democratic freedom, the equal rights of all men. No man, however learned he may be, however great in all the senses of greatness, viewed simply as an individual, who does not entertain this great idea, who does not love it, and struggle to realize it in all our social institutions, in our whole practical life, can be a contributor to American literature. We care not how much he may write; how rapid and extensive a sale his works may find; how beautifully in point of style they may be written; how much they may be praised in reviews, or admired in saloons; they shall not live and be placed among the national classics. They have no vitality for the nation, for they meet no great national want, satisfy no national craving.

In order to rear up American scholars, and produce a truly American literature, we would not do as the author of the oration before us, declaim against American literature as it is, against the servility, and want of originality and independence of the American mind; nor would we impose a specific discipline on the aspirants to scholarship. We would talk little about the want of freedom; we would not trouble ourselves at all about literature, as such. We would engage heart and soul in the great American work. We would make all the young men around us see and feel that there is here a great work, a glorious work, to be done. We would show them a work *they* can do, and fire them with the zeal and energy to do it. We would present them a great kindling cause to espouse; wake up in them a love for their like, make them see a divine worth in every brother man, long to raise up every man to the true position of a man, to secure the complete triumph of the democracy, and to enable every man to comprehend and respect himself, and be a man. If we can succeed in doing this, we can make them true scholars, and scholars who shall do honor to their country, and add glory to Humanity. When our educated men acquire faith in democratic institutions, and a love for the Christian doctrine of the brotherhood of the human race, we shall have scholars enough, and a literature which will disclose to the whole world the superiority of freedom over slavery.

Let Mr. Emerson, let all who have the honor of their country or of their race at heart, turn their whole attention to the work of convincing the educated and the fashionable, that democracy is worthy of their sincerest homage, and of making them feel the longing to labor in its ennobling cause; and then he and they may cease to be anxious as to the literary results. It will be because a man has felt with the American people, espoused their cause, bound himself to it for life or for death, time or eternity, that he becomes able to adorn American literature; not because he has lived apart, refused "to serve society," held lone reveries, and looked on sunsets, and sunrise. If he speak a word, "posterity shall not willingly let die," it will not be because he has prepared himself to speak, by a scholastic astheticism, but by loving his countrymen and sympathizing with them.

Jones Very

"Religious Sonnets," *Western Messenger*, 6 (March 1839): 308-314.

> *Jones Very's poetry was both Transcendental and religious in nature. He believed in a willless existence, and totally submerged his own voice to what he felt was the voice of God speaking through him in his poetry. At the time that James Freeman Clarke published Very's sonnets in the* Western Messenger, *Very was feared to be insane, having told friends that he embodied the second coming of Christ (more likely he had suffered a nervous breakdown). Clarke directly alluded to this in his introduction, when he said "that the intercourse we have ourselves had with him has given no evidence even of such partial derangement." Of all the Transcendentalists who chose poetry as a medium of expression, Very probably wrote the verses of finest technical merit. (For further information on this Harvard tutor and Unitarian minister, see the entry for Very in* DLB 1, The American Renaissance in New England.*)*

We received, last month, twenty-seven sonnets of a spiritual nature chiefly, from the gentleman whose name stands at the head of this article. They were accompanied by the following note:

> *Rev. J. F. Clarke, Editor Western Messenger:*
>
> Hearing of your want of matter for your Messenger, I was moved to send you the above sonnets; that they may help those in affliction for Christ's name is ever the prayer of me his disciple, called to be witness of his sufferings and an expectant of his glory. If you should ask for more as I have them so will they be communicated freely. Amen.
> The hope of Jesus be with you when you are called to be a partaker of his temptations.
> JONES VERY.

We propose to communicate a part of them in this number, reserving the remainder for the next. They have been read by ourselves with no common emotions of interest, and we trust will be equally interesting to our readers.

We hope it will not be considered indelicate if we introduce them with a few words about their author, as some acquaintance with his mental history and experience seems indispensable to a just comprehension of their meaning. If possible, we should place ourselves upon his standing point of thought, in order to be aware of their significance.

Photograph of Jones Very, Transcendentalist poet

We had the pleasure of meeting Mr. Very, a few months since, in the city of Boston. We had heard of him before, from various quarters, as a young man of much intelligence and of a remarkably pure character, whose mind had become extremely interested within a few months, upon the subject of religion. He was said to have adopted some peculiar views on this important theme, and to consider himself inspired by God to communicate them. Such pretensions had excited the fears of his friends, and by many he was supposed to be partially deranged. The more intelligent and larger sort of minds, however, who had conversed with him, dissented from this view, and although they might admit a partial derangement of the lower intellectual organs, or perhaps an extravagant pushing of some views to their last results, were disposed to consider his main thoughts deeply important and vital.

And here we may remark that the charge of Insanity is almost always brought against any man who endeavours to introduce to the common mind any very original ideas. And especially is this the case with moral and religious truths. He who insists on taking us out of that sphere of thought which is habitual to us, into a higher and purer one, is regarded by us with alarm and dissatisfaction. We must either yield ourselves to him, and suffer our minds to be taken out of their customary routine, which is always painful–or we must find some way to set aside his appeals to our reason and conscience and disarm them of their force. The easiest way is to call him insane. It is a short and ready explanation of his whole conduct. It relieves us at once of all further trouble about him. Nobody is obliged to attend to the "insane ravings" of a maniac. The moment therefore this word is applied to a man, were he sage, prophet or apostle–were he Socrates or Solon, were he Jesus or Paul–all men are authorised to look down upon him with pity. And it is so much more soothing to our vanity to look down than to look up, that it is no wonder that the worldlyminded, the men of sluggish and shallow intellects, and those who have arranged and systematised their opinions, are pleased with this excuse for pitying the man whom they ought to reverence. With them too go all those teachers, priests and prophets, who have attained an influence over the public mind, and love the exercise of that better than the attainment of new truth. The fear of innovation, error, change allies itself to these other motives, and so by common consent the prophet is declared a maniac. "He has a devil, and is mad, why hear ye him?"

was said of the saviour of men. "Paul, thou art beside thyself, much learning has made thee mad." And so have many other earnest souls, who spurned the worldly and mean thoughts and practices of those about them, who longed for an introduction of a brighter day into the darkness of time; reformers and enthusiastic philanthropists, Wesleys, Penns, Foxes, been called delirious by their own age, and been deified by the following one. "Your fathers stone the prophets, and ye build their sepulchres."

It is also, however, to be remarked, that the intense contemplation of any vast theme is apt to disturb the balance of the lower intellectual faculties. While the Reason, which contemplates absolute truth, is active and strong; the understanding which arranges and gives coherence to our thoughts, may be weakened or reduced to a state of torpor. When this reaches an extreme point, it becomes delirium or mono-mania.

But even in these cases it may be a question which is the *worst* delirium, that by which a man, possessing some great truth, has lost the use of his practical intellect–or that other wide-spread delirium, in which the mind is enslaved to the lowest cares and meanest aims, and all that is loftiest and greatest in the soul is stupified and deadened in worldliness. When, for instance, we have seen a man in whose intellect all other thoughts have become merged in the great thought of his connexion with God, we have had the feeling very strongly, which we once heard thus expressed, "Is this MONOMANIA, or is it MONOSANIA?"

With respect to Mr. Very, we have only to say that the intercourse we have ourselves had with him has given no evidence even of such partial derangement. We have heard him converse about his peculiar views of religious truth, and saw only the workings of a mind absorbed in the loftiest contemplations, and which utterly disregarded all which did not come into that high sphere of thought. We leave it to our readers to decide whether there is any thing of unsoundness in these sonnets. To us, they seem like wells of thought, clear and pellucid, and coming up from profound depths.

Mr. Very's views in regard to religion, as we gathered them from himself, were not different from those heretofore advocated by many pure and earnest religionists. He maintains, as did Fenelon, Mme. Guion and others, that all sin consists in self-will, all holiness in an unconditional surrender of our own will to the will of God. He believes that one whose object is not to do his own will in any thing, but constantly to obey God, is led by Him, and taught of him in all things. He is a Son of God, as Christ was *the* Son, because he *always* did the things which pleased his Father. He professes to be himself guided continually by this inward light, and he does not conjecture, speculate or believe, but he *knows* the truth which he delivers. In this confidence however there is nothing of arrogance, but much modesty of manner.

THE RAIL ROAD.

Thou great proclaimer to the outward eye,
Of what the spirit too would seek to tell,
Onward thou go'st, appointed from on high
The other warnings of the Lord to swell;
Thou art the voice of one that through the world
Proclaims in startling tones, "prepare the way;"
The lofty mountain from its seat is hurled,
The filthy rocks thine onward march obey;
The vallies lifted from their lowly bed
O'ertop the hills that on them frowned before,
Thou passest where the living seldom tread,
Through forests dark, where tides beneath thee roar,
And bidst man's dwelling from thy track remove,
And would with warning voice his crooked paths reprove.

THE WOLF AND THE LAMB SHALL FEED TO-GETHER.

The wolf, why heeds he not the sportive lamb,
But lies at rest beside him on the plain?
The lion feeds beside the browsing ram,
The tyger's rage is curbed without a chain;
The year of peace has on the earth begun!
And see ye not bestowed the promised sign,
The prophets by the spirit moved have sung,
To close the world's long strife with day benign?
Look not abroad, it comes not with the eye;
Nor can the ear its welcome tidings hear;
Nor seek ye Christ below, nor yet on high,
Behold the Word to thee is also near;
E'en at thy heart it speaks. Repent! Obey!
And thine eye too shall hail the rising day.

BEHOLD HE IS AT HAND THAT DOTH BETRAY ME.

Why come you out to me with clubs and staves,
That you on every side have fenced me so?
In every act you dig for me deep graves;
In which my feet must walk where'er I go;

You speak and in your words my death I find,
Pierced through with many sorrows to the core;
And none that will the bleeding spirit bind,
But at each touch still freer flows the gore;
But with my stripes your deep-dyed sins are healed,
For I must show my master's love for you;
The cov'nant that he made, forever sealed,
By blood is witnessed to be just and true;
And you in turn must bear the stripes I bear,
And in his sufferings learn alike to share.

HE WAS ACQUAINTED WITH GRIEF.

I cannot tell the sorrows that I feel
By the night's darkness, by the prison's gloom;
There is no sight that can the death reveal,
The spirit suffers in earth's living tomb;
There is no sound of grief that mourners raise,
No moaning of the wind, or dirge-like sea;
Nor hymns though prophet tones inspire the lays,
That can the spirit's grief awake in thee;
Thou too must suffer as it suffers here,
The death in Christ to know the Father's love;
Then in the strains that angels love to hear,
Thou too shalt hear the spirit's song above;
And learn in grief what these can never tell,
A note too deep for earthly voice to swell.

THE WINTER RAIN.

The rain comes down, it comes without our call;
Each pattering drop knows well its destined place,
And soon the fields whereon the blessings fall,
Shall change their frosty look for Spring's sweet face;
So fall the words thy Holy Spirit sends,
Upon the heart where Winter's robe is flung;
They shall go forth as certain of their ends,
As the wet drops from out thy vapors wrung;
Spring will not tarry, though more late its rose
Shall bud and bloom upon the sinful heart;
Yet when it buds, forever there it blows,
And hears no Winter bid its bloom depart;
It strengthens with his storms, and grows more bright,
When o'er the earth is cast his mantle white.

FORBEARANCE.

The senseless drops can feel no pain, as they

In ceaseless measure strike the barren ground;
But o'er its trodden surface constant play,
Without a pang that there no life is found;
Yet oft the word must fall on stony fields,
And where the weeds have shot their rankness high;
And nought the seed to him who sows it yields,
But bitter tears and the half-uttered sigh;
But these are rife with precious stores of love,
For him who bears them daily in his breast;
For so the Father bids him hence remove,
And so attain His everlasting rest;
For thus He bore with thee when thou wast blind,
And so He bids thee bear wouldst thou his presence find.

THE FRAGMENTS.

I would weigh out my love with nicest care,
Each moment shall make large the sum I give,
That all who want may find yet some to share;
And bless the crumb of bread that helps them live;
Or thy rich stores how much has wasted been,
Of all Thou giv'st me daily to divide;
I will in future count it for my sin,
If e'en a morsel from the poor I hide;
Help me to give them all Thou giv'st to me,
That I a faithful steward may be found;
That I may give a good account to Thee,
Of all the seed Thou sowest in my ground;
That nought of all Thou givest may remain,
That can a hungry soul in life sustain.

THE FRUIT.

Thou ripenest the fruits with warmer air,
That Summer brings around thy goodly trees;
And Thou wilt grant a summer to my prayer,
And fruit shall glisten from these fluttering leaves;
A fruit that shall not with the winter fail,
He knows no winter who of it shall eat;
But on it lives though outward storm assail,
Till it becomes in time his daily meat;
Then he shall in the fruit I give abound,
And hungry pilgrims hasten to the bough;
Where the true bread of life shall then be found,
Though nought they spy to give upon it now;
But pass it by, with sorrowing hearts that there
But leaves have grown where they the fruit would share.

TO HIM THAT HATH SHALL BE GIVEN.

Why readest thou? thou canst not gain the life
The spirit leads, but by the spirit's toil;
The labor of the body is not strife,
Such as will give to thee the wine and oil;
To him who hath, to him my verse shall give,
And he the more from all he does shall gain;
The spirit's life he too shall learn to live,
And share on earth in hope the spirit's pain;
Be taught of God; none else can learn thee aught;
He will thy steps forever lead aright,
The life is all that He his sons has taught,
Obey within, and thou shalt see its light;
And gather from its beams a brighter ray,
To cheer thee on along thy doubtful way.

[John A. Heraud]
"A Response from America," *Monthly Magazine*, 3d ser., 2 (September 1839): 344-352.

John A. Heraud's Monthly Magazine *provided a strong voice of support in England for the Transcendentalists and their writings. Indeed, when the subject of the Transcendentalists having their own journal was broached in 1839, Bronson Alcott mentioned Heraud's journal as a possible model. (Later, Heraud would review the* Dial *and give it his seal of approval by proclaiming its ideas the "same as those proposed by ourselves in the* Monthly Magazine.*") Here, Heraud reveals the "spirit of Coleridge, Wordsworth, and Thomas Carlyle" in Alcott's* The Doctrine and Disciple of Human Culture *(1836), which served as the preface to* Conversations on the Gospels; *Emerson's* Nature *(1836) and "The American Scholar"; and the October 1838 number of Brownson's* Boston Quarterly Review.

We have received from Boston the books . . . which, we perceive, are connected with a class of thinking that sufficiently interprets why they are sent to us. The spirit of Coleridge, Wordsworth, and Thomas Carlyle, has spread beyond the Atlantic, and we hear the echoes thereof from afar. Among these books are some by Mr. Alcott, sent unconsciously that we had already seen them, and had in consequence, in our Prize Essay contained in the EDUCATOR, lately published by the Central Society of Education, mentioned their author with emphatic honour. Time sufficient has not elapsed for the transmission of that volume across the Atlantic, and therefore we are not indebted to that for the works before us. No! we are indebted to the Oration on Coleridge and the Lecture on Poetic Genius for their transmission. No sooner has time sufficient passed for the circulation in America of the MONTHLY MAGAZINE, under better auspices, than we are thus welcomed, as fellow-workers for good, by the apostles of human developement in the New World.

We have long well known what influence by the elect of the school, in which we have matriculated, had been acquired over the growing intelligence of a rising country. We have rejoiced that the light of true philosophy had visited the unfettered intellect of a republican land; and while we rejoiced for their sakes, we regretted for our own, that similar principles received but slow acknowledgement under our own free institutions.

The leading article of the Fourth Number of the Boston Quarterly Review, would solve this enigma for us in its own way. It tells us, that the progress of civilisation and the association of men of letters is with the democracy. There is considerable brilliancy in this article. It tells us that the material world changes not–but that the intellectual world is subject to progress. Matter is passive–mind is active. There is a spirit in man–not in the privileged few; not in those of us only, who by the favour of Providence have been nursed in public schools, IT IS IN MAN; it is the attribute of the race.

"Reason," proceeds the writer, "exists within every breast. I mean not that faculty which deduces inferences from the experience of the senses, but that higher faculty, which, from the infinite treasures of its own consciousness, originates truth, and assents to it by the force of intuitive evidence; that faculty which raises us beyond the control of time and space, and gives us faith in things eternal and invisible. There is not the difference between one mind and another, which the pride of philosophy might conceive. To Plato or Aristotle, to Liebnitz and Locke, there was no faculty given, no intellectual function conceded, which did not belong to the meanest of their countrymen. In them there could not spring up a truth, which did not equally have its source in the mind of every one. They had not the power of creation: they could but reveal what God has implanted in the breast of every

[124]

one. On their minds not a truth could dawn, of which the seed did not equally live in every heart."

It is for the natural equality of the human powers, not of human attainments that the Boston critic contends. The latter are capable of improvement and progress. But, if it be granted, that the gifts of mind and heart are universally diffused, if the sentiments of truth, justice, love, and beauty exist in every one, then it follows, as a necessary consequence, that the common judgement in politics, morals, character and taste, is the highest authority on earth, and the nearest possible approach to an infallible decision.

Such is a regular republican conclusion from the premises, in favour of public opinion. It must be conceded to the writer, that "Absolute error can have no existence in the public mind. Whereever you see men clustering together to form a party, you may be sure that however much error may be there, truth is there also. Apply this principle boldly; it contains a lesson of candour, and a voice of encouragement. Yes, there never was a school of philosophy, nor a clan in the world of opinion, but carried along with it some important truth. To know the seminal principle of every prophet and leader of a sect, is to gather all the wisdom of the world."

We submit the above to our friend Alerist and his admirers. The following is a startling reflection.

> "Who are the best judges in matters of taste? Do you think the cultivated individual? Undoubtedly not; but the collective mind. The public is wiser than the wisest critic. In Athens, where the arts were carried to perfection, it was done when 'the fierce democracie' was in the ascendant; the temple of Minerva and the works of Phidias were invented and perfected to please the common people. When Greece yielded to tyrants, her genius for excellence in arts expired; or rather purity of taste disappeared; because the artist then endeavoured to please the individual, and therefore humoured his caprice; while before he had endeavoured to please the race."

After bringing down his instances to the present day, the reviewer concludes, that the fullest confidence may be put in the capacity of the human race for political advancement. The absence of the prejudices of the old world leaves to Americans the opportunity of consulting independent truth; and man is left to apply the instinct of freedom to every social relation and public inter-

est. They have approached so near to nature, that they can hear her gentlest whispers; they have made humanity their lawgiver and their oracle; and, therefore, principles, which in Europe the wisest receive with distrust, are the common property of their public mind. The spirit of the nation receives and vivifies every great doctrine, of which the application is required: no matter how abstract it may be in theory, or how remote in its influence, the intelligence of the multitude embraces, comprehends, and enforces it. Freedom of mind, freedom of the seas, freedom of industry, each great truth is firmly grasped; and wherever a great purpose has been held up, or a useful reform proposed, the national mind has calmly, steadily, and irresistibly pursued its aim.

To certain extent, whatever the reason, the fact doubtless is so. We find in the *Boston Quarterly Review*, what in the *London Quarterly Review* we should look for in vain–a Review of Carlyle's French Revolution–a high-toned, wise and discriminating review; and we know that she possesses, as we have shown in our *Educator Essay*, an unrivalled schoolmaster in Mr. Alcott. This gentleman's opinions on human culture are also canvassed in the number before us–well and impartially, and recommended, not however without certain mischievous reservations. The reason of this, as we learn not only from certain hints in the body of the review, but from a private letter, is, that notwithstanding the extolled tendency of the democratic mind to truth, Mr. Alcott is now suffering for truth's sake. It seems that those very inquiries which are quoted in our *Educator Essay* have brought him into trouble and want. The point is thus touched on in the review before us.

> All the functions of the body, as we call them, but which are really functions of the soul, are holy, and should be early surrounded with holy and purifying associations: hence the Conversations in the volumes before us with the children, on the mysterious phenomena attending the production and birth of a new member to the human family, or what Mr. Alcott calls the Incarnation of Spirit,–Conversations which have caused him much reproach, and done him, for the moment, we fear, no little injury. His motives were pure and praiseworthy, and his theory seemed to require him to take the course he did, and he should not be censured; but–

And then the writer puts the American prejudice, so ludicrously exhibited by Mrs. Trollope, in its strangest form. But we forbear to quote, where we must either blame or laugh.

On Mr. Alcott's *Conversations with Children,* we shall have something to say when we come to consider the great subject of education and the educator, and perhaps shall even make it the theme of a separate article–such as it deserves; for the book is a miracle! In the meantime, we shall, in this paper, say something on a little volume, which, from the style, we doubt not to be his, but which we now see for the first time, and which is entitled simply and boldly–

"NATURE,"

with this epigraph:–

> Nature is but an image or imitation of wisdom, the last thing of the soul; nature being a thing which doth only do, but not know.   PLOTINUS.

This little work consists of eight short chapters, and an introduction altogether as brief. It begins manfully.

> Our age is retrospective. It builds the sepulchres of the fathers. It writes biographies, histories, and criticism. The foregoing generations beheld God and Nature face to face; we, through their eyes. Why should not we also enjoy our original relation to the universe? Why should a man have a poetry and philosophy of insight and not of tradition, and a religion by revelation to us, and not the history of them?

Yes–even to this demand the perusal of Coleridge and Wordsworth has excited the American mind: to it, it is a possibility. A direct revelation to these times! Has the old world lost the faith in it, and is it reserved for the new? "The Sun," says Alcott, truly, "shines to day also!"

The universe, according to Alcott, is composed of Nature and the Soul. Strictly speaking, therefore, all that is separate from us, all which philosophy distinguishes as the NOT ME, that is, both Nature and Art, all other men and my own body, must be ranked under this name, Nature.

He begins his contemplation of this Nature with recognising the beauty of the stars, and the reverence that, from their inaccessibility, we feel for them. "All natural objects" says he, "make a kindred impression, when the mind is open to their influence. Neither does the wisest man extort all her secrets, and lose his curiosity by finding out all her perfection. Nature never became a toy to a wise spirit. The flowers, the animals, the mountains, reflected all the wisdom of his best hour, as much as they had delighted the simplicity of his childhood. Yet the delight that we feel in Nature is not owing to Nature. The delight resides in man, or in the harmony of him and Nature. To a man labouring under calamity, the heat of his own fire hath sadness in it. Then there is a kind of contempt of the landscape felt by him who has just lost by death a dear friend. The sky is less grand as it shuts down over less worth in the creation."

We cannot read such passages, without recollecting *Wordsworth's Ode on Immortality* and *Coleridge's Ode on Dejection.*

The analysis of the rest of the Book is indicated in two sentences. "Whoever considers the final cause of the world, will discern a multitude of uses that enter as parts into that result. They all admit of being thrown into one of the following classes; Commodity, Beauty, Language, and Discipline."

Commodity embraces our sensuous advantages.

> Nature, in its ministry to man, is not only the material, but is also the process and the result. All the parts necessarily work into each other's hands for the profit of man. The wind sows the seed; the rain evaporates the seed; the wind blows the vapour to the field; the ice, on the other side of the planet, condenses rain on this; the rain feeds the plant; the plant feeds the animal; and thus the endless circulations of the divine charity nourish man.
>
> The useful arts are but reproductions or new combinations by the wit of man, of the same natural benefactors. He no longer waits for favouring gales, but by means of steam, he realizes the fable of Æolus's bag, and carries the two and thirty winds in the boiler of his boat. To diminish friction, he paves the road with iron bars, and mounting a coach with a ship-load of men, animals and merchandise behind him, he darts through the country, from town to town, like an eagle or a swallow through the air. By the aggregate of these aids, how is the face of the world changed, from the era of Noah to that of Napoleon. The private poor man hath cities, ships, canals, bridges, built for him. He goes to

the post office, and the human race run on his errands; to the book shop, and human race read and write of all that happens for him; to the courthouse, and nations repair his wrongs. He sets his house upon the road, and the human race go forth every morning, and shovel out the snow, and cut a path for him.

Beauty, the author considers in a three-fold manner.–The simple perception of natural forms–the mark that God sets upon virtue–and the relations of things to thought. Touching the second, we are told, that, in proportion to the energy of his thought and will, man takes up the world into himself. "All those things for which men plough, build, or sail, obey virtue;" said an ancient historian. "The winds and waves," said Gibbon, "are always on the side of the ablest navigators." So are the sun and moon, and all the stars of heaven. When a noble set is done,–perchance in a scene of great natural beauty; when Leonidas and his three hundred martyrs consume one day in dying, and the sun and moon come each, and look at them once in the deep defile of Thermopylæ; when Arnold Winkelried, in the High Alps, under the shadow of the avalanche, gathers in his side a sheaf of Austrian spears to break the line for his comrades; are not these heroes entitled to add the beauty of the scene, to the beauty of the deed? When the bark of Colombus nears the shore of America;–before it the beach lined with savages, fleeing out of all their huts of cane; the sea behind; and the purple mountains of the Indian Archipelago around, can we separate the man from the living picture? Does not the new world clothe his form with her palm-groves and savannahs to fit drapery? Ever does natural beauty steal in like air, and envelope great actions. When Sir Harry Vane was dragged up the Towerhill, sitting on a sled, to suffer death, as the champion of the English laws, one of the multitude cried out to him, "You never sate on so glorious a seat." Charles II., to intimidate the citizens of London, caused the patriot Lord Russel to be drawn in an open coach, through the principal streets of the city, on his way to the scaffold. "But," to use the simple narrative of his biographer, "the multitude imagined they saw Liberty and Virtue sitting by his side." In private places, among sordid objects, an act of truth or heroism seems at once to draw to itself the sky as its temple, the sun as its candle. Nature stretches out her arms to embrace man: only let his thoughts be of equal greatness. Willingly does she follow his steps with the rose

and violet, and bind her lines of grandeur and grace to the decoration of her darling child: only let his thoughts be of equal scope, and the frame will suit the picture. A virtuous man is in unison with her works, and makes the central figure of the visible sphere. Homer, Pindar, Socrates, Phocion, associate themselves fitly in our memory with the whole geography and climate of Greece. The visible heavens and earth sympathise with Jesus. And in common life, who ever has seen a person of powerful character and happy genius, will have remarked how easily he took all things with him–the persons, the opinions, and the day–and Nature became ancillary to a man.

The love of beauty is Taste–the creation of beauty is Art.

In treating of language, the writer also considers it in threefold wise; *i.e.*

1. Words are signs of natural facts.

2. Particular natural facts are symbols of particular spiritual facts.

3. Nature is the symbol of spirit.

Whence it follows that nature is only the language of spirit.

This relation between the mind and matter is not fancied by some poets, but stands in the will of God, and so is free to be known of all men. It appears to men, or it does not appear. When in fortunate hours we ponder this miracle, the wise man doubts, if, at all other times, he is not blind and deaf;

"Can these things be,
And overcome us like a summer's cloud,
Without our special wonder?"

for the universe becomes transparent, and the light of higher laws than its own shines through it. It is the standing problem which has exercised the wonder and the study of every fine genius since the world began, from the era of the Egyptians and the Brahmins, to that of Pythagoras, of Plato, of Bacon, of Leibnitz, of Swedenborg. There sits the sphinx at the road-side, and from age to age, as each prophet passes by, he tries his fortune at reading her riddle. There seems to be a necessity in spirit to manifest itself in material forms; and day and night, river and storm, beast and bird, acid and alkali, preexist in necessary ideas in the mind of God, and are what they are by virtue of preceding affections in the world of spirits. A fact is the end or last issue of spirits. The visible creation is the terminus or the circumference of the invisible world. "Material objects," said a French philosopher,"are necessarily kinds of *scoriæ* of the substantial thoughts of the Creator, which must always preserve an exact relation to their first origin; in other words, visible nature must have a spiritual and moral side."

From the significance of nature, is inferrible nature as a discipline–for the exercise of the understanding–the will–the reason–the conscience. But in all there is the same central unity. Also to the one end of discipline, all parts of Nature conspire. Is this end the final cause of the universe? and does not nature outwardly exist? "It is," says Alcott, "a sufficient account of that appearance we call the world, that God will teach a human mind, and so makes it the receiver of a certain number of congruent sensations, which we call sun and moon, man and woman, house and trade. In my utter impotence to test the authenticity of the report of my senses, to know whether the impressions they make on me correspond with outlying objects, what difference does it make, whether Orion is up there in heaven, or some god paints the image in the firmament of the soul?" He would reduce all the apocalypse of the mind, without fear, since the active powers of man predominate so much over the reflective, as to induce him in general to resist with indignation, any hint that nature is more short-lived or mutable than spirit. Meanwhile, the best, the happiest moments of life, are those delicious awakenings of the higher powers, and the reverential withdrawing of nature before its God, which happen to the idealist, who is both a philosopher and a poet.

Nature, speaking of spirit, suggests the absolute–it is a perpetual effect–a great shadow pointing always to the sun behind us. "Idealism saith matter is a phenomenon not a substance. Idealism acquaints us with the total disparity between the evidence of our non-being, and the evidence of the world's being. The one is perfect, the other incapable of any assurance; the mind is a part of the nature of things; the world is a divine dream, from which we may presently awake to the glories and certainties of day?"

Spirit, according to Alcott, does not act upon us from without, that is, in space and time, but spiritually, or through ourselves. Therefore, that spirit, that is, the Supreme Being, does not build up nature around us, but puts it forth through us, as the life of the tree puts forth new branches and leaves through the pores of the old. As a plant upon the earth, so a man rests upon the bosom of God; he is nourished by unfailing fountains, and draws, at his need, inexhaustible power.

The highest reason is the truest–empirical science clouds the sight–the savant becomes unpoetic–the best-read naturalist is deficient in that knowledge which teaches the relations between things and thoughts. He has to learn that a guess is often more fruitful than an indisputable affirmation, and that a dream may let us deeper into the secret of nature than a hundred concerted experiments. Poetry, says Plato, comes nearer to vital truth than history.

Meditating which things, Alcott concludes his very excellent essay with some traditions of man and nature which, he says, a certain poet sang to him; and which, as they have always been in the world, and perhaps reappear to every bard, may be both history and prophecy.

The foundations of man are not in matter, but in spirit. But the element of spirit is eternity. To it, therefore, the longest series of events, the oldest chronologies are young and recent. In the cycle of the universal man, from which the known individuals proceed, centuries are points, and all history is but the epoch of one degradation.

We distrust and deny inwardly our sympathy with nature. We own and disown our relation to it by turns. We are, like Nebuchadnezzar, dethroned, bereft of reason, and eating grass like an ox. But who can set limits to the remedial force of spirit?

A man is a god in ruins. When men are innocent, life shall be longer, and shall pass into the immortal as gently as we awake from dreams. Now, the world would be insane and rabid, if these disorganizations should last for hundreds of years. It is kept in check by death and infancy. Infancy is the perpetual Messiah, which comes into the arms of fallen men, and pleads with them to return to paradise.

Man is the dwarf of himself. Once he was permeated and dissolved by spirit. He filled nature with his overflowing currents, out of him sprang the sun and moon; from man the sun; from woman the moon. The laws of his mind, the period of his actions, externised themselves into day and night, into the year and the seasons. But, having made for himself this huge shell, his waters retired; he no longer fills the veins and veinlets; he is shrunk to a drop. He sees that the structure still fits him, but fits him colossally. Say rather, once it fitted him, now it corresponds to him from far and on high. He adores timidly his own work. Now is man the follower of the sun, and woman the follower of the moon. Yet sometimes he starts in his slumber, and wonders at himself and his house, and muses strangely at the resemblance betwixt him and it. He perceives that if his law is still paramount, if still he have elemental power,"if his word is sterling yet in nature," it is not conscious power, it is not inferior but superior to his will. It is instinct. Thus my Orphic poet sang.

Alcott indulges in the liveliest hopes of man's prospects. Understanding and reason are ever reconquering nature, though inch by inch. The problem of restoring to the world original and eternal beauty, he finds is solved by the redemption of the soul. Prayer is a study of truth–a sally of the soul into the unfound infinite. No man ever prayed heartily without learning something. But when a faithful thinker, resolute to detach every object from personal relations, and see in the light of thought, shall, at the same time, kindle science with the fire of the holiest affections, then will God go forth anew into the creation.

> Then shall come to pass what my poet said; *"Nature is not fixed but fluid.* Spirit alters, moulds, makes it. The immobility or bruteness of nature is the absence of spirit; to pure spirit, it is fluid, it is volatile, it is obedient. Every spirit builds itself a house, and beyond its house a world, and beyond its world a heaven. Know then, that the world exists for you. For you the phenomena is perfect. What we are that only can we see. All that Adam had, all that Cæsar could, you have and can do. Adam called his house heaven and earth. Cæsar called his house Rome. You, perhaps, call yours a cobbler's trade, a hundred acres of ploughed land, or a scholar's garret. Yet line for line, and point for point, your dominion is as great as theirs, though without fine names. Build, therefore, your own world. As fast as you conform your life to the pure idea in your mind, that will unfold its great proportions. A correspondent revolution in things will attend the influx of the spirit. So fast will disagreeable appearances, swine, spiders, snakes, pests, mad-houses, prisons, enemies, vanish; they are temporary, and shall be no more seen. The odours and filths of nature the sun shall dry up and the wind exhale. As when the summer comes from the south, the snow-banks melt, and the face of the earth becomes green before it, so shall the advancing spirit create its ornaments along its path, and carry with it the beauty it visits, and the song which enchants it; it shall draw beautiful faces, and warm hearts, and wise discourse, and heroic acts around its way, until evil is no more seen. The kingdom of man over nature which cometh not with observation,–a dominion such as is now beyond his dream of God,–he shall enter without more wonder than the blind man feels who is gradually restored to perfect sight.

So much at present for Mr. Alcott. In regard to Mr. Emerson's *Oration,* we shall not imitate the *Boston Quarterly Review* on his *Address,* in being critical on the production. The *Address* was certainly remarkable as being delivered by a clergyman in a Divinity College to a class of young candidate preachers. The ethical rule laid down by Mr. Emerson is misinterpreted by the critic. The orator meant not by "Follow thy instincts" and "Obey thyself"–Follow your inclinations–Live as thou listest; but the contrary. The inclinations are not man's self nor his instincts, but acts of rebellion against both–against man's true personality, and the moral laws within him.

The reviewer, however, sees in all this but a system of pure egotism, such as runs through the writings of Thomas Carlyle and Carlyle's poet, Göthe. Now such critics misunderstand the individual good proposed by such authors. It is a good so deep and central as to be as one with the catholic spirit of humanity. It is the identity of the individual and the general. Hence can Mr. Emerson say with truth of the scholar, that "the instinct is sure, which prompts him to tell his brother what he thinks. He then learns, that in going down into the secrets of his own mind, he has descended into the secrets of all minds. He learns that he who has mastered any law in his private thoughts, is master to that extent of all men whose language he speaks, and of all into whose language his own can be translated. The poet, in utter solitude remembering his spontaneous thoughts and recording them, is found to have recorded that, which men in "cities vast" find true for them also. The orator distrusts at first the fitness of his frank confessions,–his want of knowledge of the persons he addresses,–until he finds that he is the complement of his hearers;–that they drink his words because he fulfils for them their own nature; the deeper he dives into his privatest, secretest presentiment, to his wonder he finds, this is the most acceptable, most public, and universally true. The people delight in it; the better part of every man feels, this is my music—this is myself."

We have invariably found in our experience, that democratic minds dislike above all things this doctrine. Wisdom with them resides in the multitude, not of councillors, but in the multitude as a multitude. They apprehend it as a result from the collision of minds, instead as the one spirit in the midst of every mind, whether two or three only or three thousand be gathered together.

The books before us shew that in America philosophy, relatively to a few minds, has travelled on the *à priori* road; but it was against the grain of public opinion nevertheless. It is some comfort, however, that in combating Mr. Emerson, Göthe, and Carlyle, the Boston reviewer uses Coleridge as his text book. We have the original of the following passage in our mind's eye.

The moral sentiment leads us up merely to universal order; the religious sentiment leads us up to God, the Father of universal order. Religious ideas always carry us into a region far above that of moral ideas. Religion gives the law to ethics, not ethics to religion. Religion is the communion of the soul with God, morality is merely the *cultus exterior,* the outward worship of God, the expression of the life of God in the soul; as James has it, "pure religion," external worship,— for so should we understand the original—"and undefiled before God and the Father is this, to visit the fatherless and widows in their affliction, and to keep himself unspotted from the world."

It is well that the American mind can meet such a position with such an argument. It shows the influence exerted beyond the Atlantic by Coleridge's *Aids to Reflection,* from which work the thought is borrowed. When shall we in England substitute that volume for Locke's *Essay on the Human Understanding?* The progress made in America will react on England— and this notice will not be in vain.

---

1. We have said in a previous article, that we cherish no literary jealousy, in proof of which, we have lent these Boston volumes to a critic in a contemporary Magazine for an article which will appear on the same day with this. Why not? Yet, we believe, that others would have acted on the *exclusive* system.

G[eorge]. E. E[llis].

"The New Controversy Concerning Miracles," *Monthly Miscellany of Religion and Letters,* 2 (June 1840): 327-336.

Ellis' critical survey of the publications following Emerson's Divinity School Address is a use-ful view of how contemporaries could see "the controversy of the day" in a measured fashion, and what they felt were the important publications and issues involved.

A series of pamphlets has lately appeared, all of which bear upon a controversy, which if for no other reason than the number of publications it has called forth, may be considered as *the* controversy of the day, or the year. Some of the readers of the Miscellany may have seen advertisements and extracts from the successive publications, without the time or the inclination to peruse them all. For such readers we will endeavour to give a brief sketch of the controversy, as far as regards the pamphlets we have enumerated below, without entering at length into the great subjects which they involve.

A new movement had for some time been creating a degree of interest in our little theological world, in which a new mode and use of individual speculation had been brought to bear upon the evidence of Christianity. Mr. Norton had once or twice expressed himself strongly in opposition to the character and tendency of some opinions publicly advanced among us. As far as we ourselves were informed, it was to give an opportunity to this gentleman, who holds so honourable a place in our denomination, to express and maintain his well considered judgement, upon the new movement, that he was invited to deliver the first address before a newly formed Association of the graduates of the Cambridge Theological School.

1. The occasion appropriately suggested Mr. Norton's subject. Fathers and brethren devoted to the study and the public exposition of Christianity were gathered after separation, in a spot consecrated in their memories. Reminded of early pursuits and friendships, of disappointed hopes and worldly trials, they cling to a cheerful faith. The value and the interests of their religion are the subjects of their thoughts, and the desire to be faithful to it, to comprehend it and to sustain it

amidst the ferment of this revolutionary age, demands that a serious and thoughtful attention be given to its present aspect. The characteristics of the times and some prevalent opinions which are at war with a belief in Christianity are to be considered. By a belief in Christianity, says Mr. Norton, "we mean the belief that Christianity is a revelation by God of the truths of religion; and that the divine authority of him whom God commissioned to speak to us in his name was attested, in the only mode in which it could be, by miraculous displays of his power." An imperfect understanding of Christianity and its ancient and various corruptions have led to the present tendency of the age, which is to reject Christianity. Political commotions over the whole world contribute to this tendency. Established power is upheld by misrepresentations of Christianity; our country sympathises with Europe, and while we are flooded by light and pernicious literature from abroad, we have among us no controlling power of intellect. The old leaven of infidelity is still working under a new form. It is now characterised by the use of holy names deprived of their essential meaning; it assumes the Christian title, while it strikes at the roots of all faith by denying the miracles which attest the divine mission of Jesus Christ. Spinoza was the first to deny the possibility of miracles, while at the same time he affected religious language and concern. Mr. Norton then discusses the subject of miracles, showing that they are the essential and primary evidence that a truth has been revealed by God to man, that they are possible, capable of proof, that they are so interwoven with the character and doctrine of Christ as to be inseparable from the Christian records, that they are a firm basis of transmitted evidence, the pillar and ground of a probable faith. The train of thought which he has followed, leads him to conclude his discourse by imploring any one, who professes to be a Christian teacher and yet disbelieves the divine origin and authority of Christianity, to stop short in a course which is ruinous to the faith of others, and disgraceful to himself. Two Notes are subjoined to the Discourse. The first, containing some remarks on the characteristics of the modern German School of Infidelity, is now designed to justify the assertion in the Discourse, that infidelity is now disguised under the name of Christianity. De Wette and Schleiermacher are quoted as examples, the influence of whose writings is covertly ruinous to Christian faith. The second Note is an answer to the objection to faith in Christianity as resting on historical facts and critical learning.

2. Under the name of an Alumnus of the Cambridge Theological School, Rev. George Ripley animadverted upon Mr. Norton's Discourse in a pamphlet of 160 pages. He too begins with a reference to the occasion. He considers Mr. Norton's Discourse inappropriate to an occasion which brought together the members of a body among us, but he brings the force of his arguments to bear against the doctrine of the impossibility of miracles, of which doctrine, says Mr. Ripley, we have not a single advocate. Mr. Norton is charged with an exclusive spirit inconsistent with his former well known labors, viz. in denying the Christian name to some who claim it, because in his view they fail in the conditions of being entitled to it. This exclusiveness is unjustifiable, however true and important the doctrine which is insisted upon may be, but Mr. Ripley adds, the doctrine may be shown to be almost peculiar to Mr. N.–This doctrine is, that miracles are the only proof of religious truths as revealed by God to man. Mr. R. does not question the Christian miracles, nor their validity as credentials of a Divine messenger; but he disputes the statement that miracles are the ONLY evidence of the Divine origin of Christianity. Here, it seems to us, a misunderstanding commences on the part of Mr. Ripley. As Mr. Norton delivered his Discourse, and as we now read it, we then conceived, and we now conceive, that his full meaning is, that miracles are primarily or ultimately essential to the proof of the Divine revelation of Christian truths. There may be other arguments to add to or to follow from these, but there must be these; without these all others would be insufficient. A landowner or an extensive manufacturer may for a time leave the country, and commit his business to the care of an agent. That agent may make it

probable to us that he is the authorized agent of the absent principal, by scheming and planning as the principal was known to scheme and plan, by an honest and open way of proceeding, by doing many things opportunely, and by doing all things well. But let him undertake to pull down and build up, to issue notes of hand and promise of payment and to transfer deeds in the name of the absent owner, and we believe that Mr. Ripley, though he thinks as little of profit and loss, and has as good an opinion of human nature as any man living, would think it essential that the agent should exhibit the seal and signature of his master. Certainly a court of justice would demand such credentials. A pretended Divine messenger without miracles would be precisely like the agent without credentials. Again, if the pretended Divine messenger offered as miracles some strange phenomena which might all be explained without any thing supernatural being involved, he would resemble an agent who exhibited forged credentials. In this latter case, however well the pretended agent might scheme and plan, he would certainly be in a worse position with his forged credentials than without any. Again, we may suppose ourselves sitting in a room with our back to the entrance, and imagine we hear a footstep and recognise that of a friend; then the sound of his voice, the touch of his hand, may confirm our impression; but we must see him face to face, to be fully and clearly convinced that it is he. This distinction between *confirmatory* and *essential* evidence is strong in our minds, and is as we think overlooked by Mr. Ripley, though the foundation of Mr. Norton's argument.

Mr. R. thinks Mr. N. has confounded two distinct propositions,–a belief in the Divine origin of Christianity, and a belief in a certain class of its proofs. Thus, as some persons may believe in the Divine origin of Judaism before they are satisfied concerning the miracles of Moses, so there are some who believe in the Divine mission of Jesus Christ before they are satisfied concerning his miracles. Mr. R. therefore denies that miracles are the *sole* proof of a Divine revelation. To sustain his position, he glances at the different arguments and topics which have for ages been adduced as the collateral evidences of revelation, and each of which has a peculiar force to different minds. He accuses Mr. N. of an innovation in theology and reasoning. The displacing of the internal evidence which Mr. R. charges upon Mr. N., according to the former, found its first advocate in modern times in Dr.

Chalmers, who subsequently qualified his statements. Then Mr. Ripley quotes a line of Christian writers–the early Apologists for the religion, the founders of the Protestant Church, Barrow, Samuel Clark, Gerard, Dwight, Verplanck, Jacob Abbott, Buckminster, Thacher, Parker, & c.– Here again we put in a word. The passages which Mr. Ripley quotes express the confidence of the writers in the internal recommendations, the convincing truth, of Christianity, and in the collateral, or rather we should say, the consequent evidence of its Divine origin by its effect upon the heart. But we question whether any one of these writers would have maintained, that Christianity would have to all minds sufficient evidence of its containing revealed truths did not miraculous acts accompany it. The fact that it is true assures to it these consequent arguments and recommendations, but the *proof* that it is revealed truth is not to be confounded with the consequents of its truth. A story which we hear may be true, but the truth of the story is no proof that this or that individual told us of it and gave us good evidence concerning it. Thus Dr. Walker is quoted as asserting, that we need not enforce the miracles upon children or doubters until we have displayed the truth and application of the lessons which the miracles sanctioned. But Dr. Walker does not say, that the miracles need not exist upon the record, or that we could in the end be satisfied without them.

Mr. R. then reverts from human authorities to the Scriptures. These, he says, appeal to other considerations besides miracles. Some Divine messengers performed no miracles, as Samuel, Jeremiah, and John the Baptist. Other Divine messengers, though they performed miracles, did not appeal to them as the sole evidence of their mission, as Jesus Christ and Paul. Again, Mr. Ripley says, "we find express passages in the Scriptures which prove that miracles are not the only evidence of Divine revelation," and "which imply the necessity of various kinds of evidence." We are warned of the plausible claims of deceivers, of the dreams of false prophets. But does Mr. Ripley mean to assert, that miracles are here intended? He says, "Jesus declares in the most solemn manner, that the power of working miracles was so far from being the only evidence of a Divine commission, that it was not even a proof of a good character. A man, he asserts, may perform miracles in his name, may utter prophesies, may cast out devils, and at the same time be a worthless man, and rejected, at the day of judgement,

from the kingdom of heaven." We are amazed at the construction which Mr. Ripley has put on the Saviour's language. Neither he nor any one of his Apostles, or of the Prophets, has any where asserted that a bad man could perform miracles. The most which he or they assert is, that some men may *claim* miraculous power, and others may make it appear as if they possessed it. The words of the Saviour to which Mr. R. refers, bear this important preface: "Many *will say to me* in that day, have we not prophesied in thy name &c." Matt. vii. 22. To claim to be a prophet, and to be a prophet, are very different things.–In conclusion, Mr. R. alleges some bad practical consequences as following from the position that miracles are the sole evidences of a revelation. It would impair the power of preaching,–it would deny the Christian name to those whose convictions are attached to it independently of miracles,–it would take the faith from the common mind and give it up to antiquarians and scholars, for the unlearned cannot master the history of the faith. But would Mr. Ripley hesitate to cross the ocean, because he could not construct the charts and instruments nor understand the process of working a ship?–Some literary and historical questions are discussed at the close of the pamphlet, in which Mr. Ripley accuses Mr. Norton of some important errors as to the Atheism or Pantheism of Spinoza, the Pantheism or Rationalism of Schleiermacher, and the opinions of De Wette.

3. Mr. Norton replies to this pamphlet, which he considers a personal attack. In a few brief preliminary observations he again asserts the essential importance of miraculous evidence for the attestation of a miraculous message, and does justice to the vast amount of internal and collateral evidence, which may aid, but cannot supersede, the former. He then justifies the charge of Atheism which he had brought against Spinoza, and reflects with some severity upon mistranslations, misquotations, and the use of poor authorities adduced by Mr. Ripley in vindication of Spinoza. The charge against Schleiermacher of not believing in the personality of the Deity, nor in personal immortality, and of a disingenuous claim to the Christian name, is substantiated, and the alleged errors of translation from De Wette are divested of the importance which Mr. Ripley attached to them.

4. Mr. Ripley in a Second Letter complains that Mr. Norton has seen fit to shift the ground of the discussion, to reply only to the statements which concerned his personal reputation, not to the arguments in which

the whole public is interested. But since the matters of controversy are now made to be the opinions of Spinoza, Schleiermacher and De Wette, Mr. Ripley is willing to stand at issue with Mr. N. upon the correctness with which either party has stated them. This pamphlet is wholly occupied with an investigation into the opinions of Spinoza, concerning God; Mr. Ripley contending in opposition to Mr. Norton, that Spinoza believed in a God distinct from nature, in his personality and intelligence, though he departed wide from the common modes of thought upon that high theme. We shall not undertake to analyse the abstruse and learned labors of Mr. Ripley to this point. We should be glad to praise him as he deserves for the hard study and the minute earnestness which he displays.

5. In his Third Letter, which is devoted to an examination of the contested opinions of Schleiermacher and De Wette, Mr. Ripley uses the opportunity to give a more complete view of German Theology than has as yet been offered in the controversy. He acknowledges the freedom of those two theologians in the treatment of the letter of our faith, while he claims for them a sincere reverence of its spirit. This single sentiment will furnish our readers with the main purpose of the whole pamphlet. Living in a revolutionary and a skeptical age, these two scholars endeavoured by a modification of the Christian faith to enforce it upon thinking minds. Their speculations are as wild and loose as the freaks of fairies. They seem to proffer Christianity to all men together with the privilege of transfusing into it their own ideas and conceptions. Yet they preserve its spirit and its reverence. Here, to our minds, is the origin of the dark fear which we entertain concerning these rash speculations. Their authors have been educated under Christian influences. Their individual faith was formed, their principles were confirmed by clear and well grounded doctrine and discipline. They may in after life battle with words and with cunning fancies in comparative safety to themselves. But let them teach their "freedom with the letter" to their children and pupils, let them undertake to *form* a Christian faith upon their new speculations, and then we believe their labor will be futile and hopeless. They will have betrayed the faith, and the faith will forsake the hearts of their pupils.

6. The two Articles from the Princeton Review were republished in their present form by the request of Mr. Norton. The first of them traces the progress of metaphysical inquiries in New England, as founded on the philosophy of Locke, developed by Edwards, and rendered absurd by the subtilty of Emmons, and then rushing from the extreme of a cold and heartless method to utilitarianism. For the last few years thought and opinion have been making an irresistible attack against these two forlorn citadels of human speculation. Yet for this new movement we have had no great philosophical leader among ourselves. We have received the new light by instalments from France, where they have tarried awhile on their way from Germany. The writer then gives a sketch of the successive phases of German Philosophy under its changing masters, Kant, Fichte, Schelling and Hegel. These successive systems of misshapen phantasies we should fail in making intelligible to our readers. They involve terms, ideas and illustrations not yet familiar to our minds, much dark light, much abortive conception and feeble parturition. We are told that they have revived much of the old Grecian philosophy; perhaps therefore in his turn that wisest of all the wise men of Greece, who brought philosophy down from the skies, will come again, and when he has come we shall hope to understand it. Madame De Stael first introduced German philosophy into France, but its extravagancies met with little favor there until Professor Cousin in 1816 brought them into notice. After lecturing four years, his exercises having incurred the displeasure of the Government, he was suspended for seven years, when he was restored, and is still diffusing light in the College of the Sorbonne. His views of God, of the human soul, of the Scriptures, and of the principles of morals are alarmingly expounded, and severely criticised. The pamphlet classes Mr. Emerson's Address at Cambridge in the same catalogue of threatening dangers.—The second Article is a more full exposition of the characteristics and tendencies at the present school of philosophy in Germany—that of Hegel, and it concludes with an earnest warning to the students of our land.

7. Mr. Young's Discourse is a decided and uncompromising assertion of the dependence of Christian faith upon the historical tradition of the miraculous events connected with the Saviour's life. Christian institutions are the pillars which support the ark of religious refuge. The prayer and the Scriptures and the spoken sermon are the indispensable aids for the culture and instruction, yes, even for the permanent existence, of the religious sentiments. Philosophy, now as of old, proffers her assistance; and an honourable place of right belongs to her; but it is not the first place; this

belongs to the record of facts, to the transmitted testimony of the Church.

8. Levi Blodgett is a fictitious name. The writer expresses his sentiments with clearness, yet we cannot but think they are superficial and not sufficiently considered. He confines himself to the question, "Do men believe in Christianity *solely* on the ground of miracles," and he concludes that they do not, on the strength of the following considerations:–the primary elements and convictions on which religion depends are innate; and need only developement and culture; men need religious teachers not to implant religious sentiments, but to address and elevate them; men obey their teachers, and recognize them as teachers of truth, not through force of the mighty works which they do, but the recommendation of their lessons, the power of their inspiration; Christianity is the most perfect of religions, and Christ performed miracles, as other religious teachers have done; but a miracle cannot prove the truth of a doctrine, on the contrary the truth of the doctrine vouches for the reality of the miracle; finally, no one of the Saviour's miracles, except his resurrection, can be proved without difficulty. In this pamphlet likewise an argument is based upon what appears to us the absurd supposition, that a teacher of iniquity or falsehood may perform miracles. The highest praise we can give to the writer is that of having clearly expressed his opinions.

9. The last pamphlet on our list contains the most explicit and consistent statement which has as yet appeared in opposition to the doctrine of Mr. Norton's Discourse. In calling it consistent, we do not allow it to be true, nor consistent with truth, but merely consistent with itself. It starts with the assumption, "that the understanding has nothing to do with religion,"–that religion "renounces all pretensions to regulate opinion, or to interfere with morals, politics, or any of the practical business of life." And it concludes with the assertion that the Almighty has no mode of addressing or confirming the faith of an individual by a miraculous event; miracles, "even if they were performed before our very eyes, would, as evidence, be totally useless." The leading assumption implies, that it is only when an individual is withdrawn from the press of cares and of outward objects, that he can feel the sensibilities and hold the convictions of religion; in affliction and sickness alone can he be a believer. When a writer starts with an assumption like this, it is of but little consequence where he leaves off, or to what conclusion he arrives. Yet there is an equal absurdity and untruth in the conclusion which the writer before us arrives at, wholly independent of the error which vitiated his reasoning in its first step. He confounds miracles with wonders, and will admit no distinction between the act of the Saviour in raising the dead to life and the power of Zerah Colburn to solve arithmetical problems. We believe however that the writer has boldly, as well as skilfully and forcibly, stated the only alternative which is to be adopted if the principle laid down by Mr. Norton is denied. He calls upon the original mover of this controversy to answer his arguments, he charges him with having endangered the faith of Christians, and of adopting a principle which if consistently followed out will result in Atheism. We hope that Mr. Norton will favour our community with a thorough exposition of his own opinions.

---

1. A Discourse on the Latest Form of Infidelity; delivered at the request of the "Association of the Alumni of the Cambridge Theological School," on the 19th of July, 1839. With Notes. By Andrews Norton. Cambridge, John Owen, 1839. pp. 64, 8 vo.

2. "The Latest Form of Infidelity" Examined. A Letter to Mr. Andrews Norton, occasioned by his "Discourse &c." By an Alumnus of that School. Boston, James Munroe & Co., 1839. pp. 160, 8vo.

3. Remarks on a Pamphlet Entitled "The Latest Form of Infidelity Examined." By Andrews Norton. Cambridge, John Owen, 1839. pp. 72, 8 vo.

4. Defence of "The Latest Form of Infidelity" Examined. A Second Letter to Mr. Andrews Norton, occasioned by his Defence of a Discourse &c. By George Ripley. Boston, Munroe & Co., 1840. pp. 85, 8 vo.

5. Defence of "The Latest Form of Infidelity" Examined. A Third Letter to Mr. Andrews Norton, occasioned by his Defence &c. By George Ripley. Boston, Munroe & Co., 1840. pp. 154, 8vo.

6. Two Articles from the Princeton Review, concerning the Transcendental Philosophy of the Germans and of Cousin, and its Influence on Opinion in this country. Cambridge, J. Owen, 1840. pp. 100, 8 vo.

7. The Church, the Pulpit, and the Gospel. A Discourse delivered at the Ordination of Rev. George E. Ellis, as Pastor of the Harvard Church in Charlestown, March 11, 1840. By Alexander Young, Minister of the Church on Church Green, Boston. Boston, Little & Brown, 1840. pp. 64, 8 vo.

8. The Previous Question between Mr. Andrews Norton and his Alumni, moved and handled in a Letter to all those Gentlemen. By Levi Blodgett. Boston, Weeks, Jordan & Co., 1840. pp. 24, 8vo.

9. A Letter to Andrews Norton, On Miracles as the Foundation of Religious Faith. Boston, Weeks, Jordan & Co., 1840. pp. 52, 8 vo.

[Ralph Waldo Emerson]
"The Editors to the Readers." *Dial,* 1 (July 1840): 1-4.

> *The* Dial *was a quarterly magazine published between July 1840 and April 1844. Margaret Fuller edited the first eight numbers and Emerson the last eight; George Ripley was business manager through the October 1841 number; Thoreau was in charge of editing the April 1843 number in Emerson's absence; and Elizabeth Palmer Peabody served as its publisher for a year. It grew out of a meeting of the Transcendental Club on 18 September 1839 at which it was proposed that a journal "designed as the organ of views more in accordance with the Soul" be started. Alcott titled the magazine after the name he had given his thoughts which he had assembled from his journals over the past few years. As editor, Fuller tried to fairly present "all kinds of people" to have "freedom to say their say, for better, for worse"; but the reviewers chose the journal as a convenient scapegoat for all the unpopular aspects of Transcendentalism, and the public, unable to grasp or digest the varied articles, declined to buy the* Dial, *whose subscription list never rose above three hundred.*
>
> *Emerson's preface to the first number of the Dial gives a sense of the high ambitions held by its supporters:"It has all things to say, and no less than all the world for its final audience."*

We invite the attention of our countrymen to a new design. Probably not quite unexpected or unannounced will our Journal appear, though small pains have been taken to secure its welcome. Those, who have immediately acted in editing the present Number, cannot accuse themselves of any unbecoming forwardness in their undertaking, but rather of a backwardness, when they remember how often in many private circles the work was projected, how eagerly desired, and only postponed because no individual volunteered to combine and concentrate the free-will offerings of many coöperators. With some reluctance the present conductors of this work have yielded themselves to the wishes of their friends, finding something sacred and not to be withstood in the importunity which urged the production of a Journal in a new spirit.

As they have not proposed themselves to the work, neither can they lay any the least claim to an option or determination of the spirit in which it is conceived, or to what is peculiar in the design. In that respect, they have obeyed, though with great joy, the strong current of thought and feeling, which, for a few years past, has led many sincere persons in New England to make new demands on literature, and to reprobate that rigor of our conventions of religion and education which is turning us to stone, which renounces hope, which looks only backward, which suspects improvement, and holds nothing so much in horror as new views and the dreams of youth.

With these terrors the conductors of the present Journal leave nothing to do,—not even so much as a word of reproach to waste. They know that there is a portion of the youth and of the adult population of this country, who have not shared them; who have in secret or in public paid their vows to truth and freedom; who love reality too well to care for names, and who live by a Faith too earnest and profound to suffer them to doubt the eternity of its object, or to shake themselves free from its authority. Under the fictions and customs which occupied others, these have explored the Necessary, the Plain, the True, the Human,—and so gained a vantage ground, which commands the history of the past and present.

No one can converse much with different classes of society in New England, without remarking the progress of a revolution. Those who share in it have no external organization, no badge, no creed, no name. They do not vote, or print, or even meet together. They do not know each other's faces, or names. They are united only in a common love of truth, and love of its work. They are of all conditions and constitutions. Of these acolytes, if some are happily born and well bred, many are no doubt ill dressed, ill placed, ill made—with as many scars of hereditary vice as other men. Without pomp, without trumpet, in lonely and obscure places, in solitude, in servitude, in compunctions and privations, trudging beside the team in the dusty road, or drudging a hireling in other men's cornfields, schoolmas-

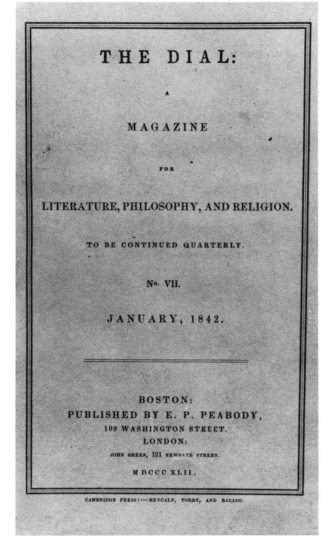

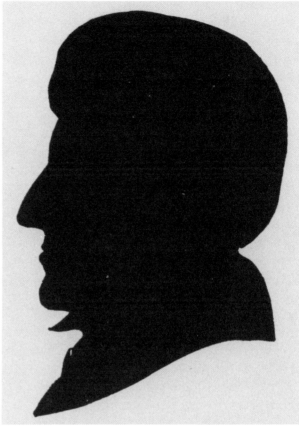

Silhouette of Emerson in the mid 1840s (David Green Haskins, Ralph Waldo Emerson: His Maternal Ancestors *[1887])*

Front wrapper of the Dial, *the penultimate issue edited by Margaret Fuller*

ters, who teach a few children rudiments for a pittance, ministers of small parishes of the obscurer sects, lone women in dependent condition, matrons and young maidens, rich and poor, beautiful and hard-favored, without concert or proclamation of any kind, they have silently given in their several adherence to a new hope, and in all companies do signify a greater trust in the nature and resources of man, than the laws or the popular opinions will well allow.

This spirit of the time is felt by every individual with some difference,—to each one casting its light upon the objects nearest to his temper and habits of thought;—to one, coming in the shape of special reforms in the state; to another, in modifications of the var-

ious callings of men, and the customs of business; to a third, opening a new scope for literature and art; to a fourth, in philosophical insight; to a fifth, in the vast solitudes of prayer. It is in every form a protest against usage, and a search of principles. In all its movements, it is peaceable, and in the very lowest marked with a triumphant success. Of course, it rouses the opposition of all which it judges and condemns, but it is too confident in its tone to comprehend an objection, and so builds no outworks for possible deference against contingent enemies. It has the step of Fate, and goes on existing like an oak or a river, because it must.

In literature, this influence appears not yet in new books so much as in the higher tone of criticism. The antidote to all narrowness is the comparision of the record with nature, which at once shames the record and stimulates to new attempts. Whilst we look at this, we wonder how any book has been thought worthy to be preserved. There is somewhat in all life untranslatable into language. He who keeps his eye on that will write better than others, and think less of his writing, and of all writing. Every thought has a certain imprisoning as well as uplifting quality, and, in proportion to its energy on the will, refuses to become an object of intellectual contemplation. Thus what is great usually slips through our fingers, and it seems wonderful how a lifelike word ever comes to be written. If our Journal share the impulses of the time, it cannot now prescribe its own course. It cannot foretell in orderly propositions what it shall attempt. All criticism should be poetic; unpredictable; superseding, as every new thought does, all foregone thoughts, and making a new light on the whole world. Its brow not wrinkled with circumspection, but serene, cheerful, adoring. It has all things to say, and no less than all the world for its final audience.

Our plan embraces much more than criticism; were it not so, our criticism would be naught. Everything noble is directed on life, and this is. We do not wish to say pretty or curious things, or to reiterate a few propositions in varied forms, but, if we can, to give expression to that spirit which lifts men to a higher platform, restores to them the religious sentiment, brings them worthy aims and pure pleasures, purges the inward eye, makes life less desultory, and through raising man to the level of nature, takes away its melancholy from the landscape, and reconciles the practical with the speculative powers.

But perhaps we are telling our little story too gravely. There are always great arguments at hand for a true action, even for the writing of a few pages. There is nothing but seems near it and prompts it,–the sphere in the ecliptic, the sap in the apple tree,–every fact, every appearance seem to persuade to it.

Our means correspond with the ends we have indicated. As we wish not to multiply books, but to report life, our resources are therefore not so much the pens of practised writers, as the discourse of the living, and the portfolios which friendship has opened to us. From the beautiful recesses of private thought; from the experience and hope of spirits which are withdrawing from all old forms, and seeking in all that is new somewhat to meet their inappeasable longins; from the secret confession of genius afraid to trust itself to aught but sympathy; from the conversation of fervid and mystical pietists; from tear-stained diaries of sorrow and passion; from the manuscripts of young poets; and from the records of youthful taste commenting on old works of

Painting of Emerson in the mid 1840s (Journals of Ralph Waldo Emerson, *edited by Edward Waldo Emerson and Waldo Emerson Forbes [1909-1914])*

art; we hope to draw thoughts and feelings, which being alive can impart life.

And so with diligent hands and good intent we set down our Dial on the earth. We wish it may resemble that instrument in its celebrated happiness, that of measuring no hours but those of sunshine. Let it be one cheerful rational voice amidst the din of mourners and polemics. Or to abide by our chosen image, let it be such a Dial, not as the dead face of a clock, hardly even such as the *Gnomon* in a garden, but rather such a Dial as in the Garden itself, in whose leaves and flowers and fruits the suddenly awakened sleeper is instantly apprised not what part of dead time, but what state of life and growth is now arrived and arriving.

[Margaret] F[uller]
"A Short Essay on Critics," *Dial,* 1 (July 1840): 5-11.

> *Fuller's essay is one of the best short statements of her philosophy of criticism. In typical Transcendentalist fashion, she moved through what Emerson called "spires of form," starting at the bottom with the "subjective" critics who "state their impressions as they rise," continuing to the "apprehensive" ones who "can go out of themselves and enter fully into a foreign existence," and closing with the "comprehensive" ones who "enter into the nature of another being and judge his work by its own law." Fuller would have agreed with Thoreau's comment in* Walden *that "Books must be read as deliberately and reservedly as they were written." (For further information, see the entry for Fuller in* DLB 1, The American Renaissance in New England.*)*

An essay on Criticism were a serious matter; for, though this age be emphatically critical, the writer would still find it necessary to investigate the laws of criticism as a science, to settle its conditions as an art. Essays entitled critical are epistles addressed to the public through which the mind of the recluse relieves itself of its impressions. Of these the only law is, "Speak the best word that is in thee." Or they are regular articles, got up to order by the literary hack writer, for the literary mart, and the only law is to make them plausible. There is not yet deliberate recognition of a standard of criticism, though we hope the always strengthening league of the republic of letters must ere long settle laws on which its Amphictyonic council may act. Meanwhile let us not venture to write on criticism, but by classifying the critics imply our hopes, and thereby our thoughts.

First, there are the subjective class, (to make use of a convenient term, introduced by our German benefactors.) These are persons to whom writing is no sacred, no reverend employment. They are not driven to consider, not forced upon investigation by the fact, that they are deliberately giving their thoughts an independent existence, and that it may live to others when dead to them. They know no agonies of conscientious research, no timidities of self-respect. They see no Ideal beyond the present hour, which makes its mood an uncertain tenure. How things affect them now they know; let the future, let the whole take care of itself. They state their impressions as they rise, of other men's spoken, written, or acted thoughts. They never dream of going out of themselves to seek the motive, to trace the law of another nature. They never dream that there are statures which cannot be measured from their point of view. They love, they like, or they hate; the book is detestable, immoral, absurd, or admirable, noble, of a most approved scope;–these statements they make with authority, as those who bear the evangel of pure taste and accurate judgment, and need be tried before no human synod. To them it seems that their present position commands the universe.

Thus the essays on the works of others, which are called criticisms, are often, in fact, mere records of impressions. To judge of their value you must know where the man was brought up, under what influences,–his nation, his church, his family even. He himself has never attempted to estimate the value of these circumstances, permanent against all influence. He is content to be the creature of his place, and to represent it by his spoken and written word. He takes the same ground with the savage, who does not hesitate to say of the product of a civilization on which he could not stand, "It is bad," or "It is good."

The value of such comments is merely reflex. They characterize the critic. They give an idea of certain influences on a certain act of men in a certain time or place. Their absolute, essential value is nothing. The long review, the eloquent article by the man of the nineteenth century are of no value by themselves considered, but only as samples of their kind. The writers were content to tell what they felt, to praise or to denounce without needing to convince us or themselves.

They sought out the divine truths of philosophy, and she proffers them not, if unsought.

Then there are the apprehensive. These can go out of themselves and enter fully into a foreign existence. They breathe its life; they live in its law; they tell what is meant, and why it so expressed its meaning. They reproduce the work of which they speak, and make it better known to us in so far as two statements are better than one. There are beautiful specimens in this kind. They are pleasing to us as bearing witness of the genial sympathies of nature. They have the ready grace of love with somewhat of the dignity of disinterested friendship. They sometimes give more pleasure than the original production of which they treat, as melodies will sometimes ring sweetlier in the echo. Besides there is a peculiar pleasure in a true response; it is the assurance of equipoise in the universe. These, if not true critics, come nearer the standard than the subjective class, and the value of their work is ideal as well as historical.

Then there are the comprehensive, who must also be apprehensive. They enter into the nature of another being and judge his work by its own law. But having done so, having ascertained his design and the degree of his success in fulfilling it, thus measuring his judgment, his energy, and skill, they do also know how to put that aim in its place, and how to estimate its relations. And this the critic can only do who perceives the analogies of the universe, and how they are regulated by an absolute, invariable principle. He can see how far that work expresses this principle as well as how far it is excellent in its details. Sustained by a principle, such as can be girt within no rule, no formula, he can walk around the work, he can stand above it, he can uplift it, and try its weight. Finally he is worthy to judge it.

Critics are poets cut down, says some one by way of jeer; but, in truth, they are men with the poetical temperament to apprehend, with the philosophical tendency to investigate. The maker is divine; the critic sees this divine, but brings it down to humanity by the analytic process. The critic is the historian who records the order of creation. In vain for the maker, who knows without learning it, but not in vain for the mind of his race.

The critic is beneath the maker, but is his needed friend. What tongue could speak but to an intelligent ear, and every noble work demands its critic. The richer the work, the more severe would be its critic; the larger its scope, the more comprehensive must be

Engraving of Margaret Fuller, pioneer feminist

his power of scrutiny. The critic is not a base cavaller, but the younger brother of genius. Next to invention is the power of interpreting invention; next to beauty the power of appreciating beauty.

And of making others appreciate it; for the universe is a scale of infinite gradation, and below the very highest, every step is explanation down to the lowest. Religion, in the two modulations of poetry and music, descends through an infinity of waves to the lowest abysses of human nature. Nature is the literature and art of the divine mind; human literature and art the criticism on that; and they, too, find their criticism within their own sphere.

The critic, then, should be not merely a poet, not merely a philosopher, not merely an observer, but tempered of all three. If he criticize the poem, he must want nothing of what constitutes the poet, except the power of creating forms and speaking in music. He must have as good an eye and as fine a sense; but if he had as fine an organ for expression also, he would make the poem instead of judging it. He must be inspired by the philosopher's spirit of inquiry and need of generalization, but he must not be constrained by the hard cemented masonry of method to which philosophers are prone. And he must have the organic acuteness of the observer, with a love of ideal perfection, which forbids him to be content with mere beauty of details in the work or the comment upon the work.

There are persons who maintain, that there is no legitimate criticism, except the reproductive; that we have only to say what the work is or is to us, never what it is not. But the moment we look for a principle, we feel the need of a criterion, of a standard; and then we say what the work is *not,* as well as what it *is;* and this is as healthy though not as grateful and gracious an operation of the mind as the other. We do not seek to degrade but to classify an object by stating what it is not. We detach the part from the whole, lest it stand between us and the whole. When we have ascertained in what degree it manifests the whole we may safely restore it to its place, and love or admire it there ever after.

The use of criticism in periodical writing is to sift, not to stamp a work. Yet should they not be "sieves and drainers for the use of luxurious readers," but for the use of earnest inquirers, giving voice and being to their objections, as well as stimulus to their sympathies. But the critic must not be an infallible adviser to his reader. He must not tell him what books are not worth reading, or what must be thought of them when read, but what he read in them. Wo to that coterie where some critic sits despotic, intrenched behind the infallible "We." Wo to that oracle who has infused such soft sleepiness, such a gentle dulness into his atmosphere, that when he opes his lips no dog will bark. It is this attempt at dictatorship in the reviewers, and the indolent acquiescence of their readers, that has brought them into disrepute. With such fairness did they make out their statements, with such dignity did they utter their verdicts, that the poor reader grew all too submissive. He learned his lesson with such docility, that the greater part of what will be said at any public or private meeting can be foretold by any one who has read the leading periodical works for twenty years. Scholars sneer at and would dispense with them altogether; and the public, grown lazy and helpless by this constant use of props and stays, can now scarce brace itself even to get through a magazine article, but reads in the daily paper laid beside the breakfast plate a short notice of the last number of the long established

and popular review, and thereupon passes its judgment and is content.

Then the partisan spirit of many of these journals has made it unsafe to rely upon them as guide-books and expurgatory indexes. They could not be content merely to stimulate and suggest thought, they have at last become powerless to supersede it.

From these causes and causes like these, the journals have lost much of their influence. There is a languid feeling about them, an inclination to suspect the justice of their verdicts, the value of their criticisms. But their golden age cannot be quite past. They afford too convenient a vehicle for the transmission of knowledge; they are too natural a feature of our time to have done all their work yet. Surely they may be redeemed from their abuses, they may be turned to their true uses. But how?

It were easy to say what they should *not* do. They should not have an object to carry or a cause to advocate, which obliges them either to reject all writings which wear the distinctive traits of individual life, or to file away what does not suit them, till the essay, made true to their design, is made false to the mind of the writer. An external consistency is thus produced, at the expense of all salient thought, all genuine emotion of life, in short, and living influences. Their purpose may be of value, but by such means was no valuable purpose ever furthered long. There are those, who have with the best intention pursued this system of trimming and adaptation, and thought it well and best to

"Deceive their country for their country's good."

But their country cannot be so governed. It misses the pure, the full tone of truth; it perceives that the voice is modulated to coax, to persuade, and it turns from the judicious man of the world, calculating the effect to be produced by each of his smooth sentences to some earnest voice which is uttering thoughts, crude, rash, ill-arranged it may be, but true to one human breast, and uttered in full faith, that the God of Truth will guide them aright.

And here, it seems to me, has been the greatest mistake in the conduct of these journals. A smooth monotony has been attained, an uniformity of tone, so that from the title of a journal you can infer the tenor of all its chapters. But nature is ever various, ever new, and so should be her daughters, art and literature. We do not want merely a polite response to what we thought before, but by the freshness of thought in other minds to have new thought awakened in our own. We do not want stores of information only, but to be roused to digest these into knowledge. Able and experienced men write for us, and we would know what they think, as they think it not for us but for themselves. We would live with them, rather than be taught by them how to live; we would catch the contagion of their mental activity, rather than have them direct us how to regulate our own. In books, in reviews, in the senate, in the pulpit, we wish to meet thinking men, not schoolmasters or pleaders. We wish that they should do full justice to their own view, but also that they should be frank with us, and, if now our superiors, treat us as if we might some time rise to be their equals. It is this true manliness, this firmness in his own position, and this power of appreciating the position of others, that alone can make the critic our companion and friend. We would converse with him, secure that he will tell us all his thought, and speak as man to man. But if he adapts his work to us, if he stifles what is distinctively his, if he shows himself either arrogant or mean, or, above all, if he wants faith in the healthy ac-

tion of free thought, and the safety of pure motive, we will not talk with him, for we cannot confide in him. We will go to the critic who trusts Genius and trusts us, who knows that all good writing must be spontaneous, and who will write out the bill of fare for the public as he read it for himself,—

"Forgetting vulgar rules, with spirit free
To judge each author by his own intent,
Nor think one standard for all minds is meant."

Such an one will not disturb us with personalities, with sectarian prejudices, or an undue vehemence in favor of petty plans or temporary objects. Neither will he disgust us by smooth obsequious flatteries and an inexpressive, lifeless gentleness. He will be free and make free from the mechanical and distorting influences we hear complained of on every side. He will teach us to love wisely what we before loved well, for he knows the difference between censoriousness and discernment, infatuation and reverence; and, while delighting in the genial melodies of Pan, can perceive, should Apollo bring his lyre into audience, that there may be strains more divine than those of his native groves.

[Frederic Henry Hedge]

"The Art of Life,–The Scholar's Calling," *Dial,* 1 (October 1840): 175-182.

Hedge's essay in the Dial's *second number addressed the idea of self-culture, what he called "the perfect unfolding of our individual nature." Self-culture, in both meanings of intellectual and spiritual development, was important to Unitarians and Transcendentalists alike: William Ellery Channing published a book on the subject and self-culture is now recognized as one of the major influences on Emerson's thought.*

Life is an art. When we consider what life may be to all, and what it is to most, we shall see how little this art is yet understood. What life may be to all is shown us in the lives of the honored few, whom we have learned to distinguish from the rest of mankind, and to worship as the heroes and saints of the world. What life is to most is seen wherever we turn our eyes. To all, life may be freedom, progress, success. To most men it is bondage, failure, defeat. Some have declared all life to be a tragedy. The life of most men is rightly so termed. What can be more tragical, than after long years of weary watching and ceaseless toil, in which all the joy and strength of our days have been wasted in pursuit of some distant good, to find, at last, that the good thus sought was a shadow, a sham, that the sum total of our endeavor, with no positive increase has left us *minus* our youth, our faculty, our hope, and that the three score years have been a live-long illusion. This is the great ground-tragedy, in which all other tragedies and sorrows and defeats of man's life are comprised. Such is the actual condition of mankind. Look at our educated men. Of the hundreds, whom every year sends forth to wander in the various paths of active life, how many are there who find or even seek the bread that alone can satisfy the hungering, dreaming heart of man? How many sell their strength and waste their days and "file their minds" for some paltry clerkship or judgeship or senatorship; or some phantom which they term a competence; or at the best some dream of Fame–"ingens gloriæ cupido quæ etiam sapientibus novissima exuitur"–and find, when the race is done and the heat is won, that they are no nearer than before the true end of their being, and that the great work of life is still to do.

The work of life, so far as the individual is concerned, and that to which the scholar is particularly called, is *self-culture,*–the perfect unfolding of our individual nature. To this end above all others the art, of which I speak, directs our attention and points our endeavor. There is no man, it is presumed, to whom this object is wholly indifferent,–who would not willingly possess this too, along with other prizes, provided the attainment of it were compatible with personal case and worldly good. But the business of self-culture admits of no compromise. Either it must be made a distinct aim or wholly abandoned.

"I respect the man," says Goethe, "who knows distinctly what he wishes. The greater part of all the mischief in the world arises from the fact, that men do not sufficiently understand their own aims. They have undertaken to build a tower, and spend no more labor on the foundation than would be necessary to erect a hut." Is not this an exact description of most men's strivings? Every man undertakes to build his tower and no one counts the cost. In all things the times are marked by a want of steady aim and patient industry. There is scheming and plotting in abundance, but no considerate, persevering effort. The young man launches into life with no definite course in view. If he goes into trade he has perhaps a general desire to be rich, but he has at the same time an equally strong desire for present gratification and luxurious living. He is unwilling to pay the price of his ambition. He endeavors to secure the present, and lets go the future. He turns seedtime into harvest, eats the corn which he ought to plant. If he goes into professional life, he sets out with a general desire to be eminent, but without considering in what particular he wishes to excel, and what is the price of that excellence. So he divides his time and talents among a great variety of pursuits; endeavoring to be all things, he becomes superficial in proportion as he is universal, and having acquired a brief reputation as worthless as it is short-lived, sinks down into hopeless insignificance.

Everything that man desires may be had for a price. The world is truer to us than we are to ourselves. In the great bargain of life no one is duped but by his own miscalculations, or baffled but by his own unstable will. If any man fail in the thing which he desires, it is because he is not true to himself, he has no sufficient inclination to the object in question. He is unwilling to pay the price which it costs.

Of self-culture, as of all other things worth seeking, the price is a single devotion to that object,—a devotion which shall exclude all aims and ends, that do not directly or indirectly tend to promote it. In this service let no man flatter himself with the hope of light work and ready wages. The work is hard and the wages are slow. Better pay in money or in fame may be found in any other path than in this. The only motive to engage in this work is its own inherent worth, and the sure satisfaction which accompanies the consciousness of progress, in the true direction towards the stature of a perfect man. Let him who would build this tower consider well the cost, whether in energy and endurance he have sufficient to finish it. Much, that he has been accustomed to consider as most desirable, he will have to renounce. Much, that other men esteem as highest and follow after as the grand reality, he will have to forego. No emoluments must seduce him from the rigor of his devotion. No engagements beyond the merest necessities of life must interfere with his pursuit. A meagre economy must be his income. "Spare fast that oft with gods doth diet" must be his fare. The rusty coat must be his badge. Obscurity must be his distinction. He must consent to see younger and smaller men take their places above him in Church and State. He must become a living sacrifice, and dare to lose his life in order that he may find it.

The scholar of these days has no encouragement from without. A cold and timid policy everywhere rebukes his aspirations. Everywhere "advice with scrupulous head" seeks to dehort and deter. Society has no rewards for him. Society rewards none but those who will do its work, which if the scholar undertake, he must straightway neglect his own. The business of society is not the advancement of the mind, but the care of the body. It is not the highest culture, but the greatest comfort. Accordingly, an endless multiplication of physical conveniences—an infinite economy has become the *cultus,* the worship of the age. Religion itself has been forced to minister in this service. No longer a divine life—an end in itself, it has become a mere instrument and condition of comfortable living, either in this earth or in some transmundane state. A more refined species of sensual enjoyment is the uttermost it holds out.

On all hands man's existence is converted into a preparation for existence. We do not properly live in these days, but, everywhere, with patent inventions and complex arrangements, are getting ready to live; like that King of Epirus, who was all his lifetime preparing to take his ease, but must first conquer the world. The end is lost in the means. Life is smothered in appliances. We cannot get to ourselves, there are so many external comforts to wade through. Consciousness stops half way. Reflection is dissipated in the circumstances of our environment. Goodness is exhausted in aids to goodness, and all the vigor and health of the soul is expended in quack contrivances to build it up. O! for some moral Alaric, one is tempted to exclaim, who should sweep away, with one fell swoop, all that has been in this kind,—all the manuals and false pretensions of modern culture, and place men once more on the eternal basis of original Nature. We are paying dearer than we imagine for our boasted improvements. The highest life,—the highest enjoyment, the point of which, after all our wanderings, we mean to land, is the life of the mind—the enjoyment of thought. Between this life and any point of outward existence, there is never but one step, and that step is an act of the will, which no aids from without can supercede or even facilitate. We travel round and round in a circle of facilities, and come at last to the point from which we set out. The mortal leap remains still to be made.

With these objects and tendencies the business of self-culture has nothing to do. Its objects are immediate and ultimate. Its aim is to live now, to live in the present, to live in the highest. The process here is one with the end. With such opposite views the scholar must expect nothing from Society, but may deem himself happy, if for the day-labor, which necessity imposes, Society will give him his hire, and beyond that leave him free to follow his proper calling, which he must either pursue with exclusive devotion, or wholly abandon. The more needful is it that he bring to the conflict the Prometheus spirit of endurance, which belongs of old to his work and line.

Besides this voluntary abstinence from temporal advantages and public affairs, the business of self-culture requires a renunciation of present notoriety, and a seclusion more or less rigorous from the public eye. The world is too much with us. We live out of doors. An all-present publicity attends our steps. Our life is in print. At every turn we are gazetted and shown up to ourselves. Society has become a chamber of mirrors, where our slightest movement is brought home to us with thousandfold reflections. The consequence is a morbid consciousness, a habit of living for effect, utterly incompatible with wholesome effort and an earnest mind. No heroic character, no depth of feeling, or clearness of insight can ever come of such a life. All that is best in human attainments springs from retirement. Whoso has conceived within himself any sublime and fruitful thought, or proposed to himself any great work or life, has been guided thereto by solitary musing. In the ruins of the capitol, Gibbon conceived his immortal "Rome." In a tavern on the banks of the Saale, Klopstock meditated his "Messiah.' In the privacy of Woolthorpe, Newton surmised the law which pervades the All. In the solitude of Erfurt, Luther received into his soul the new evangile of faith and freedom.

> "And if we would say true
> Much to the man is due
> Who from his private gardens, where
> He lived reserved and austere
> As if his highest plot
> To plant the bergamot
> Could by industrious valor climb
> To ruin the great work of time
> And cast the Kingdoms old
> Into another mould."

In retirement we first become acquainted with ourselves, our means, and ends. There no strange form interposes between us and the truth. No paltry vanity cheats us with false shows and aims. The film drops from our eyes. While we gaze the vision brightens; while we muse the fire burns. Retirement, too, is the parent of freedom. From living much among men we come to ape their views and faiths, and order our principles, our lives, as we do our coats, by the fashion of the times. Let him who aspires to popular favor and the suffrage of his contemporaries court the public eye. But whoso would perfect himself and bless the

world with any great work or example, must hide his young days in "some reclusive and religious life out of all eyes, tongues, minds, and injuries."

Whatever selfishness there may seem to be in such a discipline as this, exists only in appearance. The influence it would have upon Society would, in fact, be hardly less beneficial than its influence on the individual himself. In self-culture lies the ground and condition of all culture. Not those, who seem most earnest in promoting the culture of Society, do most effectually promote it. We have reformers in abundance, but few who, in the end, will be found to have aided essentially the cause of human improvement; either because they have failed to illustrate in themselves the benefits they wished to confer, and the lesson they wished to inculcate, or because there is a tendency in mankind to resist overt efforts to guide and control them. The silent influence of example, where no influence is intended, is the true reformer. The only efficient power, in the moral world, is attraction. Society is more benefitted by one sincere life, by seeing how one man has helped himself, than by all the projects that human policy has devised for their salvation. The Christian church–the mightiest influence the world has known–was the product of a great example.

Every period has its own wants, and different epochs require a different discipline. There are times when mankind is served by conformity; and there are times when a sterner discipline is required to revive the heroic spirit in a puny and servile age. When the Athenian mind, emasculated by the luxury which succeeded the Persian wars, and corrupted by the mischievous doctrines of the Sophists, had lost its fine sense of justice and truth; then arose, with austere front and wholesome defiance, the Cynics and the Stoics, whose fan was in their hands, and whose lives went deeper than Plato's words. That the present is a period when examples like these would not be unprofitable, no one, I think, can doubt, who has considered well its characteristic tendencies and wants–the want of courage, the want of faith, the hollowness of Church and State, the shallowness of teachers,

> "Whose lean and flashy songs
> Grate on their scrannel pipes of wretched straw,"

the hunger of the taught, who "look up and are not fed," and the frequent protest, which he who listens may hear from all the better spirits in the land. The time has come when good works are no longer of any avail. Book-teaching has become effete. No man teaches with authority. All are eager to speak, none are willing to hear. What the age requires is not books, but example, high, heroic example; not words but deeds; not societies but men,–men who shall have their root in themselves, and attract and convert the world by the beauty of their fruits. All truth must be lived before it can be adequately known or taught. Men are anterior to systems. Great doctrines are not the origin but the product, of great lives. The Cynic practice must precede the Stoic philosophy, and out of Diogenes's tub came forth in the end the wisdom of Epictetus, the eloquence of Seneca, and the piety of Antonine.

On this ground I am disposed to rejoice in those radical movements, which are everywhere springing up in the discontented spirits and misguided efforts of modern reform. Perfectionism, Grahamism, Nonresistance, and all the forms of ultraism, blind and headlong as they seem, have yet a meaning which, if it cannot command assent, must at least preclude contempt. They are the gropings of men who have waked too soon, while the rest of mankind are yet wrapt in sleep, and the new day still tarries in the East. The philosopher sees through these efforts, and knows that they are not the light that is to come; but he feels that they are sent to bear witness of the light, and hails them as the welcome tokens of approaching day. However our reason may disallow, however our taste may reject them, the thoughtful mind will perceive there the symptoms of a vitality which appears nowhere else. They are the life, however spasmodic, of this generation. There, or nowhere, beats the heart of the century. Thus the new in Church and State is always preceded by a cynical, radical spirit, which wages war with the old. Every genuine reform has its preacher in the wilderness. First the Cynic John with hair cloth and fasts, then the God-man Jesus with the bread of life.

Meanwhile the scholar has his function, too, in this baptism of repentance. For him, too, the age has its problem and its task. What other reformers are to the moral culture, he must be to the mind of his age. By taste averse, by calling exempt, from the practical movements around him, to him is committed the movement of thought. He must be a radical in speculation, an ascetic in devotion, a Cynic in independence, an anchorite in his habits, a perfectionist in discipline. Secluded from without, and nourished from within, self-sustained and self-sufficing, careless of praise or blame, intent always on the highest, he must rebuke the superficial attainments, the hollow pretensions, the feeble efforts, and trivial productions, of his contemporaries, with the thoroughness of his acquisitions, the reach of his views, the grandeur of his aims, the earnestness of his endeavor.

It is to such efforts and to such men that we must look for the long expected literature of this nation. Hitherto our literature has been but an echo of other voices and climes. Generally, in the history of nations, song has preceded science, and the feeling of a people has been sooner developed than its understanding. With us this order has been reversed. The national understanding is fully ripe, but the feeling, the imagination of the people, has found as yet no adequate expression. We have our men of science, our Franklins, our Bowditches, our Cleavelands; we have our orators our statesmen; but the American poet, the American thinker is yet to come. A deeper culture must lay the foundation for him, who shall worthily represent the genius and utter the life of this continent. A severer discipline must prepare the way for our Dantes, our Shakespeares, our Miltons. "He who would write an epic," said one of these, "must make his life an epic." This touches our infirmity. We have no practical poets,–no epic lives. Let us but have sincere livers, earnest, whole-hearted, heroic men, and we shall not want for writers and for literary fame. Then shall we see springing up, in every part of these Republics, a literature, such as the ages have not known,–a literature, commensurate with our idea, vast as our destiny and varied as our clime.

[Ralph Waldo] E[merson].
"New Poetry," *Dial,* 1 (October 1840): 220-232.

Emerson's comments on the poetry of William Ellery Channing II offer an excellent view of the non-traditional poetic theory espoused by the Transcendentalists. Here, Emerson argued for "Verses of the Portfolio," which, "not being written for publication," lacked "that finish which the conventions of literature require of authors." Supporters rejoiced in being freed from the old forms; detractors complained that Emerson was granting too much license for all sorts of what the Boston Daily Advertiser *called "a flood of crude versification" because of Emerson's notion that— as the* Advertiser *phrased it—"the failures of genius are better than victories of talent." (For further information, see the entry for Channing in* DLB 1, The American Renaissance in New England.)

The tendencies of the times are so democratical, that we shall soon have not so much as a pulpit or raised platform in any church or townhouse, but each person, who is moved to address any public assembly, will speak from the floor. The like revolution in literature is now giving importance to the portfolio over the book, but one in ten or one in five may inscribe his thoughts, or at least with short commentary his favorite readings in a private journal. The philosophy of the day has long since broached a more liberal doctrine of the poetic faculty than our fathers held, and reckons poetry the right and power of every man to whose culture justice is done. We own that, though we were trained in a stricter school of literary faith, and were in all our youth inclined to the enforcement of the straitest restrictions on the admission of candidates to the Parnassian fraternity, and denied the name of poetry to every composition in which the workmanship and the material were not equally excellent, in our middle age we have grown lax, and have learned to find pleasure in verses of a ruder strain,–to enjoy *verses of society,* or those effusions which in persons of a happy nature are the easy and unpremeditated translation of their thoughts and feelings into rhyme. This new taste for a certain private and household poetry for somewhat less pretending than the festal and solemn verses which are written for the nations really indicates, we suppose, that a new style of poetry exists. The number of writers has increased. Every child has been taught the tongues. The universal communication of the arts of reading and writing has brought the works of the great poets into every house, and made all ears familiar with the poetic forms. The progress of popular institutions has favored self-respect, and broken down that terror of the great, which once imposed awe and hesitation on the talent of the masses of society. A wider epistolary intercourse ministers to the ends of sentiment and reflection than ever existed before; the practice of writing diaries is becoming almost general; and every day witnesses new attempts to throw into verse the experiences of private life.

What better omen of true progress can we ask than an increasing intellectual and moral interest of men in each other? What can be better for the republic than that the Capitol, the White House, and the Court House are becoming of less importance than the farmhouse and the book-closet? If we are losing our interest in public men, and finding that their spell lay in number and size only, and acquiring instead a taste for the depths of thought and emotion as they may be sounded in the soul of the citizen or the countryman, does it not replace man for the state, and character for official power? Men should be treated with solemnity; and when they come to chant their private griefs and doubts and joys, they have a new scale by which to compute magnitude and relation. Art is the noblest consolation of calamity. The poet is compensated for his defects in the street and in society, if in his chamber he has turned his mischance into noble numbers. Is there not room then for a new department in poetry, namely, *Verses of the Portfolio?* We have fancied that we drew greater pleasure from some manuscript

Photograph of Ellery Channing in old age

every man's and woman's diary flying into the bookstores, yet it is to be considered, on the other hand, that men of genius are often more incapable than others of that elaborate execution which criticism exacts. Men of genius in general are, more than others, incapable of any perfect exhibition, because however agreeable it may be to them to act on the public, it is always a secondary aim. They are humble, self-accusing, moody men, whose worship is toward the Ideal Beauty, which chooses to be courted not so often in perfect hymns, as in wild ear-piercing ejaculations, or in silent musings. Their face is forward, and their heart is in this heaven. By so much are they disqualified for a perfect success in any particular performance to which they can give only a divided affection. But the man of talents has every advantage in the competition. He can give that cool and commanding attention to the thing to be done, that shall secure its just performance. Yet are the failures of genius better than the victories of talent; and we are sure that some crude manuscript poems have yielded us a more sustaining and a more stimulating diet, than many elaborated and classic productions.

We have been led to these thoughts by reading some verses, which were lately put into our hands by a friend with the remark, that they were the production of a youth, who had long passed out of the mood in which he wrote them, so that they had become quite dead to him. Our first feeling on reading them was a lively joy. So then the Muse is neither dead nor dumb, but has found a voice in these cold Cisatlantic States. Here is poetry which asks no aid of magnitude or number, of blood or crime, but finds theatre enough in the first field or brookside, breadth and depth enough in the flow of its own thought. Here is self-repose, which to our mind is stabler than the Pyramids; here is self-respect which leads a man to date from his heart more proudly than from Rome. Here is love which sees through surface, and adores the gentle nature and not the costume. Here is religion, which is not of the Church of England, nor of the Church of Boston. Here is the good wise heart, which sees that the end of culture is strength and cheerfulness. In an age too which tends with so strong an inclination to the philosophical muse, here is poetry more purely intellectual than any American verses we have yet seen, distinguished from all competition by two merits; the fineness of perception; and the poet's trust in his own grains to that degree, that there is an absence of all con-

verses than from printed ones of equal talent. For there was herein the charm of character; they were confessions; and the faults, the imperfect parts, the fragmentary verses, the halting rhymes, had a worth beyond that of a high finish; for they testified that the writer was more man than artist, more earnest than vain; that the thought was too sweet and sacred to him, than that he should suffer his ears to hear or his eyes to see a superficial defect in the expression.

The characteristic of such verses is, that being not written for publication, they lack that finish which the conventions of literature require of authors. But if poetry of this kind has merit, we conceive that the prescription which demands a rhythmical polish may be easily set aside; and when a writer has outgrown the state of thought which produced the poem, the interest of letters is served by publishing it imperfect, as we preserve studies, torsos, and blocked statues of the great masters. For though we should be loath to see the wholesome conventions, to which we have alluded, broken down by a general incontinence of publication, and

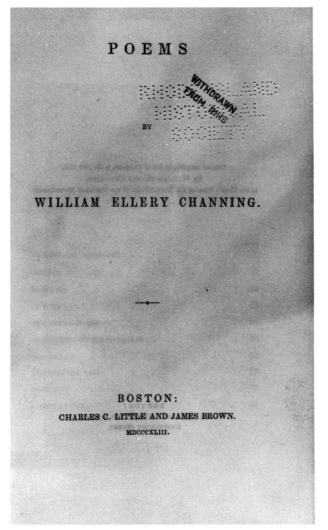

Title page for Ellery Channing's first book, for which Emerson helped to arrange publication

ventional imagery, and a bold use of that which the moment's mood had made sacred to him, quite careless that it might be sacred to no other, and might even be slightly ludicrous to the first reader.

We proceed to give our readers some selections, taken without much order from this rich pile of manuscript. We first find the poet in his boat.

BOAT SONG.

THE RIVER calmly flows,
  Through shining banks, through lonely glen,
Where the owl shrieks, though ne'er the cheer of men
    Has stirred its mute repose,
Still if you should walk there, you would go there again.

The stream is well alive;

Another passive world you see,
Where downward grows the form of every tree;
    Like soft light clouds they thrive;
Like them let us in our pure loves reflected be.

    A yellow gleam is thrown
  Into the secrets of that maze
Of tangled trees, which late shut out our gaze,
    Refusing to be known;
It must its privacy unclose,–its glories blaze.

    Sweet falls the summer air
  Over her frame who sails with me:
Her way like that is beautifully free,
    Her nature far more rare,
And is her constant heart of virgin purity.

    A quivering star is seen
  Keeping his watch above the hill,
Though from the sun's retreat small light is still
    Poured on earth's saddening mien:–
We all are tranquilly obeying Evening's will.

    Thus ever love the POWER;
  To simplest thought dispose the mind;
In each obscure event a worship find
    Like that of this dim hour,–
In lights, and airs, and trees, and in all human kind.

    We smoothly glide below
  The faintly glimmering worlds of light:
Day has a charm, and this deceptive night
    Brings a mysterious show;–
He shadows our dear earth,–but his cool stars are white.

Is there any boat song like this? any in which the harmony proceeds so manifestly from the poet's mind, giving to nature more than it receives? In the following stanzas the writer betrays a certain habitual worship of genius, which characterizes many pieces in the collection, breaking out sometimes into very abrupt expression.

OCTOBER.

DRY leaves with yellow ferns,–they are
Fit wreath of Autumn, while a star
Still, bright, and pure, our frosty air
    Shivers in twinkling points
    Of thin celestial hair,
And thus one side of heaven anoints.

I am beneath the moon's calm look
Most quiet in this sheltered nook
From trouble of the frosty wind
    Which curls the yellow blade;
    Though in my covered mind
A grateful sense of change is made.

To wandering men how dear this sight
Of a cold tranquil autumn night,
In its majestic deep repose;
    Thus will their genius be
    Not buried in high snows,
Though of as mute tranquility.

An anxious life they will not pass,
Nor, as the shadow on the grass,
Leave no impression there to stay;
    To them all things are thought;
    The blushing morn's decay,–
Our death, our life, by this is taught.

O find in every haze that shines,
A brief appearance without lines,
A single word,–no finite joy;
    For present is a Power
    Which we may not annoy,
Yet have him stronger every hour.

I would not put this sense from me,
If I could some great sovereign be;
Yet will not task a fellow man
    To feel the same glad sense.
    For no one living can
Feel–save his given influence.

WILLINGNESS.

An unendeavoring flower,–how still
Its growth from morn to eventime;
Nor signs of hasty anger fill
Its tender form from birth to prime
    Of happy will.

And some, who think these simple things
Can hear no goodness to their minds,
May learn to feel how nature brings,
Around a quiet being winds,
    And through us sings.

A stream to some is no delight,
Its element diffused around;
Yet in its unobtrusive flight
There trembles from its heart a sound
    Like that of night.

So give thy true allotment,–fair;
To children turn a social heart;
And if thy days pass clear as air,
Or friends from thy beseeching part,
    O humbly bear.

SONNETS.

I.

    The brook is eddying in the forest dell,
All full of untaught merriment,–the joy
Of breathing life is this green wood's employ.
The wind is feeling through his gentle bell;–
I and my flowers receive this music well.
Why will not man his natural life enjoy?
Can he then with his ample spirit toy?
Are human thoughts as wares now baked to sell?
All up, all round, all down, a thrilling deep,
A holy infinite salutes the sense,
And incommunicable praises leap,
Shooting the entire soul with love intense,
Throughout the All,–and can a man live on to weep?

II.

There never lived a man who with a heart
Resolved, bound up, concentred in the good,
However low or high in rank he stood,
But when from him yourself had chanced to start,
You felt how goodness alway maketh art;
And that an ever venerable mood
Of sanctity, like the deep worship of a wood,
Of its unconsciousness turns you a part.
Let us live amply in the joyous All;
We surely were not meant to ride the sea,
Skimming the wave in that so prisoned Small,
Reposing our infinite faculties utterly.
Boom like a roaring sunlit waterfall,
Humming to infinite abysms;–speak loud, speak free.

III.

Hearts of eternity,–hearts of the deep!
Proclaim from land to sky your mighty fate;
How that for you no living comes too late;
How ye cannot in Theban labyrinth creep;
How ye great harvests from small surface reap;
Shout, excellent band, in grand primeval strain,
Like midnight winds that foam along the main,
And do all things rather than pause to weep.
A human heart knows naught of littleness,
Suspects no man, compares with no man's ways,
Hath in one hour most glorious length of days,
A recompense, a joy, a loveliness,
Like eaglet keen, shoots into azure far,
And always dwelling nigh is the remotest star.

Manuscript poem by Ellery Channing (Autograph Leaves of Our Country's Authors, *edited by John Pendleton Kennedy and Alexander Bliss [1864]*)

LINES

WRITTEN IN THE EVENING OF A NOVEMBER DAY.

THEE, mild autumnal day,
I felt not for myself; the winds may steal
From any point, and seem to me alike
Reviving, soothing powers.

Like thee the contrast is
Of a new mood in a decaying man,
Whose idle mind is suddenly revived
With many pleasant thoughts.

Our earth was gratified;
Fresh grass, a stranger in this frosty time,
Peeped from the crumbling mould as welcome as
An unexpected friend.

How glowed the evening star,
As it delights to glow in summer's midst,
When not of ruddy boughs the twilight birds
Sing flowing harmony.

Peace was the will to-day,
Love in bewildering growth our joyous minds
Swelled to their widest bounds; the worldly left
All hearts to sympathize.

I felt for thee,—for thee,
Whose inward, outward life completely moves,
Surrendered to the beauty of the soul
Of this creative day.

OUR BIRTH DAYS.

I.

THESE are the solemnest days of our bright lives,
When memory and hope within exert
Delightful reign; when sympathy revives,
And that, which late was in the soul inert,
Grows warm and living, and to us alone
Are these a knowledge; nowise may they hurt,
Or cry aloud, or frightens out the tour,
Which we will strive to wear and as calm nature own.

II.

Whatever seemes our eyes once gratified,—
Those landscapes couched around our early homes,

[151]

To which our tender, peaceful heart replied,
To those our present happy feeling roams,
And takes a mightier joy than from the tomes
Of the pure scholar; those ten thousand sights
Of contrast nature flow in us, as foams
The bubbling spring; these are the true delights
Wherewith this solemn world the sorrowful requites.

These are proper Manuscript inspirations, honest, great, but crude. They have never been filed or decorated for the eye that studies surface. The writer was not afraid to write ill; he had a great meaning too much at heart to stand for trifles, and wrote lordly for his peers alone. This is the poetry of hope. Here is no French correctness, but Hans Sachs and Chaucer rather. But the minstrel can be sweet and tender also. We select from the sheaf one leaf, for which we predict a more general popularity.

A POET'S LOVE.

I CAN remember well
My very early youth,
My sumptuous Isabel,
Who was a girl of truth,
Of golden truth;–we do not often see
Those whose whole lives have only known to be.

So sunlight, very warm,
On harvest fields and trees,
Could not more sweetly form
Rejoicing melodies
For these deep things, than Isabel for me;
I lay beneath her soul as a lit tree.

That cottage where she dwelt
Was all o'er mosses green;
I still forever felt
How nothing stands between
The soul and truth; why, starving poverty

Was nothing–nothing, Isabel, to thee.

Grass beneath her faint tread
Bent pleasantly away;
From her ne'er small birds fled,
But kept at their bright play,
Not fearing her; it was her endless motion,
Just a true swell upon a summer ocean.

Those who conveyed her home,–
I mean who led her where
The spirit does not roam,–
Had such small weight to bear,

They scarcely felt; how softly was thy knell
Rung for thee that soft day, girl Isabel.

I am no more below,
My life is raised on high;
My phantasy was slow
Ere Isabel could die;
It pressed me down; but now I sail away
Into the regions of exceeding day.

And Isabel and I
Float on the red brown clouds,
That amply multiply
The very constant crowds
Of serene shapes. Play on Mortality!
Thy happiest hour is that when thou may'st die.

The second of the two following verses is of such extreme beauty, that we do not remember anything more perfect in its kind. Had the poet been looking over a book of Raffaelle's drawings, or perchance the villas and temples of Palladio, with the maiden to whom it was addressed?

TO ****.

My mind obeys the power
That through all persons breathes;
And woods are murmuring,
And fields begin to sing,
And in me nature wreathes.

Thou too art with me here,–
The best of all design;–
Of that strong purity,
Which makes it joy to be
A distant thought of thine.

But here are verses in another vein–plain, ethical, human, such as in ancient lands legislators carved on stone tablets and monuments at the roadside, or in the precincts of temples. They remind us of the austere strain in which Milton celebrates the Hebrew prophets.

"In them is plainest taught and easiest learned
What makes a nation happy and keeps so."

I.

THE Bible is a book worthy to read;
The life of those great Prophets was the life we need,
From all delusive seeming ever freed.

Be not afraid to utter what thou art;

'Tis no disgrace to keep an open heart;
A soul free, frank, and loving friends to aid,
Not even does this harm a gentle maid.

Strive as thou canst, thou wilt not value o'er
Thy life. Thou standest on a lighted shore,
And from the waves of an unfathomed sea,
The noblest impulses flow tenderly to thee;
Feel them as they arise, and take them free.

> Better live unknown,
> No heart but thy own
> Beating ever near,
> To no mortal dear
> In thy hemisphere,
> Poor and wanting bread,
> Steeped in poverty,
> Than to be a dread.
> Than to be afraid,
> From thyself to flee;
> For it is not living,
> To a soul believing,
> To change each noble joy
> Which our strength employs,
> For a state half rotten
> And a life of toys.
> Better be forgotten
> Than lose equipoise.

How shall I live? In earnestness.
What shall I do? Work earnestly.
What shall I give? A willingness.
What shall I gain? Tranquillity.
But do you mean a quietness
In which I set and no man bless?
Flash out in action infinite and free,
Action conjoined with deep tranquillity,
Resting upon the soul's true utterance,
And life shall flow as merry as a dance.

II.

Life is too good to waste, enough to prize;
Keep looking round with clear unhooded eyes;
Love all thy brothers, and for them endure
Many privations; the reward is sure.

A little thing! There is no little thing;
Through all a joyful song is murmuring;
Each leaf, each stem, each sound in winter drear
Has deepest meanings for an anxious ear.

Thou seest life is sad; the father mourns his wife and child;
Keep in the midst of heavy sorrows a fair aspect mild.

A howling fox, a shrieking owl,
A violent distracting Ghoul,

Forms of the most infuriate madness,–
These may not move thy heart to gladness,
But look within the dark outside,
Nought shalt thou hate and nought deride.

Thou meet'st a common man
With a delusive show of *can*.
His acts are petty forgeries of natural greatness,
That show a dreadful lateness
Of this life's mighty impulses; a want of truthful earnest-
ness;
He seems, not does, and in that shows
No true nobility,–
A poor ductility,
That no proper office knows,
Not even estimation small of human woes.

Be not afraid,
His understanding aid
With thy own pure content,
On highest purpose bent.

Leave him not lonely,
For that his admiration
Fastens on self and seeming only;
Make a right dedication
Of all thy strength to keep
From swelling that so ample heap
Of lives abused, of virtue given for nought,
And thus it shall appear for all in nature hast thou wrought.
If thou unconsciously perform what's good,
Like nature's self thy proper mood.

A life well spent is like a flower,
That had bright sunshine its brief hour;
It flourished in pure willingness;
Discovered strongest earnestness;
Was fragrant for each lightest wind;
Was of its own particular kind;–
Nor knew a tone of discord sharp;
Breathed alway like a silver harp;
And went to immortality
A very proper thing to die.

We will close our extracts from this rare file of blot-
ted paper with a lighter strain, which, whilst it shows
how gaily a poet can chide, gives us a new insight into
his character and habits.

TORMENTS.

YES! they torment me
Most exceedingly;–
I would I could flee.
A breeze on a river–
I listen forever;

The yellowish heather
Under cool weather,–
These are pleasures to me.

What do torment me?
Those living vacantly,
Who live but to see;
Indefinite action,
Nothing but motion,
Round stones a rolling,
No inward controlling;–
Yes! they torment me.

Some cry all the time,
Even in their prime
Of youth's flushing clime.
O! and on this sorrow!
Fear'st thou to-morrow?
Set thy legs going,
Be stamping, be rowing,–

This of life is the lime.

Hail, thou mother Earth!
Who gave me thy worth
For my portion at birth:
I walk in thy azure,
Unfond of erasure,
But they who torment me
So most exceedingly
Sit with feet on the hearth.

We have more pages from the same hand lying before us, marked by the same purity and tenderness and early wisdom as these we have quoted, but we shall close our extracts here. May the right hand that has so written never lose its cunning! may this voice of love and harmony teach its songs to the too long silent echoes of the Western Forest.

A. Bronson Alcott

"Orphic Sayings," *Dial*, 1 (January 1841): 351-361.

Alcott's "Orphic Sayings" brought down more ridicule upon the Dial *and Transcendentalism than any other single publication by the group. Alcott's unusual style bothered reviewers, as did his lack of clarity. The sayings were called "neither natural not intellectual philosophy" and the "quintesence of folly and extravagance–affected, mystical, bombastic–and, in some instances, puerile" by reviewers, who delighted in writing parodies of them over the next few years. Even Alcott called his writing "ridiculed by the general Press."*

LI. REFORM.

The trump of reform is sounding throughout the world for a revolution of all human affairs. This issue we cannot doubt; yet the cries are not without alarm. Already is the axe laid at the root of that spreading tree, whose trunk is idolatry, whose branches are covetousness, war, and slavery, whose blossom is concupiscence, whose fruit is hate. Planned by Beelzebub, it shall be rooted up. Abaddon is pouring his vail on the earth.

LII. REFORMERS.

Reformers are metallic; they are sharpest steel; they pierce whatsoever of evil or abuse they touch. Their souls are attempered in the fires of heaven; they are nailed in the might of principles, and God backs their purpose. They uproot institutions, erase traditions, revise usages, and renovate all things. They are the noblest of facts. Extant in time, they work for eternity; dwelling with men, they are with God.

LIII. ARMS.

Three qualities are essential to the reformer,–insight, veneration, valor. These are the arms with which he takes the world. He who wields these divinely shall make an encroachment upon his own age, and the centuries shall capitulate to him at last. To all else, are institutions, men, ages, invulnerable.

LIV. HERESY.

The reformer substitutes things for words, laws for usage, ideas for idols. But this is ever a deed, daring and damned, for which the culprit was aforetime cropped, exiled, or slain. In our time, his sentence is commuted to slight and starvation.

LV. SIMPLICITY.

The words of a just man are mirrors in which the felon beholds his own features, and shrinks from the portrait painted therein by the speaker. Beware of a just man, he is a limner of souls; he draws in the colors of truth. Cunning durst not sit to him.

LVI. PERSON.

Divinely speaking, God is the only person. The personality of man is partial, derivative; not perfect, not original. He becomes more personal as he partakes more largely of divinity. Holiness embosoms him in the Godhead, and makes him one with Deity.

LVII. PORTRAITS.

We are what we seek; desire, appetite, passion, draw our features, and show us whether we are gods or men, devils or beasts. Always is the soul portraying herself; the statue of our character is hewn from her affections and thoughts.–Wisdom is the soul in picture; holiness in sculpture.

[155]

LVIII. PERSONALITY.

Truth is most potent when she speaks in general and impersonal terms. Then she rebukes everybody, and all confess before her words. She draws her bow, and lets fly her arrows at broad venture into the ages, to pierce all evils and abuses at heart. She wounds persons through principles, on whose phylactery, "thou art the man," is ever written to the eye of all men.

LIX. POPULARITY.

The saints are alone popular in heaven, not on earth; elect of God, they are spurned by the world. They hate their age, its applause, its awards, their own affections even, save as these unite them with justice, with valor, with God. Whoso loves father or mother, wife or child, houses or lands, pleasures or honors, or life, more than these, is an idolater, and worships idols of sense; his life is death; his love hate; his friends foes; his fame infamy.

LX. FAME.

Enduring fame is ever posthumous. The orbs of virtue and genius seldom culminate during their terrestrial periods. Slow is the growth of great names, slow the procession of excellence into arts. institutions, life. Ages alone reflect their fulness of lustre. The great not only unseal, but create the organs by which they are to be seen. Neither Socrates nor Jesus is yet visible to the world.

LXI. TEMPTATION.

The man of sublime gifts has his temptation amidst the solitudes to which he is driven by his age as proof of his integrity. Yet nobly he withstands this trial, conquering both Satan and the world by overcoming himself. He bows not down before the idols of time, but is constant to the divine ideal that haunts his heart,—a spirit of serene and perpetual peace.

LXII. LIGHT.

Oblivion of the world is knowledge of heaven,—of sin, holiness,—of time, eternity. The world, sin, time, are interpolations into the authentic scripture of the soul, de-

Bronson Alcott at the Concord School of Philosophy, c. 1880

noting her lapse from God, innocence, heaven. Of these the child and God are alike ignorant. They have not fallen from their estate of divine intuition, into the dark domain of sense, wherein all is but shadowy reminiscence of substance and light, of innocence and clarity. Their life is above memory and hope,—a life, not of knowledge, but of sight.

LXIII. PROBITY.

The upright man holds fast his integrity amidst all reverses. Exiled by his principles from the world, a solitary amidst his age, he stands aloof from the busy haunts and low toils of his race. Amidst the general sterility he ripens for God. He is above the gauds and baits of sense. His taskmaster is in heaven; his field eternity; his wages peace. Away from him are all golden trophies, fames, honors, soft flatteries, comforts, homes, and couches in time. He lives in the smile of God; nor fears the frowns, nor courts the favor of men. With him the mint of immortal honor is not in the thronged market, but in the courts of the heart, whose awards bear not devices of applauding hosts, but of reviling soldiery,–of stakes and gibbets,–and are the guerdon not of the trial imposed, but of the valor that overcame it.

LXIV. SOPHISTRY.

Always are the ages infested with dealers in stolen treasures. Church, state, school, traffic largely in such contraband wares, and would send genius and probity, as of old, Socrates and Jesus, into the markets and thoroughfares, to higgle with publicans and sophists for their own properties. But yet the wit and will of these same vagrants is not only coin, but stock in trade for all the business of the world. Mammon counterfeits the scripture of God, and his partners, the church, the state, the school, share the profit of his peculations on mankind.

LXV. BREAD.

Fools and blind! not bread, but the lack of it is God's high argument. Wouldst enter into life? Beg bread then. In the kingdom of God are love and bread consociated, but in the realm of mammon, bread sojourns with lies, and truth is a starvling. Yet praised be God, he has bread in his exile which mammon knows not of.

LXVI. LABOR.

Labor is sweet; nor is that a stern decree that sends man into the fields to earn his bread in the sweat of his face. Labor is primeval; it replaces man in Eden,–the garden planted by God. It exalts and humanizes the soul. Life in all its functions and relations then breathes of groves and fountains, of simplicity and health. Man discourses sublimely with the divinities over the plough, the spade, the sickle, marrying the soul and the soil by the rites of labor. Sloth is the tempter that beguiles him of innocence, and exiles him from Paradise. Let none esteem himself beloved of the divine Husbandman, unless he earn the wages of peace in his vineyard. Yet now the broad world is full of idlers; the fields are barren; the age is hungry; there is no corn. The harvests are of tares and not of wheat. Gaunt is

the age; even as the seedsman winnows the chaff from the wheat, shall the winds of reform blow this vanity away.

LXVII. DIABOLUS.

Seek God in the seclusion of your own soul; the prince of devils in the midst of multitudes. Beelzebub rules masses, God individuals. *Vox populi vox dei,*–never, (save where passion and interest are silent,) but *vox populi vox diaboli.*

LXVIII. DOGMATISM.

The ages dogmatize, and would stifle the freest and boldest thought. Their language is,–our possessions skirt space, and we veto all possible discoveries of time. We are heirs of all wisdom, all excellence; none shall pass our confines; vain is the dream of a wilderness of thought to be vanquished by rebellion against us; we inherit the patrimony of God,–all goods in the gift of omnipotence.

LXIX. GENIUS AND SANCTITY.

A man's period is according to the directness and intensity of his light. Not erudition, not taste, not intellect, but character, describes his orbit and determines the worlds he shall enlighten. Genius and sanctity cast no shadow; like the sun at broad noon, the ray of these orbs pours direct intense on the world, and they are seen in their own light.

LXX. CHARACTER.

Character is the genius of conscience, as wit is of intellect. The prophet and bard are original men, and their lives and works being creations of divine art, are inimitable. Imitation and example are sepulchres in which the ages entomb their disciples. The followers of God are alone immortal.

LXXI. LIFE.
It is life, not scripture; character, not biography, that renovates mankind. The letter of life vitiates its spirit. Virtue and genius refuse to be written. The scribe weaves his own mythus of superstition always into his scripture.

The Alcotts' Orchard House with the Concord School of Philosophy at left

LXXII. BARRENNESS.

Opinions are life in foliage; deeds, in fruitage. Always is the fruitless tree accursed.

LXXIII. SCRIPTURE.

All scripture is the record of life, and is sacred or profane, as the life it records is holy or vile. Every noble life is a revelation from heaven, which the joy and hope of mankind preserve to the world. Not while the soul endures, shall the book of revelation be sealed. Her scriptures, like herself, are inexhaustible, without beginning or end.

LXXIV. SACRED BOOKS.

The current version of all sacred books is profane. The ignorance and passions of men interpolate themselves into the text, and vitiate both its doctrine and ethics. But this is revised, at successive eras, by prophets, who, holding direct communication with the source of life and truth, translate their eternal propositions from the sacred into the common speech of man, and thus give the word anew to the world.

LXXV. RESURRECTION.

A man must live his life to apprehend it. There have been few living men and hence few lives; most have lived their death. Men have no faith in life. There goes indeed a rumour through the ages concerning it, but the few, who affirm knowledge of the fact, are slain always to verify the popular doubt. Men assert, not the resurrection of the soul from the body, but of the body from the grave, as a revelation of life. Faithless and blind! the body is the grave; let the dead arise from these sepulchres of concupiscence, and know by experience that life is immortal. Only the living know that they live; the dead know only of death.

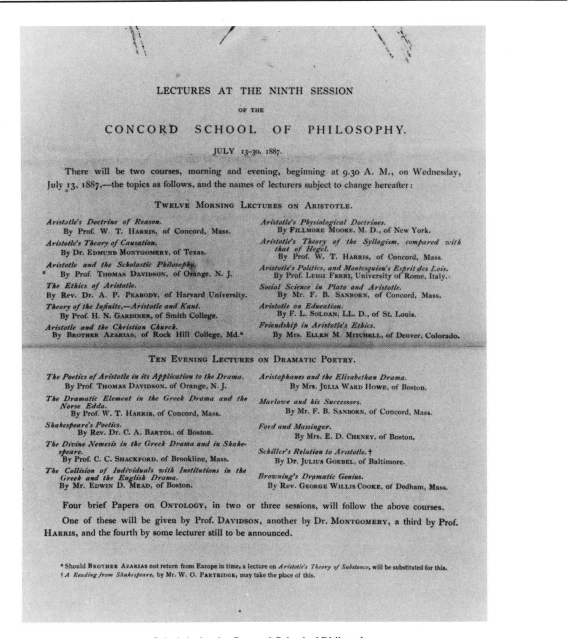

Schedule for the Concord School of Philosophy

LXXVI. MIRACLES.

To apprehend a miracle, a man must first have wrought it. He knows only what he has lived, and interprets all facts in the light of his experience. Miracles are spiritual experiences, not feats of legerdemain, not freaks of nature. It is the spiritual sight that discerns whatsoever is painted to sense. Flesh is faithless and blind.

LXXVII. FACT AND FABLE.

Facts, reported, are always false. Only sanctity and gen-

ius are eyewitnesses of the same; and their intuition, yet not their scriptures, are alone authentic. Not only all scripture, but all thought is fabulous. Life is the only pure fact, and this cannot be written to sense; it must be lived, and thus expurgate all scriptures.

LXXVIII. REVELATION.

Revelation is mediate or immediate; speculative or intuitive. It is addressed to conscience or reason,–to sight or sense. Reason receives the light through mediums and mediators; conscience direct from its source. The light of one is opake; of the other, clear. The prophet, whose eye is coincident with the celestial ray, receives this into his breast, and intensifying there, it kindles on his brow a serene and perpetual day. But the worldling, with face averted from God, reflects divinity through the obscure twilight of his own brain, and remains in the blindness of his own darkness, a deceptive meteor of the night.

LXXIX. PROPHET.

The prophet appeals direct to the heart. He addresses the divine in the breast. His influence is subtile; the reverence he inspires occult. His words are winged with marvels; his deeds mysteries; his life a miracle. Piety kneels at the shrine of his genius, and reads his mystic scriptures, as oracles of the divinity in the breasts of all men.

LXXX. TEACHER.

The true teacher defends his pupils against his own personal influence. He inspires self-trust. He guides their eyes from himself to the spirit that quickens him. He will have no disciples. A noble artist, he has visions of excellence and revelations of beauty, which he has neither impersonated in character, nor embodied in words. His life and teachings are but studies for yet nobler ideals.

LXXXI. EXPERIENCE.

A man's idea of God corresponds to his ideal of himself. The nobler he is, the more exalted his God. His own culture and discipline are a revelation of divinity. He apprehends the divine character as he comprehends his own. Humanity is the glass of divinity; experience of the soul is a revelation of God.

LXXXII. OBEDIENCE.

Obedience is the mediator of the soul. It is the organ of immediate inspiration; the hierophant of the Godhead. It is the method of revelation; the law of all culture.

LXXXIII. RETRIBUTION.

The laws of the soul and of nature are forecast and preordained in the spirit of God, and are ever executing themselves through conscience in man, and gravity in things. Man's body and the world are organs, through which the retributions of the spiritual universe are justified to reason and sense. Disease and misfortune are memoranda of violations of the divine law, written in the letter of pain and evil.

LXXXIV. WORSHIP.

The ritual of the soul is preordained in her relations to God, man, nature, herself. Life, with its varied duties, is her ordained worship; labor and meditation her sacraments. Whatsoever violates this order is idolatry and sacrilege. A holy spirit, she hallows all times, places, services; and perpetually she consecrates her temples, and ministers at the altars of her divinity. Her censer flames always toward heaven, and the spirit of God descends to kindle her devotions.

LXXXV. BAPTISM.

Except a man be born of water and of spirit, he cannot apprehend eternal life. Sobriety is clarity; sanctity is sight. John baptizes Jesus. Repent, abstain, resolve;– thus purify yourself in this laver of regeneration, and become a denizen of the kingdom of God.

LXXXVI. CARNAGE.

Conceive of slaughter and flesh-eating in Eden.

LXXXVII. TRADITION.

Tradition suckles the young ages, who imbibe health or disease, insight or ignorance, valor or pusillanimity, as the stream of life flows from urns of sobriety or luxury, from times of wisdom or folly, honor or shame.

LXXXVIII. RENUNCIATION.

Renounce the world, yourself; and you shall possess the world, yourself, and God.

ALCOTT MEMORIAL SERVICE

AT THE

Concord School of Philosophy,

SATURDAY, JUNE 16, 1888.

A Special Session of the SCHOOL OF PHILOSOPHY will be held at the Hillside Chapel in Concord, Saturday, June 16, commencing at 10 A. M. The public are invited.

The order of services will be as follows:

MORNING SESSION.

10   A. M.   Prayer by Rev. J. S. BUSH, of Concord.
10.15 A. M.   *Biographical Address* by F. B. SANBORN, of Concord.
11 A. M. to 1 P. M.   Remarks and Reminiscences by
        Rev. Dr. BARTOL, of Boston,
        Mrs. E. D. CHENEY, of Boston,
        GEORGE B. BARTLETT, of Concord,
        Rev. G. REYNOLDS, of Concord,
        Rev. Dr. F. H. HEDGE, of Cambridge,
        B. MARSTON WATSON, of Plymouth,
        W. L. GARRISON, of Boston,
        JOHN ALBEE, of New Castle, N. H.,
                and others.

AFTERNOON SESSION.

2.30 P. M.   The *Philosophy of Mr. Alcott*, by WILLIAM T. HARRIS, of Concord,
3.30 to 5 P. M.   Remarks or Letters by
        Rev. R. A. HOLLAND, S. T. D., of St. Louis,
        Prof. THOMAS DAVIDSON, of New York,
        DANIEL RICKETSON, of New Bedford,
                and others.

There will be no other Session of the Concord School of Philosophy the present Summer.

                        W. T. HARRIS,
                        S. H. EMERY, JR.,
                        F. B. SANBORN, *Secretary.*

Concord, June 2, 1888.

Memorial Service for Bronson Alcott at the Concord School of Philosophy

LXXXIX. VALOR.

Man's impotence is his pusillanimity. Duty alone is necessity; valor, might. This bridles the actual, yokes circumstance to do its bidding, and wields the arms of omnipotence. Fidelity, magnanimity, win the crown of heaven, and invest the soul with the attributes of God.

XC. MEEKNESS.

All men honor meekness; and make her their confessor. She wins all hearts; all vulgar natures do her homage. The demons flee, and the unclean Calabans and Satyrs become menials in her imperial presence. She is the potentate of the world.

XCI. GENTLENESS.

I love to regard all souls as babes, yet in their prime and innocency of being, nor would I upbraid rudely a fellow creature, but treat him as tenderly as an infant. I would be gentle alway. Gentleness is the divinest of graces, and all men joy in it. Yet seldom does is appear on earth. Not in the face of man, nor yet often in that of woman (O apostacy,) but in the countenance of childhood it sometimes lingers, even amidst the violence, the dispathy that beset it; there, for a little while, fed by divine fires, the serene flame glows, but soon flickers and dies away, choked by the passions and lusts of sense–its embers smouldering alone in the bosoms of men.

XCII. INDIVIDUALS.

Individuals are sacred: creeds, usages, institutions, as they cherish and reverence the individual. The world, the state, the church, the school, all are felons whensoever they violate the sanctity of the private heart. God, with his saints and martyrs, holds thrones, polities, hierarchies, amenable to the same, and time pours her vial of just retribution on their heads. A man is divine; mightier, holier, than rulers or powers ordained of time.

XCIII. MESSIAS.

The people look always for a political, not spiritual Messias. They desire a ruler from the world, not from heaven–a monarch who shall conform both church and state to their maxims and usages. So church and state become functions of the world, and mammon, with his court of priests and legislators, usurps the throne of conscience in the soul, to rule saints and prophets for a time.

XCIV. CHRISTENDOM.

Christendom is infidel. It violates the sanctity of man's conscience. It speaks not from the lively oracles of the soul, but reads instead from the traditions of men. It quotes history, not life. It denounces as heresy and impiety the intuitions of the individual, denies the inspiration of souls, and intrudes human dogmas and usages between conscience and God. It excludes the saints from its bosom, and with these excommunicates, as the archheretic, Jesus of Nazareth also.

XCV. CHRISTIANS.

Christians lean on Jesus, not on the soul. Such was not the doctrine of this noble reformer. He taught man's independence of all men, and a faith and trust in the soul herself. Christianity is the doctrine of self-support. It teaches man to be upright, not supine. Jesus gives his arm to none save those who stand erect, independent of church, state, or the world, in the integrity of self-insight and valor. Cast aside thy crutch, O Christendom, and by faith in the soul, arise and walk. Thy faith alone shall make thee whole.

XCVI. PENTECOST.

The pentecost of the soul draws near. Inspiration, silent long, is unsealing the lips of prophets and bards, and soon shall the vain babblings of men die away, and their ears be given to the words of the Holy Ghost; their tongues cloven with celestial eloquence.

XCVII. IMMORTALITY.

It is because the soul is immortal that all her organs decease, and are again renewed. Growth and decay, sepulture and resurrection, tread fast on the heel of the other. Birth entombs death; death encradles birth. The incorruptible is ever putting off corruption; the immortal mortality. Nature, indeed, is but the ashes of the departed soul, and the body her urn.

XCVIII. OBITUARY.

Things are memoirs of ideas; ideas the body of laws; laws the breath of God. All nature is the sepulchre of the risen soul, life her epitaph, and scripture her obituary.

XCIX. ETERNITY.

The soul doth not chronicle her age. Her consciousness opens in the dimness of traditions; she is cradled in mystery, and her infancy invested in fable. Yet a celestial light irradiates this obscurity of birth, and reveals her spiritual lineage. Ancestor of the world, prior to time, elder than her incarnation, neither spaces, times, genealogies, publish her date. Memory is the history, Hope the prophecy of her inborn eternity. Dateless, timeless, she is coeval with God.

C. SILENCE.

Silence is the initiative to wisdom. Wit is silent, and justifies her children by their reverence of the voiceless oracles of the breast. Inspiration is dumb, a listener to the oracles during her nonage; suddenly she speaks, to mock the emptiness of all speech. Silence is the dialect of heaven; the utterance of Gods.

C[hristopher]. P[earse]. C[ranch].

"Transcendentalism," *Western Messenger*, 8 (January 1841): 405-409.

Cranch, like Clarke, was an enthusiastic promoter of Transcendentalism, and he wrote this spirited defense of the movement, arguing–against all facts–for its being truly an American phenomenon which had literally transcended its sources and–more accurately–for its religious basis. (For further information on this poet and artist, see the entry for Cranch in DLB 1, The American Renaissance in New England.)

Much is said of late by persons not knowing whereof they speak, of what has been termed "Transcendentalism." Now, though not one in a hundred of these talkers can tell what this hard word means, or even explain their own vague idea of its meaning, it is a very convenient word. In the minds of most persons, it signifieth (being interpreted) "new doctrine,"–a modern synonyme for "Heresy." Strangely enough, all the "New Lights" of Philosophy and Theology, in foreign countries as well as in our own, however independent in thought, are, by a singular mode of generalizing, lumped together into a "Sect," honoured with the cognomen of "New School," and "Transcendentalists." It might amuse, almost, to see how this love of wholesale classification melts down obvious differences–persuading us that this new movement which is commencing on both sides of the Atlantic, for reviving the old well-nigh obscured truths of philosophy and theology, and is going forward in so many ways and by so many minds–is not a many headed monster, a hydra whose heads will grow again, though ever so well lopped off; but is *one*-headed, and may and must die, as only "the latest form of infidelity." It might amuse, to see how Kant, Cousin, Carlyle, Emerson, and about half Germany, are placed side by side, as if reading like schoolboys, out of the same book–stereotyping each other's thoughts–a sort of co-partnership for vending mysticisms, and turning brains. As if the "New School," as it is termed, *could* be a sect, with a fixed creed before it: as if it were not its glory that it is *many*-headed, and progressive.

Can ye not discern the signs of the times? There are some who think that they can, clearly enough, though it were through a mill-stone. They see nothing

Drawing of Christopher Pearse Cranch in 1843 by William Wetmore Story (Leonora Cranch Scott, The Life and Letters of Christopher Pearse Cranch [1917])

but darkness before them. The tendency of the age they think is to infidelity. Everything is to be dreaded from the innovations and changes, and new views

[163]

First page of a manuscript poem by Christopher Pearse Cranch

which we see around us. And especially are we warned to turn our backs on Germany, that land of darkness,

—"void of light,
Save what the glimmering of these livid flames
Casts pale and dreadful."—

But avoiding controversy, and leaving the light tone, let us look upon the new movements of the age, as we would on all great and important movements, with reverence, with faith, with hope. For there are features belonging to such movements, which we are apt to overlook. There is more here than the eye now sees. But we may see something. There is a great lesson taught us by all these periods of time, wherein the same or similar great ideas prevail; and that is that a Divine Providence is here displayed, and displayed more signally than in any other way. Thus it was with the first appearance of Christianity, in a degree never seen before or

since. Thus it was with the Reformation–thus it was with the Puritan movement–thus it was with the Unitarian movement. From time to time some grand Truth dawns like light upon nations who sat in darkness. All who are true, who are free, feel its coming, though they only *feel*, in dim, vague glimmerings of imagination and hope, but cannot *think* their dream into shape–much less speak of it. They cannot give a *reason*, either to themselves or to others, for the *hope* which is in them. They are like infants who have but a confused inarticulate language of their own, understood by none but one all-loving Parent, who will yet teach them soon an *articulate* tongue, and raise up a philosophy to translate their theology. All hearts are at such times preparing in themselves the way of the Lord: the vallies begin to be exalted, the mountains levelled, the rough places made smooth, and the crooked places straight, and when at length the voice comes crying in the wilderness, the voice which is appointed in God's Providence to be the great interpreter of hidden truths, the "Word made flesh," which in the person or teachings of some great man, comes to speak what all are yearning to hear *plainly* spoken or acted, because all feel in themselves the smouldering heat which those thoughts that breathe and words that burn, are to touch into a blaze–*then* does the light break forth:–from the hills around–from the waste places of society–from across wide seas–from language to language, the echoes of that voice reverbrate. And these echoes are not, most happily, unmeaning, barren responses or repetitions, but are turned into new modulations, into rich variations as of some mountain melody, and constantly growing richer and more varied, as they spread circling round the world.

Hence the charge we so often hear, of Imitation, and of the too enthusiastic reception which young and fresh spirits are apt to give to new views. How superficial this charge of stiff barren conservatives. How scant an insight into the deep places of human character does it betoken. How narrow a view of the forthgoings of God's Mighty Spirit upon the restless deep of human minds! Hence a certain great writer of England is accused of imitating the Germans; and another writer of our country of imitating *him;* and these writers in turn, of being imitated by others. Men cry out that a transcendental epidemic is spreading contagion through our Universities. As if this word *Imitation* settled everything. A convenient word it is, we allow, but what does it prove? Is it anything more than a superficial term for a phenomenon, to the eternal foundations of which, as it looms up from the infinite deep of the Spiritual, these narrow observers will not or cannot look? If this phenomenon–this dawning of truths over the earth, be nothing more than a paroxysm, a temporary enchantment, a spoiled child's cry after whatever is *new*– then why so eagerly received? Why so suggestive to the highest thought? Why so strengthening to the calmest and loftiest faith? I speak not now of any opinions or speculations in particular. There is every variety of such, as there should be. But I speak of that fresh, earnest, truth-loving and truth-seeking SPIRIT, which is abroad;–of that heart's-thirst, not of the fever-dream, but of the sober, waking vision of soundest health, after something *always* new and lovely and true,– something always adapted to the soul's deep demands. I allude, I repeat, not to any system, or creed, or philosophy, or party, or sect–to no men or speculations, except so far as such are types of a free, earnest, and humble love of Truth; but rather to a higher and better hope, to fast fulfilling prophecies from the heart of humanity, more wisdom-fraught than ever were the utterances of Sybils and Delphic oracles. The true Transcendentalism is that living and always new *spirit* of truth, which is ever going forth on its conquests into the world, and leading all captivity captive: but which at times arms itself as with new splendors of victory,– which is thus in the only sense *transcendental,* when it labors to *transcend* itself, and soar ever higher and nearer the great source of Truth, Himself. When we see such a spirit abroad, walking the earth in native majesty, yet not in tyranny, but in lowly freedom, like that of the Galilean Prophet, humbling itself to common life, and to fallen man, that it may be only the more exalted in the sight of God–when we see it swaying the universal Heart, as wind sways the forest with all its leaves– when we see mankind lifting up their drooping heads and opening their languid eyes, as the refreshing currents of God's providence circulate and blow around them–their thought quickened, their belief strengthened, their hope brightened, their aspiration enlarged– we cannot say,"This is the work of man–the excitement of a season–the summer-fever of prosperity–the corrupt fruit of unlicensed enquiry." It is God Himself, walking in His garden at the cool of the day. It is the Eternal Spirit breathing down on us the life-giving breeze of Almighty Grace.

It is indeed a remarkable fact, though it seems never to have been sufficiently noticed, that at certain periods, men are penetrated with the same great thoughts, or verge to the same great discoveries; and this without any sufficient cause for such unanimity presenting itself from the circle of known facts which surround us. We cannot find the source of this agreement in the events of past progress or of present excitement. Genius springs across our field of vision, like the rushing of a shooting star from the bosom of the darkness; and we are startled and awed, while we are enchanted by the unaccustomed vision, and strain our eyes in vain to track the beautiful meteor to its place of birth in the empty firmament. It is still a mystery to us.

But the mystery is not confined to solitary genius. As all the mountain tops glow in the coming day, so do all elevated minds feel the coming of a Truth. And without any preconcerted plan–without any intercommunion of minds, the sunlight of Truth seems to flash simultaneously upon lands separated by oceans, by dissimilar languages. On different shores and to insulated minds will the same aspects and applications of truth arise. This holds true in all science, physical or metaphysical, theological or political.

Thus we see Genius appearing not only as

A single silent star

Come wandering from afar."–

but in groups, in constellations; just as certain clusters of field flowers come always at certain seasons of the year. Is it said that this results from imitation–that it is a *reflected* light glancing from each to all,–that it is but the common influence of one mind kindling and quickening another. It seems to us that this principle goes but a little way to explain the phenomenon. Behind all this the mainsprings work unseen by the worldly eye. It is no less than the light from above–the spirit of God controlling the destinies of men–"the light which lighteth every man who cometh into the world." It is not ourselves. It is not the property of this man or of that woman, to be parcelled out in prismatic glimmerings, and be bought and sold like earthly possessions. It is the common daylight of the mind. It is God working within us to will and to do.

It is eminently the spirit of earnest, free, large enquiry, which is the "voice crying in the wilderness." Compared with the glowing visions which this prophetic spirit sees in the future, all the past progress of man is a mere wilderness, and it goes forth to refresh it, and make it like our lost Eden. It would leave the shadow of night behind it, and keep pace with the westering sun in its journey round the globe.

Such a spirit, we rejoice to believe, is even now abroad on the earth. Everywhere do we see its evidences. It does not confine itself to opinions; it extends to great and good *acts*. It is seen in the practical developments of our religion. It is not the bare spirit of denial and doubt, but of yearning Faith also. While it empties itself of that which it perceives to be unwholesome or noxious, it also supplies the void by fresh appropriations from the realms of truth which open upon it. So much as it sees to be good in what is old, it re-

tains. So much as it finds good in the new, it adopts. From behind and from before would it gather its treasures. They lie all around it. It has but to seek, as a merchantman seeking goodly pearls.

The friends of truth cannot but rejoice in these signs of progress: to see obstinate prejudices wearing down–old errors falling away by piecemeal–the spirit of bigotry subsiding–and the spirit of liberality extending. Let us trust it may long be so: that God may visit his people. But let it be an *active* trust. Let us prepare in our hearts and lives for the coming of the truth–and the kingdom of God will come.

Oct., 1839.

Ralph Waldo Emerson
"Self-Reliance," from *Essays: First Series* (Boston: James Munroe, 1841), pp. 36-73.

Emerson's great essay on "Self-Reliance" is one of his most widely reprinted works. In typical epigrammatic fashion, Emerson stressed the importance and divinity of the individual and the need not to conform to society, whose approval and disapproval were merely transitory. From the start, some critics have seen Emerson's doctrine as antisocial, but even more have praised his call for reforming the individual. It is important to note that Emerson's self-reliance is more properly termed "God-reliance," since he stressed that we rely upon the divinity within ourselves.

I read the other day some verses written by an eminent painter which were original and not conventional. Always the soul hears an admonition in such lines, let the subject be what it may. The sentiment they instil is of more value than any thought they may contain. To believe your own thought, to believe that what is true for you in your private heart, is true for all men,–that is genius. Speak your latent conviction and it shall be the universal sense; for always the inmost becomes the outmost,–and our first thought is rendered back to us by the trumpets of the Last Judgment. Familiar as the voice of the mind is to each, the highest merit we ascribe to Moses, Plato, and Milton, is that they set at naught books and traditions, and spoke not what men but what they thought. A man should learn to detect and watch that gleam of light which flashes across his mind from within, more than the lustre of the firmament of bards and sages. Yet he dismisses without notice his thought, because it is his. In every work of gen-

ius we recognise our own rejected thoughts: they come back to us with a certain alienated majesty. Great works of art have no more affecting lesson for us than this. They teach us to abide by our spontaneous impression with good humored inflexibility then most when the whole cry of voices is on the other side. Else, to-morrow a stranger will say with masterly good sense precisely what we have thought and felt all the time, and we shall be forced to take with shame our own opinion from another.

There is a time in every man's education when he arrives at the conviction that envy is ignorance; that imitation is suicide; that he must take himself for better, for worse, as his portion; that though the wide universe is full of good, no kernel of nourishing corn can come to him but through his toil bestowed on that plot of ground which is given to him to till. The power which resides in him is new in nature, and none but he knows what that is which he can do, nor does he know

Drawing of Emerson's mother, Ruth Haskins Emerson (Journals of Ralph Waldo Emerson, edited by Edward Waldo Emerson and Waldo Emerson Forbes [1909-1914])

Engraving of Emerson's father, the Reverend William Emerson (Journals of Ralph Waldo, edited by Edward Waldo Emerson and Waldo Emerson Forbes [1909–1914])

until he has tried. Not for nothing one face, one character, one fact makes such impression on him, and another none. It is not without preëstablished harmony, this sculpture in the memory. The eye was placed where one ray should fall, that it might testify of that particular ray. Bravely let him speak the utmost syllable of his confession. We but half express ourselves, and are ashamed of that divine idea which each of us represents. It may be safely trusted as proportionate and of good issues, so it be faithfully imparted, but God will not have his work made manifest by cowards. It needs a divine man to exhibit any thing divine. A man is relieved and gay when he has put his heart into his work and done his best; but what he has said or done otherwise, shall give him no peace. It is a deliverance which does not deliver. In the attempt his genius deserts him; no muse befriends; no invention, no hope.

Trust thyself: every heart vibrates to that iron string. Accept the place the divine Providence has found for you; the society of your contemporaries, the

connexion of events. Great men have always done so and confided themselves childlike to the genius of their age, betraying their perception that the Eternal was stirring at their heart, working through their hands, predominating in all their being. And we are now men, and must accept in the highest mind the same transcendent destiny; and not pinched in a corner, not cowards fleeing before a revolution, but redeemers and benefactors, pious aspirants to be noble clay plastic under the Almighty effort, let us advance and advance on Chaos and the Dark.

What pretty oracles nature yields us on this text in the face and behavior of children, babes and even brutes. That divided and rebel mind, that distrust of a sentiment because our arithmetic has computed the strength and means opposed to our purpose, these have not. Their mind being whole, their eye is as yet unconquered, and when we look in their faces, we are disconcerted. Infancy conforms to nobody: all conform to it, so that one babe commonly makes four or five out of the adults who prattle and play to it. So God has armed youth and puberty and manhood no less with its own piquancy and charm, and made it enviable and gracious and its claims not to be put by, if it will stand by itself. Do not think the youth has no force because he cannot speak to you and me. Hark! in the next room, who spoke so clear and emphatic? Good Heaven! It is he! It is that very lump of bashfulness and phlegm which for weeks has done nothing but eat when you were by, that now rolls out these words like bell-strokes. It seems he knows how to speak to his contemporaries. Bashful or bold, then, he will know how to make us seniors very unnecessary.

The nonchalance of boys who are sure of a dinner, and would disdain as much as a lord to do or say aught to conciliate one, is the healthy attitude of human nature. How is a boy the master of society; independent, irresponsible, looking out from his corner on such people and facts as pass by, he tries and sentences them on their merits, in the swift summary way of boys, as good, bad, interesting, silly, eloquent, troublesome. He cumbers himself never about consequences, about interests: he gives an independent, genuine verdict. You must court him: he does not court you. But the man is, as it were, clapped into jail by his consciousness. As soon as he has once acted or spoken with eclat, he is a committed person, watched by the sympathy or the hatred of hundreds whose affections must now enter into his account. There is no Lethe for this. Ah, that he could pass again into his neutral, godlike independence! Who can thus lose all pledge, and having observed, observe again from the same unaffected, unbiased, unbribable, unaffrighted innocence, must always be formidable, must always engage the poet's and the man's regards. Of such an immortal youth the force would be felt. He would utter opinions on all passing affairs, which being seen to be not private but necessary, would sink like darts into the ear of men, and put them in fear.

These are the voices which we hear in solitude, but they grow faint and inaudible as we enter into the world. Society everywhere is in conspiracy against the manhood of every one of its members. Society is a joint-stock company in which the members agree for the better securing of his bread to each shareholder, to surrender the liberty and culture of the eater. The virtue in most request is conformity. Self-reliance is its aversion. It loves not realities and creators, but names and customs.

Whoso would be a man must be a nonconformist. He who would gather immortal palms must not be hindered by the name of goodness, but must explore if it be goodness. Nothing is at last sacred but the integrity of our own mind. Absolve you to yourself, and you shall have the suffrage of the world. I remember an answer which when quite young I was prompted to make to a valued adviser who was wont to importune me with the dear old doctrines of the church. On my saying, What have I to do with the sacredness of traditions, if I live wholly from within? my friend suggested— "But these impulses may be from below, not from above." I replied, 'They do not seem to me to be such; but if I am the devil's child, I will live then from the devil.' No law can be sacred to me but that of my nature. Good and bad are but names very readily transferable to that or this; the only right is what is after my constitution, the only wrong what is against it. A man is to carry himself in the presence of all opposition as if every thing were titular and ephemeral but he. I am ashamed to think how easily we capitulate to badges and names, to large societies and dead institutions. Every decent and well-spoken individual affects and sways me more than is right. I ought to go upright and vital, and speak the rude truth in all ways. If malice and vanity wear the coat of philanthropy, shall that pass? If an angry bigot assumes this bountiful cause of Abolition, and comes to me with his last news from Barbadoes, why should I not say to him, 'Go love thy infant; love thy woodchopper: be good-natured and modest: have that grace; and never varnish your hard, uncharitable ambition with this incredible tenderness for black folk a thousand miles off. Thy love afar is spite at home.' Rough and graceless would be such greeting, but truth is handsomer than the affectation of love. Your goodness must have some edge to it—else it is none. The doctrine of hatred must be preached as the counteraction of the doctrine of love when that pules and whines. I shun father and mother and wife and brother, when my genius calls me. I would write on the lintels of the door-post, *Whim.* I hope it is somewhat better than whim at last, but we cannot spend the day in explanation. Expect me not to show cause why I seek and why I exclude company. Then, again, do not tell me, as a good man did to-day, of my obligation to put all poor men in good situations. Are they *my* poor? I tell thee, thou foolish philanthropist, that I grudge the dollar, the dime, the cent I give to such men as do not belong to me and to whom I do not belong. There is a class of persons to whom by all spiritual affinity I am bought and sold; for them I will go to prison, if need be; but your miscellaneous popular charities; the education at college of fools; the building of meeting-houses to the vain end to which many now stand; alms to sots; and the thousandfold Relief Societies;–though I confess with shame I sometimes succumb and give the dollar, it is a wicked dollar which by-and-by I shall have the manhood to withhold.

Virtues are in the popular estimate rather the exception than the rule. There is the man *and* his virtues. Men do what is called a good action, as some piece of courage or charity, much as they would pay a fine in expiation of daily non-appearance on parade. Their works are done as an apology or extenuation of their living in the world,–as invalids and the insane pay a high board. Their virtues are penances. I do not wish to expiate, but to live. My life is not an apology, but a life. It is for itself and not for a spectacle. I much prefer that it should be of a lower strain, so it be genuine and equal, than that it should be glittering and unsteady. I wish it to be sound and sweet, and not to need diet and bleeding. My life should be unique; it should be an alms, a battle, a conquest, a medicine. I ask primary evidence that you are a man, and refuse this appeal from the man to his actions. I know that for myself it makes no difference whether I do or forbear those actions which are reckoned excellent. I cannot consent to pay for a privilege where I have intrinsic right. Few and mean as my gifts may be, I actually am, and do not need for my own assurance or the assurance of my fellows any secondary testimony.

What I must do, is all that concerns me, not what the people think. This rule, equally arduous in actual and in intellectual life, may serve for the whole distinction between greatness and meanness. It is the harder, because you will always find those who think they know what is your duty better than you know it. It is easy in the world to live after the world's opinion; it is easy in solitude to live after our own; but the great man is he who in the midst of the crowd keeps with perfect sweetness the independence of solitude.

The objection to conforming to usages that have become dead to you, is, that it scatters your force. It loses your time and blurs the impression of your character. If you maintain a dead church, contribute to a dead Bible-Society, vote with a great party either for the Government or against it, spread your table like base housekeepers,–under all these screens, I have diffi-

*Silhouette of Emerson's aunt, Mary Moody Emerson (*Journals of Ralph Waldo Emerson, *edited by Edward Waldo Emerson and Waldo Emerson Forbes [1909-1914])*

culty to detect the precise man you are. And, of course, so much force is withdrawn from your proper life. But do your thing, and I shall know you. Do your work, and you shall reinforce yourself. A man must consider what a blindman's buff is this game of conformity. If I know your sect, I anticipate your argument. I hear a preacher announce for his text and topic the expediency of one of the institutions of his church. Do I not know beforehand that not possibly can he say a new and spontaneous word? Do I not know that with all this ostentation of examining the grounds of the institution, he will do no such thing? Do I not know that he is pledged to himself not to look but at one side; the permitted side, not as a man, but as a parish minister? He is a retained attorney, and these airs of the bench are the emptiest affectation. Well, most men have bound their eyes with one or another handkerchief, and attached themselves to some one of these communities of opinion. This conformity makes them not false in a

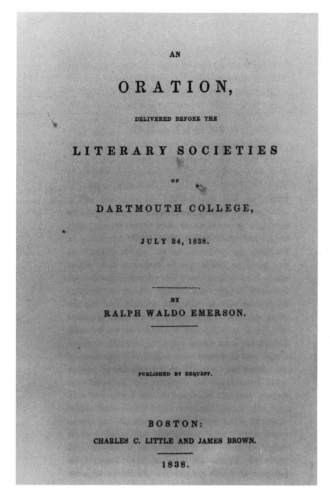

AN

ORATION,

DELIVERED BEFORE THE

LITERARY SOCIETIES

OF

DARTMOUTH COLLEGE,

JULY 24, 1838.

BY

RALPH WALDO EMERSON.

PUBLISHED BY REQUEST.

BOSTON:
CHARLES C. LITTLE AND JAMES BROWN.

1838.

Title page for "Literary Ethics," in which Emerson continued his comments on the responsibilities of the American scholar

few particulars, authors of a few lies, but false in all particulars. Their every truth is not quite true. Their two is not the real two, their four not the real four: so that every word they say chagrins us, and we know not where to begin to set them right. Meantime nature is not slow to equip us in the prison-uniform of the party to which we adhere. We come to wear one cut of face and figure, and acquire by degrees the gentlest asinine expression. There is a mortifying experience in particular which does not fail to wreak itself also in the general history; I mean, "the foolish face of praise," the forced smile which we put on in company where we do not feel at ease in answer to conversation which does not interest us. The muscles, not spontaneously moved, but moved by a low usurping wilfulness, grow tight about the outline of the face and make the most disagreeable sensation, a sensation of rebuke and warning which no brave young man will suffer twice.

For non-conformity the world whips you with its displeasure. And therefore a man must know how to estimate a sour face. The bystanders look askance on him in the public street or in the friend's parlor. If this aversation had its origin in contempt and resistance like his own, he might well go home with a sad countenance; but the sour faces of the multitude, like their sweet faces, have no deep cause,—disguise no god, but are put on and off as the wind blows, and a newspaper directs. Yet is the discontent of the multitude more formidable than that of the senate and the college. It is easy enough for a firm man who knows the world to brook the rage of the cultivated classes. Their rage is decorous and prudent, for they are timid as being very vulnerable themselves. But when to their feminine rage the indignation of the people is added, when the ignorant and the poor are aroused, when the unintelligent brute force that lies at the bottom of society is made to growl and mow, it needs the habit of magnanimity and religion to treat it godlike as a trifle of no concernment.

The other terror that scares us from self-trust is our consistency; a reverence for our past act or word, because the eyes of others have no other data for computing our orbit than our past acts, and we are loath to disappoint them.

But why should you keep your head over your shoulder? Why drag about this monstrous corpse of your memory, lest you contradict somewhat you have stated in this or that public place? It seems to be a rule of wisdom never to rely on your memory, but bring the past for judgment into the thousand-eyed present, and live ever in a new day. Trust your emotion. In your metaphysics you have denied personality to the Deity: yet when the devout motions of the soul come, yield to them heart and life, though they should clothe God with shape and color. Leave your theory as Joseph his coat in the hand of the harlot, and flee.

A foolish consistency is the hobgoblin of little minds, adored by little statesmen and philosophers and divines. With consistency a great soul has simply nothing to do. He may as well concern himself with his shadow on the wall. Out upon your guarded lips! Sew them up with packthread, do. Else, if you would be a man, speak what you think to-day in words as hard as cannon balls, and to-morrow speak what to-morrow thinks in hard words again, though it contradict every thing you said to-day. Ah, then, exclaim the aged ladies, you shall be sure to be misunderstood. Misunderstood! It is a right fool's word. Is it so bad then to be mis-

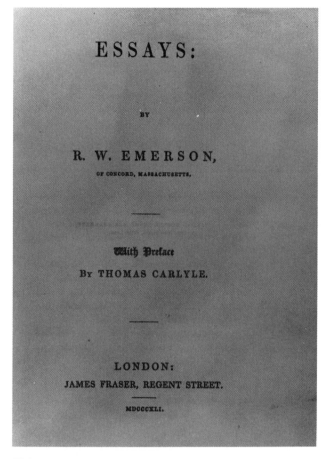

ESSAYS:

BY

R. W. EMERSON,

OF CONCORD, MASSACHUSETTS,

———

With Preface

BY THOMAS CARLYLE.

———

LONDON:

JAMES FRASER, REGENT STREET.

———

MDCCCXLI.

Title page for the first series of Essays, *with Thomas Carlyle's preface, which helped introduce English readers to his American friend*

understood? Pythagoras was misunderstood, and Socrates, and Jesus, and Luther, and Copernicus, and Galileo, and Newton, and every pure and wise spirit that ever took flesh. To be great is to be misunderstood.

I suppose no man can violate his nature. All the sallies of his will are rounded in by the law of his being as the inequalities of Andes and Himmaleh are insignificant in the curve of the sphere. Nor does it matter how you gauge and try him. A character is like an acrostic or Alexandrian stanza;–read it forward, backward, or across, it still spells the same thing. In this pleasing contrite wood-life which God allows me, let me record day by day my honest thought without prospect or retrospect, and, I cannot doubt, it will be found symmetrical, though I mean it not, and see it not. My book should smell of pines and resound with the hum of insects. The swallow over my window should interweave that thread or straw he carries in his bill into my web also. We pass for what we are. Character teaches

above our wills. Men imagine that they communicate their virtue or vice only by overt actions and do not see that virtue or vice emit a breath every moment.

Fear never but you shall be consistent in whatever variety of actions, so they be each honest and natural in their hour. For of one will, the actions will be harmonious, however unlike they seem. These varieties are lost sight of when seen at a little distance, at a little height of thought. One tendency unites them all. The voyage of the best ship is a zigzag line of a hundred tacks. This is only microscopic criticism. See the line from a sufficient distance, and it straightens itself to the average tendency. Your genuine action will explain itself and will explain your other genuine actions. Your conformity explains nothing. Act singly, and what you have already done singly, will justify you now. Greatness always appeals to the future. If I can be great enough now to do right and scorn eyes, I must have done so much right before, as to defend me now. Be it how it will, do right now. Always scorn appearances, and you always may. The force of character is cumulative. All the foregone days of virtue work their health into this. What makes the majesty of the heroes of the senate and the field, which so fills the imagination? The consciousness of a train of great days and victories behind. There they all stand and shed an united light on the advancing actor. He is attended as by a visible escort of angels go every man's eye. That is it which throws thunder into Chatham's voice, and dignity into Washington's port, and America into Adam's eye. Honor is venerable to us because it is no ephemeris. It is always ancient virtue. We worship it to-day, because it is not of to-day. We love it and pay it homage, because it is not a trap for our love and homage, but is self-dependent, self-derived, and therefore of an old immaculate pedigree, even if shown in a young person.

I hope in these days we have heard the last of conformity and consistency. Let the words be gazetted and ridiculous henceforward. Instead of the gong for dinner, let us hear a whistle from the Spartan fife. Let us bow and apologize never more. A great man is coming to eat at my house. I do not wish to please him; I wish that he should wish to please me. I will stand here for humanity, and though I would make it kind, I would make it true. Let us affront and reprimand the smooth mediocrity and squalid contentment of the times, and hurl in the face of custom, and trade, and office, the fact which is the upshot of all history, that there is a great responsible Thinker and Actor moving wherever moves a man; that a true man belongs to no other time or place, but is the centre of things. Where he is, there is nature. He measures you, and all men, and all events. You are constrained to accept his standard. Ordinarily every body in society reminds us of somewhat else or of some other person. Character, reality, reminds you of nothing else. It takes place of the whole creation. The man must be so much that he must make all circumstances indifferent,–put all means into the shade. This all great men are and do. Every true man is a cause, a country, and an age; requires infinite spaces and numbers and time fully to accomplish his thought;–and posterity seem to follow his steps as a procession. A man Cæsar is born, and for ages after, we have a Roman Empire. Christ is born, and millions of minds so grow and cleave to his genius, that he is confounded with virtue and the possible of man. An institution is the lengthened shadow of one man; as, the Reformation, of Luther; Quakerism, of Fox; Methodism, of Wesley; Abolition, of Clarkson. Scipio, Milton called "the height of Rome;" and all history resolves itself very easily into the biography of a few stout and earnest persons.

Let a man then know his worth, and keep things under his feet. Let him not peep or steal, or skulk up and down with the air of a charity-boy, a bastard, or interloper, in the world which exists for him. But the man in the street finding no worth in himself which corresponds to the force which built a tower or sculptured a marble god, feels poor when he looks on these. To him a palace, a statue, or a costly book have an alien and forbidding air, much like a gay equipage, and seem to say like that, 'Who are you, sir?' Yet they all are his, suitors for his notice, petitioners to his faculties that they will come out and take possession. The picture waits for my verdict: it is not to command me, but I am to settle its claims to praise. That popular fable of the sot who was picked up dead drunk in the street, carried to the duke's house, washed and dressed and laid in the duke's bed, and, on his waking, treated with all obsequious ceremony like the duke, and assured that he had been insane,–owes its popularity to the fact, that it symbolizes so well the state of man, who is in the world a sort of sot, but now and then wakes up, exercises his reason, and finds himself a true prince.

Our reading is mendicant and sycophantic. In history, our imagination makes fools of us, plays us false. Kingdom and lordship, power and estate are a gaudier vocabulary than private John and Edward in a small

Photograph of Emerson's son, Waldo (1836-1842), whose death–the subject of the poem "Threnody"–shook his father's early optimism

house and common day's work: but the things of life are the same to both: the sum total of both is the same. Why all this deference to Alfred, and Scanderbeg, and Gustavus? Suppose they were virtuous: did they wear our virtue? As great a stake depends on your private act to-day, as followed their public and renowned steps. When private men shall act with vast views, the lustre will be transferred from the actions of kings to those of gentlemen.

The world has indeed been instructed by its kings, who have so magnetized the eyes of nations. It has been taught by this colossal symbol the mutual reverence that is due from man to man. The joyful loyalty with which men have every where suffered the king, the noble, or the great proprietor to walk among them by a law of his own, make his own scale of men and things, and reverse theirs, pay for benefits not with money but with honor, and represent the Law in his person, was the hieroglyphic by which they obscurely signified their consciousness of their own right and comeliness, the right of every man.

The magneticism which all original action exerts is explained when we inquire the reason of self-trust. Who is the Trustee? What is the aboriginal Self on

Photograph of Emerson's second wife, Lidian, with their son, Edward, born in 1844 (Journals of Ralph Waldo Emerson, *edited by Edward Waldo Emerson and Waldo Emerson Forbes [1909-1914])*

which a universal reliance may be grounded? What is the nature and power of that science-baffling star, without parallax, without calculable elements, which shoots a ray of beauty even into trivial and impure actions if the least mark of independence appear? The inquiry leads us to that source, at once the essence of genius, the essence of virtue, and the essence of life, which we call Spontaneity or Instinct. We denote this primary wisdom as Intuition, whilst all later teachings are tuitions. In that deep force, the last fact behind which analysis cannot go, all things find their common origin. For the sense of being which in calm hours rises, we know not how, in the soul, is not diverse from things, from space, from light, from time, from man, but one with them, and proceedeth obviously from the same source whence their life and being also proceedeth. We first share the life by which things exist, and afterwards see them as appearances in nature, and forget that we have shared their cause. Here is the fountain of action and the fountain of thought. Here are the lungs of that inspiration which giveth man wisdom, of that inspiration of man which cannot be denied without impiety and atheism. We lie in the lap of immense intelligence, which makes us organs of its activity and receivers of its truth. When we discern justice, when we discern truth, we do nothing of ourselves, but allow a passage to its beams. If we ask whence this comes, if we seek to pry into the soul that causes,—all metaphysics, all philosophy is at fault. Its presence or its absence is all we can affirm. Every man discerns between the voluntary acts of his mind, and his involuntary perceptions. And to his involuntary perceptions, he knows a perfect respect is due. He may err in the expression of them, but he knows that these things are so, like day and night, not to be disputed. All my wilful actions and acquisitions are but roving;—the most trivial reverie, the faintest native emotion are domestic and divine. Thoughtless people contradict as readily the statement of perceptions as of opinions, or rather much more readily; for, they do not distinquish between perception and notion. They fancy that I choose to see this or that thing. But perception is not whimsical, but fatal. If I see a trait, my children will see it after me, and in course of time, all mankind,—although it may chance that no one has seen it before me. For my perception of it is as much a fact as the sun.

The relations of the soul to the divine spirit are so pure that it is profane to seek to interpose helps. It must be that when God speaketh, he should communicate not one thing, but all things; should fill the world with his voice; should scatter forth light, nature, time, souls, from the centre of the present thought; and new date and new create the whole. Whenever a mind is simple, and receives a divine wisdom, then old things pass away,—means, teachers, texts, temples fall; it lives now and absorbs past and future into the present hour. All things are made sacred by relation to it,—one thing as much as another. All things are dissolved to their centre by their cause, and in the universal miracle petty and particular miracles disappear. This is and must be. If, therefore, a man claims to know and speak of God, and carries you backward to the phraseology of some old mouldered nation in another country, in another world, believe him not. Is the acorn better than the oak which is its fulness and completion? Is the parent better than the child into whom he has cast his ripened being? Whence then this worship of the past? The centuries are conspirators against the sanity and majesty of the soul. Time and space are but physiological colors which the eye maketh, but the soul is light; where it is, is day; where it was, is night; and history is an impertinence and an injury, if it be anything more than a cheerful apologue or parable of my being and becoming.

Man is timid and apologetic. He is no longer upright. He dares not say 'I think,' 'I am,' but quotes some saint or sage. He is ashamed before the blade of grass or the blowing rose. These roses under my window make no reference to former roses or to better ones; they are for what they are; they exist with God today. There is no time to them. There is simply the rose; it is perfect in every moment of its existence. Before a leaf-bud has burst, its whole life acts; in the full-blown flower, there is no more; in the leafless root, there is no less. Its nature is satisfied, and it satisfies nature, in all moments alike. There is no time to it. But man postpones or remembers; he does not live in the present, but with reverted eye laments the past, or, heedless of the riches that surround him, stands on tip-toe to foresee the future. He cannot be happy and strong until he too lives with nature in the present, above time.

This should be plain enough. Yet see what strong intellects dare not yet hear God himself, unless he speak the phraseology of I know not what David, or Jeremiah, or Paul. We shall not always set so great a price on a few texts, on a few lives. We are like children who repeat by rote the sentences of grandames and tutors, and, as they grow older, of the men of talents and character they chance to see,–painfully recollecting the exact words they spoke; afterwards, when they come into the point of view which those had who uttered these sayings, they understand them, and are willing to let the words go; for, at any time, they can use words as good, when occasion comes. So was it with us, so will it be, if we proceed. If we live truly, we shall see truly. It is as easy for the strong man to be strong, as it is for the weak to be weak. When we have new perception, we shall gladly disburthen the memory of its hoarded treasures as old rubbish. When a man lives with God, his voice shall be as sweet as the murmur of the brook and the rustle of the corn.

And now at last the highest truth on this subject remains unsaid; probably, cannot be said; for all that we say is the far off remembering of the intuition. That thought, by what I can now nearest approach to say it, is this. When good is near you, when you have life in yourself,–it is not by any known or appointed way; you shall not see the face of man; you shall not hear any name;–the way, the thought, the good shall be wholly strange and new. It shall exclude all other being. You

take the way from man not to man. All persons that ever existed are its fugitive ministers. There shall be no fear in it. It asks nothing. There is somewhat low even in hope. We are then in vision. There is nothing that can be called gratitude nor properly joy. The soul is raised over passion. It seeth identity and eternal causation. It is a perceiving that Truth and Right are. Hence it becomes a Tranquillity out of the knowing that all things go well. Vast spaces of nature; the Atlantic Ocean, the South Sea; vast intervals of time, years, centuries, are of no account. This which I think and feel, underlay that former state of life and circumstances, as it does underlie my present, and will always all circumstance, and what is called life, and what is called death.

Life only avails, not the having lived. Power ceases in the instant of repose; it resides in the moment of transition from a past to a new state; in the shooting of the gulf; in the darting to an aim. This one fact the world hates, that the soul *becomes;* for, that forever degrades the past; turns all riches to poverty; all reputation to a shame; confounds the saint with the rogue; shoves Jesus and Judas equally aside. Why then do we prate of self-reliance? Inasmuch as the soul is present, there will be power not confident but agent. To talk of reliance, is a poor external way of speaking. Speak rather of that which relies, because it works and is. Who has more soul than I, masters me, though he should not raise his finger. Round him I must revolve by the gravitation of spirits; who has less, I rule with like facility. We fancy it rhetoric when we speak of eminent virtue. We do not yet see that virtue is Height, and that a man or a company of men plastic and permeable to principles, by the law of nature must overpower and ride all cities, nations, kings, rich men, poets, who are not.

This is the ultimate fact which we so quickly reach on this as on every topic, the resolution of all into the ever blessed ONE. Virtue is the governor, the creator, the reality. All things real are so by so much of virtue as they contain. Hardship, husbandry, hunting, whaling, war, eloquence, personal weight, are somewhat, and engage my respect as examples of the soul's presence and impure action. I see the same law working in nature for conservation and growth. The poise of a planet, the bended tree recovering itself from the strong wind, the vital resources of every vegetable and animal, are also demonstrations of the self-sufficing, and therefore self-relying soul. All history

Walter Scott painting of Emerson in 1848 (Concord Free Public Library)

from its highest to its trivial passages is the various record of this power.

Thus all concentrates; let us not rove; let us sit at home with the cause. Let us stun and astonish the intruding rabble of men and books and institutions by a simple declaration of the divine fact. Bid them rake the shoes from off their feet, for God is here within. Let our simplicity judge them, and our docility to our own law demonstrate the poverty of nature and fortune beside our native riches.

But now we are a mob. Man does not stand in awe of man, nor is the soul admonished to stay at home, to put itself in communication with the internal ocean, but it goes abroad to beg a cup of water of the urns of men. We must go alone. Isolation must precede true society. I like the silent church before the service begins, better than any preaching. How far off, how cool, how chaste the persons look, befit each one with a precinct or sanctuary. So let us always sit. Why should we assume the faults of our friend, or wife, or father, or child, because they sit around our hearth, or are said to have the same blood? All men have my blood, and I have all men's. Not for that will I adopt their petulance or folly, even to the extent of being ashamed of it. But your isolation must not be mechanical, but spiritual, that is, must be elevation. At times the whole world seems to be in conspiracy to importune you with emphatic trifles. Friend, client, child, sickness, fear, want, charity, all knock at once at thy closet door and say, 'Come out unto us.'–Do not spill thy soul; do not all descend; keep thy state; stay at home in thine own heaven; come not for a moment into their facts, into their hubbub of conflicting appearances, but let in the light of thy law on their confusion. The power men possess to annoy me, I give them by a weak curiosity. No man can come near me but through my act. "What we love that we have, but by desire we bereave ourselves of the love."

If we cannot at once rise to the sanctities of obedience and faith, let us at least resist our temptations, let us enter into the state of war, and wake Thor and Woden, courage and constancy in our Saxon breasts. This is to be done in our smooth times by speaking the truth. Check this lying hospitality and lying affection. Live no longer to the expectation of these deceived and deceiving people with whom we converse. Say to them, O father, O mother, O wife, O brother, O friend, I have lived with you after appearances hitherto. Henceforward I am the truth's. Be it known unto

you that henceforward I obey no law less than the eternal law. I will have no covenants but proximities. I shall endeavor to nourish my parents, to support my family, to be the chaste husband of one wife,–but these relations I must fill after a new and unprecedented way. I appeal from your customs. I must be myself. I cannot break myself any longer for you, or you. If you can love me for what I am, we shall be the happier. If you cannot, I will still seek to deserve that you should. I must be myself. I will not hide my tastes or aversions. I will so trust that what is deep is holy, that I will do strongly before the sun and moon whatever inly rejoices me, and the heart appoints. If you are noble, I will love you; if you are not, I will not hurt you and myself by hypocritical attentions. If you are true, but not in the same truth with me, cleave to your companions; I will seek my own. I do this not selfishly, but humbly and truly. It is alike your interest and mine and all men's, however long we have dwelt in lies, to live in truth. Does this sound harsh to-day? You will soon love what is dictated by your nature as well as mine, and if we follow the truth, it will bring us out safe at last.– But so you may give these friends pain. Yes, but I cannot sell my liberty and my power, to save their sensibility. Besides, all persons have their moments of reason when they look out into the region of absolute truth; then will they justify me and do the same thing.

The populace think that your rejection of popular standards is a rejection of all standard, and mere antinomianism; and the bold sensualist will use the name of philosophy to gild his crimes. But the law of consciousness abides. There are two confessionals, in one or the other of which we must be shriven. You may fulfil your round of duties by clearing yourself in the *direct,* or, in the *reflex* way. Consider whether you have satisfied your relations to father, mother, cousin, neighbor, town, cat, and dog; whether any of these can upbraid you. But I may also neglect this reflex standard, and absolve me to myself. I have my own stern claims and perfect circle. It denies the name of duty to many offices that are called duties. But if I can discharge its debts, it enables me to dispense with the popular code. If any one imagines that this law is lax, let him keep its commandment one day.

And truly it demands something godlike in him who has cast off the common motives of humanity, and has ventured to trust himself for a task-master. High be his heart, faithful his will, clear his sight, that he may in good earnest be doctrine, society, law to him-

Emerson's house in Concord

self, that a simple purpose may be to him as strong as iron necessity is to others.

If any man consider the present aspects of what is called by distinction *society,* he will see the need of these ethics. The sinew and heart of man seem to be drawn out, and we are become timorous desponding whimperers. We are afraid of truth, afraid of fortune, afraid of death, and afraid of each other. Our age yields no great and perfect persons. We want men and women who shall renovate life and our social state, but we see that most natures are insolvent; cannot satisfy their own wants, have an ambition out of all proportion to their practical force, and so do lean and beg day and night continually. Our housekeeping is mendicant, our arts, our occupations, our marriages, our religion we have not chosen, but society has chosen for us. We are parlor soldiers. The rugged battle of fate, where strength is born, we shun.

If our young men miscarry in their first enterprizes, they lose all heart. If the young merchant fails, men say he is *ruined.* If the finest genius studies at one of our colleges, and is not installed in an office within one year afterwards in the cities or suburbs of Boston or New York, it seems to his friends and to himself that he is right in being disheartened and in complaining the rest of his life. A sturdy lad from New Hampshire or Vermont, who in turn tries all the professions, who *teams it, farms it, peddles,* keeps a school, preaches, edits a newspaper, goes to Congress, buys a township, and so forth, in successive years, and always, like a cat, falls on his feet, is worth a hundred of these city dolls. He walks abreast with his days, and feels no shame in not 'studying a profession,' for he does not postpone his life, but lives already. He has not one chance, but a hundred chances. Let a stoic arise who shall reveal the resources of man, and tell men they are not leaning willows, but can and must detach themselves; that with the exercise of self-trust, new powers shall appear; that a man is the word made flesh, born to shed healing to the nations, that he should be ashamed of our compassion, and that the moment he acts from himself, tossing the laws, the books, idolatries, and customs out of the window,–we pity him no more but thank and revere him,–and that teacher shall restore the life of man to splendor, and make his name dear to all History.

It is easy to see that a greater self-reliance,–a new respect for the divinity in man,–must work a revolution in all the offices and relations of men; in their religion, in their education; in their pursuits; their modes of living; their association; in their property; in their speculative views.

1. In what prayers do men allow themselves! That which they call a holy office, is not so much as brave and manly. Prayer looks abroad and asks for some foreign addition to come through some foreign virtue, and loses itself in endless mazes of natural and supernatural, and mediatorial and miraculous. Prayer that craves a particular commodity–any thing less than all good, is vicious. Prayer is the contemplation of the facts of life from the highest point of view. It is the soliloquy of a beholding and jubilant soul. It is the spirit of God pronouncing his works good. But prayer as a means to effect a private end, is theft and meanness. It supposes dualism and not unity in nature and consciousness. As soon as the man is at one with God, he will not beg. He will then see prayer in all action. The prayer of the farmer kneeling in his field to weed it, the prayer of the rower kneeling with the stroke of his oar, are true prayers heard throughout nature, though for cheap ends. Caratach, in Fletcher's Bonduca, when admonished to inquire the mind of the god Audate, replies,

"His bidden meaning lies in our endeavors,
Our valors are our best gods."

Another sort of false prayers are our regrets. Discontent is the want of self-reliance: it is infirmity of will. Regret calamities, if you can thereby help the sufferer; if not, attend your own work, and already the evil begins to be repaired. Our sympathy is just as base. We come to them who weep foolishly, and sit down and cry for company, instead of imparting to them truth and health in rough electric shocks, putting them once more in communication with the soul. The secret of fortune is joy in our hands. Welcome evermore to gods and men is the self-helping man. For him all doors are flung wide. Him all tongues greet, all honors crown, all eyes follow with desire. Our love goes out to him and embraces him, because he did not need it. We solicitously and apologetically caress and celebrate him, because he held on his way and scorned our disapprobation. The gods love him because men hated him.

"To the persevering mortal," said Zoroaster, "the blessed Immortals are swift."

As men's prayers are a disease of the will, so are their creeds a disease of the intellect. They say with those foolish Israelites, 'Let not God speak to us, lest we die. Speak thou, speak any man with us, and we will obey.' Everywhere I am bereaved of meeting God in my brother, because he has shut his own temple doors, and recites fables merely of his brother's, or his brother's brother's God. Every new mind is a new classification. If it prove a mind of uncommon activity and power, a Locke, a Lavoisier, a Hutton, a Bentham, a Spurzheim, it imposes its classification on other men, and lo! a new system. In proportion always to the depth of the thought, and so to the number of the objects it touches and brings within reach of the pupil, is his complacency. But chiefly is this apparent in creeds and churches, which are also classifications of some powerful mind acting on the great elemental thought of Duty, and man's relation to the Highest. Such is Calvinism, Quakerism, Swedenborgianism. The pupil takes the same delight in subordinating every thing to the new terminology that a girl does who has just learned botany, in seeing a new earth and new seasons thereby. It will happen for a time, that the pupil will feel a real debt to the teacher,–will find his intellectual power has grown by the study of his writings. This will continue until he has exhausted his master's mind. But in all unbalanced minds, the classification is idolized, passes for the end, and not for a speedily exhaustible means, so that the walls of the system blend to their eye in the remote horizon with the walls of the universe; the luminaries of heaven seem to them hung on the arch their master built. They cannot imagine how you aliens have any right to see,–how you can see; 'It must be somehow that you stole the light from us.' They do not yet perceive, that, light unsystematic, indomitable, will break into any cabin, even into theirs. Let them chirp awhile and call it their own. If they are honest and do well, presently their neat new pinfold will be too strait and low, will crack, will lean, will rot and vanish, and the immortal light, all young and joyful, million–orbed, million–colored, will beam over the universe as on the first morning.

2. It is for want of self-culture that the idol of Travelling, the idol of Italy, of England, of Egypt, remains for all educated Americans. They who made England, Italy, or Greece venerable in the imagination, did so not by rambling round creation as a moth round a lamp,

Emerson's study

but by sticking fast where they were, like an axis of the earth. In manly hours, we feel that duty is our place, and that the merrymen of circumstance should·follow as they may. The soul is no traveller: the wise man stays at home with the soul, and when his necessities, his duties, on any occasion call him from his house, or into foreign lands, he is at home still, and is not gadding abroad from himself, and shall make men sensible by the expression of his countenance, that he goes the missionary of wisdom and virtue, and visits cities and men like a sovereign, and not like an interloper or a valet.

I have no churlish objection to the circumnavigation of the globe, for the purposes of art, of study, and benevolence, so that the man is first domesticated, or does not go abroad with the hope of finding somewhat greater than he knows. He who travels to be amused, or to get somewhat which he does not carry, travels away from himself, and grows old even in youth among old things. In Thebes, in Palmyra, his will and mind have become old and dilapidated as they. He carries ruins to ruins.

Travelling is a fool's paradise. We owe to our first journeys the discovery that place is nothing. At home I dream that at Naples, at Rome, I can be intoxicated with beauty, and lose my sadness. I pack my trunk, embrace my friends, embark on the sea, and at last wake up in Naples, and there beside me is the stern Fact, the sad self, unrelenting, identical, that I fled from. I seek the Vatican, and the palaces. I affect to be intoxicated with sights and suggestions, but I am not intoxicated. My giant goes with me wherever I go.

3. But the rage of travelling is itself only a symptom of a deeper unsoundness affecting the whole intellectual action. The intellect is vagabond, and the universal system of education fosters restlessness. Our minds travel when our bodies are forced to stay at home. We imitate; and what is imitation but the travelling of the mind? Our houses are built with foreign taste; our shelves are garnished with foreign ornaments; our opin-

Manuscript copy of Emerson's poem "Worship" (Autograph Leaves of Our Country's Authors, *edited John Pendleton Kennedy and Alexander Bliss [1864]*)

ions, our tastes, our whole minds lean, and follow the Past and the Distant, as the eyes of a maid follow her mistress. The soul created the arts wherever they have flourished. It was in his own mind that the artist sought his model. It was an application of his own thought to the thing to be done and the conditions to be observed. And why need we copy the Doric or the Gothic model? Beauty, convenience, grandeur of thought, and quaint expression are as near to us as to any, and if the American artist will study with hope and love the precise thing to be done by him, considering the climate, the soil, the length of the day, the wants of the people, the habit and form of the government, he will create a house in which all these will find themselves fitted, and taste and sentiment will be satisfied also.

Insist on yourself; never imitate. Your own gift you can present every moment with the cumulative force of a whole life's cultivation; but of the adopted talent of another, you have only an extemporaneous, half possession. That which each can do best, none but his Maker can teach him. No man yet knows what it is,

nor can, till that person has exhibited it. Where is the master who could have instructed Franklin, or Washington, or Bacon, or Newton. Every great man is unique. The Scipionism of Scipio is precisely that part he could not borrow. If any body will tell me whom the great man imitates in the original crisis when he performs a great act, I will tell him who else than himself can teach him. Shakespeare will never be made by the study of Shakespeare. Do that which is assigned thee, and thou canst not hope too much or dare too much. There is at this moment, there is for me an utterance bare and grand as that of the colossal chisel of Phidias, or trowel of the Egyptians, or the pen of Moses, or Dante, but different from all these. Not possibly will the soul all rich, all eloquent, with thousand-cloven tongue, deign to repeat itself; but if I can hear what these patriarchs say, surely I can reply to them in the same pitch of voice: for the ear and the tongue are two organs of one nature. Dwell up there in the simple and noble regions of thy life, obey thy heart, and thou shalt reproduce the Foreworld again.

4. As our Religion, our Education, our Art look abroad, so does our spirit of society. All men plume themselves on the improvement of society, and no man improves.

Society never advances. It recedes as fast on one side as it gains on the other. Its progress is only apparent, like the workers of a treadmill. It undergoes continual changes: it is barbarous, it is civilized, it is christianized, it is rich, it is scientific; but this change is not amelioration. For every thing that is given, something is taken. Society acquires new arts and loses old instincts. What a contrast between the well-clad, reading, writing, thinking American, with a watch, a pencil, and a bill of exchange in his pocket, and the naked New Zealander, whose property is a club, a spear, a mat, and an undivided twentieth of a shed to sleep under. But compare the health of the two men, and you shall see that his aboriginal strength the white man has lost. If the traveller tell us truly, strike the savage with a broad axe, and in a day or two the flesh shall unite and heal as if you struck the blow into soft pitch, and the same blow shall send the white to his grave.

The civilized man has built a coach, but has lost the use of his feet. He is supported on crutches, but loses so much support of muscle. He has got a fine Geneva watch, but he has lost the skill to tell the hour by the sun. A Greenwich nautical almanac he has, and so being sure of the information when he wants it, the man in the street does not know a star in the sky. The solstice he does not observe; the equinox he knows as little; and the whole bright calendar of the year is without a dial in his mind. His notebooks impair his memory; his libraries overload his wit; the insurance office increases the number of accidents; and it may be a question whether machinery does not encumber; whether we have not lost by refinement some energy, by a christianity entrenched in establishments and forms, some vigor of wild virtue. For every stoic was a stoic; but in Christendom where is the Christian?

There is no more deviation in the moral standard than in the standard of height or bulk. No greater men are now than ever were. A singular equality may be observed between the great men of the first and of the last ages; nor can all the science, art, religion and philosophy of the nineteenth century avail to educate greater men than Plutarch's heroes, three or four and twenty centuries ago. Not in time is the race progressive. Phocion, Socrates, Anaxagoras, Diogenes, are great men, but they leave no class. He who is really of their class

will not be called by their name, but be wholly his own man, and, in his turn the founder of a sect. The arts and inventions of each period are only its costume, and do not invigorate men. The harm of the improved machinery may compensate its good. Hudson and Behring accomplished so much in their fishing-boats, as to astonish Parry and Franklin, whose equipment exhausted the resources of science and art. Galileo, with an opera-glass, discovered a more splendid series of facts than any one since. Columbus found the New World in an undecked boat. It is curious to see the periodical disuse and perishing of means and machinery which were introduced with loud laudation, a few years or centuries before. The great genius returns to essential man. We reckoned the improvements of the art of war among the triumphs of science, and yet Napoleon conquered Europe by the Bivouac, which consisted of falling back on naked valor, and disencumbering it of all aids. The Emperor held it impossible to make a perfect army, says Las Casas, "without abolishing our arms, magazines, commissaries, and carriages, until in imitation of the Roman custom, the soldier should receive his supply of corn, grind it in his hand-mill, and bake his bread himself."

Society is a wave. The wave moves onward, but the water of which it is composed, does not. The same particle does not rise from the valley to the ridge. Its unity is only phenomenal. The persons who make up a nation to-day, next year die, and their experience with them.

And so the reliance on Property, including the reliance on governments which protect it, is the want of self-reliance. Men have looked away from themselves and at things so long, that they have come to esteem what they call the soul's progress, namely, the religious, learned, and civil institutions, as guards of property, and they deprecate assaults on these, because they feel them to be assaults on property. They measure their esteem of each other, by what each has, and not by what each is. But a cultivated man becomes ashamed of his property, ashamed of what he has, out of new respect for his being. Especially he hates what he has, if he see that it is accidental,–came to him by inheritance, or gift, or crime; then he feels that it is not having; it does not belong to him, has no root in him, and merely lies there, because no revolution or no robber takes it away. But that which a man is, does always by necessity acquire, and what the man acquires is permanent and living property, which does not wait the beck of rulers, or mobs, or revolutions, or fire, or storm, or bankruptcies, but perpetually renews itself wherever the man is put. "Thy lot or portion of life," said the Caliph Ali, "is seeking after it." Our dependence on these foreign goods leads us to our slavish respect for numbers. The political parties meet in numerous conventions; the greater the concourse, and with each new uproar of announcement, The delegation from Essex! The Democrats from New Hampshire! The Whigs of Maine! the young patriot feels himself stronger than before by a new thousand of eyes and arms. In like manner the reformers summon conventions, and vote and resolve in multitude. But not so, O friends! will the God deign to enter and inhabit you, but by a method precisely the reverse. It is only as a man puts off from himself all external support, and stands alone, that I see him to be strong and to prevail. He is weaker by every recruit to his banner. Is not a man better than a town? Ask nothing of men, and in the endless mutation, thou only firm column must presently appear the upholder of all that surrounds thee. He who knows that power is in the soul, that he is weak only because he has looked for good out of him and elsewhere, and so perceiving, throws himself unhesitatingly on his thought, instantly rights himself, stands in the erect position, commands his limbs, works miracles; just as a man who stands on his feet is stronger than a man who stands on his head.

So use all that is called Fortune. Most men gamble with her, and gain all, and lose all, as her wheel rolls. But do thou leave as unlawful these winnings, and deal with Cause and Effect, the chancellors of God. In the Will work and acquire, and thou hast chained the wheel of Chance, and shalt always drag her after thee. A political victory, a rise of rents, the recovery of your sick, or the return of your absent friend, or some other quite external event, raises your spirits, and you think good days are preparing for you. Do not believe it. It can never be so. Nothing can bring you peace but the triumph of principles.

Theodore Parker

A Discourse on the Transient and Permanent in Christianity; Preached at the Ordination of Mr. Charles C. Shackford, in the Hawes Place Church in Boston, May 19, 1814 (Boston: The Author, 1841).

Parker gave his discourse without any idea of the uproar that would follow. He had been preaching sermons containing similar ideas to his congregation in West Roxbury for some time, and without any apparent problems from his listeners. Yet this sermon contained–to the conservative–dangerous ideas, and when a few people who had heard it at the Hawes Place Church wrote the newspapers complaining of its infidelities, Parker felt it necessary to publish the text as a response. Once the document was available for all to read, the conservatives attacked Parker and the resulting controversy proved worse than that which had followed Emerson's Divinity School Address. The Unitarian Association even forbid its members to exchange pulpits with Parker. Parker's clear distinction between the transient ("the thought, the folly, the uncertain wisdom, the theological notions, the impiety of man") and the permanent ("the eternal truth of God"), and his placing religious emphasis on the teachings rather than the person of Christ, took away Christianity's status as a divinely inspired religion. This is perhaps the greatest of all the religious documents produced by the Transcendentalists. (For further information, see the entry for Parker in DLB 1, The American Renaissance in New England.)

PREFACE

This discourse is now printed in consequence of some incorrect rumors and printed statements respecting its contents. I have made a few verbal alterations, changed the order of a few sentences, omitted here and there a few words which were only repetitions of former sentences, and added a few paragraphs, which, though written in the manuscript, were necessarily omitted in consequence of the length of the discourse. But I have changed nothing in the substance or doctrine, and have made the alterations only to set the doctrine in a clearer and stronger light. The diffuse and somewhat rhetorical style, though less well adapted to reading than hearing, I could not change without exciting a suspicion of falseness. With the above exceptions, the discourse is printed just as it was delivered.

It is not necessary I should remark upon the article relating to this discourse, signed by several clergymen, and so industriously circulated by the religious journals. The thing speaks for itself. Others likewise, I find, have lifted up their heel against this discourse, or the rumor of it. I was not so vain as to expect my humble attempts to make a distinction between Religion and Theology, or to deliver Christianity from Heathen and Jewish notions–would be either acceptable or understood, by all; nor yet am I so young as to be surprised at the cry of "Infidel and Blasphemer," which has been successively raised against nearly all defenders of the Religion of Jesus, from Origen to Ralph Cudworth.

WEST ROXBURY, JUNE 17, 1841.
DISCOURSE.

LUKE XXL. 33.
HEAVEN AND EARTH SHALL PASS AWAY: BUT MY WORD SHALL NOT PASS AWAY.

In this sentence we have a very clear indication that Jesus of Nazareth believed the religion he taught would be eternal, that the substance of it would last forever. Yet there are some, who are affrighted by the faintest rustle which a heretic makes among the dry leaves of theology; they tremble lest Christianity itself should perish without hope. Ever and anon the cry is raised, "The Philistines be upon us, and Christianity is in danger." The least doubt respecting the popular theology, or the existing machinery of the church; the least

Heliotype of Theodore Parker

sign of distrust in the Religion of the Pulpit, or the Religion of the Street, is by some good men supposed to be at enmity with faith in Christ, and capable of shaking Christianity itself. On the other hand, a few bad men and a few pious men, it is said, on both sides of the water, tell us the day of Christianity is past. The latter—it is alleged—would persuade us that, hereafter, Piety must take a new form; the teachings of Jesus are to be passed by; that Religion is to wing her way sublime, above the flight of Christianity, far away, toward heaven, as the fledged eaglet leaves forever the nest which sheltered his callow youth. Let us, therefore, devote a few moments to this subject, and consider what is *Transient* in Christianity, and what *Permanent* therein. The topic seems not inappropriate to the times in which we live, or the occasion that calls us together.

Christ says, his Word shall never pass away. Yet at first sight nothing seems more fleeting than a word. It is an evanescent impulse of the most fickle element. It leaves no track where it went through the air. Yet to this, and this only, did Jesus entrust the truth wherewith he came laden, to the earth; truth for the salvation of the world. He took no pains to perpetuate his thoughts; they were poured forth where occasion found him an audience,—by the side of the lake, or a well; in a cottage, or the temple; in a fisher's boat, or the synagogue of the Jews. He founds no institution as a monument of his words. He appoints no order of men to preserve his bright and glad revelations. He only bids his friends give freely the truth they had freely received. He did not even write his words in a book. With a noble confidence, the result of his abiding faith, he scattered them, broad-cast, on the world, leaving the seed to its own vitality. He knew, that what is of God cannot fail, for God keeps his own. He sowed his seed in the heart, and left it there, to be watered and warmed by the dew and the sun which heaven sends. He felt his words were for eternity. So he trusted them to the uncertain air; and for eighteen hundred years that faithful element has held them good,—distinct as when first warm from his lips. Now they are translated into every human speech, and murmured in all earth's thousand tongues, from the pine forests of the North to the palm groves of eastern Ind. They mingle, as it were, with the roar of the populous city, and join the chime of the desert sea. Of a Sabbath morn they are repeated from church to church, from isle to isle, and land to land, till the music goes round the world. These words have become the breath of the good, the hope of the wise, the joy of the pious,—and that for many millions of hearts. They are the prayers of our churches, our better devotion by fireside and fieldside, the enchantment of our hearts. It is these words, that still work wonders, to which the first recorded miracles were nothing in grandeur and utility. It is these which guild our temples and beautify our homes. They raise our thoughts of sublimity, they purify our ideal of purity, they hallow our prayer for truth and love. They make beauteous and divine the life which plain men lead. They give wings to our aspirations. What charmers they are! Sorrow is lulled at their bidding. They take the sting out of disease, and rob adversity of his power to disappoint. They give health and wings to the pious soul, broken-hearted and shipwrecked in his voyage through life, and encourage him to tempt the perilous way once more. They make all things ours: Christ our brother; Time our servant; Death our ally and the witness of our triumph. They reveal to us the presence of God, which else we might not have seen so clearly, in the first wind-flower of spring; in the falling of a sparrow; in the distress of a nation; in the sorrow or the rapture of a world. Silence the voice of Christianity, and the world is well nigh dumb, for gone is that sweet music which kept in awe the rulers and the people; which cheers the poor widow in her lonely toil, and comes like light through the windows of morning, to men who sit stooping and feeble, with failing eyes and a hungering heart. It is gone–all gone; only the cold, bleak world left before them.

Such is the life of these Words; such the empire they have won for themselves over men's minds since they were spoken first. In the mean time, the words of great men and mighty, whose name shook whole continents, though graven in metal and stone, though stamped in institutions and defended by whole tribes of priests and troops of followers–their words have gone to the ground, and the world gives back no echo of their voice. Meanwhile the great works also of old times, castle and tower and town, their cities and empires, have perished, and left scarce a mark on the bosom of the earth to show they once have been. The philosophy of the wise, the art of the accomplished, the song of the poet, the ritual of the priest, though honored as divine in their day, have gone down, a prey to oblivion. Silence has closed over them; only their spectres now haunt the earth. A deluge of blood has swept over the nations; a night of darkness, more deep than the fabled darkness of Egypt, has lowered down upon that flood, to destroy or to hide what the deluge had spared. But through all this, the words of Christianity have come down to us from the lips of that Hebrew youth, gentle and beautiful as the light of a star, not spent by their journey through time and through space. They have built up a new civilization, which the wisest Gentile never hoped for, which the most pious Hebrew never foretold. Through centuries of wasting, these words have flown on, like a dove in the storm, and now wait to descend on hearts pure and earnest, as the Father's spirit, we are told, came down on his lowly Son. The old heavens and the old earth are indeed passed away, but the Word stands. Nothing shows clearer than this, how fleeting is what man calls great; how lasting what God pronounces true.

Looking at the Word of Jesus, at real Christianity, the pure religion he taught, nothing appears more fixed and certain. Its influence widens as light extends; it deepens as the nations grow more wise. But, looking at the history of what men call Christianity, nothing seems more uncertain and perishable. While true reli-

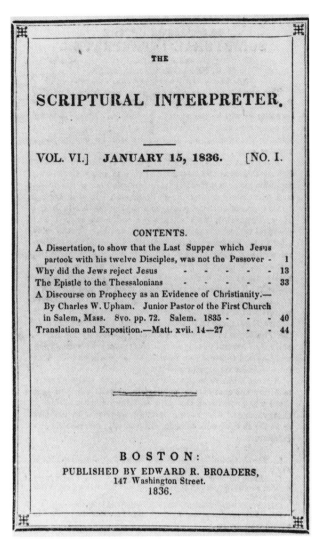

Front wrapper of the periodical edited by Theodore Parker as a divinity student at Harvard

gion is always the same thing, in each century and every land, in each man that feels it, the Christianity of the Pulpit, which is the religion taught; the Christianity of the People, which is the religion that is accepted and lived out, has never been the same thing in any two centuries or lands, except only in name. The difference between what is called Christianity by the Unitarians in our times, and that of some ages past, is greater than the difference between Mahomet and the Messiah. The difference at this day between opposing classes of Christians; the difference between the Christianity of some sects and that of Christ himself, is deeper and more vital than that between Jesus and Plato, Pagan as we call him. The Christianity of the seventh century has passed away. We recognise only the ghost of Superstition in its faded features, as it comes up at our call. It is one of the things which has been, and can be no more, for neither God nor the world goes back. Its terrors do not frighten, nor its hopes allure us. We rejoice that it has gone. But how do we know that our Christianity shall not share the same fate? Is there that difference between the nineteenth century, and some seventeen that have gone before it, since Jesus, to warrant the belief that our notion of Christianity shall last forever? The stream of time has already beat down Philosophies and Theologies, Temple and Church, though never so old and revered. How do we know that there is not a perishing element in what we call Christianity? Jesus tells us, *his* Word is the word of God, and so shall never pass away. But who tells us, that *our* word shall never pass away? that *our notion* of his Word shall stand forever?

Let us look at this matter a little more closely. In actual Christianity, that is, in that portion of Christianity which is preached and believed, there seem to have been, ever since the time of its earthly founder, two elements, the one transient, the other permanent. The one is the thought, the folly, the uncertain wisdom, the theological notions, the impiety of man; the other the eternal truth of God. These two bear perhaps the same relation to each other that the phenomena of outward nature, such as sunshine and cloud, growth, decay and reproduction, bear to the great law of nature, which underlies and supports them all. As in that case, more attention is commonly paid to the particular phenomena than to the general law, so in this case, more is generally given to the transient in Christianity than to the permanent therein.

It must be confessed, though with sorrow, that transient things form a great part of what is commonly taught as Religion. An undue place has often been assigned to forms and doctrines, while too little stress has been laid on the divine life of the soul, love to God, and love to man. Religious forms may be useful and beautiful. They are so, whenever they speak to the soul, and answer a want thereof. In our present state some forms are perhaps necessary. But they are only the accident of Christianity; not its substance. They are the robe, not the angel, who may take another robe, quite as becoming and useful. One sect has many forms; another none. Yet both may be equally Christian, in spite of the redundance or the deficiency. They are a part of the language in which religion speaks, and exist, with few exceptions, wherever man

is found. In our calculating nation, in our rationalizing sect, we have retained but two of the rites so numerous in the early Christian church, and even these we have attenuated to the last degree, leaving them little more than a spectre of the ancient form. Another age may continue or forsake both; may revive old forms, or invent new ones to suit the altered circumstances of the times, and yet be Christians quite as good as we, or our fathers of the dark ages. Whether the Apostles designed these rites to be perpetual, seems a question which belongs to scholars and antiquarians, not to us, as Christian men and women. So long as they satisfy or help the pious heart, so long they are good. Looking behind, or around us, we see that the forms and rites of the Christians are quite as fluctuating as those of the heathens; from whom some of them have been, not unwisely, adopted by the earlier church.

Again, the doctrines that have been connected with Christianity, and taught in its name, are quite as changeable as the form. This also takes place unavoidably. If observations be made upon Nature,–which must take place so long as man has senses and understanding, –there will be a philosophy of Nature, and philosophical doctrines. These will differ as the observations are just or inaccurate, and as the deductions from observed facts are true or false. Hence there will be different schools of natural philosophy, so long as men have eyes and understandings of different clearness and strength. And if men observe and reflect upon Religion,– which will be done so long as man is a religious and reflective being,–there must also be a philosophy of Religion, a theology and theological doctrines. These will differ, as men have felt much or little of religion, as they analyze their sentiments correctly or otherwise, and as they have reasoned right or wrong. Now the true system of Nature which exists in the outward facts, whether discovered or not, is always the same thing, though the philosophy of Nature, which men invent, change every month, and be one thing at London and the opposite at Berlin. Thus there is but one system of Nature as it exists in fact, though many theories of Nature, which exist in our imperfect notions of that system, and by which we may approximate and at length reach it. Now there can be but one Religion which is absolutely true, existing in the facts of human nature, and the ideas of Infinite God. That, whether acknowledged or not, is always the same thing and never changes. So far as a man has any real religion–either the principle or the sentiment thereof–so far he has

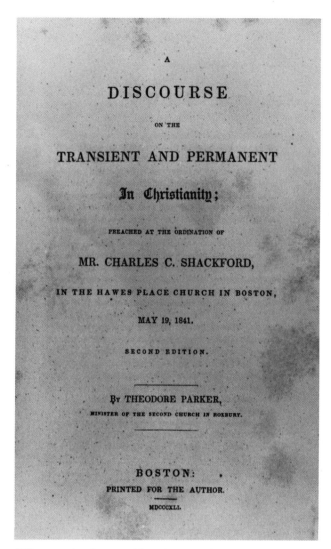

Title page for the pamphlet whose publication led to Parker's split with the Unitarian church

the solar system as it exists in fact is permanent, though the notions of Thales and Ptolemy, of Copernicus and Descartes about this system, prove transient, imperfect approximations to the true expression. So the Christianity of Jesus is permanent, though what passes for Christianity with Popes and cathechisms, with sects and churches, in the first century or in the nineteenth century, prove transient also. Now it has sometimes happened that a man took his philosophy of Nature at second hand, and then attempted to make his observations conform to his theory, and Nature ride in his panniers. Thus some philosophers refused to look at the Moon through Gallileo's telescope, for, according to their theory of vision, such an instrument would not aid the sight. Thus their preconceived notions stood up between them and Nature. Now it has often happened that men took their theology thus at second hand, and distorted the history of the world and man's nature besides, to make Religion conform to their notions. Their theology stood between them and God. Those obstinate philosophers have disciples in no small number.

What another has said of false systems of science, will apply equally to theology: "It is barren in effects, fruitful in questions, slow and languid in its improvement, exhibiting in its generality the counterfeit of perfection, but ill filled up in its details, popular in its choice, but suspected by its very promoters, and therefore bolstered up and countenanced with artifices. Even those who have been determined to try for themselves, to add their support to learning, and to enlarge its limits, have not dared entirely to desert received opinions, nor to seek the spring-head of things. But they think they have done a great thing if they intersperse and contribute something of their own: prudently considering that by their assent they can save their modesty, and by their contributions, their liberty. Neither is there, nor ever will be, an end or limit to these things. One snatches at one thing, another is pleased with another; there is no dry nor clear sight of any thing. Every one plays the philosopher out of the small treasures of his own fancy. The more sublime wits more acutely and with better success; the duller with less success but equal obstinacy, and, by the discipline of some learned men, sciences are bounded within the limits of some certain authors which they have set down, imposing them upon old men and instilling them into young. So that now, (as Tully cavilled upon Caesar's consulship) the star Lyra riseth by an

that, by whatever name he may call it. For strictly speaking there is but one kind of religion as there is but one kind of love, though the manifestations of this religion, in forms, doctrines and life, be never so diverse. It is through these, men approximate to the true expression of this religion. Now while this religion is one and always the same thing, there may be numerous systems of theology or philosophies of religion. These with their creeds, confessions and collections of doctrines, deduced by reasoning upon the facts observed, may be baseless and false, either because the observation was too narrow in extent, or otherwise defective in point of accuracy, or because the reasoning was illogical and therefore the deduction spurious. Each of these three faults is conspicuous in the systems of theology. Now edict, and authority is taken for truth and not truth for authority; which kind of order and discipline is very convenient for our present use, but banisheth those which are better."

Any one who traces the history of what is called Christianity, will see that nothing changes more age to age than the doctrines taught as Christian and insisted on as essential to Christianity and personal salvation. What is falsehood in one province passes for truth in another. The heresy of one age is the orthodox belief and "only infallible rule" of the next. Now Arius, and now Athanasius is Lord of the ascendant. Both were excommunicated in their turn; each for affirming what the other denied. Men are burned for professing what men are burned for denying. For centuries the doctrines of the Christians were no better, to say the least, than those of their contemporary pagans. The theological doctrines derived from our fathers, seem to have come from Judaism, Heathenism, and the caprice of philosophers, far more than they have come from the principle and sentiment of Christianity. The doctrine of the Trinity, the very Achilles of theological dogmas, belongs to philosophy and not religion; its subtleties cannot even be expressed in our tongue. As old religions became superannuated and died out, they left to the rising faith, as to a residuary legatee, their forms and their doctrines; or rather, as the giant in the fable left his poisoned garment to work the overthrow of his conqueror. Many tenents that pass current in our theology, seem to be the refuse of idol temples; the off-scourings of Jewish and Heathen cities, rather than the sands of virgin gold, which the stream of Christianity has worn off from the rock of ages, and brought in its bosom for us. It is wood, hay and stubble, wherewith men have built on the corner stone Christ laid. What wonder the fabric is in peril when tried by fire? The stream of Christianity, as men receive it, has caught a stain from every soil it has filtered through, so that now it is not the pure water from the well of Life, which is offered to our lips, but streams troubled and polluted by man with mire and dirt. If Paul and Jesus could read our books of theological doctrines, would they accept as their teaching, what men have vented in their name? Never till the letters of Paul had faded out of his memory; never till the words of Jesus had been torn out from the Book of Life. It is their notions about Christianity, men have taught as the only living word of God. They have piled their own rubbish against the temple of Truth where Piety comes up to

worship; what wonder the pile seems unshapely and like to fall? But these theological doctrines are fleeting as the leaves on the trees. They

> "Are found
> Now green in youth, now wither'd on the ground;
> Another race the following spring supplies;
> They fall successive and successive rise."

Like the clouds of the sky, they are here to-day; to-morrow, all swept off and vanished, while Christianity itself, like the heaven above, with its sun and moon, and uncounted stars, is always over our head, though the cloud sometimes debars us of the needed light. It must of necessity be the case that our reasonings, and therefore our theological doctrines, are imperfect and so, perishing. It is only gradually that we approach to the true system of Nature by observation and reasoning, and work out our philosophy and theology by the toil of the brain. But mean time, if we are faithful, the great truths of morality and religion, the deep sentiment of love to man and love to God, are perceived intuitively, and by instinct, as it were, though our theology be imperfect and miserable. The theological notions of Abraham, to take the story as it stands, were exceedingly gross, yet a greater than Abraham has told us Abraham desired to see my day, saw it and was glad. Since these notions are so fleeting, why need we accept the commandment of men, as the doctrine of God.

This transitoriness of doctrines appears, in many instances, of which two may be selected for a more attentive consideration. First, the doctrine respecting the origin and authority of the Old and New Testament. There has been a time when men were burned for asserting doctrines of natural philosophy, which rested on evidence the most incontestable, because those doctrines conflicted with sentences in the Old Testament. Every word of that Jewish record was regarded as miraculously inspired and therefore as infallibly true. It was believed that the Christian religion itself rested thereon, and must stand or fall with the immaculate Hebrew text. He was deemed no small sinner who found mistakes in the manuscripts. On the authority of the written Word, man was taught to believe impossible legends, conflicting assertions; to take fiction for fact; a dream for a miraculous revelation of God; an oriental poem for a grave history of miracu-

The Music Hall in Boston, where Parker preached in the 1840s

lous events; a collection of amatory idyls for a serious discourse "touching the mutual love of Christ and the Church;" they have been taught to accept a picture sketched by some glowing eastern imagination, never intended to be taken for a reality, as a proof that the Infinite God, spoke in human words, appeared in the shape of a cloud, a flaming bush, or a man who ate and drank, and vanished into smoke; that he gave counsels to-day, and the opposite to-morrow; that he violated his own laws, was angry, and was only dissuaded by a mortal man from destroying at once a whole nation—millions of men who rebelled against their leader in a moment of anguish. Questions in philosophy, questions in the Christian religion have been settled by an appeal to that book. The inspiration of its authors has been assumed as infallible. Every fact in the early Jewish history, has been taken as a type of some analogous fact in Christian history. The most distant events, even such as are still in the arms of time, were supposed to be clearly foreseen and foretold by pious Hebrews sev-

eral centuries before Christ. It has been assumed at the outset, with no shadow of evidence, that those writers held a miraculous communication with God, such as he has granted to no other man. What was originally a presumption of bigoted Jews became an article of faith, which Christians were burned for not believing. This has been for centuries the general opinion of the Christian church, both Catholic and Protestant, though the former never accepted the Bible as the *only* source of religious truth. It has been so. Still worse it is now the general opinion of religious sects at this day. Hence the attempt, which always fails, to reconcile the philosophy of our times with the poems in Genesis writ a thousand years before Christ; hence the attempt to conceal the contradictions in the record itself. Matters have come to such a pass that even now, he is deemed an infidel, if not by implication an atheist, whose reverence for the Most High forbids him to believe that God commanded Abraham to sacrifice his son, a thought at which the flesh creeps with horror; to believe it solely on the authority of an oriental story, written down no-body knows when or by whom, or for what purpose: which may be a poem, but cannot be the record of a fact unless God is the author of confusion and a lie.

Now this idolatry of the Old Testament has not al-ways existed. Jesus says that none born of a woman is greater than John the Baptist, yet the least in the king-dom of heaven was greater than John. Paul tells us the Law—the very crown of the old Hebrew revelation—is a shadow of good things, which have now come: only a schoolmaster to bring us to Christ, and when faith has come, that we are no longer under the schoolmaster: that it was a Law of sin and death, from which we are made free by the Law of the spirit of Life. Christian teachers themselves have differed so widely in their no-tion of the doctrines and meaning of those books, that it makes one weep to think of the follies deduced there-from. But modern Criticism is fast breaking to pieces this idol which men have made out of the Scriptures. It has shown that here are the most different works thrown together. That their authors, wise as they some-times were; pious as we feel often their spirit to have been, had only that inspiration which is common to other men equally pious and wise; that they were by no means infallible; but were mistaken in facts or in rea-soning; uttered predictions which time has not fulfilled; men who in some measure partook of the darkness and limited notions of their age, and were not always above its mistakes or its corruptions.

The history of opinions on the New Testament is quite similar. It has been assumed at the outset, it would seem with no sufficient reason, without the small-est pretence on its writers' part, that all of its authors were infallibly and miraculously inspired, so that they could commit no error of doctrine or fact. Men have been bid to close their eyes at the obvious difference be-tween Luke and John; the serious disagreement be-tween Paul and Peter; to believe, on the smallest evi-dence, accounts which shock the moral sense and revolt the reason, and tend to place Jesus in the same se-ries with Hercules, and Apollonius of Tyana; accounts which Paul in the Epistles never mentions, though he also had a vein of the miraculous running quite through him. Men have been told that all these things must be taken as part of Christianity, and if they accepted the reli-gion, they must take all these accessories along with it; that the living spirit could not be had without the kill-ing letter. All the books which caprice or accident had brought together, between the lids of the bible, were de-clared to be the infallible word of God, the only certain rule of religious faith and practice. Thus the Bible was made not a single channel, but the *only* certain rule of re-ligious faith and practice. To disbelieve any of its state-ments, or even the common interpretation put upon those statements, by the particular age or church in which the man belonged, was held to be infidelity if not atheism. In the name of him who forbid us to judge our brother, good men and pious men have applied these terms to others, good and pious as themselves. That state of things has by no means passed away. Men who cry down the absurdities of Paganism in the worst spirit of the French "free-thinkers," call others infidels and atheists, who point out, though reverently, other ab-surdities which men have piled upon Christianity. So the world goes. An idolatrous regard for the imperfect scripture of God's word is the apple of Atalanta, which defeats theologians running for the hand of divine truth.

But the current notions respecting the infallible in-spiration of the Bible have no foundation in the Bible it-self. Which Evangelist, which Apostle of the New Testa-ment, what Prophet or Psalmist of the Old Testament, ever claims infallible authority for himself or for oth-ers? Which of them does not in his own writings show that he was finite and with all his zeal and piety, pos-sessed but a limited inspiration, the bound whereof we can sometimes discover? Did Christ ever demand that men should assent to the doctrines of the Old Testa-ment, credit its stories, and take its poems for histo-ries, and believe equally two accounts that contradict one another? Has he ever told you that all the truths of his religion, all the beauty of a Christian life should be contained in the writings of those men, who, even after his resurrection, expected him to be a Jewish king; of men who were sometimes at variance with one another and misunderstood his divine teachings? Would not those modest writers themselves be con-founded at the idolatry we pay them? Opinions may change on these points, as they have often changed—changed greatly and for the worse since the days of Paul. They are changing now, and we may hope for the better; for God makes man's folly as well as his wrath to praise Him, and continually brings good out of evil.

Another instance of the transitoriness of doc-trines taught as Christian is found in those which relate to the nature and authority of Christ. One ancient party has told us, that he is the infinite God; another, that he is both God and man; a third, that he was a

Theodore Parker's library

man, the son of Joseph and Mary,–born as we are; tempted like ourselves; inspired, as we may be, if we will pay the price. Each of the former parties believed its doctrine on this head was infallibly true, and formed the very substance of Christianity, and was one of the essential conditions of salvation, though scarce any two distinguished teachers, of ancient or modern times, agree in their expression of this truth.

Almost every sect that has ever been, makes Christianity rest on the personal authority of Jesus, and not the immutable truth of the doctrines themselves, or the authority of God, who sent him into the world. Yet it seems difficult to conceive any reason why moral and religious truths should rest for their support on the personal authority of their revealer, any more than the truths of science on that of him who makes them known first or most clearly. It is hard to see why the great truths of Christianity rest on the personal authority of Jesus, more than the axioms of geometry rest on the personal authority of Euclid, or Archimedes. The authority of Jesus, as of all teachers, one

would naturally think, must rest on the truth of his words, and not their truth on his authority.

Opinions respecting the nature of Christ seem to be constantly changing. In the three first centuries after Christ, it appears, great latitude of speculation prevailed. Some said he was God, with nothing of human nature, his body only an illusion; others, that he was man, with nothing of the divine nature, his miraculous birth having no foundation in fact. In a few centuries it was decreed by councils that he was God, thus honoring the divine element; next, that he was man also, thus admitting the human side. For some ages the Catholic Church seems to have dwelt chiefly on the divine nature that was in him, leaving the human element to mystics and other heretical persons, whose bodies served to flesh the swords of orthodox believers. The stream of Christianity has come to us in two channels–one within the Church, the other without the Church–and it is not hazarding too much to say, that since the fourth century the true Christian life has been out of the established Church, and not in it, but rather in the ranks of dissenters. From the Reformation till the latter part of the last century, we are told, the Protestant Church dwelt chiefly on the human side of Christ, and since that time many works have been written to show how the two–perfect Deity and perfect manhood–were united in his character. But, all this time, scarce any two eminent teachers agree on these points, however orthodox they may be called. What a difference between the Christ of John Gerson and John Calvin,–yet were both accepted teachers and pious men. What a difference between the Christ of the Unitarians, and the Methodists–yet may men of both sects be true Christians and acceptable with God. What a difference between the Christ of Matthew and John–yet both were disciples, and their influence is wide as Christendom and deep as the heart of man. But on this there is not time to enlarge.

Now it seems clear, that the notion men form about the origin and nature of the scriptures; respecting the nature and authority of Christ, have nothing to do with Christianity except as its aids or its adversaries; they are not the foundation of its truths. These are theological questions, not religious questions. Their connection with Christianity appears accidental; for if Jesus had taught at Athens, and not at Jerusalem; if he had wrought no miracle, and none but the human nature had ever been ascribed to him; if the Old Testament had forever perished at his birth,–Christianity would still have been the Word of God; it would have lost none of its truths. It would be just as true, just as beautiful, just as lasting, as now it is; though we should have lost so many a blessed word, and the work of Christianity itself would have been, perhaps, a long time retarded.

To judge the future by the past, the former authority of the Old Testament can never return. Its present authority cannot stand. It must be taken for what it is worth. The occasional folly and impiety of its authors pass for no more than their value;–while the religion, the wisdom, the love, which make fragrant its leaves, will still speak to the best hearts as hitherto, and in accents even more divine, when Reason is allowed her rights. The ancient belief in the infallible inspiration of each sentence of the New Testament, is fast changing; very fast. One writer, not a skeptic, but a Christian of unquestioned piety, sweeps off the beginning of Matthew; another, of a different church and equally religious, the end of John. Numerous critics strike off several epistles. The apocalypse itself is not spared, notwithstanding its concluding curse. Who shall tell us

the work of retrenchment is to stop here; that others will not demonstrate, what some pious hearts have long felt, that errors of doctrine and errors of fact may be found in many parts of the record, here and there, from the beginning of Matthew to the end of Acts! We see how opinions have changed ever since the apostles' time; and who shall assure us that they were not sometimes mistaken in historical, as well as doctrinal matters; did not sometimes confound the actual with the imaginary, and that the fancy of these pious writers never stood in the place of their recollection?

But what if this should take place? Is Christianity then to perish out of the heart of the nations, and vanish from the memory of the world, like the religions that were before Abraham. It must be so, if it rest on a foundation which a scoffer may shake, and a score of pious critics shake down. But this is the foundation of theology, not of Christianity. That does not rest on the decision of Councils. It is not to stand or fall with the infallible inspiration of a few Jewish fishermen, who have writ their names in characters of light all over the world. It does not continue to stand through the forbearance of some critic, who can cut when he will the thread on which its life depends. Christianity does not rest on the infallible authority of the New Testament. It depends on this collection of books for the historical statement of its facts. In this we do not require infallible inspiration on the part of the writers, more than in the record of other historical facts. To me it seems as presumptuous on the one hand for the believer to claim this evidence for the truth of Christianity, as it is absurd on the other hand, for the skeptic to demand such evidence to support these historical statements. I cannot see that it depends on the personal authority of Jesus. He was the organ through which the Infinite spoke. It is God that was manifested in the flesh by him, on whom rests the truth which Jesus brought to light and made clear and beautiful in his life; and if Christianity be true, it seems useless to look for any other authority to uphold it, as for some one to support Almighty God. So if it could be proved,–as it cannot, in opposition to the greatest amount of historical evidence ever collected on any similar point, that the gospels were the fabrication of designing and artful men, that Jesus of Nazareth had never lived, still Christianity would stand firm, and fear no evil. None of the doctrines of that religion would fall to the ground, for if true, they stand by themselves. But we should lose,– oh, irreparable loss!–the example of that character, so beautiful, so divine, that no human genius could have conceived it, as none, after all the progress and refinement of eighteen centuries, seems fully to have comprehended its lustrous life. If Christianity were true, we should still think it was so, not because its record was written by infallible pens; nor because it was lived out by an infallible teacher,—but that it is true, like the axioms of geometry, because it is true, and is to be tried by the oracle God places in the breast. If it rest on the personal authority of Jesus alone, then there is no certainty of its truth, if he were ever mistaken in the smallest matter, as some Christians have thought he was, in predicting his second coming.

These doctrines respecting the scriptures have often changed, and are but fleeting. Yet men lay much stress on them. Some cling to these notions as if they were Christianity itself. It is about these and similar points that theologized battles are fought from age to age. Men sometimes use worst the choicest treasure which God bestows. This is especially true of the use men make of the Bible. Some men have regarded it as the heathen their idol, or the savage his fetish. They have subordinated Reason, Conscience, and Religion to this. Thus have they lost half the treasure it bears in its bosom. No doubt the time will come when its true character shall be felt. Then it will be seen, that, amid all the contradictions of the Old Testament; its legends, so beautiful as fictions, so appalling as facts; amid its predictions that have never been fulfilled; amid the puerile conceptions of God, which sometimes occur, and the cruel denunciations that disfigure both Psalm and Prophecy, there is a reverence for man's nature, a sublime trust in God, and a depth of piety rarely felt in these cold northern hearts of ours. Then the devotion of its authors, the loftiness of their aim and the majesty of their life, will appear doubly fair, and Prophet and Psalmist will warm our hearts as never before. Their voice will cheer the young and sanctify the gray-headed; will charm us in the toil of life, and sweeten the cup Death gives us when he comes to shake off this mantle of flesh. Then will it be seen, that the words of Jesus are the music of heaven, sung in an earthly voice, and the echo of these words in John and Paul owe their efficacy to their truth and their depth, and to no accidental matter connected therewith. Then can the Word,—which was in the beginning and now is,—find access to the innermost heart of man, and speak there as now it seldom speaks. Then shall the Bible,—which is a whole library of the deepest and most earnest thoughts and feelings, and piety and love, ever recorded in human speech,—be read oftener than ever before, not with Superstitution, but with Reason, Conscience, and Faith fully active. Then shall it sustain men bowed down with many sorrows; rebuke sin; encourage virtue; sow the world broad-cast and quick with the seed of love, that many may reap a harvest for life everlasting.

With all the obstacles men have thrown in its path, how much has the Bible done for mankind. No abuse has deprived us of all its blessings. You trace its path across the world from the day of Pentecost to this day. As a river springs up in the heart of a sandy continent, having its father in the skies and its birth-place in distant, unknown mountains; as the stream rolls on, enlarging itself, making in that arid waste, a bolt of verdure wherever it turns its way; creating palm groves and fertile plains, where the smoke of the cottager curls up at even-tide, and noble cities send the gleam of their splendor far into the sky;—such has been the course of the Bible on the earth. Despite of idolaters bowing to the dust before it, it has made a deeper mark on the world than the rich and beautiful literature of all the heathen. The first book of the Old Testament tells man he is made in the image of God; the first of the New Testament gives us the motto, Be perfect as your Father in heaven. Higher words were never spoken. How the truths of the Bible have blest us. There is not a boy on all the hills of New England; not a girl born in the filthiest cellar which disgraces a capital in Europe, and cries to God against the barbarism of modern civilization; not a boy nor a girl all Christendom through, but their lot is made better by that great book.

Doubtless the time will come when men shall see Christ also as he is. Well might he still say: "Have I been so long with you, and yet hast thou not known me." No! we have made him an idol, have bowed the knee before him, saying, "Hail, king of the Jews;" called him "Lord, Lord!" but done not the things which he said. The history of the Christian world might well be summed up in one word of the evangelist—"and there they crucified him," for there has never been an age when men did not crucify the Son of God afresh. But if error prevail for a time and grow old in the world, truth will triumph at the last, and then we shall see the Son of God as he is. Lifted up he shall draw all nations unto him. Then will men understand the Word of Jesus, which shall not pass away. Then shall we see and love the divine life that he lived. How vast has his in-

Christopher Pearse Cranch's drawing of Theodore Parker in a bookstore (Harvard University Library)

fluence been. How his spirit wrought in the hearts of the disciples, rude, selfish, bigoted, as at first, they were. How it has wrought in the world. His words judge the nations. The wisest son of man has not measured their height. They speak to what is deepest in profound men; what is holiest in good men; what is divinest in religious men. They kindle anew the flame of devotion in hearts long cold. They are Spirit and Life. His truth was not derived from Moses and Solomon; but the light of God shone through him, not colored, not bent aside. His life is the perpetual rebuke of all time since. It condemns ancient civilization; it condemns modern civilization. Wise men we have since had, and good men; but this Galilean youth strode before the world whole thousands of years,–so much of Divinity was in him. His words solve the questions of this present age. In him the Godlike and the Human

met and embraced, and a divine Life was born. Measure him by the world's greatest sons;–how poor they are. Try him by the best of men,–how little and low they appear. Exalt him as much as we may, we shall yet, perhaps, come short of the mark. But still was he not our brother; the son of man, as we are; the Son of God, like ourselves? His excellence, was it not human excellence? His wisdom, love, piety,–sweet and celestial as they were,–are they not what we also may attain? In him, as in a mirror, we may see the image of God, and go on from glory to glory, till we are changed into the same image, led by the spirit which enlightens the humble. Viewed in this way, how beautiful is the life of Jesus. Heaven has come down to earth, or, rather, earth has become heaven. The son of God, come of age, has taken possession of his birthright. The brightest revelation is this,–of what is possible for all men, if not now at least hereafter. How pure is his spirit, and how encouraging its words. "Lowly sufferer," he seems to say, "see how I bore the cross. Patient laborer, be strong; see how I toiled for the unthankful and the merciless. Mistaken sinner, see of what thou art capable. Rise up, and be blessed."

But if, as some early Christians began to do, you take a heathen view, and make him a God, the Son of God in a peculiar and exclusive sense–much of the significance of his character is gone. His virtue has no merit; his love no feeling; his cross no burden; his agony no pain. His death is an illusion; his resurrection but a show. For if he were not a man, but a god, what are all these things; what his words, his life, his excellence of achievement?–It is all nothing, weighed against the illimitable greatness of Him who created the worlds and fills up all time and space! Then his resignation is no lesson; his life no model; his death no triumph to you or me, –who are not gods, but mortal men, that know not what a day shall bring forth, and walk by faith "dim sounding on our perilous way." Alas, we have despaired of man, and so cut off his brightest hope.

In respect of doctrines as well as forms we see all is transitory. "Every where is instability and insecurity." Opinions have changed most, on points deemed most vital. Could we bring up a Christian teacher of any age,–from the sixth to the fourteenth century for example,–though a teacher of undoubted soundness of faith, whose word filled the churches of Christendom, clergymen would scarce allow him to kneel at their altar, or sit down with them at the Lord's table. His notions of Christianity could not be expressed in our forms; nor could our notions be made intelligible to his ears. The questions of his age, those on which Christianity was thought to depend,–questions which perplexed and divided the subtle doctors,–are no questions to us. The quarrels which then drove wise men mad, now only excite a smile or a tear, as we are disposed to laugh or weep at the frailty of man. We have other straws of our own to quarrel for. Their ancient books of devotion do not speak to us; their theology is a vain word. To look back but a short period, the theological speculations of our fathers during the last two centuries; their "practical divinity;" even the sermons written by genius and piety, are, with rare exceptions, found unreadable; such a change is there in the doctrines.

Now who shall tell us that the change is to stop here? That this sect or that, or even all sects united, have exhausted the river of life and received it all in their canonized urns, so that we need draw no more out of the eternal well, but get refreshment nearer at hand? Who shall tell us that another age will not smile at our doctrines, disputes and unchristian quarrels about Christianity, and make wide the mouth at men who walked brave in orthodox raiment, delighting to blacken the names of heretics, and repeat again the old charge "he hath blasphemed"? Who shall tell us they will not weep at the folly of all such as fancied Truth shone only into the contracted nook of their school, or sect, or coterie? Men of other times may look down equally on the heresy-hunters, and men hunted for heresy, and wonder at both. The men of all ages before us, were quite as confident as we, that their opinion was truth; that their notion was Christianity and the whole thereof. The men who lit the fires of persecution from the first martyr to Christian bigotry down to the last murder of the innocents, had no doubt their opinion was divine. The contest about transubstantiation, and the immaculate purity of the Hebrew and Greek text of the scriptures, was waged with a bitterness unequalled in these days. The Protestant smiles at one, the Catholic at the other, and men of sense wonder at both. It might teach us all a lesson, at least of forbearance. No doubt an age will come, in which ours shall be reckoned a period of darkness–like the sixth century– when men groped for the wall but stumbled and fell, because they trusted a transient notion, not an eternal truth; an age when temples were full of idols, set up by human folly; an age in which Christian light had scarce begun to shine into men's hearts. But while this change goes on, while one generation of opinions passes away, and another rises up, Christianity itself, that pure religion, which exists eternal in the constitution of the soul and the mind of God, is always the same. The Word that was before Abraham, in the very beginning, will not change, for that word is Truth. From this Jesus subtracted nothing; to this he added nothing. But he came to reveal it as the secret of God, that cunning men could not understand, but which filled the souls of men meek and lowly of heart. This truth we owe to God; the revelation thereof to Jesus, our elder brother, God's chosen son.

To turn away from the disputes of the Catholics and the Protestants, of the Unitarian and the Trinitarian, of Old School, and New School, and come to the plain words of Jesus of Nazareth, Christianity is a simple thing; very simple. It is absolute, pure morality; absolute, pure religion; the love of man; the love of God

Photograph of Theodore Parker

acting without let or hindrance. The only creed it lays down, is the great truth which springs up spontaneous in the holy heart–there is a God. Its watchword is, be perfect as your Father in Heaven. The only form it demands is a divine life; doing the best thing, in the best way, from the highest motives; perfect obedience to the great law of God. Its sanction is the voice of God in your heart; the perpetual presence of Him, who made us and the stars over our head; Christ and the Father abiding within us. All this is very simple; a little child can understand it; very beautiful, the loftiest mind can find nothing so lovely. Try it by Reason, Conscience and Faith–things highest in man's nature–we see no redundance, we feel no deficiency. Examine the particular duties it enjoins; humility, reverence, sobriety, gentleness, charity, forgiveness, fortitude, resignation, faith and active love; try the whole extent of Chris-

tianity so well summed up in the command, "Thou shalt love the Lord thy God with all thy heart, and with all thy soul and with all thy mind–thou shalt love thy neighbor as thyself," and is there any thing therein that can perish? No, the very opponents of Christianity have rarely found fault with the teachings of Jesus. The end of Christianity seems to be to make all men one with God as Christ was one with Him; to bring them to such a state of obedience and goodness, that we shall think divine thoughts and feel divine sentiments, and so keep the law of God by living a life of truth and love. Its means are Purity and Prayer; getting strength from God and using it for our fellow men as well as ourselves. It allows perfect freedom. It does not demand all men to *think* alike, but to think uprightly, and get as near as possible at truth; not all men to *live* alike, but to live holy and get as near as possible to a life perfectly divine. Christ set up no pillars of Hercules, beyond which men must not sail the sea in quest of Truth. He says "I have many things to say unto you, but ye cannot bear them now . . . Greater works than these shall ye do." Christianity lays no rude hand on the sacred peculiarity of individual genius and character. But there is no Christian sect which does not fetter a man. It would make all men think alike, or smother their conviction in silence. Were all men Quakers or Catholics, Unitarians or Baptists, there would be much less diversity of thought, character and life: less of truth active in the world than now. But Christianity gives us the largest liberty of the sons of God, and were all men Christians after the fashion of Jesus, this variety would be a thousand times greater than now, for Christianity is not a system of doctrines, but rather a method of attaining oneness with God. It demands, therefore, a good life of piety within, of purity without, and gives the promise that whoso does God's will, shall know of God's doctrine.

In an age of corruption as all ages are, Jesus stood and looked up to God. There was nothing between him and the Father of all; no old word, be it of Moses or Esaias, of a living Rabbi or Sanhedrim of Rabbis; no sin or perverseness of the finite will. As the result of this virgin purity of soul and perfect obedience, the light of God shone down into the very deeps of his soul, bringing all of the God-head which flesh can receive. He would have us do the same; worship with nothing between us and God; act, think feel, live, in perfect obedience to Him; and we never are *Christians* as he was the *Christ,* until we worship, as Jesus did, with no mediator, with nothing between us and the Father of all. He felt that God's word was in him; that he was one with God. He told what he saw–the Truth; he lived what he felt–a life of Love. The truth he brought to light must have been always the same before the eyes of all-seeing God, nineteen centuries before Christ, or nineteen centuries after him. A life supported by the principle and quickened by the sentiment of religion, if true to both, is always the same thing in Nazareth or New England. Now that divine man received these truths from God; was illumined more clearly by "the light that lighteneth every man"; combined and involved all the truths of Religion and Morality in his doctrine and made them manifest in his life. Then his words and example passed into the world, and can no more perish than the stars be wiped out of the sky. The truths he taught; his doctrines respecting man and God; the relation between man and man, and man and God, with the duties that grow out of that relation, are always the same and can never change till man ceases to be man, and creation vanishes into nothing. No, forms and opinions change and perish; but the Word of God cannot fail. The form Religion takes, the doctrines wherewith she is girded, can never be the same in any two centuries or two men, for since the sum of religious doctrines is both the result and the measure of a man's total growth in wisdom, virtue and piety, and since men will always differ in these respects, so religious *doctrines* and *forms* will always differ, always be transient, as Christianity goes forth and scatters the seed she bears in her hand. But the *Christianity holy men feel in the heart*–the Christ that is born within us, is always the same thing to each soul that feels it. This differs only in degree and not in kind, from age to age and man to man; there is something in Christianity which no sect from the "Ebionites" to the "latter day saints" ever entirely overlooked. This is that common Christianity, which burns in the hearts of pious men.

Real Christianity gives men new life. It is the growth and perfect action of the Holy Spirit God puts into the sons of men. It makes us outgrow any form, or any system of doctrines we have devised, and approach still closer to the truth. It would lead us to take what help we can find. It would make the Bible our servant, not our master. It would teach us to profit by the wisdom and piety of David and Solomon; but not to sin their sins, nor bow to their idols. It would make us revere the holy words spoken by "godly men of old," but

revere still more the word of God spoken through conscience, reason, and faith, as the holiest of all. It would not make Christ the despot of the soul, but the brother of all men. It would not tell us, that even he had exhausted the fulness of God, so that He could create none greater; for with him "all things are possible," and neither Old Testament or New Testament ever hints that creation exhausts the creator. Still less would it tell us, the wisdom, the piety, the love, the manly excellence of Jesus was the result of miraculous agency alone, but, that it was won, like the excellence of humbler men, by faithful obedience to Him who gave his Son such ample heritage. It would point to him as our brother, who went before, like the good shepherd, to charm us with the music of his words, and with the beauty of his life to tempt us up the steeps of mortal toil, within the gate of Heaven. It would have us make the kingdom of God on earth, and enter more fittingly the kingdom on high. It would lead us to form Christ in the heart, on which Paul laid such stress, and work out our salvation by this. For it is not so much by the Christ who lived so blameless and beautiful eighteen centuries ago, that we are saved directly, but by the Christ we form in our hearts and live out in our daily life, that we save ourselves, God working with us, both to will and to do.

Compare the simpleness of Christianity, as Christ sets it forth on the Mount, with what is sometimes taught and accepted in that honored name; and what a difference. One is of God; one is of man. There is something that will not be won, we fear, by theological battles, or the quarrels of pious men: still we may rejoice that Christ is preached in any way. The Christianity of sects, of the pulpit, of society, is ephemeral–a transitory fly. It will pass off and be forgot. Some new form will take its place, suited to the aspect of the changing times. Each will represent something of truth; but no one the whole. It seems the whole race of man is needed to do justice to the whole of truth, as "the whole church, to preach the whole gospel." Truth is entrusted for the time to a perishable Ark of human contrivance. Though often shipwrecked, she always comes safe to land, and is not changed by her mishap. That pure ideal Religion which Jesus saw on the mount of his vision, and lived out in the lowly life of a Galilean peasant; which transforms his cross into an emblem of all that is holiest on earth; which makes sacred the ground he trod, and is dearest to the best of men, most true to what is truest in them, cannot pass away.

Let men improve never so far in civilization, or soar never so high on the wings of religion and love, they can never outgo the flight of truth and Christianity. It will always be above them. It is as if we were to fly towards a Star, which becomes larger and more bright the nearer we approach, till we enter and are absorbed in its glory.

If we look carelessly on the ages that have gone by, or only on the surfaces of things as they come up before us, there is reason to fear; for we confound the truth of God with the word of man. So at a distance the cloud and the mountain seem the same. When the drift changes with the passing wind, an unpractised eye might fancy the mountain itself was gone. But the mountain stands to catch the clouds, to win the blessing they bear, and send it down to moisten the fainting violet, to form streams which gladden valley and meadow, and sweep on at last to the sea in deep channels, laden with fleets. Thus the forms of the church, the creeds of the sects, the conflicting opinions of teachers, float round the sides of the Christian mount, and swell and toss, and rise and fall, and dart their lightning, and roll their thunder, but they neither make nor mar the mount itself. Its lofty summit far transcends the tumult; knows nothing of the storm which roars below; but burns with rosy light at evening and at morn; gleams in the splendors of the mid-day sun; sees his light when the long shadows creep over plain and moorland, and all night long has its head in the heavens, and is visited by troops of stars which never set, nor veil their face to aught so pure and high.

Let then the Transient pass, fleet as it will, and may God send us some new manifestation of the Christian faith, that shall stir men's hearts as they were never stirred; some new Word, which shall teach us what we are, and renew us all in the image of God; some better life, that shall fulfil the Hebrew prophecy, and pour out the spirit of God on young men and maidens, and old men and children; which shall realize the Word of Christ, and give us the Comforter, who shall reveal all needed things. There are Simeons enough in the cottages and churches of New England, plain men and pious women, who wait for the consolation, and would die in gladness, if their expiring breath could stir quicker the wings that bear him on. There are men enough, sick and "bowed down, in no wise able to lift up themselves," who would be healed could they kiss the hand of their Savior, or touch but the hem of his garment; men who look up and are not fed, because they ask bread from heaven and water from the rock, not traditions or fancies, Jewish or heathen, or new or old, men enough who, with throbbing hearts, pray for the spirit of healing to come upon the waters, which other than angels have long kept in trouble; men enough who have lain long time sick of theology, nothing bettered by many physicians, and are now dead, too dead to bury their dead, who would come out of their graves at the glad tidings. God send us a real religious life, which shall pluck blindness out of the heart, and make us better fathers, mothers, and children; a religious life, that shall go with us where we go, and make every home the house of God, every act acceptable as a prayer. We would work for this, and pray for it, though we wept tears of blood while we prayed.

Such, then, is the Transient, and such the Permanent in Christianity. What is of absolute value never changes; we may cling round it and grow to it forever. No one can say his notions shall stand. But we may all say, the Truth, as it is in Jesus, shall never pass away. Yet there are always some even religious men, who do not see the permanent element, so they rely on the fleeting; and, what is also an evil, condemn others for not doing the same. They mistake a defence of the Truth for an attack upon the Holy of holies; the removal of a theological error for the destruction of all religion. Already men of the same sect eye one another with suspicion, and lowering brows that indicate a storm, and, like children who have fallen out in their play, call hard names. Now, as always, there is a collision between these two elements. The question puts itself to each man, "Will you cling to what is perishing, or embrace what is eternal?" This question each must answer for himself.

My friends, if you receive the notions about Christianity, which chance to be current in your sect or church, solely because they are current, and thus accept the commandment of men instead of God's truth—there will always be enough to commend you for soundness of judgment, prudence, and good sense; enough to call you Christian for that reason. But if this is all you rely upon, alas for you. The ground will shake under your feet if you attempt to walk uprightly and like men. You will be afraid of every new opinion, lest it shake down your church; you will fear "lest if a fox go up, he will break down your stone wall." The smallest contradiction in the New Testament or Old Testament, the least disagreement between the Law and the Gospel; any mistake of the Apostles, will weaken your faith. It shall be with you "as when a hungry man dreameth, and behold, he eateth; but he awaketh, and his soul is hungry.

If, on the other hand, you take the true Word of God, and live out this, nothing shall harm you. Men may mock, but their mouthfuls of wind shall be blown back upon their own face. If the master of the house were called Beelzebub, it matters little what name is given to the household. The name Christian, given in mockery, will last till the world go down. He that loves God and man, and lives in accordance with that love, need not fear what man can do to him. His Religion comes to him in his hour of sadness, it lays its hand on him when he has fallen among thieves, and raises him up, heals, and comforts him. If he is crucified, he shall rise again.

My friends, you this day receive, with the usual formalities, the man you have chosen to speak to you on the highest of all themes,–what concerns your life on earth; your life in heaven. It is a work for which no talents, no prayerful diligence, no piety, is too great. An office, that would dignify angels, if worthily filled. If the eyes of this man be holden, that he *cannot* discern between the perishing and the true, you will hold him guiltless of all sin in this; but look for light where it can be had; for his office will then be of no use to you. But if he sees the Truth, and is scared by worldly motives, and *will* not tell it, alas for him. If the watchman see the foe coming and blow not the trumpet, the blood of the innocent is on him.

Your own conduct and character, the treatment you offer this young man, will in some measure influence him. The hearer affects the speaker. There were some places where even Jesus "did not many mighty works, because of their unbelief." Worldly motives–not

seeming such–sometimes deter good men from their duty. Gold and ease have, before now, enervated noble minds. Daily contact with men of low aims, takes down the ideal of life, which a bright spirit casts out of itself. Terror has sometimes palsied tongues that, before, were eloquent as the voice of Persuasion. But thereby Truth is not holden. She speaks in a thousand tongues, and with a pen of iron graves her sentence on the rock forever. You may prevent the freedom of speech in this pulpit if you will. You may hire you servants to preach as you bid; to spare your vices and flatter your follies; to prophesy smooth things, and say, It is peace, when there is no peace. Yet in so doing you weaken and enthrall yourselves. And alas for that man who consents to think one thing in his closet and preach another in his pulpit. God shall judge him in his mercy, not man in his wrath. But over his study and over his pulpit might be writ–EMPTINESS; on his canonical robes, on his forehead and right hand–DECEIT, DECEIT.

But, on the other hand, you may encourage your brother to tell you the truth. Your affection will then be precious to him; your prayers of great price. Every evidence of your sympathy will go to baptize him anew to Holiness and Truth. You will then have his best words, his brightest thoughts, and his most hearty prayers. He may grow old in your service, blessing and blest. He will have

> "The sweetest, best of consolation,
> The thought, that he has given,
> To serve the cause of Heaven,
> The freshness of his early inspiration."

Choose as you will choose; but weal or woe depends upon your choice.

Charles Dickens

From *American Notes for General Circulation* (London: Chapman and Hall, 1842), 1:133-134.

Charles Dickens criticized America both in his American Notes, *reporting on his 1842 visit to the United States, and in his novel* The Life and Adventures of Martin Chuzzlewit *(1844), which makes his positive comments on the Transcendentalists seem quite remarkable. His comments also show the strong connection between Emerson and Thomas Carlyle which existed in the public mind.*

Painting of Charles Dickens in 1842 by Francis Alexander (Edward F. Paynè, Dickens Days in Boston [1927])

The fruits of the earth have their growth in corruption. Out of the rottenness of these things, there has sprung up in Boston a sect of philosophers known as Transcendentalists. On inquiring what this appellation might be supposed to signify, I was given to understand that whatever was unintelligible would be certainly transcendental. Not deriving much comfort from this elucidation, I pursued the inquiry still further, and found that the Transcendentalists are followers of my friend Mr. Carlyle, or, I should rather say, of a follower of his, Mr. Ralph Waldo Emerson. This gentleman has written a volume of Essays, in which, among much that is dreamy and fanciful (if he will pardon me for saying so), there is much more that is true and manly, honest and bold. Transcendentalism has its occasional vagaries (what school has not?) but it has good healthful qualities in spite of them; not least among the number a hearty disgust of Cant, and an aptitude to detect her in all the million varieties of her everlasting wardrobe. And therefore if I were a Bostonian, I think I would be a Transcendentalist.

James Murdock

From *Sketches of Modern Philosophy* (Hartford, Conn.: John C. Wells, 1842), pp. 167-188. Omitted are lengthy quotations from George Ripley, Orestes A. Brownson, Emerson, and William Dexter Wilson.

Murdock's inclusion of Transcendentalism in his history of modern philosophy shows the movement's general importance and–despite Andrews Norton–its acceptance as a system worthy of serious study. It is also a rather surprisingly objective treatment by a conservative thinker, and one of the few contemporary accounts that distinguished between the Transcendental philosophy of America and that of Kant.

That species of German Philosophy which has sprung up among the Unitarian Clergy of Massachusetts, and which is advocated especially in a recent periodical called the Dial, is known by the appellation TRANSCENDENTALISM. The propriety however of the appellation, may be questioned. Kant, who, so far as I know, first brought the term Transcendental into philosophy, would certainly not apply it to this or to any similar system. He would denominate it TRANSCENDENT, not Transcendental. The difference, according to his views, is immense. Both terms indeed denote the *surpassing* or transcending of certain limits; but the limits surpassed are entirely different. That is called *Transcendental,* which surpasses the limits of sensible or empirical knowledge and expatiates in the region of pure thought or absolute science. It is therefore truly scientific; and it serves to explain empirical truths, so far as they are explicable. On the other hand, that is called *Transcendent,* which not only goes beyond empiricism, but surpasses the boundaries of human knowledge. It expatiates in the shadowy region of imaginary truth. It is, therefore, falsely called science: it is the opposite of true philosophy. A balloon sent up by a besieging army to overlook the ramparts of a fortification, if moored by cables, whereby its elevation, its movements, and its safe return into camp are secured, is a *transcendental* thing; but if cut loose from its moorings and left to the mercy of the winds, it is *transcendent;* it has no connection with any thing stable, no regulator; it rises or descends, moves this way or that way, at hap-hazard, and it will land, no one knows where or when. Now, according to the Critical Philosophy, all speculations in physical science that attempt to go beyond phenomena, and all speculations on supersensible things which at-

tempt to explain this essential nature, are *transcendent;* that is, they overleap the boundaries of human knowledge. In violation of these canons, Fichte, Schelling, and Hegel plunged head-long into such speculations, and yet called them Transcendental; and the new German Philosophers of Massachusetts follow their example.

Waiving however this misnomer,–as every real Kantian must regard it, we will call this philosophy *Transcendental;* since its advocates choose to call it so, and seeing the name has become current in our country. And we will first inquire into its origin among us, and then proceed to notice its prominent characteristics.

ORIGIN OF TRANSCENDENTALISM

AMONG US.

According to their own representations, the believers in this philosophy are Unitarian clergymen, who had for some time been dissatisfied with the Unitarian system of the theology. They tell us, they found it to be a meagre, uninteresting system, which did not meet the religious wants of the community. While laboring to improve their system of theology or to find a better, they cast their eyes on foreign countries. There they discovered a different philosophy prevailing; a philosophy which gives an entirely new version to Christianity, invests it with a more spiritual character, with more power to move the soul, to call forth warm emotions, and to produce communion with God. This philosophy they have now embraced. Such, they inform us, was the origin of Transcendentalism among them.–But it may be more satisfactory to give their own statements on this head. . .

CHARACTERISTICS OF THE

TRANSCENDENTAL PHILOSOPHY.

None of the Transcendentalists of this country are Philosophers by profession. Nearly all of them are clergymen, of the Unitarian school; and their habits of thought, their feelings, and their aims, are manifestly theological. Nor do they give us proof that they have devoted very great attention to philosophy as a science. They have produced, I believe, no work professedly on the subject, not even an elementary treatise; and, if I do not mistake, they have brought forward no new views or principles in philosophy. So far as I can judge, they have merely taken up the philosophy of Victor Cousin, and, after comparing it according to their opportunity with that of the more recent German schools, have modified a little some of its dicta, and applied them freely to scientific and practical theology. At the same time they take little pains, to elucidate and explain the principles of their new philosophy. They address us, as if we all read and understood their favorite Cousin, and were not ignorant of the speculations of the German pantheists: and their chief aim seems to be, to shew us how much better this Gallo-Germanic philosophy explains the religion of nature and of the bible, than the old philosophy of Locke and the Scottish school. Whoever, therefore, would understand the Transcendental writers, must first understand, if he can, the French philosopher Cousin and the German pantheists.

The philosophy of Cousin, as well as that of the modern Germans, we have attempted to describe very briefly, in the preceding chapters; and to them the reader is referred.

Cousin maintains that, by taking a higher point of observation, he has brought all previous systems of philosophy to harmonize with each other. [See his Introd. to Hist. of Phil. by Linberg, page 414.] He therefore adopts, and uses at pleasure, the peculiar phraseology of all the systems, as being all suited to express his own new views. This causes his writings to exhibit, not only great variety, but apparently, if not really, great inconsistency of terminology. And hence different persons, aiming to follow him as a guide, may easily mis-

take his meaning, and adopt different principles; or, if they adopt the same principles, they may express themselves in a very different manner. And, if we suppose the same persons, with only a moderate share of philosophic learning and philosophic tact, to attempt to reconstruct the philosophy of Cousin, by comparing it with the German systems from which it is taken, and at the same time to adopt Cousin's lax use of language; we may easily conceive, what confusion of thought and obscurity of statement may appear on their pages. Now the Transcendentalists, if I do not mistake, have thus followed Cousin. Of course, they differ considerably from one another; some following Cousin more closely, and others leaning more towards some German; some preferring one set of Cousin's terms, and others another, or coining new ones to suit their fancy. After all, Linberg's translation of Cousin's Introduction to the History of Philosophy may be considered as the great store house, from which most of them–e.g. Brownson, Emerson, Parker, &c.–have derived their peculiar philosophical opinions, their modes of reasoning, and their forms of thought and expression.

The radical principle of the Transcendental philosophy, the corner stone of the whole edifice, is, Cousin's doctrine that *Spontaneous Reason* acquaints us with the true and essential nature of things. According to this doctrine, Reason, when uncontrolled by the Will, or when left free to expatiate undirected and uninfluenced by the voluntary faculty, always apprehends things as they are, or has direct and absolute knowledge of the objects of its contemplation. This *clairvoyance* of Reason, Cousin calls "an instinctive perception of truth, an entirely instinctive development of thought,"–"an original, irresistible, and unreflective perception of truth," "pure apperception, and spontaneous faith,"–"the absolute affirmation of truth, without reflection,–inspiration,–veritable revelation."–[Introd. &c. pages 163, 167, 172, 166.] The characteristics of this kind of knowledge, as being *immediate,* and *infallible,* though not always perfectly distinct at first, and as being *divine,* or as coming from God either directly or indirectly, all Transcendentalists maintain. But in what manner, or by what mode of action, our Reason acquires this knowledge, they do not distinctly inform us. Whether our Creator has endowed us with an intellectual *instinct,* a power of rational intuition; or whether the rational soul, as itself partaking of the divine nature, has this *inherent sagacity* in and of itself; or whether the divine Being, God himself, is always present in the soul and acting in it by way of *inspiration,* these philosophers seem not to have decided. They use terms, however, which fairly imply each and all of these hypotheses, and specially the last. But however undecided on this point, which is of so much importance in a philosophic view, on the general fact that all rational beings do possess this knowledge, they are very explicit; and some of them attempt to prove it, by reasoning from the necessity of such knowledge to us, and from the current belief of mankind. [See Cousin's Psychology, Chap. vi and a writer in the Dial, vol. ii. page 86, &c.]

The effects of this principle, when carried into theology, are immense. It dispels all mysteries and all obscurities from this most profound of all sciences, and gives to human Reason absolute dominion over it. For, it makes the divine Being, his government and laws, and our relations to him, and all our religious obligations and interests,–every part of theology, theoretical or practical,–perfectly comprehensible to our Reason in its spontaneous operation. It makes all the doctrines of *natural religion* the objects of our direct, intuitive knowledge: we need no explanations and no confirmations from any books or teachers; we have only to listen to the voice of spontaneous Reason, or to the teachings of our own souls, the light that shines within us, and all will be perfectly intelligible and absolutely certain. And hence, we need no *external revelation,* no inspired teacher, to solve our doubts and difficulties, or to make any part of natural religion, or any principle of moral duty, either more plain or more certain. We are, all of us, prophets of God, all inspired through our Reason, and we need no one to instruct and enlighten us. The great Seers of ancient times, Moses and the prophets, Christ and the apostles, were no otherwise inspired than we all are; they only cultivated and listened to spontaneous Reason more than ordinary men; and this enabled them to see further and to speak and write better than other men on religious subjects. If we would determine whether the *bible* was written by inspired men, we need not pore upon the so called external evidences, miracles, prophecies, &c. but merely listen to the testimony of our own souls, the teachings of spontaneous Reason, or what is called the internal evidence, and we shall at once see the clear and infallible marks of inspiration. And *to understand the bible,* we need no aid from learned interpreters. Only give us the book in a language we can read, and the suggestions of our own inspired minds will enable us to comprehend perfectly the import of every sentence, and to

see clearly what is divine and what is human, or what originated from spontaneous Reason and what from human infirmity, in the holy scriptures. And of course, every man is competent to decide, definitely and infallibly, all the controversies among theologians and all the disputes between sects of Christians, respecting the *doctrines taught in the bible.* In short, not only the profound researches of philologists, antiquarians, and biblical commentators, but also the elaborate discussions of didactic theologians, polemic, apologetic, and metaphysical, are all of little or no value in theology. Instead of depending on them, the theological inquirer should rather retire to solitude and silence, and while musing on religious subjects, with the bible and the book of nature before him, he should refrain from giving any determinate direction to his thoughts, and allowing them to flow on spontaneously, he should listen to the voice of Reason as she expatiates freely in the open field of visions; then he will be caught up, as it were, to the third heaven, and will see all that the inspired prophets saw; his knowledge will be superhuman and divine.

But to understand more fully the metaphysics of the Transcendental writers, we must not overlook their *ontological* doctrines. If Reason acquaints us with the true and essential nature of all things, then the field of ontology is open fully to our inspection, and we may form there a perfectly solid and safe science. Accordingly, all Transcendentalists, on both sides of the Atlantic, assume some system of ontology as the basis of their speculations. The prevailing system among the modern Germans, and that to which Cousin and his American followers assent, is *pantheistic:* that is, it resolves the universe into one primordial Being, who develops himself in various finite forms: in other words, it supposes God and the developments of God, to be the only real existences, the to pay, the entire universe. But when they attempt to explain this general statement, the Germans bring forward different hypotheses. Some, following *Spinoza,* invest the primordial Being with the essential attributes of both a substance and a person; and they suppose him to create from himself, or to form out of his own substance, all rational and sentient beings and all material things. Others, with *Schelling,* suppose him to be originally neither a person nor a substance, but the elementary principle of both, which, in developing itself, becomes first a person and a substance, and then a universe of beings and things. Others follow *Hegel,* and adopt a system of pure *idealism.* They suppose concrete ideas to be the only real existences, and the logical genesis of ideas to be the physical genesis of the universe. Take the simple idea of existence, and abstract from it every thing conceivable, so that it shall become evanescent: and in that evanescent state, while fluctuating between something and nothing, it is the primitive, the generative principle of all things. For it is the most comprehensive or generical of all ideas, including all other ideas under it as subordinate genera and species; and therefore, when expanded or drawn out into the subordinate genera and species, it becomes the to pay, the universe of beings and things. Vacillating among all these theories, especially between the two last, and trying to amalgamate them all in one, Cousin, without exhibiting any very definite ideas, merely declares the Infinite to be the primitive, and all that is finite to be derivative from the Infinite, while yet both the Infinite and the finite are so inseparable that neither can exist without the other.–The appellation *Pantheists,* it appears, is unacceptable to Cousin, and to most of his American followers; but some of the latter voluntarily assume it; and they unscrupulously apply it to all Transcendentalists. That the doctrines of the Transcendentalists, as well as those of Spinoza, Schelling, and Hegel, are really and truly *pantheistic,* appears from the fact that they hold to but *one essence,* or *one substance,* in the universe. They expressly deny, that God created or produced the world *out of nothing,* or that he gave existence to beings and things the substance or matter of which had no previous existence: they say, he created or brought forth the world *from himself,* or formed it out of *his own substance;* and also, that he still exists in the created universe, and the created universe in him, thus constituting an *absolute unity,* as to essence or substance. That the epithet *pantheistic* may properly be applied to such doctrines, seems not to be deniable. [See Krug's Philos. Lexikon; art. *Pantheismus.*]

As Pantheists, the Transcendentalists must behold God, or the divine nature and essence, in every thing that exists. Of course, none of them can ever doubt the *existence of God,* or be in the least danger of atheism; for they cannot believe any thing to exist, without finding God in it: they see him, they feel him, they have sensible perception of his very substance in every object around.–Moreover, if our souls are only portions of the Divinity, if they are really God working in us, then there is solid ground for the belief that *spontaneous Reason* always sees the true nature of things, or has divine knowledge of the objects of its contemplation.

–And again, if it is the Divine Nature which lives and acts in all creatures and things, then all *their action* is *Divine action.* All created intelligences think, and feel, and act, as God acts in them; and of course, precisely as He would have them. There can, then, be nothing *wrong,* nothing *sinful,* in the character or conduct of any rational being. There may be imperfection, or imperfect action, because the whole power of God is not exerted; but every act, so far as it goes, is just what it should be, just such as best pleases God. And hence, though men may sigh over their imperfections, or may ardently desire and strive to become more perfect, yet they can have no reason for *repentance,* for sorrow and shame and self-condemnation, for any thing they have done or have omitted to do. Neither can they feel themselves to need any radical *change of character,* to make them acceptable to God; or any *Redeemer,* to rescue them from impending perdition. All they need, is, to foster the divinity within, to give it more full scope and more perfect action; then they will become all that it is possible they should be, and all they can reasonably desire.–These inferences from their principles, are not palmed upon Transcendentalists by their adversaries, but are admitted and defended by their ablest writers. Says one of them, whom we have before quoted, [Dial, vol. i. pages 423-4,] "Holding as they do but one essence of all things, which essence is God, Pantheists must deny the existence of essential evil. All evil is negative,–it is imperfection, non-growth. It is not essential, but modal. Of course there can be no such thing as hereditary sin,–a tendency positively sinful in the soul. Sin is not a wilful transgression of a righteous law, but the difficulty and obstruction which the Infinite meets with in entering into the finite. *Regeneration* is nothing but an ingress of God into the soul, before which sin disappears as darkness before the rising sun. Pantheists hold also to the atonement, or at-one-ment between the soul and God. This is strictly a unity or *oneness of essence,* to be brought about by the incarnation of the spirit of God, [in us,] which is going on in us as we grow in holiness. As we grow wise, just, and pure,– in a word, holy,–we grow to be one with him in mode, as we always were in essence. This atonement is effected by *Christ,* only in as far as he taught the manner in which it was to be accomplished more fully than any other, and gave us a better illustration of the method and result in his own person than any one else that has ever lived."

"Transcendentalism"

Yale Literary Magazine, 7 (April 1842): 269-277.

This attack on Transcendentalism by a conservative undergraduate literary magazine is a
clear indication that in those schools in which the philosophy of John Locke was still taught with
vigor, there was no room for the intuitive Transcendentalist philosophy, here compared with the
tale of the emperor's new (and invisible) clothes.

In some old book there is a story told of a cunning tailor, who proposed to a foolish king, to make him a costly garment, of such a marvelous quality, that no one, in whose veins ran any base or common blood, could see it. There was a great noise of shears, and much plying of the needle, till at length the wonderful work was done. The king found no difficulty in discerning the royal garment, though his courtiers saw plainly enough, that the tailor had been cutting nothing but air with his shears.

There is a fiction similar to this among the transcendental philosophers. They tell us that their refined and spiritual philosophy is not to be comprehended, except by a chosen *few;* that the *many* must ever slumber on in ignorance of its wonders. We are thus placed in the disagreeable dilemma of confessing that we fathom their mysteries, or that we lack

"The vision and the faculty divine."

No doubt many a man (to avoid this latter imputation) has cried out "Eureka," when there was nothing before him but a mystical cloud.

That we may be justified in making this claim of the transcendentalists a ground of argument, we will transcribe a passage from one of their highest authorities.

"But it is time to tell the truth; though it requires some courage to avow it, in an age and country in which disquisitions on all subjects, not privileged to adopt technical terms or scientific symbols, must be addressed to the public. I say, then, that it is neither possible or necessary for all men, or for many, to be philosophers. There is a philosophic consciousness which lies beneath, or (as it were) behind, the spontaneous consciousness natural to all reflecting beings. As the elder Romans distinguished their northern provinces into Cis-Alpine and Trans-Alpine, so may we divide all the objects of human knowledge into those on this side, and those on the other side of the spontaneous consciousness. The latter is exclusively by the domain of pure philosophy, and is therefore properly entitled transcendental."

This is, undoubtedly, the true idea of transcendentalism. It is this Trans-Alpine province that forms its chief peculiarity–this region of pure thought, which no influence from without can reach, no motion of the sensible world can agitate; where thought springs up from the original native vigor of the mind. This is that almost untrodden region, that lies on the other side of those lofty boundaries, that limit the consciousness of the multitude, and which the transcendentalist alone can penetrate. Let him, then, that would be a philosopher, first inquire whether nature has given him a passport into this inner realm–this province of pure thought. If not, let him mingle with the multitude, and leave these high pursuits to the gifted few. Such are the claims which the transcendentalist makes upon us, and it becomes us to consider whether they are well or ill founded.

The essential characteristic of the school of Locke, is the doctrine, that all our knowledge comes by sensation and reflection; or, in other words, "there is nothing in the mind, that has not before been in sensation." This language is to be so qualified as to include those intuitive ideas which start up in the mind at the instant of certain sensations, and which would not be revealed were it not for them. Such are the ideas of space, time, etc., which are not the direct results of sensation, but which make themselves known only on condition of it. They never reveal themselves so as to be objects of consciousness, until after the work of sensation and perception have commenced. But the pure reason of the transcendentalist is made up of intuitive truths, that depend not at all upon sensation and reflection. They are the original ideas with which the mind is furnished, existing anterior to sensation, and entirely out of the reach of its influence. In other words, could a child be born into our world, absolutely destitute of the five senses, he would still have the ideas of time, space, substance, God, and many others, and would be enabled through these to carry on processes of thought and reasoning. Such is transcendentalism, when viewed at its fountains, and if it has the coherency and compactness of a true system, such it will be in its remotest streams. A fair way to test a system of this kind is to examine its operations and results. As there is a perfect harmony in all truth, if the legitimate tendencies of any system be found to contradict reason and common sense, then we are aware that there is *something* wrong at the source. This is a mere *reductio ad absurdum* mode of reasoning, and serves only to show there is a *fallacy*, without pointing out wherein it consists.

One of the first things that meet us as objectionable in the transcendental theory is, that just so far as there is any thing in it distinct from other systems, it completely sets aside the *law of induction,* the great principle that has guided all modern investigation, and brought many of the sciences to an almost absolute perfection. For if there be this remote province in the mind—this Trans-Alpine region, lying beyond the boundaries of general consciousness, cut off from every thing without and every thing within, we surely cannot approach it by following any line of induction. Like Eneas, when he was about to enter the world of shadows, we had need consult some Sybil to guide our wanderings. The transcendentalist, in his mode of forming a philosophical system, goes back two thousand years. He follows a Grecian model. Nor does his theory differ materially from some of the notions of the Greek philosophers. Plato held that ideas, or (in other words) the forms in which things appear, had existed from eternity; and that the creative operation of the Deity consisted simply in forcing crude chaotic matter (which was also eternal) into these ideal forms. He maintained, moreover, that while the vulgar mind could only hold converse with these material sensible things, yet a chosen few, illumined by the long contemplation of truth, and freed from the slavery of every earthly passion, could come

at length to look directly upon these pure ideas—these patterns of things which had existed from eternity. Here is the same pure reason—the same aristocracy of philosophers, to which the modern transcendentalist lays claim. Yet how little real permanent truth is there to be found among all those fine-spun theories of the Grecian schools? It was only when they made use of the law of induction, that they discovered any thing of lasting benefit to mankind. Their beautiful hypotheses, that had shone like stars during the night of the world, all vanished at the rising of the sun. Experience has fully shown that the inductive process of reasoning is the only mode that conducts us safely and certainly to the truth. We must be content to sit down and watch the phenomena of nature, and learn her secrets only as she reveals them to us in her daily operations. But if there be in the mind this pure reason, that can look directly upon truth, without sensation, or reflection, or any intervening step whatsoever, then it is manifest that so far the law of induction is not only unnecessary, but inapplicable. Every claim that infringes upon a law under which such splendid results have been obtained, should at least arouse our distrust; for if the results of the inductive principle are not true, then must we despair of ever attaining truth, and sink back into utter ignorance or doubt.

We have already adverted to the transcendental notion, that the philosophy of the mind is the heritage of a chosen few—that the mass of men cannot at all understand the operations of this pure reason. If this be interpreted to mean, that only a few men possess ability requisite to form a *system* of mental philosophy, the remark need not be published with any great parade; since nothing can be more simple and self-evident. It is no more true, however, in reference to mental philosophy, than in every other department of science. The world had waited long for a Linnaeus to classify its plants—for a Newton to find out the law of planetary motion—for a Sir Humphrey Davy to discover many splendid truths in chemistry. This class of truths all men are not competent to discover, but most are competent to understand. This claim of the transcendentalist has a deeper import than this, viz: that the multitude cannot comprehend *his* philosophy of the mind, even after it is formed into a system. We have no disposition to question the truth of this; but does it work *for* or *against* his philosophy? Before we can move one step in forming a system of mental science, it must be conceded, that there is a common ground-work in all minds—

that the differences of mind are differences of degree, not of kind. How else can the mental philosopher make himself the representative of his race? The field of his study lies within him. He watches and classifies his own mental phenomena, never doubting that in so doing he classifies the mental phenomena of his fellow-man, however far remote from him. If an individual can be found, the ground-work of whose mind differs from that of other men, it is manifest he belongs not to our race. He is of another order of being, and the philosophy of his mind is not a philosophy to be comprehended by man. If this be so, (and it cannot be doubted), the transcendentalist has no premises, out of which he can weave *his* system, other than those which every mind presents. Why, then, cannot his system be understood? How does it differ, in this respect, from the various physical sciences, except in being more favorable to a perfect comprehension? And surely it is more favorable; for the philosopher of the physical world often finds his most important premises in the secret places of nature, where the common eye never looks. He travels, it may be, from land to land, to find the facts on which he builds his conclusion; and when we study his system, we *trust* rather than *know,* that he has laid down his premises aright. Take any one of the physical sciences. To the common student how many things pass behind the curtain? How frequently is he called upon to exercise faith in other men's honesty? Yet he comes to the grand conclusion with no distrust. But in the study of mental science, the premises on which the system is built all lie within himself. They are the mental phenomena, that have been passing before his mind's eye day after day, through the whole period of his existence. Though the common man may have no power to define and systematize these mental facts, yet, when the system is once formed and spread out before him, can he not see that this is but the counterpart of himself? Ask the wildest savage, when he rises from sickness, and takes down again his hunting bow, if it does call back his forest wanderings–the trophies he has gained in the chase–and the old companions of his sports. Though he has never thought of the law of Association, will he not see that you are describing a state of mind that he has often felt? Whenever, then, a system of mental philosophy be clearly presented to the common mind, if there be not this answering voice from within, we may be sure that the system is wrong. When, therefore, the transcendentalist talks of a Trans-Alpine province, into

which the vulgar crowd cannot come, but which, like the most holy place in the Jewish tabernacle, these high priests of nature alone can enter, we may conclude that he is describing a region of fancy.

Another reason we have for believing transcendentalism a mere hypothesis, is, that it shows a different form under different circumstances. Like the chameleon, it takes its color from what it feeds upon. True science is everywhere the same. It has a unity–a compactness, that is not broken by moving it from place to place. Teach it perfectly to men in the remotest corners of the earth, and they have the same essential idea of it, as he in whose mind it originated. But when you present to men a thing of fancy–something that no man knows–there will be as many different conceptions of it, as there are minds to contemplate it. Each one will seek to represent it to himself, and in so doing, will combine the disjointed fragments of his knowledge into a new idea, which he supposes may stand for the given thing. Poetry is made up of examples of this kind. Take, for instance, the conclave of infernal spirits, described in the first book of Paradise Lost. No man has precisely the same idea of this as his fellow, because his conception will be modified by the whole course of his previous thought. But true philosophy is fixed and definite. Every *science* has certain legitimate natural tendencies, that give a uniform result. And if anything, claiming to be a science, has not this uniform tendency, but results in one thing here, and another there, without looking further, we are authorized to pronounce, that there is more of fancy than of fact in its ground-work. But what agreement is there in the transcendental world? What harmony of opinion exists even among the leaders of this new system! How often is the question asked, does he believe in Kant or Coleridge–Carlyle or Emerson? And if we descend to the common worshipers at the shrine of this pure reason, what do we find among them, but a set of fancies, as vague and incoherent as their nightly dreams? Everywhere transcendentalism is modified and made comformable to the institutions among which it falls–to the prevailing modes of education and thought–and to the thousand influences that affect our daily life. No doubt it would be an amusing sight, to see the American transcendentalists convocated to form a creed. Were we to witness the conflicting claims to orthodoxy, that would be urged–dreams warring against dreams–we might be satisfied to walk on still in the old beaten paths of common sense. From all this we may conclude that the geography of this Trans-Alpine province is none too well understood, even by those who are privileged to travel it–that, at best, they

"Go sounding on a dim and perilous way."

But let us pass from this general view, to a particular point. The transcendentalist derives the idea of a God from pure reason. Dr. Paley has attempted to show that this idea comes by a regular induction, the general statement of which is, that "all design argues a designer." Which of these two opinions best accords with fact? If this be an intuitive idea, then all men, without revelation, should have the same notion of the Deity; for it is impossible that an intuitive idea should be different in different minds. But if it be the result of induction, then it is easy to explain the various conceptions of the Deity, entertained by different nations. For an induction may be more or less perfect; and while all men may carry the process far enough to attain some general notion of a power above them, yet they may leave out many of the more important premises. Thus, a man who has been accustomed to look upon nature only in her wild and terrible moods–who has known of little else than storms, earthquakes, and volcanoes; though he arrives clearly at the idea of a designer, almost unconsciously clothes him with attributes of terror. On the other hand, he who lives in a more peaceful clime, where storms seldom break, and the wilder elements of nature are hushed to repose, will naturally conceive of a Deity corresponding to his experience. This view is fully confirmed by reference to those nations who have formed their notions of Deity from the light of nature. If we analyze the characters of their gods, we shall find that they are made up of elements corresponding to those phenomena of nature that forced themselves most upon the notice of the men who formed these systems. We may take, as a single example, the graphic analysis which Carlyle has given us of the Scandinavian religion. It is a complete transcript of the wild workings of nature in that stern and icy region. The actual fact then accords far better with the idea that men derive their notion of a God by an inductive process, than that it springs from pure reason. For if it be an intuition, it stops short of all practical ends. It can give, at best, but a vague and indefinite idea of a superior power, and must be filled up by induction, before it can be of the least avail. On the other hand, a perfect induction, embracing all existing prem-

ises, would undoubtedly guide us to the essential character of the Deity.

Transcendentalism, in one form or another, is infecting society far more widely than is seen at first view. There is a charm about this inner sight–this deeper vision, that bewilders and fascinates the mind. Everywhere men are beginning to look farther into the deep mysteries of the universe. Nothing so trivial or common-place, but it is filled with types and symbols. The long prevailing notion, that the men of the elder world looked with the clearest eye upon nature and her operations, is now beginning to be abandoned. Many are turning aside from the stern conflicts of real life, to waste their sensibilities in solitude, and spend their mental strength in reveries and daydreams. One hangs over a drop of water, or a flower, as though in their silent changes he expected to read the destinies of the future. Another sits all day in some solitary place, entranced in thought, and worships the God of nature. He heeds not the cry of sorrow, nor deigns to defile his hands with relieving his suffering fellow; but waits in patience till his hour shall come–till fate shall send him upon some high transcendental mission. Now what is all this, but puling sentimentality–miserable affectation? What voice is ever to call them from the dreamy cells they inhabit, into the arena of action, save the voice that now calls them with a most solemn earnestness? Who are the men to whom truth is indebted for its progress on the earth, but strong common-sense men, acting on common-sense principles? One might suppose that a new order of men had arisen, whose especial business is to watch over nature–to take her under their private care and superintendence, and see that she be not slighted: as though none discerned the beauties of the natural world, except those who are ever talking about it: as though the man covered with the dust of a well spent day, could not discover as much glory in the setting sun, as he who has followed it through all its journey.

How idle, too, is the transcendental scheme for a new organization of society, by which the miseries of our present state shall be avoided, and the sincerity and peace of the primitive Eden restored. As though the evils which beset society all spring from its form, and not from a far deeper and more hidden source. How long could an association, on this peculiar transcendental model, endure, were it not for the great world around it, from which the right materials may be gathered, and into which the filth and refuse that grow out of the system may be cast? No doubt a small community may live under some happy form of organization, in which they may shun many of the evils of our common lot, simply by casting them upon others. A State might make itself much more happy and prosperous, for a time, by collecting all its low, vicious, and dependent citizens, and sending them abroad. But what is this but the merest selfishness? If men wish to try an experiment of this kind, let them break off a fragment from the great world, that shall contain a due proportion of its corruptions, and form their society upon some lonely island, where they shall have no link of association with other men, and they will soon find that they have the same essential evils to contend with that spring up everywhere in human life. We would not be understood to mean that all organizations are equally happy, but that no one can be fortunate enough to stanch the spring and source of certain commons evils. All experiments of this sort are as idle as the long labors of the alchymist to discover a universal solvent.

The spirit of which we have been speaking infects the literature of the age. Here and there, men are starting up with new discoveries, in things that were supposed to be well understood. The characters of Shakespeare have suddenly been found to involve a deep, and as yet unexplained mystery. Who shall unfold the transcendental idea of Hamlet? Who shall explain the enigma of Othello? These are things which this age of materialism can hardly hope to find out but which a more spiritual and refined generation may per-haps bring to light. A writer in Blackwood's Magazine has recently discovered a new meaning in the works of Herodotus. "Strange," says he, "that men, in the long period that has elapsed since his time, should have persisted in calling him a historian. Herodotus was not a historian–he was a philosopher." It may be questioned whether the writings of Carlyle are not calculated to do material harm in this respect. There is about him such a natural goodness of heart, such Saxon strength in his language and style, that we can hardly fail to admire him. Yet he finds far too many "right earnest and sincere" characters in men, who played a wild and dangerous game on the earth. Mahomet is no longer an impostor, as men have all along supposed. He is the "great earnest" man sent on a high and eventful mission–struggling under misfortunes, but toiling on like one inspired. His system had as much truth in it as men could bear in that age, and was a necessary link in the great chain of development.

In our land, the dreams that go under the name of transcendentalism would find no place among men inured to vigorous action in the real business of life. The fathers of our country, when, with strong hands, they were hewing down these primitive forests, would have looked upon such notions as little better than witchcraft. It is the sickly sentiment of men who live apart from the world, and whose minds become heated with revery. Like stagnant air, it needs the strong power of a tempest to throw it into motion. If men would call it poetry, it might be better tolerated; but when it lays claim to the name of philosophy, it passes all endurance.

Charles Lane

"Transatlantic Transcendentalism," *Union*, 1 (1 August 1842): 166-168.

> *Charles Lane, an Englishman who would later join with Alcott in the Fruitlands experiment, here demonstrates why the writings of Emerson, Alcott, Theodore Parker, and Elizabeth Palmer Peabody struck such a responsive chord in his own mind. This article, published in an English reform journal, is another example of the favorable overseas response to Transcendentalism. (For further information, see the entry for Lane in* DLB 1, The American Renaissance in New England.*)*

The Yankees are famous fellows for going ahead, as everybody knows. There is nothing that they cannot do as well as, and better, if they choose, than any other nation under the sun. From a spun yarn to an illustrated poem, from a canoe to a senate-house, they are the fellows who can swallow the whole hog, tail and all. Whether they work, build, write, or speak, they accomplish each object in an entire manner. And how is this to be accounted for? Perhaps the hinderances are fewer than they are in this country. Perhaps they are more purposeful. They may know what they aim at, and have the determination to accomplish it. The nation is younger and unfettered, and, like a youth, strips off the tight coat of that tyrant tailor custom, and goes freely and fairly to the work in hand.

Be this speculation true or not, we are glad to discover in our American brethren a rivalry in something better than broad cloths and Birmingham buttons. These things we must leave to the pedlars, and talk about those things which interest *man*.

Our readers no doubt well know that there was in *olden* times, that is when the world was *young*, and vice and folly were less busy, a sort of idea that the mind was filled by an interior process, somewhat after the fashion seen in birds' eggs, and that education and the circumstances occurring in life were as the hen which hatches the egg. This Platonism was frequently combatted, and at length pretty much overturned by the Baconian philosophy, which is made answerable, though unjustly, for the doctrine that all knowledge, truth, love, and wisdom are derivable from without, and that there is no interior life and power in that curious egg, the human mind.

Again the old notion starts up, and wonderful to relate, it rises in that very country which *a priori* one would suppose to be the very head quarters of the more practical philosophy. But so it is; expectations, like dreams, generally go by contraries.

The new school, however, does not seek any authority from antiquity, the new expositors do not claim respect by quoting "wise says and *modern* instances," as old as Brama; neither do they assert any merit as new discoverers, but they seem to be happy in putting forth their revelations in the best manner they are able, which certainly is often very happy and truly eloquent.

Such *small* matters as Puseyism, Catholicism, Socialism, Paper Money, or National Prosperity, don't trouble the phrenological tenants of these enlightened heads, not less renowned for the lightness of their cares, than for their intellectual illumination. It is a curious thing to observe underlying all time, as it were, these universal principles, which ever and anon peep above the surface, here and there, just sufficient to keep before mankind a knowledge of the unitive idea, though they are not strong enough to accomplish real unity itself amongst mankind. They are the race of modern prophets, of which their predecessors formed a chain, each link knowing another all the way back to the commencement of time. These priests are no less prophetical than historical; Mr. Emerson for instance is emboldened to pronounce,

> "I am owner of the sphere,
> Of the seven stars and the solar year,
> Of Caesar's hand, and Plato's brain,
> Of Lord Christ's heart, and Shakespere's strain."

Photograph of Charles Lane

Of "Books," he says they "are the best of things, well used; abused, among the worst. What is the right use? What is the one end, which all means go to effect? They are for nothing but to inspire. I had better never see a book than be warped by its attraction clean out of my own orbit, and made a satellite instead of a system. The one thing in the world of value is the active soul,–the soul free, sovereign, active. This every man is entitled to; this every man contains within him, although, in almost all men, obstructed, and as yet unborn. The soul active sees absolute truth; and utters truth, or creates. In this action it is genius, not the privilege of here and there a favourite, but the sound estate of every man. In its essence it is progressive. The book, the college, the school of art, the institution of any kind, all these stop with some past utterance of genius. This is good, say they–let us hold by this. They pin me down. They look backward, and not forward. The eyes of man are set in his forehead, not in his hind-head. Man hopes. Genius creates."

We do not propose on this occasion to enter into an analysis of the literary productions in this school, but we cannot forbear to indulge in a few extracts from the works of Emerson, Alcott, Parker, Miss Peabody, and others, which will better inform the reader of the peculiar condition of mind they develope than any abstract we might construct. "The characteristic of a genuine heroism is its persistency. All men have wandering impulses, fits and starts of generosity. But when you have resolved to be great, abide by yourself, and do not weakly try to reconcile yourself with the world. The heroic cannot be the common, nor the common the heroic. Yet we have the weakness to expect the sympathy of people in those actions whose excellence is that they outrun sympathy, and appeal to a tardy justice. If you would serve your brother, because it is fit for you to serve him, do not take back your words when you find that prudent people do not commend you. Be true to your own act, and congratulate yourself, if you have done something strange and extravagant, and broken the monotony of a decorous age. It was a high counsel that I once heard given to a young person, 'Always do what you are afraid to do.' A simple, manly character need never make an apology."

"To speak the truth, even with some austerity, to live with some rigour of temperance, or some extremes of generosity, seems to be an asceticism, which common good-nature would appoint to those who are at ease and in plenty, in sign that they feel a brotherhood with the great multitude of suffering men. And not only need we breathe and exercise the soul by assuming the penalties of abstinence, of debt, of solitude, of unpopularity, but it behoves the wise man to look with a bold eye into those rarer dangers which sometimes invade men, and to familiarize himself with disgusting forms of disease, with sounds of execration, and the vision of violent death." *Emerson's Essays.* p.216.

LABOUR.–"Labour is sweet; nor is that a stern decree which sends man into the field to earn his bread in the sweat of his face. Labour is primeval; it replaces man in Eden–the garden planted by God. It exalts and humanizes the soul. Life in all its functions and relations then breathes of groves and fountains; of simplicity and health. Man discourses sublimely with divinity over the spade, the hoe, and the sickle; marrying the soul and the soil by the rite of labour. Sloth is the tempter that beguiles him of innocence, and exiles him from paradise. Let none esteem himself beloved by the divine husbandman, unless he earn the wages of peace in his vineyard. Yet now the broad world is full of idlers, the fields are barren, the life is hungry, there is no corn. The harvests are of tares and not of wheat." *Alcott: Orphic Sayings.*

These may be Orphic sayings in Yankee-land, but alas how sadly reversed is the picture on this side the water. Idleness is the last charge which can be brought against Englishmen, yet a plentiful harvest of tares only is to be reaped, both in literary and physical labour. Our cotton labour is much more like a certain nameless place than paradise, and even our agricultural labourers, albeit they are not confined to a factory dungeon, are more intent upon their scanty allowance of beer and bacon than the divine presence in their souls. We rejoice in hearing and imagining that these things are otherwise in America.

"ENTHUSIASM.—Believe youth that your heart is an oracle: trust her instinctive auguries, obey her divine leadings, nor listen too fondly to the uncertain echoes of your head. The heart is the prophet of the soul, and ever fulfils her prophecies. Reason is her historian, but without the prophecy the history would not be. Great is the heart; cherish her; she is big with the future; she forbodes renovation. Let the flame of enthusiasm fire always your bosom. Enthusiasm is the glory and hope of the world. It is the life of sanctity and genius: it has wrought all miracles since the beginning of time." *Alcott.*

METAPHYSICAL MOTHERS.—"There is nothing in true education which has not its germ in the maternal sentiment; and every mother would find more of the spiritual philosophy in her own affections, if her mind would but read her heart, than could be obtained by years of study in books. It indeed requires thought to get possession of principles, as well as to act upon them, and it is necessarily metaphysical thought, when the subject of attention is a child, whose essence is beyond the metaphysical nature; but every intelligent woman who will make the effort, finds, on analysing her own mind, that she knows more of metaphysics than she does of anything else." "Such is the admirable arrangement of checks and balances in the divine social institution the family, that it is astonishing to find how much of the true method of inspiration is acted out by true hearted men and women who never speculated." *Miss Peabody: Record of a School.* p.181.

A literature which does not consist in mere fine words, may thus evidently be spoken in elegant language; and it is in a literature far more satisfactory than recent times have developed amongst us, that the new and inventive idea will now be expressed. The letter, if it have any value whatever, must be made correspondent to the spirit. The old black spirit may have its antiquated black letter; the new white spirit will have its new light type. The new spirit fears not any new mode, and will somehow express itself. This outpouring of the human soul divine not even all the churches, inquisitions, governments, prisons, and persecutions upon earth shall avail in checking. The new spirit must interrogate and sift all old forms, and what it finds worthless must be cast aside. The literature which is produced from mere amusement is now fast shrinking into nothing by the side of that which is based on knowledge. In like manner, and by the same supreme authority, is it decreed, that the literature founded on knowledge, must yield to the forthcoming, which is an emanation of being.

Yes! It is a *being literature* which the world, the new world wants. An intuition of this truth pervades many minds, not in old England only, but in new England also. We hail with sincere fraternal affection the recent manifestations of this feeling on the other side the great waters. These writers are the ambassadors who shall accomplish more in the way of knitting nations together in holy brotherhood, than could ten times their number of diplomatists and financiers, if they were to make trial, which they never do. These credentials are presented to every human heart, and scarcely deserving of that honoured name must be the place where they find not a most gracious reception.

H[enry]. D[avid]. T[horeau].
"A Winter Walk," *Dial,* 4 (October 1843): 211-22.

This is arguably the best piece Thoreau published in the Dial. *It shows him as a writer of natural descriptions without many peers and acts as a showcase for the literary skills he would hone even more finely in* Walden. *(For further information, see the entry for Thoreau in* DLB 1, The American Renaissance in New England.*)*

The wind has gently murmured through the blinds, or puffed with feathery softness against the windows, and occasionally sighed like a summer zephyr lifting the leaves along the livelong night. The meadow mouse has slept in his snug gallery in the sod, the owl has sat in a hollow tree in the depth of the swamp, the rabbit, the squirrel, and the fox have all been housed. The watch-dog has lain quiet on the hearth, and the cattle have stood silent in their stalls. The earth itself has slept, as it were its first, not its last sleep, save when some street-sign or wood-house door, has faintly creaked upon its hinge, cheering forlorn nature at her midnight work.–The only sound awake twixt Venus and Mars,–advertising us of a remote inward warmth, a divine cheer and fellowship, where gods are met together, but where it is very bleak for men to stand. But while the earth has slumbered, all the air has been alive with feathery flakes, descending, as if some northern Ceres reigned, showering her silvery grain over all the fields.

We sleep and at length awake to the still reality of a winter morning. The snow lies warm as cotton or down upon the window-sill; the broadened sash and frosted panes admit a dim and private light, which enhances the snug cheer within. The stillness of the morning is impressive. The floor creaks under our feet as we move toward the window to look abroad through some clear space over the fields. We see the roofs stand under their snow burden. From the eaves and fences hang stalactites of snow, and in the yard stand stalagmites covering some concealed core. The trees and shrubs rear white arms to the sky on every side, and where were walls and fences, we see fantastic forms stretching in frolic gambols across the dusky landscape, as if nature had strewn her fresh designs over the fields by night as models for man's art.

Silently we unlatch the door, letting the drift fall in, and step abroad to face the cutting air. Already the stars have lost some of their sparkle, and a dull leaden mist skirts the horizon. A lurid brazen light in the east proclaims the approach of day, while the western landscape is dim and spectral still, and clothed in a sombre Tartarean light, like the shadowy realms. They are Infernal sounds only that you hear,–the crowing of cocks, the barking of dogs, the chopping of wood, the lowing of kine, all seem to come from Pluto's barn-yard and beyond the Styx;–not for any melancholy they suggest, but their twilight bustle is too solemn and mysterious for earth. The recent tracks of the fox or otter, in the yard, remind us that each hour of the night is crowded with events, and the primeval nature is still working and making tracks in the snow. Opening the gate, we tread briskly along the lone country road, crunching the dry and crisp snow under our feet, or aroused by the sharp clear creak of the wood-sled, just starting for the distant market, from the early farmer's door, where it has lain the summer long, dreaming amid the chips and stubble. For through the drifts and powdered windows we see the farmer's early candle, like a paled star, emitting a lonely beam, as if some severe virtue were at its matins there. And one by one the smokes begin to ascend from the chimneys amidst the trees and snows.

> The sluggish smoke curls up from some
> deep dell,
> The stiffened air exploring in the dawn,
> And making slow acquaintance with the day;
> Delaying now upon its heavenward course,
> In wreathed loiterings dallying with itself,

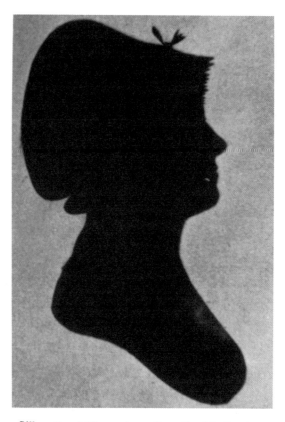

Photograph of Thoreau's father, John Thoreau, Sr. (Milton Meltzer and Walter Harding, A Thoreau Profile *[1962])*

Silhouette of Thoreau's mother, Cynthia Dunbar Thoreau (Milton Meltzer and Walter Harding, A Thoreau Profile *[1962])*

Painting of Thoreau's brother, John Thoreau, Jr. (Concord Free Public Library); his boat trip with Henry is memorialized in A Week on the Concord and Merrimack Rivers *(1849).*

Drawing of Thoreau's birthplace, near Concord

With as uncertain purpose and slow deed,
  As its half-wakened master by the hearth,
  Whose mind still slumbering and sluggish
    thoughts
  Have not yet swept into the onward current
  Of the new day;—and now it streams afar,
  The while the chopper goes with step direct,
  And mind intent to swing the early axe.
    First in the dusky dawn he sends abroad
  His early scout, his emissary, smoke,
  The earliest, latest pilgrim from the roof,
  To feel the frosty air, inform the day;
  And while he crouches still beside the hearth,
  Nor musters courage to unbar the door,
  It has gone down the glen with the light wind,
  And o'er the plain unfurled its venturous
    wreath,
  Draped the tree tops, loitered upon the hill,
  And warmed the pinions of the early bird;
  And now, perchance, high in the crispy air,
  Has caught sight of the day o'er the earth's
    edge,
  And greets its master's eye at his low door,
  As some refulgent cloud in the upper sky.

We hear the sound of wood-chopping at the farmers' doors, far over the frozen earth, the baying of the house dog, and the distant clarion of the cock. The thin and frosty air conveys only the finer particles of sound to our ears, with short and sweet vibrations, as the waves subside soonest on the purest and lightest liquids, in which gross substances sink to the bottom. They come clear and bell-like, and from a greater distance in the horizon, as if there were fewer impediments than in summer to make them faint and ragged. The ground is sonorous, like seasoned wood, and even the ordinary rural sounds are melodious, and the jingling of the ice on the trees is sweet and liquid. There is the least possible moisture in the atmosphere, all being dried up, or congealed, and it is of such extreme tenuity and elasticity, that it becomes a source of delight. The withdrawn and tense sky seems groined like the aisles of a cathedral, and the polished air sparkles as if there were crystals of ice floating in it. Those who have resided in Greenland, tell us, that, when it freezes, "the sea smokes like burning turf land, and a fog or mist arises, called frost smoke," which "cutting smoke frequently raises blisters on the face and hands, and is very pernicious to the health." But this pure stinging cold is an elixir to the lungs, and not so much a frozen mist, as a crystallized mid-summer haze, refined and purified by cold.

The sun at length rises through the distant woods, as if with the faint clashing swinging sound of cymbals, melting the air with his beams, and with such rapid steps the morning travels, that already his rays are gilding the distant western mountains. We step hastily along through the powdery snow, warmed by an inward heat, enjoying an Indian summer still, in the increased glow of thought and feeling. Probably if our lives were more conformed to nature, we should not need to defend ourselves against her heats and colds, but find her our constant nurse and friend, as do plants and quadrupeds. If our bodies were fed with pure and simple elements, and not with a stimulating and heating diet, they would afford no more pasture for cold than a leafless twig, but thrive like the trees, which find even winter genial to their expansion.

The wonderful purity of nature at this season is a most pleasing fact. Every decayed stump and moss-grown stone and rail, and the dead leaves of autumn, are concealed by a clean napkin of snow. In the bare fields and tinkling woods, see what virtue survives. In the coldest and bleakest places, the warmest charities still maintain a foot-hold. A cold and searching wind drives away all contagion, and nothing can withstand it but what has a virtue in it; and accordingly, whatever we meet with in cold and bleak places, as the tops of mountains, we respect for a sort of sturdy innocence, a Puritan toughness. All things beside seem to be called in for shelter, and what stays out must be part of the original frame of the universe, and of such valor as God himself. It is invigorating to breathe the cleansed air. Its greater fineness and purity are visible to the eye, and we would fain stay out long and late, that the gales may sigh through us too, as through the leafless trees, and fit us for the winter:—as if we hoped so to borrow some pure and steadfast virtue, which will stead us in all seasons.

At length we have reached the edge of the woods, and shut out the gadding town. We enter within their covert as we go under the roof of a cottage, and cross its threshold, all ceiled and banked up with snow. They are glad and warm still, and as genial and cheery in winter as in summer. As we stand in the midst of the pines, in the flickering and checkered light which straggles but little way into their maze, we wonder if the towns have ever heard their simple story. It seems to us that no traveller has ever explored them, and notwithstanding the wonders which science is elsewhere revealing every day, who would not like to hear

ORDER OF EXERCISES

FOR

COMMENCEMENT,

XXX AUGUST, MDCCCXXXVII.

Exercises of Candidates for the Degree of Bachelor of Arts.

[The performers will speak in the order of their names.]

1. A Salutatory Oration in Latin.
   CHARLES THEODORE RUSSELL, *Princeton.*

2. A Conference. "The Influence of Young's and Cowper's Poems."
   DANIEL WIGHT, *Natick.*
   WILLIAM PINKNEY WILLIAMS, *Baltimore, Md.*

3. An Essay. "The Effect upon Literature of a Belief in Immortality."
   JOHN FOSTER WILLIAMS LANE, *Boston.*

4. A Conference. "The Commercial Spirit of Modern Times, considered in its Influence on the Political, Moral, and Literary Character of a Nation."
   CHARLES WYATT RICE, *Brookfield.*
   DAVID HENRY THOREAU, *Concord.*
   HENRY VOSE, *Dorchester.*

5. A Literary Disquisition. "Modern Imitation of the Ancient Greek Tragedy."
   SAMUEL AUSTIN KENDALL, *Utica, N. Y.*

Music.

6. A Dissertation. "Severity of Manners in a Republic."
   CLIFFORD BELCHER, *Farmington, Me.*

7. A Philosophical Disquisition. "The Real or Supposed Decline of Science at the Present Day."
   SAMUEL TREAT, *Portsmouth, N. H.*

Program for Thoreau's graduation from Harvard

their annals? Our humble villages in the plain, are their contribution. We borrow from the forest the boards which shelter, and the sticks which warm us. How important is their evergreen to the winter, that portion of the summer which does not fade, the permanent year, the unwithered grass. Thus simply, and with little expense of altitude, is the surface of the earth diversified. What would human life be without forests, those natural cities? From the tops of mountains they appear like smooth shaven lanes, yet whither shall we walk but in this taller grass?

There is a slumbering subterranean fire in nature which never goes out, and which no cold can chill. It finally melts the great snow, and in January or July is only buried under a thicker or thinner covering. In the coldest day it flows somewhere, and the snow melts around every tree. This field of winter rye, which sprouted late last fall, and now speedily dissolves the snow, is where the fire is very thinly covered. We feel warmed by it. In the winter, warmth stands for all virtue, and we resort in thought to a trickling rill, with its bare stones shining in the sun, and to warm springs in the woods, with as much eagerness as rabbits and robins. The steam which rises from swamps and pools is as dear and domestic as that of our own kettle. What fire could ever equal the sunshine of a winter's-day, when the meadow mice come out by the wallsides, and the chickadee lisps in the defiles of the wood? The warmth comes directly from the sun, and is not radiated from the earth, as in summer; and when we feel his beams on our back as we are treading some snowy dell, we are grateful as for a special kindness, and bless the sun which has followed us into that by-place.

This subterranean fire has its altar in each man's breast, for in the coldest day, and on the bleakest hill, the traveler cherishes a warmer fire within the folds of his cloak than is kindled on any hearth. A healthy man, indeed, is the complement of the seasons, and in winter, summer is in his heart. There is the south. Thither have all birds and insects migrated, and around the warm springs in his breast are gathered the robin and the lark.

In this glade covered with bushes of a year's growth see how the silvery dust lies on every seared leaf and twig, deposited in such infinite and luxurious forms as by their very variety atone for the absence of color. Observe the tiny tracks of mice around every stem, and the triangular tracks of the rabbit. A pure elastic heaven hangs over all, as if the impurities of the summer sky refined and shrunk by the chaste winter's cold, had been winnowed from the heavens upon the earth.

Nature confounds her summer distinction at this season. The heavens seem to be nearer the earth. The elements are less reserved and distinct. Water turns to ice, rain to snow. The day is but a Scandinavian night. The winter is an arctic summer.

How much more living is the life that is in nature, the furred life which still survives the stinging nights, and, from amidst fields and woods covered with frost and snow, sees the sun rise.

"The foodless wilds
Pour forth their brown inhabitants."

The grey-squirrel and rabbit are brisk and playful in the remote glens, even on the morning of the cold Friday. Here is our Lapland and Labrador, and for our Esquimaux and Knistenaux, Dog-ribbed Indians, Novazemblaites, and Spitzbergeners, are there not the

JOHN THOREAU & CO.,
CONCORD, MASS.
MANUFACTURE
A NEW AND SUPERIOR DRAWING PENCIL,

Expressly for ARTISTS AND CONNOISSEURS, possessing in an unusual degree the qualities of the pure lead, superior blackness, and firmness of point, as well as freedom of mark, and warranted not to be affected by changes of temperature. Among numerous other testimonials are the following.

Boston, Somerset Street, June, 1844.

Dear Sir: — I have used a number of different kinds of Black-lead Pencils made by you, and find them to be of excellent quality. I would especially recommend to Engineers your fine hard pencils, as capable of giving a very fine line, the points being remarkably even and firm, which is due to the peculiar manner in which the leads are prepared. The softer kinds I find to be of good quality, and much better than any American Pencils I have used,

Respectfully,
Your Obedient Servant,
C. T. JACKSON,

Boston, June, 1844.

Sir: — Having made a trial of your pencils, I do not hesitate to pronounce them superior in every respect to any American Pencils I have yet met with, and equal to those of Rhodes, or Brookman & Langdon, London.

Respectfully Yours,
D. C. JOHNSTON,

J. THOREAU & CO. also manufacture the various other kinds of BLACK-LEAD PENCILS; the Mammoth or Large Round, the Rulers or Flat, and the Common of every quality and price; also, Lead-Points in any quantity, and plumbago Plates for Galvanic Batteries. All orders addressed to them will be promptly attended to.

Advertisement for Thoreau pencils (Concord Free Public Library)

ice-cutter and wood-chopper, the fox, muskrat, and mink?

Still, in the midst of the arctic day, we may trace the summer to its retreats, and sympathize with some contemporary life. Stretched over the brooks, in the midst of the frost-bound meadows, we may observe the submarine cottages of the caddice worms, the larvae of the Plicipennes. Their small cylindrical caves built around themselves, composed of flags, sticks, grass, and withered leaves, shells and pebbles, in form and color like the wrecks which strew the bottom—now drifting along over the pebbly bottom, now whirling in tiny eddies and dashing down steep falls, or sweeping rapidly along with the current, or else swaying to and fro at the end of some grass blade or root. Anon they will leave their sunken habitations, and crawling up the stems of plants, or floating on the surface like gnats, or perfect insects; henceforth flutter over the surface of the water, or sacrifice their short lives in the flame of our candles at evening. Down yonder little glen the shrubs are drooping under their burden, and the red alder-berries contrast with the white ground. Here are the marks of a myriad feet which have already been abroad. The sun rises as proudly over such a glen, as over the valley of the Seine or the Tiber, and it seems the residence of a pure and self-subsistent valor, such as they never witnessed; which never knew defeat nor fear. Here reign the simplicity and purity of a primitive age, and a health and hope far remote from towns and cities. Standing quite alone, far in the forest, while the wind is shaking down snow from the trees, and leaving the only human tracks behind us, we find our reflections of a richer variety than the life of cities. The chicadee and nut-hatch are more inspiring society than the statesmen and philosophers, and we shall return to these last, as to more vulgar companions. In this lonely glen, with its brook draining the slopes, its creased ice and crystals of all hues, where the spruces and hemlocks stand up on either side, and the rush and sere wild oats in the rivulet itself, our lives are more serene and worthy to contemplate.

As the day advances, the heat of the sun is reflected by the hillsides, and we hear a faint but sweet music, where flows the rill released from its fetters, and the icicles are melting on the trees; and the nut-hatch and partridge are heard and seen. The south wind melts the snow at noon, and the bare ground appears with its withered grass and leaves, and we are invigorated by the perfume which expands from it, as by the scent of strong meats.

Let us go into this deserted woodman's hut, and see how he has passed the long winter nights and the short and stormy days. For here man has lived under this south hill-side, and it seems a civilized and public spot. We have such associations as when the traveller stands by the ruins of Palmyra or Hecatompolis. Singing birds and flowers perchance have begun to appear here, for flowers as well as weeds follow in the footsteps of man. These hemlocks whispered over his head, these hickory logs were his fuel, and these pitch-pine roots kindled his fire; yonder foaming rill in the hollow, whose thin and airy vapor still ascends as busily as ever, though he is far off now, was his well. These hemlock boughs, and the straw upon this raised platform, were his bed, and this broken dish held his drink. But he has not been here this season, for the phaebes built their nest upon this shelf last summer. I find some embers left, as if he had but just gone out, where he baked his pot of beans, and while at evening he smoked his pipe, whose stemless bowl lies in the ashes, chatted with his only companion, if perchance he had any, about the depth of the snow on the morrow, already falling fast and thick without, or disputed whether the last sound was the screech of an owl, or the creak of a bough, or imagination only; and through this broad chimney-throat, in the late winter evening, ere he stretched himself upon the straw, he looked up to learn the progress of the storm, and seeing the

bright stars of Cassiopeia's chair shining brightly down upon him, fell contentedly asleep.

See how many traces from which we may learn the chopper's history. From this stump we may guess the sharpness of his axe, and from the slope of the stroke, on which side he stood, and whether he cut down the tree without going round it or changing hands; and from the flexure of the splinters we may know which way it fell. This one chip contains inscribed on it the whole history of the wood-chopper and of the world. On this scrap of paper, which held his sugar or salt, perchance, or was the wadding of his gun, sitting on a log in the forest, with what interest we read the tattle of cities, of those larger huts, empty and to let, like this, in High-streets, and Broad-ways. The eaves are dripping on the south side of this simple roof, while the titmouse lisps in the pine, and the genial warmth of the sun around the door is somewhat kind and human.

After two seasons, this rude dwelling does not deform the scene. Already the birds resort to it, to build their nests, and you may track to its door the feet of many quadrupeds. Thus, for a long time, nature overlooks the encroachment and profanity of man. The wood still cheerfully and unsuspiciously echoes the strokes of the axe that fells it and while they are few and seldom, they enhance its wildness, and all the elements strive to naturalize the sound.

Now our path begins to ascend gradually to the top of this high hill, from whose precipitous south side, we can look over the broad country, of forest, and field, and river, to the distant snowy mountains. See yonder thin column of smoke curling up through the woods from some invisible farm-house; the standard raised over some rural homestead. There must be a warmer and more genial spot there below, as where we detect the vapor from a spring forming a cloud above the trees. What fine relations are established between the traveller who discovers this airy column from some eminence in the forest, and him who sits below. Up goes the smoke as silently and naturally as the vapor exhales from the leaves, and as busy disposing itself in wreathes as the housewife on the hearth below. It is a hieroglyphic of man's life, and suggests more intimate and important things than the boiling of a pot. Where its fine column rises above the forest, like an ensign, some human life has planted itself,—and such is the beginning of Rome, the establishment of the arts, and the

Crayon portrait of Henry David Thoreau in 1854 by Samuel Rowse (Concord Free Public Library)

foundation of empires, whether on the prairies of America, or the steppes of Asia.

And now we descend again to the brink of this woodland lake, which lies in a hollow of the hills, as if it were their expressed juice, and that of the leaves, which are annually steeped in it. Without outlet or inlet to the eye, it has still its history, in the lapse of its waves, in the rounded pebbles on its shore, and on the pines which grow down to its brink. It has not been idle, though sedentary, but, like Abu Musa, teaches that "sitting still at home is the heavenly way; the going out is the way of the world." Yet in its evaporation it travels as far as any. In summer it is the earth's liquid eye; a mirror in the breast of nature. The sins of the wood are washed out in it. See how the woods form an amphitheatre about it, and it is an arena for all the genialness of nature. All trees direct the traveller to its brink, all paths seek it out, birds fly to it, quadrupeds flee to it, and the very ground inclines toward it. It is nature's saloon, where she has sat down to her toilet. Consider her silent economy and tidiness; how the sun comes with his evaporation to sweep the dust

from its surface each morning, and a fresh surface is constantly welling up; and annually, after whatever impurities have accumulated herein, its liquid transparency appears again in the spring. In summer a hushed music seems to sweep across its surface. But now a plain sheet of snow conceals it from our eyes, except when the wind has swept the ice bare, and the sere leaves are gliding from side to side, tacking and veering on their tiny voyages. Here is one just keeled up against a pebble on shore, a dry beach leaf, rocking still, as if it would soon start again. A skilful engineer, methinks, might project its course since it fell from the parent stem. Here are all the elements for such a calculation. Its present position, the direction of the wind, the level of the pond, and how much more is given. In its scarred edges and veins is its log rolled up.

We fancy ourselves in the interior of a larger house. The surface of the pond is our deal table or sanded floor, and the woods rise abruptly from its edge, like the walls of a cottage. The lines set to catch pickerel through the ice look like a larger culinary preparation, and the men stand about on the white ground like pieces of forest furniture. The actions of these men, at the distance of half a mile over the ice and snow, impress us as when we read the exploits of Alexander in history. They seem not unworthy of the scenery, and as momentous as the conquest of kingdoms.

Again we have wandered through the arches of the wood, until from its skirts we hear the distant booming of ice from yonder bay of the river, as if it were moved by some other and subtler tide than oceans know. To me it has a strange sound of home, thrilling as the voice of one's distant and noble kindred. A mild summer sun shines over forest and lake, and though there is but one green leaf for many rods, yet nature enjoys a serene health. Every sound is fraught with the same mysterious assurance of health, as well now the creaking of the boughs in January, as the soft sough of the wind in July.

> When Winter fringes every bough
>   With his fantastic wreath,
> And puts the seal of silence now
>   Upon the leaves beneath;
>
> When every stream in its pent-house
>   Goes gurgling on its way,
> And in his gallery the mouse
>   Nibbleth the meadow hay;

Manuscript poem by Thoreau (Autograph Leaves of Our Country's Authors, edited by John Pendleton Kennedy and Alexander Bliss [1864]

Methinks the summer still is nigh,
  And lurketh underneath,
As that same meadow mouse doth lie
  Snug in the last year's heath.

And if perchance the Chickadee
  Lisp a faint note anon,
The snow in summer's canopy,
  Which she herself put on.

Fair blossoms deck the cheerful trees,
  And dazzling fruits depend,
The north wind sighs a summer breeze,
  The nipping frosts to fend,

Bringing glad tidings unto me,
  The while I stand all ear,
Of a serene eternity,
  Which need not winter fear.

Out on the silent pond straightway
  The restless ice doth crack,
And pond sprites merry gambols play
  Amid the deafening rack.

Eager I hasten to the vale,
  As if I heard brave news,
How nature held high festival,
  Which it were hard to lose.

I gambol with my neighbor ice,
  And sympathizing quake,
As each new crack darts in a trice
  Across the gladsome lake.

One with the cricket in the ground,
  And faggot on the hearth,
Resounds the rare domestic sound
  Along the forest path.

Before night we will take a journey on skates along the course of this meandering river, as full of novelty to one who sits by the cottage fire all the winter's day, as if it were over the polar ice, with captain Parry or Franklin; following the winding of the stream, now flowing amid hills, now spreading out into fair meadows, and forming a myriad coves and bays where the pine and hemlock overarch. The river flows in the rear of the towns, and we see all things from a new and wilder side. The fields and gardens come down to it with a frankness, and freedom from pretension, which they do not wear on the highway. It is the outside and edge of the earth. Our eyes are not offended by violent contrasts. The last rail of the farmer's fence is some swaying willow bough, which still preserves its

freshness, and here at length all fences stop, and we no longer cross any road. We may go far up within the country now by the most retired and level road, never climbing a hill, but by broad levels ascending to the upland meadows. It is a beautiful illustration of the law of obedience, the flow of a river; the path for a sick man, a highway down which an acorn cup may float secure with its freight. Its slight occasional falls, whose precipices would not diversify the landscape, are celebrated by mist and spray, and attract the traveller from far and near. From the remote interior, its current conducts him by broad and easy steps, or by one gentle inclined plain, to the sea. Thus by an early and constant yielding to the inequalities of the ground, it secures itself the easiest passage.

No dominion of nature is quite closed to man at all times, and now we draw near to the empire of the fishes. Our feet glide swiftly over unfathomed depths, where in summer our line tempted the pout and perch, and where the stately pickerel lurked in the long corridors, formed by the bulrushes. The deep, impenetrable marsh, where the heron waded, and bittern squatted, is made pervious to our swift shoes, as if a thousand railroads had been made into it. With one impulse we are carried to the cabin of the muskrat, that earliest settler, and see him dart away under the transparent ice, like a furred fish, to his hole in the bank; and we glide rapidly over meadows where lately "the mower whet his scythe," through beds of frozen cranberries mixed with meadow grass. We skate near to where the blackbird, the pewee, and the kingbird hung their nests over the water, and the hornets builded from the maple on the swamp. How many gay warblers now following the sun, have radiated from this nest of silver birch and thistle down. On the swamp's outer edge was hung the supermarine village, where no foot penetrated. In this hollow tree the woodduck reared her brood, and slid away each day to forage in yonder fen.

In winter, nature is a cabinet of curiosities, full of dried specimens, in their natural order and position. The meadows and forests are a *hortus siccus*. The leaves and grasses stand perfectly pressed by the air without screw or gum, and the bird's nests are not hung on an artificial twig, but where they builded them. We go about dry shod to inspect the summer's work in the rank swamp, and see what a growth have got the alders, the willows, and the maples; testifying to how many warm suns, and fertilizing dews and show-

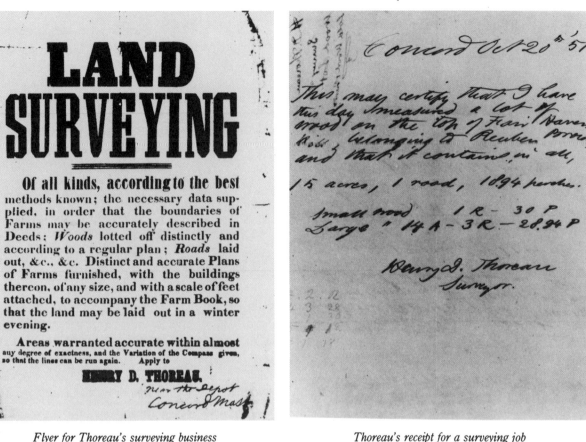

Flyer for Thoreau's surveying business   Thoreau's receipt for a surveying job

ers. See what strides their boughs took in the luxuriant summer,—and anon these dormant buds will carry them onward and upward another span into the heavens.

Occasionally we wade through fields of snow, under whose depths the river is lost for many rods, to appear again to the right or left, where we least expected; still holding on its way underneath, with a faint, stertorous, rumbling sound, as if, like the bear and marmot, it too had hibernated, and we had followed its faint summer trail to where it earthed itself in snow and ice. At first we should have thought that rivers would be empty and dry in mid winter, or else frozen solid till the spring thawed them; but their volume is not diminished even, for only a superficial cold bridges their surface. The thousand springs which feed the lakes and streams are flowing still. The issues of a few surface springs only are closed, and they go to swell the deep reservoirs. Nature's wells are below the frost. The summer brooks are not filled with snow-water, nor does the mower quench his thirst with that alone. The streams are swollen when the snow melts in the spring, because nature's work has been delayed,

the water being turned into ice and snow, whose particles are less smooth and round, and do not find their level so soon.

Far over the ice, between the hemlock woods and snow-clad hills, stands the pickerel fisher, his lines set in some retired cove, like a Finlander, with his arms thrust into the pouches of his dreadnought; with dull, snowy, fishy thoughts, himself a finless fish, separated a few inches from his race; dumb, erect, and made to be enveloped in clouds and snows, like the pines on shore. In these wild scenes, men stand about in the scenery, or move deliberately and heavily, having sacrificed the sprightliness and vivacity of towns to the dumb sobriety of nature. He does not make the scenery less wild, more than the jays and muskrats, but stands there as a part of it, as the natives are represented in the voyages of early navigators, at Nootka sound, and on the North-west coast, with their furs about them, before they were tempted to loquacity by a scrap of iron. He belongs to the natural family of man, and is planted deeper in nature and has more root than the inhabitants of towns. Go to him, ask what luck, and you will learn that he too is a worshipper of the unseen. Hear with what sincere deference and waving gesture in his tone, he speaks of the lake pickerel, which he has never seen, his primitive and ideal race of pickerel. He is connected with the shore still, as by a fish-line, and yet remembers the season when he took fish through the ice on the pond, while the peas were up in his garden at home.

But now, while we have loitered, the clouds have gathered again, and a few straggling snow-flakes are beginning to descend. Faster and faster they fall, shutting out the distant objects from sight. The snow falls on every wood and field, and no crevice is forgotten; by the river and the pond, on the hill and in the valley. Quadrupeds are confined to their coverts, and the birds sit upon their perches this peaceful hour. There is not so much sound as in fair weather, but silently and gradually every slope, and the grey walls and fences, and the polished ice, and the sere leaves, which were not buried before, are concealed, and the tracks of men and beasts are lost. With so little effort does nature reassert her rule, and blot out the traces of men. Hear how Homer has described the same. "The snow flakes fall thick and fast on a winter's day. The winds are lulled, and the snow falls incessant, covering the top of the mountains, and the hills, and the plains where the lotus tree grows, and the cultivated fields, and they are falling by the inlets and shores of the foaming sea, but are silently dissolved by the waves." The snow levels all things, and infolds them deeper on the bosom of nature, as, in the slow summer, vegetation creeps up to the entablature of the temple, and the turrets of the castle, and helps her to prevail over art.

The surly night-wind rustles through the wood, and warns us to retrace our steps, while the sun goes down behind the thickening storm, and birds seek their roosts, and cattle their stalls.

> "Drooping the lab'rer ox
> Stands covered o'er with snow, and *now* demands
> The fruit of all his toil."

Though winter is represented in the almanac as an old man, facing the wind and sleet, and drawing his cloak about him, we rather think of him as a merry woodchopper, and warm-blooded youth, as blithe as summer. The unexplored grandeur of the storm keeps up

the spirits of the traveller. It does not trifle with us, but has a sweet earnestness. In winter we lead a more inward life. Our hearts are warm and merry, like cottages under drifts, whose windows and doors are half concealed, but from whose chimneys the smoke cheerfully ascends. The imprisoning drifts increase the sense of comfort which the house affords, and in the coldest days we are content to sit over the hearth and see the sky through the chimney top, enjoying the quiet and serene life that may be had in a warm corner by the chimney side, or feeling our pulse by listening to the low of cattle in the street, or the sound of the flail in distant barns all the long afternoon. No doubt a skilful physician could determine our health by observing how these simple and natural sounds affected us. We enjoy now, not an oriental, but a boreal leisure, around warm stoves and fire-places, and watch the shadow of motes in the sunbeams.

Sometimes our fate grows too homely and familiarly serious ever to be cured. Consider how for three months the human destiny is wrapped in furs. The good Hebrew revelation takes no cognizance of all this cheerful snow. Is there no religion for the temperate and frigid zones? We know of no scripture which records the pure benignity of the gods on a New England winter night. Their praises have never been sung, only their wrath deprecated. The best scripture, after all, records but a meagre faith. Its saints live reserved and austere. Let a brave devout man spend the year in the woods of Maine or Labrador, and see if the Hebrew scriptures speak adequately of his condition and experience, from the setting in of winter to the breaking up of the ice.

Now commences the long winter evening around the farmer's hearth, when the thoughts of the indwellers travel far abroad, and men are by nature and necessity charitable and liberal to all creatures. Now is the happy resistance to cold, when the farmer reaps his reward, and thinks of his preparedness for winter and through the the glittering panes, sees with equanimity "the mansion of the northern bear," for now the storm is over,

> "The full ethereal round,
> Infinite worlds disclosing to the view,
> Shines out intensely keen; and all one cope
> Of starry glitter glows from pole to pole."

J[ames]. K[inard]., Jr.
"What is Transcendentalism? By a Thinking Man," *Knickerbocker Magazine,* 23 (March 1844): 205-211.

Not all comments on Transcendentalism were deadly serious, as is shown in this essay, in which one man tries unsuccessfully to convince another that we are all Transcendentalists.

This question has often been asked but seldom answered satisfactorily. Newspaper editors and correspondents have frequently attempted a practical elucidation of the mystery, by quoting from their own brains the rarest piece of absurdity which they could imagine, and entitling it 'Transcendentalism.' One good hit of this kind may be well enough, by way of satire upon the fogginess of certain writers who deem themselves, and are deemed by the multitude, transcendental *par excellence.* COLERIDGE however thought that to parody stupidity by way of ridiculing it, only proves the parodist more stupid than the original blockhead. Still, one such attempt may be tolerated; but when imitators of the parodist arise and fill almost every newspaper in the country with similar witticisms, such efforts become 'flat and unprofitable;' for nothing is easier than to put words together in a form which conveys no meaning to the reader. It is a cheap kind of wit, asinine rather than attic, and can be exercised as well by those who know nothing of the subject as by those best acquainted with it. Indeed, it is greatly to be doubted whether one in a hundred of these witty persons know any thing of the matter; for if they possess sense enough to make them worthy of being ranked among reasonable men, it could be proved to them in five minutes that they are themselves transcendentalists, as all thinking men find themselves compelled to be, whether they know themselves by that name or not.

'Poh!' said a friend, looking over my shoulder; 'you can't prove *me* a transcendentalist; I defy you to do it; I despise the name.'

Why so? Let us know what it is that you despise. Is it the sound of the word? Is it not sufficiently euphonious? Does it not strike your ear as smoothly as Puseyite, or Presbyterian?

'Nonsense!' said he; 'you don't suppose I am to be misled by the sound of a word; it is the meaning to which I object. I despise transcendentalism; therefore I do not wish to be called transcendentalist.'

Very well; but we shall never 'get ahead' unless you define transcendentalism according to your understanding of the word.

'That request is easily made, but not easily complied with. Have you Carlyle or Emerson at hand?'

Here I took down a volume of each, and read various sentences and paragraphs therefrom. These passages are full of transcendental ideas; do you object to them?

'No,' said my friend; 'for aught I can perceive, they might have been uttered by any one who was *not* a transcendentalist. Let me see the books.'

After turning over the leaves a long while, he selected and read about a passage from Carlyle, one of his very worst; abrupt, nervous, jerking, and at the same time windy, long-drawn-out, and parenthetical; a period filling a whole page.

'There,' said he, stopping to take breath, 'if that is not enough to disgust one with transcendentalism, then I know nothing of the matter.'

A very sensible conclusion. Bless your soul, that is *Carlyle-ism,* not transcendentalism. You said but now that you were not to be misled by the sound of a word; and yet you are condemning a principle on account of the bad style of a writer who is supposed to be governed by it. Is that right? Would you condemn Christianity because of the weaknesses and sins of one of its professors?

'Of course not,' replied he; 'I wish to be fair. I cannot express my idea of the meaning of transcendentalism without tedious circumlocution, and I begin to despair of proving my position by quotations. It is not on any particular passage that I rest my case. You have read this work, and will understand me when I say that it is to its general intent and spirit that I object, and not merely to the author's style.'

I think I comprehend you. You disregard the mere form in which the author expresses his thoughts; you go beyond and behind that, and judge him by the thoughts themselves; not by one or by two, but by the sum and *substance* of the whole. You strip off the husk to arrive at the kernel, and judge of the goodness of the crop by the latter, not the former.

'Just so,' said he; 'that's my meaning precisely. I always strive to follow that rule in every thing. 'Appearances,' you know, 'are deceitful.''

That is to say you go beyond or transcend appearances and circumstances, and divine the true meaning, the substance, the spirit of that on which you are about to decide. That is practical transcendentalism and you are a transcendentalist.

'I wish you would suggest another name for it,' said my friend, as he went out of the door; 'I detest the sound of that word.'

I wish we could, said I, but he was out of hearing; I wish we could, for it is an abominably long word to write.

'I wish we could,' mutters the printer, 'for it is an awfully long word to print.'

'I wish we could,' is the sober second thought of all; for people will always condemn transcendentalism until it is called by another name. Such is the force of prejudice.

'I have been thinking over our conversation of yesterday,' said my friend next morning, on entering my room.

'Oh, you have been writing it down, have you? Let me see it.' After looking over the sketch, he remarked:

'You *seem* to have me fast enough, but after all I believe you conquered merely by playing upon a word, and in proving me to be a transcendentalist you only proved me to be a reasonable being: one capable of perceiving, remembering, combining, comparing and deducing; one who, amid the apparent contradictions with which we are surrounded, strives to reconcile appearances and discover principles; and from the outward and visible learn the inward and spiritual; in fine, arrive at truth. Now every reasonable man claims to be all that I have avowed myself to be. If this is to be a transcendentalist, then I am one. When I read that I must hate my father and mother before I can be a disciple of JESUS, I do not understand that passage literally; I call to mind other precepts of CHRIST; I remember the peculiarities of eastern style; I compare these facts to-

gether, and deduce therefrom a very different principle from that apparently embodied in the passage quoted. When I see the Isle of Shoals doubled, and the duplicates reversed in the air above the old familiar rocks, I do not, as I stand on Rye-beach, observing the interesting phenomenon, believe there are two sets of islands there; but recalling facts which I have learned, and philosophical truths which I have acquired and verified, I attribute the appearance to its true cause, refraction of light. When in passing from room to room in the dark, with my arms outspread, I run my nose against the edge of a door, I do not therefrom conclude that my nose is longer than my arms! When I see a man stumble in the street, I do not at once set him down as a drunkard, not considering that to be sufficient evidence, although some of our Washingtonian friends do; but I compare that fact with the state of the streets, and what I know of his previous life, and judge accordingly.'

Well, said I, you are an excellent transcendentalist; one after my own heart, in morals, philosophy and religion. To be a transcendentalist is after all to be *only* a sensible, unprejudiced man, open to conviction at all times, and spiritually-minded. I can well understand that, when you condemn transcendentalism, you object not to the principle, but to the practice, in the superlative degree, of that principle. Transcendentalism is but an abstract of considering morals, philosophy, religion; an application of the principles of abstract science to these subjects. All metaphysicians are transcendentalists, and every one is transcendental so far as he is metaphysical. There are as many different modifications of the one as of the other, and probably no two transcendentalists ever thought alike; their creed is not yet written. You certainly do not condemn spiritualism, but ultra spiritualism you seem to abhor.

'Precisely so. I did not yesterday give you the meaning which I attached to transcendentalism; in truth, practically you mean one thing by that term, and I another, though I now see that in principle they are the same. The spiritualism which I like, looks through nature and revelation up to God; that which I abhor, condescends hardly to make use of nature at all, but demands direct converse with GOD, and declares that it enjoys it too; a sort of continual and *immediate* revelation. Itself is its own authority. The ultra-spiritualist contains within himself the fulness of the Godhead. He allows of nothing external, unless it be brother spirits like himself. He has abolished nature, and to the uninitiated seems to have abolished God himself, although I am charitable enough to believe that he has full faith in God, after his own fashion. He claims to be inspired; to be equal to JESUS; nay superior; for one of them lately said: 'Greater is the container than the contained, therefore I am greater than GOD, for I contain God!' The ultra-spiritualist believes only *by* and *through* and *in* his own inward light. Let him take care, as Carlyle says, that his own contemptible tar-link does not, by being held too near his eyes, extinguish to him the sun of the universe. Now the true spiritualist makes use not only of his own moral and religious instincts, but all that can be gathered by the senses from external nature, and all that can be acquired by untiring consultation with the sages who have gone before him; and from these materials in the alembic of his mind, with such power as GOD has given him, he distils truth.'

Truth! Ah, that is the very point in question. 'What is truth?' has been the ardent inquiry of every honest mind from the days of Adam to the present time, and the sneering demand of many an unbeliever. Eve sought it when she tasted the forbidden fruit. But since then, thank God! no prohibition has been uttered against the search after truth, and mankind have improved their liberty with great industry for six thousand years; and what is the truth? Is truth discovered? How much? and how much of falsehood is mixed up with what *is* known to be true? These questions are constantly suggesting themselves to thinkers, and to answer them is the labor of their lives. Let them have free scope, ultra-spiritualists and all. Even these latter go through the same operation which you have just claimed to be peculiar to the true spiritualist. All do, whether they will or not, make use of observation, learning, and the inward light. Some arrive at one result, and some at another, because the elements differ in each. If any two could be found whose external observations, learning, intellect and inward light or instincts were precisely equal in volume and proportion, can it be doubted that these two would arrive at precisely similar results? But they are *not* equal; and so one comes to believe in external authority, and the other refers every thing to a standard which he thinks he finds within himself. The latter is deemed by the public to be a representative of pure transcendentalism, and he is condemned accordingly as self-sufficient.

And privately, between you and me, my good friend, I cannot help thinking it rather ungrateful in him, after becoming so deeply indebted to his senses,

to books, and the Bible for his spiritual education, to turn round and despise these means of advancement, and declare that they are mere non-essential *circumstances,* and that a man may reach the same end by studying himself *in* himself. It is as if a man should use a ladder to reach a lofty crag, and then kick it over contemptuously, and aver that he could just as well have flown up, and ask the crowd below to break up that miserable ladder and try their wings. Doubtless they *have* wings, if they only knew it. But seriously, I am not inclined to join in the hue-and-cry against even the ultra-transcendentalist. He has truth mixed up with what I esteem objectionable, and some truth to which others have not attained; and as I deem the eclectic the only true mode of philosophy, I am willing to take truth where I can find it, whether in China or Boston, in Confucius or Emerson, Kant or Cousin, the Bible or the Koran; and though I have more reverence for one of these sources than all others, it is only because I think I find there the greatest amount of truth, sanctioned by the highest authority. To put the belief in the Bible on any other ground, is to base it on educational prejudice and superstition; on which principle the Koran should be as binding on the Mahometan as the Bible on us. Do we not all finally resort to *ourselves* in order to decide a difficult question in morals or religion? and is not the decision more or less correct accordingly as we refer it to the better or to the baser portion of our nature?

'Most certainly! I have often said I would not and could not believe in the Bible, if it commanded us to worship Sin and leave our passions unbridled.'

Well said! And in so saying, you acknowledge yourself to be governed by the same principle which actuates the ultra-transcendentalist; the moral sense or instinct, similar to the 'inward light' of the Friends. After all, I apprehend the true point in which men differ is, whether this moral sense is really an instinct, or whether it is evolved and put in operation by education. How much is due to nature? is the true question. But to solve it, is important only theoretically, for practically we all act alike; we cannot, if we would, separate the educational from the natural moral sense; we cannot *uneducate* it, and then judge by it, freed from all circumstantial bias. But whether more or less indebted either to nature or education, it is to this moral and religious sense that the ultra-transcendentalist refers every question, and passes judgment according to its verdict. It is sometimes rather vaguely called the 'Pure

Reason;' but that is only a *term*, hardly a 'mouthful of articulate wind.'

'You and I shall agree very well together, I see,' replied my friend. 'If we dispute at all, it will be foolishly about the meaning of a word. All the world have been doing that ever since the confusion of tongues at Babel. That great event prophetically shadowed forth the future; for now, as then, the confusion and disputation is greatest when we are striving most earnestly to reach heaven by our earth-built contrivances. We may draw a lesson therefrom; not to be too aspiring for our means; for our inevitable failure only makes us the more ridiculous, the higher the position we seem to have attained.'

Very true; but we should never arrive at the height of wisdom, which consists in knowing our own ignorance and weakness, unless we made full trial of our powers. The fall of which you speak should give us a modesty not to be otherwise obtained, and make us very careful how we ridicule others, seeing how open to it we ourselves are. Every man may build his tower of Babel, and if he make a right use of his failure, may in the end be nearer heaven than if he had never made the attempt. Ridicule is no argument, and should only be used by way of a *jeu d'esprit,* and never on solemn subjects. It is very hard, I know, for one who has mirthfulness strongly developed, to restrain himself on all occasions; and what is solemn to one may not be so to another; hence we should be very charitable to all; alike to the bigots, the dreamers, and the laughers; to the builders of theoretic Babel-towers, and the grovellers on the low earth.

'There is one kind of transcendentalism,' replied my friend, 'which you have not noticed particularly, which consists in believing in nothing except the spiritual existence of the unbeliever himself, and hardly that. It believes not in the external world at all.'

If you are on *that* ground, I have done. To talk of that, would be wasting our time on nothing; or 'our eternity,' for with that sect time is altogether a delusion. It *may* be true, but the believer, even in the act of declaring his faith, must practically prove himself persuaded of the falsity of his doctrine.

'You wanted a short name for Transcendentalism; if a long one will make *this* modification of it more odious, let us call it *Incomprehensibilityosityivityalityation-mentnessism!'*

My friend said this with a face nearly as long as the word, made a low bow, and departed. I took my pen and reduced our conversation to writing. I hope by this time the reader has a very lucid answer to give to the question. *What is Transcendentalism?* It will be a miracle if he can see one inch farther into the fog-bank than before. I should like to take back the boast made in the beginning of this paper, that I could prove in five minutes any reasonable man a transcendentalist. My friend disconcerted my plan of battle, by taking command of the enemy's forces, instead of allowing me to marshal them on paper to suit myself; and so a mere friendly joust ensured, instead of the utter demolition of my adversary, which I had intended.

And this little circumstance has led me to think, what a miserable business controversialists would make of it, if each had his opponent looking over his shoulder, pointing out flaws in his arguments, suggesting untimely truths, and putting every possible impediment in the path of his logic; and if, moreover, he were obliged to mend every flaw, prove every such truth a falsehood, and remove every impediment before he could advance a step. Were such the case, how much less would there be of fine-spun theory and specious argument; how much more of practical truth! Always supposing the logical combatants did not lose their patience and resort to material means and knockdown arguments; of which, judging by the spirit sometimes manifested in theological controversies, there would really seem to be some danger. Oh! it is a very easy thing to sit in one's study and demolish an opponent who after all is generally no opponent at all, but only a man of straw, dressed up for the occasion with a few purposely-tattered shreds of the adversary's castoff garments.

NOTE BY THE 'FRIEND.'–The foregoing is a *correct* sketch of our conversations, especially as the reporter has, like his congressional brother, corrected most of the bad grammar, and left out some of the vulgarisms and colloquialisms, and given me the better side of the argument in the last conversation; it is *very* correct. But it seems to me that the question put at the commencement is as far from being solved as ever. It is as difficult to be answered as the question, What is Christianity? to which every sect will return a different reply, and each prove all the others wrong.

Margaret Fuller

From *Summer on the Lakes, in 1843* (Boston: Charles C. Little and James Brown, 1844), pp. 43-69.

Fuller's first book is perhaps the best example of the small body of Transcendentalist travel writing, for she uses her trip as the occasion for launching into discussions of many ideas. In Summer on the Lakes, *Fuller showed her concerns about the relentless forcing back of the Indian and the frontier, how the settlers had ceased to be able to view the beauties of nature, and the ways in which young women were being raised with eastern manners and ideas which were quite inappropriate for the land in which they lived.*

CHAPTER III.

In the afternoon of this day we reached the Rock river, in whose neighborhood we proposed to make some stay, and crossed at Dixon's ferry.

This beautiful stream flows full and wide over a bed of rocks, traversing a distance of near two hundred miles, to reach the Mississippi. Great part of the country along its banks is the finest region of Illinois, and the scene of some of the latest romance of Indian warfare. To these beautiful regions Black Hawk returned with his band "to pass the summer," when he drew upon himself the warfare in which he was finally vanquished. No wonder he could not resist the longing, unwise though its indulgence might be, to return in summer to this home of beauty.

Of Illinois, in general, it has often been remarked that it bears the character of country which has been inhabited by a nation skilled like the English in all the ornamental arts of life, especially in landscape gardening. That the villas and castles seem to have been burnt, the enclosures taken down, but the velvet lawns, the flower gardens, the stately parks, scattered at graceful intervals by the decorous hand of art, the frequent deer, and the peaceful herd of cattle that make picture of the plain, all suggest more of the masterly mind of man, than the prodigal, but careless, motherly love of nature. Especially is this true of the Rock river country. The river flows sometimes through these parks and lawns, then betwixt high bluffs, whose grassy ridges are covered with fine trees, or broken with crumbling stone, that easily assumes the forms of buttress, arch and clustered columns. Along the face of such crumbling rocks, swallows' nests are clustered, thick as cities, and eagles and deer do not disdain their summits.

One morning, out in the boat along the base of these rocks, it was amusing, and affecting too, to see these swallows put their heads out to look at us. There was something very hospitable about it, as if man had never shown himself a tyrant near them. What a morning that was! Every sight is worth twice as much by the early morning light. We borrow something of the spirit of the hour to look upon them.

The first place where we stopped was one of singular beauty, a beauty of soft, luxuriant wildness. It was on the bend of the river, a place chosen by an Irish gentleman, whose absenteeship seems of the wisest kind, since for a sum which would have been but a drop of water to the thirsty fever of his native land, he commands a residence which has all that is desirable, in its independence, its beautiful retirement, and means of benefit to others.

His park, his deer-chase, he found already prepared; he had only to make an avenue through it. This brought us by a drive, which in the heat of noon seemed long, though afterwards, in the cool of morning and evening, delightful, to the house. This is, for that part of the world, a large and commodious dwelling. Near it stands the log-cabin where its master lived while it was building, a very ornamental accessory.

In front of the house was a lawn, adorned by the most graceful trees. A few of these had been taken out to give a full view of the river, gliding through banks such as I have described. On this bend the bank is high and bold, so from the house or the lawn the view was very rich and commanding. But if you descended a ravine at the side to the water's edge, you found there a long walk on the narrow shore, with a

SUMMER ON THE LAKES,

IN 1843.

BY

S. M. FULLER.

BOSTON:
CHARLES C. LITTLE AND JAMES BROWN.
NEW YORK:
CHARLES S. FRANCIS AND COMPANY.

MDCCCXLIV.

*Title page for Margaret Fuller's first book, an account of her
Western travels*

wall above of the richest hanging wood, in which they said the deer lay hid. I never saw one, but often fancied that I heard them rustling, at daybreak, by these bright clear waters, stretching out in such smiling promise, where no sound broke the deep and blissful seclusion, unless now and then this rustling, or the plash of some fish a little gayer than the others; it seemed not necessary to have any better heaven, or fuller expression of love and freedom than in the mood of nature here.

Then, leaving the bank, you would walk far and far through long grassy paths, full of the most brilliant,

also the most delicate flowers. The brilliant are more common on the prairie, but both kinds loved this place.

Amid the grass of the lawn, with a profusion of wild strawberries, we greeted also a familiar love, the Scottish harebell, the gentlest, and most touching form of the flower-world.

The master of the house was absent, but with a kindness beyond thanks had offered us a resting place there. Here we were taken care of by a deputy, who would, for his youth, have been assigned the place of a page in former times, but in the young west, it seems he was old enough for a steward. Whatever be called his function, he did the honors of the place so much in harmony with it, as to leave the guests free to imagine themselves in Elysium. And the three days passed here were days of unalloyed, spotless happiness.

There was a peculiar charm in coming here, where the choice of location, and the unobtrusive good taste of all the arrangements, showed such intelligent appreciation of the spirit of the scene, after seeing so many dwellings of the new settlers, which showed plainly that they had no thought beyond satisfying the grossest material wants. Sometimes they looked attractive, the little brown houses, the natural architecture of the country, in the edge of the timber. But almost always when you came near, the slovenliness of the dwelling and the rude way in which objects around it were treated, when so little care would have presented a charming whole, were very repulsive. Seeing the traces of the Indians, who chose the most beautiful sites for their dwellings, and whose habits do not break in on that aspect of nature under which they were born, we feel as if they were the rightful lords of a beauty they forbore to deform. But most of these settlers do not see it at all; it breathes, it speaks in vain to those who are rushing into its sphere. Their progress is Gothic, not Roman, and their mode of cultivation will, in the course of twenty, perhaps ten, years, obliterate the natural expression of the country.

This is inevitable, fatal; we must not complain, but look forward to a good result. Still, in travelling through this country, I could not but be struck with the force of a symbol. Wherever the hog comes, the rattlesnake disappears; the omnivorous traveller, safe in its stupidity, willingly and easily makes a meal of the most dangerous of reptiles, and one whom the Indian looks on with a mystic awe. Even so the white settler pursues the Indian, and is victor in the chase. But I shall say more upon the subject by-and-by.

While we were here we had one grand thunder storm, which added new glory to the scene.

One beautiful feature was the return of the pigeons every afternoon to their home. Every afternoon they came sweeping across the lawn, positively in clouds, and with a swiftness and softness of winged motion, more beautiful than anything of the kind I ever knew. Had I been a musician, such as Mendelsohn, I felt that I could have improvised a music quite peculiar, from the sound they made, which should have indicated all the beauty over which their wings bore them. I will here insert a few lines left at this house, on parting, which feebly indicate some of the features.

Familiar to the childish mind were tales
  Of rock-grit isles amid a desert sea,
Where unexpected stretch the flowery vales
  To soothe the shipwrecked sailor's misery.
Fainting, he lay upon a sandy shore,
And fancied that all hope of life was o'er;
But let him patient climb the frowning wall,
Within, the orange glows beneath the palm
    tree tall,
And all that Eden boasted waits his call.

Almost these tales seem realized to-day,
When the long dullness of the sultry way,
Where "independent" settlers' careless cheer
Made us indeed feel we were "strangers"
here,
  Is cheered by sudden sight of this fair spot,
On which "improvement" yet has made no
    blot,
But Nature all-astonished stands, to find
Her plan protected by the human mind.

Blest be the kindly genius of the scene;
  The river, bending in unbroken grace,
The stately thickets, with their pathways
    green,
  Fair lonely trees, each in its fittest place.
Those thickets haunted by the deer and fawn;
Those cloudlike flights of birds across the
    lawn;
The gentlest breezes here delight to blow,
And sun and shower and star are emulous
    to deck the show.

Wondering, as Crusoe, we survey the land;
Happier than Crusoe we, a friendly band;
Blest be the hand that reared this friendly
    home,
The heart and mind of him to whom we owe
Hours of pure peace such as few mortals
    know;

May he find such, should he be led to roam;
Be tended by such ministering sprites–
Enjoy such gaily childish days, such hopeful
    nights!
And yet, amid the goods to mortals given,
To give those goods again is most like heaven.

  Hazelwood, Rock River, June 30th, 1843.

The only really rustic feature was of the many coops of poultry near the house, which I understood it to be one of the chief pleasures of the master to feed.

Leaving this place, we proceeded a day's journey along the beautiful stream, to a little town named Oregon. We called at a cabin, from whose door looked out one of those faces which, once seen, are never forgotten; young, yet touched with many traces of feeling, not only possible, but endured; spirited, too, like the gleam of a finely tempered blade. It was a face that suggested a history, and many histories, but whose scene would have been in courts and camps. At this moment their circles are dull for want of that life which is waning unexcited in this solitary recess.

The master of the house proposed to show us a "short cut," by which we might, to especial advantage, pursue our journey. This proved to be almost perpendicular down a hill, studded with young trees and stumps. From these he proposed, with a hospitality of service worthy an Oriental, to free our wheels whenever they should get entangled, also, to be himself the drag, to prevent our too rapid descent. Such generosity deserved trust; however, we women could not be persuaded to render it. We got out and admired, from afar, the process. Left by our guide–and prop! we found ourselves in a wide field, where, by playful quips and turns, an endless "creek," seemed to divert itself with our attempts to cross it. Failing in this, the next best was to whirl down a steep bank, which feat our charioteer performed with an air not unlike that of Rhesus, had he but been as suitably furnished with chariot and steeds!

At last, after wasting some two or three hours on the "short cut," we got out by following an Indian trail, –Black Hawk's! How fair the scene through which it led! How could they let themselves be conquered, with such a country to fight for!

Afterwards, in the wide prairie, we saw a lively picture of nonchalance, (to speak in the fashion of dear Ireland.) There, in the wide sunny field, with neither tree nor umbrella above his head, sat a pedler, with his

Daguerreotype of Margaret Fuller in 1846

pack, waiting apparently for customers. He was not disappointed. We bought, what hold in regard to the human world, as unmarked, as mysterious, and as important an existence, as the infusoria to the natural, to wit, pins. This incident would have delighted those modern sages, who, in imitation of the sitting philosophers of ancient Ind, prefer silence to speech, waiting to going, and scornfully smile in answer to the motions of earnest life,

> "Of itself will nothing come,
> That ye must still be seeking?"

However, it seemed to me to-day, as formerly on these sublime occasions, obvious that nothing would come, unless something would go; now, if we had been as sublimely still as the pedler, his pins would have tarried in the pack, and his pockets sustained an aching void of pence!

Passing through one of the fine, park-like woods, almost clear from underbrush and carpeted with thick grasses and flowers, we met, (for it was Sunday,) a little congregation just returning from their service, which had been performed in a rude house in its midst.

It had a sweet and peaceful air as if such words and thoughts were very dear to them. The parents had with them all their little children; but we saw no old people; that charm was wanting, which exists in such scenes in older settlements, of seeing the silver bent in reverence beside the flaxen head.

At Oregon, the beauty of the scene was of even a more sumptuous character than at our former "stopping place." Here swelled the river in its boldest course, interspersed by halcyon isles on which nature had lavished all her prodigality in tree, vine, and flower, banked by noble bluffs, three hundred feet high, their sharp ridges as exquisitely definite as the edge of a shell; their summits adorned with those same beautiful trees, and with buttresses of rich rock, crested with old hemlocks, which wore a touching and antique grace amid the softer and more luxuriant vegetation. Lofty natural mounds rose amidst the rest, with the same lovely and sweeping outline, showing everywhere the plastic power of water,–water, mother of beauty, which, by its sweet and eager flow, had left such lineaments as human genius never dreamt of.

Not far from the river was a high crag, called the Pine Rock, which looks out, as our guide observed, like a helmet above the brow of the country. It seems as if the water left here and there a vestige of forms and materials that preceded its course, just to set off its new and richer designs.

The aspect of this country was to me enchanting, beyond any I have ever seen, from its fullness of expression, its bold and impassioned sweetness. Here the flood of emotion has passed over and marked everywhere its course by a smile. The fragments of rock touch it with a wildness and liberality which give just the needed relief. I should never be tired here, though I have elsewhere seen country of more secret and alluring charms, better calculated to stimulate and suggest. Here the eye and heart are filled.

How happy the Indians must have been here! It is not long since they were driven away, and the ground, above and below, is full of their traces.

> "The earth is full of men."

You have only to turn up the sod to find arrow-heads and Indian pottery. On an island, belonging to our host, and nearly opposite his house, they loved to stay, and, no doubt, enjoyed its lavish beauty as much as the myriad wild pigeons that now haunt its flower-

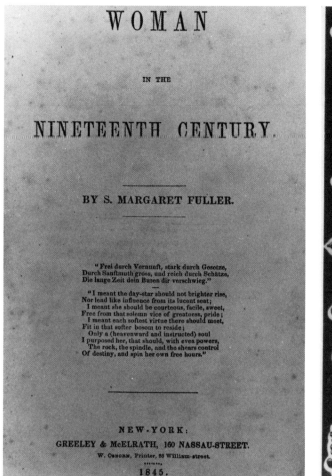

WOMAN

IN THE

NINETEENTH CENTURY.

BY S. MARGARET FULLER.

"Frei durch Vernunft, stark durch Gesetze,
Durch Sanftmuth gross, und reich durch Schätze,
Die lange Zeit dein Busen dir verschwieg."

"I meant the day-star should not brighter rise,
Nor lead like influence from its lucent seat;
    I meant she should be courteous, facile, sweet,
Free from that solemn vice of greatness, pride;
    I meant each softest virtue there should meet,
Fit in that softer bosom to reside;
    Only a (heavenward and instructed) soul
I purposed her, that should, with even powers,
    The rock, the spindle, and the shears control
Of destiny, and spin her own free hours."

NEW-YORK:
GREELEY & McELRATH, 160 NASSAU-STREET.
W. Osborn, Printer, 88 William-street.
1845.

Front wrapper for Fuller's most famous book, a call for women's equality

Engraved title page, Fuller's first book published in England (1845)

filled shades. Here are still the marks of their tomahawks, the troughs in which they prepared their corn, their caches.

A little way down the river is the site of an ancient Indian village, with its regularly arranged mounds. As usual, they had chosen with the finest taste. It was one of those soft shadowy afternoons when we went there, when nature seems ready to weep, not from grief, but from an overfull heart. Two prattling, lovely little girls, and an African boy, with glittering eye and ready grin, made our party gay; but all were still as we entered their little inlet and trod those flowery paths. They may blacken Indian life as they will, talk of its dirt, its brutality. I will ever believe that the men who chose that dwelling-place were able to feel emotions of noble happiness as they returned to it, and so were the women that received them. Neither were the children sad or dull, who lived so familiarly

with the deer and the birds, and swam that clear wave in the shadow of the Seven Sisters. The whole scene suggested to me a Greek splendor, a Greek sweetness, and I can believe that an Indian brave, accustomed to ramble in such paths, and be bathed by such sunbeams, might be mistaken for Apollo, as Apollo was for him by West. Two of the boldest bluffs are called the Deer's Walk, (not because deer do *not* walk there,) and the Eagle's Nest. The latter I visited one glorious morning; it was that of the fourth of July, and certainly I think I had never felt so happy that I was born in America. Wo to all country folks that never saw this spot, never swept an enraptured gaze over the prospect that stretched beneath. I do believe Rome and Florence are suburbs compared to this capital of nature's art.

The bluff was decked with great bunches of a scarlet variety of the milkweed, like cut coral, and all starred with a mysterious-looking dark flower, whose cup rose lonely on a tall stem. This had, for two or three days, disputed the ground with the lupine and phlox. My companions disliked, I liked it.

Here I thought of, or rather saw, what the Greek expresses under the form of Jove's darling, Ganymede, and the following stanzas took form.

GANYMEDE TO HIS EAGLE,

SUGGESTED BY A WORK OF THORWALDBEN'S.

Composed on the height called the Eagle's Nest, Oregon, Rock River,

July 4th, 1843.

Upon the rocky mountain stood the boy,
   A goblet of pure water in his hand,
His face and form spoke him one made for joy,
   A willing servant to sweet love's command,
But a strange pain was written on his brow,
And thrilled throughout his silver accents
    now–

"My bird," he cries, "my destined brother
    friend,
   O whither fleets to-day thy wayward flight?
Hast thou forgotten that I here attend,
   From the full noon until this sad twilight?
A hundred times, at least, from the clear
    spring,
   Since the full noon o'er hill and valley
    glowed,
I've filled the vase which our Olympian king
   Upon my care for thy sole use bestowed;
That at the moment when thou should'st
    descend,
A pure refreshment might thy thirst attend.

Hast thou forgotten earth, forgotten me,
   Thy fellow bondsman in a royal cause,
Who, from the sadness of infinity,
   Only with thee can know that peaceful pause
In which we catch the flowing strain of love,
Which binds our dim fates to the throne of
    Jove?

Before I saw thee, I was like the May,
   Longing for summer that must mar its
    bloom,
Or like the morning star that calls the day,
   Whose glories to its promise are the tomb;

And as the eager fountain rises higher
   To throw itself more strongly back to earth,
Still, as more sweet and full rose my desire,
   More fondly it reverted to its birth,
For, what the rosebud seeks tells not the rose,
The meaning foretold by the boy the man can
   not disclose.

I was all Spring, for in my being dwelt
   Eternal youth, where flowers are the fruit,
Full feeling was the thought of what was felt,
   Its music was the meaning of the lute;
But heaven and earth such life will still deny,
For earth, divorced from heaven, still asks
   the question
   Why?

Upon the highest mountains my young feet
   Ached, that no pinions from their lightness
    grew,
My starlike eyes the stars would fondly greet,
   Yet win no greeting from the circling blue;
Fair, self-subsistent each in its own sphere,
   They had no care that there was none for
    me;
Alike to them that I was far or near,
   Alike to them, time and eternity.

But, from the violet of lower air,
   Sometimes an answer to my wishing came,
Those lightning births my nature seemed to
    share,
   They told the secrets of its fiery frame,
The sudden messengers of hate and love,
The thunderbolts that arm the hand of Jove,
And strike sometimes the sacred spire, and
    strike the sacred grove.

Come in a moment, in a moment gone,
They answered me, then left me still more
    lone,
They told me that the thought which ruled
    the world,
As yet no sail upon its course had furled,
That the creation was but just begun,
New leaves still leaving from the primal one,
But spoke not of the goal to which *my* rapid
    wheels would run.

Still, still my eyes, though tearfully, I strained
To the far future which my heart contained,
And no dull doubt my proper hope profaned.

At last, O bliss, thy living form I spied,
   Then a mere speck upon a distant sky,
Yet my keen glance discerned its noble pride,
   And the full answer of that sun-filled eye;

I knew it was the wing that must upbear
My earthlier form into the realms of air.

Thou knowest how we gained that beauteous
   height,
Where dwells the monarch of the sons of light,
Thou knowest he declared us two to be
The chosen servants of his ministry,
Thou as his messenger, a sacred sign
Of conquest, or with omen more benign,
To give its due weight to the righteous cause,
To express the verdict of Olympian laws.

And I to wait upon the lonely spring,
   Which slakes the thirst of bards to whom
   'tis given
The destined dues of hopes divine to sing,
   And weave the needed chain to bind to
   heaven.
Only from such could be obtained a draught
For him who in his early home from Jove's
own cup has
   quaffed.

To wait, to wait, but not to wait too long,
Till heavy grows the burthen of a song;
O bird! too long hast thou been gone to-day,
My feet are weary of their frequent way,
The spell that opes the spring my tongue no
   more can say.

If soon thou com'st not, night will fall around,
My head with a sad slumber will be bound,
And the pure draught be split upon the
   ground.

Remember that I am not yet divine,
Long years of service to the fatal Nine
Are yet to make a Delphian vigor mine.

O, make them not too hard, thou bird of Jove,
Answer the stripling's hope, confirm his love,
Receive the service in which he delights,
And bear him often to the serene heights,
Where hands that were so prompt in serving
   thee,
Shall be allowed the highest ministry,
And Rapture live with bright Fidelity.

The afternoon was spent in a very different manner. The family, whose guests we were, possessed a gay and graceful hospitality that gave zest to each moment. They possessed that rare politeness which, while fertile in pleasant expedients to vary the enjoyment of a friend, leaves him perfectly free the moment he wishes to be so. With such hosts, pleasure may be combined with repose. They lived on the bank opposite the town, and, as their house was full, we slept in the town, and passed three days with them, passing to and fro morning and evening in their boats. (To one of these, called the Fairy, in which a sweet little daughter of the house moved about lighter than any Scotch Ellen ever sung, I should indite a poem, if I had not been guilty of rhyme on the very last page.) At morning this was very pleasant; at evening, I confess I was generally too tired with the excitements of the day to think it so.

Their house—a double log cabin—was, to my eye, the model of a Western villa. Nature had laid out before it grounds which could not be improved. Within, female taste had veiled every rudeness—availed itself of every sylvan grace.

In this charming abode what laughter, what sweet thoughts, what pleasing fancies, did we not enjoy! May such never desert those who reared it and made us so kindly welcome to all its pleasures!

Fragments of city life were dexterously crumbled into the dish prepared for general entertainment. Ice creams followed the dinner drawn by the gentlemen from the river, and music and fireworks wound up the evening of days spent on the Eagle's Nest. Now they had prepared a little fleet to pass over to the Fourth of July celebration, which some queer drumming and fifing, from the opposite bank, had announced to be "on hand."

We found the free and independent citizens there collected beneath the trees, among whom many a round Irish visage dimpled at the usual puffs of Ameriky.

The orator was a New Englander, and the speech smacked loudly of Boston, but was received with much applause, and followed by a plentiful dinner, provided by and for the Sovereign People, to which Hail Columbia served as grace.

Returning, the gay flotilla hailed the little flag which the children had raised from a log-cabin, prettier than any president ever saw, and drank the health of their country and all mankind, with a clear conscience.

Dance and song wound up the day. I know not when the mere local habitation has seemed to me to afford so fair a chance of happiness as this. To a person of unspoiled tastes, the beauty alone would afford stimulus enough. But with it would be naturally associated all kinds of wild sports, experiments, and the studies of natural history. In these regards, the poet, the sportsman, the naturalist, would alike rejoice in this wide range of untouched loveliness.

Then, with a very little money, a ducal estate may be purchased, and by a very little more, and moderate labor, a family be maintained upon it with raiment, food and shelter. The luxurious and minute comforts of a city life are not yet to be had without effort disproportionate to their value. But, where there is so great a counterpoise, cannot these be given up once for all? If the houses are imperfectly built, they can afford immense fires and plenty of covering; if they are small, who cares?–with such fields to roam in. In winter, it may be borne; in summer, is of no consequence. With plenty of fish, and game, and wheat, can they not dispense with a baker to bring "muffins hot" every morning to the door to their breakfast?

Here a man need not take a small slice from the landscape, and fence it in from the obtrusions of an uncongenial neighbor, and there cut down his fancies to miniature improvements which a chicken could run over in ten minutes. He may have water and wood and land enough, to dread no incursions on his prospect from some chance Vandal that may enter his neighborhood. He need not painfully economise and manage how he may use it all; he can afford to leave some of it wild, and to carry out his own plans without obliterating those of nature.

Here, whole families might live together, if they would. The sons might return from their pilgrimages to settle near the parent hearth; the daughters might find room near their mother. Those painful separations, which already desecrate and desolate the Atlantic coast, are not enforced here by the stern need of seeking bread; and where they are voluntary, it is no matter. To me, too, used to the feelings which haunt a society of struggling men, it was delightful to look upon a scene where nature still wore her motherly smile and seemed to promise room not only for those favored or cursed with the qualities best adapting for the strifes of competition, but for the delicate, the thoughtful, even the indolent or eccentric. She did not say, Fight or starve; nor even, Work or cease to exist; but, merely showing that the apple was a finer fruit than the wild crab, gave both room to grow in the garden.

A pleasant society is formed of the families who live along the banks of this stream upon farms. They are from various parts of the world, and have much to communicate to one another. Many have cultivated minds and refined manners, all a varied experience,

while they have in common the interests of a new country and a new life. They must traverse some space to get at one another, but the journey is through scenes that make it a separate pleasure. They must bear inconveniences to stay in one another's houses; but these, to the well-disposed, are only a source of amusement and adventure.

The great drawback upon the lives of these settlers, at present, is the unfitness of the women for their new lot. It has generally been the choice of the men, and the women follow, as women will, doing their best for affection's sake, but too often in heartsickness and weariness. Beside it frequently not being a choice or conviction of their own minds that it is best to be here, their part is the hardest, and they are least fitted for it. The men can find assistance in field labor, and recreation with the gun and fishing-rod. Their bodily strength is greater, and enables them to bear and enjoy both these forms of life.

The women can rarely find any aid in domestic labor. All its various and careful tasks must often be performed, sick or well, by the mother and daughters, to whom a city education has imparted neither the strength nor skill now demanded.

The wives of the poorer settlers, having more hard work to do than before, very frequently become slatterns; but the ladies, accustomed to a refined neatness, feel that they cannot degrade themselves by its absence, and struggle under every disadvantage to keep up the necessary routine of small arrangements.

With all these disadvantages for work, their resources for pleasure are fewer. When they can leave the housework, they have not learnt to ride, to drive, to row, alone. Their culture has too generally been that given to women to make them "the ornaments of society." They can dance, but not draw; talk French, but know nothing of the language of flowers; neither in childhood were allowed to cultivate them, lest they should tan their complexions. Accustomed to the pavement of Broadway, they dare not tread the wildwood paths for fear of rattlesnakes!

Seeing much of this joylessness, and inaptitude, both of body and mind, for a lot which would be full of blessings for those prepared for it, we could not but look with deep interest on the little girls, and hope they would grow up with the strength of body, dexterity, simple tastes, and resources that would fit them to enjoy and refine the western farmer's life.

But they have a great deal to war with in the habits of thought acquired by their mothers from their own early life. Everywhere the fatal spirit of imitation, of reference to European standards, penetrates, and threatens to blight whatever of original growth might adorn the soil.

If the little girls grow up strong, resolute, able to exert their faculties, their mothers mourn over the want of fashionable delicacy. Are they gay, enterprising, ready to fly about in the various ways that teach them so much, these ladies lament that "they cannot go to school, where they might learn to be quiet." They lament the want of "education" for their daughters, as if the thousand needs which call out their young energies, and the language of nature around, yielded no education.

Their grand ambition for their children, is to send them to school in some eastern city, the measure most likely to make them useless and unhappy at home. I earnestly hope that, ere long, the existence of good schools near themselves, planned by persons of sufficient thought to meet the wants of the place and time, instead of copying New York or Boston, will correct this mania. Instruction the children want to enable them to profit by the great natural advantages of their position; but methods copied from the education of some English Lady Augusta, are as ill suited to the daughter of an Illinois farmer, as satin shoes to climb the Indian mounds. An elegance she would diffuse around her, if her mind were opened to appreciate elegance; it might be of a kind new, original, enchanting, as different from that of the city belle as that of the prairie torchflower from the shopworn article that touches the cheek of that lady within her bonnet.

To a girl really skilled to make home beautiful and comfortable, with bodily strength to enjoy plenty of exercise, the woods, the streams, a few studies, music, and the sincere and familiar intercourse, far more easily to be met here than elsewhere, would afford happiness enough. Her eyes would not grow dim, nor her cheeks sunken, in the absence of parties, morning visits, and milliner's shops.

As to the music, I wish I could see in such places the guitar rather than the piano, and good vocal more than instrumental music.

The piano many carry with them, because it is the fashionable instrument in the eastern cities. Even there, it is so merely from the habit of imitating Europe, for not one in a thousand is willing to give the labor requisite to ensure any valuable use of the instrument.

But, out here, where the ladies have so much less leisure, it is still less desirable. Add to this, they never know how to tune their own instruments, and as persons seldom visit them who can do so, these pianos are constantly out of tune, and would spoil the ear of one who began by having any.

The guitar, or some portable instrument which requires less practice, and could be kept in tune by themselves, would be far more desirable for most of these ladies. It would give all they want as a household companion to fill up the gaps of life with a pleasant stimulus or solace, and be sufficient accompaniment to the voice in social meetings.

Singing in parts is the most delightful family amusement, and those who are constantly together can learn to sing in perfect accord. All the practice it needs, after some good elementary instruction, is such as meetings by summer twilight, and evening firelight naturally suggest. And, as music is an universal language, we cannot but think a fine Italian duet would be as much at home in the log cabin as one of Mrs. Gore's novels.

The sixth July we left this beautiful place. It was one of those rich days of bright sunlight, varied by the purple shadows of large sweeping clouds. Many a backward look we cast, and left the heart behind.

Our journey to-day was no less delightful than before, still all new, boundless, limitless. Kinmont says, that limits are sacred; that the Greeks were in the right to worship a god of limits. I say, that what is limitless is alone divine, that there was neither wall nor road in Eden, that those who walked there lost and found their way just as we did, and that all the gain from the Fall was that we had a wagon to ride in. I do not think, either, that even the horses doubted whether this last was any advantage.

Everywhere the rattlesnake-weed grows in profusion. The antidote survives the bane. Soon the coarser plantain, the "white man's footstep," shall take its place.

We saw also the compass plant, and the western tea plant. Of some of the brightest flowers an Indian girl afterwards told me the medicinal virtues. I doubt not those students of the soil knew a use to every fair emblem, on which we could only look to admire its hues and shape.

After noon we were ferried by a girl, (unfortunately not of the most picturesque appearance) across the Kishwaukie, the most graceful stream, and on whose bosom rested many full-blown water-lilies, twice as large as any of ours. I was told that, *en revanche,* they were scentless, but I still regret that I could not get at one of them to try.

Query, did the lilied fragrance which, in the miraculous times, accompanied visions of saints and angels, proceed from water or garden lilies?

Kishwaukie is, according to tradition, the scene of a famous battle, and its many grassy mounds contain the bones of the valiant. On these waved thickly the mysterious purple flower, of which I have spoken before. I think it springs from the blood of the Indians, as the hyacinth did from that of Apollo's darling.

The ladies of our host's family at Oregon, when they first went there, after all the pains and plagues of building and settling, found their first pastime in opening one of these mounds, in which they found, I think, three of the departed, seated in the Indian fashion.

One of these same ladies, as she was making bread one winter morning, saw from the window a deer directly before the house. She ran out, with her hands covered with dough, calling the others, and they caught him bodily before he had time to escape.

Here (at Kishwaukie) we received a visit from a ragged and barefoot, but bright-eyed gentleman, who seemed to be the intellectual loafer, the walking Will's coffeehouse of the place. He told us many charming snake stories; among others, of himself having seen seventeen young ones reenter the mother snake, on the intrusion of a visiter.

This night we reached Belvidere, a flourishing town in Boon county, where was the tomb, now despoiled, of Big Thunder. In this later day we felt happy to find a really good hotel.

From this place, by two days of very leisurely and devious journeying, we reached Chicago, and thus ended a journey, which one at least of the party might have wished unending.

I have not been particularly anxious to give the geography of the scene, inasmuch as it seemed to me no route, nor series of stations, but a garden interspersed with cottages, groves and flowery lawns, through which a stately river ran. I had no guidebook, kept no diary, do not know how many miles we travelled each day, nor how many in all. What I got from the journey was the poetic impression of the country at large; it is all I have aimed to communicate.

The narrative might have been made much more interesting, as life was at the time, by many piquant anecdotes and tales drawn from private life. But here courtesy restrains the pen, for I know those who received the stranger with such frank kindness would feel ill requited by its becoming the means of fixing many spyglasses, even though the scrutiny might be one of admiring interest, upon their private homes.

For many of these, too, I was indebted to a friend, whose property they more lawfully are. This friend was one of those rare beings who are equally at home in nature and with man. He knew a tale of all that ran and swam, and flew, or only grew, possessing that extensive familiarity with things which shows equal sweetness of sympathy and playful penetration. Most refreshing to me was his unstudied lore, the unwritten poetry which common life presents to a strong and gentle mind. It was a great contrast to the subtleties of analysis, the philosophic strainings of which I had seen too much. But I will not attempt to transplant it. May it profit others as it did me in the region where it was born, where it belongs. The evening of our return to Chicago the sunset was of a splendor and calmness beyond any we saw at the West. The twilight that succeeded was equally beautiful; soft, pathetic, but just so calm. When afterwards I learned this was the evening of Allston's death, it seemed to me as if this glorious pageant was not without connection with that event; at least, it inspired similar emotions,–a heavenly gate closing a path adorned with shows well worthy Paradise.

> Farewell, ye soft and sumptuous solitudes!
> Ye fairy distances, ye lordly woods,
> Haunted by paths like those that Poussin
>   knew,
> When after his all gazers eyes he drew;
> I go,–and if I never more may steep
> An eager heart in your enchantments deep
> Yet ever to itself that heart may say,
> Be not exacting; thou hast lived one day;
> Hast looked on that which matches with thy
>   mood,
> Impassioned sweetness of full being's flood,
> Where nothing checked the bold yet gentle
>   wave,
> Where nought repelled the lavish love that
>   gave.
> A tender blessing lingers o'er the scene,
> Like some young mother's thought, fond,
>   yet serene,
> And through its life new-born our lives have
>   been.
> Once more farewell,–a sad, a sweet farewell;

And, if I never must behold you more,	Fear,
In other worlds I will not cease to tell	And Gorgon critics, while the tale they hear,
The rosary I here have numbered o'er:	Shall dew their stony glances with a tear,
And bright-haired Hope will lend a	If I but catch one echo from your spell;–
gladdened ear,	And so farewell,–a grateful, sad farewell!
And Love will free him from the grasp of	

Margaret Fuller
"Emerson's Essays," *New-York Daily Tribune,* 7 December 1844, p. 1.

Fuller's review of Emerson's Essays: Second Series *(1844) represents her criticism at its best. She admires Emerson but is not afraid to find fault with him. Indeed, when she had received the volume from him, her response was that in "expression it seems far more adequate than the former volume* [Essays: First Series, 1841], *has more glow, more fusion. Two or three cavils I should make at present, but will not, till I have examined further if they be correct."*

At the distance of three years this volume follows the first series of Essays, which have already made to themselves a circle of readers, attentive, thoughtful, more and more intelligent, and this circle is a large one if we consider the circumstances of this country, and of England, also, at this time.

In England it would seem there are a larger number of persons waiting for an invitation to calm thought and sincere intercourse than among ourselves. Copies of Mr. Emerson's first published little volume called "Nature," have there been sold by thousands in a short time, while one edition has needed seven years to get circulated here. Several of his Orations and Essays from "The Dial" have also been republished there, and met with a reverent and earnest response.—

We suppose that while in England the want of such a voice is as great as here, a larger number are at leisure to recognize that want; a far larger number have set foot in the speculative region and have ears refined to appreciate these melodious accents.

Our people, heated by a partisan spirit, necessarily occupied in these first stages by bringing out the material resources of the land, not generally prepared by early training for the enjoyment of books that require attention and reflection, are still more injured by a large majority of writers and speakers, who lend all their efforts to flatter corrupt tastes and mental indolence, instead of feeling it their prerogative and their duty to admonish the community of the danger and arouse it to nobler energy. The aim of the writer or lecturer is not to say the best he knows in as few and well-chosen words as he can, making it his first aim to do justice to the subject. Rather he seeks to beat out a thought as thin as possible, and to consider what the audience will be most willing to receive.

The result of such a course is inevitable. Literature and Art must become daily more degraded; Philosophy cannot exist. A man who feels within his mind some spark of genius, or a capacity for the exercises of talent, should consider himself as endowed with a sacred commission. He is the natural priest, the shepherd of the people. He must raise his mind as high as he can toward the heaven of truth, and try to draw up with him those less gifted by nature with ethereal lightness. If he does not so, but rather employs his powers to flatter them in their poverty, and to hinder aspiration by useless words, and a mere seeming of activity, his sin is great, he is false to God, and false to man.

Much of this sin indeed is done ignorantly. The idea that literature calls men to the genuine hierarchy is almost forgotten. One, who finds himself able, uses his pen, as he might a trowel, solely to procure himself bread, without having reflected on the position in which he thereby places himself.

Apart from the troop of mercenaries, there is one, still larger, of those who use their powers merely for local and temporary ends, aiming at no excellence other than may conduce to these. Among these, rank persons of honor and the best intentions, but they neglect the lasting for the transient, as a man neglects to furnish his mind that he may provide the better for the house in which his body is to dwell for a few years.

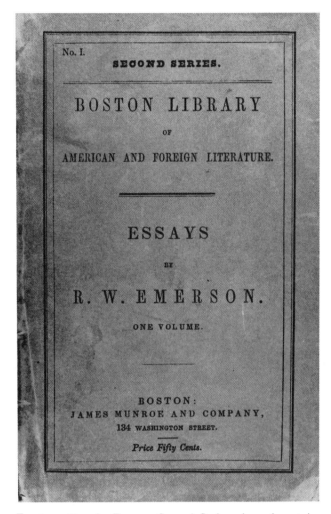

Front wrapper for Essays: Second Series, *in a format intended for popular reading*

When these sins and errors are prevalent, and threaten to become more so, how can we sufficiently prize and honor a mind which is quite pure from such? When, as in the present case, we find a man whose only aim is the discernment and interpretation of the spiritual laws by which we live and move and have our being, all whose objects are permanent, and whose every word stands for a fact.

If only as a representative of the claims of individual culture in a nation which tends to lay such stress on artificial organization and external results, Mr. Emerson would be invaluable here. History will inscribe his name as a father of the country, for he is one who pleads her cause against herself.

If New-England may be regarded as a chief mental focus to the New World, and many symptoms seem to give her this place, as to the other centres the charac-

teristics of heart and lungs to the body politic; if we may believe, as the writer does not believe, that what is to be acted out in the country at large is, most frequently, first indicated there, as all the phenomena of the nervous system in the fantasies of the brain, we may hail as an auspicious omen the influence Mr. Emerson has there obtained, which is deep-rooted, increasing, and, over the younger portion of the community, far greater than that of any other person.

His books are received there with a more ready intelligence than elsewhere, partly because his range of personal experience and illustration applies to that region, partly because he has prepared the way for his books to be read by his great powers as a speaker.

The audience that waited for years upon the lectures, a part of which is incorporated into these volumes of Essays, was never large, but it was select, and it was constant. Among the hearers were some, who though, attracted by the beauty of character and manner, they were willing to hear the speaker through, always went away discontented. They were accustomed to an artificial method, whose scaffolding could easily be retraced, and desired an obvious sequence of logical inferences. They insisted there was nothing in what they had heard, because they could not give a clear account of its course and purport. They did not see that Pindar's odes might be very well arranged for their own purpose, and yet not bear translating into the methods of Mr. Locke.

Others were content to be benefitted by a good influence without a strict analysis of its means. "My wife says it is about the elevation of human nature, and so it seems to me;" was a fit reply to some of the critics. Many were satisfied to find themselves excited to congenial thought and nobler life, without an exact catalogue of the thoughts of the speaker.

Those who believed no truth could exist, unless encased by the burrs of opinion, went away utterly baffled. Sometimes they thought he was on their side, then presently would come something on the other. He really seemed to believe there were two sides to every subject, and even to intimate higher ground from which each might be seen to have an infinite number of sides or bearings, an impertinence not to be endured! The partisan heard but once and returned no more.

But some there were, simple souls, whose life had been, perhaps, without clear light, yet still a search after truth for its own sake, who were able to receive what followed on the suggestion of a subject in a ible and haunted by many modulations, as even instruments of wood and brass seem to become after they have been long played on with skill and taste; how much more so the human voice! In the more expressive passages it uttered notes of silvery clearness, winning, yet still commanding. The words uttered in those tones, floated awhile above us, then took root in the memory like winged seed.

In the union of an even rustic plainness with lyric inspirations, religious dignity with philosophic calmness, keen sagacity in details with boldness of view, we saw what brought to mind the early poets and legislators of Greece–men who taught their fellows to plow and avoid moral evil, sing hymns to the gods and watch the metamorphoses of nature. Here in civic Boston was such a man–one who could see man in his original grandeur and his original childishness, rooted in simple nature, raising to the heavens the brow and eyes of a poet.

And these lectures seemed not so much lectures as grave didactic poems, theogonies, perhaps, adorned by odes when some Power was in question whom the poet had best learned to serve, and with eclogues wisely portraying in familiar tongue the duties of man to man and "harmless animals."

Such was the attitude in which the speaker appeared to that portion of the audience who have remained permanently attached to him.–They value his words as the signets of reality; receive his influence as a help and incentive to a nobler discipline than the age, in its general aspect, appears to require; and do not fear to anticipate the verdict of posterity in claiming for him the honors of greatness, and, in some respects, of a Master.

In New-England he thus formed for himself a class of readers, who rejoice to study in his books what they already know by heart. For, though the thought has become familiar, its beautiful garb is always fresh and bright in hue.

A similar circle of like-minded the books must and do form for themselves, though with a movement less directly powerful, as more distant from its source.

The Essays have also been obnoxious to many charges. To that of obscurity, or want of perfect articulation. Of 'Euphuism,' as an excess of fancy in proportion to imagination, and an inclination, at times, to subtlety at the expense of strength, has been styled. The human heart complains of inadequacy, either in the nature or experience of the writer, to represent its full vo-

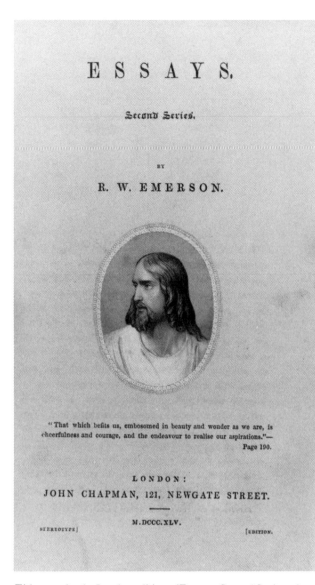

Title page for the London edition of Essays: Second Series, *demonstrating Emerson's continuing popularity in England*

natural manner, as a stream of thought. These recognized, beneath the veil of words, the still small voice of conscience, the vestal fires of lone religious hours, and the mild teachings of the summer woods.

The charm of the elocution, too, was great. His general manner was that of the reader, occasionally rising into direct address or invocation in passages where tenderness or majesty demanded more energy. At such times both eye and voice called on a remote future to give a worthy reply. A future which shall manifest more largely the universal soul as it was then manifest to this soul. The tone of the voice was a grave body tone, full and sweet rather than sonorous, yet flex-

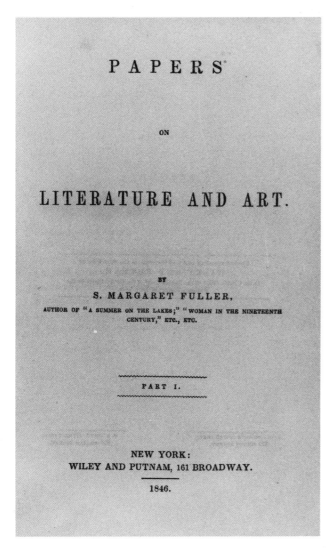

Title page for Fuller's last book published during her lifetime

cation and its deeper needs. Sometimes it speaks of this want as "under-development" or a want of expansion which may be remedied; sometimes doubts whether "in this mansion there be either hall or portal to receive the loftier of the Passions." Sometimes the soul is deified at the expense of nature, then again nature at that of man, and we are not quite sure that we can make a true harmony by balance of the statements.– This writer has never written one good work, if such a work be one where the whole commands more attention than the parts. If such an one be produced only where, after an accumulation of materials, fire enough be applied to fuse the whole into one new substance. This second series is superior in this respect to the former, yet in no one essay is the main stress so obvious as to produce on the mind the harmonious effect of a

noble river or a tree in full leaf. Single passages and sentences engage our attention too much in proportion. These essays, it has been justly said, tire like a string of mosaics or a house built of medals. We miss what we expect in the work of the great poet, or the great philosopher, the liberal air of all the zones: the glow, uniform yet various in tint, which is given to a body by free circulation of the heart's blood from the hour of birth. Here is, undoubtedly, the man of ideas, but we want the ideal man also; want the heart and genius of human life to interpret it, and here our satisfaction is not so perfect. We doubt this friend raised himself too early to the perpendicular and did not lie along the ground long enough to hear the secret whispers of our parent life. We could wish he might be thrown by conflicts on the lap of mother earth, to see if he would not rise again with added powers.

All this we may say, but it cannot excuse us from benefitting by the great gifts that have been given, and assigning them their due place.

Some painters paint on a red ground. And this color may be supposed to represent the ground work most immediately congenial to most men, as it is the color of blood and represents human vitality. The figures traced upon it are instinct with life in its fulness and depth.

But other painters paint on a gold ground. And a very different but no less natural, because also a celestial beauty, is given to their works who choose for their foundation the color of the sunbeam, which nature has preferred for her most precious product, and that which will best bear the test of purification, gold.

If another simile may be allowed, another no less apt is at hand. Wine is the most brilliant and intense expression of the powers of earth.–It is her potable fire, her answer to the sun. It exhilarates, it inspires, but then it is liable to fever and intoxicate too the careless partaker.

Mead was the chosen drink of the Northern gods. And this essence of the honey of the mountain bee was not thought unworthy to revive the souls of the valiant who had left their bodies on the fields of strife below.

Nectar should combine the virtues of the ruby wine, the golden mead, without their defects or dangers.

Two high claims our writer can vindicate on the attention of his contemporaries. One from his sincerity. You have his thought just as it found place in the life of his own soul. Thus, however near or relatively distant

Painting of Margaret Fuller by Thomas Hicks done when she was in Rome in 1849

its approximation to absolute truth, its action on you cannot fail to be healthful. It is a part of the free air.

He belongs to that band of whom there may be found a few in every age, and who now in known human history may be counted by hundreds, who worship the one God only, the God of Truth. They worship, not saints, nor creeds, nor churches, nor reliques, nor idols in any form. The mind is kept open to truth, and life only valued as a tendency toward it. This must be illustrated by acts and words of love, purity and intelligence. Such are the salt of the earth; let the minutest crystal of that salt be willingly by us held in solution.

The other is through that part of his life, which, if sometimes obstructed or chilled by the critical intellect, is yet the prevalent and the main source of his power. It is that by which he imprisons his hearer only to free him again as a "liberating God" (to use his own words). But indeed let us use them altogether, for none other, ancient or modern, can more worthily express how, making present to us the courses and destinies of nature, he invests himself with her serenity and animates us with her joy.

"Poetry was all written before time was, and whenever we are so finely organized that we can penetrate into that region where the air is music, we hear those primal warblings, and attempt to write them down, but we lose ever and anon a word, or a verse, and substitute something of our own, and thus miswrite the poem. The men of more delicate ear write down these cadences more faithfully, and these transcripts, though imperfect, become the songs of the nations."

*Manuscript poem by Margaret Fuller (*Autograph Leaves from Our Country's Author's, *edited by John Pendleton Kennedy and Alexander Bliss [1894])*

"As the eyes of Lyncaeus were said to see through the earth, so the poet turns the world to glass, and shows us all things in their right series and procession. For, through that better perception, he stands one step nearer to things, and sees the flowing or metamorphosis; perceives that thought is multiform; that within the form of every creature is a force impelling it to ascend into a higher form; and following with his eyes the life, uses the forms which express that life, and so the speech flows with the flowing of nature."

Thus have we in a brief and unworthy manner indicated some views of these books. The only true criticism of these, or any good books, may be gained by making them the companions of our lives. Does every accession of knowledge or a juster sense of beauty makes us prize them more? Then they are good, indeed, and more immortal than mortal. Let that test be applied to these; essays which will lead to great and complete poems–somewhere.

Henry David Thoreau
"Resistance to Civil Government," *Aesthetic Papers* (Boston: E. P. Peabody, 1849), pp. 189-211.

> *Thoreau's most famous essay, this is better-known as "Civil Disobedience," a title bestowed after Thoreau's death when it was collected in* A Yankee in Canada *(1866). Mahatma Gandhi and Martin Luther King, Jr., were both influenced by Thoreau's ideas that government by majority is really government by the physically stronger not the morally superior, and that unjust laws should be fought with noncompliance rather than with physical action. This essay appeared in the first and only issue of Elizabeth Palmer Peabody's series of* Aesthetic Papers.

I heartily accept the motto,–"That government is best which governs least;" and I should like to see it acted up to more rapidly and systematically. Carried out, it finally amounts to this, which also I believe,–"That government is best which governs not at all;" and when men are prepared for it, that will be the kind of government which they will have. Government is at best but an expedient; but most governments are usually, and all governments are sometimes, inexpedient. The objections which have been brought against a standing army, and they are many and weighty, and deserve to prevail, may also at last be brought against a standing government. The standing army is only an arm of the standing government. The government itself, which is only the mode which the people have chosen to execute their will, is equally liable to be abused and perverted before the people can act through it. Witness the present Mexican war, the work of comparatively a few individuals using the standing government as their tool; for, in the outset, the people would not have consented to this measure.

This American government,–what is it but a tradition, though a recent one, endeavoring to transmit itself unimpaired to posterity, but each instant losing some of its integrity? It has not the vitality and force of a single living man; for a single man can bend it to his will. It is a sort of wooden gun to the people themselves; and, if ever they should use it in earnest as a real one against each other, it will surely split. But it is not the less necessary for this; for the people must have some complicated machinery or other, and hear its din, to satisfy that idea of government which they have. Governments show thus how successfully men can be imposed on, even impose on themselves, for their own advantage. It is excellent, we must all allow; yet this government never of itself furthered any enterprise, but by the alacrity with which it got out of its way. *It* does not keep the country free. *It* does not settle the West. *It* does not educate. The character inherent in the American people has done all that has been accomplished; and it would have done somewhat more, if the government had not sometimes got in its way. For government is an expedient by which men would fain succeed in letting one another alone; and, as has been said, when it is most expedient, the governed are most let alone by it. Trade and commerce, if they were not made of India rubber, would never manage to bounce over the obstacles which legislators are continu-

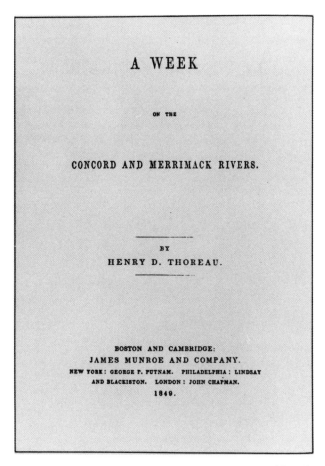

A WEEK

ON THE

CONCORD AND MERRIMACK RIVERS.

BY

HENRY D. THOREAU.

BOSTON AND CAMBRIDGE:
JAMES MUNROE AND COMPANY.
NEW YORK: GEORGE P. PUTNAM.   PHILADELPHIA : LINDSAY
AND BLACKISTON.   LONDON : JOHN CHAPMAN.
1849.

Title page for Thoreau's first book. When 706 unsold copies (out of a printing of 1,000) were returned to him in 1853, Thoreau wrote in his journal that he now had "a library of nearly nine hundred volumes, over seven hundred of which I wrote myself."

ally putting in their way; and, if one were to judge these men wholly by the effects of their actions, and not partly by their intentions, they would deserve to be classed and punished with those mischievous persons who put obstructions on the railroads.

But, to speak practically and as a citizen, unlike those who call themselves no-government men, I ask for, not at once no government, but *at once* a better government. Let every man make known what kind of government would command his respect, and that will be one step toward obtaining it.

After all, the practical reason why, when the power is once in the hands of the people, a majority are permitted, and for a long period continue, to rule, is not because they are most likely to be in the right, nor because this seems fairest to the minority, but because they are physically the strongest. But a government in which the majority rule in all cases cannot be based on justice, even as far as men understand it. Can there not be a government in which majorities do not virtually decide right and wrong, but conscience?– in which majorities decide only those questions to which the rule of expediency is applicable? Must the citizen ever for a moment, or in the least degree, resign his conscience to the legislator? Why has every man a conscience, then? I think that we should be men first, and subjects afterward. It is not desirable to cultivate a respect for the law, so much as for the right. The only obligation which I have a right to assume, is to do at any time what I think right. It is truly enough said, that a corporation has no conscience; but a corporation of conscientious men is a corporation *with* a conscience. Law never made men a whit more just; and, by means of their respect for it, even the well-disposed are daily made the agents of injustice. A common and natural result of an undue respect for law is, that you may see a file of soldiers, colonel, captain, corporal, privates, powder-monkeys and all, marching in admirable order over hill and dale to the wars, against their wills, aye, against their common sense and consciences, which makes it very steep marching indeed, and produces a palpitation of the heart. They have no doubt that it is a damnable business in which they are concerned; they are all peaceably inclined. Now, what are they? Men at all? or small moveable forts and magazines, at the service of some unscrupulous man in power? Visit the Navy Yard, and behold a marine, such a man as an American government can make, or such as it can make a man with its black arts, a mere shadow and reminiscence of humanity, a man laid out alive and standing, and already, as one may say, buried under arms with funeral accompaniments, though it may be

"Not a drum was heard, nor a funeral note,
　As his corse to the ramparts we hurried;
Not a soldier discharged his farewell shot
　O'er the grave where our hero we buried."

The mass of men serve the State thus, not as men mainly, but as machines, with their bodies. They are the standing army, and the militia, jailers, constables, *posse comitatus,* &c. In most cases there is no free exercise whatever of the judgment or of the moral sense; but they put themselves on a level with wood and earth and stones; and wooden men can perhaps be

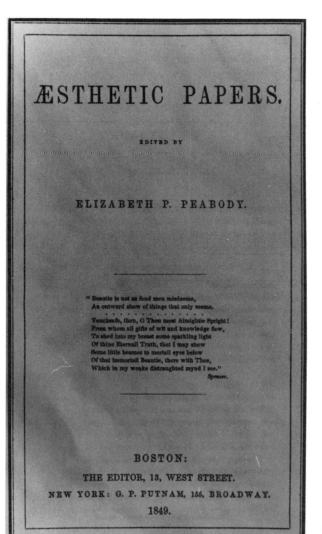

ÆSTHETIC PAPERS.

EDITED BY

ELIZABETH P. PEABODY.

" Beautie is not as fond men misdeeme,
An outward show of things that only seeme.
. . . .
Vouchsafe, then, O Thou most Almightie Spright!
From whom all gifts of wit and knowledge flow,
To shed into my breast some sparkling light
Of thine Eternall Truth, that I may show
Some little beames to mortall eyes below
Of that immortall Beautie, there with Thee,
Which in my weake distraughted mynd I see."
                                    Spenser.

BOSTON:
THE EDITOR, 13, WEST STREET.
NEW YORK: G. P. PUTNAM, 155, BROADWAY.
1849.

Title page for the collection known today for the first publication of Thoreau's essay on civil disobedience

manufactured that will serve the purpose as well. Such command no more respect than men of straw, or a lump of dirt. They have the same sort of worth only as horses and dogs. Yet such as these even are commonly esteemed good citizens. Others, as most legislators, politicians, lawyers, ministers, and office-holders, serve the State chiefly with their heads; and, as they rarely make any moral distinctions, they are as likely to serve the devil, without intending it, as God. A very few, as heroes, patriots, martyrs, reformers in the great sense, and *men,* serve the State with their consciences also, and so necessarily resist it for the most part; and they are commonly treated by it as enemies. A wise man will only be useful as a man, and will not submit to be "clay," and "stop a hole to keep the wind away," but leave that office to his dust at least:–

"I am too high-born to be propertied,
To be a secondary at control,
Or useful serving-man and instrument
To any sovereign state throughout the world."

He who gives himself entirely to his fellow-men appears to them useless and selfish; but he who gives himself partially to them is pronounced a benefactor and philanthropist.

How does it become a man to behave toward this American government to-day? I answer that he cannot without disgrace be associated with it. I cannot for an instant recognize that political organization as *my* government which is the *slave's* government also.

All men recognize the right of revolution; that is, the right to refuse allegiance to and to resist the government, when its tyranny or its inefficiency are great and unendurable. But almost all say that such is not the case now. But such was the case, they think, in the Revolution of '75. If one were to tell me that this was a bad government because it taxed certain foreign commodities brought to its ports, it is most probable that I should not make an ado about it, for I can do without them: all machines have their friction; and possibly this does enough good to counterbalance the evil. At any rate, it is a great evil to make a stir about it. But when the friction comes to have its machine, and oppression and robbery are organized, I say, let us not have such a machine any longer. In other words, when a sixth of the population of a nation which has undertaken to be the refuge of liberty are slaves, and a whole country is unjustly overrun and conquered by a foreign army, and subjected to military law, I think that it is not too soon for honest men to rebel and revolutionize. What makes this duty the more urgent is the fact, that the country so overrun is not our own, but ours is the invading army.

Paley, a common authority with many on moral questions, in his chapter on the "Duty of Submission to Civil Government," resolves all civil obligation into expediency; and he proceeds to say, "that so long as the interest of the whole society requires it, that is, so long as the established government cannot be resisted or changed without public inconveniency, it is the will of God that the established government be obeyed, and no longer."–"This principle being admitted, the justice of every particular case of resistance is reduced to a computation of the quantity of the danger and griev-

Daniel Ricketson's sketch of Thoreau in 1854 (Daniel Ricketson and His Friends, edited by Anna Ricketson and Walton Ricketson [1902])

ance on the one side, and of the probability and expense of redressing it on the other." Of this, he says, every man shall judge for himself. But Paley appears never to have contemplated those cases to which the rule of expediency does not apply, in which a people, as well as an individual, must do justice, cost what it may. If I have unjustly wrested a plank from a drowning man, I must restore it to him though I drown myself. This, according to Paley, would be inconvenient. But he that would save his life, in such a case, shall lose it. This people must cease to hold slaves, and to make war on Mexico, though it cost them their existence as a people.

In their practice, nations agree with Paley; but does any one think that Massachusetts does exactly what is right at the present crisis?

"A drab of state, a cloth-o'-silver slut,
To have her train borne up, and her soul trail in the dirt."

Practically speaking, the opponents to a reform in Massachusetts are not a hundred thousand politicians at the South, but a hundred thousand merchants and farmers here, who are more interested in commerce and agriculture than they are in humanity, and are not prepared to do justice to the slave and to Mexico, *cost what it may.* I quarrel not with far-off foes, but with those who, near at home, co-operate with, and do the bidding of those far away, and without whom the latter would be harmless. We are accustomed to say, that the mass of men are unprepared; but improvement is slow, because the few are not materially wiser or better than the many. It is not so important that many should be as good as you, as that there be some absolute goodness somewhere; for that will leaven the whole lump. There are thousands who are *in opinion* opposed to slavery and to the war, who yet in effect do nothing to put an end to them; who, esteeming themselves children of Washington and Franklin, sit down with their hands in their pockets, and say that they know not what to do, and do nothing; who even postpone the question of freedom to the question of free-trade, and quietly read the prices-current along with the latest advices from Mexico, after dinner, and, it may be, fall asleep over them both. What is the price-current of an honest man and patriot today? They hesitate, and they regret, and sometimes they petition; but they do nothing in earnest and with effect. They will wait, well disposed, for others to remedy the evil, that they may no longer have it to regret. At most, they give only a cheap vote, and a feeble countenance and Godspeed, to the right, as it goes by them. There are nine hundred and ninety-nine patrons of virtue to one virtuous man; but it is easier to deal with the real possessor of a thing than with the temporary guardian of it.

All voting is a sort of gaming, like chequers or backgammon, with a slight moral tinge to it, a playing with right and wrong, with moral questions; and betting naturally accompanies it. The character of the voters is not staked. I cast my vote, perchance, as I think right; but I am not vitally concerned that that right should prevail. I am willing to leave it to the majority.

Its obligation, therefore, never exceeds that of expediency. Even voting *for the right* is *doing* nothing for it. It is only expressing to men feebly your desire that it should prevail. A wise man will not leave the right to the mercy of chance, nor wish it to prevail through the power of the majority. There is but little virtue in the action of masses of men. When the majority shall at length vote for the abolition of slavery, it will be because they are indifferent to slavery, or because there is but little slavery left to be abolished by their vote. *They* will then be the only slaves. Only *his* vote can hasten the abolition of slavery who asserts his own freedom by his vote.

I hear of a convention to be held at Baltimore, or elsewhere, for the selection of a candidate for the Presidency, made up chiefly of editors, and men who are politicians by profession; but I think, what is it to any independent, intelligent, and respectable man what decision they may come to, shall we not have the advantage of his wisdom and honesty, nevertheless? Can we not count upon some independent votes? Are there not many individuals in the country who do not attend conventions? But no: I find that the respectable man, so called, has immediately drifted from his position, and despairs of his country, when his country has more reason to despair of him. He forthwith adopts one of the candidates thus selected as the only *available* one, thus proving that he is himself *available* for any purposes of the demagogue. His vote is of no more worth than that of any unprincipled foreigner or hireling native, who may have been bought. Oh for a man who is a *man,* and, as my neighbor says, has a bone in his back which you cannot pass your hand through! Our statistics are at fault: the population has been returned too large. How many *men* are there to a square thousand miles in this country? Hardly one. Does not America offer any inducement for men to settle here? The American has dwindled into an Odd Fellow,—one who may be known by the development of his organ of gregariousness, and a manifest lack of intellect and cheerful self-reliance; whose first and chief concern, on coming into the world, is to see that the alms-houses are in good repair; and, before yet he has lawfully donned the virile garb, to collect a fund for the support of the widows and orphans that may be; who, in short, ventures to live only by the aid of the mutual insurance company, which has promised to bury him decently.

It is not a man's duty, as a matter of course, to devote himself to the eradication of any, even the most enormous wrong; he may still properly have other concerns to engage him; but it is his duty, at least, to wash his hands of it, and, if he gives it no thought longer, not to give it practically his support. If I devote myself to other pursuits and contemplations, I must first see, at least, that I do not pursue them sitting upon another man's shoulders. I must get off him first, that he may pursue his contemplations too. See what gross inconsistency is tolerated. I have heard some of my townsmen say, "I should like to have them order me out to help put down an insurrection of the slaves, or to march to Mexico,—see if I would go;" and yet these very men have each, directly by their allegiance, and so indirectly, at least, by their money, furnished a substitute. The soldier is applauded who refuses to serve in an unjust war by those who do not refuse to sustain the unjust government which makes the war; is applauded by those whose own act and authority he disregards and sets at nought; as if the State were penitent to that degree that it hired one to scourge it while it sinned, but not to that degree that it left off sinning for a moment. Thus, under the name of order and civil government, we are all made at last to pay homage to and support our own meanness. After the first blush of sin, comes its indifference; and from immoral it becomes, as it were, *un*moral, and not quite unnecessary to that life which we have made.

The broadest and most prevalent error requires the most disinterested virtue to sustain it. The slight reproach to which the virtue of patriotism is commonly liable, the noble are most likely to incur. Those who, while they disapprove of the character and measures of a government, yield to it their allegiance and support, are undoubtedly its most conscientious supporters, and so frequently the most serious obstacles to reform. Some are petitioning the State to dissolve the Union, to disregard the requisitions of the President. Why do they not dissolve it themselves,—the union between themselves and the State,—and refuse to pay their quota into its treasury? Do not they stand in the same relation to the State, that the State does to the Union? And have not the same reasons prevented the State from resisting the Union, which have prevented them from resisting the State?

How can a man be satisfied to entertain an opinion merely, and enjoy *it?* Is there any enjoyment in it, if his opinion is that he is aggrieved? If you are cheated out of a single dollar by your neighbor, you do not rest satisfied with knowing that you are cheated, or with say-

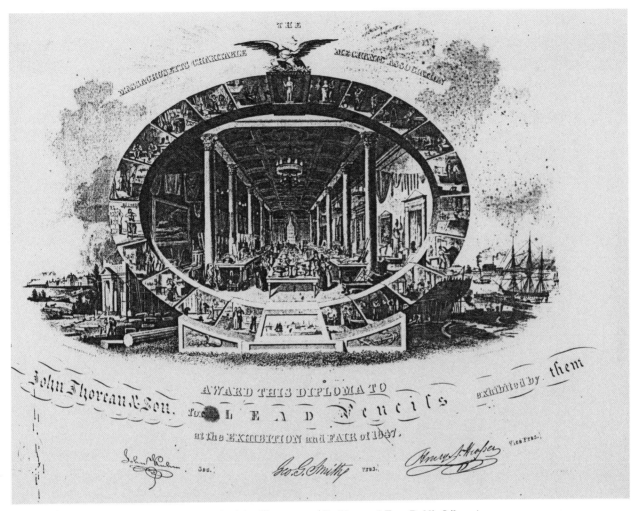

Award received for Thoreau pencils (Concord Free Public Library)

ing that you are cheated, or even with petitioning him to pay you your due; but you take effectual steps at once to obtain the full amount, and see that you are never cheated again. Action from principle,–the perception and the performance of right,–changes things and relations; it is essentially revolutionary, and does not consist wholly with any thing which was. It not only divides states and churches, it divides families; aye, it divides the *individual,* separating the diabolical in him from the divine.

Unjust laws exist: shall we be content to obey them, or shall we endeavor to amend them, and obey them until we have succeeded, or shall we transgress them at once? Men generally, under such a government as this, think that they ought to wait until they have persuaded the majority to alter them. They think that, if they should resist, the remedy would be worse than the evil. But it is the fault of the government it-

self that the remedy *is* worse than the evil. *It* makes it worse. Why is it not more apt to anticipate and provide for reform? Why does it not cherish its wise minority? Why does it cry and resist before it is hurt? Why does it not encourage its citizens to be on the alert to point out its faults, and *do* better than it would have them? Why does it always crucify Christ, and excommunicate Copernicus and Luther, and pronounce Washington and Franklin rebels?

One would think, that a deliberate and practical denial of its authority was the only offence never contemplated by government; else, why has it not assigned its definite, its suitable and proportionate penalty? If a man who has no property refuses but once to earn nine shillings for the State, he is put in prison for a period unlimited by any law that I know, and determined only by the discretion of those who placed him there; but if he should steal ninety times nine shillings from

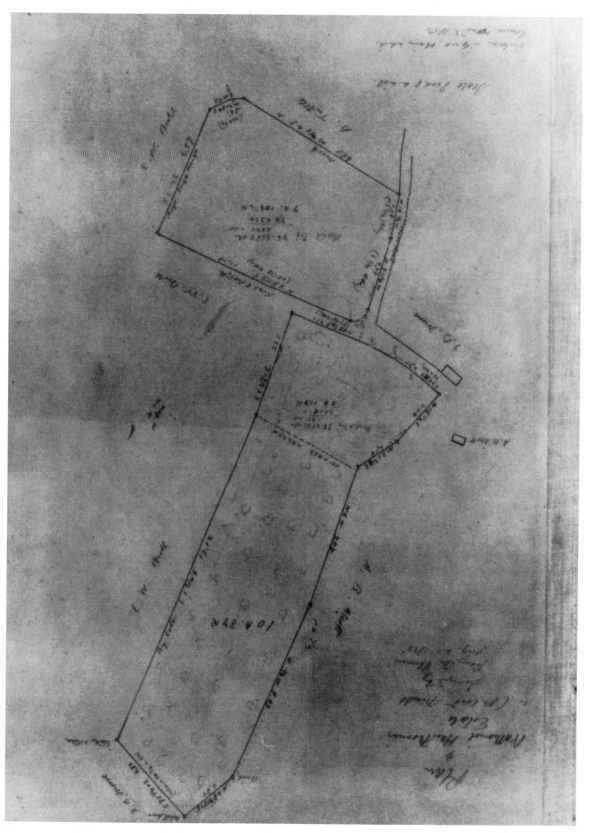

Thoreau's survey of Nathaniel Hawthorne's Concord property (Concord Free Public Library)

the State, he is soon permitted to go at large again.

If the injustice is part of the necessary friction of the machine of government, let it go, let it go: perchance it will wear smooth,—certainly the machine will wear out. If the injustice has a spring, or a pulley, or a rope, or a crank, exclusively for itself, then perhaps you may consider whether the remedy will not be worse than the evil; but if it is of such a nature that it requires you to be the agent of injustice to another, then, I say, break the law. Let your life be a counter friction to stop the machine. What I have to do is to see, at any rate, that I do not lend myself to the wrong which I condemn.

As for adopting the ways which the State has provided for remedying the evil, I know not of such ways. They take too much time, and a man's life will be gone. I have other affairs to attend to. I came into this world, not chiefly to make this a good place to live in, but to live in it, be it good or bad. A man has not every thing to do, but something; and because he cannot do *every thing*, it is not necessary that he should do *something* wrong. It is not my business to be petitioning the governor or the legislature any more than it is theirs to petition me; and, if they should not hear my petition, what should I do then? But in this case the State has provided no way: its very Constitution is the evil. This may seem to be harsh and stubborn and unconciliatory; but it is to treat with the utmost kindness and consideration the only spirit that can appreciate or deserves it. So is all change for the better, like birth and death which convulse the body.

I do not hesitate to say, that those who call themselves abolitionists should at once effectually withdraw their support, both in person and property, from the government of Massachusetts, and not wait till they constitute a majority of one, before they suffer the right to prevail through them. I think that it is enough if they have God on their side, without waiting for that other one. Moreover, any man more right than his neighbors, constitutes a majority of one already.

I meet this American government, or its representative the State government, directly, and face to face, once a year, no more, in the person of its tax-gatherer; this is the only mode in which a man situated as I am necessarily meets it; and it then says distinctly, Recognize me; and the simplest, the most effectual, and, in the present posture of affairs, the indispensablest mode of treating with it on this head, of expressing your little satisfaction with and love for it,

is to deny it then. My civil neighbor, the tax-gatherer, is the very man I have to deal with,—for it is, after all, with men and not with parchment that I quarrel,—and he has voluntarily chosen to be an agent of the government. How shall he ever know well what he is and does as an officer of the government, or as a man, until he is obliged to consider whether he shall treat me, his neighbor, for whom he has respect, as a neighbor and well-disposed man, or as a maniac and disturber of the peace, and see if he can get over this obstruction to his neighborliness without a ruder and more impetuous thought or speech corresponding with his action? I know this well, that if one thousand, if one hundred, if ten men whom I could name,—if ten *honest* men only,—aye, if *one* HONEST man, in this State of Massachusetts, *ceasing to hold slaves,* were actually to withdraw from this copartnership, and be locked up in the county jail therefor, it would be the abolition of slavery in America. For it matters not how small the beginning may seem to be: what is once well done is done for ever. But we love better to talk about it: that we say is our mission. Reform keeps many scores of newspapers in its service, but not one man. If my esteemed neighbor, the State's ambassador, who will devote his days to the settlement of the question of human rights in the Council Chamber, instead of being threatened with the prisons of Carolina, were to sit down the prisoner of Massachusetts, that State which is so anxious to foist the sin of slavery upon her sister,—though at present she can discover only an act of inhospitality to be the ground of a quarrel with her,—the Legislature would not wholly waive the subject the following winter.

Under the government which imprisons any unjustly, the true place for a just man is also a prison. The proper place to-day, the only place which Massachusetts has provided for her freer and less desponding spirits, is in her prisons, to be put out and locked out of the state by her own act, as they have already put themselves out by their principles. It is there that the fugitive slave, and the Mexican prisoner on parole, and the Indian come to plead the wrongs of his race, should find them; on that separate, but more free and honorable ground, where the State places those who are not *with* her but *against* her,—the only house in a slave-state in which a free man can abide with honor. If any think that their influence would be lost there, and their voices no longer afflict the ear of the State, that they would not be as an enemy within its walls, they do not know by how much truth is stronger than error, not how much more eloquently and effectively he can combat injustice who has experienced a little in his own person. Cast your whole vote, not a strip of paper merely, but your whole influence. A minority is powerless while it conforms to the majority; it is not even a minority then; but it is irresistible when it clogs by its whole weight. If the alternative is to keep all just men in prison, or give up war and slavery, the State will not hesitate which to choose. If a thousand men were not to pay their tax-bills this year, that would not be a violent and bloody measure, as it would be to pay them, and enable the State to commit violence and shed innocent blood. This is, in fact, the definition of a peaceable revolution, if any such is possible. If the tax-gatherer, or any other public officer, asks me, as one has done, "But what shall I do?" my answer is, "If you really wish to do any thing, resign your office." When the subject has refused allegiance, and the officer has resigned his office, then the revolution is accomplished. But even suppose blood should flow. Is there not a sort of blood shed when the conscience is wounded? Through this wound a man's real manhood and immortality flow out, and he bleeds to an everlasting death. I see this blood flowing now.

I have contemplated the imprisonment of the offender, rather than the seizure of his goods,–though both will serve the same purpose,–because they who assert the purest right, and consequently are most dangerous to a corrupt State, commonly have not spent much time in accumulating property. To such the State renders comparatively small service, and a slight tax is wont to appear exorbitant, particularly if they are obliged to earn it by special labor with their hands. If there were one who lived wholly without the use of money, the State itself would hesitate to demand it of him. But the rich man–not to make any invidious comparison–is always sold to the institution which makes him rich. Absolutely speaking, the more money, the less virtue; for money comes between a man and his objects, and obtains them for him; and it was certainly no great virtue to obtain it. It puts to rest many questions which he would otherwise be taxed to answer; while the only new question which it puts is the hard but superfluous one, how to spend it. Thus his moral ground is taken from under his feet. The opportunities of living are diminished in proportion as what are called the "means" are increased. The best thing a man can do for his culture when he is rich is to endeavour to carry out those schemes which he entertained

when he was poor. Christ answered the Herodians according to their condition. "Show me the tribute-money," said he;–and one took a penny out of his pocket;–If you use money which has the image of Cæsar on it, and which he has made current and valuable, that is, *if you are men of the State,* and gladly enjoy the advantages of Cæsar's government, then pay him back some of his own when he demands it; "Render therefore to Cæsar that which is Cæsar's, and to God those things which are God's,"–leaving them no wiser than before as to which was which; for they did not wish to know.

When I converse with the freest of my neighbors, I perceive that, whatever they may say about the magnitude and seriousness of the question, and their regard for the public tranquillity, the long and the short of the matter is, that they cannot spare the protection of the existing government, and they dread the consequences of disobedience to it to their property and families. For my own part, I should not like to think that I ever rely on the protection of the State. But, if I deny the authority of the State when it presents its tax-bill, it will soon take and waste all my property, and so harass me and my children without end. This is hard. This makes it impossible for a man to live honestly and at the same time comfortably in outward respects. It will not be worth the while to accumulate property; that would be sure to go again. You must hire or squat somewhere, and raise but a small crop, and eat that soon. You must live within yourself, and depend upon yourself, always tucked up and ready for a start, and not have many affairs. A man may grow rich in Turkey even, if he will be in all respects a good subject of the Turkish government. Confucius said,–"If a State is governed by the principles of reason, poverty and misery are subjects of shame; if a State is not governed by the principles of reason, riches and honors are the subjects of shame." No: until I want the protection of Massachusetts to be extended to me in some distant southern port, where my liberty is endangered, or until I am bent solely on building up an estate at home by peaceful enterprise, I can afford to refuse allegiance to Massachusetts, and her right to my property and life. It costs me less in every sense to incur the penalty of disobedience to the State, than it would to obey. I should feel as if I were worth less in that case.

Some years ago, the State met me in behalf of the church, and commanded me to pay a certain sum toward the support of a clergyman whose preaching my father attended, but never I myself. "Pay it," it said, "or be locked up in the jail." I declined to pay. But, unfortunately, another man saw fit to pay it. I did not see why the schoolmaster should be taxed to support the priest, and not the priest the schoolmaster; for I was not the State's schoolmaster, but I supported myself by voluntary subscription. I did not see why the lyceum should not present its tax-bill, and have the State to back its demand, as well as the church. However, at the request of the selectmen, I condescended to make some such statement as this in writing:–"Know all men by these presents, that I, Henry Thoreau, do not wish to be regarded as a member of any incorporated society which I have not joined." This I gave to the town-clerk; and he has it. The State, having thus learned that I did not wish to be regarded as a member of that church, has never made a like demand on me since; though it said that it must adhere to its original presumption that time. If I had known how to name them, I should then have signed off in detail from all the societies which I never signed on to; but I did not know where to find a complete list.

I have paid no poll-tax for six years. I was put into a jail once on this account, for one night; and, as I stood considering the walls of solid stone, two or three feet thick, the door of wood and iron, a foot thick, and the iron grating which strained the light, I could not help being struck with the foolishness of that institution which treated me as if I were mere flesh and blood and bones, to be locked up. I wondered that it should have concluded at length that this was the best use it could put me to, and had never thought to avail itself of my services in some way. I saw that, if there was a wall of stone between me and my townsmen, there was a still more difficult one to climb or break through, before they could get to be as free as I was. I did not for a moment feel confined, and the walls seemed a great waste of stone and mortar. I felt as if I alone of all my townsmen had paid my tax. They plainly did not know how to treat me, but behaved like persons who are underbred. In every threat and in every compliment there was a blunder; for they thought that my chief desire was to stand the other side of that stone wall. I could not but smile to see how industriously they locked the door on my meditations, which followed them out again without let or hindrance, and *they* were really all that was dangerous. As they could not reach me, they had resolved to punish my body; just as boys, if they cannot come at some person against

whom they have a spite, will abuse his dog. I saw that the State was half-witted, that it was timid as a lone woman with her silver spoons, and that it did not know its friends from its foes, and I lost all my remaining respect for it, and pitied it.

Thus the State never intentionally confronts a man's sense, intellectual or moral, but only his body, his senses. It is not armed with superior wit or honesty, but with superior physical strength. I was not born to be forced. I will breathe after my own fashion. Let us see who is the strongest. What force has a multitude? They only can force me who obey a higher law than I. They force me to become like themselves. I do not hear of *men* being *forced* to live this way or that by masses of men. What sort of life were that to live? When I meet a government which says to me, "Your money or your life," why should I be in haste to give it my money? It may be in a great strait, and not know what to do: I cannot help that. It must help itself; do as I do. It is not worth the while to snivel about it. I am not responsible for the successful working of the machinery of society. I am not the son of the engineer. I perceive that, when an acorn and a chestnut fall side by side, the one does not remain inert to make way for the other, but both obey their own laws, and spring and grow and flourish as best they can, till one, perchance, overshadows and destroys the other. If a plant cannot live according to its nature, it dies; and so a man.

The night in prison was novel and interesting enough. The prisoners in their shirt-sleeves were enjoying a chat and the evening air in the door-way, when I entered. But the jailer said, "Come, boys, it is time to lock up;" and so they dispersed, and I heard the sound of their steps returning into the hollow apartments. My room-mate was introduced to me by the jailer, as "a first-rate fellow and a clever man." When the door was locked, he showed me where to hang my hat, and how he managed matters there. The rooms were whitewashed once a month; and this one, at least, was the whitest, most simply furnished, and probably the neatest apartment in the town. He naturally wanted to know where I came from, and what brought me there; and, when I had told him, I asked him in my turn how he came there, presuming him to be an honest man, of course; and, as the world goes, I believe he was. "Why," said he, "they accuse me of burning a barn; but I never did it." As near as I could discover, he had probably gone to bed in a barn when drunk, and smoked his pipe there; and so a barn was burnt. He had the reputation of being a clever man, had been there some three months waiting for his trial to come on, and would have to wait as much longer; but he was quite domesticated and contented, since he got his board for nothing, and thought that he was well treated.

He occupied one window, and I the other; and I saw, that, if one stayed there long, his principal business would be to look out the window. I had soon read all the tracts that

Thoreau's flute and spyglass

were left there, and examined where former prisoners had broken out, and where a grate had been sawed off, and heard the history of the various occupants of that room; for I found that even here there was a history and a gossip which never circulated beyond the walls of the jail. Probably this is the only house in the town where verses are composed, which are afterward printed in a circular form, but not published. I was shown quite a long list of verses which were composed by some young men who had been detected in an attempt to escape, who avenged themselves by singing them.

I pumped my fellow-prisoner as dry as I could, for fear I should never see him again; but at length he showed me which was my bed, and left me to blow out the lamp.

It was like travelling into a far country, such as I had never expected to behold, to lie there for one night. It seemed to me that I never had heard the town-clock strike before, nor the evening sounds of the village; for we slept with the windows open, which were inside the grating. It was to see my native village in the light of the middle ages, and our Concord was turned into a Rhine stream, and visions of old burghers that I heard in the streets. I was an involuntary spectator and auditor of whatever was done and said in the kitchen of the adjacent village-inn,–a wholly new and rare experience to me. It was a closer view of my native town. I was fairly inside of it. I never had seen its institutions before. This is one of its peculiar institutions; for it is a shire town. I began to comprehend what its inhabitants were about.

In the morning, our breakfasts were put through the hole in the door, in small oblong-square tin pans, made to fit, and holding a pint of chocolate, with brown bread, and an iron spoon. When they called for the vessels again, I was green enough to return what bread I had left; but my comrade seized it, and said that I should lay that up for lunch or dinner. Soon after, he was let out to work at haying in a neighboring field, whither he went every day, and would not be back till noon; so he bade me good-day, saying that he doubted if he should see me again.

When I came out of prison,–for some one interfered, and paid the tax,–I did not perceive that great changes had taken place on the common, such as he observed who went in a youth, and emerged a tottering and gray-headed man; and yet a change had to my eyes come over the scene,–the town, and State, and country,–greater than any that mere time could effect. I saw yet more distinctly the State in which I lived. I saw to what extent the people among whom I lived could be trusted as good neighbors and friends; that their friendship was for summer weather only; that they did not greatly purpose to do right; that they were a distinct race from me by their prejudices and superstitions, as the Chinamen and Malays are; that, in their sacrifices to humanity, they ran no risks, not even to their property; that, after all, they were not so noble but they treated the thief as he had treated them, and hoped, by a certain outward observance and a few prayers, and by walking in a particular straight though useless path from time to time, to save their souls. This may be to judge my neighbors harshly; for I believe that most of them are not aware that they have such an institution as the jail in their village.

It was formerly the custom in our village, when a poor debtor came out of jail, for his acquaintances to salute him, looking through their fingers, which were crossed to represent the grating of a jail window, "How do ye do?" My neighbors did not thus salute me, but first looked at me, and then at one another, as if I had returned from a long journey. I was put into jail as I was going to the shoemaker's to get a shoe which was mended. When I was let out the next morning, I proceeded to finish my errand, and, having put on my mended shoe, joined a huckleberry party, who were impatient to put themselves under my conduct; and in half an hour,– for the horse was soon tackled,–was in the midst of a huckleberry field, on one of our highest hills, two miles off; and then the State was nowhere to be seen.

This is the whole history of "My Prisons."

I have never declined paying the highway tax, because I am as desirous of being a good neighbor as I am of being a bad subject; and, as for supporting schools, I am doing my part to educate my fellow-countrymen now. It is for no particular item in the tax-bill that I refuse to pay it. I simply wish to refuse allegiance to the State, to withdraw and stand aloof from it effectually. I do not care to trace the course of my dollar, if I could, till it buys a man, or a musket to shoot one with,—the dollar is innocent,—but I am concerned to trace the effects of my allegiance. In fact, I quietly declare war with the State, after my fashion, though I will still make what use and get what advantage of her I can, as is usual in such cases.

If others pay the tax which is demanded of me, from a sympathy with the State, they do but what they have already done in their own case, or rather they abet injustice to a greater extent than the State requires. If they pay the tax from a mistaken interest in the individual taxed, to save his property or prevent his going to jail, it is because they have not considered wisely how far they let their private feelings interfere with the public good.

This, then, is my position at present. But one cannot be too much on his guard in such a case, lest his action be biassed by obstinacy, or an undue regard for the opinions of men. Let him see that he does only what belongs to himself and to the hour.

I think sometimes, Why, this people mean well; they are only ignorant; they would do better if they knew how: why give your neighbors this pain to treat you as they are not inclined to? But I think, again, this is no reason why I should do as they do, or permit others to suffer much greater pain of a different kind. Again, I sometimes say to myself, When many millions of men, without heat, without ill-will, without personal feeling of any kind, demand of you a few shillings only, without the possibility, such is their constitution, of retracting or altering their present demand, and without the possibility, on your side, of appeal to any other millions, why expose yourself to this overwhelming brute force? You do not resist cold and hunger, the winds and the waves, thus obstinately; you quietly submit to a thousand similar necessities. You do not put your head into the fire. But just in proportion as I regard this as not wholly a brute force, but partly a human force, and consider that I have relations to those millions as to so many millions of men, and not of mere brute or inanimate things, I see that appeal is possible,

first and instantaneously, from them to the Maker of them, and, secondly, from them to themselves. But, if I put my head deliberately into the fire, there is no appeal to fire or to the Maker of fire, and I have only myself to blame. If I could convince myself that I have any right to be satisfied with men as they are, and to treat them accordingly, and not according, in some respects, to my requisitions and expectations of what they and I ought to be, then, like a good Mussulman and fatalist, I should endeavor to be satisfied with things as they are, and say it is the will of God. And, above all, there is this difference between resisting this and a purely brute or natural force, that I can resist this with some effect; but I cannot expect, like Orpheus, to change the nature of the rocks and trees and beasts.

I do not wish to quarrel with any man or nation. I do not wish to split hairs, to make fine distinctions, or set myself up as better than my neighbors. I seek rather, I may say, even an excuse for conforming to the laws of the land. I am but too ready to conform to them. Indeed I have reason to suspect myself on this head; and each year, as the tax-gatherer comes round, I find myself disposed to review the acts and position of the general and state governments, and the spirit of the people, to discover a pretext for conformity. I believe that the State will soon be able to take all my work of this sort out of my hands, and then I shall be no better a patriot than my fellow-countrymen. Seen from a lower point of view, the Constitution, with all its faults, is very good; the law and the courts are very respectable; even this State and this American government are, in many respects, very admirable and rare things, to be thankful for, such as a great many have described them; but seen from a point of view a little higher, they are what I have described them; seen from a higher still, and the highest, who shall say what they are, or that they are worth looking at or thinking of at all?

However, the government does not concern me much, and I shall bestow the fewest possible thoughts on it. It is not many moments that I live under a government, even in this world. If a man is thought-free, fancy-free, imagination-free, that which *is not* never for a long time appearing *to be* to him, unwise rulers or reformers cannot fatally interrupt him.

I know that most men think differently from myself; but those whose lives are by profession devoted to the study of these or kindred subjects, content me as little as any. Statesmen and legislators, standing so completely within the institution, never distinctly and nakedly behold it. They speak of moving society, but have no resting-place without it. They may be men of a certain experience and discrimination, and have no doubt invented ingenious and even useful systems, for which we sincerely thank them; but all their wit and usefulness lie within certain not very wide limits. They are wont to forget that the world is not governed by policy and expediency. Webster never goes behind government, and so cannot speak with authority about it. His words are wisdom to those legislators who contemplate no essential reform in the existing government; but for thinkers, and those who legislate for all time, he never once glances at the subject. I know of those whose serene and wise speculations on this theme would soon reveal the limits of his mind's range and hospitality. Yet, compared with the cheap professions of most reformers, and the still cheaper wisdom and eloquence of politicians in general, his are almost the only sensible and valuable words, and we thank Heaven for him. Comparatively, he is always strong, original, and, above all, practical. Still his quality is not wisdom, but prudence. The lawyer's truth is not Truth, but consistency, or a consistent expediency. Truth is always in harmony with herself, and is not concerned chiefly to reveal the justice that may consist with wrong-doing. He well deserves to be called, as he has been called, the Defender of the Constitution. There are really no blows to be given by him but defensive ones. He is not a leader, but a follower. His leaders are the men of '87. "I have never made an effort," he says, "and never propose to make an effort; I have never countenanced an effort, and never mean to countenance an effort, to disturb the arrangement as originally made, by which the various States came into the Union." Still thinking of the sanction which the Constitution gives to slavery, he says, "Because it was a part of the original compact,– let it stand." Notwithstanding his special acuteness and ability, he is unable to take a fact out of its merely political relations, and behold it as it lies absolutely to be disposed of by the intellect,–what, for instance, it behoves a man to do here in America to-day with regard to slavery, but ventures, or is driven, to make some such desperate answer as the following, while professing to speak absolutely, and as a private man,–from which what new and singular code of social duties might be inferred?–"The manner," says he, "in which the government of those States where slavery exists

are to regulate it, is for their own consideration, under their responsibility to their constituents, to the general laws of propriety, humanity, and justice, and to God. Associations formed elsewhere, springing from a feeling of humanity, or any other cause, have nothing whatever to do with it. They have never received any encouragement from me, and they never will."[1]

They who know of no purer sources of truth, who have traced up its stream no higher, stand, and wisely stand, by the Bible and the Constitution, and drink at it there with reverence and humility; but they who behold where it comes trickling into this lake or that pool, gird up their loins once more, and continue their pilgrimage toward its fountain-head.

No man with a genius for legislation has appeared in America. They are rare in the history of the world. There are orators, politicians, and eloquent men, by the thousand; but the speaker has not yet opened his mouth to speak, who is capable of settling the much-vexed questions of the day. We love eloquence for its own sake, and not for any truth, which it may utter, or any heroism it may inspire. Our legislators have not yet learned the comparative value of free-trade and of freedom, of union, and of rectitude, to a nation. They have no genius or talent for comparatively humble questions of taxation and finance, commerce and manufactures and agriculture. If we were left solely to the wordy wit of legislators in Congress for our guidance, uncorrected by the seasonable experience and the effectual complaints of the people, America would not long retain her rank among the nations. For eighteen hundred years, though perchance I have no right to say it, the New Testament has been written; yet where is the legislator who has wisdom and practical talent enough to avail himself of the light which it sheds on the science of legislation?

The authority of government, even such as I am willing to submit to,–for I will cheerfully obey those who know and can do better than I, and in many things even those who neither know nor can do so well,–is still an impure one: to be strictly just, it must have the sanction and consent of the governed. It can have no pure right over my person and property but what I concede to it. The progress from an absolute to a limited monarchy, from a limited monarchy to a democracy, is a progress toward a true respect for the individual. Is a democracy, such as we know it, the last improvement possible in government? Is it not possible to take a step further towards recognizing and organizing the rights of man? There will never be a really free and enlightened State, until the State comes to recognize the individual as a higher and independent power, from which all its own power and authority are derived, and treats him accordingly. I please myself with imagining a State at last which can afford to be just to all men, and to treat the individual with respect as a neighbor; which even would not think it inconsistent with its own repose, if a few were to live aloof from it, not meddling with it, not embraced by it, who fulfilled all the duties of neighbors and fellow-men. A State which bore this kind of fruit, and suffered it to drop off as fast as it ripened, would prepare the way for a still more perfect and glorious State, which also I have imagined, but not yet anywhere seen.

1.   These extracts have been inserted since the Lecture was read.

Henry David Thoreau

"Where I Lived, and What I Lived For," from *Walden* (Boston: Ticknor and Fields, 1854), pp. 88-107.

> *The second chapter in* Walden, *this piece is central to an understanding of the entire book. Here, Thoreau proposed to "brag as lustily as chanticleer in the morning, standing on his roost, if only to wake my neighbors up," told his readers that "I went to the woods because I wished to live deliberately, to front only the essential facts of life," and gave his credo: "Simplify, simplify."*

At a certain season of our life we are accustomed to consider every spot as the possible site of a house. I have thus surveyed the country on every side within a dozen miles of where I live. In imagination I have bought all the farms in succession, for all were to be bought, and I knew their price. I walked over each farmer's premises, tasted his wild apples, discoursed on husbandry with him, took his farm at his price, at any price, mortgaging it to him in my mind; even put a higher price on it,–took every thing but a deed of it,–took his word for his deed, for I dearly love to talk,–cultivated it, and him too to some extent, I trust, and withdrew when I had enjoyed it long enough, leaving him to carry it on. This experience entitled me to be regarded as a sort of real-estate broker by my friends. Wherever I sat, there I might live, and the landscape radiated from me accordingly. What is a house but a *sedes*, a seat?–better if a country seat. I discovered many a site for a house not likely to be soon improved, which some might have thought too far from the village, but to my eyes the village was too far from it. Well, there I might live, I said; and there I did live, for an hour, a summer and a winter life; saw how I could let the years run off, buffet the winter through, and see the spring come in. The future inhabitants of this region, wherever they may place their houses, may be sure that they have been anticipated. An afternoon sufficed to lay out the land into orchard, woodlot, and pasture, and to decide what fine oaks or pines should be left to stand before the door, and whence each blasted tree could be seen to the best advantage; and then I let it lie, fallow perchance, for a man is rich in proportion to the number of things which he can afford to let alone.

My imagination carried me so far that I even had the refusal of several farms,–the refusal was all I wanted, –but I never got my fingers burned by actual possession. The nearest that I came to actual possession was when I bought the Hollowell place, and had begun to sort my seeds, and collected materials with which to make a wheelbarrow to carry it on or off with; but before the owner gave me deed of it, his wife–every man has such a wife–changed her mind and wished to keep it, and he offered me ten dollars to release him. Now, to speak the truth, I had but ten cents in the world, and it surpassed my arithmetic to tell, if I was that man who had ten cents, or who had a farm, or ten dollars, or all together. However, I let him keep the ten dollars and the farm too, for I had carried it far enough; or rather, to be generous, I sold him the farm for just what I gave for it, and, as he was not a rich man, made him a present of ten dollars, and still had my ten cents, and seeds, and materials for a wheelbarrow left. I found thus that I had been a rich man without any dam-

Daguerreotype of Henry David Thoreau in 1856

age to my poverty. But I retained the landscape, and I have since annually carried off what it yielded without a wheelbarrow. With respect to landscapes,–

> "I am monarch of all I survey,
> My right there is none to dispute."

I have frequently seen a poet withdraw, having enjoyed the most valuable part of a farm, while the crusty farmer supposed that he had got a few wild apples only. Why, the owner, does not know it for many years when a poet has put his farm in rhyme, the most admirable kind of invisible fence, has fairly impounded it, milked it, skimmed it, and got all the cream, and left the farmer only the skimmed milk.

The real attractions of the Hollowell farm, to me, were; its complete retirement, being about two miles from the village, half a mile from the nearest neighbor, and separated from the highway by a broad field; its bounding on the river, which the owner said protected it by its fogs from frosts in the spring, though that was

nothing to me; the gray color and ruinous state of the house and barn, and the dilapidated fences, which put such an interval between me and the last occupant; the hollow and lichen-covered apple trees, gnawed by rabbits, showing what kind of neighbors I should have; but above all, the recollection I had of it from my earliest voyages up the river, when the house was concealed behind a dense grove of red maples, through which I heard the house-dog bark. I was in haste to buy it, before the proprietor finished getting out some rocks, cutting down the hollow apple trees, and grubbing up some young birches which had sprung up in the pasture, or, in short, had made any more of his improvements. To enjoy these advantages I was ready to carry it on; like Atlas, to take the world on my shoulders, –I never heard what compensation he received for that,– and do all those things which had no other motive or excuse but that I might pay for it and be unmolested in my possession of it; for I knew all the while that it would yield the most abundant crop of the kind I wanted if I could only afford to let it alone. But it turned out as I have said. All that I could say, then, with respect to farming on a large scale, (I have always cultivated a garden,) was, that I had had my seeds ready. Many think that seeds improve with age. I have no doubt that time discriminates between the good and the bad; and when at last I shall plant, I shall be less likely to be disappointed. But I would say to my fellows, once for all, As long as possible live free and uncommitted. It makes but little difference whether you are committed to a farm or the county jail. Old Cato, whose "De Re Rusticâ" is my "Cultivator," says, and the only translation I have seen makes sheer nonsense of the passage,"When you think of getting a farm, turn it thus in your mind, not to buy greedily; nor spare your pains to look at it, and do not think it enough to go round it once. The oftener you go there the more it will please you, if it is good." I think I shall not buy greedily, but go round and round it as long as I live, and be buried in it first, that it may please me the more at last.

The present was my next experiment of this kind, which I purpose to describe more at length; for convenience, putting the experience of two years into one. As I have said, I do not propose to write an ode to dejection, but to brag as lustily as chanticleer in the morning, standing on his roost, if only to wake my neighbors up.

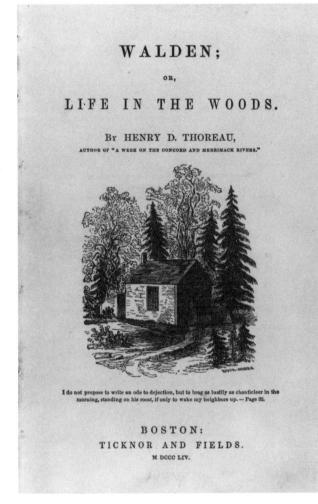

WALDEN;

OR,

LIFE IN THE WOODS.

By HENRY D. THOREAU,

AUTHOR OF "A WEEK ON THE CONCORD AND MERRIMACK RIVERS."

I do not propose to write an ode to dejection, but to brag as lustily as chanticleer in the morning, standing on his roost, if only to wake my neighbors up. — Page 92.

BOSTON:

TICKNOR AND FIELDS.

M DCCC LIV.

Title page for Thoreau's most famous book

When first I took up my abode in the woods, that is, began to spend my nights as well as days there, which, by accident, was on Independence day, or the fourth of July, 1845, my house was not finished for winter, but was merely a defense against the rain, without plastering or chimney, the walls being of rough weather-stained boards, with wide chinks, which made it cool at night. The upright white hewn studs and freshly planed door and window casings gave it a clean and airy look, especially in the morning, when its timbers were saturated with dew, so that I fancied that by noon some sweet gum would exude from them. To my imagination it retained throughout the day more or less of this auroral character, reminding me of a certain house on a mountain which I had visited the year before. This was an airy and unplastered cabin, fit to entertain a travelling god, and where a goddess might trail her garments. The winds which passed over my dwelling

were such as sweep over the ridges of mountains, bearing the broken strains, or celestial parts only, of terrestrial music. The morning wind forever blows, the poem of creation is uninterrupted; but few are the ears that hear it. Olympus is but the outside of the earth every where.

The only house I had been the owner of before, if I except a boat, was a tent, which I used occasionally when making excursions in the summer, and this is still rolled up in my garret; but the boat, after passing from hand to hand, has gone down the stream of time. With this more substantial shelter about me, I had made some progress toward settling in the world. This frame, so slightly clad, was a sort of crystallization around me, and reacted on the builder. It was suggestive somewhat as a picture in outlines. I did not need to go out doors to take the air, for the atmosphere within had lost none of its freshness. It was not so much within doors as behind a door where I sat, even in the rainiest weather. The Harivansa says, "An abode without birds is like a meat without seasoning." Such was not my abode, for I found myself suddenly neighbor to the birds; not by having imprisoned one, but having caged myself near them. I was not only nearer to some of those which commonly frequent the garden and the orchard, but to those wilder and more thrilling songsters of the forest which never, or rarely, serenade a villager,–the woodthrush, the veery, the scarlet tanager, the field-sparrow, the whippoorwill, and many others.

I was seated by the shore of a small pond, about a mile and a half south of the village of Concord and somewhat higher than it, in the midst of an extensive wood between that town and Lincoln, and about two miles south of that our only field known to fame, Concord Battle Ground; but I was so low in the woods that the opposite shore, half a mile off, like the rest, covered with wood, was my most distant horizon. For the first week, whenever I looked out on the pond it impressed me like a tarn high up on the side of a mountain, its bottom far above the surface of other lakes, and, as the sun arose, I saw it throwing off its nightly clothing of mist, and here and there, by degrees, its soft ripples or its smooth reflecting surface was revealed, while the mists, like ghosts, were stealthily withdrawing in every direction into the woods, as at the breaking up of some nocturnal conventicle. The very dew seemed to hang upon the trees later into the day than usual, as on the sides of mountains.

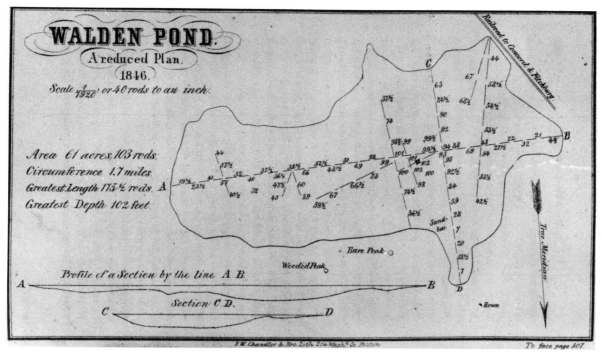

Map of Walden Pond printed in the first edition of Walden

This small lake was of most value as a neighbor in the intervals of a gentle rain storm in August, when, both air and water being perfectly still, but the sky overcast, midafternoon had all the serenity of evening, and the woodthrush sang around, and was heard from shore to shore. A lake like this is never smoother than at such a time; and the clear portion of the air above it being shallow and darkened by clouds, the water, full of light and reflections, becomes a lower heaven itself so much the more important. From a hill top near by, where the wood had been recently cut off, there was a pleasing vista southward across the pond, through a wide indentation in the hills which form the shore there, where their opposite sides sloping toward each other suggested a stream flowing out in that direction through a wooded valley, but stream there was none. That way I looked between and over the near green hills to some distant and higher ones in the horizon, tinged with blue. Indeed, by standing on tiptoe I could catch a glimpse of some of the peaks of the still bluer and more distant mountain ranges in the north-west, those true-blue coins from heaven's own mint, and also of some portion of the village. But in other directions, even from this point, I could not see over or beyond the woods which surrounded me. It is well to have some water in your neighborhood, to give buoyancy to and float the earth. One value even of the smallest

well is, that when you look into it you see that earth is not continent but insular. This is as important as that it keeps butter cool. When I looked across the pond from this peak toward the Sudbury meadows, which in time of flood I distinguished elevated perhaps by a mirage in their seething valley, like a coin in a basin, all the earth beyond the pond appeared like a thin crust insulated and floated even by this small sheet of intervening water, and I was reminded that this on which I dwelt was but *dry land.*

Though the view from my door was still more contracted, I did not feel crowded or confined in the least. There was pasture enough for my imagination. The low shrub-oak plateau to which the opposite shore arose, stretched away toward the prairies of the West and the steppes of Tartary, affording ample room for all the roving families of men. "There are none happy in the world but beings who enjoy freely a vast horizon," –said Damodara, when his herds required new and larger pastures.

Both place and time were changed, and I dwelt nearer to those parts of the universe and to those eras in history which had most attracted me. Where I lived was as far off as many a region viewed nightly by astronomers. We are wont to imagine rare and delectable places in some remote and more celestial corner of the system, behind the constellation of Cassiopeia's Chair,

Manuscript title page for Walden *from the 1909 Bibliophile Society edition; the surviving manuscript is at the Henry E. Huntington Library and Art Gallery*

far from noise and disturbance. I discovered that my house actually had its site in such a withdrawn, but forever new and unprofaned, part of the universe. If it were worth the while to settle in those parts near to the Pleiades or the Hyades, to Aldebaran or Altair, then I was really there, or at an equal remoteness from the life which I had left behind, dwindled and twinkling with as fine a ray to my nearest neighbor, and to be seen only in moonless nights by him. Such was that part of creation where I had squatted;–

> "There was a shepherd that did live,
> And held his thoughts as high
> As were the mounts whereon his flocks
> Did hourly feed him by."

What should we think of the shepherd's life if his flocks always wandered to higher pastures than his thoughts?

Every morning was a cheerful invitation to make my life of equal simplicity, and I may say innocence, with Nature herself. I have been as sincere a worshipper of Aurora as the Greeks. I got up early and bathed in the pond; that was a religious exercise, and one of the best things which I did. They say that characters were engraven on the bathing tub of king Tching-thang to this effect: "Renew thyself completely each day; do it again, and again, and forever again." I can understand that. Morning brings back the heroic ages. I was as much affected by the faint hum of a mosquito making its invisible and unimaginable tour through my apartment at earliest dawn, when I was sitting with door and windows open, as I could be by any trumpet that ever sang of fame. It was Homer's requiem; itself an Iliad and Odyssey in the air, singing its own wrath and wanderings. There was something cosmical about it; a standing advertisement, till forbidden, of the everlasting vigor and fertility of the world. The morning, which

Revised page proof from Walden *with corrections in Thoreau's hand (reproduced from the 1909 Bibliophile Society edition); the surviving proof sheets are at the Henry E. Huntington Library and Art Gallery*

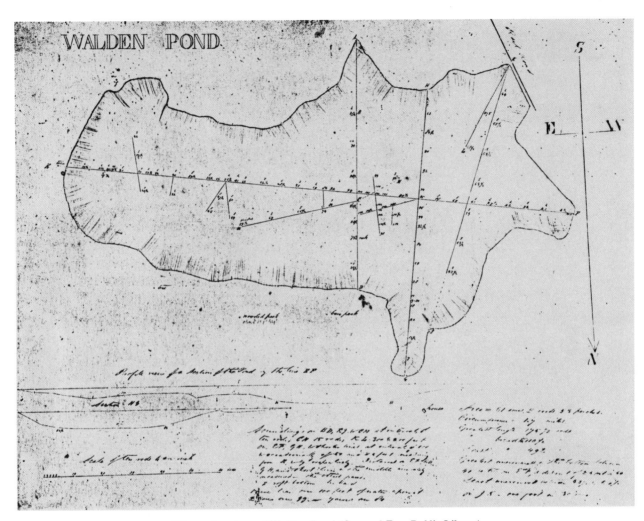

Thoreau's survey of Walden Pond (Concord Free Public Library)

is the most memorable season of the day, is the awakening hour. Then there is least somnolence in us; and for an hour, at least, some part of us awakes which slumbers all the rest of the day and night. Little is to be expected of that day, if it can be called a day, to which we are not awakened by our Genius, but by the mechanical nudgings of some servitor, are not awakened by our own newly-acquired force and aspirations from within, accompanied by the undulations of celestial music, instead of factory bells, and a fragrance filling the air—to a higher life than we fell asleep from; and thus the darkness bear its fruit, and prove itself to be good, no less than the light. That man who does not believe that each day contains an earlier, more sacred, and auroral hour than he has yet profaned, has despaired of life, and is pursuing a descending and darkening way. After a partial cessation of his sensuous life, the soul of man, or its organs rather, are reinvigorated

each day, and his Genius tries again what noble life it can make. All memorable events, I should say, transpire in morning time and in a morning atmosphere. The Vedas say, "All intelligences awake with the morning." Poetry and art, and the fairest and most memorable of the actions of men, date from such an hour. All poets and heroes, like Memnon, are the children of Aurora, and emit their music at sunrise. To him whose elastic and vigorous thought keeps pace with the sun, the day is a perpetual morning. It matters not what the clocks say or the attitudes and labors of men. Morning is when I am awake and there is a dawn in me. Moral reform is the effort to throw off sleep. Why is it that men give so poor an account of their day if they have not been slumbering? They are not such poor calculators. If they had not been overcome with drowsiness they would have performed something. The millions are awake enough for physical labor; but only one in a

Site of Thoreau's cabin at Walden Pond

million is awake enough for effective intellectual exertion, only one in a hundred millions to a poetic or divine life. To be awake is to be alive. I have never yet met a man who was quite awake. How could I have looked him in the face?

We must learn to reawaken and keep ourselves awake, not by mechanical aids, but by an infinite expectation of the dawn, which does not forsake us in our soundest sleep. I know of no more encouraging fact that the unquestionable ability of man to elevate his life by a conscious endeavor. It is something to be able to paint a particular picture, or to carve a statue, and so to make a few objects beautiful; but it is far more glorious to carve and paint the very atmosphere and medium through which we look, which morally we can do. To affect the quality of the day, that is the highest of arts. Every man is tasked to make his life, even in its details, worthy of the contemplation of his most elevated and critical hour. If we refused, or rather used up, such paltry information as we get, the oracles would distinctly inform us how this might be done.

I went to the woods because I wished to live deliberately, to front only the essential facts of life, and see if I could not learn what it had to teach, and not, when I came to die, discover that I had not lived. I did not wish to live what was not life, living is so dear; nor did I wish to practice resignation, unless it was quite necessary. I wanted to live deep and suck out all the marrow of life, to live so sturdily and Spartan-like as to put to rout all that was not life, to cut a broad swath and shave close, to drive life into a corner, and reduce it to its lowest terms, and, if it proved to be mean, why then to get the whole and genuine meanness of it, and publish its meanness to the world; or if it were sublime, to know it by experience, and be able to give a true account of it in my next excursion. For most men, it appears to me, are in a strange uncertainty about it, whether it is of the devil or of God, and have *somewhat hastily* concluded that it is the chief end of man here to "glorify God and enjoy him forever."

Still we live meanly, like ants; though the fable tells us that we were long ago changed into men; like pygmies we fight with cranes; it is error upon error, and clout upon clout, and our best virtue has for its occasion a superfluous and evitable wretchedness. Our life is frittered away by detail. An honest man has hardly need to count more than his ten fingers, or in extreme cases he may add his ten toes, and lump the rest. Sim-

Reconstruction of Thoreau's cabin at Walden Pond

plicity, simplicity, simplicity! I say, let your affairs be as two or three, and not a hundred or a thousand; instead of a million count half a dozen, and keep your accounts on your thumb nail. In the midst of this chopping sea of civilized life, such are the clouds and storms and quicksands and thousand-and-one items to be allowed for, that a man has to live, if he would not founder and go to the bottom and not make his port at all, by dead reckoning, and he must be a great calculator indeed who succeeds. Simplify, simplify. Instead of three meals a day, if it be necessary eat but one; instead of a hundred dishes, five; and reduce other things in proportion. Our life is like a German Confederacy, made up of petty states, with its boundary forever fluctuating, so that even a German cannot tell you how it is bounded at any moment. The nation itself, with all its so called internal improvements, which, by the way, are all external and superficial, is just such an unwieldy and overgrown establishment, cluttered with furniture and tripped up by its own traps, ruined by luxury and heedless expense, by want of calculation and a worthy aim, as the million households in the land; and the only cure for it as for them is in a rigid economy, a stern and more than Spartan simplicity of life and elevation of

purpose. It lives too fast. Men think that it is essential that the *Nation* have commerce, and export ice, and talk through a telegraph, and ride thirty miles an hour, without a doubt, whether *they* do or not; but whether we should live like baboons or like men, is a little uncertain. If we do not get out sleepers, and forge rails, and devote days and nights to the work, but go to tinkering upon our *lives* to improve *them*, who will build railroads? And if railroads are not built, how shall we get to heaven in season? But if we stay at home and mind our business, who will want railroads? We do not ride on the railroad; it rides upon us. Did you ever think what those sleepers are that underlie the railroad? Each one is a man, an Irishman, or a Yankee man. The rails are laid on them, and they are covered with sand, and the cars run smoothly over them. They are sound sleepers, I assure you. And every few years a new lot is laid down and run over; so that, if some have the pleasure of riding on a rail, others have the misfortune to be ridden upon. And when they run over a man that is walking in his sleep, a supernumerary sleeper in the wrong position, and wake him up, they suddenly stop the cars, and make a hue and cry about it, as if this were an exception. I am glad to know that it takes a

Ambrotype of Henry David Thoreau in 1861

gang of men for every five miles to keep the sleepers down and level in their beds as it is, for this is a sign that they may sometimes get up again.

Why should we live with such hurry and waste of life? We are determined to be starved before we are hungry. Men say that a stitch in time saves nine, and so they take a thousand stitches to-day to save nine tomorrow. As for *work,* we haven't any of any consequence. We have the Saint Vitus' dance, and cannot possibly keep our heads still. If I should only give a few pulls at the parish bell-rope, as for a fire, that is, without setting the bell, there is hardly a man on his farm in the outskirts of Concord, notwithstanding that press of engagements which was his excuse so many times this morning, nor a boy, nor a woman, I might almost say, but would forsake all and follow that sound, not mainly to save property from the flames, but, if we will confess the truth, much more to see it burn, since burn it must, and we, be it known, did not set it on fire,—or to see it put out, and have a hand in it, if that is done as handsomely; yes, even if it were the parish church itself. Hardly a man takes a half hour's nap after dinner, but when he wakes he holds up his head and asks, "What's the news?" as if the rest of mankind had stood his sentinels. Some give directions to be waked every

half hour, doubtless for no other purpose; and then, to pay for it, they tell what they have dreamed. After a night's sleep the news is as indispensable as the breakfast. "Pray tell me any thing new that has happened to a man any where on this globe,"—and he reads it over his coffee and rolls, that a man has had his eyes gouged out this morning on the Wachito River; never dreaming the while that he lives in the dark unfathomed mammoth cave of this world, and has but the rudiment of an eye himself.

For my part, I could easily do without the post-office. I think that there are very few important communications made through it. To speak critically, I never received more than one or two letters in my life—I wrote this some years ago—that were worth the postage. The penny-post is, commonly, an institution through which you seriously offer a man that penny for his thoughts which is so often safely offered in jest. And I am sure that I never read any memorable news in a newspaper. If we read of one man robbed, or murdered, or killed by accident, or one house burned, or one vessel wrecked, or one steamboat blown up, or one cow run over on the Western Railroad, or one mad dog killed, or one lot of grasshoppers in the winter,—we never need read of another. One is enough. If you are acquainted with the principle, what do you care for a myriad instances and applications? To a philosopher all *news,* as it is called, is gossip, and they who edit and read it are old women over their tea. Yet not a few are greedy after this gossip. There was such a rush, as I hear, the other day at one of the offices to learn the foreign news by the last arrival, that several large squares of plate glass belonging to the establishment were broken by the pressure,–news which I seriously think a ready wit might write a twelvemonth or twelve years beforehand with sufficient accuracy. As for Spain, for instance, if you know how to throw in Don Carlos and the Infanta, and Don Pedro and Seville and Granada, from time to time in the right proportions,–they may have changed the names a little since I saw the papers,–and serve up a bull-fight when other entertainments fail, it will be true to the letter, and give us as good an idea of the exact state or ruin of things in Spain as the most succinct and lucid reports under this head in the newspapers; and as for England, almost the last significant scrap of news from that quarter was the revolution of 1649; and if you have learned the history of her crops for an average year, you never need attend to that thing again, unless your speculations are of a merely pecuniary character. If one may judge who rarely looks into the newspapers, nothing new does ever happen in foreign parts, a French revolution not excepted.

What news! how much more important to know what that is which was never old! "Kieou-he-yu (great dignitary of the state of Wei) sent a man to Khoung-tseu to know his news. Khoung-tseu caused the messenger to be seated near him, and questioned him in these terms: What is your master doing? The messenger answered with respect: My master desires to diminish the number of his faults, but he cannot come to the end of them. The messenger being gone, the philosopher remarked: What a worthy messenger! What a worthy messenger!" The preacher, instead of vexing the ears of drowsy farmers on their day of rest at the end of the week,–for Sunday is the fit conclusion of an ill-spent week, and not the fresh and brave beginning of a new one,–with this one other draggletail of a sermon, should shout with thundering voice,–"Pause! Avast!

The house in Concord where Thoreau died

STANZAS:

Written to be sung at the funeral of Henry D. Thoreau, of Concord, Massachusetts,

Friday, May 9th, 1862.

Hearest thou the sobbing breeze complain
How faint the sunbeams light the shore,—
His heart more fixed than earth or main,
Henry! that faithful heart is o'er.

O weep not thou thus vast a soul,
O do not mourn this lordly man,
As long as Walden's waters roll,
And Concord river fills a span.

For thoughtful minds in Henry's page
Large welcome find and bless his verse,
Drawn from the poet's heritage,
From wells of right and nature's source.

Fountains of hope and faith! inspire
Most stricken hearts to lift this cross,
His perfect trust shall keep the fire,
His glorious peace disarm all loss!

Broadside of Ellery Channing's "Stanzas" sung at Thoreau's funeral

Why so seeming fast, but deadly slow?"

Shams and delusions are esteemed for soundest truths, while reality is fabulous. If men would steadily observe realities only, and not allow themselves to be deluded, life, to compare it with such things as we know, would be like a fairy tale and the Arabian Nights' Entertainments. If we respected only what is inevitable and has a right to be, music and poetry would resound along the streets. When we are unhurried and wise, we perceive that only great and worthy things have any permanent and absolute existence,–that petty fears and petty pleasures are but the shadow of the reality. This is always exhilarating and sublime. By closing the eyes and slumbering, and consenting to be deceived by shows, men establish and confirm their daily life of routine and habit every where, which still is built on purely illusory foundations. Children, who play life, discern its true law and relations more clearly than men, who fail to live it worthily, but who think that they are wiser by experience, that is, by failure. I have read in a Hindoo book, that "there was a king's son, who, being expelled in infancy from his native city, was brought up by a forester, and, growing up to

maturity in that state, imagined himself to belong to the barbarous race with which he lived. One of his father's ministers having discovered him, revealed to him what he was, and the misconception of his character was removed, and he knew himself to be a prince. So soul," continues the Hindoo philosopher, "from the circumstances in which it is placed, mistakes its own character, until the truth is revealed to it by some holy teacher, and then it knows itself to be *Brahme.*" I perceive that we inhabitants of New England live this mean life that we do because our vision does not penetrate the surface of things. We think that that *is* which *appears* to be. If a man should walk through this town and see only the reality, where, think you, would the "Mill-dam" go to? If he should give us an account of the realities he beheld there, we should not recognize the place in his description. Look at a meeting-house, or a court-house, or a jail, or a shop, or a dwelling-house, and say what that thing really is before a true gaze, and they would all go to pieces in your account of them. Men esteem truth remote, in the outskirts of the system, behind the farthest star, before Adam and after the last man. In eternity there is indeed some-

Henry D. Thoreau.

Died at Concord, on Tuesday, 6 May, Henry D Thoreau, aged 44 years.

The premature death of Mr. Thoreau is a bitter disappointment to many friends who had set no limit to their confidence in his power and future performance. He is known to the public as the author of two remarkable books, "A Week on the Concord and Merrimack Rivers," published in 1849, and "Walden, or Life in the Woods," published in 1854. These books have never had a wide circulation, but are well known to the best readers, and have exerted a powerful influence on an important class of earnest and contemplative persons.

Mr. Thoreau was born in Concord, in 1817; was graduated at Harvard University, in 1837. Resisting the example of his companions, and the advice of friends, he declined entering either of the learned professions, and for a long time pursued his studies as his genius led him, without apparent method. But being a good mathematician and with an early and controlling love of nature, he afterwards came by imperceptible steps into active employment as a land-surveyor,—whose art he had first learned in the satisfaction of his private questions,—a profession which gave him lucrative work, and not too much of it, and in the running of town lines and the boundaries of farms and woodlands, carried him precisely where he wished to go,- to the homes of new plants, and of swamp and forest birds, as well as to wild landscape, and Indian relics. A man of simple tastes, hardy habits, and of preternatural powers of observation, he became a patient and successful student of nature in every aspect, and obtained an acquaintance with the history of the river on whose banks he lived, and with the habits of plants and animals, which made him known and valued by naturalists. He gathered a private museum of natural curiosities, and has left a large collection of manuscript records of his varied experiments and observations, which are much more than scientific value. His latest studies were in forest trees, the succession of forest growths, and the annual increment of wood. He knew the literature of natural history, from Aristotle and Pliny, down to the English writers on his favorite departments.

But his study as a naturalist, which went on increasing, and had no vacations, was less remarkable than the power of his mind and the strength of his character. He was a man of stoic temperament, highly intellectual, of a perfect probity, full of practical skill, an expert woodsman and boatman, acquainted with the use of tools, a good planter and cultivator, when he saw fit to plant, but without any taste for luxury, without the least ambition to be rich, or to be popular, and almost without sympathy in any of the common motives of men around him. He led the life of a philosopher, subordinating all other pursuits and so-called duties to his pursuit of knowledge and to his own estimate of duty. He was a man of firm mind and direct dealing, never disconcerted, and not to be bent by any inducement from his own course. He had a penetrating insight into men with whom he conversed, and was not to be deceived or used by any party, and did not conceal his disgust at any duplicity. As he was incapable of any the least dishonesty or untruth, he had nothing to hide, and kept his haughty independence to the end. And when we now look back at the solitude of this erect and spotless person, we lament that he did not live long enough for all men to know him.   E.

Emerson's obituary for Thoreau in the Boston Daily Advertiser *(8 May 1862)*

thing true and sublime. But all these times and places and occasions are now and here. God himself culminates in the present moment, and will never be more divine in the lapse of all the ages. And we are enabled to apprehend at all what is sublime and noble only by the perpetual instilling and drenching of the reality that surrounds us. The universe constantly and obediently answers to our conceptions; whether we travel fast or slow, the track is laid for us. Let us spend our lives in conceiving then. The poet or the artist never yet had so fair and noble a design but some of his posterity at least could accomplish it.

Let us spend one day as deliberately as Nature, and not be thrown off the track by every nutshell and mosquito's wing that falls on the rails. Let us rise early and fast, or break fast, gently and without perturbation; let company come and let company go, let the bells ring and the children cry,–determined to make a day of it. Why should we knock under and go with the stream? Let us not be upset and overwhelmed in that terrible rapid and whirlpool called a dinner, situated in the meridian shallows. Weather this danger and you are safe, for the rest of the way is down hill. With unrelaxed nerves, with morning vigor, sail by it, looking another way, tied to the mast like Ulysses. If the engine whistles, let it whistle till it is hoarse for its pains. If the bell rings, why should we run? We will consider what kind of music they are like. Let us settle ourselves, and work and wedge our feet downward through the mud and slush of opinion, and prejudice, and tradition, and delusion, and appearance, that alluvion which covers the globe, through Paris and London, through New York and Boston and Concord, through church and state, through poetry and philosophy and religion, till we come to a hard bottom and rocks in place, which we can call *reality,* and say, This is, and no mistake; and then begin, having a *point d'appui,* below freshet and frost and fire, a place where you might found a wall or a state, or set a lamp-post safely, or perhaps a gauge, not a Nilometer, but a Realometer, that future ages might know how deep a freshet of shams and appearances had gathered from time to time. If you stand right fronting and face to face to a fact, you will see the sun glimmer on both its surfaces, as if it were a cimeter, and feel its sweet edge dividing you through the heart and marrow, and so you will happily conclude your mortal career. Be it life or death, we crave only reality. If we are really dying, let us hear the rattle in our throats and feel cold

The Thoreau family plot in Sleepy Hollow Cemetery, Concord

in the extremities; if we are alive, let us go about our business.

Time is but the stream I go a-fishing in. I drink at it; but while I drink I see the sandy bottom and detect how shallow it is. Its thin current slides away, but eternity remains. I would drink deeper; fish in the sky, whose bottom is pebbly with stars. I cannot count one. I know not the first letter of the alphabet. I have always been regretting that I was not as wise as the day I was born. The intellect is a cleaver; it discerns and rifts its way into the secret of things. I do not wish to be any more busy with my hands than is necessary. My head is hands and feet. I feel all my best faculties concentrated in it. My instinct tells me that my head is an organ for burrowing, as some creatures use their snout and fore-paws, and with it I would mine and burrow my way through these hills. I think that the richest vein is somewhere hereabouts; so by the divining rod and thin rising vapors I judge; and here I will begin to mine.

BROOK FARM

Brook Farm, a community established by George and Sophia Ripley at West Roxbury, Massachusetts, near Boston, lasted from April 1841 to September 1847. One of America's most famous communal experiments, it was the best representation of the social aspect of Transcendentalism. When Ripley began the community, he wrote Emerson:

> Our objects . . . are to insure a more natural union between intellectual and manual labor than now exists; to combine the thinker and the worker, as far as possible, in the same individual; to guarantee the highest mental freedom, by providing all with labor, adapted to their tastes and talents, and securing to them the fruits of their industry; to do away [with] the necessity of menial services, by opening the benefits of education and the profits of labor to all; and thus to prepare a society of liberal, intelligent, and cultivated persons, whose relations with each other would permit a more simple and wholesome life, than can be led amidst the pressure of our competitive institutions.

Emerson declined to join the community, and his reply shows a basic difference between the two men: "It seems to me a circuitous & operose way of relieving myself of any irksome circumstances, to put on your community the task of my emancipation which I ought to take on myself." That is, while Ripley felt that just laws and good living would produce good people, Emerson believed that the individual must first be reformed and that just people would then–and only then–make just laws.

Ripley had planned to raise some $50,000 capital, but soon lowered his goal to $30,000. Yet when he purchased the 170-acre Ellis Farm in West Roxbury for $10,500, he immediately had to take out additional mortgages. In September 1841, the "Brook Farm Institute of Agriculture and Education" was chartered, with twenty-four shares at $500 apiece pledged, one-third of that sum in cash. Each shareholder was to receive free tuition for his children in the Brook Farm school or five per cent annual interest. Membership in the community would be granted by a two-thirds vote after a two-month probationary period. Those who worked received free board; those who did not paid four dollars a week.

The early period of Brook Farm went fairly well. Ripley envisioned a community where everyone shared in the work and in the profits, yet had time for contemplation and artistic endeavors. Not everyone found it possible to do all these things, and Nathaniel Hawthorne, an original shareholder, left when he discovered that his work load was too heavy to permit him time to write. (He later fictionalized Brook Farm in his novel, *The Blithedale Romance*.) Activities were distributed in these areas: teaching in the school, farming, working in the manufacturing shops (such as the shoemaker's), domestic tasks (such as waiting on tables), maintenance of buildings and grounds, and group recreation. Of these, the only unqualified successes were the school and recreation. Life was hard but pleasant, and visitors included Bronson Alcott, Orestes Brownson, Emerson, Margaret Fuller, and Theodore Parker.

A dramatic change of direction occurred in March 1845, when the community was re-organized as the "Brook Farm Phalanx." Patterned after the ideal community of the French utopian thinker, Charles Fourier, the phalanx structured its life around various "groups." Each person served in a number of groups–Dinner Waiters, Farmers, Washers, Printers, and so on–and, in theory, could work in any of them. The strict regimentation brought about by this change upset many people, and the community's fortunes declined. The death blow was delivered in March 1846, when the new central building being constructed, the Phalanstery, caught fire and burned to the ground, for an uninsured loss of

Buildings at Brook Farm

$7,000. Brook Farm never recovered, and it ended in September 1847.

One reason for the community's demise was the declining public interest in the late 1840s in utopian and communitarian ventures. Another–and more important– reason was Brook Farm's shaky financial base. Immediately after buying the land for Brook Farm, Ripley took out two mortgages, one for $6,000 and another for $5,000; that is, he mortgaged the property for $500 more than he paid for it. A third mortgage of $1,000 was taken out in April 1843 and a fourth mortgage of $2,500 in August 1845. With the loss of the Phalanstery– and the money invested in it–the end of the community was not far off. Ripley sold his library to help pay off the debts (Theodore Parker bought much of it) and eventually paid all his creditors personally. (For further information, see the entry for Ripley in *DLB 1, The American Renaissance in New England.*)

Nathaniel Hawthorne

From The American Notebooks, ed. Claude M. Simpson (Columbus: Ohio State University Press, 1972), pp. 196-222.

Hawthorne's stay at Brook Farm is well documented in these passages from the private journal which he kept while there, which describe both the physical setting and some of the people at the community. (For further information, see the entry for Hawthorne in DLB 1, The American Renaissance in New England.)

[1] [Sunday], September 26th, 1841.

A walk this morning along the Needham road. A clear, breezy morning, after nearly a week of cloudy and showery weather. The grass is much more fresh and vivid than it was last month, and trees still retain much of their verdure; though here and there there is a shrub or bough arrayed in scarlet and gold. Along the road, in the midst of the beaten track, I saw mushrooms or toad-stools, which had sprung, probably, during the night.

The houses in this vicinity are many of them quite antique, with long sloping roofs, commencing at a few feet from the ground, and ending in a lofty peak. Some of them have huge old elms, overshadowing the yard. You may see the family sleigh near the door, having stood there all through the summer sunshine, and perhaps with weeds sprouting up through the crevices of its bottom, the growth of the months since snow departed. Old barns, patched, and supported by timbers leaned against the sides, and stained with the dung of past ages.

[2] September 26th, continued.–A walk in the forenoon, along the edge of the meadow towards Cow Island. Large trees, almost a wood, principally of pine, with the green pasture glades intermixed, and cattle feeding. They cease grazing when an intruder appears, and look at him with long and wary observation. Then bend their necks to the pasture again. Where the firm ground of the pasture ceases, the meadow begins–loose, spungy, yielding to the tread, sometimes permitting the foot to sink into black mud, or perhaps over ancles in water. Cattle paths, somewhat firmer than the general surface, traverse the dense shrubbery which here overgrows the meadow. This shrubbery consists of small birch, elders, maples, and other trees, with here and there white pines of larger growth. The whole is tangled and wild, thick-set, so that it is necessary to part the rustling stems and branches, and go crashing through. There are creeping plants of various sorts, which clamber up the trees; and some of them have changed color in the slight frosts which already have befallen these low grounds; so that you see a spiral wreath of scarlet leaves twining up to the tip-top of a green tree, intermingling its bright hues with the ver[3]dure, as if all were of one piece. Sometimes, instead of scarlet, the spiral wreath is of a golden yellow.

Within the verge of the meadow, mostly near the firm shore of pasture ground, I found several grape vines, hung with abundance of large purple grapes. The vines had caught hold of maples and alders, and climbed to the top, curling round and interwreathing their twisted folds in so intimate a manner, that it was not easy to tell the parasite from the supporting tree or shrub. Sometimes the same vine had enveloped several shrubs, and caused a strange tangled confusion, converting all these poor plants to the purposes of its own support, and hindering them growing to their own benefit and convenience. The broad vine-leaves, some of them yellow or yellowish-tinged, were seen apparently growing on the same stems with the silver maple leaves, and those of the other shrubs, thus married against their will by this conjugal twine; and the purple clusters of grapes hung down from above and in the midst, so that a man might gather grapes, if not of thorns, yet of as alien bushes. One vine had [4] as-

The Old Manse in Concord, where both Emerson and Hawthorne lived in the 1830s and 1840s

cended almost to the tip-top of a large white pine tree, spreading its leaves and hanging its purple clusters among all its boughs–still climbing and clambering, as if it would not be content till it crowned the very summit of the tree with a wreath of its own foliage and a cluster of grapes. I mounted high into the tree, and ate grapes there, while the vine wreathed still higher into the depths of the tree, above my head. The grapes were sour, being not yet fully ripe; some of them, however, were sweet and pleasant. The vine embraces the trees like a serpent.

[Monday], September 27th, [1841].

A ride to Brighton yesterday morning, it being the day of the weekly cattle fair. William Allen and myself went in a wagon, carrying a calf, to be sold at the fair. The calf had not had his breakfast, as his mother had preceded him to Brighton; and he kept expressing his hunger and discomfort by loud, sonorous baa-s, especially when we passed any cattle in the fields or on the road. The cows, grazing within hearing expressed great interest, and some of them came galloping to the

Painting of Nathaniel Hawthorne by Charles Osgood in 1840 (Essex Institute, Salem, Massachusetts)

[274]

roadside to behold the calf. Little children, also, on their way to school, stopt to laugh and point at poor little Bossy. He was a prettily behaved urchin, and kept thrusting his hairy [5] muzzle between William and myself, apparently wishing to be stroked and patted. It was an ugly thought, that his confidence in human nature, and Nature in general, was to be so ill rewarded as by cutting his throat, and selling him in quarters. This, I suppose, has been his fate before now.

It was a beautiful morning, clear as chrystal, with an invigorating, but not disagreeable coolness. The general aspect of the country was as green as summer,—greener, indeed than mid or latter summer—and there were occasional interminglings of the brilliant hues of Autumn, which made the scenery more beautiful, both visibly and in sentiment. We saw no absolutely mean or poor-looking abodes along the road. There were warm and comfortable farm-houses, ancient, with the porch, the sloping roof, the antique peak, the clustered chimneys, of old times; and modern cottages, smart and tasteful; and villas, with terraces before them, and dense shade, and wooden urns on pillars, and other such tokens of gentility. Pleasant groves of oak and walnut, also, there were, sometimes stretching along vallies, sometimes ascending a hill and cloathing it [6] all round, so as to make it a great clump of verdure. Frequently, we passed people with cows, oxen, sheep or pigs, for Brighton fair.

On arriving at Brighton, we found the village thronged with people, horses, and vehicles. Probably there is no place in New England where the character of our agricultural population may be so well studied. Almost all the farmers, within a reasonable distance, make it a point, I suppose, to attend Brighton fair pretty frequently, if not on business, yet as amateurs. Then there are all the cattle-people and butchers who supply the Boston market, and dealers from far and near; and every man who has a cow or yoke of oxen, either to sell or buy, goes to Brighton on Monday. There were a thousand or two of cattle in the extensive pens, belonging to the tavern keeper, besides many standing about. You could hardly stir a step without running upon the horns of one dilemma or other, in the shape of ox, cow, bull, or ram. The yeomen appeared to be more in their element than I ever saw them anywhere else, except, indeed, at labor—more than at musterings and such gatherings of amusement. And yet this was a sort of festal day, too, as well as a day of business. Most of the people were of a bulky make, with much bone [7] and muscle, and some good store of fat, like people who lived on flesh-diet—with mottled faces, too, hard and red, as if they adhered to the good old fashion of spirit-drinking;—great round-paunched country-squires were there too, sitting under the porch of the tavern, or waddling about, whip in hand, discussing the points of the cattle. There, also, were gentle men farmers, neatly, trimly, and fashionably dressed, in handsome surtouts, and pantaloons strapt under their boots. Yeomen, too, in their black or blue sunday suits, cut by country tailors, and aukwardly worn. Others (like myself) had on the blue stuff frocks which they wear in the fields—the most comfortable garment that ever man invented. Country loafers, too, were among the throng—men who looked wistfully at the liquors in the bar, and waited for some friend to invite them to drink—poor shabby, out at elbowed devils. Also, dandies from the city, stayed and buckramed, who had come to see the humors of Brighton fair. All these, and other varieties of mankind, either thronged the spacious bar-room of the hotel, drinking, smoking, talking, bargaining; or walked about among the cattle-pens, looking with knowing eyes at the horned people. The owners [8] of the cattle stood near at hand, waiting for offers; there was something indescribable in their aspect that showed them to be the owners, though they intermixed among the crowd. The cattle, brought from a hundred separate farms, or rather a thousand, seemed to agree very well together, not quarrelling in the least. They almost all had a history, no doubt, if they could but have told it—the cows had each given their milk to support families—had roamed the pasture, and come home to the barn-yard—had been looked upon as a sort of member of the domestic circle, and was known by a name, as Brindle or Cherry. The oxen, with their necks bent by the heavy yoke, had toiled in the plough-field and in haying time, for many years, and knew their master's stall as well as the master himself did his own table. Even the young steers, and the little calves, had something of domestic sacredness about them; for children had watched their growth, and patted them, and played with them. And here they all were, old and young, gathered from their thousand homes to Brighton fair; whence the great chance was that they would go to the slaughter-house, and thence be transmitted, in sirloins, joints, and such pieces, to the tables of the Boston people.

William Allen had come to buy four little pigs, [9] to take the places of our four, who have now grown large, and are to be fatted and killed within a few weeks. There were several hundreds, in pens appropriated to their use, grunting discordantly, and apparently in no very good humor with their companions or the world at large. Most, or many, of these pigs had been imported from the state of New York. The drovers set out with a large number, and peddle them along the road, till they arrive at Brighton with the remainder. William selected four, and bought them at five cents per pound. These poor little porkers were forthwith seized by the tails, their legs tied, and they thrown into our wagon, where they kept up a continual grunt and squeal, till we got home. Two of them were yellowish, or light gold colored; the other two black and white speckled; and all four of very piggish aspect and deportment. One of them snapt at William's finger most spitefully, and bit it to the bone.

All this scene of the fair was very characteristic and peculiar—cheerful and lively, too, in the bright, warm sun. I must see it again; for it ought to be studied.

[10] [Tuesday]. September 28th, 1841.

A picnic party in the woods, yesterday, in honor of Frank Dana's birth-day, he being six years old. I strolled into the woods, after dinner, with Mr. Bradford; and in a lonesome glade, we met the apparition of an Indian chief, dressed in appropriate costume of blanket, feathers, and paint, and armed with a musket. Almost at the same time a young gipsey fortune teller came from among the trees, and proposed to tell my fortune; which while she was doing, the goddess Diana (known on earth as Miss Ellen Slade) let fly an arrow and hit me smartly in the hand. This fortune teller and goddess were a fine contrast, Diana being a blonde, fair, quiet, with a moderate composure; and the gipsey (Ora Gannet) a bright, vivacious, dark-haired, rich-complexioned damsel—both of them very pretty; at least, pretty enough to make fifteen years enchanting. Accompanied by these denizens of the wild wood, we went onward, and came to a company of fantastic figures, arranged in a ring for a dance or game. There was a Swiss girl, an Indian squaw, a negro of the Jim Crow order, one or two foresters; and several people in Christian attire; besides children of all ages. Then followed childish games, in which the grown people took part [11] with mirth enough—while I, whose nature it is to be a mere spectator both of sport and serious business, lay under the trees and looked on. Meanwhile, Mr. Emerson and Miss Fuller, who had arrived an hour or two before, came forth into the little glade where we were assembled. Here followed much talk.

The ceremonies of the day concluded with a cold collation of cakes and fruit. All was pleasant enough; "an excellent piece of work;—would 'twere done!" It has left a fantastic impression on my memory, this intermingling of wild and fabulous characters with real and homely ones, in the secluded nook of the woods. I remember them with the sunlight breaking through overshadowing branches, and they appearing and disappearing confusedly—perhaps starting out of the earth; as if the every day laws of Nature were suspended for this particular occasion. There are the children, too, laughing and sporting about, as if they were at home among such strange shapes—and anon bursting into loud uproar of lamentation, when the rude gambols of the merry-makers chance to overturn them. And, apart, with a shrewd Yankee observation of the scene, stands our friend Orange, [12] a thickset, sturdy figure, in his blue frock, enjoying the fun well enough, yet rather laughing with a perception of its nonsensicallness, than at all entering into the spirit of the thing.

This morning I have been helping to gather apples. The principal farm labors, at this time, are ploughing for winter rye, and breaking up the green sward for next year's crop of potatoes; gathering squashes—and not much else, except such year round employments as milking. The crop of rye, to be sure, is in process of being thrashed, at odd intervals.

I ought to have mentioned, among the diverse and incongruous guests of the picnic party, our two Spanish boys from Manilla—Lucas with his heavy features and almost mulatto complexion; and Jose, slighter, with rather a feminine face—not a gay-girlish one, but grave, reserved, eyeing you sometimes with an earnest, but secret expression, and causing you to question what sort of person he is. Make up the group with good, homely, sensible Mrs. Pratt, and her husband, every way fitted to her—pattern specimens of New England matrimony.

Friday, October 1st, 1841.

I have been looking at our four swine, not of the last lot, but those in process of fat[13]ting. They lie among the clean rye straw in their stye, nestling close together; for they seem to be a sensitive beast to the cold; and this is a clear, bright, chrystal, north-west windy, cool morning. So there lie these four black swine, as deep among the straw as they can burrow, the very symbols of slothful ease and sensual comfort. They seem to be actually oppressed and overburdened with comfort. They are quick to notice any one's approach to the stye, and utter a low grunt–not drawing breath for that particular purpose, but grunting with their ordinary breath–at the same time turning an observant, though dull and sluggish eye upon the visitor. They seem to be involved and buried in their own corporeal substance, and to look dimly forth at the outer world. They breathe not easily, and yet not with difficulty or discomfort; for the very unreadiness and oppression with which their breath comes, appears to make them sensible of the deep sensual satisfaction which they feel. Swill, the remnant of their last meal, remains in their trough, denoting that their food is more abundant than even a hog can demand. Anon, they fall asleep, drawing short and heavy breaths, which heave their huge sides up and down; but at the slightest [14] noise, they sluggishly unclose their eyes, and give another gentle grunt. They also grunt among themselves, apparently without any external cause, but merely to express their swinish sympathy. I suppose it is the knowledge that these four grunters are doomed to die within two or three weeks, that gives them a sort of awfulness in my conception; it makes me contrast their present gross substance of fleshly life with the nothingness speedily to come.

Meantime, the four newly bought pigs are running about the cow-yard, lean, active, shrewd, investigating everything, as their nature is. When I throw apples among them, they scramble with one another for the prize; and the successful one scampers away to eat it at leisure. They thrust their snouts into the mud, and pick a grain of corn out of the filth. Nothing within their sphere do they leave unexamined–grunting all the time, with infinite variety of expression. Their language seems to be the most copious of that of any quadruped; and, indeed, there is something deeply and indefinably interesting in the swinish race. They appear the more a mystery, the longer you gaze at them; it seems as if there was an important meaning to them, if you could but find out. One interesting trait in swine, is their perfect independence of char[15]acter. They care not for man, and will not adapt themselves to his notions, as other beasts do; but are true to themselves, and act out their hoggish nature.

[Thursday], October 7th, [1841].

Since Saturday last (it being now Thursday) I have been in Boston and Salem; and there has been a violent storm and rain during the whole time. This morning shone as bright as if it meant to make up for all the dismalness of the past days. Our brook, which in the summer was no longer a running stream, but stood in pools along its pebbly course, is now full from one grassy verge to another, and hurries along with a murmuring rush. It will continue to swell, I suppose; and in the winter and spring, it will flood all the broad meadows through which it flows–

I have taken a long walk, this forenoon, along the Needham road and across the bridge–thence pursuing a crossroad through the woods, parallel with the river, which I crossed again at Dedham bridge. Most of this road lay through a growth of young oaks principally; they still retain their verdure; though, looking closely in among them, you perceive the broken sunshine falling on a few sear or bright-hued tufts of shrubbery. In [16] low, marshy spots, on the verge of the meadows, or along the river side, there is a much more marked autumnal change. Whole ranges of shrubbery are there painted with many variegated hues, not of the brightest tint, but a sober cheerfulness. I suppose this is more owing to the late rains, than to the frost; for a heavy rain changes the foliage somewhat, at this season. The first marked frost was seen last Saturday morning; soon after sunrise, it lay white as snow over all the grass, and on the tops of the fences, and in the yard, on the heap of firewood. On Sunday, I think, there was a fall of snow; which, however, did not lie on the ground a moment.

There is no season, when such pleasant sunny and verdant spots may be lighted on, and produce so pleasant an effect on the feelings, as now in October. The sunshine is peculiarly genial, and, in sheltered places, as on the side of a bank, or of a barn or house, you become acquainted and friendly with the sunshine; it seems to be of a kindly and homely nature. And the green grass, strewn with a few withered leaves, looks the more green and beautiful for them. In summer or spring, nature is further from one's sympathies.

[17] [Friday], October 8th, 1841.

Another gloomy day, lowering with portents of rain close at hand. I have walked up into the pasture, this morning, and looked about me a little. The woods present a very diversified appearance, just now, with perhaps more varieties of tint, though less marked ones, than they are destined to wear at a somewhat later period. There are some strong yellow hues, and some deep red; there are innumerable shades of green; some few having the depth of summer; others, partially changed towards yellow, look freshly verdant, the delicate tinge of early summer, or of May. Then there is the solemn and dark green of the pines. The effect is, that every tree in the wood, and every bush among the shrubbery, seems to have a separate existence, since, confusedly intermingled, each wears its peculiar hue, instead of being lost in the universal verdure of the summer. And yet there is a oneness of effect, likewise, when we choose to look at a whole sweep of woodland, or swamp shrubbery, instead of analyzing its component trees. Scattered over the pasture, which the late rain have kept tolerably green, there are spots, or islands, of a dusky [18] red—a deep, substantial hue, very well fit to be close to the ground, while the yellow, and light fantastic shades of green, soar upward to the sky. These red spots are the blue-berry bushes. The sweet fern is changed mostly to a russet hue, but still retains its wild and delightful fragrance, when pressed by the hand. Wild china asters are scattered about, but beginning to wither. A little while ago, mushrooms or toad-stools were very numerous, along the wood-paths, and by the road sides, especially after rain. Some were of spotless white, some yellow, some scarlet. They are always mysteries, and objects of interest, to me, springing, as they do, so suddenly from no root or seed, and growing nobody can tell why. I think, too, these are rather a pretty object—little fairy tables, centre tables, standing on one leg. But their growth appears to be checked now; and they are of a brown hue, and decayed.

The farm business, to-day, is to dig potatoes. I worked a little at it. The process is first to grasp all the stems of a hill, and pull them up. A great many of the potatoes are thus pulled; clinging to the stems, and

to one another, in curious shapes, [19] long red things, and little round ones, imbedded in the earth which clings to the roots. These being plucked off, the rest of the potatoes are dug out of the hill with a hoe;–the tops being flung into a heap for the cow yard. On my way home, I paused to inspect the squash field. Some of the squashes lay in heaps, as they were gathered, presenting much variety of shape and hue–as golden yellow, like great lumps of gold, dark green, striped and variegated, &c; and some were round, and some lay curling their long necks, nestling, as it were, and seeming as if they had life. Some are regularly scalloped, and would make handsome patterns for dishes.

In my walk, yesterday forenoon, I passed an old house, which seemed to be quite deserted. It was a two-story wooden house, dark and weather-beaten. The front windows, some of them, were shattered and open to the weather, others were boarded up. Trees and shrubbery were growing neglected, so as quite to block up the lower windows. There was an aged barn, near at hand, so ruinous that it had been necessary to prop it up. There were two old carts, both of which, I believe, had lost a wheel. [20] Everything, in short, was in keeping. At first, I supposed that there could be no inhabitants in such a delapidated place; but passing on, I looked back, and saw a ruinous and infirm old man round the angle of the house, its fit occupant. The grass, however, was very green and beautiful around this house, and the sunshine falling brightly on it, the whole effect was cheerful and pleasant. It seemed as if the world was so pleasant, that this old desolate house, where there was never to be any more hope and happiness, could not at all lessen the general effect of joy.

I found a small turtle by the roadside, where he crept to warm himself in the glad sunshine. He had a sable back; underneath his shell was yellow, and at the edges, bright scarlet. His head, tail, and claws, were striped yellow, black, and red. He withdrew himself, as far as he possibly could, into his shell, and positively refused to thrust out his head, even when I put him into the water. Finally I threw him into a deep pool, and left him. These mailed gentlemen, from the size of a foot or more down to an inch, were very numerous in the spring, and now the smaller kind seem to appear again.

[21] Saturday, October 9th [1841].

Still dismal weather. Our household, being composed in great measure of children and young people, is generally a cheerful one enough, even in gloomy weather. For a week past, we have been especially gladdened with a little sempstress from Boston, about seventeen years old, but of such a petite figure that, at first view, one would take her to be hardly in her teens. She is very vivacious and smart, laughing, singing, and talking, all the time–talking sensibly, but still taking the view of matters that a city girl naturally would. If she were larger than she is, and of less pleasing aspect, I think she might be intolerable; but being so small, and with a white skin, healthy as a wild flower, she is really very agreeable; and to look at her face is like being shone upon by a ray of the sun. She never walks, but bounds and dances along; and this motion, in her small person, does not give the idea of violence. It is like a bird, hopping from twig to twig, and chirping merrily all the time. Sometimes she is a little vulgar; but even that works well enough into her character, and accords with it. On continued observation and acquaintance, you discover that she is not a little girl, but really a little woman, with [22] all the prerogatives and liabilities of a woman. This gives a new aspect to her character; while her girlish impression still continues, and is strangely combined with the sense that this frolicksome little maiden has the material for the sober character, a wife. She romps with the boys, runs races with them in the yard, and up and down the stairs, and is heard scolding laughingly at their rough play. She asks William Allen to put her "on top of that horse," whereupon he puts his large brown hands about her waist, and, swinging her to-and-fro, places her on horseback. By the bye, William threatened to rivet two horse shoes round her neck, for having clambered, with the other girls and boys, upon a load of hay; whereby the said load lost its balance, and slided off the cart. She strings the seed-berries of roses together, making a scarlet necklace of them, which she wears about her neck. She gathers everlasting flowers, to wear in her hair or bonnet, arranging them with the skill of a dress-maker. In the evening, she sits singing by the hour together, with the musical part of the establishment–often breaking into laughter, whereto she is incited by the tricks of the boys. The last thing you hear of her, she is tripping up stairs, to bed, talking lightsomely or singing; and you meet her in the morning, the very image of lightsome morn [23] itself, smiling briskly at you, so that one takes her for a promise

of cheerfulness through the day. Be it said, among all the rest, there is a perfect maiden modesty in her deportment; though I doubt whether the boys, in their rompings with her, do not feel that she has past out of her childhood.

This lightsome little maid has left us this morning; and the last thing I saw of her was her vivacious face, peeping through the curtain of the carryall, and nodding a brisk farewell to the family, who were shouting their adieus at the door. With her other merits, she is an excellent daughter, and, I believe, supports her mother by the labor of her hands. It would be difficult to conceive, beforehand, how much can be added to the enjoyment of a household by mere sunniness of temper and smartness of disposition; for her intellect is very ordinary, and she never says anything worth hearing, or even laughing at, in itself. But she herself is an expression, well worth studying.

October 9th, continued. A walk, this afternoon, to Cow Island. The clouds had broken away, towards noon, and let forth a few sunbeams, and more and more blue sky continued to appear, till at last it was really [24] warm and sunny–indeed, rather too warm, in the sheltered hollows, though it is delightful to be too warm now, after so much stormy chillness. Oh, the beauty of grassy slopes, and the hollow ways of paths, winding between hills, and the intervals between the road and a woodlot; and all such places, where Summer lingers and sits down, strewing dandelions of gold, and blue asters, as her parting gifts, and memorials! I went to a grape vine, which I have already visited several times, and found some clusters of grapes still remaining, and now perfectly ripe. Coming within view of the river, I saw several wild ducks, under the shadow of the opposite shore, which was high, and covered with a grove of pines. I should not have discovered the ducks, had they not risen, and skimmed the surface of the glassy river, breaking its dark water with a bright streak, and sweeping round gradually rose high enough to fly away. I likewise started a partridge, just within the verge of the woods; and in another place a large squirrel ran across the wood path, from one shelter of trees to the other. Small birds in flocks were flitting about the fields, seeking and finding I know not what sort of food. There are little fish also dar[25]ting in shoals through the pools and depths of the brooks, which are now replenished to their brims, and beyond, and rush towards the river with a swift, amber-colored current.

Cow Island is not an island, at least at this season; though I believe, in the season of freshets, the marshy Charles floods the meadows all roundabout it, and extends its puddle across its communication with the mainland. The path to it is a very secluded one, threading a wood of pines, and just wide enough to admit the passage of the loads of meadow hay, which are drawn from the marshy shore of the river. The island has a growth of stately pines, with tall and ponderous stems, standing at distance enough to admit the eye to travel far among them; and as there is no underbrush, the effect is somewhat like looking among the pillars of a church.

I returned home by the high-road. On my right, separated from the road by a level field, perhaps fifty yards across, was a range of young woods, dressed in their garb of autumnal glory. The sun shone directly upon them; and sunlight is like the breath of [26] life to this pomp of autumn. In its absence, you doubt whether there is any truth in what poets have told about the splendor of an American autumn; but when this charm is added, you feel that the effect is beyond description. As I beheld it to-day, there was nothing dazzling, but gentle and mild, though brilliant and diversified–it had a most quiet and pensive influence. And yet, there were some trees that seemed really made of sunshine, and others of a sunny red, and the whole picture was painted with but little relief of darksome hues–only a few evergreens. But there was nothing inharmonious; and, on closer examination, it appeared that all the hues had a relationship among themselves; and this, I suppose, is the reason, that, while Nature seems to scatter them so carelessly, they still never shock the beholder by their contrasts, nor disturb, but only soothe. The brilliant yellow, and the brilliant scarlet, are different hues of the maple leaves, and the first changes into the last. I saw one maple tree, its centre yellow as gold, set in a framework of red. The native poplars have different shades of green, verging towards yellow, and are very cheerful in the sunshine. Most of the oak-leaves have still the deep verdure of sum[27]mer; but where a change has taken place, it is of a russet red, a warm, but sober hue. These colors, infinitely diversified by the progress which different trees have made in their decay, constitute almost the whole glory of Autumnal woods; but it is impossible to conceive how much is done with such scanty materials. And, as you pass along, every tree seems to be an existence by itself.

In summer, the sunshine is thrown away upon the wide, unvaried verdure. Now, every tree seems to define and embody the sunshine. And yet, the spectator can diffuse himself throughout the scene, and receive one impression from all this painted glory.

In my whole walk, I saw only one man, and him at a distance, in the obscurity of the trees. He had a horse and wagon, and seemed to be getting a load of dry brushwood.

Sunday, October 10th, [1841].

I visited my grape vine, this afternoon, and ate the last of its clusters. This vine climbs around a young maple tree, which has now assumed the yellow leaf. The vine leaves are more decayed than those of the maple. Thence to Cow Island, a solemn and thoughtful walk. Returned from the island by [28] another path, of the width of a pair of wagon wheels, passing through a grove of hard-wood trees, the lightsome hues of which make the walk more cheerful than among the pines. The roots of oak trees emerged from the soil, and contorted themselves across the path. The sunshine, also, broke across in spots, and in other spots the shadow was deep; but still there was intermingling enough of sunshine and bright hues to keep off the gloom from the whole path.

Brooks and pools of water seem to me to have a peculiar aspect, at this season. You know that the water must be cold, and you shiver a little at the sight of it; and yet the grass about the pool is of the deepest verdure, and the sun may be shining into it. The withered leaves, which overhanging trees shed into the water, contribute much to the effect of it.

Insects have mostly vanished in the fields and woods. I hear locusts yet singing in the sunny hours; and crickets have not quite finished their song. Once in a while, I see a caterpillar–this afternoon, for instance, a red hairy one, with black hair at the head and tail. They do not appear to be active; and it makes one rather melancholy to look at them.

[29] Tuesday, October 12th, [1841].

The cawing of the crow resounds among the woods, at this season. A centinel is aware of your approach a great way off, and gives the alarm to his comrades loud and eagerly–Caw-caw-caw–. Immediately, the whole conclave replies in the same word; and you behold them rising above the trees, flapping darkly, and winging their way to deeper solitudes. Sometimes, however, they remain on a tree, till you come near enough to discern their sable gravity of aspect, each occupying a separate bough, or perhaps the blasted tip-top of a pine tree. As you approach, one after another, with loud cawing, flaps his wings and throws himself upon the air.

There is hardly a more striking feature in the landscape, now-a-days, than the red patches of blue berry bushes, as seen on a long sloping hill side, like islands among the grass, with trees growing on them; or crowning the summit of a bare, brown hill with their somewhat russet liveliness–or circling round the base of an earth-embedded rock. At a distance, this hue clothing spots and patches of the earth looks more like a picture– yet such a picture as I never saw painted–than anything else. Being a strong, [30] substantial hue, too, it serves well to be the ground-work of the picture, while the fantastic lightness of the yellow, and yellowish-green, treetops, is flung up towards the sky.

The oaks are now beginning to look sere, and their leaves have withered borders. It is pleasant to notice the wide circle of greener grass, beneath the circumference of an overshadowing oak. Passing an orchard, you hear an uneasy rustling in the trees, not as if they were struggling with the wind. Scattered about, are barrels to contain the apples; and perhaps a great heap of golden or scarlet apples is collected in one place.

Wednesday, October 13th, [1841].

A good view from an upland swell of our pasture across the valley of the river Charles. There is the meadow, as level as a floor and carpeted with green, perhaps two miles from the rising ground on this side of the river, to that on the opposite side. The river winds through the midst of this level space, without any banks at all, for it fills its bed almost to the brim, and bathes the meadow grass on either side. A tuft of shrubbery, at broken intervals, is scattered along its border; and thus the river meanders sluggishly along, without other life than what it gains from gleaming in the sun. Now, into this broad, flat meadow, as into a [31] lake, capes and headlands put themselves forth, and shores of firm woodland border it, all covered with variegated

foliage, making the contrast so much the stronger of their height and rough outline with the unvaried plane of the meadow. And beyond the river, far away, rises a long gradual swell of country, covered with an apparently dense growth of foliage, for miles, till the horizon terminates it; and here and there a house or two rises among the contiguity of trees. Every where, the trees have their autumned hue, so that the whole landscape is red, russet, orange and yellow, blending at a distance into a rich tint of brown orange, or thereabout– except the green meadow, so definitely hemmed in by the higher grounds.

I took a long walk this morning, going first nearly to Newton, thence nearly to Brighton, thence to Jamaica plains, and thence home. It was a fine northwest windy morning, cool, when facing the wind, but warm and most genially pleasant in sheltered spots; and warm enough everywhere, while in motion. I traversed most of the by-ways which offered themselves to me; and passing through one, in which there was a double line of grass between the wheel-tracks and that of the hor[32]ses feet, I came to where had once stood a farm-house, which appeared to have been recently torn down. Most of the old timber and boards had been carted away; a pile of it, however, remained. The cellar of the house was uncovered; and beside it stood the base and middle height of the chimney. The oven, in which household bread had been baked for daily food, and puddings, and cake, and jolly pumpkin pies, for festivals, opened its mouth, being deprived of its iron door. The fire-place was close at hand. All round the site of the house was a pleasant sunny green space, with old fruit trees, seemingly in pretty fair condition, though aged. There was a barn, aged, but in decent repair, and a ruinous shed, on a corner of which was nailed a boy's windmill, where it had probably been turning and clattering for years together, till now it was black with years and weather-stain. It was broken now, but still it went round, whenever the wind stirred. The spot was entirely secluded, there being no other house within a mile or two.

No language can give an idea of the beauty and glory of the trees, just at this time. It would be easy, by a process of word-daubing, to set down a confused idea of gorgeous colors, like a bunch of tangled skeins of [33] bright silk; but there is nothing, in the reality, of the glare which would thus be conveyed. And yet the splendor both of individual trees, and of whole scenes, is unsurpassable. The oaks are now far advanced in their change of hue; and, in certain positions relatively to the sun, they appear lighted up and gleaming with a most magnificent deep gold, varying, according as portions of the foliage are in shadow or sunlight. On the sides which receive the direct sunshine, the effect is altogether rich; and in other points of view, it is equally beautiful, if less brilliant. This hue of the oak is more magnificent than the lighter yellow of the maples and walnuts. The whole landscape is now covered with this indescribable magnificence; you discern it on the uplands, afar off; and Blue Hill in Milton, at the distance of several miles, actually seemed to glisten with rich, dark light–no, not glisten, nor gleam; but perhaps a subdued glow will do something towards the expression of it.

Met few people this morning–a grown girl, in company with a little boy, gathering barberries in a secluded lane–a portly autumnal gentleman, wrapped in a great coat, who asked the way to Mr. Joseph Goddard's–[34] a fish-cart from the city, the driver of which sounded his horn along the lonesome way.

Monday, October 18th, [1841].

There has been a succession of Autumnal days, cold and bright in the forenoon, and gray, sullen, and chill, towards night. The woods have now assumed a soberer tint than they wore at my last date. Many of the shrubs, which looked brightest a little while ago, are now wholly bare of leaves. The oaks have mostly a russet brown tint; although some of them are still green, as are likewise other scattered trees in the woods. The bright yellow and the rich scarlet are no more to be seen. None of the trees, scarcely, will now bear a close examination; for then they look ragged, wilted, and of faded, frost-bitten hue; but at a distance, and in the mass, and enlivened by sunshine, the woods have still somewhat of the variegated splendor which distinguished them a week ago. It is wonderful what a difference the sunshine makes; it is like varnish, bringing out the hidden veins in a piece of rich wood. In the cold gray atmosphere, such as most of our afternoons are now, the landscape lies dark-brown and unvaried, in a much deeper shadow than if it were clothed in green. But perchance a gleam of sunshine falls on a certain spot of distant shrubbery or wood[35]land; and we see it brighten forth, with varied hues, standing forth prominently from the dark mass around it. The sun-

shine gradually spreads over the whole landscape; and the whole sombre mass is changed to a variegated picture, the light bringing out many shades of color, and converting its gloom to an almost laughing cheerfulness. At such times, I almost doubt whether the foliage has lost any of its brilliancy; but the gray clouds intercept the sunshine again; and lo! old Autumn, clad in his cloak of russet brown.

Beautiful now, while the general landscape lies in shadow, looks the summit of a distant hill (say a mile off) with the sunshine brightening the trees that cover it. It is noticeable that the outlines of hills, and the whole bulk and mass of them, at the distance of several miles, become stronger, denser, and more substantial, in this autumn atmosphere, and in these autumnal tints, than they were in summer. Then they used to look blue, misty, and dim; now they show their great hump backs more evidently, as if they had drawn nearer to us.

A waste of shrubbery and small trees, such as overruns the borders of the meadows for miles together, looks much more ragged, wild, and savage, in its present brown hue, [36] than when clad in green.

I passed through a very pleasant wood-path, yesterday, quite shut in and sheltered by trees that had not yet thrown off their yellow foliage. The sun shone strongly in among these trees, and quite kindled them; so that the path seemed the brighter for their shade, than if it had been quite exposed to the sun.

In the village grave-yard, which lies contiguous to the street, I saw a man digging a grave; and one inhabitant after another turned aside from the street to look into the grave, and talk with the digger. I heard him laugh, with the hereditary mirthfulness of men of that occupation.

In a hollow of the woods, yesterday afternoon, I lay a long while watching a squirrel, who was capering about among the trees (oaks and white-pines, so close together that their branches intermingled) over my head. The squirrel seemed not to approve of my presence; for he frequently uttered a sharp, quick, angry noise, like that of a scissor-grinder's wheel. Sometimes I could see him sitting on an impending bough, with his tail over his back, looking down pryingly upon me; it seems to be a natural posture with him to sit on his hind legs, holding up his fore-paws. Anon, with a peculiarly quick start, he would scamper along the [37] branch, and be lost to sight in another part of the tree, whence his shrill chatter would again be heard. Then I would see him rapidly descending the trunk, and running along the ground; and a moment afterwards, casting my eyes upward, I beheld him flitting like a bird among the high interweaving branches, at the summits of the trees, directly over my head. After a while, he apparently became accustomed to my presence, and set about some business of his. He descended the trunk of a tree to the ground, took up a piece of a decayed bough of a tree, (a great burthen for such a small personage) and, with this in his mouth, again climbed the tree, and passed from the branches of that to those of another, and thus onward and onward, till he was out of sight. Shortly afterwards he returned for another burthen; and this he repeated several times. I suppose he was building a nest–at least, I know not what else could have been his object. Never was there such an active, cheerful, choleric, continually-in-motion fellow, as this little red squirrel–talking to himself, chattering at me, and as sociable in his own person as if he had half a dozen companions, instead of being alone in the lonesome wood. Indeed, he flitted about so quickly, and showed him[38]self in different places so suddenly, that I was in some doubt whether there were not two or three of him.

I must mention again the very beautiful effect produced by the masses of blueberry bushes (or whortleberry) lying like scarlet islands in the midst of withered pasture-ground, or crowning the tops of barren hills. Their hue, at a distance, is a lustrous scarlet; although it does not look nearly so bright and beautiful, when examined close at hand. But, at a proper distance, it is a beautiful fringe on Autumn's petticoat.

Friday, October 22d, [1841].

A continual succession of unpleasant Novembry days; and Autumn has made rapid progress in the work of decay. It is now somewhat of a rare good fortune to find a verdant grassy spot, on some slope, or in a hollow; and even such seldom seen oases are bestrewn with dried brown leaves;–which, however, methinks, make the short fresh grass look greener around them. Dry leaves are now plentiful everywhere, save where there are none but pine-trees; they rustle beneath the tread–and there is nothing more autumnal than that sound. Nevertheless, in a walk this afternoon I have seen two oak trees which retained almost the verdure of summer. They grew close to the huge Pulpit

Rock, so [39] that portions of their trunks appeared to grasp the rough surface; and they were rooted beneath it; and ascending high into the air, they overshadowed the gray crag with fresh foliage. Other oaks, here and there, have a few green leaves or boughs, among their rustling and russet shade.

Yet, dreary as the woods are in a bleak, sullen day, there is a very peculiar sense of warmth, and a sort of richness of effect, in the sheltered spots, on the slope of a bank, where bright sunshine falls, and where the brown oaken foliage is gladdened by it, and where green grass is seen among withered leaves. There is then a feeling of shelter and comfort, and consequently a heart-warmth, which cannot be experienced in summer.

I walked, this afternoon, along a pleasant wood-path, gently winding, so that but little of its course could be seen at a time, and going up and down small slopes, now plunging into a denser shadow, and now emerging from it. Part of the way, it was strewn with the dusky yellow leaves of white pines–the cast off garments of last year; part of the way with green grass, close cropt and very fresh for the season. Sometimes the trees met across it; sometimes it was bordered, on one side, [40] by an old rail fence, of moss grown cedar, with bushes sprouting beneath it, and thrusting their branches through it; sometimes by a stone wall, of unknown antiquity,–older than the wood it bordered in. A stone wall, when shrubbery has grown around it; and trees have thrust their roots beneath it, becomes a very pleasant and meditative object; it does not belong too evidently to man, having been built so long ago; it seems a part of nature.

Yesterday, I found two mushrooms in the woods, evidently of the preceding night growth. Also, I saw a musquito, frost-pinched, and so wretched that I felt avenged for all the injuries which his tribe inflicted upon me, last summer–and so did not molest this lone survivor.

Walnuts, in their green rinds, are falling from the trees; and so are chesnut-burrs.

I found a maple leaf to-day, yellow all over, except its extremest point, which was a bright scarlet. It looked as if a drop of blood were hanging from it. The first change of the maple is to scarlet–next to yellow. Then it withers, wilts, and drops off–as most of them have already done.

[Wednesday], October 27th, [1841].

Fringed gentians, found the last, probably, that will be seen this year, growing on the margin of the brook.

[41] The device of a sun-dial for a monument over a grave—with some suitable motto.

To symbolize moral or spiritual disease by disease of the body;–thus, when a person committed any sin, it might cause a sore to appear on the body;–this to be wrought out.

A man with the right perception of things–a feeling within him of what is true and what is false. It might be symbolized by the talisman, with which, in fairy tales, an adventurer was enabled to distinquish enchantments from realities.

[Elizabeth] P[almer]. P[eabody].
"Plan of the West Roxbury Community," *Dial,* 2 (January 1842): 361-372.

Peabody's account of Brook Farm provides an interesting discussion of its principles and practices, and warns against possible excesses.

In the last number of the Dial were some remarks, under the perhaps ambitious title, of "A Glimpse of Christ's Idea of Society;" in a note to which, it was intimated, that in this number, would be given an account of an attempt to realize in some degree this great Ideal, by a little company in the midst of us, as yet without name or visible existence. The attempt is made on a very small scale. A few individuals, who, unknown to each other, under different disciplines of life, reacting from different social evils, but aiming at the same object,–of being wholly true to their natures as men and women; have been made acquainted with one another, and have determined to become the Faculty of the Embryo University.

In order to live a religious and moral life worthy the name, they feel it is necessary to come out in some degree from the world, and to form themselves into a community of property, so far as to exclude competition and the ordinary rules of trade;–while they reserve sufficient private property, or the means of obtaining it, for all purposes of independence, and isolation at will. They have bought a farm, in order to make agriculture the basis of their life, it being the most direct and simple in relation to nature.

A true life, although it aims beyond the highest star, is redolent of the healthy earth. The perfume of clo-

Painting of Elizabeth Palmer Peabody by Charles C. Burleigh, Jr. in 1878 (Essex Institute, Salem, Massachusetts)

ver lingers about it. The lowing of cattle is the natural bass to the melody of human voices.

On the other hand, what absurdity can be imagined greater than the institution of cities? They originated not in love, but in war. It was war that drove men together in multitudes, and compelled them to stand so close, and build walls around them. This crowded condition produces wants of an unnatural character, which resulted in occupations that regenerated the evil, by creating artificial wants. Even when that thought of grief,

> "I know, where'er I go
> That there hath passed away a glory from the Earth,"

came to our first parents, as they saw the angel, with the flaming sword of self-consciousness, standing between them and the recovery of spontaneous Life and Joy, we cannot believe they could have anticipated a time would come, when the sensuous apprehension of Creation–the great symbol of God–would be taken away from their unfortunate children,–crowded together in such a manner as to shut out the free breath and the Universal Dome of Heaven, some opening their eyes in the dark cellars of the narrow, crowded streets of walled cities. How could they have believed in such a conspiracy against the soul, as to deprive it of the sun and sky, and glorious apparelled Earth!–The growth of cities, which were the embryo of nations hostile to each other, is a subject worthy the thoughts and pen of the philosophic historian. Perhaps nothing would stimulate courage to seek, and hope to attain social good, so much, as a profound history of the origin, in the mixed nature of man, and the exasperation by society, of the various organized Evils, under which humanity groans. Is there anything, which exists in social or political life, contrary to the soul's Ideal? That thing is not eternal, but finite, saith the Pure Reason. It has a beginning, and so a history. What man has done, man may *undo*. "By man came death; by man also cometh the resurrection from the dead."

The plan of the Community, as an Economy, is in brief this; for all who have property to take stock, and receive a fixed interest thereon; then to keep house or board in commons, as they shall severally desire, at the cost of provisions purchased at wholesale, or raised on the farm; and for all to labor in community, and be paid at a certain rate an hour, choosing their own number of hours, and their own kind of work. With the results of this labor, and their interest, they are to pay their board, and also purchase whatever else they require at cost, at the warehouses of the Community, which are to be filled by the Community as such. To perfect this economy, in the course of time they must have all trades, and all modes of business carried on among themselves, from the lowest mechanical trade, which contributes to the health and comfort of life, to the finest art which adorns it with food or drapery for the mind.

All labor, whether bodily or intellectual, is to be paid at the same rate of wages; on the principle, that as the labor becomes merely bodily, it is a greater sacrifice to the individual laborer, to give his time to it; because time is desirable for the cultivation of the intellect, in exact proportion to ignorance. Besides, intellectual labor involves in itself higher pleasures, and is more its own reward, than bodily labor.

Another reason, for setting the same pecuniary value on every kind of labor, is, to give outward expression to the great truth, that all labor is sacred, when done for a common interest. Saints and philosophers already know this, but the childish world does not; and very decided measures must be taken to equalize labors, in the eyes of the young of the community, who are not beyond the moral influences of the world without them. The community will have nothing done within its precincts, but what is done by its own members, who stand all in social equality;–that the children may not "learn to expect one kind of service from Love and Goodwill, and another from the obligation of others to render it,"–a grievance of the common society stated, by one of the associated mothers, as destructive of the soul's simplicity. Consequently, as the Universal Education will involve all kinds of operation, necessary to the comforts and elegances of life, every associate, even if he be the digger of a ditch as his highest accomplishment, will be an instructer in that to the young members. Nor will this elevation of bodily labor be liable to lower the tone of manners and refinement in the community. The "children of light" are not altogether unwise in their generation. They have an invisible but all-powerful guard of principles. Minds incapable of refinement, will not be attracted into this association. It is an Ideal community, and only to the ideally inclined will it be attractive; but these are to be found in every rank of life, under every shadow of circumstance. Even among the diggers in the ditch are to be found some, who through religious cultivation, can look down, in meek superiority, upon the outwardly refined, and the book-learned.

Besides, after becoming members of this community, none will be engaged merely in bodily labor. The hours of labor for the Association will be limited by a general law, and can be curtailed at the will of the individual still more; and means will be given to all for intellectual improvement and for social intercourse, calculated to refine and expand. The hours redeemed from labor by community, will not be reapplied to the acquisition of wealth, but to the production of intellectual goods. This community aims to be rich, not in the metallic representative of wealth, but in the wealth itself, which money should represent; namely, LEISURE TO LIVE IN ALL THE FACULTIES OF THE SOUL. As a community, it will traffic with the world at large, in the products of Agricultural labor; and it will sell education to as many young persons as can be domesticated in the families, and enter into the common life with their own children. In the end, it hopes to be enabled to provide–not only all the necessaries, but all the elegances desirable for bodily and for spiritual health; books, apparatus, collections for science, works of art, means of beautiful amusement. These things are to be common to all; and thus that object, which alone gilds and refines the passion for individual accumulation, will no longer exist for desire, and whenever the Sordid passion appears, it will be seen in its naked selfishness. In its ultimate success, the community will realize all the ends which selfishness seeks, but involved in spiritual blessings, which only greatness of soul can aspire after.

And the requisitions on the individuals, it is believed, will make this the order forever. The spiritual good will always be the condition of the temporal. Every one must labor for the community in a reasonable degree, or not taste its benefits. The principles of the organization therefore, and not its probable results in future time, will determine its members. These principles are cooperation in social matters, instead of competition or balance of interests; and individual self-unfolding, in the faith that the whole soul of humanity is in each man and woman. The former is the application of the love of man; the latter of the love of God, to life. Whoever is satisfied with society, as it is; whose sense of justice is not wounded by its common action, institutions, spirit of commerce, has no business with this community; neither has any one who is willing to have other men (needing more time for intellectual cultivation than himself) give their best hours and strength to bodily labor, to secure himself immunity therefrom. And whoever does not measure what society owes to its members of cherishing and instruction, by the needs of the individuals that compose it, has no lot in this new society. Whoever is willing to receive from his fellow men that, for which he gives no equivalent, will stay away from its precincts forever.

But whoever shall surrender himself to its principles, shall find that its yoke is easy and its burden light. Everything can be said of it, in a degree, which Christ said of his kingdom, and therefore, it is believed that in some measure it does embody his Idea. For its Gate of entrance is strait and narrow. It is literally a pearl *hidden in a field.* Those only who are willing to lose their life for its sake shall find it. Its voice is that which sent the young man sorrowing away. "Go sell all thy goods and give to the poor, and then come and follow me." "Seek first the kingdom of Heaven, and its righteousness, and all other things shall be added to you."

This principle, with regard to labor, lies at the root of moral and religious life; for it is not more true that "money is the root of all evil," than that *labor is the germ of all good.*

All the work is to be offered for the free choice of the members of the community, at stated seasons, and such as is not chosen, will be hired. But it is not anticipated that any work will be set aside to be hired, for which there is actual ability in the community. It is so desirable that the hired labor should be avoided, that it is believed the work will all be done freely, even though at voluntary sacrifice. If there is some exception at first, it is because the material means are inadequate to the reception of all who desire to go. They cannot go, unless they have shelter; and in this climate, they cannot have shelter unless they can build houses; and they cannot build houses unless they have money. It is not here as in Robinson Crusoe's Island, or in the prairies and rocky mountains of the far west, where the land and the wood are not appropriated. A single farm, in the midst of Massachusetts, does not afford range enough for men to create out of the Earth a living, with no other means; as the wild Indians, or the United States Army in Florida may do.

This plan, of letting all persons choose their own departments of action, will immediately place the Genius of Instruction on its throne. Communication is the life of spiritual life. Knowledge pours itself out upon ignorance by a native impulse. All the arts crave response. "WISDOM CRIES." If every man and woman taught only what they loved, and so many hours as they could naturally communicate, instruction would cease to be a drudgery, and we may add, learning would be no longer a task. The known accomplishments of many of the members of this association have already secured it an interest in the public mind, as a school of literary advantages quite superior. Most of the associates have had long practical experience in the details of teaching, and have groaned under the necessity of taking their method and law from custom and caprice, when they would rather have found it in the nature of the thing taught, and the condition of the pupil to be instructed. Each instructor appoints his hours of study or recitation, and the scholars, or the parents of the children, or the educational committee, choose the studies, for the time, and the pupils submit, as long as they pursue their studies with any teacher, to his regulations.

As agriculture is the basis of their external life, scientific agriculture, connected with practice, will be a prominent part of the instruction from the first. This obviously involves the natural sciences, mathematics, and accounts. But to classical learning justice is also to be done. Boys may be fitted for our colleges there, and even be carried through the college course. The particular studies of the individual pupils, whether old or young, male or female, are to be strictly regulated, according to their inward needs. As the children of the community can remain in the community after they become of age, as associates, if they will; there will not be an entire subserviency to the end of preparing the means of earning a material subsistence, as is frequently the case now. Nevertheless, as they will have had an opportunity, in the course of their minority, to earn three or four hundred dollars, they can leave the community at twenty years of age, if they will, with that sufficient capital, which, together with their extensive education, will gain *a subsistence* anywhere, in the best society of the world. It is this feature of the plan, which may preclude from parents any question as to their right to go into this community, and forego forever all hope of great individual accumulation *for their children;* a customary plea for spending life in making money. Their children will be supported at free board, until they are ten years of age; educated gratuitously; taken care of in case of their parents' sickness and death; and they themselves will be supported, after seventy years of age, by the community, unless their accumulated capital supports them.

There are some persons who have entered the community without money. It is believed that these will be able to support themselves and dependents, by less work, more completely, and with more ease than elsewhere; while their labor will be of advantage to the community. It is in no sense an eleemosynary establishment, but it is hoped that in the end it will be able to receive all who have the spiritual qualifications.

It seems impossible that the little organization can be looked on with any unkindness by the world without it. Those, who have not the faith that the principles of Christ's kingdom are applicable to real life in the world, will smile at it, as a visionary attempt. But even they must acknowledge it can do no harm, in any event. If it realizes the hope of its founders, it will immediately become a manifold blessing. Its moral *aura* must be salutary. As long as it lasts, it will be an example of the beauty of brotherly love. If it succeeds in uniting successful labor with improvement in mind and manners, it will teach a noble lesson to the agricultural population, and do something to check that rush from the country to the city, which is now stimulated by ambition, and by something better, even a desire for learning. Many a young man leaves the farmer's life, because only by so doing can he have intellectual companionship and opportunity; and yet, did he but know it, professional life is ordinarily more unfavorable to the perfection of the mind, than the farmer's life; if the latter is lived with wisdom and moderation, and the labor mingled as it might be with study. This community will be a school for young agriculturalists, who may learn within its precincts, not only the skilful practice, but the scientific reasons of their work, and be enabled afterwards to improve their art continuously. It will also prove the best of normal schools, and as such, may claim the interest of those, who mourn over the inefficiency of our common school system, with its present ill-instructed teachers.

It should be understood also, that after all the working and teaching, which individuals of the community may do, they will still have leisure, and in that leisure can employ themselves in connexion with the world around them. Some will not teach at all; and those especially can write books, pursue the Fine Arts, for private emolument if they will, and exercise various functions of men.–From this community might go forth preachers of the gospel of Christ, who would not have upon them the odium, or the burthen, that now diminishes the power of the clergy. And even if *pastors* were to go from this community, to reside among congregations as now, for a salary given, the fact that they would have something to retreat upon, at any moment, would save them from that virtual dependence on their congregations, which now corrupts the relation. There are doubtless beautiful instances of the old true relation of pastor and people, even of teacher and taught, in the decaying churches around us, but it is in vain to attempt to conceal the ghastly fact, that many a taper is burning dimly in the candlestick, no longer silver or golden, because compassion forbids to put it quite out. But let the spirit again blow "where it listeth," and not circumscribe itself by salary and other commodity,–and the Preached word might reassure the awful Dignity which is its appropriate garment; and though it sit down with publicans and sinners, again speak "with authority and not as the scribes."

We write, as is evident perhaps, not as members, which we are not, but interested spectators of the growth of this little community. It is due to their modesty to apologize for bringing out so openly, what they have done simply and without pretension. We rest on the spirit of the day, which is that of communication. No sooner does the life of man become visible, but it is a part of the great phenomenon of nature, which never seeks display, but suffers all to speculate thereon. When this speculation is made in respect, and in love of truth, it is most to be defended. We shall now proceed to make some observations that may sound like criticism, but this we do without apology, for earnest seekers of a true life are not liable to be petulant.

The very liberality, and truth to nature of the plan, is a legitimate reason for fearing it will not succeed as a special community in any given time. The vineyard does not always yield according to the reasonable expectation of its Lord. When he looks for grapes, behold it brings forth wild grapes. For outward success there must always be compromise, and where it is so much the object to avoid the dangers of compromise, as there very properly is here, there is perhaps danger of not taking advantage of such as nature offers.

One of these is the principle of antagonism. It is fair to take advantage of this in one respect. The members may be stimulated to faithfulness and hope, by the spectacle of society around them, whose unnecessary evils can be clearly seen to be folly, as well as sin, from their retreat. The spirit of liberality must be discriminated from the spirit of accommodation. Love is a stern principle, a severe winnower, when it is one with the pure Reason; as it must be, to be holy, and to

be effective. It is a very different thing from indulgence. Some persons have said that in order to a true experiment, and to enact a really generous faith in man, there should be any neighborhood taken without discrimination, with the proportion that may happen to be in it, of the good and bad, the strong and weak. But we differ as to the application in this instance. They are so little fenced about with rules and barriers, that they have no chance but by being strong in the spirit. "Touch not, taste not, handle not," must be their watchword, with respect to the organized falsehoods they have protested against; and with respect to means of successful manifestation, the aphorism of St. Augustine, "God is patient because he is Eternal."

To be a little more explicit. The men and women of the world, as they rise, are not at the present moment wise enough, in the Hebrew sense of the word wisdom, even if they are good-intentioned enough, to enter into a plan of so great mutual confidence. To all the evils arising from constitutional infirmity and perversion they must, especially at first, be exposed. There will always be natures too cold to satisfy the warmhearted, too narrow for the enjoyment of the widevisioned, some will be deficient in reason, and some in sensibility, and there will be many who, from defect of personal power, will let run to waste beautiful hearts, and not turn to account great insight of natural wisdom. Love, justice, patience, forbearance, every virtue under heaven, are always necessary in order to do the social duties. There is no knot that magnanimity cannot untie; but the Almighty Wisdom and Goodness will not allow any tower to be builded by the children of men, where they can understand one another *without* this solvent magnanimity. There must ever be sincerity of good design, and organic truth, for the evolution of Beauty.

Now there can be only one way of selecting and winnowing their company. The power to do this must be inherent in their constitution; they must keep sternly true to their principles.

In the first place, they must not compromise their principle of labor, in receiving members. Every one, who has any personal power, whether bodily or mental, must bring the contribution of personal service, no matter how much money he brings besides. This personal service is not to amount to drudgery in any instance, but in every able-bodied or sound-minded person, it should be at least equivalent to the care of their own persons. Exchange, or barter of labor, so as to distribute to each according to his genius, is to be the means of ease, indefinitely, but no absolute dispensation should be given, except for actual infirmity. "My Father worketh hitherto, and I work," is always the word of the divine humanity.

But granting that they keep the gate of entrance narrow, as the gate of life, which is being as liberal as the moral Law, a subtle temptation assails them from the side of their Organization. Wo be unto them if they lean upon it; if they ever forget that it is only what they have made it, and what they sustain it to be. It not only must be ever instinct with spirit, but it must never be thought, even then, to circumscribe the spirit. It can do nothing more, even if it work miracles, than make bread out of stones, and after all, man liveth not by bread alone, but by *every word that proceedeth out of the mouth of God.* Another temptation assails them, clothed as an angel of light. The lover of man finds in his benevolence a persuasive advocate, when the Devil proposes to him to begin by taking possession of the kingdoms of this world, according to his ability. In their ardor for means of success, they may touch the mammon of unrighteousness. They will be exposed to endowment. Many persons, enlightened enough to be unwilling to let the wealth, they have gained by the accident of birth or of personal talent, go to exasperate the evil of present society, will be disposed to give it, or to leave it as a legacy to this community, and it would be asceticism to refuse it absolutely. But they should receive it greatly. "Thou shalt worship the Lord thy God, and Him *only* shalt thou *serve.*" No person who proposes to endow the community as a University, or as the true system of life, understands what he does, unless he surrenders what he gives, unconditionally, in the same spirit of faith, with which the members throw themselves in, with their lives, their property, and sacred honor. At all events it would violate their principle of progress to accept anything with conditions; unless indeed it may be considered a condition, that they remain an association, governed by the majority of members, according to its present general constitution.

It were better even to forego the advantage of good buildings, apparatus, library, than to have these shackles.–Though space cannot now be given to do more than state these points, it might be demonstrated that to keep to them is essential to independence, and can alone justify the conscience of endower and endowed.

Another danger which should be largely treated is the spirit of coterie. The breadth of their platform, which admits all sects; and the generality of their plan, which demands all degrees of intellectual culture to begin with, is some security against this. But the ultimate security must be in numbers. Some may say, "already this taint has come upon them, for they are doubtless *transcendentalists.*" But to mass a few protestants together and call them transcendentalists, is a popular cant. Transcendentalism belongs to no sect of religion, and no social party. It is the common ground to which all sects may rise, and be purified of their narrowness; for it consists in seeking the spiritual ground of all manifestations. As already in the pages of this periodical, Calvinist, and Unitarian, and Episcopalian, and Baptist, and Quaker, and Swedenborgian, have met and spoken in love and freedom, on this common basis; so it would be seen, if the word were understood, that transcendentalism, notwithstanding its name is taken in vain by many moonshiny youths and misses who assume it, would be the best of all guards against the spirit of coterie. Much as we respect our friends of the community, we dare not hope for them quite so much, as to aver that they *transcend,* as yet, all the limitations that separate men from love and mutual trust.

Serene will be our days and bright,
And happy will our nature be,
When Love is an unerring light
And Joy its own security.
And blest are they who in the main
This faith, even now, do entertain;
Live in the spirit of this creed;
Yet find the *strength of Love* according to their need!

We had intended to subjoin some further remarks, by way of inquiry, into the possibility of other portions of society, not able to emancipate themselves from the thraldom of city life, beginning also to act, in a degree, on the principles of cooperation. Ameliorations of present evils, initiations into truer life, may be made we believe everywhere. Worldly wisdom, for its own purposes, avails itself of what is outward in the community plan; at least of the labor-saving element. Why may not the children of light be equally wise?

There may be some persons, at a distance, who will ask, to what degree has this community gone into operation? We cannot answer this with precision, for we do not write as organs of this association, and have reason to feel, that if we applied to them for information, they would refuse it, out of their dislike to appear in public. We desire this to be distinctly understood. But we can see, and think we have a right to say, that it has purchased the Farm, which some of its members cultivated for a year with success, by way of trying their love and skill for agricultural labor;–that in the only house they are as yet rich enough to own, is collected a large family, including several boarding scholars, and that all work and study together. They seem to be glad to know of all, who desire to join them in the spirit, that at any moment, when they are able to enlarge their habitations, they may call together those that belong to them.

[Orestes A. Brownson]

"Brook Farm," *United States Magazine, and Democratic Review,* 11 (November 1842): 481-496.

> *Bronson's article (from which material not related to Brook Farm has been omitted) includes a positive letter from a visitor to the community which gives a good picture of the daily life there.*

The subjoined letter from a highly esteemed friend and distinguished literary lady, giving some notice of Brook Farm, or the Community at West Roxbury, Mass., was addressed to me while Editor of the Boston Quarterly Review, and would have appeared in the last number of that journal, but for the want of room. This will explain its personal address and allusions. It is laid before the readers of the Democratic Review, because its details can hardly fail to interest them, and because it gives me an opportunity to offer some additional remarks on the importance of establishments like that of Brook Farm, in working out the moral, intellectual, and physical amelioration of mankind, especially of the poorest and most numerous class.

. . . .

It is proper, however, to remark, that Brook Farm is not an establishment for the indolent, nor for those who are in need of charity. It is an INDUSTRIAL ESTABLISHMENT. Industry is its basis and its object. It is established on the principle that man must obtain his bread by the sweat of his face. This must be borne in mind in attempting like establishments. The founder of this establishment very justly remarks: "Every community should have its leading purpose, some one main object to which it directs its energies. We are a company of teachers. The branch of industry which we pursue as our primary object, and chief means of support, is teaching. Others may be companies of manufacturers or of agriculturists; or may engage in some particular branch of manufacture or of agriculture. Whatever the branch of industry agreed upon, it will be necessary to make that the principal object of pursuit, as the only way in which unity and efficiency can be secured to the labors of the community."

Of the advantages of associated and attractive industry there is no occasion to speak. They are well known, and have been ably presented by Mr. Brisbane, in the pages of this Journal and elsewhere. The common merit, and the chief merit of the schemes of Owen and Fourier, is in their proposing associated and attractive industry. These Mr. Ripley secures at Brook Farm, without their complicated machinery, and multiplicity of details,–of details often frivolous; at any rate foreign to the habits, tastes, and convictions of the American people. Families of moderate means associating in this way, by their union and cooperation may obtain an industrial and pecuniary independence to which they cannot aspire under existing social relations. What we most want, is such an arrangement as shall secure to every man a competence as the reward of his industry, and which shall render industry in any or all of its branches compatible with the highest moral and intellectual culture, and the greatest delicacy and refinement of manners. This we cannot have as things are; but this by means of association on the principles of the Brook Farm establishment we may have. And when once this is obtained, when I am once sure that by the labor of my hands I can earn an honest and *honorable* livelihood, and without being obliged to forego any of the real advantages, pleasures, and refinements of society and social intercourse, I shall no longer feel that I was cursed by my Maker, when he commanded me to "eat my bread in the sweat of my face."

. . . .

"August, 1842.

"MY DEAR SIR: I have made my visit to the Community, as it is called, at West Roxbury, and find that it more than answers the expectation held out in that account of it, which appeared in the Dial last January. I mean that the degree of success already attained, is greater than it was there intimated it could be, for many years to come. In a pecuniary point of view it is not failing, and that is success, considering the great embarrassments under which they began. There are seventeen associates. Had each of these been able to contribute one thousand dollars a-piece, they would be at this moment under no embarrassment at all, but instead of that, not one third of the sum was contributed. For the cost of their farm, as I understood it, they are paying interest; but by means of the farm and the school, they are able to pay this interest and to *feed* themselves; although there are seventy people already there, and the number will be one hundred in the course of the winter. The joining of a few associates or even one with some money, would render them quite independent. But they feel they have gained so much morally and intellectually, by having been so poor, as to have had none join but those to whom the accomplishment of the *Idea* appears worth working and suffering for, that it is no longer to be feared, that they will be tempted to receive among them any, of whom money is the chief recommendation. They prefer to sacrifice many conveniences, to endangering the social and ideal character of their company. Several mechanics who have been hired to do jobs upon the place, I mean carpenters, blacksmiths, shoemakers, tailors, have at first expressed themselves amazed, that people should go together, of such apparent inequality, and make a common cause, and share the fruits of their labors equally among themselves; but after seeing the operation for weeks, they have desired to join, and to forego some of the income they were already receiving from their trades, in order to have the enjoyment, the moral advantage, and the intellectual improvement, of a social life on principles so consistently democratic and Christian; and more especially, in order to have all their children have every advantage of education to which their abilities can do jus-

tice. I speak of facts. The association has actually under consideration such propositions. Also, one of the farmers, the most thriving one, whose farm joins theirs, has for the sake of his children made them the offer, if they can meet him half way, of throwing in his farm and becoming one. He would be richer in dollars and cents to remain as he is, but this additional money could not buy for him that education of all his children, which he must receive in this community, if he is one of them; to say nothing of his own enjoyment and improvement. To me, it is an inspiring thought, that they have already showed to the agricultural population around them, that with the cultivation of the earth may be combined an intellectual and tasteful life, and that the true democratic equality may be obtained by *levelling up*, instead of *levelling down*.

But let me speak of the education in detail, and show that the children of the actual associates have even greater advantages than those sent there, though for the latter, it is, I think, the best school I ever saw. I will begin with the a-b-c-d-arians. There is one lady among the associates, who loves to keep a regular school on the old-fashioned plan, with a kind but efficient discipline of rules and lessons. She has as many of the younger scholars as the parents wish. But some parents prefer a different system—in which their children are only confined a very short time, while they can be individually attended to by the teacher. And there are among the young women, several who take two or three at once—making one little class, and enlist their undivided, unwavering attention for an hour, or an hour and a half, and then let them play all the rest of the day. These children, in this way, get more instruction and do more intellectual work, than in ordinary schools, and yet have none of the weariness and bad physical and moral effect of confinement. They are never obliged to sit still and do nothing; nor do they in this plan become troublesome to others. There is so much room, they can spread round, and find infinite amusement on the place. I never saw children at once so happy and so little in the way of other people. There seemed to be great love for the little things, in all the men and boys, as well as the women; and I observed that when the young men went to walk in the woods, or about any out-of-door occupation, they would let two or three children go too, and keep their eye upon them, and so relieve the mothers and make the children happy, and this without troubling themselves either. Children from the ages of nine or ten up

Josiah Wolcott's painting of Brook Farm (Massachusetts Historical Society)

to thirteen and fourteen, go to the school of a gentleman who has been a very successful teacher for many years, and understands the drilling processes. But of this class also, if there are any, whose parents, on account of their health, or peculiar genius, or sex, wish to receive separate attention, there are found those who will attend to them in a very desirable way. Then there is a very fine teacher of Greek, and another of Latin, and another of Mathematics, among the gentlemen associates. Several teach German, French, Italian and Spanish, and I do not know how many other things. One lady has classes in History, Moral Philosophy, various branches of elegant literature, and with all her cares, (one of which is the care of a house of fourteen rooms), she told me she had not for more than a year set aside two recitations! This will show what real method lies under the graceful exterior, where not mathematical lines, but only the curves of beauty appear. This lady told me, too, that never in her life had she had so much leisure and enjoyment of herself, for hours together, and never had the occupations of life been so little fatiguing to her.

I would have you observe that grown up persons, as well as children, are members of these various classes. The workmen in the field partake just as much as they please, of these means of education. One man, who does as much hard work, if not more than any one on the place, and who never learnt any language, and is forty years old, a husband and father, having been engaged in a mechanical trade all his life, studied German last winter, on Ollendorf's method, with the greatest perseverance. They had eighty recitations a week, last winter. All have access also to all the books owned by any of the members, the most of them being collected in a charming room, designated as the "Library," of which all are free, young and old.

In another common parlor there is a pianoforte, and there, in the evening, the lovers of music congregate, and hear fine music from some of their number, sometimes songs, and sometimes psalms, and sometimes the deep music of Beethoven. Mr. J. S. D[wight]. superintends the musical department of the teaching. The very little children have to sing by rote; those who are old enough, are taught by the Manual of the Academy of Music. Instrumental music is also taught to all who have the ability and the desire to learn. It struck me how beautiful it would be, if some of those noble Italian exiles should go and join their number, who could throw in their music and their beautiful language, and receive in return the realization of the dreams of their youth; but all this will come in good time.

To go back to the children. The greatest advantage is, that the life is so natural, it makes a discipline without the ugly forms. Every body works and studies, and so the children work and study from imitation and in spirit. I never saw such habits of disinterestedness–so little personal selfishness. Children were requested by all parties to do all sorts of things; and if one had refused, another would only have been called upon, as the only rebuke. The punishment of appearing selfish, and not being in the general spirit, precludes all others. Of course, I do not mean to imply that any circumstances of social arrangement will destroy all moral evil. I know there are those which originate in the constitution of every finite creature, and which are only to be set aside in their principles and consequences, by a deep internal struggle, where there is no witness but God, by whose sovereign mercy alone is the great victory accomplished, and each individual introduced into "the company of the first born." But there are innumerable social vices, and deformities of character, which are exasperated, if not produced, by the unsanctified conventions of our common life, and which here do not appear; and there is no telling how much more those who are good have the advantage of their goodness, and those who are morally inferior are assisted, by living where there is such a general spirit and such habits among the adults. Country employments and country scenery, too, has an immeasurable effect upon children's tempers. I would repeat, that I am not one of those who believe that the issues of the human constitution, under any earthly circumstances, can be perfect goodness;–that finite creatures can ever be other than *pensioners* of the Love revealed in Jesus Christ; but I do believe that infancy and youth would shine with moral beauty, as a general rule, if society and education did their part. Some people seem to be dreadfully afraid that God will not have anything to forgive, and so the doctrine of forgiveness be proved unnecessary, if we admit that children can grow up, unselfish in their habits and lovely in their general characters. Such persons have, it seems to me, very little appreciation of the depth, and extent, and excellence of that Law, the violation of which is sin; for it seems to me that we may be very high in the scale of excellence, in the eyes of

our fellow creatures; your faults may be not even perceptible to them; and yet we may be so far below that Ideal, which shines into us from God, that we shall yet require all the comfort of St. Paul's doctrine of justification by faith. I see less self-righteousness likely to be generated, under the views and habits of this community, than ordinarily; and to stand a better chance of being corrected. Should man, in the progress of wisdom and love, be elevated above all social crime and wrong, there will yet, as I think, be sin possible to him, great enough to have him feel the whole opposition between the law of finite natures, and that Law of the Infinite God, which Christ mysteriously reveals to him, as a glory to be had.

This is rather an episode in my letter, dear sir, but I must needs dwell a little upon the subject, because the majority of people I hear talk, seem to be in one of two extremes, equally erroneous. One set of people make no evil but social evil, and seem to think that if wars and theft and deception, are driven from the earth, the whole holiness and glory of humanity is attained, even up to the measure of Christ Jesus; while others think, that because the Bible and the Spirit of God within us teach that man, even when pure as the heaven or heavens, is not clean BEFORE God, he must necessarily unfold, in the process of his development, all the crimes to which he can be degraded; and that a systematical effort to prevent this, by removing occasions and exasperating causes of crime, is opposing the systems of Providence, and practically denying the philosophy of Christianity. I have heard it gravely urged against this little community, that it aimed at a state of enjoyment and general excellence, which would result, if it succeeded, in a state contrary to what the Bible declares to be the general character of human nature. I dispute the fact. I believe human nature may attain to a state of excellence that shall seem to realize Isaiah's visions of the millenium, and still the inhabitants of the earth will be even more disposed to use, with respect to themselves, the deepest language of contrition and humility which the Bible contains; for then they shall *see God*, by reason of their purity, so much more, that they shall still more earnestly feel the prayer,

"Forgive our *virtues* too–
Those lesser faults–half converts to the right."

It is because I think thus, that I do not condemn utterly that other class of errorists, who suppose evil so very superficial; and that if we could eschew bad organization of society, and act out our instincts, we should be as perfect, as human beings, as the animal creation is perfect in *its* way, and the vegetable creation in *its* way. In their faith in the better issues of human instincts under favorable circumstances, they go upon a fact. Human nature is capable of great excellence, beauty, and purity, when it draws only upon the original gifts of the good God of nature, common to all men; and there is a sort of blasphemy to me, in speaking irreverently of the virtues of Solon and Aristides, Anaxagoras, and Plato, and Socrates; of Regulus, and Brutus, and the Antonines; and even of many a beautiful child and adult of the present day, although he has not yet entered into all the depths of the unsearchable riches of Christ. To be arrested at the point of attainment of any of these persons, would indeed be *to be damned,* (if I may use old-fashioned phraseology). Such minds we may call *a sort of heaven.* But I think these persons would say, that to be condemned to an everlasting self-development in that same heaven, and receive nothing from without, or from the deeper *within* which is *a without* to the individual; in short, to have no more grace of God, would make it to them a hell. Indeed, the Swedenborgian hells are neither more nor less than for the individual to be given up to his individuality; and so Swedenborg says that the damned are often not without their enjoyments; which whole system shows how deeply he looked into things. But what is such enjoyment to the action upon an infinite good? The joy of immortality, and the only doctrine of immortality which is not a misnomer, consists in believing that man never is absorbed in the Infinite, but is CONSCIOUSLY RELATIVE for ever and ever. This is, if I read it aright, your own doctrine of life, as you have stated it in your letter to Dr. Channing, which I believe people do not understand, because you have couched it so much in theological formulas, that they do not see it to be something they have not thought.

At Brook Farm there may be more inclination to the error of believing that self-development, on the original stock of human nature, is the true way, than to the equal error of supposing it necessary to undervalue and be unfaithful to this original stock, which prevails in the world. But there are those there, who are the predominating life and strength of the place, who transcend both errors; and there is nothing in the plan of their life which favors either.

But I will leave moralizing and theologizing, and return to an account of what I saw in my visit.

With respect to the labor, which is the material wealth of the establishment, and the body of its life, they intend to have all trades and occupations which contribute to necessities and healthy elegancies, within their own borders, so as not to buy them from without, which is too expensive; but at present their labor is agriculture, and the simplest housekeeping. They have above a dozen cows that they take care of, and sell all their milk at the door; they cultivate vegetables extensively, and sell them in the markets of Roxbury and Boston, and this branch of their industry may be almost indefinitely extended. They cultivate grass also, and sell hay very profitably. I do not know about their grain, not being wise enough in those matters to understand what I saw. The farm is not wholly under cultivation, because they have not yet force enough to do all they wish. Fifty more men might be profitably employed on it. Teachers, scholars, and all, work. Their Greek teacher spends several hours a day in taking care of the fruit, which hereafter, they think, will constitute a great part of their wealth. Every one prescribes his own hours of labor, controlled only by his conscience, and the spirit of place, which tends to great industry, and almost to too much exertion. A drone would soon find himself isolated and neglected, and could not live there. The new comers, especially if they come from the city, have to begin gradually, but soon learn to increase the labor of one hour a day in the field, to six or seven hours, and some work all day long; but there can be no drudgery where there is no constraint. As all eat together, they change their dress for their meals; and so after tea they are all ready for grouping, in the parlors of the ladies, or in the library, or in the music-room, or they can go to their private rooms, or into the woods, or anywhere. They visit a good deal; and when they have business out of the community, nothing seems more easy than for them to arrange with others of their own number, to take their work or teaching for the time being; so that while they may work more than people out of the community, none seem such prisoners of their duties. The association of labor makes distribution according to taste and ability easy, and this takes the sting out of fatigue. Then I believe bodily labor does not fatigue so much, when the mind is active and elevated by noble sentiments; and certainly, intelligence and the spirit of improvement, give the advantage of saving themselves drudgery, by all the devices of our mechanical age. Perhaps they might go into vagaries in labor-saving expedients, but that their narrow pecuniary means checks all freakishness of mind in this respect. They put their hands to the plough in good earnest, and do their work by main strength, and not by stratagem. As the pupils work more or less, it makes the school a most desirable one for farmers' children; and I hope many a young man will be saved to the healthy pursuits of agricultural life, by this establishment, whose laudable desire for intellectual improvement and for bettering his condition in life, would drive him into our crowded professions and city warehouses.

For the women, there is, besides many branches of teaching, washing and ironing, housekeeping, sewing for the other sex, and for the children, and conducting all the social life. They have to hire one washerwoman now, but hope, bye and bye, to do all the washing within themselves. By the wide distribution of these labors, no one has any great weight of any one thing. They iron every forenoon but one; but they take turns, and each irons as long as she thinks right. The care of the houses is also distributed among those who are most active, in a way mutually satisfactory. And so of the cooking. In nothing did they seem to feel so immediate a desirableness of improvement, as in the kitchen department, and the eating rooms. These are all in the old house, and not at all convenient. Their next building is to be a kitchen establishment, and convenient dining hall, which will enable them to appear much more to advantage; besides leaving the old house, which they called *"the Hive,"* to be entirely used for sleeping rooms and parlors. A more spacious and convenient dining-hall will enable them to be less confused and more elegant at table, than which nothing is more important for the general tone of manners. There is no vulgarity now, because all the people have the sentiment and desire of improvement; but many have not been in society, and these need to have things so arranged that the table manners of the more educated and best bred should have a chance to be observed, and do their work of refinement. The manners of the children also can then be more easily attended to; and when this is brought about it seems to me that in the article of elegance they will not fall behind the rest of the world. Without any wearisome etiquette there would be the beauty that naturally hovers round "plain living and high thinking"; and of which nothing now hinders the full development, but their crowded and inconvenient

eating apartments. I ought to say that though a common table is preferable to most, yet any individual family, by taking the trouble on themselves, can have some or all of their meals at their own rooms; and now any individuals who wish, on account of ill health or for any other reason, to take a meal alone, can easily do so; and constantly there are those who are thus favored. You would hardly imagine that so many individuals should have their own way so constantly without clashing. For a time they did not have any regular housekeeper, but this office passed from one to the other; for they were afraid that the pride and tyranny of office might interfere with the freedom of individuals, and they preferred the inconveniences of frequent change, to the evil of that fixed vexation. But at last a housekeeper appeared, so *fit,* that they created for her the office! This woman went out to sew for them a week as a sempstress, during which time she used her eyes and ears and mind to such purpose that at the end of the week she wanted to join. The associates proposed that she should remain two months, without committing herself; and then, if she continued in the same mind, she should be considered to have joined from the first. During these two months she employed herself variously, and showed so much delicacy and tact, as well as ability and housekeeping talent, that they all agreed that she should be queen in that department, and they would obey. I do not know what measures they would take to dethrone her if she should grow naughty, but at present she reigns by the greatest of King Alfred's titles, the divine right of might and virtue.

I do not seem to myself to have told you a moiety of the good which I saw; I have only indicated some of it. But is it not enough to justify me in saying they have succeeded? It seems to me, if their highest objects were appreciated, they would challenge some of the devotedness which makes the Sisters of Charity throw large fortunes into their institution, and give themselves, body and soul, to its duties. It is truly a most religious life, and does it not realize in miniature that identity of church and state which you think is the deepest idea of our American government? It seems to me that this community, point by point, corresponds with the great community of the Republic, whose divine lineaments are so much obscured by the rubbish of reported abuses (that, however, only lie on the surface, and may be shaken off, "like dewdrops from the lion's mane";) and whose divine proportions are now lost to our sight by the majestic grandeur with which they tower beyond the apprehension of our time-bound senses. For the theory of our government also proposes education (the freest development of the individual, according to the law of God) as its main end; an equal distribution of the results of labor among the laborers, as its means; and a mutual respect of each man by his neighbor as the basis. Only in America, I think, could such a community have so succeeded as I have described, composed of persons coming by chance, as it were, from all circumstances of life, and united only by a common idea and plan of life. They have succeeded, because they are the children of a government the ideal of which is the same as their own, although, as a mass, we are unconscious of it; so little do we understand our high vocation, and act up to it. But these miniatures of the great original shall educate us to the apprehension and realization of it, as a nation.

Some people make objection to this community, because it has no chapel in it. But I think this is an excellent feature of it. There are churches all round it, to which any can go as they please; and there has been service within it, which such might attend as were not pleased with any neighboring church; and this might be resumed if there were not seen to be a general preference in the church-goers to go out. The children are gathered on Sundays spontaneously, to sing hymns, the natural devotion of children, and to be read to by those who wish to do so; and there is a perfect freedom to do anything for social religious worship, that is felt desirable, by any, provided only nothing is prescribed to another authoritatively.

I meant to have asked you in some detail whether it would not be possible for this community system to be introduced into our cities by persons of different employments who were willing to associate, and thrown in their small capitals, combining and living together in some large hotel, or block of houses, agreeably situated, and perhaps having a country house attached? I have no head to make arrangements, but I should like much to have such a thing planned out. What do you think?

I am truly your friend, &c., &c.

Charles Lane.
"American Correspondence," *New Age,* 1 (1 September 1843): 90.

This letter from Lane describes his visit to Brook Farm with Alcott and refers to their own work at Fruitlands.

Our friend Charles Lane writes to us, from Fruitlands, Harvard, Massachusetts, dated July 30, 1843, as follows, which we trust will be interesting to many of our readers:–

"Mr. Alcott and I returned last evening from a short visit to Boston, to purchase a few articles; and while there we went out one evening to Roxbury, where there are eighty or ninety persons playing away their youth and day-time in a miserably joyous frivolous manner. There are not above four or five who could be selected as really and truly progressing beings. Most of the adults are there to pass "a good time"; the children are taught languages, &c. The animals occupy a prominent position, there being no less than sixteen cows, besides four oxen, a herd of swine, a horse or two, &c. The milk is sold in Boston, and they buy butter, to the extent of 500 dollars a year. We had a pleasant summer evening conversation with many of them, but it is only in a few individuals that anything deeper than ordinary is to be found. The Northampton Community is one of industry–the one at Hopedale aims at practical theology–this of Roxbury is one of taste; yet it is the best which exists here, and perhaps we shall have to say it is the best which can exist. At all events, we can go no further than to keep open fields, and, as far as we have it, open house to *all* comers. We know very well that if they come not in the right name and nature, they will not long remain. Our dietetic system is a test quite sufficient for many. As far as acres of fine land are concerned, you may offer their free use to any free souls who will come here and work them, and any aid we can offer shall be freely given. The aid of sympathetic companionship is not small, and that at least we can render. To bridge the Atlantic is a trifle, if the heart is really set on the attainment of better conditions. Here are they freely presented, at a day's walk from the shore, without a long and expensive journey to the West. Please to advertize these facts to all youthful men and women, for such are much wanted here. There is now a certain opportunity for planting a love colony, the influence of which may be felt for many generations, and more than felt: it may be the beginning for a state of things which shall far transcend itself. They to whom our work seems not good enough, may come and set out a better.

"I could send you a description of works and crops–our mowing, hoeing, reaping, ploughing in tall crops of clover and grass for next year's manure, and various other operations; but although they have some degree of relation to the grand principle to which they are obedient, they are worth little in the exoteric sense alone. Perhaps the internal revelations of success ought always to be kept secret, for every improvement discovered is only turned to a money-Bmaking account, and to the further degradation of man, as we see in the march of science to this very moment. If we knew how to double the crops of the earth, it is scarcely to be hoped that any good would come by revealing the mode. On the contrary, the bounties of God are already made the means by which man debases himself more and more. We will, therefore, say little concerning the sources of external wealth, until man is himself secured to the End which rightly uses these means."

Should any of our friends consider emigration a favourable step towards human elevation, and be disposed to avail themselves of the above invitation of our friend Charles Lane, we shall be happy to advise with such parties, and enter into such arrangements as will render the undertaking easy to be put in practice.– *Editor.*

C[harles] L[ane]

"Brook Farm," *Dial,* 4 (January 1844); 351-357.

Lane complains here about the lack of "oneness of spirit" in the Brook Farm community, but this
may simply be a projection of his own feelings about the impending failure of Fruitlands.

Wherever we recognize the principle of progress, our sympathies and affections are engaged. However small may be the innovation, however limited the effort towards the attainment of pure good, that effort is worthy of our best encouragement and succor. The Institution at Brook Farm, West Roxbury, though sufficiently extensive in respect to number of persons, perhaps is not to be considered an experiment of large intent. Its aims are moderate; too humble indeed to satisfy the extreme demands of the age; yet, for that reason probably, the effort is more valuable, as likely to exhibit a larger share of actual success.

Though familiarly designated a "Community," it is only so in the process of eating in commons; a practice at least, as antiquated, as the collegiate halls of old England, where it still continues without producing, as far as we can learn, any of the Spartan virtues. A residence at Brook Farm does not involve either a community of money, of opinions, or of sympathy. The motives which bring individuals there, may be as various as their numbers. In fact, the present residents are divisible into three distinct classes; and if the majority in numbers were considered, it is possible that a vote in favor of self-sacrifice for the common good would not be strongly carried. The leading portion of the adult inmates, they whose presence imparts the greatest peculiarity and the fraternal tone to the household, believe that an improved state of existence would be developed in association, and are therefore anxious to promote it. Another class consists of those who join with the view of bettering their condition, by being exempted from some portion of worldly strife. The third portion, comprises those who have their own development or educaton, for their principal object. Practically, too, the institution manifests a threefold improvement over the world at large, corresponding to these three motives. In consequence of the first, the companionship, the personal intercourse, the social bearing are of a marked, and very superior character. There may possibly, to some minds, long accustomed to other modes, appear a want of homeness, and of the private fireside; but all observers must acknowledge a brotherly and softening condition, highly conducive to the permanent, and pleasant growth of all the better human qualities. If the life is not of a deeply religious cast, it is at least not inferior to that which is exemplified elsewhere; and there is the advantage of an entire absence of assumption and pretence. The moral atmosphere so far is pure; and there is found a strong desire to walk ever on the mountain tops of life; though taste, rather than piety, is the aspect presented to the eye.

In the second class of motives, we have enumerated, there is a strong tendency to an important improvement in meeting the terrestrial necessities of humanity. The banishment of servitude, the renouncement of hireling labor, and the elevation of all unavoidable work to its true station, are problems whose dissociate systems have in vain sought remedies for this unfavorable portion of human condition. It is impossible to introduce into separate families even one half of the economies, which the present state of science furnished to man. In that particular, it is probable that even the feudal system is superior to the civic; for its combinations permit many domestic arrangements of an economic character, which are impractible in small households. In order to economize labor, and dignify the laborer, it is absolutely necessary that men should cease to work in the present isolate competitive mode, and adopt that of cooperative union or association. It is as ruinous to call any man 'master' in secular business, as

Margaret Fuller Cottage at Brook Farm

it is in theological opinions. Those persons, therefore, who congregate for the purpose, as it is called, of bettering their outward relations, on principles so high and universal as we have endeavored to describe, are not engaged in a petty design, bounded by their own selfish or temporary improvement. Every one who is here found giving up the usual chances of individual aggrandizement, may not be thus influenced; but whether it be so or not, the outward demonstration will probably be equally certain.

In education, Brook Farm appears to present greater mental freedom than most other institutions. The tuition being more heart-rendered, is in its effects more heart-stirring. The younger pupils as well as the more advanced students are held, mostly if not wholly, by the power of love. In this particular, Brook farm is a much improved model for the oft-praised schools of New England. It is time that the imitative and book-learned systems of the latter should be superseded or liberalized by some plan, better calculated to excite originality of thought, and the native energies of the mind. The deeper, kindly sympathies of the heart, too,

should not be forgotten; but the germination of these must be despaired of under a rigid hireling system. Hence, Brook farm, with its spontaneous teachers, presents the unusual and cheering condition of a really "free school."

By watchful and diligent economy, there can be no doubt that a community would attain greater pecuniary success, than is within the hope of honest individuals working separately. But Brook Farm is not a Community, and in the variety of motives with which persons associate there, a double diligence, and a watchfulness perhaps too costly, will be needful to preserve financial prosperity. While, however, this security is an essential element in success, riches would, on the other hand, be as fatal as poverty to the true progress of such an institution. Even in the case of those foundations which have assumed a religious character, all history proves the fatality of wealth. The just and happy mean between riches and poverty is, indeed, more likely to be attained when, as in this instance, all thought of acquiring great wealth in a brief time, is necessarily abandoned, as a condition of membership. On the other hand, the presence of many persons, who congregate merely for the attainment of some individual end, must weigh heavily and unfairly upon those whose hearts are really expanded to universal results. As a whole, even the initiative powers of Brook Farm have, as is found almost every where, the design of a life much too objective, too much derived from objects in the exterior world. The subjective life, that in which the soul finds the living source and the true communion within itself, is not sufficiently prevalent to impart to the establishment the permanent and sedate character it should enjoy. Undeniably, many devoted individuals are there; several who have as generously as wisely relinquished what are considered great social and pecuniary advantages; and by throwing their skill and energies into a course of the most ordinary labors, at once prove their disinterestedness, and lay the foundation of industrial nobility.

An assemblage of persons, not brought together by the principles of community, will necessarily be subject to many of the inconveniences of ordinary life, as well as to burdens peculiar to such a condition. Now Brook Farm is at present such an institution. It is not a community: it is not truly an association: it is merely an aggregation of persons, and lacks that oneness of spirit, which is probably needful to make it of deep and lasting value to mankind. It seems, even after three years continuance, uncertain, whether it is to be resolved more into an educational, or an industrial institution, or into one combined of both. Placed so near a large city, and in a populous neighborhood, the original liability for land, &c. was so large, as still to leave a considerable burden of debt. This state of things seems fairly to entitle the establishment to re-draw from the old world in fees for education, or in the sale of produce, sufficient to pay the annual interest of such liabilities. Hence the necessity for a more intimate intercourse with the trading world, and a deeper involvement in money affairs than would have attended a more retired effort of the like kind. To enter into the corrupting modes of the world, with the view of diminishing or destroying them, is a delusive hope. It will, notwithstanding, be a labor of no little worth, to induce improvements in the two grand departments of industry and education. We say *improvement,* as distinct from *progress;* for with any association short of community, we do not see how it is possible for an institution to stand so high above the present world, as to conduct its affairs on principles entirely different from those which now influence men in general.

There are other considerations also suggested by a glance at Brook Farm, which are worthy the attention of the many minds now attracted by the deeply interesting subject of human association. We are gratified by observing several external improvements during the past year; such as a larger and a more convenient dining room, a labor-saving cooking apparatus, a purer diet, a more orderly and quiet attendance at the refections, superior arrangements for industry, and generally an increased seriousness in respect to the value of the example, which those who are there assembled may constitute to their fellow beings.

Of about seventy persons now assembled there, about thirty are children sent thither for education; some adult persons also place themselves there chiefly for mental assistance; and in the society there are only four married couples. With such materials it is almost certain that the sensitive and vital points of communication cannot well be tested. A joint-stock company, working with some of its own members and with others as agents, cannot bring to issue the great question, whether the existence of the marital family is compatible with that of the universal family, which the term "Community" signifies. This is now the grand problem. By mothers it has ever been felt to be so. The maternal instinct, as hitherto educated, has declared itself so strongly in favor of the separate fire-side, that association, which appears so beautiful to the young and unattached soul, has yet accomplished little progress in the affections of that important section of the human race—the mothers. With fathers, the feeling in favor of the separate family is certainly less strong; but there is an undefinable tie, a sort of magnetic *rapport,* an invisible, inseverable, umbilical chord between the mother and child, which in most cases circumscribes her desires and ambition to her own immediate family. All the accepted adages and wise saws of society, all the precepts of morality, all the sanctions of theology, have for ages been employed to confirm this feeling. This is the chief corner stone of present society; and to this maternal instinct have, till very lately, our most heartfelt appeals been made for the progress of the human race, by means of a deeper and more vital education. Pestalozzi and his most enlightened disciples are distinguished by this sentiment. And are we all at once to abandon, to deny, to destroy this supposed stronghold of virtue? Is it questioned whether the family arrangement of mankind is to be preserved? Is it discovered that the sanctuary, till now deemed the holiest on earth, is to be invaded by intermeddling skepticism, and its altars sacrilegiously destroyed by the rude hands of innovating progress? Here "social science" must be brought to issue. The question of association and of marriage are one. If, as we have been popularly led to believe, the individual or separate family is in the true order of Providence, then the associative life is a false effort. If the associative life is true, then is the separate family a false arrangement. By the maternal feeling, it appears to be decided that the coexistence of both is incompatible, is impossible. So also say some religious sects. Social science ventures to assert their harmony. This is the grand problem now remaining to be solved, for at least, the enlightening, if not for the vital elevation of humanity. That the affections can be divided or bent with equal ardor on two objects, so opposed as universal and individual love, may at least be rationally doubted. History has not yet exhibited such phenomena in an associate body, and scarcely perhaps in any individual. The monasteries and convents, which have existed in all ages, have been maintained solely by the annihilation of that peculiar affection on which the separate family is based. The Shaker families, in which the two sexes are not entirely dissociated, can yet only maintain their union by forbidding and preventing the growth of personal affection other than that of a spiritual character. And this in fact is not personal in the sense of individual, but ever a manifestation of universal affection. Spite of the speculations of hopeful bachelors and aesthetic spinsters, there is somewhat in the marriage bond which is found to counteract the universal nature of the affections, to a degree tending at least to make the considerate

pause, before they assert that, by any social arrangements whatever, the two can be blended into one harmony. The general condition of married persons at this time is some evidence of the existence of such a doubt in their minds. Were they as convinced as the unmarried of the beauty and truth of associate life, the demonstration would be now presented. But might it not be enforced that the two family ideas really neutralize each other? Is it not quite certain that the human heart cannot be set in two places; that man cannot worship at two altars? It is only the determination to do what parents consider the best for themselves and their families, which renders the o'er populous world such a wilderness of selfhood as it is. Destroy this feeling, they say, and you prohibit every motive to exertion. Much truth is there in this affirmation. For to them, no other motive remains, nor indeed to any one else, save that of the universal good, which does not permit the building up of supposed self-good; and therefore, forecloses all possibility of an individual family.

These observations, of course, equally apply to all the associative attempts, now attracting so much public attention; and perhaps most especially to such as have more of Fourier's designs than are observable at Brook Farm. The slight allusion in all the writers of the "Phalansterian" class, to the subject of marriage, is rather remarkable. They are acute and eloquent in deploring Woman's oppressed and degraded position in past and present times, but are almost silent as to the future. In the mean while, it is gratifying to observe the successes which in some departments attend every effort, and that Brook Farm is likely to become comparatively eminent in the highly important and praiseworthy attempts, to render labor of the hands more dignified and noble, and mental education more free and loveful.

[George Ripley]
"Introductory Notice," *Harbinger*, 1 (14 June 1845): 8-10.

The Harbinger *was the official paper of the Brook Farm community. Eight volumes were published between 14 June 1845 and 10 February 1849, the last three volumes by the American Union of Associationists in New York City, as Brook Farm collapsed. George Ripley was its primary editor. Unfortunately for students of the history of Brook Farm, the* Harbinger *was more interested in promoting associationism–the organization of men into harmonious working groups–than it was in promoting Brook Farm, and articles on the community itself are scarce. In this piece, Ripley articulates his objectives and goals for the paper.*

In meeting our friends, for the first time, in the columns of the Harbinger, we wish to take them by the hand with cheerful greetings, to express the earnest hope that our intercourse may be as fruitful of good, as it will be frank and sincere, and that we to-day may commence a communion of spirit, which shall mutually aid us in our progress towards the truth and beauty, the possession of which is the ultimate destiny of man. We address ourselves to the aspiring and free minded youth of our country; to those whom long experience has taught the emptiness of past attainments and inspired with a better hope; to those who cherish a living faith in the advancement of humanity, whose inner life consists not in doubting, questioning, and denying, but in believing; who, resolute to cast off conventional errors and prejudices, are hungering and thirsting for positive truth; and who, with reliance on the fulfilment of the prophetic voice in the heart of man, and on the Universal Providence of God, look forward to an order of society founded on the divine principles of justice and love, to a future age of happiness, harmony, and of great glory to be realized on earth. We have attained, in our own minds, to firm and clear convictions, in regard to the problems of human destiny; we believe that principles are now in operation, which will produce as great a change on the face of society, as that which caused beauty and order to arise from the chaos of the primitive creation by the movings of the divine Spirit; and to impart these convictions and principles to the hearts of our readers, will be our leading purpose in the columns of this paper.

It will be, then, in the light of positive ideas, not of fanciful conceptions that we shall criticise the cur-

Engraving of George Ripley, the founder of Brook Farm

rent literature, the political movements, the social phenomena of the day; and without inquiring how far we may be in accordance with the prevailing standards of fashion or popular opinion, speak our minds on the subjects we shall discuss, with entire independence of outward authority.

Our faith in the high destiny of man is too profound to allow us to cherish the spirit of antagonism:

we would not destroy but reconstruct; and if our readers expect to find in these pages, the fierce ebullitions of Jacobinical wrath, to be entertained with the virulence of invective against the evils which we condemn, or to be stimulated with the sallies of personal abuse, they will certainly be disappointed. Those who wish to indulge a taste for such condiments, must look elsewhere for its gratification. We trust that ruffian and reformer are not convertible terms;–if they be, we lay no claim to the title of the latter.

We mean to dispense all questions of public interest, with the utmost freedom, and with a single eye to the finding of the whole Truth, being well assured that the whole Truth and the highest Good, are connected in indissoluble union. But we have no desire wantonly to violate any cherished convictions, nor to maintain what is new simply because it is new.–It is our belief that there is much good, mingled with much error, in all the parties and sects both of the Church and of the State, and it is the duty of all persons who sincerely desire to aid in the progress of the human race, not to abandon themselves blindly to one particular doctrine, but to try all and to hold fast that which is good. The time has come for politicians and philanthropists to break the restraints of a barren, one-sided sectarianism, to assume some higher and broader ground, which will enable them to select the good of all partial creeds, to combine it in a consistent and glorious whole. Nor can this process degenerate into a meagre and barren Eclecticism, whenever we take our stand on the broad and universal principles, which the true science of human nature unfolds.

With a deep reverence for the Past, we shall strive so to use its transmitted treasures as to lay in the Present, the foundation of a better Future. Our motto is, the elevation of the whole human race, in mind, morals, and manners, and the means, which in our view are alone adapted to the accomplishment of this end, are not violent outbreaks and revolutionary agitations, but orderly and progressive reform.

In Politics, it will be our object to present fair discussions of the measures of political parties, taking the principles of Justice to all men as our standard of judgment. By sympathy and conviction we are entirely democratic; our faith in democracy is hardly inferior to our faith in humanity; but by democracy we do not understand a slavish adherence to "regular nominations," nor that malignant mobocracy which would reduce to its

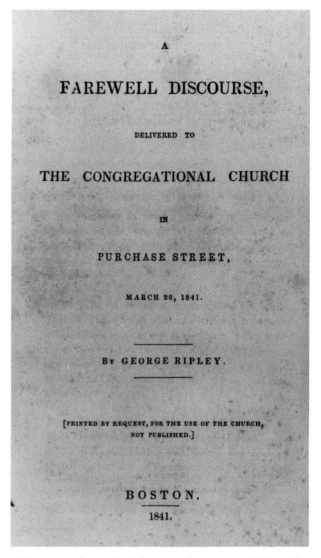

Title page for George Ripley's resignation sermon (1841), delivered when he left to begin Brook Farm

own meanness all who aspire to nobler ends than itself, but that benevolent, exalting, and refining creed, which holds that the great object of government, should be to secure the blessings of Liberty, Intelligence, and Good Order, to the whole people. We believe in the Rights of Man,–best summed up in the right to a perfect development of his whole nature, physical, intellectual, and moral,–and shall oppose partial or class legislation as inconsistent with the fundamental principles of Republican Institutions. Yet we shall take sides with no party, but proceed from time to time to remark upon all parties, with the frankness and independence which our position fully enables us to exercise. If our politicians take offence at what we shall say, the fault will be their own, and our only apology will be a little more severity.–Foreign politics, which are too much neglected by the journals of the country, will be regularly treated by us, in the form of well-digested reviews of the English, French, and German press.

In Literature, besides elaborate notices of new publications, with the aim to inform and improve the taste of the public, and not to gratify the cupidity of booksellers, it is our wish to keep a faithful record of literary intelligence, noticing the most important works that are issued in Europe and this country, and giving brief sketches of the matter of those most generally interesting to the American reader.

The Fine Arts too shall have due honor done them. Music, the Art most appreciable to the many, most associated with the hopes of Humanity, and most flourishing always where Humanity is most alive, we shall watch with almost jealous love; striving not only by criticism of all important musical performances, schools and publications, but also by historical and philosophical essays on the principles of the Art itself, and the creations of its master minds, to keep it true to the standard of pure taste, true to the holy end for which the passion of hearing harmonies was given to man. Painting, Sculpture, Architecture, the Drama, and all arts which seek the Good, by way of the Beautiful, will, we hope, be criticised in practice, and interpreted in theory from the same humanitary and universal point of view. For this end, we shall have correspondents in our principal cities, on whose taste and power of communication we can rely. Summaries of intelligence under this head from Europe too, from countries where Art has a home, will occasionally be offered to our readers. Musical criticism is a thing which has not hitherto existed in our country. Instead of the unmeaning praise, and petty partial censure with which all concerts are alike served up in our newspaper, we would humbly hope to contribute something, if only by our sincerity and impartiality, toward a sound and profitable criticism.

In Science, as far as the limits of a weekly newspaper permit, we shall preserve a record of the most important improvements and discoveries, considered with especial reference to their bearing on the great object of all our labors, the progressive well-being of man.

The interests of Social Reform, will be considered as paramount to all others, in whatever is admitted into the pages of the Harbinger. We shall suffer no attachment to literature, no taste for abstract discussion, no love of purely intellectual theories, to seduce us from our devotion to the cause of the oppressed, the down-trodden, the insulted and injured masses of our fellow men. Every pulsation of our being vibrates in sympathy with the wrongs of the toiling millions, and every wise effort for their speedy enfranchisement will find in us resolute and indomitable advocates. If any imagine from the literary tone of the preceding remarks, that we are indifferent to the radical movement for the benefit of the masses, which is the crowning glory of the nineteenth century, they will soon discover their egregious mistake. To that movement, consecrated by religious principle, sustained by an awful sense of justice, and cheered by the brightest hopes of future good, all our powers, talents, and attainments are devoted. We look for an audience among the refined and educated circles, to which the character of our paper will win its way; but we shall also be read by the swart and sweaty artizan; the laborer will find in us another champion; and many hearts, struggling with the secret hope which no weight of care and toil can entirely suppress, will pour on us their benedictions as we labor for the equal rights of All.

We engage in our enterprise, then, with faith in our cause, with friendship for our readers, with an exulting hope for Humanity, and with a deep conviction which long years of experience have confirmed, that every sincere endeavor for a universal end will not fail to receive a blessing from all that is greatest and holiest in the universe. In the words of the illustrious Swedenborg, which we have selected for the motto of the Harbinger, "all things, at the present day, stand provided and prepared, and await the light. The ship is in the harbor; the sails are swelling; the east wind blows; let us weigh anchor, and put forth to sea."

[George Ripley]
"Fire at Brook Farm," *Harbinger*, 2 (14 March 1846): 220-222.

*Here, Ripley tells the sad story of the fire at the Phalanstery. Brook Farm would come to
an end a year and a half later.*

Our readers have no doubt been informed before
this, of the severe calamity with which the Brook
Farm Association has been visited, by the destruction
of the large unitary edifice which it has been for some
time erecting on its domain. Just as our last paper was
going through the press, on Tuesday evening the 3d
inst., the alarm of fire was given at about a quarter before nine, and it was found to proceed from the "Phalanstery;" in a few minutes, the flames were bursting
through the doors and windows of the second story;
the fire spread with almost incredible rapidity throughout the building; and in about an hour and a half the
whole edifice was burned to the ground. The members
of the Association were on the spot in a few moments,
and made some attempts to save a quantity of lumber
that was in the basement story; but so rapid was the
progress of the fire, that this was found to be impossible, and they succeeded only in rescuing a couple of tool-
chests that had been in use by the carpenters.

The neighboring dwelling-house called the "Eyry"
was in imminent danger, while the fire was at its
height, and nothing but the stillness of the night, and
the vigilance and activity of those who were stationed
on its roof preserved it from destruction. The vigorous
efforts of our nearest neighbors, Mr. T. J. Orange,
and Messrs. Thomas and George Palmer were of
great service in protecting this building, as a part of
our force were engaged in another direction, watching
the workshops, barn, and principal dwelling house.

In a short time, our neighbors from the village of
West Roxbury, a mile and a half distant arrived in
great numbers with their Engine, which together with
the Engines from Jamaica Plain, Newton, and Brook-
line, rendered valuable assistance in subduing the flaming ruins, although it was impossible to check the progress of the fire, until the building was completely

Front page from the official publication of Brook Farm

destroyed. We are under the deepest obligations to
the Fire Companies, which came, some of them, five
or six miles, through deep snow on cross roads, and
did every thing in the power of skill or energy, to preserve our other buildings from ruin. Many of the Engines from Boston came four or five miles from the

city, but finding the fire going down, returned without reaching the spot. The engines from Dedham, we understand, made an unsuccessful attempt to come to our aid, but were obliged to turn back on account of the condition of the roads. No efforts, however, would have probably been successful in arresting the progress of the flames. The building was divided into nearly a hundred rooms in the upper stories, most of which had been lathed for several months, without plaster, and being almost as dry as tinder, the fire flashed through them with terrific rapidity.

There had been no work performed on this building during the winter months, and arrangements had just been made to complete four out of the fourteen distinct suites of apartments into which it was divided, by the first of May. It was hoped that the remainder would be finished during the summer, and that by the first of October, the edifice would be prepared for the reception of a hundred and fifty persons, with ample accommodations for families, and spacious and convenient public halls and saloons. A portion of the second story had been set apart for a Church or Chapel, which was to be finished in a style of simplicity and elegance, by private subscription, and in which it was expected that religious services would be performed by our friend William H. Channing, whose presence with us, until obliged to retire on account of ill health, has been a source of unmingled satisfaction and benefit.

On the Saturday previous to the fire, a stove was put up in the basement story for the accommodation of the carpenters, who were to work on the inside; a fire was kindled in it on Tuesday morning, which burned till four o'clock in the afternoon; at half past eight in the evening, the building was visited by the night watch, who found every thing apparently safe; and at about a quarter before nine, a faint light was discovered in the second story, which was supposed at first to have proceeded from a lamp, but, on entering, to ascertain the fact, the smoke at once showed that the interior was on fire. The alarm was immediately given, but almost before the people had time to assemble, the whole edifice was wrapped in flames. From a defect in the construction of the chimney, a spark from the stove pipe had probably communicated with the surrounding wood work; and from the combustible nature of the materials, the flames spread with a celerity that made every effort to arrest their violence without effect.

This edifice was commenced in the summer of 1844, and has been in progress from that time until No-

vember last, when the work was suspended for the winter, and resumed, as before stated, on the day in which it was consumed. It was built of wood, one hundred and seventy-five feet long, three stories high, with spacious attics, divided into pleasant and convenient rooms for single persons. The second and third stories were divided into fourteen houses, independent of each other, with a parlor and three sleeping rooms in each, connected by piazzas which ran the whole length of the building on both stories. The basement contained a large and commodious kitchen, a dining-hall capable of seating from three to four hundred persons, two public saloons, and a spacious hall or lecture room. Although by no means a model for the Phalanstery, or unitary edifice of a Phalanx, it was well adapted for our purposes at present, situated on a delightful eminence which commanded a most extensive and picturesque view, and affording accommodations and conveniences in the Combined Order, which in many respects, would gratify even a fastidious taste. The actual expenditure upon the building, including the labor performed by the Associates, amounted to about $7,000, and $3,000 more, it was estimated, would be sufficient for its completion. As it was not yet in use by the Association, and until the day of its destruction, not exposed to fire, no insurance had been effected. It was built by investments in our loan stock, and the loss falls upon the holders of partnership stock and the members of the Association.

It is some alleviation of the great calamity which we have sustained, that it came upon us at this time rather than at a later period. The house was not endeared to us by any grateful recollections; the tender and hallowed associations of home had not yet begun to cluster around it; and although we looked upon it with joy and hope as destined to occupy an important sphere in the social movement to which it was consecrated, its destruction does not rend asunder those sacred ties, which bind us to the dwellings that have thus far been the scene of our toils and of our satisfactions. We could not part with either of the houses in which we have operation; and not a look or expression of despondency could have been perceived. The calamity is felt to be great; we do not attempt to conceal from ourselves its consequences; but it has been met with a calmness and high trust, which gives us a new proof of the power of Associated life to quicken the best elements of character, and to prepare men for every emergency.

We shall be pardoned for entering into these almost personal details, for we know that the numerous friends of Association, in every part of our land, will feel our misfortune, as if it were a private grief of their own. We have received nothing but expressions of the most generous sympathy from every quarter, even from those who might be supposed to take the least interest in our purposes; and we are sure that our friends in the cause of Social Unity will share with us the affliction that has visited a branch of their own fraternity.

We have no wish to keep out of sight the magnitude of our loss. In our present infant state, it is a severe trial of our strength. We cannot now calculate its ultimate effect. It may prove more than we are able to bear; or like other previous calamities, it may serve to bind us more closely to each other, and to the holy cause to which we are devoted. We await the result with calm hope, sustained by our faith in the Universal Providence, whose social laws we have endeavored to ascertain and embody in our daily lives.

It may not be improper to state, as we are speaking of our own affairs more fully than we have felt at liberty to do before in the columns of our paper, that, whatever be our trials of an external character, we have every reason to rejoice in the internal condition of our Association. For the few last months, it has more nearly than ever approached the idea of a truly social order. The greatest harmony prevails among us; not a discordant note is heard; a spirit of friendship, of brotherly kindness, of charity, dwells with us and blesses us; our social resources have been greatly multiplied; and our devotion to the cause which has brought us together, receives new strength every day. Whatever may be in reserve for us, we have an infinite satisfaction in the true relations which have united us, and the assurance that our enterprise has sprung from a desire to obey the divine law. We feel assured that no outward disappointment or calamity can chill our zeal for the realization of a divine order of society, or abate our efforts in the sphere which may be pointed out in our best judgment as most favorable to the cause which we have at heart.

[John S. Dwight]
"How Stands the Cause?" *Harbinger,* 3 (7 November 1846): 348-351.

> *Dwight was Ripley's chief assistant at Brook Farm, and his article is a fine example of the be-*
> *lief in social progress which many of the Transcendentalists possessed. (For further information*
> *on this reformer and music critic, see the entry for Dwight in* DLB 1, The American Renais-
> *sance in New England.)*

Since the first flush of enthusiasm with which the idea of Association was newly received in this country, by so many earnest seekers after light respecting the true social destiny of man; since the first memorable conventions in New York and Boston, and the impulse thereby given to thousands who rushed into practical experiments in various parts of the land; much, no doubt, has happened to moderate expectations, much has been suffered, and a new aspect has come over the movement which it requires some insight to define. Practical trials in almost every instance have been failures, as those best acquainted with the true principles and conditions of the associative organization could have predicted and indeed did predict. But Association is like Christianity itself, it triumphs in its failures; where it is trampled upon, there it most effectually plants itself, and its seeds are now silently taking root even in the hearts of those who outwardly reject it. The world has been gradually growing up to this conviction, reached it may be by but few minds now; while *all* minds, consciously or unconsciously, are on the way to it. In France, where Fourier wrote, the working classes are too ignorant, too utterly ground down, to have intelligence or energy of mind to seize upon so great a hope; besides which, public meetings and popular lectures and discussions are prohibited by law. The other class, the nobles and the savans and the money-getters, could not be supposed so disinterested as all at once to think of exchanging their present advantages for the chance of increased prosperity to all, through a more equitable and more productive system. And yet, remarkable as it may appear, the attention of statesmen and philosophers in France is now more earnestly turned to the great social problem, than in any other part of the civilized world, and the doctrines of Fourier are rapidly gaining ground among many of the most influential minds of that nation, to the extent that they already are beginning to influence politics. The Associative School there wisely wait their time; they have accumulated large funds for a systematic promulgation of their ideas through the public press, and are preparing the convictions of the best men and through them of the government, at the same time that they are raising by a gradual and steady increase the requisite material means for commencing a Model Phalanx, in some suitable place, and on the proper scale.

In Germany, socialism is rife; but the philosophic mind of that country, which generally goes to the bottom of every matter, has not yet fastened upon the Social Science as it will do, and with incalculable results. In England, the popular restlessness is growing wiser, and there is a tendency, though not in name, of every popular movement to grope its way out into the full light of Association.

But here in the free soil of America is the true home and first land of promise for this grand movement of Humanity. Here the whole tendency of thought, and of the practical working of our institutions is towards it. When its light first broke upon a few earnest minds, already thoroughly persuaded of the vicious circle in which civilization travels, and of the impossibility of attaining to anything like *real* freedom and equality; *real* opportunities of education, fortune, influence, congenial labor and society to all, without a radical change in the whole social framework; then for a time that light was almost too strong to bear; enthusiasm overflowed the bounds of practical restraining wisdom; glimpses (however incomplete) of truth were

Painting of John Sullivan Dwight, Ripley's chief assistant at Brook Farm (George Willis Cooke, John Sullivan Dwight [1898])

taken for clear knowledge, and nothing was esteemed too great to undertake or to expect; the remedy of all ol wrongs, the conditions of universal happiness and elevation, in a word the Divine Order of Society seemed understood and practicable at any moment. Then the movement had its Pentecost. And since then it has had its trials. Multitudes of little Associations, commenced without science, without money, without men, have struggled through their little day and peaceably subsided. The sceptical world bestows a smile of mingled triumph and compassion on the predicted failure, and still goes its way. But how is it with the actors in these experiments? Their faith in the principles and in the reality of the movement is stronger by every effort and by every failure. The conviction has taken root and withstood the droughts and winds of discouragement. The speculative idea has acquired the weight and earnestness of an idea which men can work for and suffer for, and wait for through long periods of apparent failure and defeat. It has spoken all the more eloquently by this fact to others. The *necessity* of a change has not been refuted by any of these failures, and more and

more have turned hopelessly away from existing politics and philosophies and institutions, and have been compelled to examine this one only solution ever offered to the whole length and breadth and depth of the social problem. We verily believe that no moral movement in the history of man has ever made such progress, in a few short years, as has this doctrine of Association in the minds of all classes of men and women in these United States. Our failures we account as nothing; the experience we have gained by them is pure success. They have drawn attention to the subject, as no other method could have done at this stage of the movement. They have knit lasting bonds of union between hundreds of earnest souls, who, though they could not in all cases contrive materially to hold together, are yet pledged to one another and to this most holy cause of Unity, while life lasts. Each of these little practical attempts at true societies has been a nucleus and rallying-point for minds possessed with this idea; each has been a centre of discussion and study, where one enlightened, warmed and stimulated another, and the result has been an incalculable increase of knowledge and of faith. We all know better what we want, what the cause demands, and what are the preliminary conditions to a true Association; and the hope is not at all abated that we shall live to see and to co-operate with a society formed after the image of the heavenly kingdom. That Association is the thing that is wanted–association of families instead of isolated households; association of Labor, and of Labor with Capital, instead of the free competition now prevailing; association of tastes, opinions, creeds, religious, moral or philosophical, into one great serial whole, instead of the exclusiveness and mutual denial by which each partizan deprives himself of what his rival, or more properly his complement, has to give–is proved beyond a doubt by these very abortive attempts at Association. The theory of Association accounts for the failure, better than the criticisms of the world can. The conditions to an experiment were wanting, and thus the failure, if it proved anything, proved the theory true.

The movement, then, is going on. It *is* a movement–every day more widely recognized, more deeply felt. There is earnest thinking on this subject where but a little while ago where was undisturbed persuasion of the impossibility of mending or improving the existing order, or where there were only sneers and passing smiles at the idle, amiable vision. It enters largely onto the conversation of all thinking circles. It has become the life-long hope and study of some who have every thing personally to hope from the present form of society, except that which only truth can give. It forces itself upon the attention of the working-classes, who are rising in their turn, as the middling classes rose before them, to constitute the soul of society and settle the destiny of nations. It is the freshest subject on the carpet, and yet not the newest; it still justifies consideration and still demands it, where the political and other interests and hobbies of the day, and even other schemes of reform, have ceased to promise anything. It still rings out livelily and clearly to the blow, where these have long since returned nothing but a flat and deadened sound.–And now what for action? And where stands the movement? If there is not a fully organized Association for us to go into, or an attempt at one of sufficient magnitude and promise to warrant the concentration of all the means and energies of all friends of the cause upon it, yet there is no necessity for standing utterly aloof; there are channels opened into which belief may flow to feel the gratifying sense of action; there are nuclei of permanent and useful measures formed, about which Associationists may gather and feel their strength not lost. There is enough to do, the worth of which and way to which can be made plain. We will mention three things, which we trust it will become the settled policy of all Associationists to regard and aid as most important agencies, and as mutually dependent branches of the movement. We think the relation which they sustain each to each must soon be seen by all, as it is seen by us, and then we shall not longer feel that we are waiting and wandering in the dark, but travelling by routes agreed upon and definite to the same definite end.

1. In the first place we have overstated the failure of actual attempts at Association. The North American Phalanx, the Wisconsin and several other Phalanxes at the West, still exhibit decided symptoms of progress. Their industry, organized so far as it can be with small numbers on Associative principles, proves abundantly productive; and social harmony, though without the full accords of more varied elements of character and culture, rewards their faithful efforts. That they are succeeding in their way is evident. The only question is, in what light these little industrial families are to be regarded. With the utmost success of which they are capable, or to which they aspire, they would be far enough from Fourier's conception of a Phalanx. But they are an important part of the machinery by

which the elements for future Association are providentially training themselves. They are so many groups, or primary elements, of the great organic system which is to be. Each of these little Associations will have its special tone, and to some extent its special occupations, to distinguish it from others. Each is nourishing the corporate spirit, and the habit of combined activity in a little band or group, which finally will affiliate itself with other kindred or related groups, until by degrees and by an almost unconscious process of natural attraction, series of series will be formed, expanding gradually into full Association. This is one process by which it is reasonable to suppose that the new Order will engraft itself upon the old, absorbing all its energy into its own better forms. It may be called the Synthetic mode, and is analogous with nature's growth. The practical bands of workers trained in these little independent unions, will come with a wealth of experience and a self-relying power, to take their places in the complete social unity when sufficient means and science call for the experiment. And without such tried bands, who have already worked together under disadvantage in the name of Social Unity, we doubt if any science, wealth or numbers would be adequate to the initiation of the first living centre of Industrial and Social Order.

2. There is at the same time a tendency to the opposite mode of realization, or what may be called the Analytic, which enumerates and provides beforehand all the elements, constructs the seales of industrial and passional varieties, contrives the various affinities and contrasts, of the complete model Phalanx, and having first cast the material mould, then introduces the life and sets it all in motion. The elements are brought together in proper proportions and varieties, and the whole is then left to attraction as in the coalescing of any chemical compound. For the laws of passional attraction are strictly analogous to those of material attraction. Given the right circumstances, and instantly the social elements will disengage themselves from artificial and constrained combinations, and flow together into willing harmony and beauty. There is truth in this also: but the greatest hope is in the meaning of both these counter-processes. Nature's methods are composite and not simple: and these many ways are leading to the same result.

To the successful organization, however, of a model Association, by whatever means arrived at, we all naturally look forward as the consummation of our efforts. Let the small Associations grow up to it if they will; yet not the less must all Associationists make this the end and focus of all their practical measures. The world awaits this proof, before it will be convinced of the soundness of our social doctrines; it asks to *see* the thing in practice; and we know too well that all we can do now with our small means is *not* that thing. A great work must be gone through first; the work of propagation and indoctrination. The idea must be set before the collective mind and conscience of this nation; the destructive tendencies of modern society and modern conservatism must be exposed to those who, wise enough in many things, are but the blind slaves of habit and authority in all that regards the vital interests of society, the property *commonwealth;* the fallacy of all this talk about perfectability, while the gulf grows wider all the time between the heartless practice and the Christian theory of society, must be urged to every one who flatters himself that he is promoting the elevation of the race by vague, vain methods. A larger portion of the world must be converted speculatively, before the means will be forthcoming to convert the whole by a practical demonstration. This, then, is the great work for Associationists at this day: to indoctrinate the people; and this requires instrumentalities and organization, not to be sustained without a liberal dedication of the means. The commencement of such an organization has been made, upon the principle of affiliated societies, which may save and draw to operative centres the scattered means and energies of all who cherish the same hope with us. Friends of Association! will you hesitate to use these channels by which you all in your degrees may help the cause? Shall not this organization be made effective? Shall not "The American Union of Associationists" command by its very name the earnest co-operation every where of those whom it is intended to unite? Shall it wait till it becomes a by-word, before the means be given it to send forth its corps of lecturers, and establish its presses, and fill up its lists of contributions to a permanent fund for the great practical experiment?

We are happy, however, to announce that several liberal pledges have been already made, and that money enough is already in hand to set on foot some lecturing expeditions this winter. We believe these projects will not end in words. Before long there will be an affiliated active brotherhood and sisterhood of believers and workers in this great cause of Heaven and Humanity, all quickened by one life, and responsive to each other's calls through all parts of the land. The printed word, the living voice shall go forth freely and return not unanswered. But first of all, the most devoted workers in this business, those who are prepared to teach it and to preach it, and who have consecrated their whole lives to it without consideration of reward, must be united: and this leads us to consider a third branch which we hold essential to our policy, and which we only ask Associationists to prize as fully as they ever have done.

3. We believe it to be essential to the cause that there should be an associative home and rallying-point, an intellectual and moral nucleus of the faith, preserved at Brook Farm. Many speculations and inquiries are afloat respecting the condition and probable fate of this earliest and most cherished little associative institution. Reports of its failure and approaching dissolution are by no means unfrequent. We cannot say that as an Industrials Association it has succeeded, or offers at the present time much promise of success. Its position is ambiguous and precarious. Yet there is the strongest clinging to the life among those of its members who have been enabled to remain, and it is felt to be like death to give it up. There is a feeling, both within and without the institution, that it is thus far the sacred citadel of the Associative cause, humble as may be its importance in other points of view, that if it should be abandoned, the most devoted advocates and soldiers of the cause would be scattered, there would be no constant reunion of so many of them again, where they could meet each other upon true associative ground and inspire each other to the study and diffusion of the doctrine; and that the sympathies of Associationists generally would find no common spot to rest upon; the cause would be identified no longer with a society, a life, which, notwithstanding business mistakes and failures, has been a beautiful and hope-sustaining thing, more beautiful in all its poverty than aught with civilization can afford.

What has been the mission of Brook Farm, and is that mission yet accomplished? These are the questions which we wish to have considered.

It is almost needless to review the history of the institution. Originally commenced without any purpose of Association on a large scale, without capital and in debt, its experience daily proved the need of organization like that in the mind of Fourier: then it partook of the first enthusiasm of the Associative movement to which we have referred above, and set to work with zeal to enlarge its industry and expand into a great industrial Phalanx. In this it failed; and it now is held in existence only by the considerable reduction in its numbers to which it has submitted, and by a modification of its internal arrangements, whereby every branch of business, and indeed every member, is made responsible for self-support, until there shall be nothing left that does not pecuniarily aid the institution. In this way so far as it goes, it must be sound; whether it will survive, however, remains to be seen. Of course we cannot enter here into all the details of its present arrangements and workings. But what is the motive which makes this life so clung to, in spite of so many discouragements and losses? It is the conviction of the important influence which it has always had upon the cause. How much of the impulse which has been given to the whole movement, by lectures, publications, discussions, conversations, has proceeded from this centre! It has been the nursery and school of Associationists; the social centre and strong-hold of those who are engaged in the great work of propagation. This it may yet be; and while we would do nothing to preclude any possibilities of enlarged and various industry, on associative principles, still we think that the peculiar providential mission of Brook Farm has been, to be the intellectual and moral centre of the movement. This has been the essential and central fact of its existence; and all the rest should always have been considered incidental. The outward husk, the incidental part has failed; but the essential *fact* survives; the inspiring and uniting influence which may still proceed from this little school or centre, will be greater and better than ever, provided only that its true character and worth be generally recognized by all friends of the cause. We do not ask for it any pecuniary aid; we simply ask that it shall not be *considered* a failure, because in one point of view it has failed; we ask that its true importance to the movement may be understood and recognized, and that it be not judged by any false standard. If it should be dissolved tomorrow, would not our plans for propagation, to be at all efficient, instantly demand the establishment of another such centre? And could another be created in years which would have the sacredness, the wealth of experience and of cherished associations, and that binding power between many souls, which this has?– At present the only printed organ which we have, proceeds from this place, and would cease with it; it is an educational resort also to young and old, who breathe here the hopeful spirit of humanity and all their lessons of literature and science; it has sent forth nearly every lecturer, and been the main-spring of nearly every meeting and convention from which the cause has gained new impulse; it has brought together manual industry with refined scholarship and culture, and taught the two elements to live and share together in equal honor; and even in its lowest estate, amid its worst embarrassments as a pecuniary and business operation, there is a feeling, so long as it lasts, that the cause of Association is not without "a local habitation and a name:" is not without its holy-land, where pilgrimages may be made, with hope of more than the imaginery influence of seeing the spot where the dead Lord was laid, but of being quickened by a living spirit, warmed to a new hope, and filled with a clearer light, about the destinies of society and the duty of each towards so great a movement.

We can but hint at this idea, and here we leave it for the present, to the earnest and candid consideration of all who work and pray with us for the coming of the great day of Unity.

FRUITLANDS

Main house at Fruitlands

Fruitlands, a Utopian experiment begun by Bronson Alcott at Harvard, Massachusetts, near Concord, lasted from June 1843 to January 1844. Alcott first conceived of such a venture while in England in the summer of 1842 and definitely decided upon it when he returned to Concord that fall with two English reformers, Charles Lane and Henry G. Wright. In May 1843, Lane bought the ninety-acre Wyman Farm at Harvard for $1,800, receiving the house and barn rent-free for a year. The Alcotts, Lane, Wright, and a few others moved in on 1 June. Alcott proposed to "take charge of the agricultural and educational departments, assist too in household labours, and carry forward the literary work with Mr. Lane, as far as I have time." As summer wore on, though, the project started falling apart. No one, especially Alcott and Lane, knew much about agriculture, and their farming habits were erratic at best. Mrs. Alcott had early developed a strong dislike for Lane. He was an egotistical and overbearing man, one who held his financial backing of the community–Alcott had had no money of his own to put up–over the Alcotts' heads; who attempted to convert Alcott to his own belief in celibacy and thus drive a wedge between him and Mrs. Alcott; and who strictly enforced a vegetarian dietary regimen of fruit, nuts, bread, and water that made Mrs. Alcott ill. Things became worse when, in September, the harvesting season, Lane and Alcott left on a lecture trip, leaving the women to bring in the crops.

Alcott finally began to have his doubts. The lack of privacy bothered both him and his wife. More important, Lane wanted a true communitarian organization, one where the individual's own needs and desires were secondary to the good of the group, and this contrasted sharply with Alcott's Transcendentalist belief in individualism. By the end of the year, open dissent broke out, and Lane left to join a Shaker community. On 16 January 1844, Alcott, ill and depressed, called it quits and departed with his family to board with friends nearby. The failure nearly broke him–never again would he risk so much on his beliefs–and he wrote his brother after arriving at Concord: "the ways of God, are less clear to me, at times, than at former periods . . . Such a disproportion between my desires and deeds!"

[Charles Lane]
"Fruitlands," *Dial,* 4 (July 1843): 135-136.

> *The following letter, which Lane composed both for himself and for Alcott, was purely and simply a promotional piece for Fruitlands.*

We have received a communication from Messrs. Alcott and Lane, dated from their farm, *Fruitlands,* in Harvard, Massachusetts, from which we make the following extract.

"We have made an arrangement with the proprietor of an estate of about a hundred acres, which liberates this tract from human ownership. For picturesque beauty both in the near and the distant landscape, the spot has few rivals. A semi-circle of undulating hills stretches from south to west, among which the Wachusett and Monadnoc are conspicuous. The vale, through which flows a tributary to the Nashua, is esteemed for its fertility and ease of cultivation, is adorned with groves of nut-trees, maples, and pines, and watered by small streams. Distant not thirty miles from the metropolis of New England, this reserve lies in a serene and sequestered dell. No public thoroughfare invades it, but it is entered by a private road. The nearest hamlet is that of Stillriver, a field's walk of twenty minutes, and the village of Harvard is reached by circuitous and hilly roads of nearly three miles.

"Here we prosecute our effort to initiate a Family in harmony with the primitive instincts in man. The present buildings being ill placed and unsightly as well as inconvenient, are to be temporarily used, until suitable and tasteful buildings in harmony with the natural scene can be completed. An excellent site offers itself on the skirts of the nearest wood, affording shade and shelter, and commanding a view of the lands of the estate, nearly all of which are capable of spade culture. It is intended to adorn the pastures with orchards, and to supersede ultimately the labor of the plough and cattle, by the spade and the pruning knife.

"Our planting and other works, both without and within doors, are already in active progress. The present Family numbers ten individuals, five being children of the founders. Ordinary secular farming is not our object. Fruit, grain, pulse, garden plants and herbs, flax and other vegetable products for food, raiment, and domestic uses, receiving assiduous attention, afford at once ample manual occupation, and chaste supplies for the bodily needs. Consecrated to human freedom, the land awaits the sober culture of devout men.

"Beginning with small pecuniary means, this enterprise must be rooted in a reliance on the succors of an ever bounteous Providence, whose vital affinities being secured by this union with uncorrupted fields and un-

The library at Fruitlands

worldly persons, the cares and injuries of a life of gain are avoided.

"The inner nature of every member of the Family is at no time neglected. A constant leaning on the living spirit within the soul should consecrate every talent to holy uses, cherishing the widest charities. The choice Library (of which a partial catalogue was given in Dial No. XII.) is accessible to all who are desirous of perusing these records of piety and wisdom. Our plan contemplates all such disciplines, cultures, and habits, as evidently conduce to the purifying and edifying of the inmates. Pledged to the spirit alone, the founders can anticipate no hasty or numerous accession to their numbers. The kingdom of peace is entered only through the gates of self-denial and abandonment; and felicity is the test and the reward of obedience to the unswerving law of Love."

June 10, 1843.

From Joel Myerson

"William Harry Harland's 'Bronson Alcott's English Friends,' " *Resources for American Literary Study,* 8 (Spring 1978): 24-60.

These letters from Lane to William Oldham, a friend in England, provide one of the best day-to-day accounts of life at Fruitlands.

Concord, Mass.
May 31, 1843

My Dear friend,

. . . . Mr. Alcott and I walked up the river to a place called the Cliffs where is a young orchard of 16 acres and woodland below. He came home with his head full of poetic schemes for a Cottage, &c., on this spot. I, however, came home first and found that a man had been sent by the young man who walked with me to Southborough, having a farm to sell at Harvard, 14 miles off. He proposed to take me directly to see it, but I was fatigued, so Samuel Larnard, the visitor who came up with Mr Wright, went in the waiting vehicle. The next morning being very fine Mr Alcott and I walked there, not knowing his name but we ascertained it to be Wyman; we saw his place, consisting of 90 acres, 14 of them wood, a few apple and other fruit trees, plenty of nuts and berries, much of the land very good; the prospect from the highest part very sublime. The house and the barn very poor, but the Water excellent and plentiful. The capabilities are manifold, but the actualities humble. For the whole he asked 2,700 dollars, which being beyond my means we had much talk when he offered to sell the land for 1,000 dollars and to lend us the buildings gratis for a year. I should observe it is extremely retired, there being no road to it. On these terms we have closed. He gives us the few crops he has just planted and grass to a considerable amount will soon be cut. I have slept a night or two there. William and two friends (Larnard and Abraham called "The Plain Man" in *The Vt. Telegraph*) and a hired man remain there, and the family are to start early to-morrow morning, so now for plenty of work of all sorts. Ninety acres; much of it first rate; some worth 100 dollars per acre, the whole at 20 dollars per acre; would that some of the English honest half-starved were on it!

This, I think you will admit, looks like an attempt at something which will entitle transcendentalism to some respect for its practicality. . . .

We have very much to do but the occasions are opportune. I think Mr Emerson is not so well pleased with our departure as he would be with our company but as he did nothing to keep us we must go. It appeared to me that for the hopefulness of many it was needful we should make a movement of some kind this year, even though we fail; and Providence seems really to have worked for us. . . .

I thank you very much for the £10; the note arrived very opportunely to enable Mr A. to quit Concord, to do which all his debts must be paid and I need not tell you on whom that falls. Our transactions at present leave me about 500 dollars in debt, but everyone says we have made a good bargain in the purchase of the Land. I seriously hope we are forming the basis for something really progressive, call it family or community, or what you will. . . .

We have now plenty of work to do and how we get on I shall faithfully report though the pen will not do much at present . . . Believe me dear friend,

Yours stedfastly in the spirit,
CHARLES LANE.

Fruitlands

The Alcotts' bedroom at Fruitlands

Harvard,
Mass.
June 16, 1843.

My Dear Friend,

The morning being rainy I took advantage of the suspension of out door labours to sit down and have a little chat with you of and concerning our doings and progress. The day after I wrote you last all the household effects and all the household were mounted on wheels and trundled to this place; the old little cottage being left as clean as a new book by Mrs Alcott's great energy. The day was sharp and cold for the season, but the weather has since come out fine and warm, some days hot. We have been all busily engaged in manual operations in the field, house, wood yard, &c. Planting, ploughing, sowing, cleaning fruit trees, gardening, chopping, sawing, fitting up, &c., &c., have gone on at a rapid rate, as the place was in a very slovenly condition. When tired we have taken a look round the estate to see what was growing, learn the shape of it,

and its capabilities with more minuteness. It seems to be agreed on all hands, and we have opinions from many practical men, that we have not made a bad exchange, even in the commercial sense, of our cash for land. Only think, brother Oldham, ninety acres, every one of which may, in a short time, and without much outlay, be brought into a state fit for spade culture; and much of it very good land, obtained at the rate of 20 dollars or only *four pounds per acre freehold.* Recollect, too, this includes fuel and some building material, for there are 14 acres of wood, including many trees of edible nuts. And still only 30 miles from a metropolitan city of 110,000 inhabitants. The land is most beautifully disposed in hill and valley, and the scenery is of a sublime and elevating character. Water abundant and excellent and the springs being on the hill, it may be conveyed anywhere about the place for irrigation, &c. As is common in this district, the principal part is meadow and pasture; but we shall go on ploughing up as much as possible, sowing crops of clover or buck wheat, and turning them in, so as to redeem the land without animal manures, which in practice I find to be as filthy as in idea. The use of them is disgusting in the extreme. At present, we have about 4 acres in Maize, 1 1/2 in Rye, 1 1/2 in Oats, 1 Barley, 2 in Potatoes, nearly 1 in Beans, Peas, Melons, Squashes, &c.; there will be some Buckwheat, Turnips, &c., making in all about 11 acres arable. We have no Wheat this year. The grass promises well, and we may possibly cut 200 dollars' worth; but by hired teams we are now turning up one piece of 8 or 9, and another of 5 acres, and means to attack another 4 or 5 for our next year's homestead or garden, should we obtain the means of building. The hill side of 12 or 14 acres pasture is also to be ploughed, directly if we can; so that the work of reclamation will go rapidly forward. There is a large piece of peat land, as black as ink, which, mixed with sand, makes a most productive soil, valued at 200 to 300 dollars per acre; and there is sand on our lot within 100 yards. We have been much plagued, and a little cheated, with the cattle, but our stock is now reduced to one yoke of oxen.

Besides Mr Alcott, his Wife and Children, myself and William, who is very efficient and active, we have only a Mr Larnard and Abraham—who appears in *The Vermont Telegraph* as the "Plain Man". Larnard was many months at West Roxbury, is only about 20 years of age, his father was a merchant and he has been a counting house man and is what the world calls genteel. Abraham is about 42, a cooper by trade, but an excellent assistant here, very faithful to every work he undertakes, very serious, has had rather deep experience, having been imprisoned in a mad house by his relations because he had a little property, but still he is not a spiritual being, at least not consciously and wishfully so.

I have exchanged more letters with Samuel Bower and he promises to come here to-morrow. If his real state bears out his writings I think he may be added to the family, otherwise he thinks of looking at Roxbury for the purpose of finding a home there. . . .

Mr. Alcott is as persevering in practice as last year we found him to be in idea. To do better and better, to *be* better and better, is the constant theme. His hand is every where, like his mind. He had held the plough with great efficiency, sometimes for the whole day, and by the straightness of his furrow may be said to be giving lessons to the professed ploughmen, who work in a slovenly manner. We have called in the aid of a carpenter who has made simple shelves for our books and for the first time our library stands upright as it should do. It occupies about 100 feet of shelves.

June 28, 1843

On the 19th I received your very kind and newsful letter of the 1st instant enclosed in Mrs. C[hichester]'s. Mr Bower having kept his promise was here and I read much of it at breakfast, having also another visitor from Brook Farm, Mr Hoecker. All were much interested in the facts reported and Saml. Bower heard your remembrances fresh from your pen. You affect him more than any other person. In your next you will perhaps devote a slip to him and I will forward it. He, Larnard and Hecker visited the Shakers and were much attracted by them. Larnard who, on common report, used to oppose them, talks of joining them so pleasant is their society; at least at first. . . .

If I were not at this moment surrounded by so much that is beautiful in the present, hopeful in the future and ennobling in the act, your affectionate invitation to Ham would seriously touch me. But by God's blessing something shall be done *here* which shall reach you *there. If we can aid the people in any way to let self be conquered we shall do something. Lust abounds and love is deserted. Lust of money, of food, of sexuality, of books, of music, of art—while Love demands the powers devoted to these false ends.* I thank you for your hint respecting worldliness. I believe I am getting on safe ground if I am not already landed. From or in England you say I

should expect nothing, and I am now in the same predicament here. Every farthing I had is now either put in or involved in this affair, and more, for I have put my hand to two rather large bills; silly enough, you will say. In a few weeks I expect to be literally pennyless, and even unable for want of stage hire to travel to Boston if you send me ever so many orders, of which you discover I have been so neglectful. No; I think I am now out of the money world. Let my privation be ever so great I will never make any property claim on this effort. It is an offering to the Eternal Spirit, and I consider that I have no more right than any other person; and I have arranged the title deeds, as well as I could, to meet that end. I could only consent to return to England on condition of being held free, like a child, from all money entanglements. As no person or association can guarantee this for me, I think it would be better to remain here where the simple wants can be so easily met, and where there is much opportunity for doing good and more hope as the outward conditions are so beautifully free. Would that you were here for a month; we have now the most delightful steady weather we can conceive; we are all dressed in our linen tunics, Abraham is ploughing, Larnard bringing some turf about the house, Alcott doing a thousand things, Bower and I have well dug a sandy spot for carrots, the children and Lady are busy in their respective ways, and some hirelings are assisting. . . .

Now that something, though little, is doing, you will find my expressions more peaceful. Con-fi-dence in Love I hope will ne'er be wanting in your affectionate friend.

CHARLES LANE.

Fruitlands,
Harvard,
Mass.
July 30, 1843.

Dear Friend,

. . . . A few days after I wrote you Samuel Bower joined us and has steadily and zealously entered into all the works and speculations we have in hand and in mind. Mr. Hecker, a very spiritually minded young man, also has been with us. He is partner with his brothers at New York in a very extensive baking and corn mill business. He has resided several months at W. Roxbury but is by no means satisfied with their school-boy dilletante spiritualism. He will, I believe, go to New York to clear up if possible with his family as to the relation on which they are in future to stand to each other. They appear to be so loving and united a family with such strong humane attachments that although he has done much towards breaking away, I fear that in the desire to bring his brothers further into the inner world he will himself be detained.

Mr Alcott and I returned last evening from a short visit to Boston to purchase a few articles and while there we went out one evening to Roxbury where there are 80 or 90 persons playing away their youth and day time in a miserably joyous frivolous manner. There are not above four or five who could be selected as really and truly progressing beings. Most of the adults are there to pass "a good time"; the children are taught languages &c., the animals (in consequence I believe solely of Mr Ripley's tendency) occupy a prominent position, there being no less than 16 cows, besides 4 oxen, a herd of swine, a horse or two, &c. The milk is sold in Boston, and they buy butter to the extent of 500 dollars a year. We had a pleasant summer evening conversation with many of them, but it is only in a few individuals that anything deeper than ordinary is to be found. The Northampton Community is one of industry, the one at Hopedale aims at practical theology, this of Roxbury is one of taste, yet it is the best which exists here, and perhaps we shall have to say it is the best which can exist. At all events we can go no further than to keep open fields, and as far as we have it, open house to *all* comers. We know very well that if they come not in the right name and nature they will not long remain. Our dietetic system is a test quite sufficient for many. As far as acres of fine land are concerned you may offer their free use to any free souls who will come here and work them, and any aid we can afford shall be freely given. The aid of sympathetic companionship is not small, and that at least we can render. To bridge the Atlantic is a trifle if the heart is really set on the attainment of better conditions. Here are they freely presented, at a day's walk from the shore, without a long and expensive journey to the West. Please to advertize these facts to all youthful men and women; for such are much wanted here. There is now a certain opportunity for planting a love colony the influence of which may be felt for many generations, and more than felt; it may be the beginning for a

state of things which shall far transcend itself. They to whom our work seems not good enough may come and set out a better.

I should mention to you that passing his door Mr Theodore Parker came to the Community in the evening and again in the morning. He is a very popular man at present and has a congregation at Roxbury, but being unwell by reason of close study, he will sail to Europe on the 1st Sept. He will remain in Germany for three or four months, and afterwards as long in England. No doubt you will see him and render him all the service you can. . . .

At present we are not sought by many persons, but the value in our enterprise depends not upon numbers so much as upon the spirit from which we can live outwardly and in all relations true to the intuitions which are gifted to us. We must not forget how great have been the works done by individuals, and in the absence of what are usually called facilities. Our obstacles are, I suppose, chiefly within, and as these are subdued we shall triumph in externalities. I could send you a description of works and crops, our mowing, hoeing, reaping, ploughing in tall crops of clover and grass for next year's manure, and various other operations, but although they have some degree of relation to the grand principle to which they are obedient they are worth little in the exoteric sense alone. Perhaps the external revelations of success ought always to be kept secret, for every improvement discovered is only turned to a money making account and to the further degradation of man, as we see in the march of science to this very moment. If we knew how to double the crops of the earth it is scarcely to be hoped that any good would come by revealing the mode. On the contrary the bounties of God are already made the means by which man debases himself more and more. We will therefore say little concerning the sources of external wealth until man is himself secured to the End which rightly uses these means. . . .

Mr Wheeler, the eminent Greek student, who went from here to Germany last summer, died at Liepsic in June, age 26. He was one of Mr. Emerson's great hopes.

Samuel Bower continues with us, but he is not so happy in body or mind as he ought to be: a letter from you in the universal spirit would cheer him up. He confesses to the possession of a little Nomadic blood in his veins. He thinks Mr Alcott is arbitrary or despotic, as some others do, but I shall endeavour

The small dining room at Fruitlands

(and I think not in vain) to urge him to the noblest conduct of which our position is capable. He must not complain nor walk off, but cheerfully amend whatever is amiss. I suppose your letter has failed at the post somewhere, but I have inquired fully on this side. With assurances of continued affection to yourself and all friends on the divine ground,

I remain, Dr. Oldham,
truly yours,
CHARLES LANE.

Fruitlands,
Harvard,
Mass.
September 29, 1843.

My Dear Friend,

I have been such a gad-about during the past month and have so recently returned to the pen that I shall be scarcely settled and calm enough to write anything worthy your acceptance. Moreover our future is again uncertain. For a few days at least it remains undecided whether or not the man with the beard will complete the arrangements by which our bodies are to be transferred to Leominster if thiter they are to go. A simple narrative of peregrinations I can however submit to you. Miss Page having desired to go as far as Providence to make arrangements respecting her furniture we hired a vehicle and she, Mr Alcott and I went as far as that city which we found in a considerable bustle from its being the commencement day of the college or university. The friend there, Mr Clarke, who married one of the Chase family, had just buried their infant, so that we made little progress in gathering any of them into our circle, as we somewhat expected for two of the young women, for they found enough employment in comforting each other. We had however an evening conversation at Mrs Newcomb's during which Mr Alcott said that as competition had made the facilities so great we might take that opportunity to go on to New York. I replied there was no other objection than the want of means. On which the company proffered them. Whereupon the next afternoon we went by the Rail Road and one of the magnificent Steamboats furnished with nearly 400 beds, through Long Island Sound and arrived at New York City at about 6 o'clock in the morning. We went to the Graham House to breakfast where we found some people half if not quite alive. Afterwards we sought out Edward Palmer who after living two or three years without using money is making pills &c. with a Dr Beach, a progressive man in medicine. Edward Palmer is a man of extreme gentleness but pretty firm, though lately he has been somewhat hopeless of seeing anything better than the present order upon earth. Wm. Chase, who is now studying law, has exercised an unfavourable influence upon him. We also saw Mrs Black and her mother, both mystic characters. They were busily at work for their bread on the Sunday. Parke Godwin of *The Pathfinder* we saw– Whitley president of the Sylvania Association, which is busily at work with the rough of a commencement–Dr Valhec, who is the Greaves of New York, if there be one–Mr and Mrs Green of New Jersey–Mr Wm. Emerson–Mr and Mrs Child–Wm. H. Channing– Brisbane–Mr Daniel, and others. The number of living persons in the 300,000 inhabitants of N.Y. is very small. Channing's meetings are moderately attended–at one which he had on purpose to bring us out we discoursed on the deepest topics in a very crowded and attentive room. . . .

Our friend and sometime inmate, Isaac Hecker, entertained us most hospitably at N.Y. where he and his brothers carry on an extensive baking and corn grinding business. He has invented a new article he calls pearled wheat, which is much admired, but I think it too intense for frequent use. . . .

On our return from N.Y. instead of going by the usual route through Stonington, &c., we went by Steamer to New Haven, Connecticut, where Yale College is situated, a neat small city; thence by coach to Waterbury, the township adjoining Wolcott where Mr Alcott was born. This is the most wretched agricultural place I have seen, and the farmer Norton to whom Mr A's sister is married, living on the paternal estate on Spindle Hill, once so well managed, is the puniest fellow in the place. We saw Dr Alcott's father and mother and tho' he is past work his farm is in fair order. . . .

On our arrival at home we learnt that in our absence several friends and strangers had called, amongst them S. Bower, Parker Pilsbury, and an acquaintance, Mr. Hamond of New Ipswich in New Hampshire State. Thinking the latter worth seeing we went to visit him, a distance of about 25 miles. He is married to an exoteric wife of some good household qualities, he has built with his own hands a smart cottage, being an expert workman, and has moreover a respectable talent for portrait painting which he estimates humbly without a consciousness of humility. Next to Edward Palmer, he is a person who, I should think, would make one with us. He introduced us at two houses to four females who vitally considered constitute with himself the whole of the town. Our visit there will do some good, for though they have read my letters printed last winter in the newspapers, yet the presence of the living person is much more real a thing. I saw their good intentions were greatly encouraged. I could not dissuade the oldest from promising never to taste flesh again, which I was rather inclined to on account of her years. . . .

On Saturday last Anna Alcott most magnanimously walked her little legs fourteen miles in about five hours down to old Concord, where our friends appear to have been pretty somnolent since our departure. On Tuesday we returned on foot, and accomplished somewhat towards the liberation of the animals by a heroine of 13. Mr Emerson is I think quite stationary: he is off the Railroad of progress, and merely an elegant, kindly observer of all who pass onwards, and notes down their aspect while they remain in sight; of course when they arrive at a new station they are gone from and for him. I see Mr Sterling dedicates his new tragedy of Strafford to him: no very alarming honor! I suppose that Thos. Carlyle with all his famous talking does not yet *actually* lead the people out of their troubles. These worthy and enlightened scribblers will do little to save the nations. Some there are I hope of more real solid metal. . . .

Samuel Bower has not yet had your note as I am not sure where he is. He could not, it seems, long endure Joseph Palmer's offer of land, &c., it was so solitary. He called here when we were on our long journey on his way to Lowell, the Manchester of New England. If his aims are high and his head clear or his hands effective he will not be able to wander far from us; but a wanderer it is certain he must allowed to be. Abraham comes and goes with some regard to the law within him; he is now busy with our latter hay, the maize, buck wheat, &c.

What is to be our destiny I can in no wise guess. Mr Alcott makes such high requirements of all persons that few are likely to stay, even of his own family, unless he can become more tolerant of defect. He is an artist in human character requiring every painter to be a Michael Angelo. He also does not wish to keep a hospital, nor even a school, but to be surrounded by Masters–Masters of Arts, of the one grand Art of human life. I suppose such a standard would soon empty your Concordium as well as every other house, which I suppose you call by insinuation "Discordiums", or more elegantly "Discordia". I purpose to pass at least another winter in New England to know more averagingly what they are, as the last was particularly severe. I have gone about on these several journies in the simple tunic and linen garments and mean to keep them on as long as I can. We have had a fine summer of three months, and a fine autumn seems on hand. Sharp frost this morning yet we took our bath as usual out of doors in the gray of the morn at 1/2 past 5. Health, the grand external condition, still attends me, every stranger rating me 10 or 12 years younger than I am; so that if such are the effects of climate I may indeed be happy, for my youthfulness is not all appearance–I *feel* as buoyant and as boyish as I look, which I find a capital endorsement to my assertions about diet, &c. It staggers the sceptical and sets their selfish thoughts to work. . . .

Hoping that all minds are thus laboring, let us, my dear friend, act as if all good progress depended upon us and unfailingly present a clean breast to Eternal Love, shedding forth our full measure in the clearest Light; in which I am thine truly

CHAS. LANE

Abraham just notifies me there is work in the field, so I must go.

Joseph Palmer and his team have come to day, but what he has done about the new place I have not yet learnt.

Fruitlands,
Harvard,
Massachusetts.
Octr. 30/43.

My Dear friend,

Thank heaven you will not die of stagnation this year, though you may be much harassed by over exertion. A true consociate, it seems, you have not found though partial associates several; else, I think, your labours would have been less severe. It would appear to be almost as vain to address you for calm advice as the prime minister, yet, as whatever one receives from you will, at least, be sincere, I shall as usual lay myself open before you whatever my state may be. I cannot recall the tone of my letter to Mrs C[hichester] but I dare say your remark is just and that you attributed any altered appearance to the right cause. At present I am situated thus–all the persons who have joined us during the summer have from some cause or other quitted; they say in consequence of Mr Alcott's despotic manner, which he interprets as their not being equal to the Spirit's demands. Joseph Palmer, who has done, and is doing, our farm work for love, still remains in the same relation he ever did as he never proposed to dwell with us. He is still willing to give the free use of $2,000 worth of land and house, but the place having been disposed of which he had in view, he wishes to have time to find another; he also would prefer it should be in Leominster, while Mr. Alcott desires to be near Boston, and the apprehension of being shut in here during the winter now that he has an impulse towards talking makes him rather impatient. He would willingly let me reclaim this place as property and spend it all in a year or two in housekeeping in or near town, by which process, he prognosticates, persons would be drawn to an appreciation and support of something better than is yet proposed in any of the popular schemes. I am not inclined to this dissipation, or if it is to be done I think I could do it better myself, and Palmer says that having once declared this land free we should never go back, at least until the world has been fairly tested. Under all this it should be stated that Mrs Alcott has no spontaneous inclination towards a larger family than her own natural one; of spiritual ties she knows nothing though to keep all together she does and would go through a good deal of exterior and interior toil. I hoped I had done with pecuniary affairs, but it seems I am not to be let off. The crops, I believe, will not discharge all the obligations they were expected to liquidate, and against going farther into debt I am most determinately settled. Add to these that we ought to be out of this house by the 1st of May next,

The buildings at Fruitlands today

even if we are able to buy it, and you will perceive that I have, like yourself, a small peck of troubles; not quite heavy enough to drive me to a junction with our friends, the Shakers, but sufficiently so to put the thought into one's head, as you perceive. In the midst of all these events, and of William's illness, who is in bed 8 or 10 days with a sort of bilious fever, I am not without the consolitary hope that some measure of Spirit utility is bound up with our obscure doings. . . .

Expecting your kind and sincere advice in all matters, I remain, dear brother,

Yours most affectionately,
CHARLES LANE.

At a late visit on foot to Roxbury I found the numbers at Brook Farm had considerably diminished. I don't know what they will say to my letter if they see the N.A. but never mind.

Harvard,
Massachusetts.
[26-29] November 1843.

Dear Friend,

. . . .The Liverpool steam packet arrived several days ago, but not a letter or printed paper for me from you or any one else. Very good. I am not sorry that my valuelessness is discovered. Or, if you think that sentiment savors of offended pride, let me say that I rejoice that you and all friends are too well employed to have any leisure for writing. I would that the suspension of my pen had as good a reason. But it has not. What with agitations of mind and ills of body, I have passed a less happy time than usual. William was ill a whole month with a low fever so that he could not even sit up in bed for one minute. I had to nurse him while plagued with hands so chapped and sore that I was little more capable than the patient. Then came Mr May's announcement that he should not pay the note to which he had put his hand; so that money affairs and individual property came back again upon me for a season. Thereupon ensued endless discussions, doubts, and anticipations concerning our destiny. These still hang over us. But in the midst of them Mrs Alcott gives notice that she concedes to the wishes of her friends and shall withdraw to a house which they will provide for herself and her four children. As she will take all the furniture with her, this proceeding necessarily leaves me alone and naked in the new world. Of course Mr A. and I could not remain together without her. To be "that devil come from Old England to separate husband and wife", I will not be, though it might gratify New England to be able to *say* it. So that you will perceive a separation is possible. Indeed, I believe that under any external circumstances it is now inevitable. Every person who has tried to join us has been so treated that junction was impossible; the last instance, that of Anne Page appearing to me a little short of a kicking out of doors chiefly on the part of Mrs A. who vows that her own family is all she lives for or wishes to live for. I do not desire to live for so narrow a purpose and if there was on the part of any one the design to bend me and my appurtenances to that end, upon the cunning ones let the consequences fall. In conversation the other day Mr A. put it to me thus–"You think that before the outlay of money began I expressed certain high moral principles, that during the expenditure these principles were for lower and selfish ends suppressed; and that now the money is all expended I recur to the higher moral principles formerly avowed". I trust it was mere speculation and not consciousness which suggested this thought to him. His conduct is certainly liable to such interpretation, but I deem him rather wayward and notional than wicked or acquisitive, and more borne down by his wife and family than wishful to abandon any affirmation he may make. He one day spontaneously put this question to me–"Can a man act continually for the universal end while he co-habits with a wife?" How different a state of mind must this thought have issued from to that which caused him to shed tears on the same subject eighteen months ago at Ham!! Hopeful prospect! Poor fellow; between his cherished idiosyncracies and his sec-

ular or social difficulties, his high moral principles have a sad time of it. In my further connexion with him be assured I shall try to help the latter to a larger expansion, and to contract the two former as much as I can. The mere thought of separation is painful to him. Personally he will feel, as I shall, a great loss of hopeful friendship; pecuniarily I expect he will feel somewhat, for I do not wholly excuse him from the parasite nature; but how to explain it to the public is his greatest puzzle, for after all his defiance of orthodox opinions I have felt justified in telling him many times that he regards too much the question "what will Mrs Grundy say?" Amidst this conflict in small matters I trust I shall not act self-willedly, but wait to be guided aright. Would that you were here a little while; but I suppose I shall have to act before your advice can reach me. . . .

I believe I have followed out this experiment to the ultimate. The future will be merely repetitions of the past. In the absence of sincere advisers I shall, however, act with all possible deliberation. So far as outward delay denotes inner calmness I can ensure that by the almanac. I have little feeling of disappointment; events and characters are laid open to me more in sorrow than in anger, and I entertain more hope than either of these feelings. Everything about me, both within doors and without, convinces me more and more that the individual family life must soon cease. Common sense, economy and good feeling must put an end to the separation of man from man which only the grossest selfishness and ignorance could tolerate for one hour, especially in a country where human action is so free as here it is. The pulpit, the "devil's citadel" is, I believe, one of the greatest hinderances to true progress; the press unfortunately is the next; politics, I think, are less obstructive than either, though they are bad enough. May humanity be soon delivered from the oppression of the trinity of pulpit, press and politics.

With kindest remembrances to all companions and friends, I continue, Dear Oldham,

Yours faithfully in the Spirit,
CHARLES LANE.

Louisa May Alcott
"Transcendental Wild Oats," *Independent,* 25 (18 December 1873): 1569-1571.

Louisa May Alcott was unhappy during much of her time at Fruitlands, and she gained a measure of satiric revenge on some of the participants in this fictionalized account of her venture. In her story, Abel Lamb is Bronson Alcott, Hope Lamb is Mrs. Alcott, and Timon Lion is Charles Lane. (For further information about the author of Little Women, *see the entry for Alcott in* DLB 1, The American Renaissance in New England.)

A CHAPTER FROM AN UNWRITTEN

ROMANCE

On the first day of June, 184-, a large wagon, drawn by a small horse and containing a motley load, went lumbering over certain New England hills, with the pleasing accompaniments of wind, rain, and hail. A serene man with a serene child upon his knee was driving, or rather being driven, for the small horse had it all his own way. A brown boy with a William Penn style of countenance sat beside him, firmly embracing a bust of Socrates. Behind them was an energetic-looking woman, with a benevolent brow, satirical mouth, and eyes brimful of hope and courage. A baby reposed upon her lap, a mirror leaned against her knee, and a basket of provisions danced about at her feet, as she struggled with a large, unruly umbrella. Two blue-eyed little girls, with hands full of childish treasures, sat under one old shawl, chatting happily together.

In front of this lively party stalked a tall, sharp-featured man, in a long blue cloak; and a fourth small girl trudged along beside him through the mud as if she rather enjoyed it.

The wind whistled over the bleak hills; the rain fell in a despondent drizzle, and twilight began to fall. But the calm man gazed as tranquilly into the fog as if he beheld a radiant bow of promise spanning the gray sky. The cheery woman tried to cover every one but herself with the big umbrella. The brown boy pillowed his head on the bald pate of Socrates and slumbered peacefully. The little girls sang lullabies to their dolls in soft, maternal murmurs. The sharp-nosed pedestrian marched steadily on, with the blue cloak streaming out

Daguerreotype of Louisa May Alcott in the early 1850s

behind him like a banner; and the lively infant splashed through the puddles with a duck-like satisfaction pleasant to behold.

Thus these modern pilgrims journeyed hopefully out of the old world, to found a new one in the wilderness.

The editors of *The Transcendental Tripod* had received from Messrs. Lion & Lamb (two of the afore-

[325]

said pilgrims) a communication from which the following statement is an extract:-

"We have made arrangements with the proprietor of an estate of about a hundred acres which liberates this tract from human ownership. Here we shall prosecute our effort to initiate a Family in harmony with the primitive instincts of man.

"Ordinary secular farming is not our object. Fruit, grain, pulse, herbs, flax, and other vegetable products, receiving assiduous attention, will afford ample manual occupation, and chaste supplies for the bodily needs. It is intended to adorn the pastures with orchards, and to supersede the labor of cattle by the spade and the pruning-knife.

"Consecrated to human freedom, the land awaits the sober culture of devoted men. Beginning with small pecuniary means, this enterprise must be rooted in a reliance on the succors of an ever-bounteous Providence, whose vital affinities being secured by this union with uncorrupted field and unworldly persons, the cares and injuries of a life of gain are avoided.

"The inner nature of each member of the Family is at no time neglected. Our plan contemplates all such disciplines, cultures, and habits as evidently conduce to the purifying of the inmates.

"Pledged to the spirit alone, the founders anticipate no hasty or numerous addition to their numbers. The kingdom of peace is entered only through the gates of self-denial; and felicity is the test and the reward of loyalty to the unswerving law of Love."

This prospective Eden at present consisted of an old red farmhouse, a dilapidated barn, many acres of meadow-land, and a grove. Ten ancient apple-trees were all the "chaste supply" which the place offered as yet; but, in the firm belief that plenteous orchards were soon to be evoked from their inner consciousness, these sanguine founders had christened their domain Fruitlands.

Here Timon Lion intended to found a colony of Latter Day Saints, who, under his patriarchal sway, should regenerate the world and glorify his name for ever. Here Abel Lamb, with the devoutest faith in the high ideal which was to him a living truth, desired to plant a Paradise, where Beauty, Virtue, Justice, and Love might live happily together, without the possibility of a serpent entering in. And here his wife, unconverted but faithful to the end, hoped, and after many wanderings over the face of the earth, to find rest for herself and a home for her children.

"There is our new abode," announced the enthusiast, smiling with a satisfaction quite undampened by the drops dripping from his hatbrim, as they turned at length into a cart-path that wound along a steep hillside into a barren-looking valley.

"A little difficult of access," observed his practical wife, as she endeavored to keep her various household goods from going overboard with every lurch of the laden ark.

"Like all good things. But those who earnestly desire and patiently seek will soon find us," placidly responded the philosopher from the mud, through which he was now endeavoring to pilot the much-enduring horse.

"Truth lies at the bottom of a well, Sister Hope," said Brother Timon, pausing to detach his small comrade from a gate, whereon she was perched for a clearer gaze into futurity.

"That's the reason we so seldom get at it, I suppose," replied Mrs. Hope, making a vain clutch at the mirror, which a sudden jolt sent flying out of her hands.

"We want no false reflections here," said Timon, with a grim smile, as he crunched the fragments under foot in his onward march.

Sister Hope held her peace, and looked wistfully through the mist at her promised home. The old red house with a hospitable glimmer at its windows cheered her eyes; and, considering the weather, was a fitter refuge than the sylvan bowers some of the more ardent souls might have preferred.

The new-comers were welcomed by one of the elect precious,–a regenerate farmer, whose idea of reform consisted chiefly in wearing white cotton raiment and shoes of untanned leather. This costume, with a snowy beard, gave him a venerable, and at the same time a somewhat bridal appearance.

The goods and chattels of the Society not having arrived, the weary family reposed before the fire on blocks of wood, while Brother Moses White regaled them with roasted potatoes, brown bread and water, in two plates, a tin pan, and one mug; his table service being limited. But, having cast the forms and vanities of a depraved world behind them, the elders welcomed hardship with the enthusiasm of new pioneers, and the children heartily enjoyed this foretaste of what they believed was to be a sort of perpetual picnic.

During the progress of this frugal meal, two more brothers appeared. One a dark, melancholy man, clad in homespun, whose peculiar mission was to turn

Louisa May Alcott's bedroom in Orchard House in Concord

his name hind part before and use as few words as possible. The other was a bland, bearded Englishman, who expected to be saved by eating uncooked food and going without clothes. He had not yet adopted the primitive costume, however; but contented himself with meditatively chewing dry beans out of a basket.

"Every meal should be a sacrament, and the vessels used should be beautiful and symbolical," observed Brother Lamb, mildly, righting the tin pan slipping about on his knees. "I priced a silver service when in town, but it was too costly; so I got some graceful cups and vases of Brittania ware."

"Hardest things in the world to keep bright. Will whiting be allowed in the community?" inquired Sister Hope, with a housewife's interest in labor-saving institutions.

"Such trivial questions will be discussed at a more fitting time," answered Brother Timon, sharply, as he burnt his fingers with a very hot potato. "Neither sugar, molasses, milk, butter, cheese, nor flesh

are to be used among us, for nothing is to be admitted which has caused wrong or death to man or beast."

"Our garments are to be linen till we learn to raise our own cotton or some substitute for woolen fabrics," added Brother Abel, blissfully basking in an imaginery future as warm and brilliant as the generous fire before him.

"Haou abaout shoes?" asked Brother Moses, surveying his own with interest.

"We must yield that point till we can manufacture an innocent substitute for leather. Bark, wood, or some durable fabric will be invented in time. Meanwhile, those who desire to carry out our idea to the fullest extent can go barefooted," said Lion, who liked extreme measures.

"I never will, nor let my girls," murmured rebellious Sister Hope, under her breath.

"Haou do you cattle'ate to treat the ten-acre lot? Ef things ain't 'tended to right smart, we shan't hev no crops," observed the practical patriarch in cotton.

"We shall spade it," replied Abel, in such perfect

good faith that Moses said no more, though he indulged in a shake of the head as he glanced at hands
that had held nothing heavier than a pen for years. He
was a paternal old soul and regarded the younger men
as promising boys on a new sort of lark.

"What shall we do for lamps, if we cannot use
any animal substance? I do hope light of some sort is
to be thrown upon the enterprise," said Mrs. Lamb,
with anxiety, for in those days kerosene and camphene
were not, and gas unknown in the wilderness.

"We shall go without till we have discovered
some vegetable oil or wax to serve us," replied
Brother Timon, in a decided tone, which caused Sister
Hope to resolve that her private lamp should be always
trimmed, if not burning.

"Each member is to perform the work for which
experience, strength, and taste best fit him," continued Dictator Lion. "Thus drudgery and disorder will be
avoided and harmony prevail. We shall rise at dawn,
begin the day by bathing, followed by music, and then
a chaste repast of fruit and bread. Each one finds congenial occupation till the meridian meal; when some deep-
searching conversation gives rest to the body and development to the mind. Healthful labor again engages us
till the last meal, when we assemble in social communion, prolonged till sunset, when we retire to sweet repose, ready for the next day's activity."

"What part of the work do you incline to yourself?" asked Sister Hope, with a humorous glimmer in
her keen eyes.

"I shall wait till it is made clear to me. Being in preference to doing is the great aim, and this comes to us
rather by a resigned willingness than a wilful activity,
which is a check to all divine growth," responded
Brother Timon.

"I thought so." And Mrs. Lamb sighed audibly,
for during the year he had spent in her family Brother
Timon had so faithfully carried out his idea of "being,
not doing," that she had found his "divine growth" both
an expensive and unsatisfactory process.

Here her husband struck into the conversation,
his face shining with the light and joy of the splendid
dreams and high ideals hovering before him.

"In these steps of reform, we do not reply so
much on scientific reasoning or physiological skill as on
the spirit's dictates. The greater part of man's duty consists in leaving alone much that he now does. Shall I stimulate with tea, coffee, or wine? No. Shall I consume
flesh? Not if I value health. Shall I subjugate cattle?

*Louisa May Alcott in her study in Orchard House, Concord, c.
1870*

Shall I claim property in any created thing? Shall I
trade? Shall I adopt a form of religion? Shall I interest myself in politics? To how many of these questions—could
we ask them deeply enough and could they be heard
as having relation to our eternal welfare—would the response be 'Abstain'?"

A mild snore seemed to echo the last word of
Abel's rhapsody, for Brother Moses had succumbed to
mundane slumber and sat nodding like a massive
ghost. Forest Absalom, the silent man, and John
Pease, the English member, now departed to the barn;
and Mrs. Lamb led her flock to a temporary fold, leaving the founders of the "Consociate Family" to build castles in the air till the fire went out and the symposium
ended in smoke.

The furniture arrived next day, and was soon bestowed; for the principal property of the community consisted in books. To this rare library was devoted the
best room in the house, and the few busts and pictures
that still survived many flittings were added to beautify
the sanctuary, for here the family was to meet for
amusement, instruction, and worship.

Any housewife can imagine the emotions of Sister Hope, when she took possession of a large, dilapidated kitchen, containing an old stove and the peculiar stores out of which food was to be evolved for her little family of eleven. Cakes of maple sugar, dried peas and beans, barley and hominy, meal of all sorts, potatoes, and dried fruit. No milk, butter, cheese, tea, or meat appeared. Even salt was considered a useless luxury and spice entirely forbidden by these lovers of Spartan simplicity. A ten years' experience of vegetarian vagaries had been good training for this new freak, and her sense of the ludicrous supported her through many trying scenes.

Unleavened bread, porridge, and water for breakfast; bread, vegetables, and water for dinner; bread, fruit, and water for supper was the bill of fare ordained by the elders. No teapot profaned that sacred stove, no gory steak cried aloud for vengeance from her chaste gridiron; and only a brave woman's taste, time, and temper were sacrificed on that domestic altar.

The vexed question of light was settled by buying a quantity of bayberry wax for candles; and, on discovering that no one knew how to make them, pine knots were introduced, to be used when absolutely necessary. Being summer, the evenings were not long, and the weary fraternity found it no great hardship to retire with the birds. The inner light was sufficient for most of them. But Mrs. Lamb rebelled. Evening was the only time she had to herself, and while the tired feet rested the skilful hands mended torn frocks and little stockings, or anxious heart forgot its burden in a book.

So "mother's lamp" burned steadily, while the philosophers built a new heaven and earth by moonlight; and through all the metaphysical mists and philanthropic pyrotechnics of that period Sister Hope played her own little game of "throwing light," and none but the moths were the worse for it.

Such farming probably was never seen before since Adam delved. The band of brothers began by spading garden and field; but a few days of it lessened their ardor amazingly. Blistered hands and aching backs suggested the expediency of permitting the use of cattle till the workers were better fitted for noble toil by a summer of the new life.

Brother Moses brought a yoke of oxen from his farm,—at least, the philosophers thought so till it was discovered that one of the animals was a cow; and Moses confessed that he "must be let down easy, for he couldn't live on garden sarse entirely."

Great was Dictator Lion's indignation at this lapse from virtue. But time pressed, the work must be done; so the meek cow was permitted to wear the yoke and the recreant brother continued to enjoy forbidden draughts in the barn, which dark proceeding caused the children to regard him as one set apart for destruction.

The sowing was equally peculiar, for, owing to some mistake, the three brethren, who devoted themselves to this graceful task, found when about half through the job that each had been sowing a different sort of grain in the same field; a mistake which caused much perplexity; as it could not be remedied; but, after a long consultation and a good deal of laughter, it was decided to say nothing and see what would come of it.

The garden was planted with a generous supply of useful roots and herbs; but, as manure was not allowed to profane the virgin soil, few of these vegetable treasures ever came up. Purslane reigned supreme, and the disappointed planters ate it philosophically, deciding that Nature knew what was best for them, and would generously supply their needs, if they could only learn to digest her "sallets" and wild roots.

The orchard was laid out, a little grafting done, new trees and vines set, regardless of the unfit season and entire ignorance of the husbandmen, who honestly believed that in the autumn they would reap a bounteous harvest.

Slowly things got into order, and rapidly rumors of the new experiment went abroad, causing many strange spirits to flock thither, for in those days communities were the fashion and transcendentalism raged wildly. Some came to look on and laugh, some to be supported in poetic idleness, a few to believe sincerely and work heartily. Each member was allowed to mount his favorite hobby and ride it to his heart's content. Very queer were some of the riders, and very rampant some of the hobbies.

One youth, believing that language was of little consequence if the spirit was only right, startled newcomers by blandly greeting them with "Good-morning, damn you," and other remarks of an equally mixed order. A second irresponsible being held that all the emotions of the soul should be freely expressed, and illustrated his theory by antics that would have sent him to a lunatic asylum, if, as an unregenerate wag said, he had not already been in one. When his spirit soared, he climbed trees and shouted; when doubt assailed him, he lay upon the floor and groaned lamentably. At joyful periods, he raced, leaped, and sang; when sad, he wept aloud; and when a great thought burst upon him in the watches of night, he crowed like a jocund cockerel, to the great delight of the children and the great annoyance of the elders. One musical brother fiddled whenever so moved, sang sentimentally to the four little girls, and put a music-box on the wall when he hoed corn.

Brother Pease ground away at his uncooked food, or browsed over the farm on sorrel, mint, green fruit, and new vegetables. Occasionally he took his walks abroad, airily attired in an unbleached cotton *poncho,* which was the nearest approach to the primeval costume he was allowed to indulge in. At midsummer he retired to the wilderness, to try his plan where the woodchucks were without prejudices and huckleberry-bushes were hospitably full. A sunstroke unfortunately spoilt his plan, and he returned to semi-civilization a sadder and wiser man.

Forest Absalom preserved his Pythagorean silence, cultivated his fine dark locks, and worked like a beaver, setting an excellent example of brotherly love, justice, and fidelity by his upright life. He it was who helped overworked Sister Hope with her heavy washes, kneaded the endless succession of batches of bread, watched over the children, and did the many tasks left undone by the brethren, who were so busy discussing and defining great duties that they forgot to perform the small ones.

Moses White placidly plodded about, "chorin' raound," as he called it, looking like an old-time patriarch, with his silver hair and flowing beard, and saving the community from many a mishap by his thrift and Yankee shrewdness.

Brother Lion domineered over the whole concern; for, having put the most money into the speculation, he was resolved to make it pay,—as if anything founded on an ideal basis could be expected to do so by any but enthusiasts.

Abel Lamb simply revelled in the Newness, firmly believing that his dream was to be beautifully realized and in time not only little Fruitlands, but the whole earth, be turned into a Happy Valley. He worked with every muscle of his body, for *he* was in deadly earnest. He taught with his whole head and heart; planned and sacrificed, preached and prophesied, with a soul full of the purest aspirations, most unselfish purposes, and desires for a life devoted to God

and man, too high and tender to bear the rough usage of this world.

It was a little remarkable that only one woman ever joined this community. Mrs. Lamb merely followed wheresoever her husband led,—"as ballast for his balloon," as she said, in her bright way.

Miss Jane Gage was a stout lady of mature years, sentimental, amiable, and lazy. She wrote verses copiously, and had vague yearnings and graspings after the unknown, which led her to believe herself fitted for a higher sphere than any she had yet adorned.

Having been a teacher, she was set to instructing the children in the common branches. Each adult member took a turn at the infants; and, as each taught in his own way, the result was a chronic state of chaos in the minds of these much-afflicted innocents.

Sleep, food, and poetic musings were the desires of dear Jane's life, and she shirked all duties as clogs upon her spirit's wings. Any thought of lending a hand with the domestic drudgery never occurred to her; and when to the question, "Art there any beasts of burden on the place?" Mrs. Lamb answered, with a face that told its own tale, "Only one woman!" the buxom Jane took no shame to herself, but laughed at the joke, and let the stout-hearted sister tug on alone.

Unfortunately, the poor lady hankered after the flesh-pots, and endeavored to stay herself with private sips of milk, crackers, and cheese, and on one dire occasion she partook of fish at a neighbor's table.

One of the children reported this sad lapse from virtue, and poor Jane was publicly reprimanded by Timon.

"I only took a little bit of the tail," sobbed the penitent poetess.

"Yes, but the whole fish had to be tortured and slain that you might tempt your carnal appetite with one taste of the tail. Know ye not, consumers of flesh meat, that ye are nourishing the wolf and tiger in your bosoms?"

At this awful question and the peal of laughter which arose from some of the younger brethren, tickled by the ludicrous contrast between the stout sinner, the stern judge, and the naughty satisfaction of the young detective, poor Jane fled from the room to pack her trunk and return to a world where fishes' tails were not forbidden fruit.

Transcendental wild oats were sown broadcast that year, and the fame thereof has not yet ceased in

The Alcott family plot in Sleep Hollow Cemetery, Concord

the land; for, futile as this crop seemed to outsiders, it bore an invisible harvest, worth much to those who planted in earnest. As none of the members of this particular community have ever recounted their experiences before, a few of them may not be amiss, since the interest in these attempts has never died out and Fruitlands was the most ideal of all these castles in Spain.

A new dress was invented, since cotton, silk, and wool were forbidden as the product of slave-labor, worm-slaughter, and sheep-robbery. Tunics and trowsers of brown linen were the only wear. The women's skirts were longer, and their straw hat-brims wider than the men's, and this was the only difference. Some persecution lent a charm to the costume, and the long-haired, linen-clad reformers quite enjoyed the mild martyrdom they endured when they left home.

Money was abjured, as the root of all evil. The produce of the land was to supply most of their wants, or be exchanged for the few things they could not grow. This idea had its inconveniences; but self-denial was the fashion, and it was surprising how many things one can do without. When they desired to travel, they walked, if possible, begged the loan of a vehicle, or boldly entered car or coach, and, stating their principles to the officials, took the consequences. Usually their dress, their earnest frankness, and gentle resolution won them a passage; but now and then they met

with hard usage, and had the satisfaction of suffering for their principles.

On one of these penniless pilgrimages they took passage on a boat and, when fare was demanded, artlessly offered to talk, instead of pay. As the boat was well under way and they actually had not a cent, there was no help for it. So Brothers Lion and Lamb held forth to the assembled passengers in their most eloquent style. There must have been something effective in this conversation, for the listeners were moved to take up a contribution for these inspired lunatics, who preached peace on earth and good-will to man so earnestly, with empty pockets. A goodly sum was collected; but when the captain presented it the reformers proved that they were consistent even in their madness, for not a penny would they accept, saying, with a look at the group about them, whose indifference or contempt had changed to interest and respect, "You see how well we get on without money"; and so went serenely on their way, with their linen blouses flapping airily in the cold October wind.

They preached vegetarianism everywhere and resisted all temptations of the flesh, contentedly eating apples and bread at well-spread tables, and much afflicting hospitable hostesses by denouncing their food and taking away their appetite, discussing the "horrors of shambles," the "incorporation of the brute in man," and "on elegant abstinence the sign of a pure soul." But, when the perplexed or offended ladies asked what they should eat, they got in reply a bill of fare consisting of "bowls of sunrise for breakfast," "solar seeds of the sphere," "dishes from Plutarch's chaste table," and other viands equally hard to find in any modern market.

Reform conventions of all sorts were haunted by these brethren, who said many wise things and did many foolish ones. Unfortunately, these wanderings interfered with their harvest at home; but the rule was to do what the spirit moved, so they left their crops to Providence and went a-reaping in wider and, let us hope, more fruitful fields than their own.

Luckily, the earthly providence who watched over Abel Lamb was at hand to glean the scanty crop yielded by the "uncorrupted land," which "consecrated to human freedom," had received "the sober culture of devout men."

About the time the grain was ready to house, some call of the Oversoul wafted all the men away. An easterly storm was coming up and the yellow stacks were sure to be ruined. Then Sister Hope gathered her forces. Three little girls, one boy (Timon's son), and herself, harnessed to clothes-baskets and Russia-linen sheets, were the only teams she could command; but with these poor appliances the indomitable woman got in the grain and saved the food for her young, with the instinct and energy of a mother-bird with a brood of hungry nestlings to feed.

This attempt at regeneration had its tragic as well as comic side, though the world only saw the former.

With the first frosts, the butterflies, who had sunned themselves in the new light through the summer, took flight, leaving the few bees to see what honey they had stored for winter use. Precious little appeared beyond the satisfaction of a few months of holy living.

At first it seemed as if a chance to try holy dying also was to be offered them. Timon, much disgusted with the failure of the scheme, decided to retire to the Shakers, who seemed to be the only successful community going.

"What is to become of us?" asked Mrs. Hope, for Abel was heartbroken at the bursting of his lovely bubble.

"You can stay here, if you like, till a tenant is found. No more wood must be cut, however, and no more corn ground. All I have must be sold to pay the debts of the concern, as the responsibility rests with me," was the cheering reply.

"Who is to pay us for what we have lost? I gave all I had,–furniture, time, strength, six months of my children's lives,–and all are wasted. Abel gave himself body and soul, and is almost wrecked by hard work and disappointment. Are we to have no return for this, but leave to starve and freeze in an old house, with winter at hand, no money, and hardly a friend left; for this wild scheme has alienated nearly all we had. You talk much about justice. Let us have a little, since there is nothing else left."

But the woman's appeal met with no reply but the old one: "It was an experiment. We all risked something, and must bear our losses as we can."

With this cold comfort, Timon departed with his son, and was absorbed into the Shaker brotherhood, where he soon found that the order of things was reversed, and it was all work and no play.

Then the tragedy began for the forsaken little family. Desolation and despair fell upon Abel. As his wife said, his new beliefs had alienated many friends. Some

thought him mad, some unprincipled. Even the most kindly thought him a visionary, whom it was useless to help till he took more practical views of life. All stood aloof, saying, "Let him work out his own ideas, and see what they are worth."

He had tried, but it was a failure. The world was not ready for Utopia yet, and those who attempted to found it only got laughed at for their pains. In other days, men could sell all and give to the poor, lead lives devoted to holiness and high thought, and, after the persecution was over, find themselves honored as saints or martyrs. But in modern times these things are out of fashion. To live for one's principles, at all costs, is a dangerous speculation; and the failure of an ideal, no matter how humane and noble, is harder for the world to forgive and forget than bank robbery or the grand swindles of corrupt politicians.

Deep waters now for Abel, and for a time there seemed no passage through. Strength and spirits were exhausted by hard work and too much thought. Courage failed when, looking about for help, he saw no sympathizing face, no hand out-stretched to help him, no voice to say cheerily,

"We all make mistakes, and it takes many experiences to shape a life. Try again, and let us help you."

Every door was closed, every eye averted, every heart cold, and no way open whereby he might earn bread for his children. His principles would not permit him to do many things that others did; and in the few fields where conscience would allow him to work, who would employ a man who had flown in the face of society, as he had done?

Then this dreamer, whose dream was the life of his life, resolved to carry out his idea to the bitter end. There seemed no place for him here,–no work, no friend. To go begging conditions was as ignoble as to go begging money. Better perish of want than sell one's soul for the sustenance of his body. Silently he lay down upon his bed, turned his face to the wall, and waited with pathetic patience for death to cut the knot which he could not untie. Days and nights went by, and neither food nor water passed his lips. Soul and body were dumbly struggling together, and no word of complaint betrayed what either suffered.

His wife, when tears and prayers were unavailing, sat down to wait the end with a mysterious awe and submission; for in this entire resignation of all things there was an eloquent significance to her who knew him as no other human being did.

"Leave all to God," was his belief; and in this crisis the loving soul clung to this faith, sure that the Allwise Father would not desert this child who tried to live so near to Him. Gathering her children about her, she waited the issue of the tragedy that was being enacted in that solitary room, while the first snow fell outside, untrodden by the footprints of a single friend.

But the strong angels who sustain and teach perplexed and troubled souls came and went, leaving no trace without, but working miracles within. For, when all other sentiments had faded into dimness, all other hopes died utterly; when the bitterness of death was nearly over, when body was past any pang of hunger or thirst, and soul stood ready to depart, the love that outlives all else refused to die. Head had bowed to defeat, hand had grown weary with too heavy tasks, but heart could not grow cold to those who lived in its tender depths, even when death touched it.

"My faithful wife, my little girls,—they have not forsaken me, they are mine by ties that none can break. What right have I to leave them alone? What right to escape from the burden and the sorrow I have helped to bring? This duty remains to me, and I must do it manfully. For their sakes, the world will forgive me in time; for their sakes, God will sustain me now."

Too feeble to rise, Abel groped for the food that always lay within his reach, and in the darkness and solitude of that memorable night ate and drank what was to him the bread and wine of a new communion, a new dedication of heart and life to the duties that were left him when the dreams fled.

In the early dawn, when that sad wife crept fearfully to see what change had come to the patient face on the pillow, she found it smiling at her, saw a wasted hand outstretched to her, and heard a feeble voice cry bravely, "Hope!"

What passed in that little room is not to be recorded except in the hearts of those who suffered and endured much for love's sake. Enough for us to know that soon the wan shadow of a man came forth, leaning on the arm that never failed him, to be welcomed and cherished by the children, who never forgot the experiences of that time.

"Hope" was the watchword now; and, while the last logs blazed on the hearth, the last bread and apples covered the table, and the new commander, with recovered courage, said to her husband,—

"Leave all to God—and me. He has done this part, now I will do mine."

"But we have no money, dear."

"Yes, we have. I sold all we could spare, and have enough to take us away from this snow-bank."

"Where can we go?"

"I have engaged four rooms at our good neighbor, Lovejoy's. There we can live cheaply till spring. Then for new plans and a home of our own, please God."

"But, Hope, your little store won't last long, and we have no friends."

"I can sew and you can chop wood. Lovejoy offers you the same pay as he gives his other men; my old friend, Mrs. Truman, will send me all the work I want; and my blessed brother stands by us to the end. Cheer up, dear heart, for while there is work and love in the world we shall not suffer."

"And while I have my good angel Hope, I shall not despair, even if I wait another thirty years before I step beyond the circle of the sacred little world in which I still have a place to fill."

So one bleak December day, with their few possessions piled on an ox-sled, the rosy children perched atop, and the parents trudging arm in arm behind, the exiles left their Eden and faced the world again.

"Ah me! my happy dream. How much I leave behind that never can be mine again," said Abel, looking back at the lost Paradise, lying white and chill in its shroud of snow.

"Yes, dear, but how much we bring away," answered brave-hearted Hope, glancing from husband to children.

"Poor Fruitlands! The name was as great a failure as the rest!" continued Abel, with a sigh, as a frostbitten apple fell from a leafless bough at this feet.

But the sigh changed to a smile as his wife added, in a half-tender, half-satirical tone,—

"Don't you think Apple Slump would be a better name for it, dear?"

THE RISE OF TRANSCENDENTALISM
1815-1860

Alexander Kern

AMERICAN Transcendentalism[1] was, it now appears, an essentially indigenous movement, which, though it showed foreign influences and counterparts, developed along independent lines in response to American needs. First appearing as "The Latest Form of Infidelity," and later recognized for the importance of its literary contributions, it was perhaps the major liberating force of its period, and as such made significant contributions to a number of areas. In philosophy it was important to the development of the pragmatisms[2] of William James, Charles Saunders Peirce, and John Dewey. In religion it both spiritualized a wing of Unitarianism and gave grounds for the growth of free religion. To literature it furnished a new and significant aesthetic theory and our two best writers of nonfictional prose in Emerson and Thoreau, as well as two of our major poets in Emerson and his distant disciple Whitman. Even Hawthorne and Melville were affected by it, if negatively. In the social realm, Transcendentalism provided for its time not only the most cogent criticism of commercial materialism, but it indirectly affected American education, and though it had little immediate effect on other institutions, it reinforced Gandhi's program of nonviolent resistance, which has influenced the lives of hundreds of millions of people. Consequently the development of Transcendentalism in all these several directions can fruitfully be explored.

But in order to discover how and why Transcendentalism grew, it is necessary to find out what it was. This is difficult to do, because it was a developing movement, not a static philosophy, and because the Transcendentalists were, as separate thinkers, hardly logical system-builders, while, as a group, they were radical individualists who often disagreed with each other, however much alike they may have appeared to their opponents. For these reasons no completely successful definition of Transcendentalism has ever been worked out. Take, for example, two definitions offered by men who knew it at first hand: Emerson called Transcendentalism "Idealism as it appears in 1842,"[3] yet this accurately applied only to a certain New England group, for Poe, who was certainly an idealist, was not part of the movement. Cabot's assertion that Transcendentalism was "Romanticism on Puritan ground,"[4] is also too broad, since it would fit Hawthorne, Melville, and even Henry Wadsworth Longfellow. Nor have modern scholars been much more successful.[5] Nevertheless, by pointing out the common characteristics of the members of the group and their common ideas, it is possible to set forth a model or constructed type, like Professor Wellek's "Movement,"[6] which can increase our understanding of its inception and growth.

The names of thirty-odd of the more significant Transcendentalists whose works will be considered follow in chronological order: Dr. William Ellery Channing (1780-1842), James Marsh (1794-1842), Convers Francis (1795-1863), Amos Bronson Alcott (1799-1888), George Bancroft (1800-1891), Sampson Reed (1800-1880), William Howard Furness (1802-1896), George Ripley (1802-1880), Caleb Stetson (c. 1802-1870), Ralph Waldo Emerson (1803-1882), Orestes Brownson (1803-1876), Caleb Sprague Henry (1804-1884), Elizabeth Palmer Peabody (1804-1894), Frederic Henry Hedge (1805-1890), Sophia Ripley (c. 1807-1861), William Henry Channing (1810-1884), (Sarah) Margaret Fuller (1810-1850), Theodore Parker (1810-1860), Cyrus Bartol (1813-1900), Charles T. Brooks (1813-1883), Christopher Cranch (1813-1892), John Sullivan Dwight (1813-1893), Sylvester Judd (1813-1853), Samuel Osgood (1813-1880), Jones Very (1813-1880), Ellen Sturgis Hooper (1815-1848), Charles Stearns Wheeler (1816-1843), Henry David Thoreau (1817-1862), (William) Ellery Channing (1818-1901), Caroline Sturgis Tappan (1818-1888),

Map of Boston in 1855

John Weiss (1818-1879), Samuel Longfellow (1819-1892), Charles King Newcomb (1820-1894), Octavius B. Frothingham (1822-1895), Samuel Johnson (1822-1882), Thomas Wentworth Higginson (1823-1911), David Wasson (1823-1887), Franklin Benjamin Sanborn (1831-1917), Moncure Conway (1823-1907).

Of the less familiar figures, Marsh and Reed were precursors; Bancroft, the historian, though a Transcendentalist in philosophy, was not a member of the central group; the Sturgis sisters were poets; Henry and Osgood became Episcopal rectors; Wheeler, who influenced Thoreau, died young; and Conway, Frothingham, Higginson, Longfellow, Johnson, Sanborn, Wasson, and Weiss, members of the later movement which is not the subject of this paper, will be mentioned only in connection with the antislavery movement.

Of the central group, all were New Englanders and Unitarians, and all who attended any college attended Harvard (at least for work in divinity). All except Ellery Channing had at one time been clergymen or teachers. A number came from clerical or professional families, and most from the middle class which prized education, so that even when they were not well off, they found relatives and scholarships to support college careers. Brownson, Parker, and Alcott came from poorer families, were mainly self-educated, and significantly represent in their various ways more radical social positions. They were all serious, religious, intent on self-improvement, independent, and individualistic. Though some were more nearly mystical and others more logical, though some believed in self-reform and others more in social reform, though some remained Unitarians while others revolted against the church; they were substantially alike as intuitive idealists–moral and unworldly. With these similarities of background and temperament they produced a movement which could be identified without mistake.

Negatively they rejected the following ideas: (1) the sensationalist, anti-idealist features of Locke's philosophy;[7] (2) the associationist psychology, which denied the active shaping power of the human mind;[8] (3) the concept of a mechanical universe with a bystanding God, which derived from Newton and Paley; (4) the sensationalist and associationist features of the Scottish Common-Sense school; (5) the materialist philosophy and "pale negations" of the conservative Unitarians–their institutionalized ritual, their coolness, conservatism, and decorum illogically combined with a belief in the saving powers of Jesus and in the miracles of the New Testament; (6) the Calvinistic acceptance of total depravity, predestination, and pessimism; (7) the need to adhere to the generalized, balanced, formalized style of neoclassicism with its emphasis on fluency, structure, and careful working out of decorative details; (8) the commercial ideal of thrift, industry, profit, and "success" as attested by vulgar monetary standards; (9) the improvement of society by social legislation through the will of the majority.

Affirmatively, the Transcendentalists adopted the following concepts: (1) an intuitive idealism which accepted ideas as ultimates; (2) a view of the imagination of intuition (in their language Reason) giving a direct apprehension of reality which the logical faculties (the Understanding) could not furnish; (3) the concept of an organic universe in which Nature, suffused by an immanent God, corresponded with spirit in such a way that the connections and indeed the whole could be grasped by contemplation and intuition; (4) a living religion in which miracles seemed natural; (5) the divinity of man, who consequently did not need salvation; (6) a

Program for the Concord Lyceum in 1843

concept of Genius which could produce works of art by recording its intuitions through the use of nature symbols; (7) a freedom and spontaneity in art to permit the creation of works liberated from the artificialities produced by talent or mechanical rules alone; (8) an individual moral insight which should supersede the dollar as the standard of conduct; (9) self-improvement as the primary avenue of social improvement; (10) individualism, i.e., reliance on God, rather than conformity to the will of a political or social majority; (11) an optimism about the potentialities of individual lives and of the universe.

With this pattern of negative and affirmative concepts in mind, it is possible now to proceed by showing in successive sections certain transitions from earlier to Transcendentalist views:

I. The philosophical shift from sensationalism and materialism to intuitive idealism–from the moral sense to the direct apprehension of reality.

II. The transformation of a mechanistic universe to a vitalistic and evolving nature which serves as a symbol of the realm of the spirit.

III. The religious development from the conservative Unitarian institutionalism which combined philosophical materialism with belief in the miracles of the New Testament to the clear insistence upon the divinity of man.

IV. The literary change from neoclassical principles of correctness to the romantic use of symbol to body forth the intuited and organic vision of the genuinely creative artist.

V. The turn in social thought from emphasis upon collective natural rights to individual integrity and the freedom of each man for maximum personal development.

In this process of plotting transitions, it will be necessary to note both the leading lines of growth and the deviations and disagreements among the members of the group. It will, moreover, be necessary to take cognizance of the factors which contributed to the changes, including both the ostensible causes of dissatisfaction with the previously accepted ideas and the reading which may have furnished some of the hints followed out in the new developments. While the Transcendentalists were such wide readers that specific literary sources cannot always be isolated with assurance, still it is worth the attempt to treat the influences as critically as may be. The developmental period will be especially emphasized as well as the contributions of Emerson as the most important if not the most typical writer of the school. By this method, it is hoped, it will be possible to appreciate how the Transcendentalists, in response to a special set of psychic needs, aroused in particular by the contradictions in Unitarianism, developed an American thought pattern which though it used materials from many philosophies, avoided the religious and political conservatism of the later Coleridge and Wordsworth, the sexual license of Goethe and Byron, and the hero-worship and disdain of the masses of Carlyle.

I

The idealism of the Transcendentalists, although of course the ultimate sources of some of the Transcendental ideas were foreign, was composed finally into a distinctive American pattern. Nor can it be said that any single strand of foreign thought was primary, because the emphasis on any particular European philosopher varied from individual to individual. The new design which emerged was not purely Platonic, nor Berkeleyan, nor Kantian,[9] but a complicated interweaving.

In this turn toward idealism the American Transcendentalists were part of the Romantic movement, which met a similar problem in similar ways. Locke's *Essay Concerning Human Understanding* and the later analysis of Hume, which held that absolute knowledge of the outer world was impossible, left the problem of epistemology in a state which proved emotionally unsatisfying to a large number of thinkers of whom the Transcendentalists were only one group. They, like the Scottish Common-Sense school founded by Reid, like Kant and his followers, like Coleridge, and like the French eclectics, sought for a theory which would not only make knowledge possible and would give ideas a permanent place in the universe, but would also leave room for religion. Whether or not the new philosophy preceded the religious controversy, the real issue was philosophical and ultimately epistemological. The first dissatisfaction with Unitarianism was not with what its clergy accepted on faith–that is, its belief in revelation and miracles, but with its liberal rationalism which left it with a materialistic philosophy except in the realm of morals.

For serious thinkers of a certain temperament, dissatisfaction with the emotionally cool sensationalism, mechanism, and determinism descending from Locke was increasing. The Scottish Common-Sense philosophers, Reid,[10] Stewart,[11] and Brown,[12] had offered some amelioration, both through insisting that the dictates of universal common apprehension could not be gainsaid by any logical analysis, and more particularly through claiming that man had an innate moral sense which unerringly judged right and wrong.[13] These philosophers were taught at Harvard,[14] partly to soften Locke. Yet even this was not totally satisfactory. Thus beginning in the 1820's one of the clearest issues was the need for idealism as opposed to materialism. This was true of James Marsh; it was true not only of Emerson's *Nature*,[15] but more significantly of his lecture "The Transcendentalist,"[16] which emphasized that the new views were simply idealism; it was also true of Theodore Parker's "Transcendentalism,"[17] which sets up a long contrast between materialism and idealism. Whatever we may think now, the Transcendentalists believed that the issue was one between the old philosophy, whether Lockean or Scottish, and the new idealism.

In their various ways Joseph S. Buckminster, Edward Everett, and William Ellery Channing had begun to open windows of Boston to new winds of doctrine.

Emerson's study in Concord

to chart the new path. He it was who is said, on discovering in Jouffroy that Dr. Richard Price's *Dissertations on Matter and Spirit* had influenced German idealism, to have remarked:

> Price saved me from Locke's philosophy. He gave me the Platonic doctrine of ideas. . . . His book, probably, moulded my philosophy into the form it has always retained, and opened my mind into the *transcendental depth.* And I have always found in the accounts I have read of German philosophy in Madame de Staël, and in these later times, that it was cognate to my own. I cannot say that I have ever received a new idea from it; and the cause is obvious, if Price was alike the father of *it* and *mine.*[18]

While he claimed that Hutcheson's *Moral Philosophy* was one of the most important books he read in college, it was Coleridge to whose mind he "owed more than to the mind of any other philosophic thinker,"[19] through both the *Biographia Literaria* and personal acquaintance in 1822-1823.[20]

Perhaps Dr. Channing most closely approached Transcendentalism in his sermon "Likeness to God" in 1828, where he said:

> The divine attributes are first developed in ourselves, and thence transferred to our Creator. The idea of God, sublime and awful as it is, is the idea of our own spiritual nature, purified and enlarged to infinity. In ourselves are the elements of the Divinity. God, then, does not sustain a figurative resemblance to man. It is the resemblance of a parent to a child, the likeness of a kindred nature.[21]

Late in his life Channing seemed to think that the "new views" would tend to "loosen the tie which binds the soul to its great friend and deliverer."[22] On another occasion he said, "The danger that besets our Transcendentalists is that they sometimes mistake their individualities for the Transcendent. What is common to men and revealed by Jesus transcends every single individuality, and is the spiritual object and food of all individuals. . . . there is a danger that Emerson's followers may lapse into a kind of *egotheism.*"[23] But for all his influence upon Emerson,[24] Parker,[25] and ‚Elizabeth Peabody, Channing was both too much of a Christian and too much of a rationalist to go the whole way toward Transcendentalism himself.[26] And he was more highly regarded by Emerson and Parker for his high moral senti-

Buckminster, by establishing the Anthology Club with William Emerson, Waldo's father, and its magazine the *Monthly Anthology,* but especially by giving his large library filled with foreign books to the Boston Athenaeum, had both created interest in literature and furnished a source for new ideas. Edward Everett, the first American to study in Germany, returned in 1819 filled with eloquence and classical learning. He, however, was not influenced by German idealistic thought, and it was not until George Bancroft's return in 1821 that German romanticism was brought back to America. It was Channing who of the three did most to let in new ideas, by the personal influence of his receptivity to new ideas, by his acceptance of Price, Coleridge, and Wordsworth, and by his undogmatic spirituality.

As Dr. Channing made the first steps, he began

ment and religious personality than for his intellectual powers and ideas.[27] Nevertheless he was an attractive, liberalizing influence because of his open-mindedness, his eloquence, his high spiritual station, and his real if reluctant participation in movements of reform.[28]

Emerson and his coevals were able to develop Transcendentalist idealism much farther than Dr. Channing and to put much farther behind them the combination of sensationalism and moral sense which was taught at Harvard in the 1820's and 1830's. The growth was slow and indistinct for a time, nor did Emerson emerge as the leader until 1838. On the other hand some of the other active members of the early band lost their prominence. Hedge, less extreme in his views, withdrew not out of timidity, but out of conviction. Brownson became a Catholic in 1844, and Ripley cut himself off after the collapse of the Brook Farm experiment. Conversely, Thoreau, who was a Transcendentalist by 1837 or 1838, did not achieve prominence except among his most perceptive neighbors until after his death.

Generally speaking, the point of departure for the new movement was the sensationalist philosophy of Locke, which Alexander Hill Everett defended from the attacks of Europeans as early as 1829, before the Americans of the New School had begun to announce their views in public. Everett, in attacking Cousin and Kant, called idealism "an unsubstantial dream, which charms the infantile period of intellectual philosophy" rather than "one of the two opinions which have nearly divided the thinking men of all ages and nations."[29] In 1831 Timothy Walker continued the defense against the foreign evil in a denial of the views of the still anonymous Carlyle. Walker saw little to be feared in a mechanism which smooths down mountains, gives a concept of a supreme being by deduction from the lawful universe, and shows man's mind closest to God's in subjugating matter to laws.[30] Needless to say Walker thought that Carlyle's dislike of Locke's philosophy was definitely wrong.[31]

Frederic Henry Hedge, a vigorous little man, educated in Germany and a competent student of philosophy, achieved an early prominence apparently because, though it cannot be documented specifically, he was important in explaining various strains of German thought to the Transcendental Club, or the "Hedge Club" as Emerson called it, since it met whenever Hedge came down from Bangor, Maine, where he preached until 1850.[32] One of Hedge's major services to the move-ment was his article on Coleridge in the *Christian Examiner* in 1833. This was the first public defense of the Transcendentalist philosophy, and it went much further than its titular subject. After claiming that Coleridge was not needlessly obscure,[33] Hedge went on to say that Kant distinguished between two types of consciousness, the common, which is a passive receptor of the world, and the interior, which is active.[34] Transcendentalism, he says, seeks to find an unconditioned absolute as the ground of finite existence, and as a final step to establish a "coincidence between the facts of ordinary experience and those which we have discovered within ourselves."[35] This fine paper, commended by Emerson as a "living, leaping logos," was even approved by the Unitarian Henry Ware.[36]

More prominent in the subsequent controversy was George Ripley, a man of fine intelligence and magnificent integrity. A good scholar, indeed something of a pedant, and possibly a dull preacher, Ripley both read and knew the European philosophers. He recognized the great differences between Kant and Coleridge,[37] and pointed out that they seemed obscure only to certain kinds of minds. He was opposed to utilitarianism with its "selfish calculations" which were in constant danger of disagreeing with "the dictates of unchangeable justice."[38] An honest and vigorous fighter, Ripley sought in 1836 in his *Discourse on the Philosophy of Religion* to counter the public attack of Andrews Norton, the Unitarian "Pope." Ripley pointed out that in religion men are conversant with invisible objects, though this does not make men visionary or impractical.[39] Indeed, Ripley argued that "things which are unseen possess the only independent reality."[40] In thorough Transcendental fashion he insisted that the power for perceiving truth is Reason,[41] that man has a faculty for recognizing moral distinctions, that man is capable of disinterested love,[42] and that man possesses a power of conceiving perfection.[43] This was a strong statement of the idealistic position.

Certainly the best philosophical thinker in the early group, and one of the most energetic in mind, was Orestes Brownson, a self-educated farm boy with a pugnacious temperament, who was for years a seeker of answers. Born in Vermont, he became in turn a Presbyterian, a Universalist, an agnostic organizer of the Workingmen's Party, a Unitarian preacher, editor of the *Boston Quarterly Review* (1838-1842), and coeditor of the *Democratic Review* from 1842. In 1844 he joined the Catholic church and henceforth attacked

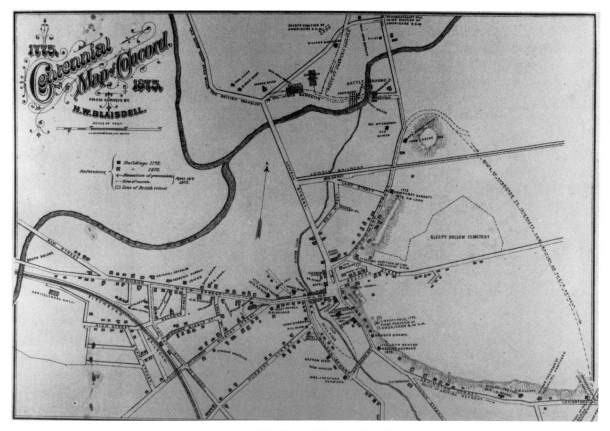

Concord in 1875 (Concord Free Public Library)

his own former views and associates. Though difficult to get along with, he was a particularly able writer in a number of fields, notably philosophical and social, where he showed learning, logical acumen, and generalizing ability along with a heavy dogmatism which may have resulted from a certain insecurity about his social and educational background.

When he became the Unitarian minister at Canton, Massachusetts, in 1834, Brownson was within reach of the Boston group of liberals and he began to write for the *Christian Examiner,* where he first made his weight felt in a disquisition on Constant's *De la réligion.* In this essay he explained that religious institutions regularly crystallize or ossify while religious sentiment progresses, and that a new religious movement must tear down the old outmoded structure to permit development of the new sentiment. Then he took up Constant's point "that religion and morality rest not on the understanding, not on logical deductions, but on an interior sentiment. Here is an important recognition,–a recognition of two distinct orders of human faculties. This recognition is not always made by metaphysicians, but it never escapes popular language."[44] And this feeling which may be aroused "when contemplating a vast and tranquil sea, distant mountains with harmonious outlines, or, when marking an act of heroism, of disinterestedness, or of generous self-sacrifice for others' welfare, rises without any dependence on the understanding."[45] Thus Brownson took a position in conscious opposition to the older school of thought. "We are aware, that the philosophy of sensation will condemn this position. Be it so," he added, for while he recognized the philosophy of sensation as the philosophy of the last half-century in America, he hoped it would not be that of the future.[46]

In his early Transcendental period, Brownson was especially affected by Cousin's thought (which he preferred to that of Kant, Schelling, and Hegel[47]) as not leading to skepticism, because he thought that it could span the deplorable breach between religion and philosophy.[48] And this he felt was true because Cousin made "psychology the foundation, but not the superstructure" of his philosophy, while by his technique of empiricism he gave objective validity to his results.[49]

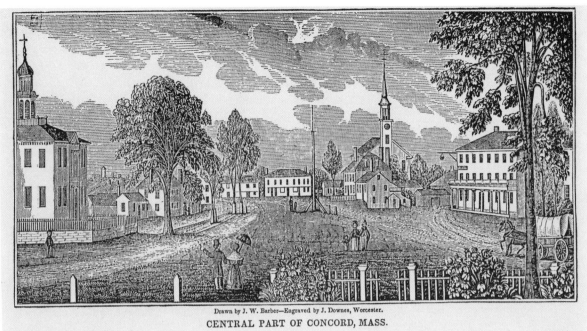

Drawn by J. W. Barber—Engraved by J. Downes, Worcester.

CENTRAL PART OF CONCORD, MASS.

The above is a northern view in the central part of Concord village. Part of the Court-House is seen on the left. Burying-ground Hill (a post of observation to the British officers in the invasion of 1775) is seen a short distance beyond. The Unitarian Church and Middlesex Hotel are seen on the right.

Concord Free Public Library

Since the reason, though appearing in us, is not our *self* but objective, according to Cousin, it is a "legitimate authority for whatever it reveals,"[50] and what it reveals is the absolute, which is given and not deducted from the relative, which it logically precedes.[51] This view, which Brownson insisted was not pantheism because according to it the universe is the effect of God and not God, permits him to hold that God appears in us as reason—a view so satisfactory to him that he recommended it to all his readers. In this way he promoted a form of Transcendentalism which insisted upon intuitive apprehension of God.

In an important pamphlet, *New Views of Christianity, Society, and the Church* (1836), Brownson moved on to a vigorous and penetrating historical analysis of Unitarianism which put both the United States and Unitarianism into the stream of Western history as a part of the Atlantic civilization. This he did by setting up two contrasting social systems, the spiritual and the material, or heavenly and worldly, which are constantly at war with each other and need to be harmonized. First one predominates and then the other, materialism under Greece and Rome and spiritualism in the Middle Ages, with materialism triumphing again in Protestantism, which "brought up the state, civil liberty, human reason, philosophy, industry, all the temporal interests."[52] As a sort of premonition of his later conversion, he continued, "Properly speaking, Protestantism has no religious character" and "is, in fact, only Catholicism continued" and watered down.[53] That Brownson really means the religion of the Enlightenment by Protestantism is indicated by his assertion that the arts showed the same tendency–the familiar marks of neoclassicism, exaltation of the material order and a patterning after the Greeks and Romans.[54] Protestantism and industrialism were by Brownson associated in terms anticipating Weber and Tawney,[55] and so also were civil and political liberty. Indeed he saw the American Revolution and Unitarianism as parts of what may be called the Enlightenment.[56] But all this materialism he saw declining with the failure of the French Revolution and the consequent despotism of Napoleon. Despair of things on earth caused men to seek refuge in heaven. While certain oversimplifications in this picture could be pointed out, it is clear that Brownson was declaring that Unitarianism, whatever its humane virtues, was attached to a dying past, though from it must come the reconciliation of the future in terms of the spiritual philosophy. This attack on all sides is significant, but at this point it is necessary to emphasize the attack on the sensational philosophy as antiquated and outmoded.

Much more immediate reaction was occasioned by the publication of Amos Bronson Alcott's *Record of Conversations on the Gospels held in Mr. Alcott's School, Unfolding the Doctrine and Discipline of Human Culture,* December, 1836. Alcott, born at Spindle Hill, Connecticut, was reared on a farm, served a period as a peddler in the South, and then turned to school teaching. Though he had been a Lockean,[57] Alcott was by temperament inclined toward idealism of an extremely intuitional sort, a tendency which was reinforced by his friendship with Dr. Channing and his reading of Reed's *Growth of the Mind* in 1829, Cousin in 1831, Coleridge's *Aids to Reflection* in 1832, and in 1833 the *Biographia Literaria,* some Plato, Proclus, and Plotinus, *Wilhelm Meister,* some Carlyle, Wordsworth's *Excursion,* Okely's life of Boehme, and an abstract of Kant. In 1834 he opened the Temple School in Boston and in 1835 became acquainted with Emerson. By this time, as his journals show, he was a thorough Transcendentalist, and indeed he influenced Emerson's *Nature,* which apparently as a consequence goes farther in the direction of absolute idealism (that is, in reducing everything to spirit) than his writing usually does.

Though Alcott had published an article on his Cheshire School in William Russell's *American Journal of Education* at the end of 1827, it was the publication of Peabody's *Record of a School* (1835) which first made his work widely known. But it was his own *Record of Conversations on the Gospels Held in Mr. Alcott's School, Unfolding the Doctrine and Discipline of Human Culture* (Vol. 1, 1836; Vol. II, 1837) which called down public denunciation upon him. This book, harmless enough in twentieth-century eyes, was vigorously attacked. "Mr. Alcott should hide his head in shame," wrote a parent to the Boston *Courier;* the editor called it "indecent and obscene" and quoted a clergyman, apparently Andrews Norton, who said the book was one-third "absurd, one-third blasphemous, and one-third obscene."[58] This response was due in part to the book's religious quality (Ripley indicated that the clergy felt their territory was invaded),[59] to its romantic assumption that children were not only naturally good but closer to God, and to its supposed frankness.[60] Properly speaking, it was, of course, a threat both to the "spare the rod and spoil the child" theory of education and to conservative Unitarianism because it assumed that *"Christianity is grounded in the essential Nature of Man."*[61]

Another important Transcendentalist publication of 1836 was W. H. Furness's *Remarks on the Four Gospels,* in which he argued that if the world were considered and understood from a spiritual point of view which recognized that scientific knowledge was incomplete and fragmentary, then there was nothing miraculous about even the resurrection of Jesus; the supernatural was "everywhere in the natural."[62] And this rather than the sensational philosophy was for Furness the most desirable because it was the broadest position.

Though it took time for the fact to become evident, it was Emerson's *Nature* which was the great book of the year 1836, for even though it did not completely unfold Emerson's mature thought, it possessed a breadth and depth which gradually made itself felt. *Nature,* Emerson's first published work, gave the impression that its author was always a Transcendentalist, but this was of course not true; like the others, Emerson began with the older views. Indeed, despite the fact that his father had been a Unitarian minister, Emerson was brought up in an atmosphere to which his Aunt Mary Moody Emerson contributed a large supply of Calvinism with a moral though not a doctrinal effect. Moreover, Emerson was taught Locke at Harvard and in addition the Scottish philosophers of the Common-Sense school, and the latter especially influenced his thought. It appears that Emerson had an inclination toward idealism which was not completely submerged even by his formal education, with the result often a mixture of systems or a conflict between them.

This tendency toward idealism is significantly made manifest in Emerson's college essay on "The Character of Socrates," which won a Bowdoin second prize in 1820. His subject lay outside the topics most acceptable at Harvard and met with a partial rebuke from President Kirkland, who thought Emerson should be "a better Locke, Stewart, and Paley scholar."[63] But the line of this essay lay in the direction of Waldo's future development. It is easy to see some ironical reflections on the self-satisfied state of his professors in the introduction:

> The increasing notice which it [the philosophy of the human mind] obtains is owing much to the genius of those men who have raised themselves with the science to general regard, but chiefly, as its patrons contend, to the uncontrolled progress of human improvement. The zeal of its advocates, however, in other respects commendable, has sinned in one particular,–they

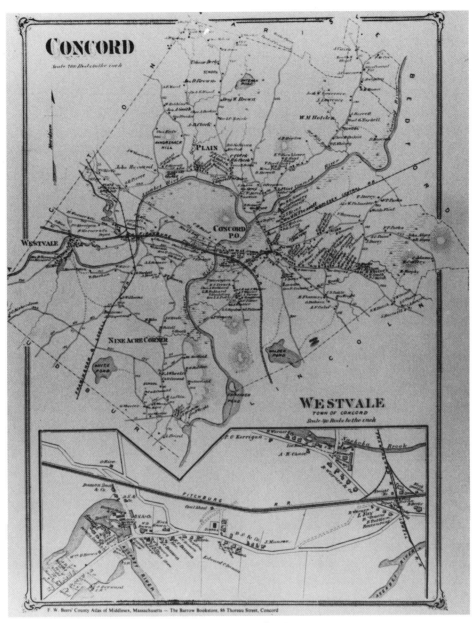

Map of Concord in 1875

have laid a little too much self-complacent stress on the merit and success of their own unselfish exertions, and in their first contempt of the absurd and trifling speculations of former metaphysicians, appear to have confounded sophists and true philosophers, and to have been disdainful of some who have enlightened the world and marked out a path of future advancement.

Indeed the giant strength of modern improvement is more indebted to the early wisdom of Thales and Socrates and Plato than is generally allowed, or perhaps than modern philosophers have been well aware.[64]

Emerson's emphasis upon the moral courage of Socrates in disagreeing with conventional religion[65] is also significant as a premonition of Self-Reliance; his emphasis upon Socrates' abstemious life and cheerful acceptance of poverty for the sake of cultivating his soul indicates Emerson's own ideal; his insistence that Socrates is higher in character than in intellect[66] points to his future belief that character is above intellect. Emerson's quotation:

"Let us not, then, refuse to believe even what we do not behold, and let us supply the defect of our corporeal eyes by using those of the soul; but especially let us learn to render the just homage of respect and veneration to that Divinity whose will it seems to be that we should have no other perception of him but by his effects in our favor . . . by doing his will"[67]

indicates here an approval of intuition as well as of following it, which again prepares for his later doctrine of reliance upon the Over-Soul. His emphasis upon the "moral perfection" of a man who did not enjoy the advantages of Christian "revelation"[68] shows his own boldness in religious areas. His emphasis on Socrates' view that the soul was a form of eternal beauty in the divine mind and was most nearly approached by beautiful mortals,[69] foreshadows some of his later views of both friendship and aesthetics. Thus a number of later doctrines and centers of interest are adumbrated in this early essay, which shows a certain characteristic boldness of speculation.

The Scottish Common-Sense philosophers who were taught at Harvard along with Locke, as has already been pointed out, offered a halfway station on the road to idealism. Dugald Stewart's *Elements of the Philosophy of the Human Mind* and Thomas Brown's *Lectures* were part of the curriculum,[70] but perhaps more important for Emerson was the fact that he read independently in 1820-1821 Stewart's *Outlines of Moral Philosophy,* which maintained that a moral sense was inborn in each child and was a mainspring of his mental powers. These ideas were reinforced by Levi Hedge, who Ripley thought followed the moral-sense school,[71] and Levi Frisbie, professor of logic, whose lecture notes were later published by Andrews Norton,[72] although Frisbie thought that the moral sense needed cultivation.

Emerson was, in 1821, pondering these ideas which anticipated his later views. Meanwhile, at the instance of his vigorous and influential Aunt Mary, he was reading Price's *Morals* with some perplexity and on March 14 recorded in his *Journal,* "Dr. Price says that right and wrong are not determined by any reasoning or deduction, but by the ultimate perception of the human mind. It is to be desired that this was capable of satisfactory proof, but, as it is in direct opposition to the skeptical philosophy, it cannot stand unsupported by strong and sufficient evidence. I will however read more. . . ."[73]

Beneath the apparent certainty of his senior paper, "The Present State of Ethical Philosophy," which again won a Bowdoin second prize, there is some ambivalence with reference to both Hume and the Scottish school. If Emerson were attempting to win a first award by treating a more conventionally acceptable subject, he was too honest to claim more than he actually felt, and this work is more important for its somewhat confused examination of the subject than for its positive answers. Proceeding with the logical organization which characterized his early work, Emerson briefly sketches the history of moral philosophy up to Clarke, Price, Butler, Reid, Paley, Smith, and Stewart.[74] Evidently distinguishing between the common-sense and moral-sense aspects of the school, he says that ethical science's "fundamental principles are taught by the moral sense, and no advancement of time can improve them,"[75] since only natural science and not moral intuitions are progressive.[76] "The object of these reasonings," he continues, "is to confirm the decisions of the moral faculty, which is recognized as an original principle of our nature,–an intuition by which we directly determine the merit or demerit of an action."[77] On the other hand, the common sense of the Scottish group does not seem perfect to him, since its "reasonings as yet want the neatness and conclusiveness of a system," and have not removed "the terror which attached to the name of Hume";[78] nevertheless he thinks that the first true advance must be made in the Scottish school through the use of moral maxims rather than ultimate principles. Also ambivalent is his attitude toward Hume. On the one hand, Hume's claim that happiness lies in the condition of the mind, not in an external quality, represents "sagacity,"[79] and his skepticism is "manly" and does not deserve a "*sneer.*"[80] On the other hand, he calls Hume's dissolution of moral laws an "outrage."[81] Though not satisfied completely with Reid and Stewart and not yet having developed his own solution, Emerson states (anticipating his later individualism) that the chief benefit of the science of morals which has "more permanent interest than any other,"[82] lies "in its effect on the individual,"[83] and that the idea of progress cannot certainly be believed.[84]

Thus by 1821 Emerson already showed sympathies with idealism, a serious regard for honest and rigorous skeptics like Hume, acceptance of the idea of a moral sense, and some doubt of the efficacy, so far at least, of the attempts to codify morals on a practical rather than an intuitional basis. Here his permanent interest in morals is asserted, with some indication that

The Concord main street in the mid 1860s (Concord Free Public Library)

they will be built upon insight rather than upon classification or codes.

While he did not find permanent form for his ideas until 1836, as a young preacher Emerson was beginning to put forward the ideas which characterized his later thought, though couched in terms which included Christ and God. His very first sermon, "Pray without Ceasing," asserted the dual worlds of matter and spirit, the latter "more certain and stable,"[85] though most men err in following the law of the material, working for "bread and wine and dress and our houses and our furniture."[86] But as an idealist already, Emerson pointed out that men's minds are "ideas present to the mind of God," and only men's liberty could be called their own.[87] In 1829 he spoke of nature's "everlasting analogies,"[88] and especially after the shattering death of his wife Ellen, he emphasized the doctrine of compensation.[89]

Professor Rusk finds a similar premonition of Emerson's later ideas in his unpublished sermons:

A sermon against foolish, counterfeit pride said that "The good man reveres himself, re-

veres his conscience, and would rather suffer any calamity than lower himself in his own esteem." Another sermon declared that physical things were chiefly significant as symbols; another, that heaven was here and now; another, that the moral sentiment, perceiver of right and wrong and therefore the sovereign part of man's nature, existed in the mind independently of experience; another, that there was a "law of progress, that on-look of human nature, which is its distinguishing and beautiful characteristic." Others asserted freedom of the will in spite of all determination from outside, or the Quaker doctrine of the inward light with its implication that "the bible has no force but what it derives from within us." Jesus, the preacher explained, had no authority as a person. The delivery of the same truths Jesus uttered would have invested the humblest created spirit with the same authority, no more and no less. . . . "A trust in yourself . . . is the height not of pride but of piety, an unwillingness to learn of any but God himself." . . . He asserted that "What you can get of moral or intellectual excellence out of this little plot of ground you call *yourself,* by the sweat of your brow—is your portion." . . .

His hearers must have been struck by his habit of regarding man as divine.[90]

The *Journals* likewise reveal a gradual advance toward a coherent pattern of idealism. As early as 1820 Emerson saw the "properties of matter as the properties of mind,"[91] and in 1822 he wrote that the Platonist was right in his view of the war of mind and matter.[92] Though he used the Common-Sense argument that the Trinity was an invalid concept because "inconceivable," he gave the argument an idealistic slant by saying, "Infinite Wisdom established the foundations of the knowledge of the mind."[93] He continued his acceptance of a moral sense which comes from a mind that is God, and which, unlike the emotions or the human intellect, never fails and is always the same.[94] By 1828 he suggested that man was "connected to God by his conscience,"[95] which thus acted as the agency of the moral sense and furnished the basis of a self-trust which he began to proclaim in the same year.[96] Moreover, as every close reader of the *Journals* knows, they indicate a crisis of increasing proportions until his resignation as minister of the Second Church in 1832 and his departure for Europe.

Nature, while it does not give Emerson's ideas in their final form, still is a major landmark both for Emerson's thought and for Transcendentalism. Since it is well known, but especially since a number of the points it makes will be taken up in other sections of this paper dealing with scientific, religious, aesthetic, and social ideas, only a few salient aspects will come up for comment here. Certainly this intuitive idealism is more Platonic than Kantian, though one of the statements attributed to Plato is really from Kant as quoted by Coleridge.[97] Indeed the conclusion, at least, is much more Neoplatonic in its emanation theory than is usual with Emerson, because he had been reading the *Journals* of Bronson Alcott, presumably the "certain Poet" in "Prospects," whose views reinforced those of Plotinus and Proclus. The fact that Emerson emphasizes the declining slope of the great chain of being, the "degradation" of man,[98] indicates that his optimism had not yet set without cracks, that there was the dark background of death beneath this superficial optimism.[99]

That Emerson's thought had not been completely worked out is indicated by certain confusions and certain disagreements with his later ideas. Thus, while he later most characteristically maintained a dualism of matter and spirit, he here used the triple Kantian division of the senses, understanding, and reason in handling sections II to V of *Nature;* yet the modern reader is embarrassed by Emerson's handling of the spiritual element of beauty,[100] putting it below the appeal to the intellect, which is contrary to his subsequent statements of his position. Moreover, there was in the original work no indication of the evolutionary ideas which later replaced his emanationism. Nevertheless this is the most complete, if not the clearest, of the early statements of Transcendentalism.

Thoreau's early writing must be considered here to show the development of Transcendentalism, despite the facts that he did not publish any work until 1841, and that he was not seriously considered as a major member of the group until the twentieth century.[101] His college essays written for Professor Edward Channing, the Boylston Professor of Rhetoric, show the transition not only from a balanced eighteenth-century style to a looser form of prose, but from the concepts of the Scottish philosophers to those of Emerson.[102]

In Essay XIII Thoreau accepts the sensationalist concept of Locke,[103] and in No. XII he quotes Dugald Stewart on the imagination;[104] as late as 1837 he was still using the principles of the Common-Sense school to indicate the certainty of reasoning, but by this time he had separated the thought from its emotional effect, which was the element that would influence conduct.[105] Though he had characteristically emphasized self-reliance from the start,[106] his reading of *Nature* sharpened the new views and he was soon quoting from it.[107] On May 15, 1837, Thoreau wrote on the assignment, "Speak of the duty, inconvenience, and dangers of *Conformity,* in little things and great," that duty lies in conforming "to the dictates of an inward arbiter," and that "fear of displeasing the world ought not in the least to influence my actions. Were it otherwise, the principal avenue of Reform would be closed."[108] The tone of the passage indicates that Thoreau was talking about Transcendental self-reliance rather than the Scottish moral sense, but in either case there is a conflict with the approach of common sense. This makes evident a certain shift of position.

In the later exercises Transcendentalist ideas begin to supersede the earlier Common-Sense concepts; thus Thoreau is found commending Plato,[109] taking the romantic view that "The civilized man is the slave of Matter,"[110] and that truth should be sought directly by each individual, not through imitation of oth-

Concord Free Public Library (Concord Free Public Library)

ers.[111] The point is clear, then, that even so confirmed a Transcendentalist as Thoreau was not born to the view, but was first influenced by the prevailing ideas of the Lockean and Common-Sense schools before finding in his home town the philosophy which was more congenial to his mind.

By 1836 it was clear to intelligent readers in New England that an idealistic philosophy was being unmistakably propounded by a small but articulate group who were seeking to find a firmer theoretical foundation for their religious beliefs. The wide reading of this new group made it difficult to tell certainly what the sources for these ideas were, and the emphasis by different new writers on different sources did not simplify the problem. Nor is it simple today. Often the material for the accurate estimate of different philosophers as sources is lacking. Yet the influences which are clearest can be pointed out with the aid of an extensive series of scholarly studies.

Of these Platonism is of basic import since Plato is a fountainhead of philosophic idealism, but since nearly everybody read him, his specific influence is difficult to assess. If the significant criterion is similarity of thought pattern, then Emerson is the most Platonic of the Transcendentalists, for the concept of "the one and the many" was central to Emerson's thought. And even, as has been pointed out,[112] Emerson's criticisms of Plato as being too intellectual and having no system are implied self-criticisms which indicate that his problems were the same as Plato's.

However the fact that Emerson's system was not completely Platonic is indicated by the fact that he did not habitually think in certain Platonic categories which he sometimes used. Emerson generally dealt in terms of poles and did not regularly have use for the daemonic level which he derived from the *Symposium* and used in "Initial, Daemonic and Celestial Love." Moreover, his use of the "twice bisected line" gave him four categories which his other concepts did not permit him to use systematically. It is worth noting that James Freeman Clarke was able to think in Kantian terms of pure and practical reason and pure and practical understanding.[113]

Thus, while Emerson is more of a Platonist than a Kantian, a leading historian of American philosophy believes that "Things interested him neither in terms of their universal patterns nor in terms of their natural existence, but in terms of their ability to stir the poetic imagination, which he and his fellow transcendentalists called reason or spirit."[114] And Emerson was more Platonic than the others; Alcott being more influenced by the Neoplatonists, while Thoreau, for example, wrote that Plato is a dogma and that "The wood thrush is a more modern philosopher."[115]

The Transcendentalists did not get their Plato pure, however; and were somewhat misled by the translations and introductions of Thomas Taylor, who colored them with his own Neoplatonism and consequently gave Plato a more mystical interpretation than the texts alone would warrant.[116] Moreover the Transcendentalists read the Cambridge Platonists Cudworth and Henry Moore, and used them also in constructing their idealistic thought.[117]

Emerson and especially Alcott, among the more mystical of the Transcendentalists, made special use of the doctrines of the Neoplatonists. (Thoreau's mysticism was reinforced more strongly by the Hindu scriptures.) Though Emerson went through several periods when he accepted their views more wholeheartedly as in *Nature* and in essays like "The Over-Soul" and "Circles," and though he liked the imagery of Proclus, Porphyry, and Iamblichus, it was Alcott who was closer to the group of Neoplatonists, whom he first read in 1833. His doctrine of Genesis or Lapse, which contended that the world was an emanation from God through man's spirit and so on through animals down to atoms, is Neoplatonic.[118] Much of Alcott's obscurity lay in the fact that he was by temperament as well as by reading an heir of the hermetic mystical tradition.[119]

In addition to Platonism, the Oriental scriptures had some effect on the Transcendentalists, though this appeared less in the ideas specifically supplied than in the imagery furnished. The impact of the Hindu and Persian writings was not in any case made very early. For Emerson, at least, though he had read scattered bits earlier, it first was outlined in De Gerando's *Histoire Comparée des Systèmes de Philosophie,*[120] which he began to read in 1830. And, though he took up the Orientals again in the late 1830's, it was not until 1841 that he encountered the Persian poets in a German translation.[121] The emphasis upon Asia in *Representative Men* and works like "Hamatraya," "Brahma," and "Illusions" shows the depth and extent of the influence on Emerson. Alcott, who first read in the *Bhagavat-Gita* in 1846, gave conversations which included the Orientals in 1851.[122] And Charles Lane brought to Fruitlands in 1843 an extensive collection of Oriental books. Thoreau, however, was perhaps most interested. He translated some of the Ethnic Scriptures for the *Dial*[123] and found in these writings a confirmation of his own somewhat mystical temperament. Because of his interest, he was presented by the Englishman Thomas Chalmondeley with forty-four volumes of oriental writings in various languages.[124] Finally the Transcendentalists' excitement over oriental writing was channeled much later into the study of comparative religions by James Freeman Clarke in *Ten Great Religions* (1871, 1883).

Other sources for the idealism of the Transcendentalists included the writings of Swedenborg, especially as interpreted by the oracular writing of Sampson Reed. His oration on "Genius," delivered in 1821 and copied from manuscript by Emerson, and *Observations on the Growth of the Mind*[125] furnished a basis, though probably not the primary one, for the doctrine of correspondence. Emerson was considerably impressed by Swedenborg's use of natural facts as symbols of the spiritual realm and seemed close enough to becoming a disciple to have been asked to become a New Church pastor, but his lecture on Swedenborg in *Representative Men,* which was critical of both the rigidity and orthodoxy of the system, caused some objection.[126] A French disciple, G. Oegger, who wrote *The True Messiah,* was also read by Emerson in 1835 in Elizabeth Peabody's manuscript translation.[127] Swedenborg was also, as will be evident later, taken up at Brook Farm.

The German idealists were of great importance to the American Transcendentalists, particularly as interpreted by French and English intermediaries. Only a few of the New Englanders were really at home in the German language, but Frederic Henry Hedge had an excellent command of it and Brownson was also thoroughly equipped to handle German philosophy, though Emerson was neither a fluent reader of German nor an adept at the close logic of Kant or Hegel. Hedge was of special value to the Transcendental Club in explaining the meaning of the German writers, while Brownson criticized the supposed skepticism of Kant's *Critique of Pure Reason* and preferred the objective

First Parish Church in Concord

idealism he found in Cousin.[128] Some of the Transcendentalists, as will appear later, were especially affected by the writings of the German mystics and theologians.

But the German attempts to solve the epistemological problem which had been posed by Descartes were transmitted to New England principally by other thinkers. Of these Madame de Staël had an indistinct though significant effect. Her *De l'Allemagne* served mainly to interest her readers in the new German solutions since she did not give sufficient detail to do more than enliven the attention paid the Germans. Yet she performed her function well, as comments by Dr. Channing, Emerson, and Clarke, indicate.[129] More specifically important were Constant and Cousin, but especially the latter. His eclecticism had a widespread vogue among the Transcendentalists because, using the Kantian system in a way which was easily comprehensible, he rescued innate ideas while still retaining some of the empiricism from the English school. Although his mixture is singularly unpalatable to the twentieth century, it offered an easy transition to Americans who had been raised on Locke and the Common-Sense

philosophers but who demanded something more. Particularly adopted by Brownson, he was translated by Caleb Sprague Henry and George Ripley,[130] taken seriously for a time by Parker, and read (rather early) in 1829 by Emerson, who was not, however, especially enthusiastic about the specific doctrine.

Doubtless of greatest value to the Transcendentalists were the English romantics, who interpreted idealism in ways which could be helpful; and of these the first to be read, though not the most important, was Wordsworth. Emerson's response was significant, if not typical. Though he was impressed by flashes of genius, he was bothered by the fact that Wordsworth was too much the poet and too egotistical for comfort.[131] Gradually he appreciated Wordsworth's abilities, still objecting to his infelicities. Strangely, in order to appreciate the poetry, it seemed necessary to accept the philosophy, yet this was taught to the Americans mainly by other writers.

Next in order of influence and importance was Carlyle, whose ideas were known by his magazine articles on German literature and by his translations as early as

1827,[132] when he was still anonymous. The story of his effect upon Emerson and of Emerson's successful efforts to get *Sartor Resartus and Critical and Miscellaneous Writings* published are too well known to require repetition.[133] The vigor of Carlyle's interpretation, the vivid violence of his style, and eventually the optimism of "The Everlasting Yea," all had their effect. His emphasis upon Fichte's concept of "Glauben" (which was like Kant's Reason), and his treatment of the Kantian distinction between Reason and Understanding must have impressed Emerson. And even Carlyle's failure to indicate Kant's reservations on the efficacy of reason influenced Emerson further.[134]

Of course it was Coleridge who acted most vigorously on the minds of a number of the American Transcendentalists. It is only a little too strong to say that he furnished the spark which set off the intellectual reaction. The American publication by James Marsh of Vermont, with his long "Preliminary Essay," of Coleridge's *Aids to Reflection* in 1829 and of *The Friend* in 1831 was a crucial effort. Coleridge emphasized the Kantian distinction as misleadingly as did Carlyle, but unlike Carlyle he incorporated a good deal of Schelling without giving credit. It is from Schelling rather than from Kant that Coleridge's idealism derives, and it is this type of view that nature has its laws in the ground of man's own existence,[135] which is echoed by Emerson when he says in *Nature* "What we are, that only can we see."[136] The effect then of Coleridge was one of the first order, since he presented materials which were much desired by the Americans in a guise which they could recognize as good.

II

Besides changing over their philosophy from what they thought was sensualism to idealism, and besides extending the application of the moral sense from one area to the direct apprehension of reality in all areas, the American Transcendentalists also transformed the previously accepted theory of the universe. They succeeded in transmuting the mechanized universe of Paley into a vitalistic and evolutionary Nature which serves as a symbol of the spiritual world. In this again the Americans were a part of the Romantic movement, for as Professor Wellek has pointed out, "we find throughout Europe . . . the same conceptions of nature and its relation to man," as well as the same concep-

tion of "the workings and nature of the poetic imagination." and the same conception of "imagery, symbolism, and myth."[137] Probably the closest of the New Englanders to this central stream, in their attitudes toward nature, were Emerson and Thoreau, who significantly are also the writers of most lasting interest. They were able to transcendentalize the scientific universe of the Enlightenment by making it the intuitively understandable symbol of the realm of the spirit.

Emerson always saw science as important and tried to make use of it in rebuilding his philosophy. As he looked back in 1880 upon the development of Transcendentalism, he said:

> I think the paramount source of the religious revolution was Modern Science; beginning with Copernicus, who destroyed the pagan fictions of the Church, by showing mankind that the earth on which we live was not the centre of the Universe, around which the sun and stars revolved every day, and thus fitted to be the platform on which the Drama of the Divine Judgment was played before the assembled Angels of Heaven, . . . but a little scrap of a planet, rushing round the sun in our system. . . . Astronomy taught us our insignificance in Nature; showed that our sacred as our profane history had been written in gross ignorance of the laws, which were far grander than we knew; and compelled a certain extension and uplifting of our views of the Deity and his Providence. This correction of our superstitions was confirmed by the new science of Geology. . . . But we presently saw also that the religious nature in man was not affected by these errors in his understanding.

And he continued:

> Whether from these influences, or whether by a reaction of the general mind against the too formal science, religion and social life of the earlier period, there was, in the first quarter of our nineteenth century, a certain sharpness of criticism, an eagerness for reform, which showed itself in every quarter.[138]

This might be suspect as idle, if not senile, retrospection if it were not confirmed by his early views, for as early as 1831 he wrote, "The Religion that is afraid of science dishonors God and commits suicide."[139] Yet this again is only a reflection of still earlier views, at first half-formed, of the relationship between

Emerson's letter about changing publishers, which led to his signing a contract with Ticknor and Fields the world and the spirit. Thus in 1820 he wrote, "We feel . . . that eternal analogy which subsists between the external changes of nature, and scenes of good and ill that chequer human life,"[140] and in 1821 he discusses with his Aunt Mary the Swedenborgian idea "that the physical world was the basso-relievo of the moral." Furthermore he records, in 1822, "the pleasure of finding out a connection between a material image and a moral sentiment."[141] These are at least the germs of what was to become a unified theory of correspondence.

Of major significance was his reading of Coleridge's *The Friend* in 1829,[142] but in a particular way, since Emerson was led to read a number of the authors mentioned by Coleridge, e.g., Bacon and Hunter. From Coleridge, Emerson also received the distinction between the intuited Law of Science and the Theory of Scheme which was developed by the understanding.[143] Of especial importance, however, for Emerson was the Newtonian concept of a unified and ordered universe, for it was necessary to have a concept of a lawful whole before the immutable moral order could be seen as paralleling it. Yet "only when this structural dualism was represented psychologically . . . was correspondence, as the act of intuitive perception that spanned the gap of finite (outer) and infinite (inner) and unified them in the experience of the self, a necessary assumption of this thought."[144] Thus from these sources and his own thought, Emerson formulated the idea that nature mediates between man and God.

Emerson's sermon on "Astronomy," delivered May 27, 1832, indicates the extension of his ideas in one direction. First he admitted that this science "made the theological *scheme of Redemption* absolutely incredible," so, as a consequence, "Newton became a Unitarian."[145] But while astronomy tended to cause skepticism, it more significantly offered proofs of "beneficent design"; the voice of nature led to "higher truth."[146] This much was clear to Emerson, but there follow difficulties both in terminology and in logical connection. When he says that the discoveries of astronomy reconcile "the greatness of nature to the greatness of mind,"[147] this seems to be an early statement of his later view; but when he says they make "moral distinctions still more important"[148] this is a *non sequitur*. When he continues that astronomy commands all men to "repent,"[149] the difficulty is largely terminological: he is heading toward the idea that men should follow the moral law which they can intuit from the laws of celestial mechanics. Yet when he says that the enlarged

views of the solar system "can never throw the least shade upon . . . moral truth" and that the beatitudes of the Sermon on the Mount are of permanent value and agree well with "all the new and astonishing facts in the book of nature,"[150] he is not announcing anything very significant. Faith is not confirmed because a given body of science does not convert it. But again Emerson is on the trail of his later idea that physical and moral laws in some way correspond. As he wrote in *Nature*, "things are emblematic," and the "axioms of physics translate the laws of ethics."[151]

Thus while Newton was one of the sources for his philosophical synthesis, Emerson developed his ideas rather slowly, often encountering an idea several times, or in several different writers, before he was able to complete his imaginative transformation. This, of course, makes the specific influences difficult to pin down. Consequently to Newton must be added Butler's *Analogy*, Paley's *Natural Theology*, Wollaston's *Religion of Nature*, and even Bacon's *Advancement of Learning* and J. F. W. Herschel's *A Discourse of the Study of Natural Philosophy*.[152] And even this list is not complete.

In addition to being the heir of the theoretical science of the previous period, Emerson was delighted by the beauties of nature, through which he also saw the realities of the spirit, and in this was a thorough romantic.[153] It is significant that his first philosophical essay is called *Nature* rather than *Concerning the Human Understanding*, or *The Critique of Pure Reason*, or *How To Make Our Ideas Clear*, or *Pragmatism*. Yet more important than a further discussion of the science in *Nature* is an examination of his developing evolutionary idea, of which there is no hint at all in *Nature*. The original epitaph was the following quotation from Plotinus, "Nature is but an image or imitation of wisdom, the last thing of the soul; Nature being a thing which doth only do, but not know." But in 1849 the second edition of *Nature* had a different motto, the one which we know,

A subtle chain of countless rings
The next unto the farthest brings;
The eye reads omens where it goes,
And speaks all languages the rose;
And striving to be man, the worm
Mounts through all the spires of form.

The poem, of course, negates the more pessimistic aspect of the descent on the chain of being, affirms a view which is at least philosophically if not scientifically evolutionary, and illustrates the generally accepted idea that Emerson's emanation theory was transmuted into evolution.[154] The origins of this view are to be found early in Emerson's thought, though they were not to take their final form until after 1840. Again a number of influences can be pointed out as contributory to the intellectual development. As early as 1829 Emerson read in Coleridge's *Aids to Reflection,* "All things strive to ascend, and ascend in their striving."[155] He had also read some Leibniz early,[156] and had picked up some of the ideas of Linnaeus, Buffon, Cuvier, John Hunter, Erasmus Darwin, and possibly Lamarck by 1833. He was consequently prepared for his visits to the Jardin des Plantes and the Hunterian Museum in Glasgow, which displayed the various types of life in an ordered array showing "the upheaving principle of life everywhere incipient."[157] In his second public lecture in December, 1833, he reproduced these generally evolutionary ideas along with those of Sir Charles Bell.[158] In 1834 Emerson became acquainted with some of the morphological ideas of Goethe,[159] and in his lecture in 1836 on "The Humanity of Science" he again sounds as if he had seized upon a philosophical approach to evolution.

> Lamarck finds a monad of organic life common to every animal, and becoming a worm, a mastiff, or a man, according to circumstances. He says to the caterpillar, How dost thou brother? Please God, you shall yet be a philosopher. . . . The block fits. All agents, the most diverse, are pervaded by radical analogies; and in deviations and degradations we learn that the law is not only firm and eternal, but also alive. . . .[160]

Another approach to this theory of development, which is not to be confused with the specific biological hypothesis of Darwin's *Origin of Species,* indicates that Emerson as a result of the unexpected attacks upon the "Divinity School Address" put less emphasis upon self-reliance, went through a period of realistic skepticism in which he emphasized experience, and then fell back upon a dogmatic optimism and "soft determinism" which depended upon a belief in "Beneficent Tendency" and amelioration, a loosely evolutionary upward spiral.[161] By the time of "The Young American" in 1844 this tendency is strong, and from this year Emerson's *Journals* also show an evolutionary cast.[162]

Further sources for Emerson's evolutionary views included Lorenz Oken and Stallo. The former he mentioned as early as 1842,[163] in the lecture on Swedenborg, and again in "Fate," where he emphasizes the effect of environment on the development of vesicles, and he seems also to have known of Oken's evolutionary theories.[164] Between Oken and Stallo there is a curious link since it was after Alcott's discussion of his illumination that the whole world was a spine (as a result of reading Oken) that Emerson gave to Alcott the lines which now preface *Nature;* and these lines were based upon Stallo's *Principles of the Philosophy of Nature* which taught that all things mount in spirals–a negation of Alcott's view.[165]

A fairly complete doctrine of evolution set forth in Emerson's "Poetry and Imagination" in a part first delivered in 1854,[166] except for the phrase *arrested and progressive development,* which he attributed to Hunter, but which is really by Chambers.[167] When *The Origin of Species* was published Emerson was so used to the type of ideas it contained that he was not even excited. And afterwards he sought to adjust his views to Darwin's,[168] since evolution was easily acceptable to the Transcendentalists.

Thoreau's attitude toward science and his views of nature, though difficult to work out because he usually implies rather than states them, are equally significant. It is clear by now that as a young man he was interested in nature not as a scientist seeking accurate predictability on the physical level, but as a Transcendentalist seeking a way to unlock the secrets of the spirit. It is equally clear that in his final years he became increasingly interested in finding relationships among the great batches of facts which he recorded in the *Journals.* So much so, that he has properly been regarded by scientists as a pioneer limnologist and phenologist and as an ecologist before the name was even invented.[169]

In an early *Dial* paper, Thoreau made his attitude toward science perfectly clear when he wrote, "Let us not underrate the value of a fact; it will one day flower into a truth"–a sufficiently patent statement of the view of nature as a symbol, and continued:

We must look a long time before we can see. Slow are the beginnings of philosophy. He has something demoniacal in him, who can discern a law or couple two facts. We can imagine a time when "Water runs down hill" may have been taught in the schools. The true man of science will know nature better by his finer organization; he will smell, taste, see, hear, feel better than other men. His will be a deeper and finer experience. We do not learn by inference and deduc-

Photograph of Emerson in 1854

Photograph of Emerson in 1858

Drawing of Emerson in 1859

Photograph of Emerson in the 1860s

tion and the application of mathematics to philosophy, but by direct intercourse and sympathy. It is with science as with ethics—we cannot know truth by contrivance and method; the Baconian is as false as any other, and with all the helps of machinery and the arts, the most scientific will still be the healthiest and friendliest man, and possess a more perfect Indian wisdom.[170]

Thus Thoreau felt certain that ultimately the meaning lay in himself, not the physical world. "Instead of being 'wholly involved in nature,' he was subservient to the spirit within. This, and not nature, was the inspirer." But as the moments of ecstasy became fewer, the agony of this deprivation increased and, despite an almost desperate optimism, nearly shattered his sanity.[171] He fell back upon the recording of fact though he recognized that it represented a falling off. "It is impossible for the same person to see things from the poet's point of view and that of the man of science. The poet's second love may be science, not his first,—when use has worn off the bloom. I realize that men may be born to a condition of mind at which others arrive in middle age by the decay of their faculties."[172] Science is then for Thoreau, as for Emerson, only a symbol of a higher truth. Yet science was apparently as high as some men could ever get, and was perhaps as high as Thoreau could attain in his later life.

Though Thoreau still thought of science in 1860 as "always more barren and mixed up with error than our sympathies are,"[173] this was not the whole story. Even if he accepted science only as a second love, it is certain that his interest in natural phenomena increased as he grew older and that he finally began to apply a more sophisticated scientific method than most of his contemporaries. In *Walden* he already gave the impression of recording many natural facts for their own sakes rather than for an ulterior meaning, and this indicated an important unconscious swing in the direction of philosophical realism.[174] The last three volumes of the *Journals* also convey the fact that Thoreau was becoming increasingly scientific in his interests, seeking relations between plants and their habitats, and explaining the succession of forest trees. He turned to the counting of tree rings and the examination of the age of oak roots with a gusto which belied his sneers at science.

To the other Transcendentalists celestial laws proved to be of somewhat less interest. As romantics they were inspired by nature to poetic expression, but most of them concentrated on their literary and theological positions. Certain pseudo sciences did, however, prove of considerable interest to them, particularly phrenology. Dr. Kaspar Spurtzheim's doctrine of the relation of mental faculties to cranial shapes was first popularized by the publication of George Combe's *The Constitution of Man* in Boston, 1829, and Spurtzheim himself lectured there in the early 1830's. James Freeman Clarke became quite interested in this science, as did Margaret Fuller and Horace Mann, though the latter was not a Transcendentalist. Instead of accepting the view that the theory was deterministic in the sense of showing mind related to and shaped by the cranium, the Transcendentalists accepted the interpretation that moral truths could be taught and character so trained as to minimize the defects.[175] Without necessarily accepting the doctrine, Emerson, Parker, and Margaret Fuller attested to its effects.[176]

Thus it may be said that the Transcendentalists, dissatisfied with the mechanical universe of Paley and of the materialistic scientists, moved towards a romantic view of nature which accepted facts and laws as symbols of a spiritual or divine truth.[177] Their emphasis was not upon deduction of a God from the universe, *à la* Tom Paine,[178] but upon the direct perception of divine law. The views of Emerson and Thoreau were at times tinged with pantheism, yet this was not the whole story. As Bartol pointed out, "Pantheism is said to sink man and nature in God, Materialism to sink God and man in nature, and Transcendentalism to sink God and nature in man,"[179] though he cautioned that this definition was too neat. In his major period from *Nature* through *Essays, Second Series* Emerson was not an avowed pantheist, yet it appears that as his illuminated moments became less frequent, he put more emphasis upon natural law and the beneficent tendency of evolution, he made all natural instead of supernatural, and by this change of terminology and emphasis, he perhaps reverted to a clearer pantheism.[180] But no such thing should be said of Furness, Clarke, Parker, Hedge, and Alcott, who all adhered to concepts of the personality of God. At any rate it was the greatest of the Transcendentalists, Emerson, who was able to make the greatest use of previous science and to interpret an ordered universe as the basis for correspondence between matter and mind.

Photograph of Emerson with his children, Edward and Ellen

Photograph of Emerson in 1868

Photograph of Emerson in the 1870s

Photograph of Emerson in old age

III

In the field of religion the Transcendentalists caused the first immediate excitement by substituting for institutional traditionalism and belief in the revelation of God through the miracles of the New Testament, the direct intuition of a spiritual and immanent God who was still operative in the soul of each individual man. The initial conflict arose between the apostles of "The Newness" and the conservative Unitarians who were forced to a still more conservative position in the contest which followed. Many of the Transcendentalists remained within the Unitarian church, organized as it was on the Congregational system, since it had no machinery for rejecting heretics. This combat, in which Theodore Parker came to the fore, resulted later in the Free Religious Movement, which split into two wings, the Transcendentalists and the more rationalistic Scientific Theists. But this latter development lies outside the scope of this plan of discussion.

When James Marsh published Coleridge's *Aids to Reflection* in 1829, he hoped to swing the Congregational church back to idealism. But the major effect was upon a group of Unitarians who felt that religion had become too icy. This new group of divines began to find itself chilled by the "corpse-cold" institution and emotionally starved by the "pale negations" of a rationalistic religion which was more notable for the doctrines of the sovereignty of God, providence, original sin, predestination, election, and revelation through the Bible which it rejected than for positive beliefs to which it adhered. While evangelical religion had burst forth by 1801 in the Great Revival in the West, the growth of the warmer wing of Unitarianism which emerged as Transcendentalism later supplied the need for enthusiasm in the more intellectual and more sophisticated clergy.

The Unitarianism which the young and ardent group found wanting was remarkably conservative. Its members were former Federalists who did not want to be bothered by theological and social questions,[181] and though they gave up the rigorous predestinarianism and election of Puritanism, they were not unreservedly optimistic about the goodness of the nature of man, whom the Reverend Nathaniel Frothingham called a "poor worm."[182] Whigs in politics,[183] the typical Unitarians were skeptical about the value of reform and conveniently felt that society could be improved only by the gradual influence of virtuous men, which they knew themselves to be. Consequently the laymen were able

to rationalize their bourgeois interests in terms of a religion which bolstered their "social conservatism."[184] (Yet it is worth noting that Emerson and Thoreau adhered in the main to the view that the regeneration of society could come only through the regeneration of individuals.) Thus a conservative Unitarian theologian like Orville Dewey was forced, in response to liberal attacks, to accept a belief in human depravity and to suggest that Unitarians employ the terms "Father, Son, and Holy Ghost."[185]

The generally glacial quality of the Unitarian Church after the disagreement emerged is made clear by Henry Adams, who from the age of ten attended Dr. Nathaniel Frothingham's First Church:

> Nothing quieted doubt so completely as the mental calm of the Unitarian clergy. In uniform excellence of life and character, moral and intellectual, the score of Unitarian clergymen about Boston, who controlled society and Harvard College, were never excelled. They proclaimed as their merit that they insisted on no doctrine, but taught, or tried to teach, the means of leading a virtuous, useful, unselfish life, which they held to be sufficient for salvation. For them, difficulties might be ignored; doubts were waste of thought; nothing exacted solution. Boston had solved the universe; or had offered and realized the best solution yet tried. The problem was worked out.
>
> Of all the conditions of his youth which afterwards puzzled the grown-up man, this disappearance of religion puzzled him most. . . . That the most powerful emotion of man next to the sexual, should disappear, might be a personal defect of his own; but that the most intelligent society, led by the most intelligent clergy, in the most moral conditions he ever knew, should have solved all the problems of the universe so thoroughly as to have quite ceased making itself anxious about past or future, and should have persuaded itself that all the problems which had convulsed human thought from earliest recorded time, were not worth discussing, seemed to him the most curious social phenomenon he had to account for in a long life.[186]

With this background it is easy to understand why the "liberal" views of the rationalistic Unitarians hardened into conservative dogma under the impact of the Transcendentalists. Indeed the Unitarians were particularly irritated because the Calvinists' prediction that Unitarianism would result in further heresy[187] turned out to be accurate.

The break of the Transcendentalists from previous Unitarian beliefs came from two principal causes: the growth of intuitive idealism and the growth of intellectual skepticism. Of these the first, probably the crucial factor, has already been dealt with in section I, while the second deserves more attention. Together they outline the paradoxical position of the Transcendentalists, who were simultaneously more spiritual than their opponents and also more doubtful of the need of revealed or institutional religion.

The inspiration of the new group was Dr. Channing, who was both an idealist and a warm and emotional advocate of personal religion—a man whose loftiness of character permitted him to say things that would be attacked in others. But Dr. Channing was never doubtful of the miracles of Jesus. Consequently it is Emerson, the first of the "New School" to resign his ministry, who deserves more careful consideration. As has been suggested earlier, his philosophy was already idealistic by the time he resigned as pastor of the Second Church, but this fact alone did not bring about his change of view. He found himself increasingly restless about the institution of the church. In 1831 he wrote, "Calvinism stands, fear I, by pride and ignorance; and Unitarianism, as a sect, stands by the opposition of Calvinism. It is cold and cheerless, the mere creature of the understanding, until controversy makes it warm with fire got from below."[188] Early in 1832 he said "It is the best part of a man, I sometimes think, that revolts most against his being a minister." The difficulty was that accommodation to ready-made institutions caused a loss of "integrity and . . . power."[189] Consequently he felt that "in order to be a good minister, it was necessary to leave the ministry."[190]

In his crisis over the administration of the Lord's Supper, a rite in which he no longer believed, he retired to the mountains, where he found that his first thoughts were best; and reinforcing himself with accounts of George Fox's integrity and courage,[191] he decided, himself, to be genuine and to stand on principle. This was the most important act of his career, for it gave him the moral right to speak of Self-Reliance, that is, reliance upon the intuitions of the Over-Soul. While the break did not seem necessarily final, for afterwards Emerson often preached, it was this decision which freed him from what he regarded as bondage and gave him a larger audience.

Emerson's decision was based upon a number of factors. For one thing his skepticism of dogma and of the infallibility of religious institutions was doubtless increased by his reading of Montaigne.[192] For Emerson, skepticism was the vestibule of the Temple, the clearing away of debris before building the foundations of the new belief; so he could respect Montaigne for his skepticism as well as for his sturdy individualism and independence of judgment. Furthermore, he was considerably impressed by the doctrines and character of a number of Quakers. A part of his sermon on "The Lord's Supper," the issue which he strategically picked for his congregation, was based upon Thomas Clarkson's *A Portraiture of the Society of Friends.*[193] And immediately upon his return from Europe he preached at New Bedford, where a number of Hicksite Quakers had joined the Unitarian congregation. Here he was especially impressed by Deborah Brayton and Mary Rotch.[194] He also talked of Stubler, another Quaker he had known, and of Lucretia Mott, whom he met in Philadelphia and whose wholehearted zeal he much admired.[195]

Undoubtedly Emerson was also influenced by the experience of his older brother William, who had gone to Göttingen to study for the ministry, but whose religious doubts had caused him to turn to law instead. When William talked over his problem with Goethe, the sage told him to "preach to the people what they wanted," since "his personal belief was no business of theirs."[196] But Waldo, like his brother, felt that integrity demanded the separation. Thus he left the church for a series of reasons. Had he been trained in another type of faith, his skepticism of ritual, sacrament, and institution might not have occurred, for Unitarian rationalism encouraged the sort of questioning which beset him. Or if he had been reared in a faith which accepted enthusiasm more freely, he might also have found an avenue for his abilities within the fold.

Emerson was not alone in his dissatisfaction with conventional Unitarianism, and the differences between the New School and the old were deep. The issue around which they crystallized was the value of miracles, for, as the Transcendentalists were quick to point out, it was inconsistent of a church which followed a rationalistic or common-sense philosophy to insist on the miracle as the sole sanction of religion. This controversy must be briefly sketched.

Although Paine had attacked miracles earlier, among the Unitarians the issue was first raised by Ripley in 1835 in a discussion of Herder in the *Christian Examiner.* Here the point was made that Herder thought it impossible "to establish the truth of any reli-

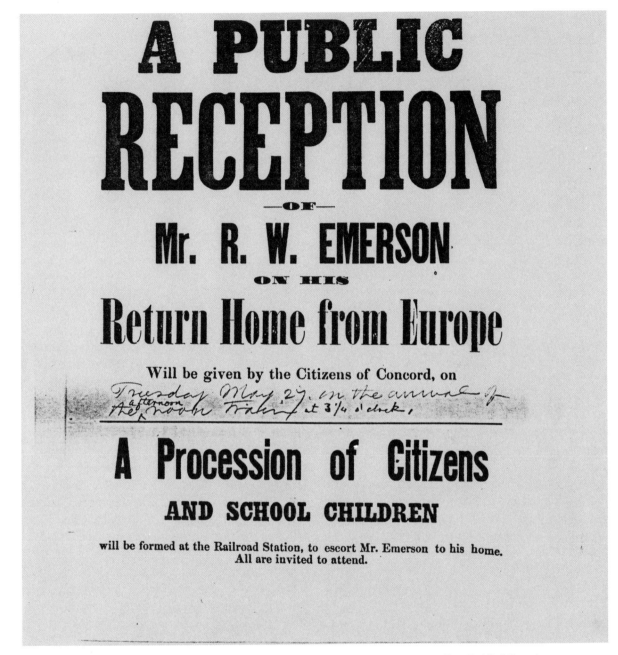

Broadside announcing Emerson's return from Europe in 1873 (Concord Free Public Library)

gion, merely on the ground of miracles." A miracle may call attention to a doctrine, or give authority to the teacher, but it cannot prove the truth of the assertion.[197] Such a view was potentially serious, though both Herder and Ripley themselves believed in miracles, and, as has already been noted, Furness held a rather similar view. In November, 1836, Ripley took up the subject again and added a slightly new idea, that there was no way to tell a religious miracle from a natural power without faith in the divinity of the per-

former.[198]

The conservative Unitarians soon began to reply to these arguments, marshaling their strength under the leadership of Andrews Norton, who led the attack by disavowing in an insulting manner responsibility for the printing of Ripley's views in the *Christian Examiner*.[199] Ripley of course rejoined with all the arts of controversy, but made it clear that the basic issue was one of philosophy. Meanwhile Martin Hurlbut's review of Furness's *Remarks* defined the issue clearly. Hurlbut thought that it would be impossible to have revelation without miracles; and he continued, "If the miracles of the Gospel are to be regarded as 'natural facts,' capable of being reduced to natural laws, and explained by them, it does appear to us, that Christianity, as a system of revealed truth, ceases to be. We are thrown back upon *mere naturalism.*"[200]

At this point Emerson's "Divinity School Address" (1838) caused great excitement on both sides. Because of his serene confidence in reason, Emerson said little in favor of historical Christianity which, because it used the understanding, misinterpreted Jesus and insisted on his personality as a divinity. Here Emerson went much further than a mere denial of specific miracles; by saying that all men had in them the same access to the divine, he denied the entire miracle of the New Testament as it was understood by the conservative Unitarians.

These sensational views were, of course, the occasion of a vigorous exchange, though Emerson himself refused to indulge in further argument. When Henry Ware, Jr., sought to draw him into a logical discussion, Emerson simply withdrew. But there was no lack of support. Andrews Norton's *Discourse on the Latest Form of Infidelity,* which was more dignified than his immediate rejoinder in the Boston *Daily Advertiser,* drew a reply from Ripley, who insisted that "The doctrine that miracles are the only evidence of divine revelation, if generally admitted, would impair the religious influence of the Christian ministry."[201] Meanwhile Brownson had challenged Norton by saying that his position showed a lack of faith in the people.[202]

At this point Theodore Parker, who was to prove himself the most important of the Transcendentalists who remained a preacher, issued a pamphlet under the pseudonym "Levi Blodgett." Parker, a Lexington man, reared in poverty and too poor to attend Harvard as an undergraduate, though he took and passed all the examinations, showed a powerful mind and prodigious energy in all his activities. Widely read—he claimed command of twenty languages—forthright and courageous, he poured forth a constant stream of expansive rhetoric, but he was also a skilled logician and a masterly conductor of argument. Though he believed personally in the miracles of Jesus, he did not see "how a miracle proves a doctrine."[203] And by appealing to the ordinary capacities of ordinary people, he hoped to prove that the conservatives were wrong, for in his writing there were no lofty mysteries.

To such straits were the conservatives reduced that Andrews Norton, laying aside for a time the old conflict between Calvinists and Unitarians, published under the title *Transcendentalism of the Germans and of Cousin and Its Influence on the Opinion in This Country* (Cambridge, Mass., 1840), two articles by the Princeton professors J. W. Alexander, Albert Dod, and Charles Hodge from the *Biblical Repertory and Princeton Review* for January, 1839. This vigorous analysis, after ridiculing Cousin, describes "the nonsense and impiety" of the "Divinity School Address" and decides that even Deism is "to be preferred to German insanity."[204]

Probably the most cogent of the series of defenses of Transcendentalist views was Parker's famous and controversial sermon on the "Transient and Permanent in Christianity," which announced his concept of "Absolute Religion," the doctrine that the human soul can intuit the permanent part of Christianity, while churches, creeds, ritual, revelation, and secondhand beliefs all partake of the transient.[205] This was of course taking the matter farther than Dr. Channing could go. Yet Parker always personally insisted that the Christian religion was the absolute religion, and it was only after the Civil War that the final doubt of even this was raised by those men who went farther than Parker—the apostles of Free Religion such as F. E. Abbott.

Without doubt the New School employed the works of German philosophers, theologians, and Biblical scholars in developing and defending their views, and they considered the Germans a liberalizing influence. Dr. Nathaniel Frothingham, one of the staunch conservatives, was asked to one of the first meetings of the "Transcendentalist Club,"[206] presumably because he was a reader of German critical works. The parade of German authors, especially theological, read by Parker and Ripley in particular is impressive: Herder, Schleiermacher, Jacobi, Eichhorn, Strauss, Steudlin, Ammon, Gabler Hase, Wegscheider, Bauer, and especially De Wette. Parker translated and annotated De Wette in *A Critical and Historical Introduction to the Canonical Scriptures of the Old Testament* in two volumes, while James Freeman Clarke translated De Wette's *Theodore* in two volumes,[207] and Samuel Osgood translated De Wette's *Ethics,* again in two volumes, the last two being parts of Ripley's series, *Specimens of Foreign Standard Literature* (14 volumes, 1838-1842).

But neither a listing nor a detailed analysis of the use of the German theologians should be taken to indicate that Transcendentalism depended entirely upon German sources. As Brownson asserted, "The movement is really of American origin, and the prominent actors in it were carried away by it before ever they formed any acquaintance with French or German metaphysics; and their attachment to the literatures of France and Germany is the effect of their connection with the movement, not the cause."[208] When an article in the *Western Messenger* agreed that there was a New School, it also agreed that the common ground among the members was not any specific doctrine or influence, but was rather a desire for more "LIFE."[209] No one foreign theologian influenced the whole group, and no one foreign theologian was wholly accepted by any of the group. The common cause of the Transcendentalists lay in a common need that was variously satisfied in detail. In general, they all felt the necessity of moving from adherence to a cold, negative, institutionalized religion, based upon an unhappy union of materialistic philosophy and belief in certain miracles, to the positive acceptance of a spiritual philosophy of a God with whom they could come into immediate and direct contact, whether or not he was held to be personal or impersonal. Their rejection of miracles as the grounding of belief in the New Testament laid them open to the claim that they were infidels and pantheists, yet they could argue that they and not the Norton camp were the more deeply religious. At any rate they were right in contending that they were not merely conservative and defensive.

IV

Another crucial transition involved the change from neoclassical concepts of correctness, generality, and imitation in art to the romantic or Transcendental use of symbol as bodying forth the intuitive vision of the genuinely creative artist in an organic fusion of content and form. The Transcendentalists' basically religious problem was solved by a philosophical concept of the world as symbol of the mind, and the corollary of this idea of symbol carried over into their aesthetic theories and expressions. Their replacement of a mechanistic concept of nature by a vitalistic and creative concept was paralleled by the replacement of a mechanical and formalistic aesthetic theory by an organic concept of the unfolding of form from within outward. While some, like Margaret Fuller and John Sullivan Dwight, were primarily critics, Emerson and Thoreau, though

they may have thought of themselves as seers, were primarily concerned with the problems of finding expressive forms in their prose and verse to articulate their insights and ideas.

Of this development Dr. Channing's "Remarks on a National Literature" were in at least one respect prophetic. For besides claiming that democratic institutions were favorable, he said that the new and higher literature would come from a new and higher religious principle. No man, he continued, can "put forth all his powers . . . till he has risen to communion with the Supreme Mind . . . till he regards himself as the recipient and minister of the Infinite Spirit."[210] Certainly it was the consciousness of such intuitions of the divine which furnished much of the fire to the Transcendentalists' literary work. And Channing's advocacy of the use of images from nature to body forth artistically the inner life of the spirit, coming after the predominantly pictorial or surface writing of Knickerbockers such as Irving, is especially important. Channing, the friend of Coleridge, pleaded for "a poetry which pierces beneath the exterior life to the depths of the soul, and which lays open its mysterious working, borrowing from the whole outward creation fresh images and correspondences, with which to illuminate the secrets of the world within us."

Of course the Transcendentalists were not born with the new concept of literature, and both Emerson and Thoreau had to break away from the emphasis on formalized structure which had been inculcated by their Harvard teacher of rhetoric, E. T. Channing, and from the Latinate diction, abstract vocabulary, and windy parallelisms which appeared in their Harvard textbooks. What they lost in perspicuity of argument they more than made up in vividness of expression. Thoreau, in particular, in his less successful later passages even shows reversion to the flat, balanced style of his college days.

Emerson's *Nature* contains the basis of his artistic as well as of his philosophical and religious ideas, but, as has already been pointed out, some of the germs appeared earlier. In 1822 he connected a material image with a moral sentiment; later he learned from Goethe the balance between form and idea (pushed in the direction of the primacy of the idea by Emerson);[211] and from 1835 he made use of Cudworth's *The True Intellectual System of the Universe*. From the latter he gained the idea of a plastic nature, *natura naturans,* which imposed the divine will on matter, and which he equated with man's ability, when he showed genius, to do the same.[212] This idea he worked out between the two essays on "Art" (1836 and 1840): in the first he emphasized the inferiority of the art object to the beholder's intuition of the divine;[213] in the second he gave Art some of the quality of *natura naturans*.[214] The first decried modern art; the second said the best art derives from the flow of the divine spirit through the artist's passive soul. Thus Emerson put a good deal of emphasis upon an inspiration that was beyond the power of the artist, and for him poetry was not meter, but "metre-making argument."[215]

Emerson had a fairly complete theory of art in which the poet by intuition seized facts from the flux of the many to set forth the one, of which truth and goodness were aspects or parts.[216] The art thus created was organic in the sense that form and content were fused, though thought was prior to form;[217] this implies a primacy of thought which may explain why Emerson is said to have called Poe "that jingle man." Yet art was not final but only initial. The creation of man was its end. Thus the audience was to be kept in the artist's mind as well, not just the work. This explains why Emerson thought that art should cheer and ennoble, and why when he was asked about *The Scarlet Letter,* he is said to have commented, "Ghastly, Ghastly!"[218]

On the question of traditionalism as opposed to innovation, he is open to more than one interpretation. Emerson saw the moral identity of all men and felt that men do not progress in time.[219] Emphasis upon this aspect of his thought puts him into the stream from the past, and in fact with his Yankee caution he never stepped too far out of the path of tradition. Yet it is worth noting that instead of saying, If what is true for you is true of all men, then you are a genius; he actually said, "To believe your own thought, to believe that what is true for you in your private heart is true for all men,– that is genius."[220] And though it is to be admitted that Emerson's Self-Reliance he felt to be God-Reliance[221] and not romantic individualism, still he was calling for the new poet who could capture the divine meaning by using as symbols "Small and mean things" and "Bare lists of words."[222] His acceptance, however qualified, of Whitman's work would seem to bear out this interpretation.[223] Emerson was at least a theoretical rebel, as his ringing declaration in *The American Scholar* makes clear. Yet his assumption that the intuition of the Over-Soul was unconditioned by either environment or personality permitted him to apply his radical insights in a conservative manner.

The same considerations must also be applied in answering the question of how rigidly moralistic his aesthetic theories were. But here he gradually overcame some of his Puritan moral background. On the other hand Emerson sometimes seemed to be descended from a long line of moralist ministers; his worry that Shakespeare had no central view of life[224] is part of this heritage. Yet he was able to accept Montaigne despite his "semisavage indecency,"[225] and from Goethe, despite his lack of moral rigor, Emerson was able to learn that a ballet should be viewed objectively and a painting as a painting.[226]

Emerson's aesthetic ideal was a controlled insight which could give a communicable experience, an experience based upon more than association of ideas as Alison's *Essay on Taste* suggested, and communicated by symbols which are more than the mannerly metaphors recommended by Blair's *Lectures on Rhetoric.*[227] While Emerson was not opposed to revision in order to improve the expression of the poet's insights, he did not approve of the imitation of fashionable styles. Instead of being worked up by talent, art should be organic; and if it is organic, it will be recognized by readers as the genuine production of genius.

Thoreau's ideals were not too markedly different from Emerson's, since he was also interested in conveying to others his communicable insights. He too believed in the organic concept of art,[228] but with stronger emphasis upon the effects of character and training upon the genius of the artist. He believed that some physical labor was desired,[229] that a man should write as if he held a plow in his hand, and that there should be boulders in his style. In addition, Thoreau put greater emphasis upon precise expression (for him there was no such thing as a translation), and upon concreteness of fact, for he was convinced that every fact was a potential symbol.

There was in Trancendentalist literary theory a certain amount of nationalism, which went naturally with the youthful exuberance of an expanding America in a romantic period. Thoreau was, for example, content not to go to Europe with Hecker, and instead traveled extensively in Concord. Emerson, who said, "We have listened too long to the courtly muses of Europe,"[230] was certain that America would yet produce a poet. Indeed he suggested that American literature face westward and turn out more writing with the tang of Daniel Boone and Davy Crockett.[231] One of the clear aims of a group of Transcendentalists was to publish

The Emerson family in the 1870s, including his wife Lidian, children Edward, Ellen, and Edith, and grandchildren (Concord Free Public Library)

and encourage a nonimitative American literature. Certainly the *Dial* was set up with such an aim in mind, and the verse of Ellery Channing could hardly have appeared anywhere else.

The new group also hoped to develop society by educating it through the art of criticism, an aspect of the movement which shows it at perhaps its most ambitious. Despite the fact that there was relatively little painting and sculpture in the country and that public musical performances were fairly new, an attempt was bravely made to develop a criticism. Of the general critics of the arts, Margaret Fuller deserves the most attention, as leader of the "arty" group of which John S. Dwight was second in command. Intelligent, emotional, and highly trained, partly out of place in the Boston environment, she had a remarkably warm personality attractive to many women and men, and was a wonderful conversationalist. Though she never felt completely at home in writing, she was nevertheless the critic of the New York *Tribune* from 1844 to 1846, after the failure of the *Dial*, of which she was the original editor.

Margaret Fuller made a vigorous attempt to establish an objective system of criticism based upon fixed laws, though in practice she had great difficulty avoiding impressionism of a markedly emotional variety. In "A Short Essay on Critics" she tried to work out an operating theory. The first class of critics rejected by her was the subjective group, which without knowing anything about art still judges it by preconceptions. The second class she called the apprehensive, a class which would today be called impressionistic–useful popularizers but with no standards except their own responses. The right kind she considered the comprehensive critics who could feel into a work of art, but who also maintained principles and canons of judgment.[232] Unfortunately she herself vacillated between two types, the transcendental and the naturistic romantic. In the one mood she saw art as the expression of the spiritual ideal; in the other she saw the work of art as the highest growth of nature, as the ultimate goal of man.[233] But in either she was usually emotional and impressionistic.

She accepted the theory that there was a parallel between the succession of forest trees and the succession of dominant forms of art,[234] the latter expressing the dominant spirit of the age. Thus, for the Greeks and Elizabethans drama was dominant, and for other ages lyrical poetry, art, or sculpture.[235] In her own age these were of low quality, and she looked toward the ballet and especially music as the great arts. Typical of the romantic tendency, she placed music at the top because of its perfect fusion of form and content,[236] and also doubtless because it offered release to her tortured and repressed emotions. Again typically, the Beethoven of the Second, Fifth, Sixth, and Ninth Symphonies was her ideal, with Handel, Bach, and Haydn following in that order.

The most celebrated music critic of the Transcendentalists was John Sullivan Dwight, who was rather a failure as a Unitarian minister, but a success as the music and Latin teacher at Brook Farm and later as a musical arbiter. From 1852 to 1881 he edited the first long-lived musical journal in the country, *Dwight's Journal of Music.* He too was an admirer to Beethoven, the transcendental composer.

While criticism was applied to all the arts by members of the new group,[237] the major emphasis was in the long run placed upon literature. With their belief in intuition as the source for inspiration, they lacked the ability or interest to work out the complex symbols required in the structure of the novel. Sylvester Judd, who wrote *Margaret* (1845), was the only Transcendental novelist. Emerson and Thoreau, in fact, did not even regard the novel very highly as an art form.[238] But though the organic theory of art offered little means for structural analysis, Emerson, at least, worked out an aesthetic theory, including the aspects of creation, of the work of art, and of the response of the audience, which embodied the theory of correspondence with some success. This theory was a radical departure from the neoclassical standards of balance, restraint, generality, correctness, and imitation which had dominated European and American taste in the previous period.

V

The Trancendentalists in the economic, political, and social sphere tended to transfer their emphasis from the natural social rights of the previous age to individual integrity and the freedom of each man for maximum personal development. As a group they showed little uniformity, however, in their ideas of how this development was to take place, varying from the early reforming zeal of Brownson through the associationism of Ripley and the emphases on education of Emerson and Alcott to the extreme individualism of Thoreau's one-man revolution. Yet for all their differences–often conscious disagreements as to methods–they were in fairly close agreement in their reasons for desiring social change and advancement. They all tended to use as the standard for measuring society their intuitions of what was best, a standard of which the existing institutions always fell short. And in light of such an ideal which showed up the deficiencies of the actual, they also tended to disregard the justifications of history, of tradition, and of the past which were often adduced by conservatives who, if they did not think this the best of all possible worlds, nevertheless argued against any vigorous attempt at change.

Transcendentalism actually offered justification for opposing tendencies in American society when different aspects of the doctrine were stressed, democracy as opposed to individualism, for example, or equality as opposed to liberty. Transcendentalism, emphasizing as it did the ability of each person to come into contact with the ultimate truth, justified democracy rather than aristocracy. In this it broke with the Calvinist concept of the regenerate "elect" and the damned, who as individuals in the eyes of New England leaders were often equated with the prosperous (who were rewarded by Providence on this earth), and the poor (who were getting as much as they deserved). When given this emphasis, Trancendentalism could be a justification for majority rule and for the rights of the laboring classes. It could be argued that if all men had access to ultimate truth, the decision of a majority legislated the closest approximation of that truth, and this is the line John Dewey was emphasizing when he called Emerson the philosopher of democracy.[239] On the other hand it was fairly clear to most of the Transcendentalists that most men were not actually following the moral law or, more probably, were not permitting themselves to become conscious of it. Disagreements with a man's intuitions of the absolute tended to be proof of the error or perhaps even sin of the majority. And when looking from this angle, Transcendentalism saw that political democracy was far from ultimate and that the Jacksonians showed the evils of rule by the uneducated mass;

Contemporary engraving of Emerson's funeral, which appeared in Harper's Weekly
(13 May 1882)

while the Democrats had the best principles, Emerson sided with the Whigs, who had the best man.[240]

Here was an ineluctable paradox in Transcendentalist political thought, since either equality or liberty, either democracy or individualism could be emphasized, but ultimately all the Transcendentalists were for improving man; the question was how this was to be done. At least four separate and distinct techniques were suggested varying all the way from (1) legislation of improvement, through (2) voluntary association and (3) education to (4) self-reform and individual action.

All four were at one time or another advocated and employed.

The Transcendentalists, as vigorous individualists, departed widely from the eighteenth-century concept of social rights and the social contract. As heirs of Boston Federalism most of them failed to recognize America's revolutionary tradition. Thus there was little emphasis upon democracy in the political sense. *The Federalist* was taught at Harvard,[241] and the majority of the group were in the Federalist-Whig tradition and opposed to Jacksonian democracy. But for individualists and conservatives alike, at the end of the period the issue of slavery assumed such proportions that all showed a willingness to take group and even legislative action.

To this general attitude Bancroft and Brownson were conspicuous exceptions. George Bancroft, as a result of his education in Germany, returned to America an adherent of the Transcendentalist philosophy.[242] After a period of proving himself an advanced educator at Round Hill and a successful popularizer of German literature, he became a New England leader of the Democratic party and a dispenser of its patronage,[243] and began to write his *History of the United States* (1834ff.), proclaiming the thesis that democracy was ordained by Providence. The proof of this thesis he thought was scientific, though a more historical view would recognize it as philosophic. In a famous passage on Kant and the early Quakers he showed his Transcendentalism.

> The professor of Königsberg, like Fox and Barclay and Penn, derived philosophy from the voice in the soul; like them, he made the oracle within the categorical rule of practical morality, the motive of disinterested virtue; like them, he esteemed the Inner Light, which discerns universal and necessary truths, an element of humanity; and therefore his philosophy claims for humanity the right of ever renewed progress and reform.[244]

Bancroft really meant social reform when he used the word *reform;* for him reforms could be effected only "through the masses of the people."[245] But he was never a central member of the Transcendental group, although he repeatedly praised Emerson.

Brownson, who came from a home of poverty and who did not remain a Transcendentalist, was the most vigorous politically and the most prophetic political thinker of the group. Having been influenced by Frances Wright and the Owens, he endeavored to organize a Workingman's Party about 1830.[246] His *Boston Quarterly Review* (1838-1842) was even too closely tied to the Democratic party for the taste of the Transcendentalists, who turned down his offer to make it into an organ for the group. Convinced that the election of 1840 was of crucial importance, he wrote his celebrated two-part essay on "The Laboring Classes," which, though it stirred up a hurricane of criticism at the time, is now recognized as a brilliant piece of social thought.

Brownson saw the real conflict in society as between the operative and the employer, with all advantages in the latter's hands.[247] The conditions of the laborer were getting worse since, as the frontier moved west, it became more difficult economically to take up new land.[248] The evil lay in the social arrangements, not the characters of either group, and could be eliminated only by changing the institutions. His program started with the premise that the power of the priesthood must be broken. Then the "proletaries" must turn to legislative enactments, first by repealing discriminatory laws and abolishing banks and other monopolies. Then must come positive laws aiding the poor. Here he went too far for the times by suggesting the end of the inheritance of property, an idea he derived from the Saint-Simonians.[249] Having tried to demonstrate that capitalism was worse than slavery, in the second article Brownson answered his critics and pushed his views even further.[250] To the idea that the poor can rise, he correctly replied that it was possible only for a few at the expense of the many, while he demanded equality as a "natural right." And if force were needed to enforce the right, as inspection of the past would indicate, then it would be forthcoming, though force might not prove necessary.

This does not seem Transcendental doctrine, though it was no less intuited than Emerson's social restraint. It was not, however, typical, and even Brownson, disillusioned in the people by the election of the Whig Harrison (1840), retreated to the view that the people, unable to see their own interests, must be protected by the operation of a Calhoun-type system of concurrent majorities.[251]

The nature and effect of voluntary associations must be considered next, leaving the question of slavery in all its ramifications until last. Such associated groups which included informal clubs like the "Transcendental" Club, occasional meetings like the Chardon Street Convention, societies in favor of peace, temperance, and women's rights, lyceums, and the Associationist groups like Brook Farm and Fruitlands were a characteristic of the age. They were by no means confined to the Transcendentalists, and many of the peculiar persons whose activities gave rise to the term "Transcendental nonsense" were not members of the group. The significance of these associations lies in the fact that falling as they did between legislative action and individual isolation, they furnished an outlet for the reforming ferment of the times. Some Transcendentalists were involved in each of the above movements, but only the communitarian groups can be treated here.

Of these Brook Farm is justly the most famous. George Ripley, who became increasingly dissatisfied with preaching to his Purchase Street congregation on subjects which did not closely concern him, was convinced that some form of social action was necessary. In his letter to his church on his resignation, he wrote:

> There is a class of persons who desire a reform in the prevailing philosophy of the day. These are called Transcendentalists, because they believe in an order of truths which transcends the sphere of the external senses. Their leading idea is the supremacy of mind over matter. . . . These views I have always adopted. . . . There is another class of persons who are devoted to the removal of the abuses that prevail in modern society. They witness the oppressions that are done under the sun, and they cannot keep silence . . . [and] they look forward to a more pure, more lovely, more divine state of society than was ever realized on earth. With these views, I rejoice to say, I strongly and entirely sympathize.[252]

Though these were not fire-eating words, the action based upon them was more drastic than many would take. While Emerson probably came close to consenting orally to participating in the venture, he finally withdrew, saying that there was little point in moving from a small prison to a larger one.

Brook Farm, founded in 1841 upon the idea of having the scholar do some labor and thus escape some of the evils of industrialism, never flourished economically, but its school, to which Bancroft and Brownson sent sons,[253] was excellent. However, its emphasis shifted when Albert Brisbane, who had been convinced by Fourier's doctrines of a highly organized phalanx,[254] used his influence and persuasion to change Brook Farm over to the new form of organization in 1844.[255] This helped seal its doom, since the school attracted fewer pupils when it became associated with the more radical system.[256] Interestingly, there was a mixture of Fourier and Swedenborg in the periodical the *Harbinger* (1845-1849), which was launched at Brook Farm. This may have been the result of a need for balancing a mechanical system with a mystical religion, or simply because the complicated gradations in each fit the other.[257]

Only a shade less well known was the tragicomic experiment at Fruitlands (1842-1843). The individualistic Alcott must have been persuaded by Charles Lane to become involved in this venture, which combined many faddisms from vegetarianism and disapproval of using animals for work (or even for wool) to nudism.[258]

These experiments are difficult to assess. Products of the depression in 1837,[259] they seem to represent an attempt to escape the evident evils of industrialism by trying to return to an earlier, semifeudalistic form of organization.[260] Brook Farm, despite its poor land, might have succeeded as a school, but the collapse of all the communities indicates how much they were going against the main stream.

Not quite like any of their other avenues of expression was the Transcendentalists' emphasis upon education, though it fitted well with the view that individual development was better than political action. Alcott applied a mixture of theories to his highly efficient teaching. As a Lockean (at first) and an associationist, he believed in improving the surroundings of his schools; as a Transcendentalist he believed in bringing out the spirit of his pupils; as a New Englander he emphasized introspection. Later in life he decided perhaps too conservatively, along with Greaves, that inherited constitution was a major factor.[261] Associated with him in the Temple School in 1835-1837 was Elizabeth Peabody, who preferred the Froebel technique of developing outward activity and handicraft creativity, ideas which she later applied as the founder of the American kindergarten movement.[262]

Of profound importance in this area of education was Pestalozzi, whose works were read with interest in America. Emerson cited with approval Pestalozzi's conclusion that "the amelioration of outward circumstances will be the effect, but never can be the means of mental and moral improvement."[263] And the Emersonian belief that "Education is the drawing out of the soul"[264] seems to have had a similar basis. Moreover the teaching technique which used kindness in place of corporal punishment–a technique successfully adopted by Alcott, Thoreau, and Ripley–was taken over from or was consonant with the practices of the Swiss educator.

The Transcendentalist emphasis upon individualism had its effect in another branch of education by influencing the subsequent elective system introduced much later at Harvard by Charles W. Eliot. The New Group had found it necessary to employ their own elective system at Harvard when they gained their real edu-

Emerson's grave in Sleepy Hollow Cemetery, Concord

cation by independent reading rather than from the stagnant curriculum.[265] Emerson urged that the object of education should be to remove obstructions and let "natural force have free play and exhibit its peculiar product."[266] He was also a member of the Board of Overseers which elected Eliot to the presidency, while Eliot for his part always believed that it was the Transcendentalist spirit which was the force behind the change to free election. Emerson's statement, "I would have the studies elective,"[267] was the spirit acknowledged by Eliot.

Certainly no less characteristic of "The Newness" was the emphasis upon self-reform, individual action, and individualism. A logical deduction from the doctrine of direct contact with God as Conscious Law, it formed the most characteristic mode of action, though it was clearly not the only one. Dr. Channing had held to the view so completely that he believed each individual should perfect himself before attempting social activity of any sort.[268] Such an emphasis, while it might help the character of the person, could actually hinder social change. Emerson's position, though less extreme, dis-

turbed some of his more activist associates when he pursued his separate path. As he expressed it, "the only right is what is after my constitution," and he sought to practice his individualistic principle, "Every one to his chosen work."[269] His lectures on "The Times," "The Conservative," and "The Transcendentalist" took him out of social reform activity just at the instant when his associates were taking it up,[270] yet it is difficult to say that given his personality he was wrong.

The most extreme form of individualist protest was of course that of Thoreau, who wanted a minimum of government and who came as close to seceding from the state as a person can. His signing off from the church and his refusal to pay a poll tax or to vote were no less individualistic than his advocacy of the cause of John Brown. Since he wrote about his activities and thus achieved an ultimate effect through his published works, he cannot simply be called a quixotic skulker. Without claiming more than Emerson that others should follow his example–and there is never any danger of having too many Thoreaus–he offered a cogent criticism of his society by his very extremism.

The slavery crisis finally involved nearly all the Transcendentalists, whatever their previous theories of social amelioration. Even Emerson and Thoreau were so affected that they were unable to hold aloof. For this fact their very theories were responsible. Emerson with his theoretical anarchism had claimed that it was immoral to try to bind another man to anyone's insights,[271] and this seemed particularly true when the law controverted his own higher intuitions. Thus the passage of the Fugitive Slave Law (1850) came as a personal shock which jolted him out of a rather more passive objection to slavery. Since it was a moral wrong, the blot must be removed before society could be improved. He was even moved to action in the extreme form of a political speech for which he was shouted down.[272] Thoreau also felt the need of active rather than passive resistance and even helped one of John Brown's raiders to escape. Such actions were not consistent with the extreme reluctance of these men to engage in group activity, but more basic was their feeling of the need to follow the dictates of their insights in whatever direction they commanded.

The leader of the group in the antislavery movement was Theodore Parker, who clearly saw that Transcendentalism had social consequences. While Parker normally used his eloquence to call on offending groups to repent rather than to call on legislatures to pass prohibitory laws,[273] he both denounced slavery and actively opposed it. His attack on Daniel Webster for his seventh of March speech, which advocated the Fugitive Slave Law, surpassed all others in vehemence.[274] Parker also took a personal part in opposing this law. He tried to whip up a crowd to attempt the rescue of the recaptured fugitive slave Sims, and Anthony Burns was close to being freed by a mob which Parker organized. (Bronson Alcott was also there.) Indeed, the opposition attempted to indict Parker for obstructing the Fugitive Slave Act, but without success.

In economic emphases the Transcendentalists varied between the extremes of Brownson's legislative reform and Thoreau's individual protest against materialism by reducing his wants. In the midground lay the ambiguous views of Emerson, who has been variously regarded as a petty bourgeois apologist and as an outstanding critic of materialism, with some evidence to back both interpretations. The question is from what part of the essay the views are extracted, since Emerson regularly constructed his lectures by ascending from the material to the moral laws. Since he felt that the laws of both levels should be obeyed, he could on the physical level emphasize a conservative laissez faire which came close to justifying the free competition of classical economics. Thus he could say that "Gravitation is Nature's Grand Vizier and prime favorite. . . . In morals, again, Gravity is the *laissez-faire* principle, or Destiny, or Optimism, than which nothing is wiser or stronger."[275] And on this level of law for thing, Emerson opposed charity[276] and accepted more fully than Adam Smith the view that beneficent social laws would cause a free economy to improve.[277] But even when sounding most like *Poor Richard's Almanac,* Emerson ascended by the end of a lecture to the higher realm of spirit; and it was this that made him a sharp critic of American materialism, and made the other Transcendentalists almost equally trenchant in their discussions of American society.

The prevailing individualism, the optimism, the expansionism, the manifest destiny of Jacksonian America had its echoes in the thought of the Transcendentalists too. Though the direct effect of the frontier on Emerson's ideas has been overemphasized,[278] since his thought was well worked out before he went to the West, still in a general way he, like the rest of the group, was influenced by the American intellectual climate. The exuberance which accompanied the expanding economy was part of the atmosphere which the Tran-

scendentalists breathed. But aside from this broad influence, their ideas had been formed before the problem of society came to their attention; and the ideas they had already developed were merely carried over into the social sphere. Here their views showed a long jump from the socially rather than individually centered theories of the eighteenth century, but their individualism was both ethical and responsible. Even the most conservative members of the group looked radical at times to the local New England public.

VI

The Transcendentalists of New England were not pale reflections of a European movement, but an indigenous group who met American problems in a distinctive way. While they used ideas where they found them, the minds of the abler men among them were distinguished by great imaginative ability which adapted their sources to their needs with results which were strikingly different from those of their European forebears. These rebels and idealists were New Englanders, heirs also of the moral intensity and the practical ability of the earlier era. Not for nothing was Emerson called a "winged Franklin." Even such commercially unsuccessful men as Alcott had a remarkably keen judgment of people. Even so ardent an apostle of self-culture as Margaret Fuller became an equally ardent champion of the rights of women as well as of tyrannized Italy. Far from being blind visionaries, they knew what they were combating.

Most immediately they were in reaction against the sterile repudiations and cold complacency of Unitarianism. They pierced the joints in its armor as no other group was able to do. They saw clearly that the rationalistic philosophy and the acceptance of miraculous authority did fit, that the defense of human nature against the charges of total depravity was weak if not false, when the doctrine of the mediation of Christ between man and God was still required. The New Group also attacked the sensationalism, the scientific rationalism, the common-sense realism, and the bourgeois commercialism associated with Unitarianism, though in almost every case some part of the older beliefs was transformed into something more usable.

The intuitive Transcendentalists reacted strongly against the philosophy of the Enlightenment as symbolized by Locke's *Essay Concerning Human Understand-*

Daniel Chester French statue of Emerson in the Concord Free Public Library (Concord Free Public Library)

ing. Locke was impressive but unsatisfactory. Though mentioned by Emerson in "The American Scholar" as one of the able young men in a library,[279] Locke was also held by Emerson to be one of the marks of "the decline and not the rise of a just philosophy. With him disappeared the class of laborious philosophers who had studied Man with Plato in the belief that Man existed in connexion with the Divine Mind. . . ."[280] The tenderer minds of the Transcendentalists could not follow Locke, and they rejected the sensationalist theories; had they been offered no ground for a new position, they would have had to invent it.

While the Transcendentalists as idealists abandoned the Lockean epistemology, with its sensationalism and associationism, they were able to build upon the foundations rather than the ruins of the eighteenth-century faith in reason, because of the romantic character of American material progress.[281] They could use Newton's laws as the basis for correspondence; and at the same time Emerson, at least on one level, could accept the doctrines of beneficent social laws. Indeed, through his dualism between physical law and moral

law, Emerson could both accept the natural basis of societal laws and reject those laws as not of ultimate validity.

The major tenets and theological dogmas of the Puritans were flatly rejected. The belief in the personal sovereign God, in predestination, in original sin, in salvation of only the elect by Divine grace, in a capricious Providence, and in the Divine inspiration of the Bible were all abandoned in favor of belief in an immanent Over-Soul, in the divinity of the individual soul which could gain contact with the absolute by an intuitive process, in freedom of the will, and in the view that nature as symbol can reveal the moral laws.

Though the relationship of Puritanism and Transcendentalism still requires further study, a number of positive influences can now be pointed out. While the Transcendentalists escaped most of the dogma and theology of Calvinism, they shared its emotional qualities. Much of the zeal, introspection, soul-searching, journal keeping, industry, distrust of fiction, and moral restraint of the Puritan tradition left its mark and set the limits which prevented the Transcendentalists from imitating the less disciplined conduct of the European romantics. While retaining the intensity and exaltation of earlier New England, the Transcendentalists cast off the sense of sin and inadequacy and the terror of eternal damnation whenever they could do so. Emerson, though he did not suffer from fear of Hell, certainly felt as a young man that he was inadequate in personality– cold, mean, silly.[282] On the other hand Theodore Parker, who was terrified as a child by the doctrine of eternal damnation,[283] gave up this idea, even though he was never able to abandon the exacting regimen of the Puritans which brought him to an early grave. It has been well said of the Transcendentalists that they gave to all men what the Calvinists had reserved to the elect.[284]

But in Emerson particularly the later economic doctrines have some relationship to the Puritan views which, whether engendered by early Calvinism or by the stern necessities of the struggle for existence on a bleak frontier, emphasized the qualities of thrift, industry, and prudence.[285] On the level of law for thing he opposed charity and felt that wealth was a sign of virtue.[286] Though this was not his final position, it shows an important Puritan survival in his attitudes.[287]

Finally it is worth noting that the enthusiasm which Edwards defended against the more respectable and more nearly Unitarian Chauncey is one of the more important aspects of Transcendentalism.[288] While rejecting Edwards's philosophy, for none of the Transcendentalists returned to Calvinism, they kept his emotional warmth as intuitionists of a semimystical or super-rational type.

Moreover Transcendentalism was a part of a rebellion against the cultural dominance of Europe. Edward Everett had called for an American literature,[289] and Dr. Channing had held up the ideal of an American writing which should do more than express the utilitarian side of American life.[290] Emerson not only predicted an American literature, but also in poems like "Hamatraya" broke radically not only from the neoclassical, but also from the romantic tradition. The opening lines,

> Bulkeley, Hunt, Willard, Hosmer, Merriam, Flint,
> Possessed the land which rendered to their toil
> Hay, corn, roots, hemp, flax, apples, wool and
>   wood.[291]

strike a new note in American poetry. In the *Dial,* Emerson gave space to Jones Very, Ellery Channing, and Thoreau, whose "Natural History of Massachusetts" also opened up a fresh field for development. And Emerson also brought to a boil the American poet who, in *Leaves of Grass,* was most unmistakably different from recent foreign literature.

In social theory the Transcendentalists also differed from the Enlightenment, although both rejected a society of status sanctioned by revelation. The difference can perhaps be most easily stated in terms of the greater importance given by Transcendentalism to the individual, who had within him the potentiality of direct contact with ultimate reality. Consequently the loss of individual as opposed to social rights seemed the greater danger to the Transcendentalist who talked less of social contract. This difference was due in part to the fact that the American nation was based upon natural rights which represented a triumph of the Enlightenment, and the successors were able to carry the process a step further by claiming the extreme that no individual could properly bind another by passing a law. Nor did the groups agree on the perfectibility of the world. If, as the Enlightenment held, ideas were the results of sensations, then man could be improved by giving him a better environment. But if, as the Transcendentalists believed, men's ideas came from insights into an eternal realm of total truth, then society could improve only as individuals improve. Thoreau's statement that "The sun is but a morning star" does not imply the idea of material progress. And Parker, instead of call-

ing upon the public to pass more stringent laws to limit business, called upon the merchants to reform themselves and turn their power to goodness. These statements indicate the direction of the revolt from the more logical and mechanical theories of the Enlightenment.

Finally, whether as individuals they believed in social reform or self-reform, the Transcendentalists reacted against a bourgeois commercial money-society where position was dependent upon wealth, and not on family or culture or the intrinsic value of the individual. Emerson understood this when he said that the same sort of thinking which falling on Roman times made Stoic philosophers, "falling on Unitarian and commercial times, makes the peculiar shades of idealism which we know."[292] And Parrington felt that the absence of a commercial mentality in the South was one of the factors which prevented the appearance of a Transcendental movement there. Moreover the Transcendentalists of the clerical group, which if Veblen is right, was a sort of vicarious leisure class attached to the older aristocracy, opposed Jacksonianism partly on the above ground and partly because they unconsciously recognized the threat to their previous position of dominance. But on the positive side Transcendentalism represented the kind of rebellion against Philistinism which is vitally needed in a commercial or industrial society if its civilization is not to die.

American Transcendentalism arose in response to domestic needs and was partly shaped by the native environment. Basically the problem solved by the "Newness" was the unsatisfying coolness, rationalism, and skepticism of the Enlightenment and of American Unitarianism. In order to work out a satisfactory set of beliefs the Transcendentalists found it necessary to make a number of shifts in thought. (1) They abandoned Lockean sensationalism and Scottish Common-Sense philosophy in favor of intuitive idealism–intuitive because they were not as a group logicians. (2) Finding a mechanical universe an inadequate expression of an immanent God, they used the harmony of nature as the basis for a theory of correspondence in which phenomena became symbols of spiritual unity. (3) In religion they substituted for formal institutionalism and sterile rationalism an insistence upon the divinity of the individual soul and the validity of its apprehension of reality as superior to the sanctions of historically recorded miracles. (4) In the aesthetic realm, using seventeenth century and romantic writings as examples, they decided that the organic expression of the intuitions of the reason was superior to regular and correct expression according to codified rules. (5) During a period of increasing democracy and individualism, they emphasized the development of the potentialities of each man as he was able to perceive them with his highest capacities, without necessarily considering either material prosperity or majority will as the controlling factor of central importance. In producing this loose pattern of thought the Transcendentalists made significant contributions to American culture, in philosophy, in the interpretation of science, in religious thought, in the theory and creation of art, and in social and economic thought and application.

1. Basic references for major aspects of the movement include Arthur E. Christy, *The Orient in American Transcendentalism* (New York, 1932); George W. Cooke, *The Poets of Transcendentalism: An Anthology* (Boston, 1903); Octavius B. Frothingham, *Transcendentalism in New England: A History* (New York, 1876); Harold C. Goddard, *Studies in New England Transcendentalism* (New York, 1908); Clarence L. F. Gohdes, *The Periodicals of American Transcendentalism* (Durham, N.C., 1931); Perry Miller, *The Transcendentalists: An Anthology* (Cambridge, Mass., 1950); Henry A. Pochmann, *New England Transcendentalism and St. Louis Hegelianism* (Philadelphia, 1948); Lindsay Swift, *Brook Farm* (New York, 1900).

2. A. O. Lovejoy, "The Thirteen Pragmatisms," *Journal of Philosophy*, V (1908), 1-12; 29-39; F. I. Carpenter, "Points of Comparison between Emerson and William James," *New England Quarterly*, II (1929), 458-474; F. I. Carpenter, "William James and Emerson," *American Literature*, XI (1939), 39-57; C. S. Peirce, *Collected Papers*, ed. Hartshorne and Weiss (Cambridge, Mass., 1931-1935), VI, 86-87; John Dewey, "Emerson," *Characters and Events* (New York, 1929), I, 69-77.

3. Ralph Waldo Emerson, *The Complete Works of Ralph Waldo Emerson*, ed. E. W. Emerson (Boston, 1903-1904) (hereinafter cited as Emerson, *Works*), I, 329.

4. J. E. Cabot, *A Memoir of Ralph Waldo Emerson* (Boston, 1887), I, 248.

5. Gohdes, *op cit.*, H. G. Townsend, *Philosophical Ideas in the United States* (New York, 1934), p. 86.

6. René Wellek, "Periods and Movements," *English Institute Annual, 1940* (New York, 1941), pp. 90-91.

7. For Locke's sensationalism, see Harold Höffding, *A History of Modern Philosophy* (London, 1924), I, 383-387.

8. *Ibid.*, I, 447.

9. H. W. Schneider, *A History of American Philosophy* (New York, 1946), p. 284; H. D. Gray, *Emerson, A Statement of New England Transcendentalism as Expressed in the Philosophy of its Chief Exponent* (Stanford Univ., 1917), p. 66. Cf. W. H. Werkmeister, *A History of Philosophical Ideas in America* (New York, 1949), p. 41.

10. Thomas Reid (1710-1796), preacher and professor at Aberdeen and Glasgow, published his principal work, *Inquiry into the Human Mind on the Principles of Common Sense*, in 1764.

11. Dugald Stewart (1753-1858) published *Elements of the Philosophy of the Human Mind* from 1792 to 1827, and *Outlines of Moral Philosophy* in 1793.

12. Thomas Brown (1778-1820) published posthumously *Physiology of the Human Mind* (1820) and *Lectures on the Philosophy of the Human Mind* (1822).

13. Höffding, *op.cit.*, I, 451.

14. E. W. Todd, "Philosophical Ideas at Harvard College, 1817-1837," *New England Quarterly*, XVI (1943), 64.

15. Emerson's technique is here, as it is generally, affirmative rather than negative, yet it emphasizes the contrast between material and ideal (*Works*, I, 8, 47).

16. *Ibid.*, I, 329-333.

17. In George F. Whicher (ed.), *The Transcendentalist Revolt against Materialism* (Boston, 1949), pp. 68 ff.

18. Elizabeth Palmer Peabody, *Reminiscences of Rev. William Ellery Channing, D.D.* (Boston, 1880), p. 368.

19. *Ibid.*, p. 75.

20. Goddard, *op.cit.*, p. 43 n.

21. William Ellery Channing, *Works* (Boston, 1886), p. 293.

22. Letter of Channing to Elizabeth Peabody, August, 1841, in Peabody, *op. cit.*, p. 432.

23. *Ibid.*, p. 365. Though Miss Peabody quotes this from memory, it is unlikely, despite the fact that she was a Transcendentalist, that she was distorting the views of her hero, Channing.

24. Ralph L. Rusk, *The Life of Ralph Waldo Emerson* (New York, 1949), p. 103; cf. Lenthiel H. Downs, "Emerson and Dr. Channing," *New England Quarterly*, XX (Dec., 1947), 516-534.

25. Goddard, *op. cit.*, p. 84.

26. Arthur I. Ladu, "Channing and Transcendentalism," *American Literature*, XI (1939), 134. Cf. Channing, *Works*, p. 297.

27. Ladu, *op. cit.*, pp. 135-136.

28. Letter to Lydia M. Child, March, 1842, in *Letters of Lydia Maria Child* (Boston, 1883), p. 46.

29. Alexander Hill Everett, review of Victor Cousin, *North American Review*, XXIX (1829), 109. Fear of human skepticism had caused the new idealists, thought Everett, to throw out the baby with the bath, under the assumption that complete negation of the possibility of knowledge was a necessary consequence of Locke. But the new was "transitory," and the public would "settle down again in the conclusions of Locke and Aristotle" (*ibid.*, p. 119).

30. Timothy Walker, "Defence of Mechanical Philosophy," *North American Review*, XXXIII (1831), 123, 126.

31. *Ibid.*, p. 130.

32. Goddard, *op. cit.*, p. 35.

33. Frederic Hedge, review of Coleridge's works, *Christian Examiner*, XIV (1833), 116.

34. *Ibid.*, XIV, 119.

35. *Ibid.*, XIV, 121.

36. R. V. Wells, *Three Christian Transcendentalists: James Marsh, Caleb Sprague Henry, Frederic Henry Hedge* (New York, 1943), p. 97 n.

37. George Ripley, review of Charles Follen, "Inaugural Discourse," *Christian Examiner*, XI (1832), 375.

38. George Ripley, review of James Mackintosh, "A General View of the Progress of Ethical Philosophy," *Christian Examiner*, XIII (1833), 332.

39. George Ripley, *Discourses on the Philosophy of Religion* (Boston, 1836), in Miller, *op. cit.*, p. 133.

40. *Ibid.*, p. 135.

41. *Ibid.*, p. 137.

42. *Ibid.*, p. 139.

43. *Ibid.*, p. 140.

44. Orestes Brownson, review of Benjamin Constant, *Christian*

Examiner, XVII (1834), 70.

45. *Ibid.*, XVII, 71.

46. *Loc. cit.*

47. René Wellek, "The Minor Transcendentalists and the German Philosophy," *New England Quarterly*, XV (1942), 669.

48. Orestes Brownson, article on Cousin, *Christian Examiner*, XXI (1836), 34-35.

49. *Ibid.*, XXI, 40.

50. *Ibid.*, XXI, 45.

51. *Ibid.*, XXI, 46.

52. Orestes A. Brownson, *The Works of Orestes A Brownson*, ed. H. F. Brownson (Detroit, 1883), IV, 17.

53. *Ibid.*, IV, 22.

54. *Ibid.*, IV, 17-19, 23.

55. *Ibid.*, IV, 17-23.

56. *Ibid.*, IV, 39-40. Following Cousin's eclecticism as a pattern, Brownson predicts a religious eclecticism which will combine the best features of both spiritualism and materialism. Of this a prototype is Dr. Channing (*ibid.*, IV, 46).

57. Odell Shepard, *Pedlar's Progress* (Boston, 1937), p. 133.

58. *Ibid.*, pp. 193-195; Hubert H. Hoeltje, *Sheltering Tree* (Durham, N.C., 1943), pp. 31-32.

59. *The Journals of Bronson Alcott*, ed. Odell Shepard (Boston, 1938), p. 80.

60. Shepard, *Pedlar's Progress*, p. 194.

61. *Record of Conversations on the Gospels held in Mr. Alcott's School* (Boston, 1837), Introduction.

62. Miller, *op. cit.*, p. 128.

63. Rusk, *op. cit.*, p. 80.

64. Edward Everett Hale, *Ralph Waldo Emerson: Together with Two Early Essays of Emerson* (Boston, 1904), pp. 57-58.

65. *Ibid.*, p. 87.

66. *Ibid.*, p. 73.

67. *Ibid.*, p. 81.

68. *Ibid.*, p. 59.

69. *Ibid.*, p. 75.

70. Merrill R. Davis, "Emerson's Reason and the Scottish Philosphers," *New England Quarterly*, XVII (1944), 214-215; Todd, *op. cit.*, XVI, 64.

71. Rusk, *op. cit.*, p. 82.

72. *Ibid.*, pp. 81-82.

73. *Journals of Ralph Waldo Emerson*, ed. E. W. Emerson and W. E. Forbes (Boston, 1909), I, 78.

74. Hale, *op. cit.*, p. 112.

75. *Loc. cit.*

76. *Ibid.*, p. 115.

77. *Ibid.*, p. 116.

78. *Ibid.*, p. 122-123.

79. *Ibid.*, p. 121.

80. *Ibid.*, p. 123.

81. *Ibid.*, p. 122.

82. *Ibid.*, p. 135.

83. *Ibid.*, p. 134.

84. *Ibid.*, p. 130.

85. A. C. McGiffert, Jr. (ed.), *Young Emerson Speaks: Unpublished Discourses on Many Subjects* (Boston, 1938), p. 1.

86. *Ibid.*, p. 2.

87. *Ibid.*, p. 4.

88. *Ibid.*, p. 44.

89. *Ibid.*, p. 209.

90. Rusk, *op. cit.*, p. 158.

91. *Journals*, I, 60.

92. *Ibid.*, I, 148.

93. *Ibid.*, I, 104.

94. *Ibid.*, I, 187-188.

95. *Ibid.*, II, 248.

96. *Ibid.*, II, 242, 249.

97. John S. Harrison, *The Teachers of Emerson* (New York, 1910), pp. 41-42.

98. Emerson, *Works*, I, 70-71.

99. *Ibid.*, I, 9, 11, 16.

100. Henry Pochmann and Gay Allen, *Masters of American Literature* (New York, 1949), I, 678; Emerson, *Works*, I, 19-24.

101. Neither Frothingham nor Goddard treats Thoreau in detail.

102. Joseph J. Kwiat, "Thoreau's Philosophical Apprenticeship," *New England Quarterly*, XVIII (1945), 51-69.

103. Frank B. Sanborn, *The Life of Henry David Thoreau, Including Many Essays Hitherto Unpublished* (Boston, 1917), pp. 117-118.

104. *Ibid.*, pp. 115-116.

105. *Ibid.*, pp. 157.

106. *Ibid.*, p. 66-67; 74.

107. *Ibid.*, p. 137. Cf. Emerson, *Works*, I, 56.

108. Sanborn, *op. cit.*, pp. 150-152.

109. *Ibid.*, p. 176.

110. *Ibid.*, p. 180.

111. *Ibid.*, pp. 183-184.

112. S. G. Brown, "Emerson's Platonism," *New England Quarterly*, XVIII (1945), 325-345.

113. John W. Thomas, *James Freeman Clarke: Apostle of German Culture to America* (Boston, 1949), p. 161.

114. Schneider, *op. cit.*, p. 284.

115. Bradford Torrey and F. H. Allen (eds.), *The Journal of Henry D. Thoreau* (Boston, 1906), I, 171.

116. F. I. Carpenter, *Emerson and Asia* (Cambridge, Mass., 1930), p. 43.

117. Harrison, *op. cit.*, pp. 80-83.

118. Shepard, *Pedlar's Progress*, pp. 453-462.

119. Austin Warren, "The Orphic Sage: Bronson Alcott," *American Literature*, III (1931), 13.

120. Emerson, *Journals*, II, 329.

121. Carpenter, *Emerson and Asia*, p. 20.

122. Christy, *op. cit.*, p. 246.

123. *Dial*, III (1843), 493-494; IV (1843), 59-62; 205-210; 402-404.

124. Sanborn, *op. cit.*, p. 305; Christy, *op. cit.*, pp. 46-47.

125. Kenneth W. Cameron, *Emerson the Essayist* (Raleigh, N.C., 1945), pp. 3-31.

126. Clarence Hotson, "Emerson and the Swedenborgians," *Studies in Philology*, XXVII (1930), 517-545.

127. Cameron, *op. cit.*, II, 83-101.

128. René Wellek, "The Minor Transcendentalists and German Philosophy," *New England Quarterly*, XV (1942), 669.

129. Peabody, *Reminiscences*, p. 368; Emerson, *Journals*, II, 129; Thomas, *Clarke*, p. 73.

130. "Philosophical Miscellanies from the French of Cousin, Jouffroy, Constant," *Speciments of Foreign Standard Literature*, I, II (Boston, 1838).

131. Emerson, *Journals*, II, 232, 429-430.

132. Rusk, *op. cit.*, p. 522 n.

133. Frank L. Thompson, "Emerson and Carlyle," *Studies in Philology*, XXIV (1927), 438-453.

134. Rusk, *op. cit.*, 206.

135. Joseph Warren Beach, *The Concept of Nature in Nineteenth-Century English Poetry* (New York, 1936), p. 328.

136. Emerson, *Works*, I, 76.

137. René Wellek, "The Concept of Romanticism in Literary History," *Comparative Literature*, I (1949), 147.

138. Emerson, *Works*, X, 335-337.
139. Emerson, *Journals*, II, 362.
140. *Ibid.*, I, 26.
141. *Ibid.*, I, 105.
142. Beach, *op. cit.*, p. 327.
143. Sherman Paul, *Emerson's Angle of Vision: Man and Nature in American Experience* (Cambridge, Mass., 1952), pp. 40-41.
144. Paul, *op. cit.*, p. 35.
145. McGiffert, *op. cit.*, pp. 174-175.
146. *Ibid.*, p. 177.
147. *Ibid.*, p. 176.
148. *Ibid.*, p. 177.
149. *Ibid.*, p. 178.
150. *Loc. cit.*
151. Emerson, *Works*, I, 20, 33.
152. Harry Hayden Clark, "Emerson and Science," *Philological Quarterly*, X (1931), 225-260.
153. Norman Foerster, *Nature in American Literature* (New York, 1923), pp. 37-68.
154. Gray, *op. cit.*, p. 45.
155. Coleridge, *Aids to Reflection*, Comments on Aphorism No. 74.
156. Emerson, *Journals*, I, 298.
157. *Ibid.*, III, 163.
158. Cabot, *op. cit.*, I, 224. *Ibid.*, II, 329 misdates the lecture as 1832.
159. Emerson, *Journals*, III, 293.
160. Cabot, *op. cit.*, II, 343.
161. Stephen Whicher, "The Lapse of Uriel: A Study of the Evolution of Emerson's Thought" (unpublished dissertation, Harvard University, 1943), pp. 401-403.
162. Emerson, *Journals*, VII, 8-9, 26, 53.
163. *The Letters of Ralph Waldo Emerson*, ed. Ralph L. Rusk (New York, 1939), III, 76-77.
164. Beach, *op. cit.*, pp. 342-343.
165. Emerson, *Journals*, VIII, 77; Alcott, *Journals*, p. 211 n.
166. Emerson, *Works*, VIII, 358.
167. Beach, *op. cit.*, p. 342.
168. Pochmann and Allen, *op. cit.*, I, 678; Stow Persons, *Evolutionary Thought in America* (New Haven, 1950), p. 440.
169. E. S. Deevey, "A Re-examination of Thoreau's *Walden*," *Quarterly Review of Biology*, XVII (1942), I-II; Raymond Adams, "Thoreau's Science," *Scientific Monthly*, LX (1945), 379-382; Philip and Kathryn Whitford, "Thoreau: Pioneer Ecologist and Conservationist," *Scientific Monthly*, LXXIII (1951), 291-296.
170. Thoreau, *Writings*, V, 130-131.
171. Foerster, *op. cit.*, p. 127. For Thoreau's mental strains, see Ethel Seybold, *Thoreau, the Quest and the Classics* (New Haven, 1951), p. 68; Sherman Paul, "The Wise Silence: Sound as the Agency of Correspondence in Thoreau," *New England Quarterly*, XXII (1949), 523.
172. Thoreau, *Journals*, III, 311-312.
173. *Ibid.*, XIII, 169.
174. William Drake, "A Formal Study of H. D. Thoreau," University of Iowa (1948), p. 68.
175. James Freeman Clarke, *Autobiography* (Boston, 1892), p. 49; Merle Curti, *The Social Ideas of American Educators* (New York, 1935), pp. 110-112.
176. Miller, *op. cit.*, pp. 75-77.
177. Schneider, *op. cit.*, p. 261.
178. H. H. Clark, "An Historical Interpretation of Thomas Paine's Religion," *University of California Chronicle*, XXXV (1933), 56-87.
179. C. A. Bartol, *Radical Problems* (Boston, 1872), p. 83.
180. Stephen Whicher, *op. cit.*, p. 402.
181. Stow Persons, *Free Religion, An American Faith* (New Haven, 1947), p. 3.
182. O. B. Frothingham, *Boston Unitarianism, 1820-50* (New York, 1890), p. 13.
183. Frothingham, *Transcendentalism*, p. 110.
184. G. W. Cooke, *Unitarianism in America* (Boston, 1910), p. 158.
185. Orville Dewey, *Discourses and Reviews* (written in the 1840's) in Persons, *Free Religion*, pp. 7-8.
186. Henry Adams, *The Education of Henry Adams* (New York, 1931, Mod. Lib. ed.), p. 34.
187. Clarence H. Faust, "The Background of Unitarian Opposition to Transcendentalism," *Modern Philology*, XXXV (1938), 317.
188. Emerson, *Journals*, II, 424.
189. *Ibid.*, 448-449.
190. *Ibid.*, II, 491.
191. *Ibid.*, II, 497-500.
192. Emerson, *Works*, IV, 172; Charles L. Young, *Emerson's Montaigne* (New York, 1941), p. 17.
193. M. C. Turpie, "A Quaker Source for Emerson's Sermon on the Lord's Supper," *New England Quarterly*, XVII (1944), 95-101.
194. Emerson, *Journals*, III, 258-260.
195. *Ibid.*, III, 228; VIII, 110; Cf. Paul W. Barrus, "Emerson and Quakerism," University of Iowa (1949).
196. Rusk, *op. cit.*, p. 113.
197. George Ripley, review of Herder, *Christian Examiner*, XIX (1835), 195-197.
198. Miller, *op. cit.*, p. 131.
199. *Ibid.*, p. 159.
200. *Christian Examiner*, XXII (1837), 122.
201. Miller, *op. cit.*, p. 217.
202. *Ibid.*, p. 208.
203. *Ibid.*, p. 229.
204. *Ibid.*, pp. 238-240.
205. *Ibid.*, pp. 273-281.
206. Alcott, *Journals*, pp. 78-79.
207. De Wette furnished the model for Clarke's novel, *The Legend of Thomas Didymus, the Jewish Skeptic* (Boston, 1881).
208. Miller, *op. cit.*, p. 243. Brownson here as elsewhere goes too far; e.g., neither he nor Parker was totally unaffected by his reading of European books. In fact this rather negative statement may need revision on the appearance of Professor Henry Pochmann's forthcoming study of the influences of German thought in America.
209. *Ibid.*, p. 203.
210. Channing, *Works*, p. 136.
211. Vivian C. Hopkins, *Spires of Form* (Cambridge, Mass., 1951), p. 74.
212. *Ibid.*, p. 64.
213. Emerson, *Works*, II, 356, 365.
214. *Ibid.*, VII, 39.
215. *Ibid.*, III, 9.
216. *Ibid.*, I, 24.
217. *Ibid.*, III, 10.
218. Edwin C. Mead, *The Influence of Emerson* (Boston, 1903), p. 243.
219. Mildred Silver, "Emerson and the Idea of Progress," *American Literature*, XII (1940), 1-19.
220. Emerson, *Works*, II, 45.
221. *Ibid.*, X, 65-66.
222. *Ibid.*, III, 17.
223. Hopkins, *op. cit.*, p. 142.
224. Robert P. Falk, "Emerson and Shakespeare," *PMLA*, LVI (1941), 532-543.
225. Emerson, *Journals*, II, 440.

226. Hopkins, *op. cit.*, p. 135.
227. Sherman Paul, *Emerson's Angle of Vision*, p. 131; William Charvat, *The Origins of American Cultural Thought* (Philadelphia, 1936), pp. 29-30, 48-52.
228. Fred Lorch, "Thoreau and the Organic Principle in Poetry," *PMLA*, LIII (1938), 286-302.
229. Thoreau, *Writings*, VI, 171.
230. Emerson, *Works*, I, 114.
231. Hopkins, *op. cit.*, p. 144.
232. Margaret Fuller, "A Short Essay on Critics," *Dial*, I (1841), 5-11.
233. Roland C. Burton, "Margaret Fuller's Criticism, Theory and Practice," unpublished dissertation, University of Iowa (1941), pp. 148-149.
234. Margaret Fuller, "The Modern Drama," *Dial*, IV (1844), 310.
235. Margaret Fuller, "Lives of the Great Composers," *Dial*, II (1842), 150.
236. *Ibid.*, II, 152.
237. G. W. Cooke, *John Sullivan Dwight* (Boston, 1898), p. 150.
238. J. T. Flanagan, "Emerson as a Critic of Fiction," *Philological Quarterly*, XV (1936), 30.
239. John Dewey, *op. cit.*, I, 76.
240. See John C. Gerber, "Emerson's Economics," unpublished dissertation, University of Chicago, 1941.
241. Merrill Davis, *op. cit.*, pp. 214-215 n.
242. Orie Long, *Literary Pioneers* (Cambridge, Mass., 1935), p. 134; Russel B. Nye, *George Bancroft: Brahmin Rebel* (New York, 1944), p. 101.
243. Arthur M. Schlesinger, Jr., *Orestes A. Brownson* (Boston, 1939), p. 72.
244. George Bancroft, *History of the United States*, II (1837), in Miller, *op. cit.*, p. 423.
245. In Miller, *op. cit.*, p. 428.
246. Schlesinger, *op. cit.*, pp. 19-23.
247. Orestes A. Brownson, "The Laboring Classes," *Boston Quarterly Review*, III (1840), 370.
248. *Ibid.*, III, 373-374.
249. Schlesinger, *op. cit.*, p. 94.
250. Brownson, "The Laboring Classes," *Boston Quarterly Review*, III (1840), 420-512.
251. Schlesinger, *op. cit.*, p. 120.
252. O. B. Frothingham, *George Ripley* (Boston, 1882), pp. 85-86.
253. John T. Codman, *Brook Farm: Historic and Personal Memoirs* (Boston, 1894), p. 57; Schlesinger, *Brownson*, p. 151.
254. Lindsay Swift, *Brook Farm*, p. 263.
255. *Ibid.*, p. 279.
256. Codman, *op. cit.*, p. 214.
257. Zoltan Harazsti, *The Idyll of Brook Farm as Revealed by Unpublished Letters in the Boston Public Library* (Boston, 1937), p. 44.
258. Clara E. Sears, *Bronson Alcott's Fruitlands* (Boston, 1915), pp. 39-40.
259. Harazsti, *op. cit.*, p. 11.

260. William Chavat, "American Romanticism and the Depression of 1837," *Science and Society*, II (1937), 80.
261. Alcott, *Journals*, pp. 173 n., 174 n.
262. Louise Hall Tharp, *The Peabody Sisters of Salem* (Boston, 1950), p. 319.
263. Emerson, *Journals*, II, 416.
264. *Ibid.*, II, 412.
265. Clarke, *Autobiography*, p. 38.
266. Emerson, *Journals*, III, 416.
267. Hazen Carpenter, "Emerson, Eliot, and the Elective System," *New England Quarterly*, XXIV (1951), 23.
268. Schlesinger, *op. cit.*, p. 78.
269. Emerson, *Works*, II, 50; "Ode Inscribed to W. H. Channing."
270. Stephen Whicher, "The Lapse of Uriel," pp. 393 ff.
271. Emerson, *Works*, III, 214-215.
272. M. M. Moody, "The Evolution of Emerson as an Abolitionist," *American Literature*, XVII (1945), 18.
273. Theodore Parker, "A Sermon of Merchants," in Miller, *op. cit.*, pp. 455, 456.
274. H. S. Commager, *Theodore Parker* (Boston, 1936), pp. 226-321.
275. Emerson, *Journals*, VIII, 8-9.
276. Emerson, *Works*, II, 52.
277. John C. Gerber, "Emerson and the Political Economists," *New England Quarterly*, XXII (1949), 340.
278. See Ernest Marchand, "Emerson and the Frontier," *American Literature*, III (1931), 149-174; Lucy Hazard, *The Frontier in American Literature* (New York, 1927), pp. 150-162; Arthur I. Ladu, "Emerson: Whig or Democrat," *New England Quarterly*, XIII (1940), 434-437.
279. Emerson, *Works*, I, 89.
280. Rusk, *op. cit.*, p. 239.
281. Schneider, *op. cit.*, p. 261.
282. Emerson, *Journals*, I, 362.
283. John Weiss, *Theodore Parker*, (New York, 1864), I, 30, 38.
284. O. B. Frothingham, *Transcendentalism in New England* (New York, 1876), p. 108.
285. Alexander C. Kern, "Emerson and Economics," *New England Quarterly*, XIII (1940), 683.
286. Emerson, *Works*, VI, 100.
287. Kern, *op. cit.*, pp. 682-683.
288. Perry Miller, "Jonathan Edwards to Emerson," *New England Quarterly*, XIII (1940), 609.
289. Edward Everett, "The Circumstances Favorable to the Progress of Literature in America," in J. L. Blau (ed.), *American Philosophic Addresses* (New York, 1946), pp. 60-93.
290. William Ellery Channing, *Works*, pp. 124-138.
291. Emerson, *Works*, IX, 35.
292. *Ibid.*, I, 339. The diversity of opinion produced by this individualistic emphasis on shades of idealism was expressed freely in the magazine contributions of the members. For details, see Gohdes, *op. cit., passim.*

BOOKS FOR FURTHER READING

Albanese, Catherine L. *Corresponding Motion: Transcendental Religion and the New America.* Philadelphia: Temple University Press, 1977.

Allen, Joseph Henry. *Our Liberal Movement in Theology.* Boston: Roberts Brothers, 1882.

Allen. *Sequel to "Our Liberal Movement."* Boston: Roberts Brothers, 1897.

Anagnos, Julia R. *Philosophiae Quaestor: or, Days in Concord.* Boston: D. Lothrop, 1885.

Ando, Shoei. *Zen and American Transcendentalism.* Tokyo: Hokuseido, 1970.

Barbour, Brian M., ed. *American Transcendentalism: An Anthology of Criticism.* Notre Dame: University of Notre Dame Press, 1973.

Boller, Paul F., Jr. *American Transcendentalism, 1830–1860: An Intellectual Inquiry.* New York: Putnams, 1974.

Bridgman, Raymond L., ed. *Concord Lectures on Philosophy: Comprising Outlines of All the Lectures at the Concord Summer School of Philosophy in 1882.* Boston: Moses King, 1883.

Brown, Jerry Wayne. *The Rise of Biblical Criticism in America, 1800–1870: The New England Scholars.* Middletown, Conn.: Wesleyan University Press, 1969.

Buell, Lawrence. *Literary Transcendentalism: Style and Vision in the American Renaissance.* Ithaca: Cornell University Press, 1973.

Buell, *New England Literary Culture: From Revolution to Renaissance.* New York: Cambridge University Press, 1986.

Burton, Katherine. *Paradise Planters: The Story of Brook Farm.* London: Longmans, Green, 1939.

Cameron, Kenneth Walter, ed. *Concord Harvest,* 2 vols. Hartford, Conn.: Transcendental Books, 1970.

Cameron, ed. *Responses to Transcendental Concord.* Hartford, Conn.: Transcendental Books, 1974.

Cameron, ed. *Transcendental Climate,* 3 vols. Hartford, Conn.: Transcendental Books, 1973.

Cameron, ed. *Transcendental Epilogue,* 3 vols. Hartford, Conn.: Transcendental Books, 1965.

Cameron, ed. *Transcendental Log.* Hartford, Conn.: Transcendental Books, 1973.

Cameron, ed. *Transcendental Reading Patterns.* Hartford, Conn.: Transcendental Books, 1970.

Cameron, ed. *The Transcendentalists and Minerva,* 3 vols. Hartford, Conn.: Transcendental Books, 1958.

Charvat, William. *The Origins of American Critical Thought, 1810–1835.* Philadelphia: University of Pennsylvania Press, 1936.

Christy, Arthur. *The Orient in American Transcendentalism.* New York: Columbia University Press, 1932.

Clark, Annie M. L. *The Alcotts in Harvard.* Lancaster, Mass.: J. C. L. Clark, 1902.

Codman, John Thomas. *Brook Farm: Historic and Personal Memoirs.* Boston: Arena, 1894.

Cooke, George Willis. *An Historical and Biographical Introduction to Accompany* The Dial, 2 vols. Cleveland: Rowfant Club, 1902.

Cooke. *Unitarianism in America.* Boston: American Unitarian Association, 1902.

Cooke, ed. *The Poets of Transcendentalism.* Boston: Houghton, Mifflin, 1903.

Dall, Caroline H. *Transcendentalism: A Lecture.* Boston: Roberts Brothers, 1897.

Delano, Sterling F. *The* Harbinger *and New England Transcendentalism: A Portrait of Associationism in America.* Rutherford, N.J.: Fairleigh Dickinson University Press, 1983.

Diehl, Carl. *Americans and German Scholarship 1770–1870.* New Haven: Yale University Press, 1978.

Dwight, Marianne. *Letters from Brook Farm*

1844–1847, ed. Amy L. Reed. Poughkeepsie, N.Y.: Vassar College, 1928.

Eliot, Samuel A., ed. *Heralds of a Liberal Faith,* vols. 2–3. Boston: American Unitarian Association, 1910.

Ellis, Charles Mayo. *An Essay on Transcendentalism.* Boston: Crocker and Ruggles, 1842.

Feidelson, Charles, Jr. *Symbolism and American Literature.* Chicago: University of Chicago Press, 1953.

Flower, Elizabeth, and Murray G. Murphey. *A History of Philosophy in America,* 2 vols. New York: Putnams, 1977.

Frothingham, Octavius Brooks. *Boston Unitarianism 1820–1850.* New York: Putnams, 1890.

Frothingham. *Transcendentalism in New England: A History.* New York: Putnams, 1876.

Gilmore, Michael T. *American Romanticism and the Marketplace.* Chicago: University of Chicago Press, 1985.

Goddard, Harold Clarke. *Studies in New England Transcendentalism.* New York: Columbia University Press, 1908.

Goetzmann, William H., ed. *The American Heglians: An Intellectual Episode in the History of Western America.* New York: Knopf, 1973.

Gohdes, Clarence L. F. *The Periodicals of American Transcendentalism.* Durham: Duke University Press, 1931.

Greene, William B. *Transcendentalism.* West Brookfield, Mass.: Oliver S. Cooke, 1849.

Gura, Philip F. *The Wisdom of Words: Language, Theology, and Literature in the New England Renaissance.* Middletown, Conn.: Wesleyan University Press, 1981.

Gura, and Joel Myerson, eds. *Critical Essays on American Transcendentalism.* Boston: G. K. Hall, 1982.

Habich, Robert D. *Transcendentalism and the* Western Messenger: *A History of the Magazine and Its Contributors, 1835–1841.* Rutherford, N.J.: Fairleigh Dickinson University Press, 1985.

Haraszti, Zoltan. *The Idyll of Brook Farm as Revealed by Unpublished Letters in the Boston Public Library.* Boston: Trustees of the Public Library, 1937; enl. ed., 1940.

Herbst, Jurgen. *The German Historical School in American Scholarship.* Ithaca: Cornell University Press, 1965.

Herreshoff, David. *American Disciples of Marx.* Detroit: Wayne State University Press, 1967; rpt.

as *The Origins of American Marxism* (New York: Pathfinder, 1973).

Hochfield, George, ed. *Selected Writings of the American Transcendentalists.* New York: New American Library, 1966.

Hovenkamp, Herbert. *Science and Religion in America 1800–1860.* Philadelphia: University of Pennsylvania Press, 1978.

Howe, Daniel Walker. *The Unitarian Conscience: Harvard Moral Philosophy, 1805–1861.* Cambridge: Harvard University Press, 1970.

Howe, Irving. *The American Newness: Culture and Politics in the Age of Emerson.* Cambridge: Harvard University Press, 1986.

Hutchison, William R. *The Transcendentalist Ministers: Church Reform in the New England Renaissance.* New Haven: Yale University Press, 1959.

Jackson, Carl T. *The Oriental Religions and American Thought: Some Nineteenth-Century Explorations.* Westport, Conn.: Greenwood, 1981.

Kaplan, Nathaniel, and Thomas Katsaros. *Origins of American Transcendentalism in Philosophy and Mysticism.* New Haven: College and University Press, 1975.

Kirby, Georgiana Bruce. *Years of Experience: An Autobiographical Narrative.* New York: Putnams, 1887. [On Brook Farm]

Koster, Donald N. *Transcendentalism in America.* Boston: Twayne, 1975.

Kuklick, Bruce. *The Rise of American Philosophy.* New Haven: Yale University Press, 1977.

Lader, Lawrence. *The Bold Brahmins: New England's War Against Slavery, 1831–1863.* New York: Dutton, 1961.

Leighton, Walter L. *French Philosophers and New England Transcendentalism.* Charlottesville: University of Virginia, 1908.

Lowance, Mason I. *The Language of Canaan: Metaphor and Symbol in New England from the Puritans to the Transcendentalists.* Cambridge: Harvard University Press, 1980.

McKinsey, Elizabeth R. *The Western Experiment: New England Transcendentalists in the Ohio Valley.* Cambridge: Harvard University Press, 1973.

Matthiessen, F. O. *American Renaissance: Style and Vision in the Age of Emerson and Whitman.* New York: Oxford University Press, 1941.

Miller, Perry, ed. *The American Transcendentalists:*

Their Poetry and Prose. New York: Doubleday, 1957.

Miller, ed. *The Transcendentalists: An Anthology.* Cambridge: Harvard University Press, 1950.

Myerson, Joel. *Brook Farm: An Annotated Bibliography and Resources Guide.* New York: Garland, 1978.

Myerson. *The New England Transcendentalists and the Dial: A History of the Magazine and Its Contributors.* Rutherford, N.J.: Fairleigh Dickinson University Press, 1980.

Myerson, ed. *The American Renaissance in New England, DLB 1.* Detroit: Gale, 1978.

Myerson, ed. *The Brook Farm Book: A Collection of First–Hand Accounts of the Community.* New York: Garland, 1987.

Myerson, ed. *The Transcendentalists: A Review of Research and Criticism.* New York: Modern Language Association, 1983.

Nye, Russel Blaine. *Society and Culture in America 1830–1860.* New York: Harper, 1974.

Persons, Stow. *Free Religion: An American Faith.* New Haven: Yale University Press, 1947.

Pochmann, Henry A. *German Culture in America, 1600–1900: Literary and Philosophical Influences.* Madison: University of Wisconsin Press, 1957.

Pochmann. *New England Transcendentalism and St. Louis Hegelianism.* Philadelphia: Carl Schurz Foundation, 1948.

Richardson, Robert D., Jr. *Myth and Literature in the American Renaissance.* Bloomington: Indiana University Press, 1978.

Robinson, David. *The Unitarians and the Universalists.* Westport, Conn.: Greenwood, 1985.

Rosa, Alfred. *Salem, Transcendentalism, and Hawthorne.* Rutherford, N.J.: Fairleigh Dickinson University Press, 1980.

Rose, Ann C. *Transcendentalism as a Social Movement, 1830–1850.* New Haven: Yale University Press, 1981.

Sams, Henry W., ed. *Autobiography of Brook Farm.* Englewood Cliffs, N.J.: Prentice–Hall, 1958.

Sanborn, F. B. *Bronson Alcott at Alcott House, England, and Fruitlands, New England (1842–1844).* Cedar Rapids, Iowa: Torch Press, 1908.

Sears, Clara Endicott. *Bronson Alcott's Fruitlands.* Boston: Houghton Mifflin, 1915.

Sears, John Van Der Zee. *My Friends at Brook Farm.* New York: Desmond FitzGerald, 1912.

Simon, Myron, and Thornton H. Parsons, eds. *Transcendentalism and Its Legacy.* Ann Arbor: University of Michigan Press, 1966.

Spencer, Benjamin T. *The Quest for Nationality: An American Literary Campaign.* Syracuse: Syracuse University Press, 1957.

Stange, Douglas C. *Patterns of Antislavery Among American Unitarians, 1831–1860.* Rutherford, N.J.: Fairleigh Dickinson University Press, 1977.

Stoehr, Taylor. *Nay–Saying in Concord.* Hamden, Conn.: Archon, 1979.

Swift, Lindsay. *Brook Farm: Its Members, Scholars, and Visitors.* New York: Macmillan, 1900.

Vogel, Stanley M. *German Literary Influences on the American Transcendentalists.* New Haven: Yale University Press, 1955.

Waggoner, Hyatt H. *American Poets from the Puritans to the Present.* Boston: Houghton Mifflin, 1968.

Whicher, George F., ed. *The Transcendentalist Revolt Against Materialism.* Boston: D. C. Heath, 1949; Gail Kennedy, ed. revised edition, *The Transcendentalist Revolt* (1968).

Williams, George Huntston. *The Harvard Divinity School: Its Place in Harvard University and in American Culture.* Boston: Beacon, 1954.

Wright, Conrad. *The Beginnings of Unitarianism in America.* Boston: Starr King Press, 1955.

Wright. *The Liberal Christians.* Boston: Beacon, 1970.

Wright, ed. *A Stream of Light: A Sesquicentennial History of American Unitarianism.* Boston: Beacon, 1975.

Ziff, Larzer. *Literary Democracy: The Declaration of Cultural Independence in America.* New York: Viking, 1981.

The following journals are the best places to look for articles dealing with Transcendentalism:

American Transcendental Quarterly (1969–   )
Concord Saunterer (1965–   )
Emerson Society Quarterly (1955–1971)
ESQ: A Journal of the American Renaissance (1972–   )
Studies in the American Renaissance (1977–   )
Thoreau Journal Quarterly (1969–1981)
Thoreau Society Bulletin (1941–   )

Cumulative Index

Dictionary of Literary Biography, Volumes 1-67
Dictionary of Literary Biography Yearbook, 1980-1986
Dictionary of Literary Biography Documentary Series, Volumes 1-5

Cumulative Index

DLB before number: *Dictionary of Literary Biography,* Volumes 1-67
Y before number: *Dictionary of Literary Biography Yearbook,* 1980-1986
DS before number: *Dictionary of Literary Biography Documentary Series,* Volumes 1-5

A

E

F

G

H

L

N

O

Oakes, Urian circa 1631-1681 .... DLB-24

Oates, Joyce Carol 1938- DLB-2, 5; Y-81

Oberholtzer, Ellis Paxson 1868-1936 .... DLB-47

O'Brien, Edna 1932- DLB-14

O'Brien, Kate 1897-1974 .... DLB-15

O'Brien, Tim 1946- Y-80

O'Casey, Sean 1880-1964 .... DLB-10

Ochs, Adolph S. 1858-1935 .... DLB-25

O'Connor, Flannery 1925-1964 .... DLB-2; Y-80

O'Dell, Scott 1903- DLB-52

Odell, Jonathan 1737-1818 .... DLB-31

Odets, Clifford 1906-1963 ....DLB-7, 26

O'Faolain, Julia 1932- DLB-14

O'Faolain, Sean 1900- DLB-15

O'Flaherty, Liam 1896-1984 .... DLB-36; Y-84

Off Broadway and Off-Off-Broadway DLB-7

Off-Loop Theatres DLB-7

Ogilvie, J. S., and Company DLB-49

O'Grady, Desmond 1935- DLB-40

O'Hara, Frank 1926-1966 ....DLB-5, 16

O'Hara, John 1905-1970 .... DLB-9; DS-2

O. Henry (see Porter, William S.)

Old Franklin Publishing House DLB-49

Older, Fremont 1856-1935 .... DLB-25

Oliphant, Laurence 1829?-1888 .... DLB-18

Oliphant, Margaret 1828-1897 .... DLB-18

Oliver, Chad 1928- DLB-8

Oliver, Mary 1935- DLB-5

Olsen, Tillie 1913?- DLB-28; Y-80

Olson, Charles 1910-1970 ....DLB-5, 16

Olson, Elder 1909- DLB-48, 63

On Art in Fiction (1838), by
    Edward Bulwer DLB-21

On Some of the Characteristics of Modern
    Poetry and On the Lyrical Poems of Alfred
    Tennyson (1831), by Arthur Henry
    Hallam DLB-32

"On Style in English Prose" (1898), by Frederic

Harrison DLB-57

"On Style in Literature: Its Technical Elements"
    (1885), by Robert Louis Stevenson DLB-57

"On the Writing of Essays" (1862),
    by Alexander Smith...................... DLB-57

Ondaatje, Michael 1943- DLB-60

O'Neill, Eugene 1888-1953 ....DLB-7

Oppen, George 1908-1984 ....DLB-5

Oppenheim, James 1882-1932................. DLB-28

Oppenheimer, Joel 1930- DLB-5

Optic, Oliver (see Adams, William Taylor)

Orlovitz, Gil 1918-1973 .... DLB-2, 5

Orlovsky, Peter 1933- DLB-16

Ormond, John 1923- DLB-27

Ornitz, Samuel 1890-1957 ....DLB-28, 44

Orton, Joe 1933-1967 .... DLB-13

Orwell, George 1903-1950.................... DLB-15

The Orwell Year Y-84

Osbon, B. S. 1827-1912...................... DLB-43

Osborne, John 1929- DLB-13

Osgood, Herbert L. 1855-1918 .... DLB-47

Osgood, James R., and Company............. DLB-49

O'Shaughnessy, Arthur 1844-1881 .... DLB-35

O'Shea, Patrick [publishing house] DLB-49

Oswald, Eleazer 1755-1795 .... DLB-43

Otis, James (see Kaler, James Otis)

Otis, James, Jr. 1725-1783.................... DLB-31

Otis, Broaders and Company................. DLB-49

Ottendorfer, Oswald 1826-1900 .... DLB-23

Ouellette, Fernand 1930- DLB-60

Ouida 1839-1908 .... DLB-18

Outing Publishing Company.................. DLB-46

Outlaw Days, by Joyce Johnson............... DLB-16

The Overlook Press DLB-46

Overview of U.S. Book Publishing, 1910-1945...DLB-9

Owen, Guy 1925- DLB-5

Owen, John [publishing house]............... DLB-49

Owen, Wilfred 1893-1918 .... DLB-20

Owsley, Frank L. 1890-1956.................. DLB-17

Ozick, Cynthia 1928- DLB-28; Y-82

P

Q

R

Cumulative Index

U

V

Cumulative Index

W